Michael Augustine Corrigan

**The New Testament of our Lord and Saviour Jesus Christ**

Michael Augustine Corrigan

**The New Testament of our Lord and Saviour Jesus Christ**

ISBN/EAN: 9783741112942

Manufactured in Europe, USA, Canada, Australia, Japa

Cover: Foto ©Lupo / pixelio.de

Manufactured and distributed by brebook publishing software (www.brebook.com)

Michael Augustine Corrigan

**The New Testament of our Lord and Saviour Jesus Christ**

THE

# NEW TESTAMENT

OF

## OUR LORD AND SAVIOUR JESUS CHRIST.

TRANSLATED FROM

### THE LATIN VULGATE,

DILIGENTLY COMPARED WITH THE ORIGINAL GREEK,

AND FIRST PUBLISHED BY THE ENGLISH COLLEGE AT RHEIMS,
A.D. 1582.

WITH ANNOTATIONS, REFERENCES,

AND

AN HISTORICAL AND CHRONOLOGICAL INDEX.

WITH THE IMPRIMATUR OF
MOST REV. M. A. CORRIGAN, D.D.,
ARCHBISHOP OF NEW YORK.

WITH 100 ILLUSTRATIONS.

NEW YORK, CINCINNATI, CHICAGO:
**BENZIGER BROTHERS,**
*Printers to the Holy Apostolic See.*
1897

# CONTENTS.

## THE GOSPEL ACCORDING TO ST. MATTHEW.

| | | |
|---|---|---|
| Chap. I. p. 3 | Chap. X. p. 17 | Chap. XIX. p. 36 |
| II. p. 4 | XI. p. 19 | XX. p. 38 |
| III. p. 6 | XII. p. 21 | XXI. p. 40 |
| IV. p. 7 | XIII. p. 24 | XXII. p. 42 |
| V. p. 8 | XIV. p. 27 | XXIII. p. 44 |
| VI. p. 11 | XV. p. 28 | XXIV. p. 46 |
| VII. p. 13 | XVI. p. 31 | XXV. p. 49 |
| VIII. p. 14 | XVII. p. 33 | XXVI. p. 51 |
| IX. p. 16 | XVIII. p. 34 | XXVII. p 55 |

Chap. XXVIII. p. 58.

## THE GOSPEL ACCORDING TO ST. MARK.

| | | |
|---|---|---|
| Chap. I. p. 59 | Chap. VI. p. 68 | Chap. XI. p. 80 |
| II. p. 61 | VII. p. 71 | XII. p. 81 |
| III. p. 63 | VIII. p. 73 | XIII. p. 84 |
| IV. p. 64 | IX. p. 75 | XIV. p. 86 |
| V. p. 66 | X. p. 77 | XV. p. 89 |

Chap. XVI. p. 91.

## THE GOSPEL ACCORDING TO ST. LUKE.

| | | |
|---|---|---|
| Chap. I. p. 96 | Chap. IX. p. 113 | Chap. XVII. p. 131 |
| II. p. 97 | X. p. 117 | XVIII. p. 133 |
| III. p. 99 | XI. p. 119 | XIX. p 135 |
| IV. p. 101 | XII. p. 122 | XX. p. 137 |
| V. p. 103 | XIII. p. 124 | XXI. p. 139 |
| VI. p. 105 | XIV. p 126 | XXII. p. 141 |
| VII. p. 108 | XV. p. 128 | XXIII. p. 145 |
| VIII. p. 110 | XVI. p. 130 | XXIV. p. 147 |

## THE GOSPEL ACCORDING TO ST. JOHN.

| | | |
|---|---|---|
| Chap. I. p. 150 | Chap. VIII. p. 166 | Chap. XV. p. 181 |
| II. p. 152 | IX. p. 169 | XVI. p. 182 |
| III. p. 153 | X. p. 170 | XVII. p. 184 |
| IV. p. 155 | XI. p. 172 | XVIII. p. 185 |
| V. p. 158 | XII. p. 175 | XIX. p. 187 |
| VI. p. 160 | XIII. p. 177 | XX. p. 189 |
| VII. p. 164 | XIV. p. 179 | XXI. p. 191 |

## CONTENTS.

### THE ACTS OF THE APOSTLES.

| | | |
|---|---|---|
| Chap. I. p. 193 | Chap. X. p. 211 | Chap. XIX. p. 228 |
| II. p. 195 | XI. p. 213 | XX. p. 230 |
| III. p. 197 | XII. p. 215 | XXI. p. 232 |
| IV. p. 198 | XIII. p. 216 | XXII. p. 235 |
| V. p. 200 | XIV. p. 219 | XXIII p. 236 |
| VI. p. 202 | XV. p. 220 | XXIV p. 238 |
| VII. p. 203 | XVI. p. 222 | XXV. p. 239 |
| VIII. p. 206 | XVII. p. 225 | XXVI. p. 241 |
| IX. p. 208 | XVIII. p. 227 | XXVII. p. 243 |

Chap. XXVIII. p. 245.

### EPISTLE OF ST. PAUL TO THE ROMANS.

| | | |
|---|---|---|
| Chap. I. p. 247 | Chap. VI. p. 255 | Chap. XI. p. 263 |
| II. p. 249 | VII p. 256 | XII. p. 265 |
| III. p. 250 | VIII. p. 257 | XIII p 266 |
| IV. p. 252 | IX. p. 260 | XIV. p. 267 |
| V. p. 253 | X p. 262 | XV. p. 269 |

Chap. XVI. p. 270.

### FIRST EPISTLE OF ST. PAUL TO THE CORINTHIANS.

| | | |
|---|---|---|
| Chap. I. p. 272 | Chap. VI. p. 278 | Chap. XI p. 285 |
| II. p. 273 | VII p. 279 | XII. p. 287 |
| III. p. 274 | VIII. p. 281 | XIII p 288 |
| IV. p. 276 | IX. p. 282 | XIV. p 289 |
| V. p. 277 | X p 283 | XV. p. 291 |

Chap. XVI. p. 294.

### SECOND EPISTLE OF ST. PAUL TO THE CORINTHIANS.

| | | |
|---|---|---|
| Chap. I p. 295 | Chap. V. p. 299 | Chap. IX. p 303 |
| II. p 297 | VI. p 301 | X. p. 304 |
| III. p. 298 | VII p. 301 | XI. p. 305 |
| IV. p. 298 | VIII p. 302 | XII. p. 307 |

Chap. XIII p. 308.

### EPISTLE OF ST. PAUL TO THE GALATIANS.

| | | |
|---|---|---|
| Chap. I p. 309 | Chap. III. p. 312 | Chap. V. p. 315 |
| II. p. 310 | IV. p. 813 | VI. p. 316 |

### EPISTLE OF ST. PAUL TO THE EPHESIANS.

| | | |
|---|---|---|
| Chap. I. p. 317 | Chap. III. p. 319 | Chap. V. p. 322 |
| II. p. 318 | IV. p. 320 | VI. p. 323 |

## CONTENTS.

### EPISTLE OF ST. PAUL TO THE PHILIPPIANS.

Chap. I. p. 325 | Chap. II p. 326 | Chap III. p. 328
Chap. IV. p. 329.

### EPISTLE OF ST. PAUL TO THE COLOSSIANS.

Chap. I. p. 330 | Chap. II. p. 332 | Chap. III. p. 333
Chap. IV. p. 335.

### FIRST EPISTLE OF ST. PAUL TO THE THESSALONIANS.

Chap. I. p. 336 | Chap. III. p 338 | Chap. V. p. 339
II. p. 337 | IV. p. 339

### SECOND EPISTLE OF ST PAUL TO THE THESSALONIANS.

Chap. I. p. 341 | Chap. II. p. 342 | Chap. III. p. 343

### FIRST EPISTLE OF ST. PAUL TO TIMOTHY.

Chap. I. p. 344 | Chap. III. p. 346 | Chap. V. p. 348
II. p. 345 | IV. p. 347 | VI p 349

### SECOND EPISTLE OF ST. PAUL TO TIMOTHY.

Chap. I. p. 350 | Chap. II p. 351 | Chap. III. p. 352
Chap IV. p. 353.

### EPISTLE OF ST. PAUL TO TITUS.

Chap. I. p. 355 | Chap. II. p. 356 | Chap. III. p. 356

### EPISTLE OF ST. PAUL TO PHILEMON.

Chap. I. p. 358.

### EPISTLE OF ST. PAUL TO THE HEBREWS.

Chap. I. p. 359 | Chap V p. 363 | Chap IX. p. 367
II. p. 360 | VI. p. 364 | X. p. 369
III. p. 361 | VII. p. 365 | XI. p. 371
IV. p. 362 | VIII p 366 | XII. p. 373
Chap. XIII. p. 375.

### CATHOLIC EPISTLE OF ST. JAMES THE APOSTLE.

Chap. I. p. 377 | Chap. III. p. 380 | Chap. V. p. 382
II. p. 378 | IV. p. 381

## CONTENTS.

### FIRST EPISTLE OF ST. PETER THE APOSTLE.

Chap. I. p. 383 | Chap. III. p. 386 | Chap. V. p. 388
II. p. 385 | IV. p. 387 |

### SECOND EPISTLE OF ST. PETER THE APOSTLE.

Chap. I. p. 389 | Chap. II. p. 391 | Chap. III. p. 392

### FIRST EPISTLE OF ST. JOHN THE APOSTLE.

Chap. I. p. 394 | Chap. III. p. 396 | Chap. V. p. 390
II. p. 395 | IV. p. 398 |

### SECOND EPISTLE OF ST. JOHN THE APOSTLE.

Chap. I. p. 402.

### THIRD EPISTLE OF ST. JOHN THE APOSTLE.

Chap. I. p. 403.

### CATHOLIC EPISTLE OF ST. JUDE THE APOSTLE.

Chap. I. p. 404.

### APOCALYPSE OF ST. JOHN THE APOSTLE.

Chap. I. p. 407 | Chap. VIII. p. 415 | Chap. XV. p. 424
II. p. 408 | IX. p. 416 | XVI. p. 424
III. p. 410 | X. p. 418 | XVII. p. 426
IV. p 411 | XI. p. 419 | XVIII p. 427
V. p. 412 | XII. p. 420 | XIX. p. 429
VI. p. 413 | XIII p 421 | XX. p. 430
VII. p. 414 | XIV. p. 422 | XXI. p. 431
Chap. XXII. p. 433.

|  | PAGE |
|---|---|
| HISTORICAL AND CHRONOLOGICAL INDEX | 435 |
| A TABLE OF REFERENCES | 440 |
| A TABLE OF ALL THE EPISTLES AND GOSPELS FOR ALL SUNDAYS AND HOLIDAYS IN THE YEAR | 444 |

# LIST OF ILLUSTRATIONS.

|   | PAGE |
|---|---|
| The Angel Announces the Birth of St. John | 4 |
| The Annunciation | 8 |
| Mary Visits Elizabeth | 12 |
| Birth of St. John the Baptist | 16 |
| The Angels Announce the Birth of Christ | 20 |
| The Shepherds Adoring the New-Born Saviour | 24 |
| The Shepherds Announce the Birth of Christ | 28 |
| The Adoration of the Magi | 32 |
| The Presentation in the Temple | 36 |
| Joseph is Warned to Flee into Egypt | 40 |
| The Flight into Egypt | 44 |
| Massacre of the Holy Innocents | 48 |
| Jesus among the Doctors in the Temple | 52 |
| St. John the Baptist Preaching in the Desert | 56 |
| The Baptism of Jesus in the Jordan | 60 |
| The Temptation of Christ | 64 |
| St. John Gives Testimony of Our Lord | 68 |
| The Disciples of Jesus | 72 |
| The Miracle at Cana | 76 |
| Christ Purging the Temple | 80 |
| Christ's Discourse with Nicodemus | 84 |
| Jesus and the Samaritan Woman | 88 |
| The Miraculous Draught of Fishes | 92 |
| Christ Healing the Man Sick of the Palsy | 96 |
| The Sermon on the Mount | 100 |
| Jesus Casting Out Devils | 104 |
| The Raising of the Widow's Son | 108 |
| The Sins of Mary Magdalen are Forgiven | 112 |
| Cure of the Man Sick for Thirty-Eight Years | 116 |
| The Apostles are Sent Out to Preach | 120 |
| The Parable of the Cockle | 124 |

## LIST OF ILLUSTRATIONS.

|  | PAGE |
|---|---|
| Jesus Sleeping during the Tempest | 128 |
| The Woman Taken in Adultery | 132 |
| Jesus Restores the Daughter of Jairus | 136 |
| Two Blind Men are Restored to Sight | 140 |
| Beheading of St. John the Baptist | 144 |
| Jesus Supporting St. Peter on the Water | 148 |
| The Multiplication of the Loaves and Fishes | 152 |
| The Primacy Conferred on St. Peter | 156 |
| The Transfiguration of Our Lord | 160 |
| "He that Shall Receive one such Little Child in My Name Receiveth Me" | 164 |
| The Good Samaritan | 168 |
| "Mary Hath Chosen the Better Part" | 172 |
| The Good Shepherd | 176 |
| The Prodigal Son | 180 |
| Lazarus and Dives | 184 |
| Jesus Cures the Man Born Blind | 188 |
| One of Ten Lepers Returns to give Thanks | 192 |
| The Pharisee and the Publican | 196 |
| The Rich Young Man | 200 |
| The Laborers in the Vineyard | 204 |
| Christ Blessing Little Children | 208 |
| The Raising of Lazarus | 212 |
| Mary Magdalen Anointing the Head of Jesus | 216 |
| Christ's Entry into Jerusalem | 220 |
| The Coin of Tribute | 224 |
| The Parable of the Man without a Wedding Garment | 228 |
| The Wise and the Foolish Virgins | 232 |
| Jesus Washes His Disciples' Feet | 236 |
| The Last Supper | 240 |
| The Agony in the Garden | 244 |
| Judas Betrays his Master | 248 |
| Christ Before the High-Priest Annas | 252 |
| St. Peter Denies Our Lord | 256 |
| Jesus before Caiphas | 260 |
| Jesus before Herod | 264 |
| Jesus is Crowned with Thorns | 268 |

# LIST OF ILLUSTRATIONS.

|   | PAGE |
|---|---|
| Jesus is Given to be Crucified | 272 |
| The Death of Judas | 276 |
| Jesus is Led Away to be Crucified | 280 |
| The Crucifixion | 284 |
| The Burial of Christ | 288 |
| The Resurrection of Christ | 292 |
| The Angel Declaring the Resurrection of Christ | 296 |
| Mary Magdalen at the Sepulchre | 300 |
| Christ Appears to Mary Magdalen | 304 |
| Jesus and the Two Disciples of Emmaus | 308 |
| Christ Appears to His Disciples at the Sea of Tiberias | 312 |
| Jesus Appears to St. Thomas and the Other Disciples | 316 |
| St. Peter is Appointed Chief Pastor | 322 |
| The Ascension of Christ | 328 |
| The Descent of the Holy Ghost | 334 |
| St. Peter Curing the Lame Man | 340 |
| The Martyrdom of St. Stephen | 346 |
| The Conversion of the Eunuch | 352 |
| The Conversion of St. Paul | 358 |
| "That which God hath Cleansed, do not thou call Common" | 364 |
| St. Peter Speaking of Jesus Christ to the Centurion | 370 |
| St. Peter is Delivered from Prison | 376 |
| St. Peter Addressing the Council of Jerusalem | 382 |
| SS. Paul and Barnabas Taken for Gods by the People of Lystra | 388 |
| St. Paul Preaches to the Athenians | 394 |
| St. Paul's Departure from Ephesus | 400 |
| Paul and Silas in Prison—The Prison-Keeper Believes | 406 |
| St. Paul's Arrival in Rome | 412 |
| Revelation of Jesus Christ to St. John (Apoc. i.) | 418 |
| The Book Sealed with Seven Seals is opened by the Lamb (Apoc. v.) | 424 |
| The Seventh Seal of the Book is Opened (Apoc. viii.) | 430 |
| The Archangel Michael's Victory Over the Dragon (Apoc. xii.) | 436 |
| The New Jerusalem (Apoc. xxi.) | 442 |

# THE HOLY GOSPEL OF JESUS CHRIST,

## ACCORDING TO ST. MATTHEW

*St. Matthew, one of the twelve Apostles, who from being a publican, that is, a tax-gatherer, was called by our Saviour to the Apostleship; in that profession his name was Levi: (Luke v. 27, and Mark ii. 14.) He was the first of the Evangelists that wrote the Gospel, and that in Hebrew, or Syro-Chaldaic, which the Jews in Palestine spoke at that time. The original is not now extant, but as it was translated in the time of the Apostles into Greek, that version was of equal authority. He wrote about six years after our Lord's Ascension.*

## CHAP. I.

*The genealogy of Christ: he is conceived and born of a virgin.*

THE book of the generation of JESUS CHRIST, the son of *a* David, the son of Abraham:

2 *b* Abraham begot *c* Isaac. And Isaac begot Jacob. *d* And Jacob begot Judas and his brethren.

3 *e* And Judas begot Phares and Zara of Thamar. *f* And Phares begot Esron. And Esron begot Aram.

4 And Aram begot Aminadab. *g* And Aminadab begot Naasson. And Naasson begot Salmon.

5 And Salmon begot Booz of Rahab. *h* And Booz begot Obed of Ruth. And Obed begot Jesse.

6 *i* And Jesse begot David the king. *k* And David the king begot Solomon, of her that had been *the wife* of Urias.

7 *l* And Solomon begot Roboam. *m* And Roboam begot Abia. *n* And Abia begot Asa.

8 And Asa begot Josaphat. And Josaphat begot Joram. And Joram begot Ozias.

9 *o* And Ozias begot Joatham. *p* And Joatham begot Achaz. *q* And Achaz begot Ezechias.

10 *r* And Ezechias begot Manasses. *s* And Manasses begot Amon. *t* And Amon begot Josias.

11 *u* And Josias begot Jechonias and his brethren in the transmigration of Babylon.

12 And after the transmigration of Babylon, Jechonias begot Salathiel. And Salathiel begot Zorobabel.

13 And Zorobabel begot Abiud. And Abiud begot Eliacim. And Eliacim begot Azor.

14 And Azor begot Sadoc. And Sadoc begot Achim. And Achim begot Eliud.

15 And Eliud begot Eleazar. And Eleazar begot Mathan. And Mathan begot Jacob.

*a* Luke 3. 31.—*b* Gen. 21. 2.—*c* Gen. 25. 25.—*d* Gen. 29. 35.—*e* Gen. 38. 29. 1 Par. 2. 4.—*f* Ruth 4. 18. 1 Par. 2. 5.—*g* Num. 7. 12.—*h* Ruth 4. 22.—*i* 1 Kings 16. 1.—*k* 2 Kings 12. 24.—*l* 3 Kings 11. 43.

*m* 3 Kings 14. 31.—*n* 3 Kings 15. 8.—*o* 2 Par. 26. 23.—*p* 2 Par. 27. 9.—*q* 2 Par. 28. 27.—*r* 2 Par. 32. 33.—*s* 2 Par. 33. 20.—*t* 2 Par. 33. 25.—*u* 2 Par. 36. 2.

16 And Jacob begot Joseph the husband of Mary, of whom was born JESUS, who is called CHRIST.

17 So all the generations from Abraham to David, are fourteen generations. And from David to the transmigration of Babylon, are fourteen generations; and from the transmigration of Babylon to Christ are fourteen generations.

18 Now the generation of CHRIST was in this wise. *a* When as his mother Mary was espoused to Joseph, before they came together, she was found with child, of the Holy Ghost.

19 Whereupon Joseph her husband, being a just man, and not willing publicly to expose her, was minded to put her away privately.

20 But while he thought on these things, behold the Angel of the Lord appeared to him in his sleep, saying: Joseph, son of David, fear not to take unto thee Mary thy wife, for that which is conceived in her, is of the Holy Ghost.

21 And she shall bring forth a son : *b* and thou shalt call his name JESUS. For he shall save his people from their sins.

22 Now all this was done that it might be fulfilled which the Lord spoke by the prophet, saying :

23 *c* *Behold a virgin shall be*

*a* Luke 1. 27. — *b* Luke 1. 31. — *c* Acts 4. 12. — *c* Isaias 7. 14.

CHAP. I. Ver. 16 *The husband of Mary.* The Evangelist gives us rather the pedigree of St. *Joseph*, than that of the blessed Virgin, to conform to the custom of the *Hebrews*, who in their genealogies took no notice of women; but as they were near akin, the pedigree of the one shewed that of the other.

4

*with child, and bring forth a son, and they shall call his name Emmanuel*, which being interpreted is, *God with us.*

24 And Joseph rising up from sleep, did as the Angel of the Lord had commanded him, and took unto him his wife.

25 And he knew her not till she brought forth her first-born son : and he called his name JESUS.

## CHAP. II.

*The offerings of the wise men : the flight into Egypt : the massacre of the Innocents.*

WHEN *d* JESUS therefore was born in Bethlehem of Juda, in the days of king Herod, be-

*d* A.M. 4000. Being four years before the coming : account called Anno Domini. Luke 2. 7.

Ver. 25. *Till she brought forth her first-born son.* From these words Helvidius and other heretics most imply us v inferred that the blessed Virgin Mary had other children besides Christ ; but St. Jerome shews, by divers examples, that this expression of the Evangelist was a manner of speaking usual among the *Hebrews*, to denote by the word *until*, only what is done, without any regard to the future : Thus it is said, Gen. chap. viii. ver. 6 and 7. That *Noe sent forth a raven, which went forth, and did not return* TILL *the waters were dried up on the earth.* That is, did not return any more. Also *Isaias.* chap. xlvi. ver. 4. God says : *I am* TILL *you grow old.* Who dare infer that God should then cease to be ? Also in the first book of *Machabees* chap. v. ver. 54. *And they went up to mount Sion with joy, and gladness, and offered holocausts, because not one of them was slain till they had returned in peace.* That is, not one was slain, before or after they had returned. God saith to his divine Son : *Sit on my right hand* TILL *I make thy enemies thy footstool.* Shall he sit no longer after his enemies are subdued ? Yea and for all eternity. St. Jerome also proves by Scripture examples, that an *only begotten* son was also called first-born, or *first-begotten*: because according to the

THE ANGEL ANNOUNCES THE BIRTH OF ST. JOHN.

hold, there came wise men from the East to Jerusalem.

2 Saying: Where is he that is born King of the Jews? For we have seen his star in the East, and are come to adore him.

3 And king Herod hearing this, was troubled, and all Jerusalem with him.

4 And assembling together all the chief priests and the Scribes of the people, he inquired of them where Christ should be born.

5 But they said to him: In Bethlehem of Juda. For so it is written by the prophet:

6 *And thou Bethlehem the land of Juda art not the least among the princes of Juda: for out of thee shall come forth the captain that shall rule my people Israel.*

7 Then Herod privately calling the wise men learned diligently of them the time of the star which appeared to them;

8 And sending them into Bethlehem, said: Go and diligently inquire after the child; and when you have found him, bring me word again, that I also may come and adore him.

9 Who having heard the king, went their way; and behold the star which they had seen in the East, went before them, until it came and stood over where the child was.

10 And seeing the star they rejoiced with exceeding great joy.

11 And entering into the house, they found the child with Mary his mother, and falling down they adored him: *b* and opening their treasures, they offered him gifts; gold, frankincense, and myrrh.

12 And having received an answer in sleep that they should not return to Herod, they went back another way into their country.

13 And after they were departed, behold an Angel of the Lord appeared in sleep to Joseph, saying: Arise, and take the child and his mother, and fly into Egypt: and be there until I shall tell thee. For it will come to pass that Herod will seek the child to destroy him.

14 Who arose, and took the child and his mother, by night, and retired into Egypt: and he was there until the death of Herod.

15 That it might be fulfilled which the Lord spoke by the prophet, saying: *c Out of Egypt have I called my son.*

16 Then Herod perceiving that he was deluded by the wise men, was exceeding angry: and sending killed all the men-children that were in Bethlehem, and in all the borders thereof, from two years old and under, according to the time which he had diligently inquired of the wise men.

17 Then was fulfilled that which was spoken by Jeremias the prophet, saying:

18 *d A voice in Rama was heard, lamentation and great mourning; Rachel bewailing her children, and would not be comforted, because they are not.*

19 But when Herod was dead, behold an Angel of the Lord

---

*a* Mich. 5. 2. John 7. 42.

law, the *first-born* males were to be consecrated to God: *Sanctify unto me, saith the Lord, every first-born that openeth the womb among the children of Israel, &c.* Exod. chap. xiii. ver. 2.

*b* Ps. 71. 10. — *c* Osee 11. 1. — *d* Jer. 31. 15.

appeared in sleep to Joseph in Egypt,

20 Saying: Arise, and take the child and his mother, and go into the land of Israel. For they are dead that sought the life of the child.

21 Who arose, and took the child and his mother, and came into the land of Israel.

22 But hearing that Archelaus reigned in Judea in the room of Herod his father, he was afraid to go thither: and being warned in sleep retired into the quarters of Galilee.

23 And coming he dwelt in a city called Nazareth: that it might be fulfilled which was said by the prophets: That he shall be called a Nazarite.

## CHAP. III.

*The preaching of John: Christ is baptised.*

AND [a] in those days cometh John the Baptist preaching in the desert of Judea.

2 And saying; [b] Do penance: for the kingdom of heaven is at hand.

3 For this is he that was spoken of by Isaias the prophet, saying: [c] *A voice of one crying in the desert, Prepare ye the way of the Lord, make straight his paths.*

4 And the same John had his garment of camels' hair, and a leathern girdle about his loins: and his meat was locusts and wild honey.

5 [d] Then went out to him Jerusalem and all Judea, and all the country about Jordan:

6 And were baptized by him in the Jordan confessing their sins.

7 And seeing many of the Pharisees and Sadducees *coming to his baptism, he said to them: Ye brood of vipers, who hath shewed you to flee from the wrath to come?

8 Bring forth therefore fruit worthy of penance.

9 And think not to say within yourselves, [f] We have Abraham for our father. For I tell you that God is able of these stones to raise up children to Abraham.

10 For now the axe is laid to the root of the trees. Every tree therefore that doth not yield good fruit, shall be cut down, and cast into the fire.

11 [g] I indeed baptize you in water unto penance, but he that shall come after me, is mightier than I, whose shoes I am not worthy to bear; he shall baptize you in the Holy Ghost and fire.

12 Whose fan is in his hand, and he will thoroughly cleanse his floor: and gather his wheat into the barn, but the chaff he will burn with unquenchable fire.

13 [h] Then cometh JESUS from Galilee to the Jordan, unto John, to be baptized by him.

---

[a] A.D. 28.—[b] Mark 1. 4. Luke 3. 3.—[c] Isaias 40. 3. Mark 1. 3. Luke 3. 4.

CHAP. III. Ver. 2. *Do penance.* 'Pœnitentiam agite,' μετανοειτε. Which word, according to the use of the scriptures and the holy fathers, does not only sign'fy repentance and amendment of life, but also punishing past sins by fasting, and such like penitential exercises.

[d] Mark 1. 5.—[e] Luke 3. 7.—[f] John 8. 39.—[g] Mark 1. 8. Luke 3. 16. John 1. 26. Acts 1. 5.—[h] Mark 1. 9.

Ver. 7. *Pharisees and Sadducees.* These were two sects among the Jews: of which the former were for the most part notorious hypocrites; the latter a kind of free-thinkers in matters of religion.

14 ᵃ But John stayed him, saying: I ought to be baptized by thee, and comest thou to me? 

15 And JESUS answering, said to him: Suffer it to be so now. For so it becometh us to fulfil all justice. Then he suffered him.

16 And JESUS being baptized, forthwith came out of the water: and lo, the heavens were opened to him: and he saw the ᵇ Spirit of God descending as a dove, and coming upon him.

17 ᶜ And behold a voice from heaven, saying: This is my beloved Son, in whom I am well pleased.

## CHAP. IV.

*Christ's fast of forty days: he is tempted. He begins to preach, to call disciples to him, and to work miracles.*

THEN ᵈ JESUS was led by the spirit into the desert, to be tempted by the devil.

2 And when he had fasted forty days and forty nights, afterwards he was hungry.

3 And the tempter coming said to him: If thou be the Son of God, command that these stones be made bread.

4 Who answered and said: It is written, ᵉ *Not in bread alone doth man live, but in every word that proceedeth from the mouth of God.*

5 Then the devil took him up into the holy city, and set him upon the pinnacle of the temple,

6 And said to him: If thou be the Son of God, cast thyself down, for it is written: ᶠ *That he hath given his Angels charge over thee, and in their hands shall they bear thee up, lest perhaps thou dash thy foot against a stone.*

---
ᵃ A. D. 30.—ᵇ Luke 3. 22.—ᶜ Mark 1. 11. Luke 3. 22. 9 Pet. L 17.—ᵈ A.D. 30. Luke 4. 1.—ᵉ Deut. 8. 3. Luke 4. 4.—ᶠ Ps. 90. 11.

7 JESUS said to him, It is written again: ᵍ *Thou shalt not tempt the Lord thy God.*

8 Again the devil took him up into a very high mountain: and shewed him all the kingdoms of the world, and the glory of them.

9 And said to him: All these will I give thee, if falling down thou wilt adore me.

10 Then JESUS saith to him: Begone, Satan: for it is written: ʰ *The Lord thy God shalt thou adore, and him only shalt thou serve.*

11 Then the devil left him: and behold Angels came and ministered to him.

12 And when JESUS had heard that John was delivered up, ⁱ he retired into Galilee:

13 And leaving the city Nazareth, he came and dwelt in Capharnaum on the sea coast, in the borders of Zabulon and of Nephthalim:

14 That it might be fulfilled which was said by Isaias the prophet:

15 ᵏ *Land of Zabulon and land of Nephthalim, the way of the sea beyond the Jordan, Galilee of the gentiles:*

16 *The people that sat in darkness, hath seen great light: and to them that sat in the region of the shadow of death, light is sprung up.*

17 ˡ From that time JESUS began to preach, and to say:

---
ᵍ Deut. 6. 16.—ʰ Deut. 6. 13.—ⁱ Mark 1. 14. Luke 4. 14. John 4. 43.—ᵏ Isaias 9. 1.—ˡ Mark 1. 15.

CHAP. IV. Ver. 6. *Shewed him, &c.* That is, pointed out to him where each kingdom lay; and set for h in words what was most glorious and admirable in each of them. Or also set before his eyes, as it were in a large map, a lively representation of all those kingdoms.

7

Do penance, for the kingdom of heaven is at hand.

18 And JESUS walking by the sea of Galilee, *saw two brethren, Simon who is called Peter, and Andrew his brother, casting a net into the sea (for they were fishers).

19 And he saith to them: Come ye after me, and I will make you to be fishers of men.

20 And they immediately leaving their nets, followed him.

21 And going on from thence, he saw other two brethren, James the son of Zebedee, and John his brother, in a ship with Zebedee their father, mending their nets: and he called them.

22 And they forthwith left their nets and father, and followed him.

23 And JESUS went about all Galilee, teaching in their synagogues, and preaching the gospel of the kingdom: and healing all manner of sickness and every infirmity, among the people.

24 And his fame went throughout all Syria, and they presented to him all sick people that were taken with divers diseases and torments, and such as were possessed by devils and lunatics, and those that had the palsy, and he cured them:

25 *b* And much people followed him from Galilee, and from Decapolis, and from Jerusalem, and from Judea, and from beyond the Jordan.

## CHAP. V.

*Christ's sermon upon the mount. The eight beatitudes.*

AND *c* seeing the multitudes, he went up into a mountain, and when he was set down, his disciples came unto him.

*a* Mark 1. 16. Luke 5. 2.—*b* Mark 3. 7. Luke 6. 17.—*c* A.D. 31.

2 And opening his mouth he taught them, saying:

3 *d* Blessed are the poor in spirit: for theirs is the kingdom of heaven.

4 *e* Blessed are the meek: for they shall possess the land.

5 *f* Blessed are they that mourn: for they shall be comforted.

6 Blessed are they that hunger and thirst after justice: for they shall have their fill.

7 Blessed are the merciful: for they shall obtain mercy.

8 *g* Blessed are the clean of heart: for they shall see God.

9 Blessed are the peacemakers: for they shall be called the children of God.

10 *h* Blessed are they that suffer persecution for justice sake: for theirs is the kingdom of heaven.

11 Blessed are ye when they shall revile you, and persecute you, and speak all that is evil against you, untruly, for my sake;

12 Be glad and rejoice, for your reward is very great in heaven. For so they persecuted the prophets that were before you.

13 You are the salt of the earth. *i* But if the salt lose its savour, wherewith shall it be salted? It is good for nothing any more but to be cast out, and to be trodden on by men.

14 You are the light of the world. A city seated on a mountain cannot be hid.

*d* Luke 6. 20.—*e* Ps. 36. 11.—*f* Isaias 61. 2.—*g* Ps. 23. 4.—*h* 1 Pet. 2. 20. and 3. 14. and 4. 14.—*i* Mark 9. 49. Luke 14. 43.

CHAP. V. Ver. 3. *The poor in spirit.* That is, the humble; and they whose spirit is not set upon riches.

THE ANNUNCIATION.

15 ᵃNeither do men light a candle and put it under a bushel, but upon a candlestick, that it may shine to all that are in the house.

16 So let your light shine before men, ᵇthat they may see your good works, and glorify your Father who is in heaven.

17 Do not think that I am come to destroy the law, or the prophets. I am not come to destroy, but to fulfil.

18 ᶜFor amen I say unto you, till heaven and earth pass, one jot, or one tittle shall not pass of the law, till all be fulfilled.

19 ᵈHe therefore that shall break one of these least commandments, and shall so teach men, shall be called the least in the kingdom of heaven. But he that shall do and teach, he shall be called great in the kingdom of heaven.

20 For I tell you, that unless your justice abound ᵉmore than that of the Scribes and Pharisees, you shall not enter into the kingdom of heaven.

21 You have heard that it was said to them of old: ᶠThou shalt not kill. And whosoever shall kill, shall be in danger of the judgment.

22 But I say to you, that whosoever is angry with his brother, shall be in danger of the judgment. And whosoever shall say to his brother, Raca, shall be in danger of the council. And whosoever shall say, Thou fool, shall be in danger of hell fire.

23 If therefore thou offer thy gift at the altar, and there thou remember that thy brother hath anything against thee;

24 Leave there thy offering before the altar, and go first to be reconciled to thy brother, and then coming thou shalt offer thy gift.

25 ᵍBe at agreement with thy adversary betimes, whilst thou art in the way with him; lest perhaps the adversary deliver thee to the judge, and the judge deliver thee to the officer, and thou be cast into prison.

26 Amen I say to thee, thou shalt not go out from thence till thou repay the last farthing.

27 You have heard that it

---

ᵃ Mark 4. 21. Luke 8. 16. and 11. 33.—ᵇ 1 Pet. 2. 12.—ᶜ Luke 16. 17.—ᵈ Jas. 2. 10.—ᵉ Luke 11. 39.—ᶠ Exod. 20. 13. Deut. 5. 17.

Ver. 17. *To fulfil.* By accomplishing all the figures and prophecies; and perfecting all that was imperfect.

Ver. 18. *Amen.* That is, *assuredly, of a truth.* This Hebrew word, *Amen,* is here retained by the example and authority of all the four evangelists, who have retained it. It is used by our Lord as a strong asseveration, and affirmation of the truth.

Ver. 20. *The Scribes and Pharisees.* The *Scribes* were the doctors of the law of Moses: the *Pharisees* were a precise set of men, making profession of a more exact observance of the law: and upon that account greatly esteemed among the people.

Ver. 21. *Shall be in danger of the judgment:* That is, shall deserve to be

ᵍ Luke 12. 58.

punished by that lesser tribunal among the Jews, called the *Judgment,* which took cognizance of such crimes.

Ver. 22. *Raca:* A word expressing great indignation or contempt. *Shall be in danger of the council:* that is, shall deserve to be punished by the highest court of Judicature, called the *Council,* or *Sanhedrim,* consisting of seventy-two persons, where the highest causes were tried and judged, which was at Jerusalem.—Ibid. *Thou fool.* This was then looked upon as a heinous injury, when uttered with contempt, spite, or malice; and therefore is here so severely condemned. *Shall be in danger of hell fire:* literally, according to the Greek, shall deserve to be cast into the *Gehenna of fire.* Which words our Saviour made use of to express the fire and punishment of hell.

was said to them of old: <sup>a</sup>Thou shalt not commit adultery.

28 But I say to you, that whosoever shall look on a woman to lust after her, hath already committed adultery with her in his heart.

29 <sup>b</sup> And if thy right eye scandalize thee, pluck it out and cast it from thee. For it is expedient for thee that one of thy members should perish, rather than thy whole body be cast into hell.

30 And if thy right hand scandalize thee, cut it off, and cast it from thee: for it is expedient for thee that one of thy members should perish, rather than that thy whole body go into hell.

31 And it hath been said,<sup>c</sup> Whosoever shall put away his wife, let him give her a bill of divorce.

32 But I say to you, <sup>d</sup> that whosoever shall put away his wife, excepting the cause of fornication, maketh her to commit adultery: and he that shall marry her that is put away, committeth adultery.

33 Again you have heard that it was said to them of old, <sup>e</sup>Thou shalt not forswear thyself: but thou shalt perform thy oaths to the Lord.

34 But I say to you not to swear at all, neither by heaven, for it is the throne of God:

35 Nor by the earth, for it is his footstool; nor by Jerusalem, for it is the city of the great king:

36 Neither shalt thou swear by thy head, because thou canst not make one hair white or black.

37 <sup>f</sup> But let your speech be yea, yea: no, no: and that which is over and above these is of evil.

38 You have heard that it hath been said: <sup>g</sup> An eye for an eye, and a tooth for a tooth.

39 But I say to you not to resist evil: <sup>h</sup> but if one strike thee on thy right cheek, turn to him also the other:

40 <sup>i</sup> And if a man will contend with thee in judgment, and take away thy coat, let go thy cloak also unto him.

41 And whosoever will force thee one mile, go with him other two

42 <sup>k</sup> Give to him that asketh of thee, and from him that would borrow of thee turn not away.

43 You have heard that it hath been said, <sup>l</sup>Thou shalt love thy neighbour, and hate thy enemy.

---

<sup>a</sup> Exod. 20. 14.—<sup>b</sup> Mark 9. 46. Infra. 18. 9.—<sup>c</sup> Deut. 24. 1. Infra. 19. 7.—<sup>d</sup> Mark 10. 11. Luke 16. 18. 1 Cor. 7. 10.—<sup>e</sup> Exod. 20. 7. Lev. 19. 12. Deut. 5. 11. Jas. 5. 12.

<sup>f</sup> Jas. 5. 12.—<sup>g</sup> Exod. 21. 24. Lev. 24. 20. Deut. 19. 21.—<sup>h</sup> Luke 6. 29.—<sup>i</sup> 1 Cor. 6. 7.—<sup>k</sup> Deut. 15. 8.—<sup>l</sup> Lev. 19. 18.

Ver. 29. *Scandalize thee.* That is, if it be a stumbling-block, or occasion of sin, to thee. By which we are taught to fly the immediate occasions of sin, though they be as dear to us, or as necessary to us, as a hand or an eye.

Ver. 34. *Not to swear at all.* 'Tis not forbid to swear in truth, justice, and judgment; to the honour of God, or our own or neighbour's just defence: but only to swear rashly, or profanely, in common discourse, and without necessity.

Ver. 39. *Not to resist evil,* &c. What is here commanded is a christian patience under injuries and affronts, and to be willing even to suffer still more rather than to indulge the desire of revenge: but what is further added does not strictly oblige according to the letter, for neither did Christ nor St. Paul turn the other cheek. St. John xviii. and Acts xxiii.

44 But I say to you, *a* Love your enemies, *b* do good to them that hate you: *c* and pray for them that persecute and calumniate you:

45 That you may be the children of your Father who is in heaven, who maketh his sun to rise upon the good, and bad, and raineth upon the just and the unjust.

46 For if you love them that love you, what reward shall you have? do not even the publicans this?

47 And if you salute your brethren only, what do you more? do not also the heathens this?

48 Be you therefore perfect, as also your heavenly Father is perfect.

## CHAP. VI.

*A continuation of the sermon on the mount.*

TAKE heed that you do not your justice before men, to be seen by them: otherwise you shall not have a reward of your Father who is in heaven.

2 Therefore when thou dost an alms-deed, sound not a trumpet before thee, as the hypocrites do in the synagogues and in the streets, that they may be honoured by men. Amen I say to you, they have received their reward.

3 But when thou dost alms,

*a* Luke 6. 27.—*b* Rom. 12. 20.—*c* Luke 23. 34. Acts 7. 59.

let not thy left hand know what thy right hand doth.

4 That thy alms may be in secret, and thy Father who seeth in secret will repay thee.

5 And when ye pray, you shall not be as the hypocrites, that love to stand and pray in the synagogues and corners of the streets, that they may be seen by men: Amen I say to you, they have received their reward.

6 But thou when thou shalt pray, enter into thy chamber, and having shut the door, pray to thy Father in secret: and thy Father who seeth in secret will repay thee.

7 And when you are praying, speak not much, as the heathens. For they think that in their much speaking they may be heard.

8 Be not you therefore like to them, for your Father knoweth what is needful for you, before you ask him.

9 Thus therefore shall you pray: *d* Our Father who art in heaven, hallowed be thy name,

10 Thy kingdom come. Thy will be done on earth as it is in heaven.

11 Give us this day our supersubstantial bread.

12 And forgive us our debts, as we also forgive our debtors.

13 And lead us not into temptation. But deliver us from evil. Amen.

*d* Luke 11. 2.

Ver. 44. *The Publicans.* These were the gatherers of the public taxes: a set of men odious and infamous among the Jews for their extortions and injustice.

CHAP. VI. Ver. 1. *Your justice,* i.e. *Works of justice,* viz. fasting, prayer, and almsdeeds: which ought to be performed not out of ostentation, or a view to please men, but solely to please God.

Ver. 11. *Supersubstantial bread.* In St *Luke* the same word is rendered *daily bread.* It is understood of the bread of life, which we receive in the Blessed Sacrament.

Ver. 13. *Lead us not into temptation.* That is, suffer us not to be overcome by temptation.

CHAP. VI.   ST. MATTHEW.   CHAP. VI.

14 <sup>a</sup> For if you will forgive men their offences, your heavenly Father will forgive you also your offences.

15 But if you will not forgive men, neither will your Father forgive you your offences.

16 And when you fast, be not as the hypocrites, sad. For they disfigure their faces, that they may appear unto men to fast. Amen I say to you, they have received their reward.

17 But thou, when thou fastest anoint thy head, and wash thy face:

18 That thou appear not to men to fast, but to thy Father who is in secret: and thy Father who seeth in secret, will repay thee.

19 Lay not up to yourselves treasures on earth: where the rust, and moth consume, and where thieves break through, and steal.

20 <sup>b</sup> But lay up to yourselves treasures in heaven: where neither the rust nor moth doth consume, and where thieves do not break through, nor steal.

21 For where thy treasure is, there is thy heart also.

22 <sup>c</sup> The light of thy body is thy eye. If thy eye be single thy whole body shall be lightsome.

23 But if thy eye be evil thy whole body shall be darksome. If then the light that is in thee, be darkness: the darkness itself how great shall it be?

24 <sup>d</sup> No man can serve two masters. For either he will hate the one, and love the other: or he will sustain the one, and despise the other. You cannot serve God and mammon.

25 <sup>e</sup> Therefore I say to you, be not solicitous for your life, what you shall eat, nor for your body what you shall put on. Is not the life more than the meat: and the body more than the raiment?

26 Behold the birds of the air, for they neither sow, nor do they reap, nor gather into barns: and your heavenly Father feedeth them. Are not you of much more value than they?

27 And which of you by taking thought, can add to his stature one cubit?

28 And for raiment why are you solicitous? Consider the lilies of the field how they grow: they labour not, neither do they spin.

29 But I say to you, that not even Solomon in all his glory was arrayed as one of these.

30 And if the grass of the field, which is to-day, and tomorrow is cast into the oven, God doth so clothe: how much more you, O ye of little faith?

31 Be not solicitous therefore, saying: What shall we eat: or what shall we drink, or wherewith shall we be clothed?

32 For after all these things do the heathens seek. For your Father knoweth that you have need of all these things.

33 Seek ye therefore first the kingdom of God, and his justice, and all these things shall be added unto you.

34 Be not therefore solicitous for to-morrow; for the morrow will be solicitous for itself. Sufficient for the day is the evil thereof.

<sup>a</sup> Eccli. 28. 3, 4, & 5. Infra, 18. 35. Mark 11. 25.—<sup>b</sup> Luke 12. 33. 1 Tim. 6. 19.—<sup>c</sup> Luke 11. 34.—<sup>d</sup> Luke 16. 13.

Ver. 24. *Mammon.* That is, riches, worldly interest.

<sup>e</sup> Ps. 54. 23. Luke 12. 22. Phil. 4. 6. 1 Tim. 6. 7. 1 Pet. 5. 7.

MARY VISITS ELIZABETH.

## CHAP. VII.

*The third part of the sermon on the mount.*

JUDGE ᵃnot, that you may not be judged.

2 For with what judgment you judge, you shall be ᵇjudged: and with what measure you mete, it shall be measured to you again.

3 And why seest thou the mote that is in thy brother's eye; and seest not the beam that is in thy own eye?

4 Or how sayest thou to thy brother: Let me cast the mote out of thy eye; and behold a beam is in thy own eye?

5 Thou hypocrite, cast out first the beam out of thy own eye, and then shalt thou see to cast out the mote out of thy brother's eye.

6 Give not that which is holy to dogs; neither cast ye your pearls before swine, lest perhaps they trample them under their feet, and turning upon you they tear you.

7 ᶜAsk and it shall be given you: seek and you shall find: knock, and it shall be opened to you.

8 For every one that asketh, receiveth: and he that seeketh, findeth: and to him that knocketh, it shall be opened.

9 ᵈOr what man is there among you, of whom if his son shall ask bread, will he reach him a stone?

10 Or if he shall ask him a fish, will he reach him a serpent?

11 If you then being evil, know how to give good gifts to your children: how much more will your Father who is in heaven, give good things to them that ask him?

12 ᵉAll things therefore whatsoever ye would that men should do to you, do you also to them. For this is the law and the prophets.

13 ᶠEnter ye in at the narrow gate: for wide is the gate, and broad is the way that leadeth to destruction, and many there are who go in thereat.

14 How narrow is the gate, and strait is the way that leadeth to life: and few there are that find it.

15 Beware of false prophets, who come to you in the clothing of sheep, but inwardly they are ravening wolves.

16 By their fruits you shall know them. Do men gather grapes of thorns, or figs of thistles?

17 Even so every good tree bringeth forth good fruit, and the evil tree bringeth forth evil fruit.

18 A good tree cannot bring forth evil fruit, neither can an evil tree bring forth good fruit.

19 ᵍEvery tree that bringeth not forth good fruit, shall be cut down and shall be cast into the fire.

20 Wherefore by their fruits you shall know them.

21 ʰNot every one that saith to me, Lord, Lord, shall enter into the kingdom of heaven; but he that doth the will of my Father who is in heaven, he shall enter into the kingdom of heaven.

22 Many will say to me in that day: Lord, Lord, have not we prophesied in thy name, ⁱand cast out devils in thy name, and done many miracles in thy name?

---

ᵃ Luke 6. 37. Rom. 2. 1.—ᵇ Mark 4. 24.—ᶜInfra, 21. 22. Mark 11. 24. Luke 11. 9. John 14. 13. Jas. 1. 6.—ᵈLuke 11. 11.

ᵉTobias 4. 16. Luke 6. 31.—ᶠLuke 13. 24.—ᵍSupra, 3. 10.—ʰInfra, 25. 11. Luke 6. 46.—ⁱActs 19. 13.

13

23 And then will I profess unto them, I never knew you: *a* depart from me, you that work iniquity.

24 *b* Every one therefore that heareth these my words, and doth them, shall be likened to a wise man that built his house upon a rock.

25 And the rain fell, and the floods came, and the winds blew, and they beat upon that house, and it fell not, for it was founded on a rock.

26 And every one that heareth these my words, and doth them not, shall be like a foolish man that built his house upon the sand.

27 And the rain fell, and the floods came, and the winds blew, and they beat upon that house, and it fell, and great was the fall thereof.

28 And it came to pass when JESUS had fully ended these words, the people were in admiration at his doctrine.

29 *c* For he was teaching them as one having power, and not as their scribes and Pharisees.

## CHAP. VIII.

*Christ cleanses the leper, heals the centurion's servant, Peter's mother-in-law, and many others: he stills the storm at sea, drives the devils out of two men possessed, and suffers them to go into the swine.*

AND *d* when he was come down from the mountain, great multitudes followed him:

2 *e* And behold a leper came and adored him, saying: Lord, if thou wilt, thou canst make me clean.

3 And JESUS stretching forth his hand, touched him, saying: I will, be thou made clean. And forthwith his leprosy was cleansed.

4 And JESUS saith to him: See thou tell no man: but go, *f* show thyself to the priest, and offer the gift which Moses commanded, for a testimony unto them.

5 *g* And when he had entered into Capharnaum, there came to him a centurion, beseeching him,

6 And saying, Lord, my servant lieth at home sick of the palsy, and is grievously tormented.

7 And JESUS saith to him: I will come and heal him.

8 And the centurion, making answer, said: *h* Lord, I am not worthy that thou shouldst enter under my roof; but only say the word, and my servant shall be healed.

9 For I also am a man subject to authority, having under me soldiers; and I say to this, Go, and he goeth, and to another, Come, and he cometh, and to my servant, Do this, and he doeth it.

10 And JESUS hearing this, marvelled; and said to them that followed him: Amen I say to you, I have not found so great faith in Israel.

11 And I say to you that many shall come from the east and the west, and shall sit down with Abraham, and Isaac, and Jacob in the kingdom of heaven:

12 But the children of the kingdom shall be cast out into the exterior darkness: there shall be weeping and gnashing of teeth.

---

*a* Ps. 6. 9. Infra, 25. 41. Luke 13. 27.
—*b* Luke 6. 46. Rom. 2. 13. Jas. 1. 22.
—*c* Mark 1. 22. Luke 4. 32.—*d* A.D. 31.
—*e* Mark 1. 40. Luke 5. 21.

*f* Lev. 14. 2.—*g* Luke 7. 1.—*h* Luke 7. 6.—*i* Mal. 1. 11.

13 And JESUS said to the centurion: Go, and as thou hast believed, so be it done to thee. And his servant was healed at the same hour.

14 And when JESUS was come into Peter's house, he saw his wife's mother lying, and sick of a fever.

15 And he touched her hand, and the fever left her, and she arose and ministered to them.

16 *And when evening was come, they brought to him many that were possessed with devils: and he cast out the spirits with his word: and all that were sick he healed.

17 That it might be fulfilled, which was spoken by the prophet *Isaias saying: *He took our infirmities, and bore our diseases.*

18 And JESUS seeing great multitudes about him, gave orders to pass over the water.

19 And a certain scribe came and said to him: Master, I will follow thee whithersoever thou shalt go.

20 And JESUS saith to him: *The foxes have holes, and the birds of the air nests; but the son of man hath not where to lay his head.

21 And another of his disciples said to him: Lord, suffer me first to go and bury my father.

22 But JESUS said to him: Follow me, and let the dead bury their dead.

23 *And when he entered into the boat, his disciples followed him:

24 And behold a great tempest arose in the sea, so that the boat was covered with waves, but he was asleep,

25 And they came to him, and awaked him, saying: Lord, save us, we perish.

26 And JESUS saith to them: Why are you fearful, O ye of little faith? Then rising up he commanded the winds, and the sea, and there came a great calm.

27 But the men wondered, saying: What manner of man is this, for the winds and the sea obey him?

28 *And when he was come on the other side of the water, into the country of the Gerasens, there met him two that were possessed with devils, coming out of the sepulchres, exceeding fierce, so that none could pass by that way.

29 And behold they cried out saying: What have we to do with thee, JESUS Son of God? art thou come hither to torment us before the time?

30 *And there was, not far from them, an herd of many swine feeding.

31 And the devils besought him saying: If thou cast us out hence, send us into the herd of swine.

32 And he said to them: Go. But they going out went into the swine, and behold the whole herd ran violently down a steep place into the sea: and they perished in the waters.

33 And they that kept them fled: and coming into the city, told everything, and concerning them that had been possessed by the devils.

34 And behold the whole city went out to meet JESUS, *and when they saw him, they besought him that he would depart from their coast.

## CHAP. IX.

*Christ heals one sick of the palsy: calls Matthew: cures the issue of blood: raises to life the daughter of Jairus: gives sight to two blind men: and heals a dumb man possessed by the devil.*

AND entering into a boat, he passed over the water and came into his own city.

2 *a* And behold they brought to him one sick of the palsy lying in a bed. And JESUS seeing their faith, said to the man sick of the palsy: Be of good heart, son, thy sins are forgiven thee.

3 And behold some of the scribes said within themselves: He blasphemeth.

4 And JESUS seeing their thoughts, said: Why do you think evil in your hearts?

5 Whether is easier, to say, Thy sins are forgiven thee: or to say, Arise and walk?

6 But that you may know that the son of man hath power on earth to forgive sins, (then said he to the man sick of the palsy,) Arise, take up thy bed, and go into thy house.

7 And he arose, and went into his house.

8 And the multitude seeing it, feared, and glorified God that gave such power to men.

9 *b* And when JESUS passed on from thence, he saw a man sitting in the custom-house, named Matthew; and he saith to him: Follow me. And he arose up and followed him.

10 And it came to pass as he was sitting at meat in the house, behold many publicans and sinners came, and sat down with JESUS and his disciples.

11 And the Pharisees seeing it, said to his disciples: Why doth your master eat with publicans and sinners?

12 But JESUS hearing it, said: They that are in health need not a physician, but they that are ill.

13 Go then and learn what this meaneth, *c I will have mercy, and not sacrifice.* For I am not come to call the just, *d* but sinners.

14 Then came to him the disciples of John, saying: *e* Why do we and the Pharisees fast often, but thy disciples do not fast?

15 And JESUS said to them: Can the children of the bridegroom mourn, as long as the bridegroom is with them? But the days will come, when the bridegroom shall be taken away from them, and then they shall fast.

16 And nobody putteth a piece of raw cloth unto an old garment. For it taketh away the fulness thereof from the garment, and there is made a greater rent.

17 Neither do they put new wine into old bottles. Otherwise the bottles break, and the wine runneth out, and the bottles perish. But new wine they put into new bottles: and both are preserved.

18 *f* As he was speaking these things unto them, behold a certain ruler came up, and adored him, saying: Lord, my

---

*c* Osee 6. 6. Infra, 12. 7.—*d* 1 Tim. 1. 15.—*e* Mark 2. 18. Luke 5. 33.—*f* Mark 5. 22. Luke 8. 41.

CHAP. IX. Ver. 15. *Can the children of the bridegroom.* This, by a Hebraism, signifies the *friends* or companions of the bridegroom.

---

*a* Mark 2. 3. Luke 5. 18.—*b* Mark 2. 14. Luke 5. 27.

BIRTH OF ST. JOHN THE BAPTIST.

daughter is even now dead; but come, lay thy hand upon her, and she shall live.

19 And JESUS rising up followed him, with his disciples.

20 *a* And behold a woman who was troubled with an issue of blood twelve years, came behind him, and touched the hem of his garment.

21 For she said within herself: If I shall touch only his garment, I shall be healed.

22 But JESUS turning and seeing her, said: Be of good heart, daughter, thy faith hath made thee whole. And the woman was made whole from that hour.

23 And when JESUS was come into the house of the ruler, and saw the minstrels and the multitude making a rout,

24 He said: Give place, for the girl is not dead, but sleepeth. And they laughed him to scorn.

25 And when the multitude was put forth, he went in, and took her by the hand. And the maid arose.

26 And the fame hereof went abroad into all that country.

27 And as JESUS passed from thence, there followed him two blind men crying out and saying, Have mercy on us, O Son of David.

28 And when he was come to the house, the blind men came to him. And JESUS saith to them, Do you believe, that I can do this unto you? They say to him, Yea, Lord.

29 Then he touched their eyes, saying, According to your faith, be it done unto you.

30 And their eyes were opened, and JESUS strictly charged them, saying, See that no man know this.

31 But they going out, spread his fame abroad in all that country.

32 And when they were gone out, *b* behold they brought him a dumb man, possessed with a devil.

33 And after the devil was cast out, the dumb man spoke, and the multitudes wondered saying, Never was the like seen in Israel.

34 But the Pharisees said, By the prince of devils he casteth out devils.

35 *c* And JESUS went about all the cities and towns, teaching in their synagogues, and preaching the gospel of the kingdom, and healing every disease, and every infirmity.

36 And seeing the multitudes, he had compassion on them, because they were distressed, and lying like sheep that have no shepherd.

37 Then he saith to his disciples, *d* The harvest indeed is great, but the labourers are few.

38 Pray ye therefore the Lord of the harvest, that he send forth labourers into his harvest.

## CHAP. X.

*Christ sends out his twelve apostles, with the power of miracles. The lessons he gives them.*

AND *e* having called his twelve disciples together, he gave them power over unclean spirits, to cast them out, and to heal all manner of diseases, and all manner of infirmities.

2 And the names of the twelve Apostles are these: The

---

*a* Mark 5. 25. Luke 8. 43.
*b* Infra, 12. 22. Luke 11. 14.—*c* Mark 6. 6.—*d* Luke 10. 2.—*e* Mark 3. 13. Luke 6. 13. and 9. 1.

first, Simon, who is called Peter, and Andrew his brother.

3 James the son of Zebedee, and John his brother, Philip and Bartholomew, Thomas and Matthew the publican, and James *the son* of Alpheus, and Thaddeus.

4 Simon the Cananean, and Judas Iscariot, who also betrayed him.

5 These twelve JESUS sent: commanding them, saying: Go ye not into the way of the gentiles, and into the cities of the Samaritans enter ye not:

6 But go ye rather *a*to the lost sheep of the house of Israel.

7 And going preach, saying: The kingdom of heaven is at hand.

8 Heal the sick, raise the dead, cleanse the lepers, cast out devils: freely have you received, freely give.

9 *b* Do not possess gold, nor silver, nor money in your purses.

10 Nor scrip for your journey, nor two coats, nor shoes, nor a staff; for the workman is worthy of his meat.

11 And into whatsoever city or town you shall enter, inquire who in it is worthy, and there abide till you go thence.

12 And when you come into the house, salute it, saying: Peace be to this house.

13 And if that house be worthy, your peace shall come upon it; but if it be not worthy, your peace shall return to you.

14 And whosoever shall not receive you, nor hear your words: going forth out of that house or city shake off the dust from your feet.

15 Amen I say to you, it shall be more tolerable for the land of Sodom and Gomorrha in the day of judgment, than for that city.

16 *c* Behold I send you as sheep in the midst of wolves. Be ye therefore wise as serpents and simple as doves.

17 But beware of men. For they will deliver you up in councils, and they will scourge you in their synagogues.

18 And you shall be brought before governors, and before kings for my sake, for a testimony to them and to the gentiles:

19 But when they shall deliver you up, *d* take no thought how or what to speak: for it shall be given you in that hour what to speak.

20 For it is not you that speak, but the Spirit of your Father that speaketh in you.

21 The brother also shall deliver up the brother to death, and the father the son; and the children shall rise up against their parents, and shall put them to death.

22 And you shall be hated by all men for my name's sake: but he that shall persevere unto the end, he shall be saved.

23 And when they shall persecute you in this city, flee into another. Amen I say to you, you shall not finish all the cities of Israel, till the son of man come.

24 *e* The disciple is not above the master, nor the servant above his lord.

25 It is enough for the dis-

---

*c* Luke 10. 3.—*d* Luke 12. 11.—*e* Luke 6. 40. John 13. 16 and 15. 20.

CHAP. X. Ver. 16. *Simple.* That is, harmless, plain, sincere, and without guile.

---

*a* Acts 13. 46.—*b* Mark 6. 8. Luke 9. 3. and 10. 4.

ciple that he be as his master, and the servant as his lord. If they have called the good-man of the house Beelzebub, how much more them of his household?

26 Therefore fear them not. *a* For nothing is covered that shall not be revealed; nor hid, that shall not be known.

27 That which I tell you in the dark, speak ye in the light: and that which you hear in the ear, preach ye upon the housetops.

28 And fear ye not them that kill the body, and are not able to kill the soul: but rather fear him that can destroy both soul and body into hell.

29 *b* Are not two sparrows sold for a farthing: and not one of them shall fall on the ground without your Father.

30 But the very hairs of your head are all numbered.

31 Fear not therefore: better are you than many sparrows.

32 *c* Every one therefore that shall confess me before men, I will also confess him before my Father who is in heaven.

33 But he that shall deny me before men, I will also deny him before my Father who is in heaven.

34 *d* Do not think that I came to send peace upon earth: I came not to send peace, but the sword.

35 For I came to set a man at variance against his father, and the daughter against her mother, and the daughter-in-law against her mother-in-law.

36 *e* And a man's enemies shall be they of his own household.

37 *f* He that loveth father or mother more than me, is not worthy of me; and he that loveth son or daughter more than me, is not worthy of me.

38 *g* And he that taketh not up his cross, and followeth me, is not worthy of me.

39 He that findeth his life, shall lose it: *h* and he that shall lose his life for me, shall find it.

40 *i* He that receiveth you, receiveth me: and he that receiveth me, receiveth him that sent me.

41 He that receiveth a prophet in the name of a prophet, shall receive the reward of a prophet: and he that receiveth a just man in the name of a just man, shall receive the reward of a just man.

42 *k* And whosoever shall give to drink to one of these little ones a cup of cold water only in the name of a disciple, amen I say to you, he shall not lose his reward.

## CHAP. XI.

*John sends his disciples to Christ, who upbraids the Jews with their incredulity, and calls to him such as are sensible of their burdens.*

AND it came to pass: when Jesus had made an end of commanding his twelve disci-

---

*a* Mark 4. 22. Luke 8. 17, and 12. 2.—*b* 2 Kings 14. 11. Acts 27. 35.—*c* Mark 8. 33. Luke 9. 26. and 12. 8. 2 Tim. 2. 12.—*d* Luke 12. 51.

Ver. 35. *I came to set a man at variance, &c.* Not that this was the end or design of the coming of our Saviour; but that his coming, and his doctrine would have this effect, by

*e* Mich. 7. 6.—*f* Luke 14. 26.—*g* Infra, 16. 24. Mark 8. 34. Luke 14. 27.—*h* Luke 9. 24. and 17. 33. John 12. 25.—*i* Luke 10. 16. John 13. 20.—*k* Mark 9. 40.

reason of the obstinate resistance that many would make, and of their persecuting all such as should adhere to him.

ples, he passed from thence, to teach and preach in their cities.

2 ᵃ Now when John had heard in prison the works of Christ: sending two of his disciples he said to him:

3 Art thou he that art to come, or look we for another?

4 And JESUS making answer said to them: Go and relate to John what you have heard and seen.

5 ᵇ The blind see, the lame walk, the lepers are cleansed, the deaf hear, the dead rise again, ᶜ the poor have the gospel preached to them.

6 And blessed is he that shall not be scandalized in me.

7 ᵈ And when they went their way, JESUS began to say to the multitudes concerning John: What went you out into the desert to see? a reed shaken with the wind?

8 But what went you out to see? a man clothed in soft garments? Behold they that are clothed in soft garments, are in the houses of kings.

9 But what went you out to see? a prophet? yea I tell you, and more than a prophet.

10 For this is he of whom it is written: ᵉ *Behold I send my Angel before thy face, who shall prepare thy way before thee.*

11 Amen I say to you, there hath not risen among them that are born of women a greater than John the Baptist: yet he that is the lesser in the kingdom of heaven is greater than he.

12 And from the days of John the Baptist until now, the kingdom of heaven suffereth violence, and the violent bear it away.

13 For all the prophets and the law prophesied until John:

14 And if you will receive it, he is Elias that is to come.

15 He that hath ears to hear, let him hear

16 But whereunto shall I esteem this generation to be like? It is like to children sitting in the market-place.

17 Who crying to their companions say: We have piped to you, and you have not danced: we have lamented, and you have not mourned.

18 For John came neither eating nor drinking: and they say: He hath a devil.

19 The son of man came eating and drinking, and they say: Behold a man that is a glutton and a wine-drinker, a friend of publicans and sinners. And wisdom is justified by her children.

20 Then began he to upbraid the cities, wherein were done the most of his miracles, for that they had not done penance.

21 ᵍ Wo to thee, Corozain, wo to thee, Bethsaida: for if in Tyre and Sidon had been wrought the miracles that have been wrought in you, they had long ago done penance in sackcloth and ashes.

22 But I say unto you, it shall be more tolerable for Tyre and

---

ᵃ Luke 7. 18.—ᵇ Isaias 35. 5.—ᶜ Isaias, 61. 1.—ᵈ Luke 7. 24.—ᵉ Mal. 3. 1. Mark 1. 2. Luke 7. 27.

ᶠ Mal. 4. 5.—ᵍ Luke 10. 13.

---

CHAP. XI. Ver. 6. *Scandalized in me.* That is, who shall not take occasion of scandal or offence from my humility, and the disgraceful death of the cross which I shall endure.

Ver. 12. *Suffereth violence,* &c. It is not to be obtained but by main force, by using violence upon ourselves, by mortification and penance, and resisting our perverse inclinations.

Ver. 14. *He is Elias,* &c. Not in person, but in spirit.—*Luke* 1. 17.

THE ANGELS ANNOUNCE THE BIRTH OF CHRIST.

Sidon in the day of judgment, than for you.

23 And thou Capharnaum, shalt thou be exalted up to heaven? thou shalt go down even unto hell. For if in Sodom had been wrought the miracles that have been wrought in thee, perhaps it had remained unto this day.

24 But I say unto you, that it shall be more tolerable for the land of Sodom in the day of judgment, than for thee.

25 At that time Jesus answered and said: I confess to thee, O Father, Lord of heaven and earth, because thou hast hid these things from the wise and prudent, and hast revealed them to little ones.

26 Yea, Father; for so hath it seemed good in thy sight.

27 All things are delivered to me by my Father. *a* And no one knoweth the Son, but the Father: neither doth any one know the Father, but the Son, and he to whom it shall please the Son to reveal *him.*

28 Come to me, all you that labour, and are burdened, and I will refresh you.

29 Take up my yoke upon you, and learn of me, because I am meek, and humble of heart: *b* And you shall find rest to your souls.

30 *c* For my yoke is sweet and my burden light.

## CHAP. XII.

*Christ reproves the blindness of the Pharisees, and confutes their attributing his miracles to satan.*

AT *d* that time Jesus went through the corn on the sabbath: and his disciples being hungry, began to pluck the ears, and to eat.

2 And the Pharisees seeing them, said to him: Behold thy disciples do that which is not lawful to do on the sabbath-days.

3 But he said to them: Have you not read *e* what David did when he was hungry, and they that were with him:

4 How he entered into the house of God, and did eat the loaves of proposition, which it was not lawful for him to eat, nor for them that were with him, *f* but for the priests only?

5 Or have ye not read in the law, *g* that on the sabbath-days the priests in the temple break the sabbath, and are without blame?

6 But I tell you that there is here a greater than the temple.

7 And if you knew what this meaneth: *h I will have mercy, and not sacrifice:* you would never have condemned the innocent.

8 For the son of man is Lord even of the sabbath.

9 And when he had passed from thence, he came into their synagogue.

10 *i* And behold there was a man who had a withered hand, and they asked him, saying: Is it lawful to heal on the sabbath-days? that they might accuse him.

11 But he said to them:

---

*a* John 4. 44. 7. 28. 8. 19. and 10. 15.—*b* Jer. 6. 16.—*c* 1 John 5. 3.—*d* Mark 2. 23. Luke 6. 1.

*e* 1 Kings 21. 6.—*f* Lev. 24. 9.—*g* Num. 28. 9.—*h* 1 Kings 15. 22. Eccle. 4. 17. Osee 6. 6. Supra, 9. 13.—*i* Mark 3. 1. Luke 6. 6.

CHAP. XII. Ver. 4. *The loaves of proposition.* So were called the twelve loaves which were placed before the sanctuary in the temple of God.

* What man shall there be among you, that hath one sheep: and if the same fall into a pit on the sabbath-day, will he not take hold on it and lift it up?

12 How much better is a man than a sheep? Therefore it is lawful to do a good deed on the sabbath-days.

13 Then he saith to the man: Stretch forth thy hand, and he stretched it forth, and it was restored to health even as the other.

14 And the Pharisees going out made a consultation against him, how they might destroy him.

15 But JESUS knowing it, retired from thence: and many followed him, and he healed them all.

16 And he charged them that they should not make him known.

17 That it might be fulfilled which was spoken by Isaias the prophet, saying:

18 *b Behold my servant whom I have chosen, my beloved in whom my soul hath been well pleased. I will put my Spirit upon him, and he shall show judgment to the gentiles.*

19 *He shall not contend, nor cry out, neither shall any man hear his voice in the streets.*

20 *The bruised reed he shall not break, and smoking flax he shall not extinguish: till he send forth judgment unto victory.*

21 *And in his name the gentiles shall hope.*

22 Then was offered to him one possessed with a devil, blind and dumb: and he healed him, so that he spoke and saw.

23 And all the multitudes were amazed, and said: Is not this the son of David?

24 *c* But the Pharisees hearing it, said: This man casteth not out devils but by Beelzebub the prince of the devils.

25 And JESUS knowing their thoughts, said to them: *d Every kingdom divided against itself shall be made desolate: and every city or house divided against itself shall not stand.*

26 And if satan cast out satan, he is divided against himself: how then shall his kingdom stand?

27 And if I by Beelzebub cast out devils, by whom do your children cast them out? Therefore they shall be your judges.

28 But if I by the Spirit of God cast out devils, then is the kingdom of God come upon you.

29 Or how can any one enter into the house of the strong, and rifle his goods, unless he first bind the strong? and then he will rifle his house.

30 He that is not with me, is against me: and he that gathereth not with me, scattereth.

31 *e* Therefore I say to you:

*c Supra, 9. 34. Mark 3. 22. Luke 11. 15.—d Luke 11. 17.—f Mark 3. 28. and 29. Luke 12. 10.*

Ver. 31. *The blasphemy of the Spirit.* The sin here spoken of is that blasphemy, by which the Pharisees attributed the miracles of Christ, wrought by the Spirit of God, to Beelzebub the prince of devils. Now, this kind of sin is usually accompanied with so much obstinacy, and such wilful opposing the Spirit of God, and the known truth, that men who are guilty of it, are seldom or ever converted: and therefore are never forgiven, because they will not repent. Otherwise there is no sin, which God cannot or will not forgive to such as sincerely repent, and have recourse to the keys of the church.

*a Deut. 22. 4.—b Isaias 42. 1.*

Every sin and blasphemy shall be forgiven men, but the blasphemy of the Spirit shall not be forgiven.

32 And whosoever shall speak a word against the son of man, it shall be forgiven him: but he that shall speak against the Holy Ghost, it shall not be forgiven him neither in this world, nor in the world to come.

33 Either make the tree good and its fruit good: or make the tree evil, and its fruit evil. For by the fruit the tree is known.

34 O generation of vipers, how can you speak good things, whereas you are evil? ᵃfor out of the abundance of the heart the mouth speaketh.

35 A good man out of a good treasure bringeth forth good things: and an evil man out of an evil treasure bringeth forth evil things.

36 But I say unto you, that every idle word that men shall speak, they shall render an account for it in the day of judgment.

37 For by thy words thou shalt be justified, and by thy words thou shalt be condemned.

38 Then some of the Scribes and Pharisees answered him, saying: Master, we would see a sign from thee.

39 Who answering said to them: ᵇAn evil and adulterous generation seeketh a sign: and a sign shall not be given it, ᶜbut the sign of Jonas the prophet.

40 For as Jonas was in the whale's belly three days and three nights: so shall the son of man be in the heart of the earth three days and three nights.

41 ᵈThe men of Ninive shall rise in judgment with this generation, and shall condemn it: because they did penance at the preaching of Jonas. And behold a greater than Jonas here.

42 The queen of the south shall rise in judgment with this generation, and shall condemn it: ᵉbecause she came from the ends of the earth to hear the wisdom of Solomon, and behold a greater than Solomon here.

43 ᶠAnd when an unclean spirit is gone out of a man he walketh through dry places seeking rest, and findeth none.

44 Then he saith: I will return into my house from whence I came out. And coming he findeth it empty, swept, and garnished.

45 Then he goeth, and taketh with him seven other spirits more wicked than himself, and they enter in and dwell there: ᵍand the last state of that man is made worse than the first. So shall it be also to this wicked generation.

---

ᵃ Luke 6. 45.

ᵇ Infra. 16. 4. Luke 11. 29. 1 Cor. 1. 22.—ᶜJonas 2. 1.—ᵈJonas 3. 5.—ᵉ3 Kings 10. 1. 2 Par. 9. 1.—ᶠLuke 11. 24.—ᵍ2 Pet. 2. 20.

Ver. 32. *Nor in the world to come.* From these words St. *Augustine* (De Civ. l. xxi. c. 13.) and St. *Gregory* (Dialog. iv. c. 39.) gather, that some sins may be remitted in the world to come: and, consequently, that there is a purgatory or a middle place.

Ver. 36. *Every idle word.* This shews there must be a place of temporal punishment hereafter where these slighter faults shall be punished.

Ver. 38. *A sign.* That is, a miracle from heaven. St. Luke xi. 16.

Ver. 40. *Three days, &c.* Not complete days and nights; but part of three days, and three nights, taken according to the way that the Hebrews counted their days and nights, viz., from evening to evening.

23

46 ᵃ As he was yet speaking to the multitudes, behold his mother and his brethren stood without, seeking to speak to him.

47 And one said unto him: Behold thy mother and thy brethren stand without, seeking thee.

48 But he answering him that told him, said: Who is my mother, and who are my brethren?

49 And stretching forth his hand towards his disciples, he said: Behold my mother and my brethren.

50 For whosoever shall do the will of my Father, that is in heaven, he is my brother, and sister, and mother.

## CHAP. XIII.

*The parables of the sower and the cockle; of the mustard-seed, &c.*

THE same day JESUS going out of the house, sat by the sea side.

2 ᵇ And great multitudes were gathered together unto him, so that he went up into a boat and sat: and all the multitude stood on the shore.

3 And he spoke to them many things in parables, saying: Behold the sower went forth to sow.

4 And whilst he soweth some fell by the way side, and the birds of the air came and ate them up.

5 And other some fell upon stony ground, where they had not much earth: and they sprung up immediately, because they had no deepness of earth.

6 And when the sun was up they were scorched: and because they had not root, they withered away.

7 And others fell among thorns: and the thorns grew up and choked them.

8 And others fell upon good ground: and they brought forth fruit, some an hundred fold, some sixty fold, and some thirty fold.

9 He that hath ears to hear let him hear.

10 And his disciples came and said to him: Why speakest thou to them in parables?

11 Who answered and said to them: Because to you it is given to know the mysteries of the kingdom of heaven: but to them it is not given.

12 ᶜ For he that hath, to him shall be given, and he shall abound: but he that hath not, from him shall be taken away that also which he hath.

13 Therefore do I speak to them in parables: because seeing they see not, and hearing they hear not, neither do they understand.

14 And the prophecy of Isaias is fulfilled in them, who saith: ᵈ *By hearing you shall hear, and shall not understand: and seeing you shall see, and shall not perceive.*

15 *For the heart of this people is grown gross, and with their ears they have been dull of hear-*

---

ᵃ Mark 8. 31. Luke 8. 19.—ᵇ Mark 4. 1. Luke 8. 4.

Ver. 48. *Who is my mother?* This was not spoken by way of slighting his mother, but to show that we are never to suffer ourselves to be taken from the service of God, by any inordinate affection to our earthly parents: and that which our Lord chiefly regarded in his mother, was her doing the will of his Father in heaven. It may also further allude to the reprobation of the Jews, his carnal kindred, and the election of the Gentiles.

ᶜ Infra, 25. 29.—ᵈ Isaias 6. 9. Mark 4. 12. Luke 8. 10. John 12. 40. Acts 28. 26. Rom. 11. 8.

THE SHEPHERDS ADORING THE NEW-BORN SAVIOUR.

ing, and their eyes they have shut: lest at any time they should see with their eyes, and hear with their ears, and understand with their heart, and be converted, and I should heal them.

16 But blessed are your eyes, because they see, and your ears, because they hear.

17 ᵃ For, amen I say to you, many prophets and just men have desired to see the things that you see, and have not seen them: and to hear the things that you hear and have not heard them.

18 Hear you therefore the parable of the sower.

19 When any one heareth the word of the kingdom, and understandeth it not, there cometh the wicked one, and catcheth away that which was sown in his heart: this is he that received the seed by the way side.

20 And he that received the seed upon stony ground: this is he that heareth the word, and immediately receiveth it with joy.

21 Yet hath he not root in himself, but is only for a time: and when there ariseth tribulation and persecution because of the word, he is presently scandalized.

22 And he that received the seed among thorns: is he that heareth the word, and the care of this world and the deceitfulness of riches choketh up the word, and he becometh fruitless.

23 But he that received the seed upon good ground: this is he that heareth the word, and understandeth, and beareth fruit, and yieldeth the one an hundred fold, and another sixty and another thirty.

24 ᵇ Another parable he proposed to them, saying: The kingdom of heaven is likened to a man that sowed good seed in his field.

25 But while men were asleep, his enemy came and oversowed cockle among the wheat, and went his way.

26 And when the blade was sprung up, and had brought forth fruit, then appeared also the cockle.

27 And the servants of the good-man of the house coming said to him: Sir, didst thou not sow good seed in thy field? whence then hath it cockle?

28 And he said to them: An enemy hath done this. And the servants said to him: Wilt thou that we go and gather it up?

29 And he said: No, lest perhaps, gathering up the cockle, you root up the wheat also together with it.

30 Suffer both to grow until the harvest, and in the time of the harvest I will say to the reapers: Gather up first the cockle, and bind it into bundles to burn, but the wheat gather ye into my barn.

31 ᶜ Another parable he proposed to them, saying: The kingdom of heaven is like to a grain of mustard-seed, which a man took and sowed in his field.

32 Which is the least indeed of all seeds, but when it is grown up, it is greater than all herbs, and becometh a tree, so that the birds of the air come and dwell in the branches thereof.

33 Another parable he spoke

---

ᵃ Luke 10. 24.   ᵇ Mark 4. 26.—ᶜ Mark 4. 31. Luke 13. 19.

to them: *a* The kingdom of heaven is like to leaven, which a woman took and hid in three measures of meal, until the whole was leavened.

34 All these things Jesus spoke in parables to the multitudes: and without parables he did not speak to them.

35 That it might be fulfilled which was spoken by the prophet, saying: *b I will open my mouth in parables, I will utter things hidden from the foundation of the world.*

36 *c* Then having sent away the multitudes, he came into the house, and his disciples came to him, saying: Expound to us the parable of the cockle of the field.

37 Who made answer and said to them: He that soweth the good seed is the son of man.

38 And the field is the world. And the good seed are the children of the kingdom. And the cockle, are the children of the wicked one.

39 And the enemy that sowed them, is the devil. *d* But the harvest is the end of the world. And the reapers are the Angels.

40 Even as cockle therefore is gathered up, and burnt with fire: so shall it be at the end of the world.

41 The son of man shall send his Angels, and they shall gather out of his kingdom all scandals, and them that work iniquity.

42 And shall cast them into the furnace of fire: There shall be weeping and gnashing of teeth.

43 *e* Then shall the just shine as the sun, in the kingdom of their Father. He that hath ears to hear, let him hear.

44 The kingdom of heaven is like unto a treasure hidden in a field. Which a man having found, hid it, and for joy thereof goeth, and selleth all that he hath, and buyeth that field.

45 Again the kingdom of heaven is like to a merchant seeking good pearls.

46 Who when he had found one pearl of great price, went his way, and sold all that he had, and bought it.

47 Again the kingdom of heaven is like to a net cast into the sea, and gathering together of all kinds of fishes.

48 Which, when it was filled, they drew out, and sitting by the shore, they chose out the good into vessels, but the bad they cast forth.

49 So shall it be at the end of the world. The Angels shall go out, and shall separate the wicked from among the just.

50 And shall cast them into the furnace of fire: there shall be weeping and gnashing of teeth.

51 Have ye understood all these things? They say to him: Yes.

52 He said unto them: Therefore every scribe instructed in the kingdom of heaven, is like to a man that is a householder, who bringeth forth out of his treasure new things and old.

53 And it came to pass: when Jesus had finished these parables, he passed from thence.

54 *f* And coming into his own country, he taught them in their synagogues, so that they wondered and said How came this

*a* Luke 13. 21.—*b* Ps. 77. 2.—*c* Mark 4. 34.—*d* Apoc. 14. 15.—*e* Wisd. 3. 7. Dan. 12. 3.

*f* Mark 6. 1. Luke 4. 16.

man by this wisdom and miracles?

55 ᵃIs not this the carpenter's son? Is not his mother called Mary, and his brethren James, and Joseph, and Simon, and Jude:

56 And his sisters, are they not all with us? Whence therefore hath he all these things?

57 And they were scandalized in his regard. But JESUS said to them: A prophet is not without honour, save in his own country, and in his own house.

58 And he wrought not many miracles there, because of their unbelief.

## CHAP. XIV.

*Herod puts John to death. Christ feeds five thousand in the desert. He walks upon the sea, and heals all the diseased with the touch of his garment.*

AT ᵇthat time Herod the Tetrarch heard the fame of JESUS.

2 And he said to his servants: This is John the Baptist: he is risen from the dead, and therefore mighty works shew forth themselves in him.

3 ᶜFor Herod had apprehended John and bound him, and put him into prison, because of Herodias, his brother's wife.

4 For John said to him: It is not lawful for thee to have her.

5 And having a mind to put him to death, he feared the people: ᵈbecause they esteemed him as a prophet.

6 But on Herod's birth-day, the daughter of Herodias danced before them: and pleased Herod.

7 Whereupon he promised with an oath, to give her whatsoever she would ask of him.

8 But she being instructed before by her mother, said: Give me here in a dish the head of John the Baptist.

9 And the king was struck sad: yet because of his oath, and for them that sat with him at table, he commanded it to be given.

10 And he sent, and beheaded John in the prison.

11 And his head was brought in a dish: and it was given to the damsel, and she brought it to her mother.

12 And his disciples came and took the body, and buried it, and came and told JESUS.

13 ᵉ Which when JESUS had heard, he retired from thence by a boat, into a desert place apart, and the multitudes having heard of it, followed him on foot out of the cities.

14 And he coming forth saw a great multitude, and had compassion on them, and healed their sick.

15 And when it was evening, his disciples came to him, saying: This is a desert place, and the hour is now passed: send away the multitudes, that going into the towns, they may buy themselves victuals.

---

ᵃ John 6. 42.—ᵇ Mark 6. 14. Luke 9. 7. A.D. 32.—ᶜ Mark 6. 17. Luke 3. 19.

CHAP. XIII. Ver. 55. *His brethren.* These were the children of *Mary,* the wife of *Cleophas,* sister to our Blessed Lady (St. Matt. xxvii. 56: St. John xix. 25), and therefore, according to the usual style of the Scripture, they were called *brethren,* that is, *near relations* to our Saviour.

CHAP. XIV. Ver. 1. *Tetrarch.* This word, derived from the Greek, signifies one that rules over the fourth part of a kingdom: as *Herod* then ruled over *Galilee,* which was but the fourth part of the kingdom of his father.

ᵈ Infra. 21. 26.—ᵉ Mark 6. 31. Luke 9. 10. John 6. 3.

16 But Jesus said to them, They have no need to go: give you them to eat.

17 They answered him: We have not here but five loaves, and two fishes.

18 Who said to them: Bring them hither to me.

19 And when he had commanded the multitude to sit down upon the grass, he took the five loaves and the two fishes, and looking up to heaven, he blessed, and brake, and gave the loaves to his disciples, and the disciples to the multitudes.

20 And they did all eat, and were filled. And they took up what remained, twelve full baskets of fragments.

21 And the number of them that did eat, was five thousand men, besides women and children.

22 ᵇ And forthwith JESUS obliged his disciples to go up into the boat, and to go before him over the water, till he dismissed the people.

23 And having dismissed the multitude, ᶜ he went up into a mountain alone to pray. And when it was evening, he was there alone.

24 But the boat in the midst of the sea was tossed with the waves: for the wind was contrary.

25 And in the fourth watch of the night, he came to them walking upon the sea.

26 And they seeing him walking upon the sea, were troubled, saying: It is an apparition. And they cried out for fear.

27 And immediately JESUS spoke to them, saying: Be of good heart: It is I, fear ye not.

28 And Peter making answer said: Lord, if it be thou, bid me come to thee upon the waters.

29 And he said: Come. And Peter going down out of the boat, walked upon the water to come to Jesus.

30 But seeing the wind strong, he was afraid: and when he began to sink, he cried out, saying: Lord, save me.

31 And immediately JESUS stretching forth his hand took hold of him, and said to him: O thou of little faith, why didst thou doubt?

32 And when they were come up into the boat, the wind ceased.

33 And they that were in the boat came and adored him, saying: Indeed thou art the Son of God.

34 ᵈ And having passed the water, they came into the country of Genesar.

35 And when the men of that place had knowledge of him, they sent into all that country, and brought to him all that were diseased.

36 And they besought him that they might touch but the hem of his garment. And as many as touched, were made whole.

## CHAP. XV.

*Christ reproves the scribes. He cures the daughter of the woman of Canaan; and many others: and feeds four thousand with seven loaves.*

THEN ᵃ came to him from Jerusalem scribes and Pharisees, saying:

---

ᵃ John 6. 9.—ᵇ Mark 6. 45.—ᶜ John 6. 15. Mark 6. 46.

ᵈ Mark 6. 53.—ᵉ Mark 7. 1.

THE SHEPHERDS ANNOUNCE THE BIRTH OF CHRIST.

ST. MATTHEW.

2 *Why do thy disciples transgress the tradition of the ancients? For they wash not their hands when they eat bread.
3 But he answering, said to them: Why do you also transgress the commandment of God for your tradition? For God said:
4 *Honour thy father and mother: *And: He that shall curse father or mother, let him die the death.
5 But you say: Whosoever shall say to father or mother, The gift whatsoever proceedeth from me, shall profit thee.
6 And he shall not honour his father or his mother; and you have made void the commandment of God for your tradition.
7 Hypocrites, well hath Isaias prophesied of you, saying:
8 *This people honoureth me with their lips: but their heart is far from me.
9 And in vain do they worship me, teaching doctrines and commandments of men.

*Mark 7. 5.—*Exod. 20. 12. Deut. 5. 16. Ephes. 6. 2.—*Exod. 21. 17. Lev. 20. 9. Prov. 20. 20.—*Isaias 29. 13. Mark 7. 6.

CHAP. XV. Ver. 5. *The gift, &c.* That is, the offering that I shall make to God, shall be instead of that which should be expended for thy profit. This tradition of the Pharisees was calculated to enrich themselves; by exempting children from giving any further assistance to their parents, if they once offered to the temple and the priests, that which should have been the support of their parents. But this was a violation of the law of God, and of nature, which our Saviour here condemns.
Ver. 9. *Commandments of men.* The doctrines and commandments here reprehended are such as are either contrary to the law of God (as that of neglecting parents, under pretence of giving to God), or at least are frivolous, unprofitable, and no ways conducing to true piety, as that of often

10 And having called together the multitudes unto him, he said to them: Hear ye and understand.
11 Not that which goeth into the mouth, defileth a man: but what cometh out of the mouth, this defileth a man.
12 Then came his disciples, and said to him: Dost thou know that the Pharisees, when they heard this word, were scandalized?
13 But he answering said:* Every plant which my heavenly Father hath not planted, shall be rooted up.

*John 15. 2.

washing hands, &c., without regard to the purity of the heart. But as to the rules and ordinances of the holy church, touching fasts, festivals, &c., these are no ways repugnant to, but highly agreeable to God's holy word, and all christian piety: neither are they to be counted among the doctrines and commandments of men; because they proceed not from mere human authority; but from that which Christ has established in his Church; whose pastors he has commanded us to hear and obey, even as himself. St. Luke x. 16. St. Matt. xviii. 17.
Ver. 11. *Not that which goeth into, &c.* No uncleanness in meat, nor any dirt contracted by eating it with unwashed hands, can defile the soul: but sin alone; or a disobedience of the heart to the ordinance and will of God. And thus when Adam took the forbidden fruit, it was not the apple, which entered into the mouth, but the disobedience to the law of God which defiled him. The same is to be said if a Jew, in the time of the old law, had eaten swine's flesh, or a christian convert, in the days of the Apostles, contrary to their ordinance, had eaten blood; or if any of the faithful at present should transgress the ordinance of God's Church, by breaking the fasts: For in all these cases the soul would be defiled; not indeed by that which goeth into the mouth: but by the disobedience of the heart, in wilfully transgressing the ordinance of God, or of those who have their authority from him.

14 Let them alone: <sup>a</sup>they are blind, and leaders of the blind. And if the blind lead the blind, both fall into the pit.

15 <sup>b</sup> And Peter answering said to him: Expound to us this parable.

16 But he said: Are you also yet without understanding?

17 Do you not understand, that whatsoever entereth into the mouth, goeth into the belly, and is cast out into the privy?

18 But the things which proceed out of the mouth, come forth from the heart, and those things defile a man.

19 For from the heart come forth evil thoughts, murders, adulteries, fornications, thefts, false testimonies, blasphemies.

20 These are the things that defile a man. But to eat with unwashed hands doth not defile a man.

21 <sup>c</sup> And Jesus went from thence, and retired into the coasts of Tyre and Sidon.

22 And behold a woman of Canaan who came out of those coasts, crying out, said to him: Have mercy on me, O Lord, thou son of David: my daughter is grievously troubled by a devil.

23 Who answered her not a word. And his disciples came and besought him, saying: Send her away, for she crieth after us:

24 And he answering, said: I was not sent <sup>d</sup> but to the sheep that are lost of the house of Israel.

25 But she came and adored him, saying: Lord, help me.

26 Who answering, said: It is not good to take the bread of the children, and to cast it to the dogs.

27 But she said: Yea, Lord: for the whelps also eat of the crumbs that fall from the table of their masters.

28 Then Jesus answering, said to her: O woman, great is thy faith: be it done to thee as thou wilt: and her daughter was cured from that hour.

29 And when Jesus had passed away from thence, he came nigh the sea of Galilee: and going up into a mountain, he sat there.

30 <sup>e</sup> And there came to him great multitudes, having with them the dumb, the blind, the lame, the maimed, and many others: and they cast them down at his feet, and he healed them:

31 So that the multitudes marvelled seeing the dumb speak, the lame walk, the blind see: and they glorified the God of Israel.

32 <sup>f</sup> And Jesus called together his disciples, and said: I have compassion on the multitudes, because they continue with me now three days, and have not what to eat: and I will not send them away fasting, lest they faint in the way.

33 And the disciples say unto him: Whence then should we have so many loaves in the desert, as to fill so great a multitude?

34 And Jesus said to them: How many loaves have you? But they said: Seven, and a few little fishes.

35 And he commanded the multitude to sit down upon the ground.

36 And taking the seven loaves and the fishes, and giving thanks,

---

<sup>a</sup> Luke 6. 39.—<sup>b</sup> Mark 7. 17.—<sup>c</sup> Mark 7. 24.—<sup>d</sup> Supra, 10. 6. John 10. 3.

<sup>e</sup> Isaias 35. 5.—<sup>f</sup> Mark 8. 1.

he brake, and gave to his disciples, and the disciples gave to the people.

37 And they did all eat, and had their fill. And they took up, seven baskets full, of what remained of the fragments.

38 And they that did eat, were four thousand men, besides children and women.

39 And having dismissed the multitude, he went up into a boat, and came into the coasts of Magedan.

## CHAP. XVI.

*Christ refuses to show the Pharisees a sign from heaven. Peter's confession is rewarded. He is rebuked for opposing Christ's passion. All his followers must deny themselves.*

AND *a* there came to him the Pharisees and Sadducees tempting: and they asked him to show them a sign from heaven.

2 But he answered and said to them: *b* When it is evening, you say: It will be fair weather, for the sky is red.

3 And in the morning: To-day *there will be* a storm, for the sky is red and lowering: You know then how to discern the face of the sky: and can you not know the signs of the times?

4 *c* A wicked and adulterous generation seeketh after a sign: and a sign shall not be given it, *d* but the sign of Jonas the prophet. And he left them and went away.

5 And when his disciples were come over the water, they had forgotten to take bread.

6 Who said to them: *e* Take heed and beware of the leaven of the Pharisees and Sadducees.

7 But they thought within themselves, saying: Because we have taken no bread.

8 And JESUS knowing it, said: Why do you think within yourselves, O ye of little faith, for that you have no bread?

9 Do you not yet understand, neither do you remember *f* the five loaves among five thousand men, and how many baskets you took up?

10 *g* Nor the seven loaves, among four thousand men, and how many baskets you took up?

11 Why do you not understand that it was not concerning bread I said to you: Beware of the leaven of the Pharisees and Sadducees?

12 Then they understood that he said not that they should beware of the leaven of bread, but of the doctrine of the Pharisees and Sadducees.

13 *h* And JESUS came into the quarters of Cesarea Philippi: and he asked his disciples, saying: Whom do men say that the son of man is?

14 But they said: 'Some John the Baptist, and other some Elias, and others Jeremias, or one of the prophets.

15 JESUS saith to them: But whom do you say that I am?

16 Simon Peter answered and said: *k* Thou art Christ the Son of the living God.

17 And JESUS answering, said to him: Blessed art thou, Simon Bar-Jona: because flesh and blood hath not revealed it to thee, but my Father who is in heaven.

---

*a* Mark 8. 11.—*b* Luke 12. 54.—*c* Supra, 12. 39.—*d* Jonas 2. 1.—*e* Mark 8. 15. Luke 12. 1. *f* Supra, 14. 17. John 6. 9.—*g* Supra, 15. 34.—*h* Mark 8. 27.—*i* Mark 6. 28. Luke 9. 19.—*k* John 6. 70.

18 <sup>a</sup> And I say to thee: That thou art Peter; and upon this rock I will build my church, and the gates of hell shall not prevail against it.

19 <sup>b</sup> And I will give to thee the keys of the kingdom of heaven. <sup>c</sup> And whatsoever thou shalt bind upon earth, it shall be bound also in heaven: and whatsoever thou shalt loose on earth, it shall be loosed also in heaven.

20 Then he commanded his disciples, that they should tell no one that he was JESUS the CHRIST.

21 From that time JESUS began to show to his disciples, that he must go to Jerusalem, and suffer many things from the ancients and scribes and chief priests, and be put to death, and the third day rise again.

22 And Peter taking him, began to rebuke him, saying: Lord, be it far from thee, this shall not be unto thee.

23 Who turning said to Peter: <sup>d</sup> Go behind me, satan, thou art a scandal unto me: because thou savourest not the things that are of God, but the things that are of men.

24 Then JESUS said to his disciples: <sup>e</sup> If any man will come after me, let him deny himself, and take up his cross, and follow me

25 <sup>f</sup> For he that will save his

---

<sup>a</sup> John 12. 42.—<sup>b</sup> Isaias 22. 22.

CHAP. XVI. Ver. 18. *Thou art Peter, &c.* As St. *Peter*, by divine revelation, here made a solemn profession of his faith of the divinity of Christ; so in recompense of this faith and profession, our Lord here declares to him the dignity to which he is pleased to raise him: *Viz.*, that he, to whom he had already given the name of *Peter*, signifying a rock, St. John 1. 42, should be a rock indeed, of invincible strength, for the support of the building of the Church; in which building he should be, next to Christ himself, the chief foundation stone, in quality of chief pastor, ruler, and governor; and should have accordingly all fulness of ecclesiastical power, signified by the keys of the kingdom of heaven.—Ibid. *Upon this rock, &c.* The words of Christ to *Peter*, spoken in the vulgar language of the *Jews* which our Lord made use of, were the same as if he had said in *English, Thou art a Rock, and upon this rock I will build my church.* So that, by the plain course of the words, *Peter* is here declared to be the rock, upon which the church was to be built: Christ himself being both the principal foundation and founder of the same. Where also note, that Christ, by building his house, that is, his church, upon a rock, has thereby secured it against all storms and floods, like the wise builder, St. *Matt.* vii. 24. 25.—Ibid. *The gates of hell, &c.* That is, the powers of darkness, and whatever satan can do, either by himself, or his agents. For as the church is here likened to a house, or fortress, built on a rock; so the adverse powers are likened to a contrary house or fortress, the gates of which, i.e., the whole strength, and all the efforts it can make, will never be able to prevail over the city or church of Christ. By this promise we are fully assured, that neither idolatry, heresy, nor any pernicious error whatsoever shall at any time prevail over the church of Christ.

Ver. 19. *Loose on earth.* The loosing the bands of temporal punishments due to sins, is called an indulgence, the power of which is here granted.

<sup>c</sup> John 20. 23.—<sup>d</sup> Mark 8. 33.—<sup>e</sup> Supra, 10. 38. Luke 9. 23. and 14. 27.—<sup>f</sup> Luke 17. 33. John 12. 25.

Ver. 22. *And Peter taking him.* That is, taking him aside, out of a tender love, respect and zeal for his Lord and Master's honour, began to expostulate with him, as it were to rebuke him, saying, Lord, far be it from thee to suffer death: but the Lord said to Peter, ver. 23, *Go behind me, satan.* These words may signify, begone from me; but the holy fathers expound them otherwise, that is, *come after me,* or *follow me;* and by these words the Lord would have Peter to follow him in his suffering, and not to oppose the divine will by contradiction; for the word *satan* means in Hebrew an *adversary,* or one that opposes.

THE ADORATION OF THE MAGI.

life, shall lose it: and he that shall lose his life for my sake, shall find it.

26 For what doth it profit a man, if he gain the whole world, and suffer the loss of his own soul? Or what exchange shall a man give for his soul?

27 For the son of man shall come in the glory of his Father with his Angels: *a* and then will he render to every man according to his works.

28 Amen I say to you, *b* there are some of them that stand here, that shall not taste death, till they see the son of man coming in his kingdom.

## CHAP. XVII.

*The transfiguration of Christ: He cures the lunatic child, foretells his passion: and pays the didrachma.*

AND *c* after six days JESUS taketh unto him Peter and James, and John his brother, and bringeth them up into a high mountain apart:

2 And he was transfigured before them. And his face did shine as the sun: and his garments became white as snow.

3 And behold there appeared to them Moses and Elias talking with him.

4 And Peter answering, said to JESUS: Lord, it is good for us to be here: if thou wilt, let us make here three tabernacles, one for thee, and one for Moses, and one for Elias.

5 And as he was yet speaking, behold a bright cloud overshaded them. *d* And lo a voice out of the cloud, saying: This is my beloved Son, in whom I am well pleased: hear ye him.

6 And the disciples hearing, fell upon their face, and were very much afraid.

7 And JESUS came and touched them: and said to them: Arise, and fear not.

8 And they lifting up their eyes, saw no one, but only JESUS.

9 And as they came down from the mountain, JESUS charged them, saying: Tell the vision to no man, till the son of man be risen from the dead.

10 And his disciples asked him, saying: *e* Why then do the Scribes say that Elias must come first?

11 *f* But he answering, said to them: Elias indeed shall come, and restore all things.

12 But I say to you, *g* that Elias is already come, and they knew him not, *h* but have done unto him whatsoever they had a mind. So also the son of man shall suffer from them.

13 Then the disciples understood, that he had spoken to them of John the Baptist.

14 *i* And when he was come to the multitude, there came to him a man falling down on his knees before him, saying: Lord, have pity on my son, for he is a lunatic, and suffereth much: for he falleth often into the fire, and often into the water.

15 And I brought him to thy disciples, and they could not cure him.

16 Then JESUS answered and said: O unbelieving and perverse generation, how long shall I be with you? how long shall I suffer you? Bring him hither to me.

---

*a* Acts 17. 31. Rom. 2. 6.—*b* Mark 8. 39. Luke 9. 42.—*c* Mark 9. 1. Luke 9. 28.—*d* Supra, 3. 17. 2 Pet. 1. 17.

*e* Mark 9. 10.—*f* Mal. 4. 5.—*g* Supra. 11 14.—*h* Supra, 14. 10.—*i* Mark 9. 16. Luke 9. 38.

17 And Jesus rebuked him, and the devil went out of him, and the child was cured from that hour.

18 Then came the disciples to Jesus secretly, and said: Why could not we cast him out?

19 Jesus said to them: Because of your unbelief. *a* For, amen I say to you, if you have faith as a grain of mustard-seed, you shall say to this mountain, Remove from hence hither, and it shall remove: and nothing shall be impossible to you.

20 But this kind is not cast out but by prayer and fasting.

21 And when they abode together in Galilee, Jesus said to them: *b* The son of man shall be betrayed into the hands of men:

22 And they shall kill him, and the third day he shall rise again. And they were troubled exceedingly.

23 And when they were come to Capharnaum, they that received the didrachmas, came to Peter, and said to him: Doth not your master pay the didrachma?

24 He said: Yes. And when he was come into the house, Jesus prevented him, saying: What is thy opinion, Simon? The kings of the earth, of whom do they receive tribute or custom? of their own children, or of strangers?

25 And he said: Of strangers. Jesus said to him: Then the children are free.

26 But that we may not scandalize them, go to the sea, and cast in a hook: and that fish which shall first come up, take: and when thou hast opened its mouth, thou shalt find a stater: take that, and give it to them for me and thee.

### CHAP. XVIII.

*Christ teaches humility, to beware of scandal, and to flee the occasions of sin: to denounce to the church incorrigible sinners, and to look upon such as refuse to hear the church as heathens. He promises to his disciples the power of binding and loosing; and that he will be in the midst of their assemblies. No forgiveness for them that will not forgive.*

AT *c* that hour the disciples came to Jesus, saying: Who, thinkest thou, is the greater in the kingdom of heaven?

2 *d* And Jesus calling unto him a little child, set him in the midst of them.

3 And said: Amen I say to you, *e* unless you be converted, and become as little children, you shall not enter into the kingdom of heaven

4 Whosoever therefore shall humble himself as this little child, he is the greater in the kingdom of heaven.

5 And he that shall receive one such little child in my name, receiveth me.

6 *f* But he that shall scandalize one of these little ones

---

*a* Luke 17. 6.—*b* Infra, 20. 18. Mark 9. 30. Luke 9. 44.

CHAP. XVII. Ver. 19. *As a grain of mustard-seed. That is, a perfect faith; which in its properties, and its fruits, resembles the grain of mustard-seed, in the parable, chap. xii. 31.*

Ver. 23. *The didrachmas. A didrachma was half a sickle, or half a stater; that is, about 15d. English; which was a tax laid upon every head for the service of the temple.*

*c* Mark 9. 33. Luke 9. 46.—*d* Infra, 19. 14.—*e* 1 Cor. 14. 20.—*f* Mark 9. 41. Luke xvii. 2

CHAP. XVIII. Ver. 6. *Shall scandalize. That is, shall put a stumblingblock in their way, and cause them to fall into sin.*

that believe in me, it were better for him that a millstone should be hanged about his neck, and that he should be drowned in the depth of the sea.

7 Wo to the world because of scandals. For it must needs be that scandals come: but nevertheless wo to that man by whom the scandal cometh.

8 *And if thy hand, or thy foot, scandalize thee, cut it off, and cast it from thee. It is better for thee to go into life, maimed or lame, than having two hands or two feet, to be cast into everlasting fire.

9 And if thy eye scandalize thee, pluck it out, and cast it from thee. It is better for thee having one eye to enter into life, than having two eyes to be cast into hell fire.

10 See that you despise not one of these little ones: for I say to you, *b* that their Angels in heaven always see the face of my Father who is in heaven.

11 *c* For the son of man is come to save that which was lost.

12 *d* What think you? If a man have an hundred sheep, and one of them should go astray: doth he not leave the ninety-nine in the mountains, and goeth to seek that which is gone astray?

13 And if it so be that he find it: Amen I say to you, he rejoiceth more for that, than for the ninety-nine that went not astray.

14 Even so it is not the will of your Father, who is in heaven, that one of these little ones should perish.

15 *e* But if thy brother shall offend against thee, go, and rebuke him between thee and him alone. If he shall hear thee, thou shalt gain thy brother.

16 And if he will not hear thee, take with thee one or two more: *f* that in the mouth of two or three witnesses every word may stand.

17 *g* And if he will not hear them: tell the church. And if he will not hear the church, let him be to thee as the heathen and publican.

18 *h* Amen I say to you, whatsoever you shall bind upon earth, shall be bound also in heaven: and whatsoever you shall loose upon earth shall be loosed also in heaven.

19 Again I say to you, that if two of you shall consent upon earth, concerning anything whatsoever they shall ask, it shall be done to them by my Father who is in heaven.

20 For where there are two or three gathered together in my name, there am I in the midst of them.

21 Then came Peter unto him and said: *i* Lord, how often shall my brother offend against me, and I forgive him? till seven times?

---

*a* Supra, 5. 30. Mark 9. 42.—*b* Ps. 33. 8.—*c* Luke 19. 10.—*d* Luke 15. 4.

Ver. 7. *It must needs be, &c.* Viz. considering the wickedness and corruption of the world.

Ver. 8. *Scandalize thee.* That is, cause thee to offend.

*e* Lev. 19. 17. Eccli. 19. 13. Luke 17. 3. Jas. 5. 19.—*f* Deut. 19. 15. John 8. 17. 2 Cor. 13. 1. Heb. 10. 28.—*g* 1 Cor. 5. 9. 2 Thess. 3. 14.—*h* John 20. 23.—*i* Luke 17. 4.

Ver. 20. *There am I in the midst of them.* This is understood of such assemblies only, as are gathered in the name and authority of Christ; and in unity of the church of Christ. St. Cyprian *de Unitate Ecclesiæ.*

35

CHAP. XVIII.    ST. MATTHEW.    CHAP. XIX.

22 JESUS saith to him: I say not to thee, till seven times; but till seventy times seven times.

23 Therefore is the kingdom of heaven likened to a king, who would take an account of his servants.

24 And when he had begun to take the account, one was brought to him, that owed him ten thousand talents.

25 And as he had not wherewith to pay it, his lord commanded that he should be sold, and his wife and children, and all that he had, and payment to be made.

26 But that servant falling down, besought him, saying: Have patience with me, and I will pay thee all.

27 And the lord of that servant being moved with pity, let him go and forgave him the debt.

28 But when that servant was gone out, he found one of his fellow-servants that owed him an hundred pence: and laying hold of him, he throttled him, saying: Pay what thou owest.

29 And his fellow-servant, falling down, besought him, saying: Have patience with me, and I will pay thee all.

30 And he would not: but went and cast him into prison, till he paid the debt.

31 Now his fellow-servants seeing what was done, were very much grieved, and they came, and told their lord all that was done.

32 Then his lord called him: and said to him: Thou wicked servant, I forgave thee all the debt, because thou besoughtest me:

33 Shouldst not thou then have had compassion also on thy fellow-servant, even as I had compassion on thee?

34 And his lord being angry, delivered him to the torturers until he paid all the debt.

35 So also shall my heavenly Father do to you, if you forgive not every one his brother from your hearts.

CHAP. XIX.

*Christ declares matrimony to be indissoluble: he recommends the making one's-self an eunuch for the kingdom of heaven; and parting with all things for him. He shews the danger of riches, and the reward of leaving all to follow him.*

AND it came to pass when JESUS had ended these words he departed from Galilee, <sup>a</sup> and came into the coasts of Judea, beyond Jordan.

2 And great multitudes followed him: and he healed them there.

3 <sup>b</sup> And there came to him the Pharisees tempting him, saying: Is it lawful for a man to put away his wife for every cause?

4 Who answering, said to them: Have ye not read, that he <sup>c</sup> who made man from the beginning, *made them male and female?* And he said:

5 <sup>d</sup> *For this cause shall a man leave father and mother, and shall cleave to his wife, and they two shall be in one flesh.*

---

Ver. 24. *Talents.* A talent was seven hundred and fifty ounces of silver, which at the rate of five shillings to the ounce is a hundred and eighty-seven pounds ten shillings sterling.

Ver. 28. *Pence.* The Roman penny was the eighth part of an ounce, that is, about sevenpence halfpenny English.

<sup>a</sup> Mark 10. 1.—<sup>b</sup> Mark 10. 2.—<sup>c</sup> Gen. 1. 27.—<sup>d</sup> Gen. 2. 24. 1 Cor. 6. 16. Ephes. 5. 31.

THE PRESENTATION IN THE TEMPLE.

CHAP. XIX. ST. MATTHEW. CHAP. XIX.

6 Therefore now they are not two, but one flesh. What therefore God hath joined together, let no man put asunder.

7 They say to him: *a* Why then did Moses command to give a bill of divorce, and to put away?

8 He saith to them: Because Moses by reason of the hardness of your heart permitted you to put away your wives: but from the beginning it was not so.

9 *b* And I say to you, that whosoever shall put away his wife, except it be for fornication, and shall marry another, committeth adultery; and he that shall marry her that is put away, committeth adultery.

10 His disciples say unto him: If the case of a man with his wife be so, it is not expedient to marry.

11 Who said to them: All men take not this word, but they to whom it is given.

12 For there are eunuchs, who were born so from their mother's womb: and there are eunuchs, who were made so by men: and there are eunuchs, who have made themselves eunuchs for the kingdom of heaven. He that can take, let him take it.

13 *c* Then were little children presented to him, that he should impose hands upon them and pray. And the disciples rebuked them.

14 But JESUS said to them: *d* Suffer the little children, and forbid them not to come to me: for the kingdom of heaven is for such.

15 And when he had imposed hands upon them, he departed from thence.

16 And behold one came and said to him: Good master, what good shall I do that I may have life everlasting?

17 Who said to him: Why askest thou me concerning good? One is good, God. But if thou wilt enter into life, keep the commandments.

18 He said to him: Which? And JESUS said: *e* Thou shalt do no murder, Thou shalt not commit adultery, Thou shalt not steal, Thou shalt not bear false witness.

19 *Honour thy father and thy mother:* and, *Thou shalt love thy neighbour as thyself.*

20 The young man saith to him: All these have I kept from my youth, what is yet wanting to me?

21 JESUS saith to him: If thou wilt be perfect, go sell what

---

*a* Deut. 24. 1.—*b* Supra, 5. 32. Mark 10. 11. Luke 16. 18. 1 Cor. 7. 10.

CHAP. XIX. Ver. 9. *Except it be, &c.* In the case of fornication, that is, of adultery, the wife may b put away; but even then the husband cannot marry another as long as the wife is living.

Ver. 11. *All men take not this word.* That is, all receive not the gift of living singly and chastely, unless they pray for the grace of God to enable them to live so, and for some it may be necessary to that end to fast as well as pray: and to these it is given from above.

Ver. 12. *There are eunuchs, who have made themselves eunuchs for the kingdom of heaven.* This text is not

*c* Mark 10. 13. Luke 18. 15.—*d* Supra, 18. 3.—*e* Exod. 20. 13.

to be taken in the literal sense; but means, that there are such, who have taken a firm and commendable resolution of leading a single and chaste life, in order to serve God in a more perfect state than those who marry: as St. Paul clearly shews, 1 Cor. chap vii. vers. 37, 38.

thou hast, and give to the poor, and thou shalt have treasure in heaven: and come, follow me.

22 And when the young man had heard this word, he went away sad: for he had great possessions.

23 Then JESUS said to his disciples: Amen I say to you, that a rich man shall hardly enter into the kingdom of heaven.

24 And again I say to you: It is easier for a camel to pass through the eye of a needle, than for a rich man to enter into the kingdom of heaven.

25 And when they had heard this, the disciples wondered very much, saying: Who then can be saved?

26 And JESUS beholding said to them: With men this is impossible: but with God all things are possible.

27 Then Peter answering, said to him: Behold we have left all things, and have followed thee: what therefore shall we have?

28 And JESUS said to them: Amen I say to you, that you, who have followed me, in the regeneration, when the son of man shall sit on the seat of his majesty, you also shall sit on twelve seats judging the twelve tribes of Israel.

29 And every one that hath left house, or brethren, or sisters, or father, or mother, or wife, or children, or lands for my name's sake; shall receive an hundred fold, and shall possess life everlasting.

30 *a* And many that are first, shall be last: and the last shall be first.

*a* Infra, 20. 16. Mark 10. 31. Luke 13. 30.

## CHAP. XX.

*The parable of the labourers in the vineyard. The ambition of the two sons of Zebedee. Christ gives sight to two blind men.*

THE kingdom of heaven is like to an householder, who went out early in the morning to hire labourers into his vineyard.

2 And having agreed with the labourers for a penny a day, he sent them into his vineyard.

3 And going out about the third hour, he saw others standing in the market-place idle,

4 And he said to them: Go you also into my vineyard, and I will give you what shall be just.

5 And they went their way. And again he went out about the sixth and the ninth hour: and did in like manner.

6 But about the eleventh hour he went out and found others standing, and he saith to them: Why stand you here all the day idle?

7 They say to him: Because no man hath hired us. He saith to them: Go ye also into my vineyard.

8 And when evening was come, the lord of the vineyard saith to his steward: Call the labourers and pay them their hire, beginning from the last even to the first.

9 When therefore they were come that came about the eleventh hour, they received every man a penny.

10 But when the first also came, they thought that they should receive more: and they also received every man a penny.

11 And receiving it they murmured against the master of the house,

12 Saying: These last have

worked *but* one hour, and thou hast made them equal to us, that have borne the burden of the day and the heats.

13 But he answering said to one of them: Friend, I do thee no wrong: didst thou not agree with me for a penny?

14 Take what is thine, and go thy way: I will also give to this last even as to thee.

15 Or, is it not lawful for me to do what I will? is thy eye evil, because I am good?

16 *a* So shall the last be first, and first last. For many are called, but few chosen.

17 And JESUS going up to Jerusalem, took the twelve disciples apart, and said to them:

18 Behold we go up to Jerusalem, and the son of man shall be betrayed to the chief priests and the scribes, and they shall condemn him to death.

19 And shall deliver him to the gentiles to be mocked, and scourged, and crucified, and the third day he shall rise again.

20 *b* Then came to him the mother of the sons of Zebedee with her sons, adoring and asking something of him.

21 Who said to her: What wilt thou? She saith to him: Say that these my two sons may sit, the one on thy right hand, and the other on thy left, in thy kingdom.

22 And JESUS answering, said: You know not what you ask. Can you drink the chalice that I shall drink? They say to him: We can.

23 He saith to them: My chalice indeed you shall drink: but to sit on my right or left hand, is not mine to give to you, but to them for whom it is prepared by my Father.

24 *c* And the ten hearing it, were moved with indignation against the two brethren.

25 *d* But JESUS called them to him, and said: You know that the princes of the gentiles lord it over them: and they that are the greater, exercise power upon them.

26 It shall not be so among you, but whosoever will be the greater among you, let him be your minister.

27 And he that will be first among you, shall be your servant.

28 *e* Even as the son of man is not come to be ministered unto, but to minister, and to give his life a redemption for many.

29 *f* And when they went out from Jericho, a great multitude followed him.

30 And behold two blind men sitting by the way side, heard that JESUS passed by, and they cried out, saying: O Lord, thou son of David, have mercy on us.

31 And the multitude rebuked them that they should hold their peace. But they cried out the more, saying: O Lord, thou son of David, have mercy on us.

32 And JESUS stood, and called them, and said: What will ye that I do to you?

33 They say to him: Lord, that our eyes be opened.

34 And JESUS having com-

---

*a* Supra, 19. 30. Mark 10. 31. Luke 13. 30.—*b* Mark 10. 35.

CHAP. XX. Ver. 14. *What I will.* Viz. with my own, and in matters that depend on my own bounty.

*c* Mark 10. 41.—*d* Luke 22. 25.—*e* Phil. 2. 7.—*f* Mark 10. 46. Luke 18. 35.

passion on them, touched their eyes. And immediately they saw, and followed him.

## CHAP. XXI.

*Christ rides into Jerusalem upon an ass: he casts the buyers and sellers out of the temple: curses the fig-tree: and puts to silence the priests and scribes.*

AND ⁿ when they drew nigh to Jerusalem, and were come to Bethphage, unto Mount Olivet, then JESUS sent two disciples,

2 Saying to them: Go ye into the village that is over against you, and immediately you shall find an ass tied and a colt with her: loose *them* and bring them to me:

3 And if any man shall say anything to you, say ye, that the Lord hath need of them: and forthwith he will let them go.

4 Now all this was done that it might be fulfilled which was spoken by the prophet, saying:

5 ᵇ *Tell ye the daughter of Sion: Behold thy king cometh to thee, meek, and sitting upon an ass, and a colt the foal of her that is used to the yoke.*

6 And the disciples going did as JESUS commanded them.

7 And they brought the ass and the colt, and laid their garments upon them, and made him sit thereon.

8 And a very great multitude spread their garments in the way: and others cut boughs from the trees, and strewed them in the way:

9 And the multitudes that went before and that followed, cried, saying: *Hosanna to the son of David:* ᶜ *Blessed is he that cometh in the name of the Lord: Hosanna in the highest.*

10 And when he was come into Jerusalem, the whole city was moved, saying: Who is this?

11 And the people said: This is JESUS the prophet, from Nazareth of Galilee.

12 ᵈ And JESUS went into the temple of God, and cast out all them that sold and bought in the temple, and overthrew the tables of the money-changers, and the chairs of them that sold doves.

13 And he saith to them: It is written, ᵉ *My house shall be called the house of prayer: but you have made it a den of thieves.*

14 And there came to him the blind, and the lame in the temple; and he healed them.

15 And the chief priests and scribes seeing the wonderful things that he did, and the children crying in the temple, and saying, *Hosanna to the son of David;* were moved with indignation,

16 And said to him: Hearest thou what these say? And JESUS said to them: Yea, have you never read: ᶠ *Out of the mouth of infants and of sucklings thou hast perfected praise.*

17 And leaving them, he went out of the city into Bethania, and remained there.

18 And in the morning returning into the city he was hungry.

19 ᵍ And seeing a certain fig-tree by the way side, he came to it, and found nothing on it but

---
ᵃ Mark 11.1. Luke 19. 29.—ᵇ Isaias 62. 11. Zach. 9. 9. John 12. 15.—ᶜ Ps. 117. 26. Mark 11. 10. Luke 19. 38.

ᵈ Mark 11. 15. Luke 19. 45. John 2. 14.—ᵉ Isaias 56. 7. Jer. 7. 11. Luke 19. 46.—ᶠ Ps. 8. 3.—ᵍ Mark 11. 13.

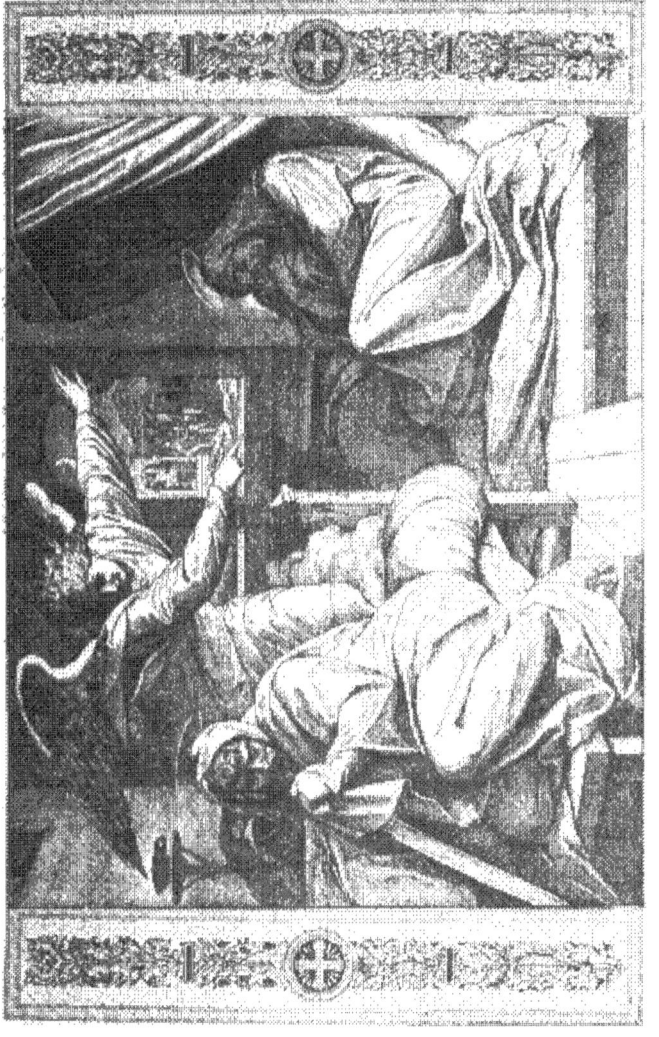

JOSEPH IS WARNED TO FLEE INTO EGYPT.

leaves only, and he said to it: May no fruit grow on thee henceforward for ever. And immediately the fig-tree withered away.

20 ᵃ And the disciples seeing it, wondered, saying: How is it presently withered away?

21 And JESUS answering said to them: Amen I say to you, if you shall have faith, and stagger not, not only this of the fig-tree shall you do, but also if you shall say to this mountain, Take up and cast thyself into the sea, it shall be done.

22 ᵇ And all things whatsoever you shall ask in prayer believing, you shall receive.

23 And when he was come into the temple, there came to him as he was teaching, the chief priests and ancients of the people, saying: ᶜ By what authority dost thou these things? and who hath given thee this authority?

24 JESUS answering said to them: I also will ask you one word, which if you shall tell me, I will also tell you by what authority I do these things.

25 The baptism of John whence was it? from heaven, or from men? But they thought within themselves, saying:

26 If we shall say from heaven, he will say to us: Why then did you not believe him? But if we shall say from men, we are afraid of the multitude: ᵈ for all held John as a prophet.

27 And answering JESUS they said: We know not. He also said to them: Neither do I tell you by what authority I do these things.

28 But what think you? A certain man had two sons, and coming to the first, he said: Son, go work to-day in my vineyard.

29 And he answering, said: I will not. But afterwards, being moved with repentance, he went.

30 And coming to the other, he said in like manner. And he answering, said: I go, Sir, and went not:

31 Which of the two did the father's will? They say to him: The first. JESUS said to them: Amen I say to you, that the publicans and the harlots shall go into the kingdom of God before you.

32 For John came to you in the way of justice and you did not believe him. But the publicans and the harlots believed him: but you seeing it, did not even afterwards repent, that you might believe him.

33 Hear ye another parable: ᵉ There was a man a householder who planted a vineyard, and made a hedge round about it, and dug in it a press, and built a tower, and let it out to husbandmen: and went into a strange country.

34 And when the time of the fruits drew nigh, he sent his servants to the husbandmen, that they might receive the fruits thereof.

35 And the husbandmen laying hands on his servants, beat one, and killed another, and stoned another.

36 Again he sent other servants more than the former: and they did to them in like manner.

---

ᵃ Mark 11. 20.—ᵇ Supra, 7. 7. Mark 11. 24. John 14. 13. 16. 23.—ᶜ Mark 11. 28. Luke 20. 2.—ᵈ Supra, 14. 6.

ᵉ Isaias 5. 1. Jer. 2. 21. Mark 11. 22. Luke 20. 9.

37 And last of all he sent to them his son, saying: They will reverence my son.

38 But the husbandmen seeing the son, said among themselves: *a* This is the heir, come, let us kill him, and we shall have his inheritance.

39 And taking him they cast him forth out of the vineyard, and killed him.

40 When therefore the lord of the vineyard shall come, what will he do to those husbandmen?

41 They say to him: He will bring those evil men to an evil end: and will let out his vineyard to other husbandmen, that shall render him the fruit in due season.

42 JESUS saith to them: Have you never read in the Scriptures: *b* *The stone which the builders rejected, the same is become the head of the corner? By the Lord this has been done, and it is wonderful in our eyes.*

43 Therefore I say to you, that the kingdom of God shall be taken from you, and shall be given to a nation yielding the fruits thereof.

44 And whosoever shall fall on this stone, shall be broken: but on whomsoever it shall fall, it shall grind him to powder.

45 And when the chief priests and Pharisees had heard his parables, they knew that he spoke of them.

46 And seeking to lay hands on him, they feared the multitudes: because they held him as a prophet.

---

*a* Infra, 26. 3. and 27. 2. John 11. 53.
—*b* Ps. 117. 22. Acts 4. 11. Rom. 9. 33. 1 Pet. 2. 7.

42

## CHAP. XXII.

*The parable of the marriage feast: Christ orders tribute to be paid to Cesar; he confutes the Sadducees: shews which is the first commandment in the law: and puzzles the Pharisees.*

AND *c* JESUS answering, spoke again in parables to them, saying:

2 *d* The kingdom of heaven is likened to a king, who made a marriage for his son.

3 And he sent his servants, to call them that were invited to the marriage: and they would not come.

4 Again he sent other servants, saying: Tell them that were invited: Behold, I have prepared my dinner; my beeves and fatlings are killed, and all things are ready: come ye to the marriage.

5 But they neglected, and went their ways, one to his farm, and another to his merchandise.

6 And the rest laid hands on his servants, and having treated them contumeliously put them to death.

7 But when the king had heard of it, he was angry, and sending his armies, he destroyed those murderers, and burnt their city.

8 Then he saith to his servants: The marriage indeed is ready: but they that were invited, were not worthy.

9 Go ye therefore into the high-ways: and as many as you shall find, call to the marriage.

10 And his servants going forth into the ways, gathered together all that they found,

---

*c* A.D. 33.—*d* Luke 14. 16. Apoc. 19. 9.

both bad and good: and the marriage was filled with guests.

11 And the king went in to see the guests: and he saw there a man who had not on a wedding garment.

12 And he saith to him: Friend, how camest thou in hither not having on a wedding garment? But he was silent.

13 Then the king said to the waiters: *a* Bind his hands and feet, and cast him into the exterior darkness: there shall be weeping and gnashing of teeth.

14 For many are called, but few are chosen.

15 *b* Then the Pharisees going, consulted among themselves how to ensnare him in *his* speech.

16 And they sent to him their disciples with the Herodians, saying: Master, we know that thou art a true speaker, and teachest the way of God in truth, neither carest thou for any man: for thou dost not regard the person of men.

17 Tell us therefore what dost thou think, is it lawful to give tribute to Cesar, or not?

18 But JESUS knowing their wickedness, said: Why do you tempt me, ye hypocrites?

19 Shew me the coin of the tribute. And they offered him a penny.

20 And JESUS saith to them: Whose image and inscription is this?

21 They say to him, Cesar's. Then he saith to them: *c* Render therefore to Cesar the things that are Cesar's: and to God, the things that are God's.

22 And hearing *this*, they wondered, and leaving him went their ways.

23 That day there came to him the Sadducees, who say *d* there is no resurrection: and asked him,

24 Saying: Master, Moses said, *e* If a man die having no son, his brother shall marry his wife, and raise up issue to his brother.

25 Now there were with us seven brethren: and the first having married a wife, died; and not having issue, left his wife to his brother.

26 In like manner the second, and the third, and so on to the seventh.

27 And last of all the woman died also.

28 At the resurrection therefore whose wife of the seven shall she be? for they all had her.

29 And JESUS answering, said to them: You err, not knowing the scriptures, nor the power of God.

30 For in the resurrection they shall neither marry nor be married: but shall be as the Angels of God in heaven.

31 And concerning the resurrection of the dead, have you not read that which was spoken by God saying to you:

32 *f* I am the God of Abraham, and the God of Isaac, and the God of Jacob? He is not the

---

*a* Supra. 6. 12. and 13. 4. Infra. 25. 30.—*b* Mark 12. 13. Luke 20. 20.

---

CHAP. XXII. Ver. 16. *The Herodians.* That is, some that belonged to Herod, and that joined with him in standing up for the necessity of paying tribute to Cesar, that is, to the Roman emperor. Some are of opinion that there was a sect among the Jews called Herodians, from their maintaining that Herod was the Messias.

*c* Rom. 13. 7.—*d* Acts 23. 8.—*e* Deut. 25. 5. Mark 12. 19. Luke 20. 28.— *f* Exod. 3. 6.

God of the dead, but of the living.

33 And the multitudes hearing it, were in admiration at his doctrine.

34 But the Pharisees hearing that he had silenced the Sadducees, came together:

35 ᵃ And one of them a doctor of the law asked him, tempting him:

36 Master, which is the great commandment in the law?

37 JESUS said to him: ᵇ *Thou shalt love the Lord thy God with thy whole heart, and with thy whole soul, and with thy whole mind.*

38 This is the greatest and the first commandment.

39 And the second is like to this: ᶜ *Thou shalt love thy neighbour as thyself.*

40 On these two commandments dependeth the whole law and the prophets.

41 And the Pharisees being gathered together, JESUS asked them,

42 ᵈ Saying: What think you of Christ: whose son is he? They say to him: David's.

43 He saith to them: ᵉ How then doth David in spirit call him Lord; saying:

44 ᶠ *The Lord said to my Lord, sit on my right hand, until I make thy enemies thy footstool?*

45 If David then call him Lord, how is he his son?

46 And no man was able to answer him a word: neither durst any man from that day forth ask him any more questions.

---

ᵃ Mark 12. 28. Luke 10. 25.—ᵇ Deut. 6. 5.—ᶜ Lev. 19. 18. Mark 12. 31.—ᵈ Mark 12. 35. Luke 20. 41.—ᵉ Luke 20. 42.—ᶠ Ps. 109. 1.

## CHAP. XXIII.

*Christ admonishes the people to follow the good doctrine, not the bad example of the scribes and Pharisees; he warns his disciples not to imitate their ambition: and denounces divers woes against them for their hypocrisy and blindness.*

THEN JESUS spoke to the multitudes and to his disciples,

2 Saying: ᵍ The scribes and the Pharisees have sitten on the chair of Moses.

3 All things therefore whatsoever they shall say to you, observe and do: but according to their works do ye not: for they say, and do not.

4 ʰ For they bind heavy and insupportable burdens: and lay them on men's shoulders: but with a finger of their own they will not move them.

5 And all their works they do for to be seen of men. ⁱ For they make their phylacteries broad and enlarge their fringes.

6 ᵏ And they love the first places at feasts, and the first chairs in the synagogues,

7 And salutations in the market-place, and to be called by men, Rabbi.

8 ˡ But be not you called Rabbi. For one is your master, and all you are brethren.

9 ᵐ And call none your father

---

ᵍ 2 Esdras 6. 4.—ʰ Luke 11. 46. Acts 15. 10.—ⁱ Num. 15. 38. Deut. 6. 8. and 22. 12.—ᵏ Mark 12. 39. Luke 11. 43. and 20. 46.—ˡ Jas. 3. 1.—ᵐ Mal. 1. 6.

CHAP. XXIII. Ver. 5. *Phylacteries*, i.e., Parchments on which they wrote the ten commandments, and carried them on their foreheads before their eyes; which the Pharisees affected to wear broader than other men; so to seem more zealous for the law.

Ver. 9. 10. *Call none your father—Neither be ye called masters, &c.* The meaning is, that our Father in heaven

THE FLIGHT INTO EGYPT.

upon earth: for one is your father, who is in heaven.

10 Neither be ye called masters: for one is your master, Christ.

11 He that is the greatest among you shall be your servant.

12 ᵃ And whosoever shall exalt himself, shall be humbled: and he that shall humble himself shall be exalted.

13 But wo to you scribes and Pharisees, hypocrites: because you shut the kingdom of heaven against men, for you yourselves do not enter in; and those that are going in, you suffer not to enter.

14 Wo to you scribes and Pharisees, hypocrites: ᵇ because you devour the houses of widows, praying long prayers. For this you shall receive the greater judgment.

15 Wo to you scribes and Pharisees, hypocrites: because you go round about the sea and the land to make one proselyte: and when he is made, you make him the child of hell twofold more than yourselves.

16 Wo to you blind guides, that say, whosoever shall swear by the temple, it is nothing: but he that shall swear by the gold of the temple, is a debtor.

17 Ye foolish and blind: for whether is greater, the gold, or the temple, that sanctifieth the gold?

18 And whosoever shall swear by the altar, it is nothing: but whosoever shall swear by the gift that is upon it, is a debtor.

19 Ye blind: for whether is greater, the gift, or the altar, that sanctifieth the gift?

20 He therefore that sweareth by the altar, sweareth by it, and by all things that are upon it:

21 And whosoever shall swear by the temple, sweareth by it, and by him that dwelleth in it:

22 And he that sweareth by heaven, sweareth by the throne of God, and by him that sitteth thereon.

23 ᶜ Wo to you scribes and Pharisees, hypocrites: because you tithe mint, and anise, and cummin, and have left the weightier things of the law,ᵈ judgment, and mercy, and faith. These things you ought to have done, and not to leave those undone.

24 Blind guides, who strain out a gnat and swallow a camel.

25 Wo to you scribes and Pharisees, hypocrites: because you make clean the outside of the cup and of the dish: but within you are full of rapine and uncleanness.

26 Thou blind Pharisee, first make clean the inside of the cup and of the dish, that the outside may become clean.

27 Wo to you scribes and Pharisees, hypocrites: because you are like to whited sepulchres, which outwardly appear to men beautiful, but within are full of dead men's bones, and of all filthiness.

---

ᵃ Luke 14. 11. and 18. 14.—ᵇ Mark 12. 40. Luke 20. 47.

is incomparably more to be regarded, than any father upon earth: and no master to be followed, who would lead us away from Christ. But this does not hinder but that we are by the law of God to have a due respect both for our parents and spiritual fathers (1 Cor. iv. 15), and for our masters and teachers.

ᶜ Luke 11. 42.—ᵈ Mich. 6. 8. Zach. 7. 9.

28 So you also outwardly indeed appear to men just; but inwardly you are full of hypocrisy and iniquity.

29 Wo to you scribes and Pharisees, hypocrites, that build the sepulchres of the prophets, and adorn the monuments of the just.

30 And say: If we had been in the days of our fathers, we would not have been partakers with them in the blood of the prophets.

31 Wherefore you are witnesses against yourselves, that you are the sons of them that killed the prophets.

32 Fill ye up then the measure of your fathers.

33 <sup>a</sup> You serpents, generation of vipers, how will you flee from the judgment of hell?

34 Therefore behold I send to you prophets, and wise men, and scribes: and some of them you will put to death and crucify, and some you will scourge in your synagogues, and persecute from city to city:

35 That upon you may come all the just blood that hath been shed upon the earth, <sup>b</sup> from the blood of Abel the just, even unto the blood of <sup>c</sup> Zacharias the son of Barachias whom you killed between the temple and the altar.

36 Amen I say to you all these things shall come upon this generation.

37 <sup>d</sup> Jerusalem, Jerusalem, thou that killest the prophets, and stonest them that are sent unto thee, how often would I have gathered together thy children, as the hen doth gather her chickens under her wings, and thou wouldest not?

38 Behold your house sh'l. be left to you, desolate.

39 For I say to you, you shall not see me henceforth till you say: Blessed is he that cometh in the name of the Lord.

## CHAP. XXIV.

*Christ foretells the destruction of the temple: with the signs that shall come before it, and before the last judgment. We must always watch.*

AND <sup>e</sup> JESUS being come out of the temple, went away. And his disciples came to shew him the buildings of the temple.

2 And he answering said to them: Do you see all these things? Amen I say to you, there shall not be left here a stone upon a stone that shall not be destroyed.

3 And when he was sitting on mount Olivet, the disciples came to him privately, saying: Tell us when shall these things be? and what shall be the sign of thy coming, and of the consummation of the world?

4 And JESUS answering, said

---

<sup>a</sup> Supra, 3. 7.—<sup>b</sup> Gen. 4. 8. Heb. 11. 4.

Ver. 29. *Build the sepulchres, &c.* This is not blamed, as if it were in itself evil to build or adorn the monuments of the prophets: but the hypocrisy of the Pharisees is here taxed; who, whilst they pretended to honour the memory of the prophets, were persecuting even unto death the Lord of the prophets.

Ver. 35. *That upon you may come, &c.* Not that they should suffer more than their own sins justly deserved; but that the justice of God should now fall upon them with such a final vengeance, once for all, as might comprise all the different kinds of judgments and punishments, that had at any time before been inflicted for the shedding of just blood.

<sup>c</sup> 2 Par. 24. 22.—<sup>d</sup> Luke 13. 34.—<sup>e</sup> Mark 13. 1.—<sup>f</sup> Luke 19. 44.

to them: ᵃ Take heed that no man seduce you:

5 For many will come in my name saying, I am Christ: and they will seduce many.

6 And you shall hear of wars, and rumours of wars. See that ye be not troubled. For these things must come to pass, but the end is not yet.

7 For nation shall rise against nation, and kingdom against kingdom: and there shall be pestilences, and famines, and earthquakes in places:

8 Now all these are the beginnings of sorrows.

9 ᵇ Then shall they deliver you up to be afflicted, and shall put you to death: and you shall be hated by all nations for my name's sake.

10 And then shall many be scandalized: and shall betray one another: and shall hate one another.

11 And many false prophets shall rise, and shall seduce many.

12 And because iniquity hath abounded, the charity of many shall grow cold.

13 But he that shall persevere to the end, he shall be saved.

14 And this Gospel of the kingdom shall be preached in the whole world, for a testimony to all nations, and then shall the consummation come.

15 ᶜ When therefore you shall see *the abomination of desolation*, which was spoken of by ᵈ Daniel the prophet, standing in the holy place: he that readeth, let him understand.

16 Then they that are in Judea, let them flee to the mountains.

17 And he that is on the house-top, let him not come down to take any thing out of his house:

18 And he that is in the field, let him not go back to take his coat.

19 And wo to them that are with child, and that give suck in those days.

20 But pray that your flight be not in the winter, or on the ᵉ sabbath.

21 For there shall be then great tribulation, such as hath not been from the beginning of the world until now, neither shall be.

22 And unless those days had been shortened, no flesh should be saved: but for the sake of the elect those days shall be shortened.

23 ᶠ Then if any man shall say to you: Lo here is Christ, or there: do not believe him.

24 For there shall rise false Christs and false prophets, and shall show great signs and wonders, insomuch as to deceive (if possible) even the elect.

25 Behold I have told it to you, beforehand.

26 If therefore they shall say to you: Behold he is in the desert; go ye not out: Behold *he is* in the closets, believe it not.

27 For as lightning cometh out of the east, and appeareth even into the west: so shall also the coming of the son of man be.

28 ᵍ Wheresoever the body

---

ᵃ Ephes. 5. 6. Col. 2. 18.—ᵇ Supra. 10. 17. Luke 21. 12. John 16. 20. and 16. 2.—ᶜ Mark 13. 14. Luke 21. 20.—ᵈ Dan. 9. 27.

ᵉ Acts 1. 12.—ᶠ Mark 13. 31. Luke 17. 23.—ᵍ Luke 17. 37.

CHAP. XXIV. Ver. 28. *Wheresoever, &c.* The coming of Christ shall

47

CHAP. XXIV.   ST. MATTHEW.   CHAP. XXIV.

shall be, there shall the eagles also be gathered together.

29 *a* And immediately after the tribulation of those days, the sun shall be darkened, and the moon shall not give her light, and the stars shall fall from heaven, and the powers of heaven shall be moved:

30 And then shall appear the sign of the son of man in heaven: and then shall all tribes of the earth mourn: *b* and they shall see the son of man coming in the clouds of heaven with much power and majesty.

31 *c* And he shall send his Angels with a trumpet, and a great voice: and they shall gather together his elect from the four winds, from the farthest parts of the heavens to the utmost bounds of them.

32 And from the fig-tree learn a parable: when the branch thereof is now tender, and the leaves come forth, you know that summer is nigh.

33 So you also, when you shall see all these things, know ye that it is nigh *even* at the doors.

34 Amen I say to you, that this generation shall not pass, till all these things be done.

35 *d* Heaven and earth shall

---

*a* Isaias 13. 10. Ezec. 32. 7. Joel 2. 10. and 3. 15. Mark 13. 24. Luke 21. 25.— *b* Apoc. 1. 7.— *c* 1 Cor. 15. 52. 1 Thess. 4. 11.— *d* Mark 13. 31.

---

be sudden, and manifest to all the world, like lightning; and wheresoever he shall come, thither shall all mankind be gathered to him, as eagles are gathered about a dead body.
Ver. 29. *The stars.* Or flaming meteors resembling stars.
Ver. 30. *The sign,* &c. The cross of Christ.
Ver. 35. *Shall pass.* Because they shall be changed at the end of the world into a new heaven and new earth.

48

pass but my words shall not pass.

36 But of that day and hour no one knoweth, no not the Angels of heaven, but the Father alone.

37 *e* And as in the days of Noe, so shall also the coming of the son of man be.

38 For as in the days before the flood, they were eating and drinking, marrying and giving in marriage, even till that day in which Noe entered into the ark.

39 And they knew not till the flood came, and took them all away: so also shall the coming of the son of man be.

40 Then two shall be in the field: one shall be taken, and one shall be left.

41 Two women shall be grinding at the mill: one shall be taken, and one shall be left.

42 Watch ye therefore, because ye know not what hour your Lord will come.

43 But this know ye, *f* that if the good man of the house knew at what hour the thief would come, he would certainly watch, and would not suffer his house to be broken open.

44 Wherefore be you also ready, because at what hour you know not the son of man will come.

45 Who thinkest thou, is a faithful and wise servant, whom his lord hath appointed over his family, to give them meat in season?

46 *g* Blessed is that servant, whom when his lord shall come, he shall find so doing.

47 Amen I say to you, he shall place him over all his goods.

---

*e* Gen. 7. 7. Luke 17. 26.— *f* Mark 13. 33. Luke 12. 39.— *g* Apoc. 16. 15.

MASSACRE OF THE HOLY INNOCENTS.

48 But if that evil servant should say in his heart: My lord is long a coming:

49 And shall begin to strike his fellow-servants, and shall eat, and drink with drunkards:

50 The lord of that servant shall come in a day that he hopeth not, and at an hour that he knoweth not:

51 And shall separate him, and appoint his portion with the hypocrites. *a* There shall be weeping and gnashing of teeth.

## CHAP. XXV.

*The parable of the ten virgins, and of the talents. the description of the last judgment.*

THEN shall the kingdom of heaven be like to ten virgins, who taking their lamps went out to meet the bridegroom and the bride.

2 And five of them were foolish, and five wise.

3 But the five foolish, having taken their lamps, did not take oil with them:

4 But the wise took oil in their vessels with the lamps.

5 And the bridegroom tarrying, they all slumbered and slept.

6 And at midnight there was a cry made: Behold the bridegroom cometh, go ye forth to meet him.

7 Then all those virgins arose and trimmed their lamps.

8 And the foolish said to the wise: Give us of your oil, for our lamps are gone out.

9 The wise answered, saying: Lest perhaps there be not enough for us and for you, go you rather to them that sell, and buy for yourselves.

10 Now whilst they went to buy, the bridegroom came: and they that were ready, went in with him to the marriage, and the door was shut.

11 But at last come also the other virgins, saying: Lord, Lord, open to us.

12 But he answering said: Amen I say to you, I know you not.

13 *b* Watch ye therefore, because you know not the day nor the hour.

14 *c* For even as a man going into a far country, called his servants, and delivered to them his goods.

15 And to one he gave five talents, and to another two, and to another one, to every one according to his proper ability; and immediately he took his journey.

16 And he that had received the five talents, went his way, and traded with the same, and gained other five.

17 And in like manner he that had received the two gained other two.

18 But he that had received the one, going his way digged into the earth, and hid his lord's money.

19 But after a long time the lord of those servants came, and reckoned with them.

20 And he that had received the five talents coming, brought other five talents, saying: Lord, thou didst deliver to me five talents, behold I have gained other five over and above.

21 His lord said to him: Well done, good and faithful servant, because thou hast been faithful over a few things, I will place

---

*a* Supra, 13. 42. Infra, 25. 30.    *b* Mark 13. 33.—*c* Luke 10. 12.

thee over many things: enter thou into the joy of thy lord.

22 And he also that had received the two talents came and said: Lord, thou deliveredst two talents to me: behold I have gained other two.

23 His lord said to him: Well done, good and faithful servant: because thou hast been faithful over a few things, I will place thee over many things, enter thou into the joy of thy lord.

24 But he that had received the one talent, came and said: Lord, I know that thou art a hard man; thou reapest where thou hast not sown, and gatherest where thou hast not strewed.

25 And being afraid I went and hid thy talent in the earth: behold here thou hast that which is thine.

26 And his lord answering, said to him: Wicked and slothful servant, thou knewest that I reap where I sow not, and gather where I have not strewed:

27 Thou oughtest therefore to have committed my money to the bankers, and at my coming I should have received my own with usury.

28 Take ye away therefore the talent from him, and give it him that hath ten talents.

29 *a* For to every one that hath shall be given, and he shall abound: but from him that hath not, that also which he seemeth to have shall be taken away.

30 And the unprofitable servant cast ye out into the exterior darkness. There shall be weeping and gnashing of teeth.

31 And when the son of man shall come in his majesty, and all the angels with him, then shall he sit upon the seat of his majesty:

32 And all nations shall be gathered together before him, and he shall separate them one from another, as the shepherd separateth the sheep from the goats:

33 And he shall set the sheep on his right hand, but the goats on his left.

34 Then shall the king say to them that shall be on his right hand: Come, ye blessed of my Father, possess you the kingdom prepared for you from the foundation of the world.

35 *b* For I was hungry, and you gave me to eat: I was thirsty, and you gave me to drink: I was a stranger, and you took me in:

36 Naked, and you covered me: *c* sick, and you visited me: I was in prison, and you came to me.

37 Then shall the just answer him, saying: Lord, when did we see thee hungry, and fed thee; thirsty, and gave thee drink?

38 And when did we see thee a stranger, and took thee in? or naked, and covered thee?

39 Or when did we see thee sick or in prison, and came to thee?

40 And the king answering, shall say to them: Amen I say to you, as long as you did it to one of these my least brethren, you did it to me.

41 Then he shall say to them also that shall be on his left hand: *d* Depart from me, you cursed, into everlasting fire

---

*a* Supra, 13. 12. Mark 4. 25. Luke 8. 18. and 19. 26.
*b* Isaias 58. 7. Ezec. 18. 7. and 16.—*c* Eccli. 7. 39.—*d* Is. 6. 9. Supra, 7. 23. Luke 13. 27.

which was prepared for the devil and his angels.

42 For I was hungry, and you gave me not to eat: I was thirsty, and you gave me not to drink.

43 I was a stranger, and you took me not in: naked, and you covered me not: sick and in prison, and you did not visit me.

44 Then they also shall answer him, saying: Lord, when did we see thee hungry or thirsty, or a stranger, or naked, or sick, or in prison, and did not minister to thee?

45 Then he shall answer them, saying: Amen I say to you, as long as you did it not to one of these least, neither did you do it to me.

46 *a* And these shall go into everlasting punishment: but the just, into life everlasting.

## CHAP. XXVI.

*The Jews conspire against Christ. He is anointed by Mary. The treason of Judas. The last supper. The prayer in the garden. The apprehension of our Lord: his treatment in the house of Caiphas.*

AND *b* it came to pass, when JESUS had ended all these words, he said to his disciples:

2 *c* You know that after two days shall be the pasch, and the son of man shall be delivered up to be crucified:

3 Then were gathered together the chief priests and ancients of the people into the court of the high-priest, who was called Caiphas.

4 And they consulted together that by subtilty they might apprehend JESUS, and put him to death.

*a* Dan. 12. 2. John 5. 29.—*b* A.D. 33. —*c* Mark 14. 1. Luke 22. 1.

5 But they said: Not on the festival day, lest perhaps there should be a tumult among the people.

6 And when JESUS was in Bethania, in the house of Simon the leper,

7 There came to him a woman having an alabaster-box of precious ointment, *d* and poured it on his head as he was at table.

8 And the disciples seeing it, had indignation, saying: To what purpose is this waste?

9 For this might have been sold for much, and given to the poor.

10 And JESUS knowing *it*, said to them: Why do you trouble this woman? for she hath wrought a good work upon me.

11 For the poor you have always with you: but me you have not always.

12 For she in pouring this ointment upon my body, hath done it for my burial.

13 Amen I say to you, wheresoever this gospel shall be preached in the whole world, that also which she hath done, shall be told for a memory of her.

14 *e* Then went one of the twelve, who was called Judas Iscariot, to the chief priests,

15 And said to them: What will you give me, and I will deliver him unto you? But they appointed him thirty pieces of silver.

16 And from thenceforth he

*d* Mark 14. 8. John 11. 2. and 12. 3.— *e* Mark 14. 10. Luke 22. 3.

CHAP. XXVI. Ver. 11. *Me you have not always.* Viz., in a visible manner, as when conversant here on earth: and as we have the poor, whom we may daily assist and relieve.

sought opportunity to betray him.

17 ᵃ And on the first day of the Azymes the disciples came to JESUS saying: Where wilt thou that we prepare for thee to eat the pasch?

18 But JESUS said: Go ye into the city to a certain man, and say to him: The master saith, My time is near at hand, with thee I make the pasch with my disciples.

19 And the disciples did as JESUS appointed to them, and they prepared the pasch.

20 ᵇ But when it was evening, he sat down with his twelve disciples.

21 And whilst they were eating, he said: Amen I say to you, ᶜ that one of you is about to betray me.

22 And they being very much troubled, began every one to say: Is it I, Lord?

23 But he answering said: He that dippeth his hand with me in the dish, he shall betray me.

24 The son of man indeed goeth, ᵈ as it is written of him: but wo to that man, by whom the son of man shall be betrayed: It were better for him, if that man had not been born.

25 And Judas that betrayed him, answering said: Is it I, Rabbi? He saith to him: Thou hast said *it*.

26 ᵉ And whilst they were at supper, JESUS took bread, and blessed, and broke: and gave to his disciples, and said: Take ye, and eat: This is my body.

27 And taking the chalice he gave thanks: and gave to them, saying: Drink ye all of this.

28 For this is my blood of the new testament which shall be shed for many unto remission of sins.

29 And I say to you, I will not drink from henceforth of this fruit of the vine, until that day when I shall drink it with you new in the kingdom of my father.

30 And a hymn being said, they went out unto mount Olivet.

---

ᵃ Mark 14. 12. Luke 22. 7.—ᵇ Mark 14. 17. Luke 22. 14.—ᶜ John 13. 21.—ᵈ Ps. 40. 10.—ᵉ 1 Cor. 11. 24.

Ver. 17. *Azymes.* Feast of the unleavened bread.—*Pasch.* The Paschal lamb.

Ver. 26. *This is my body.* He does not say, *this is the figure of my body,* but *this is my body* (2 Council of Nice. Acts vi.) Neither does he say *in this,* or *with this is my body;* but absolutely *this is my body:* which plainly implies transubstantiation.

Ver. 27. *Drink ye all of this.* This was spoken to the twelve apostles; who were the *All* then present; and *they all drank of it,* says St. *Mark,* xiv. 23. But it no ways follows from these words spoken to the apostles, that all the faithful are here commanded to drink of the chalice; any more than that all the faithful are commanded to consecrate, offer, and administer this sacrament; because Christ upon this same occasion, and at the same time, bid the apostles do so; in these words, St. *Luke* xxii. 19, *Do this in commemoration of me.*

Ver. 28. *Blood of the new testament.* As the old testament was dedicated with the blood of victims, by *Moses,* in these words: *this is the blood of the testament, &c., Hebrews* ix. 20. So here is the dedication and institution of the new testament, in the blood of Christ, here mystically shed, by these words: *this is the blood of the new testament, &c.*

Ver. 29. *Fruit of the vine.* These words, by the account of St. *Luke,* xxii. 18, were not spoken of the sacramental cup, but of the wine that was drunk with the paschal lamb. Though the sacramental cup might also be called the *fruit of the vine,* because it was consecrated from wine, and retains the likeness, and all the accidents, or qualities of wine.

JESUS AMONG THE DOCTORS IN THE TEMPLE.

31 Then JESUS saith to them: *All you shall be scandalized in me this night. For it is written: *I will strike the shepherd, and the sheep of the flock shall be dispersed.*

32 *But after I shall be risen again, I will go before you into Galilee.

33 And Peter answering, said to him: Although all shall be scandalized in thee, I will never be scandalized.

34 JESUS said to him, *d* Amen I say to thee, that in this night before the cock crow, thou wilt deny me thrice.

35 Peter saith to him: *Yea, though I should die with thee, I will not deny thee. And in like manner said all the disciples.

36 Then JESUS came with them into a country place which is called Gethsemani: and he said to his disciples: Sit you here, till I go yonder and pray.

37 And taking with him Peter and the two sons of Zebedee, he began to grow sorrowful and to be sad.

38 Then he saith to them: My soul is sorrowful even unto death: stay you here, and watch with me.

39 And going a little further, he fell upon his face, praying, and saying: My Father, if it be possible, let this chalice pass from me. Nevertheless not as I will, but as thou *wilt.*

40 And he cometh to his disciples, and findeth them asleep, and he saith to Peter: What? Could you not watch one hour with me?

41 Watch ye, and pray that ye enter not into temptation. The spirit indeed is willing, but the flesh is weak.

42 Again the second time, he went and prayed, saying: My Father, if this chalice may not pass away, but I must drink it, thy will be done.

43 And he cometh again, and findeth them sleeping: for their eyes were heavy.

44 And leaving them he went again: and he prayed the third time, saying the self-same word.

45 Then he cometh to his disciples, and saith to them: Sleep ye now and take your rest: behold the hour is at hand, and the son of man shall be betrayed into the hands of sinners.

46 Rise, let us go: behold he is at hand that will betray me.

47 *f* As he yet spoke, behold Judas, one of the twelve, came, and with him a great multitude with swords and clubs, sent from the chief priests and the ancients of the people.

48 And he that betrayed him, gave them a sign, saying: Whomsoever I shall kiss, that is he, hold him fast.

49 And forthwith coming to JESUS, he said: Hail, Rabbi. And he kissed him.

50 And JESUS said to him: Friend, whereto art thou come? Then they came up, and laid hands on JESUS, and held him.

51 And behold one of them that were with JESUS, stretching forth his hand, drew out his sword; and striking the servant

---

*a* Mark 14. 27. John 16. 32.—*b* Zach. 13. 7.—*c* Mark 14. 28. and 16. 7.—*d* Mark 14. 30. John 13. 38.—*e* Mark 14. 31. Luke 22. 33.

Ver. 31. *Scandalized in me, &c.* Forasmuch as my being apprehended shall make you all run away and forsake me.

*f* Mark 14. 43. Luke 22. 47. John 18. 3.

of the high-priest, cut off his ear.

52 Then JESUS saith to him: Put up again thy sword into its place: *a* for all that take the sword shall perish with the sword.

53 Thinkest thou that I cannot ask my Father, and he will give me presently more than twelve legions of Angels?

54 *b* How then shall the scriptures be fulfilled, that so it must be done.

55 In that same hour JESUS said to the multitudes: You are come out as it were to a robber with swords and clubs to apprehend me. I sat daily with you teaching in the temple, and you laid not hands on me.

56 Now all this was done, that the *c* scriptures of the prophets might be fulfilled. Then the disciples *d* all leaving him, fled.

57 But they holding JESUS *e* led him to Caiphas the high-priest, where the scribes and the ancients were assembled.

58 And Peter followed him afar off, even to the court of the high-priest. And going in, he sat with the servants, that he might see the end.

59 And the chief priests and the whole council sought false witness against JESUS, that they might put him to death:

60 And they found not, whereas many false witnesses had come in. And last of all there came two false witnesses;

61 And they said: *f* This man said, I am able to destroy the temple of God, and after three days to rebuild it.

62 And the high-priest rising up, said to him: Answerest thou nothing to the things which these witness against thee?

63 But JESUS held his peace. And the high-priest said to him: I adjure thee by the living God, that thou tell us if thou be the Christ the Son of God.

64 JESUS saith to him: Thou hast said it. Nevertheless I say to you, *g* hereafter you shall see the son of man sitting on the right hand of the power of God, and coming in the clouds of heaven.

65 Then the high-priest rent his garments, saying: He hath blasphemed, what further need have we of witnesses? Behold now you have heard the blasphemy:

66 What think you? But they answering said: He is guilty of death.

67 *h* Then did they spit in his face, and buffeted him, and others struck his face with the palms of their hands,

68 Saying: Prophesy unto us, O Christ; who is he that struck thee?

69 *i* But Peter sat without in the court: and there came to him a servant-maid, saying: Thou also wast with JESUS the Galilean.

70 But he denied before them all, saying: I know not what thou sayest.

71 And as he went out of the gate, another maid saw him, and she said to them that were there: This man also was with JESUS of Nazareth.

72 And again he denied with an oath: That I know not the man.

---

*a* Gen. 9. 6. Apoc. 13. 10.—*b* Isaias 53. 10.—*c* Lam. 4. 20.—*d* Mark 14. 50. —*e* Luke 22. 54. John 18. 24.—*f* John 2. 19.

*g* Supra, 16. 27. Rom. 14. 10. 1 Thess. 4. 15.—*h* Isaias 50. 6. Mark 14. 65.—*i* Luke 22. 55. John 18. 17.

73 And after a little while they came that stood by, and said to Peter: Surely thou also art one of them: for even thy speech doth discover thee.

74 Then he began to curse and to swear that he knew not the man. And immediately the cock crew.

75 And Peter remembered the word of JESUS which he had said: Before the cock crow, thou wilt deny me thrice. And going forth he wept bitterly.

## CHAP. XXVII.

*The continuation of the history of the passion of Christ. His death and burial.*

AND when morning was come, all the chief priests and ancients of the people took counsel against JESUS, that they might put him to death.

2 ᵃ And they brought him bound, and delivered him to Pontius Pilate the governor.

3 Then Judas, who betrayed him, seeing that he was condemned; repenting himself, brought back the thirty pieces of silver to the chief priests and ancients,

4 Saying: I have sinned, in betraying innocent blood. But they said: What is that to us? look thou to it.

5 And casting down the pieces of silver in the temple, he departed: ᵇ and went and hanged himself with an halter.

6 But the chief priests having taken the pieces of silver, said: It is not lawful to put them into the corbona, because it is the price of blood.

7 And after they had consulted together, they bought with them the potter's field, to be a burying-place for strangers.

8 ᶜ For this cause that field was called haceldama, that is, the field of blood, even to this day.

9 Then was fulfilled that which was spoken by Jeremias the prophet, saying: ᵈ And they took the thirty pieces of silver, the price of him that was prized, whom they prized of the children of Israel.

10 And they gave them unto the potter's field, as the Lord appointed to me.

11 And JESUS stood before the governor, ᵉ and the governor asked him, saying: Art thou the king of the Jews? JESUS saith to him: Thou sayest it.

12 And when he was accused by the chief priests and ancients, he answered nothing.

13 Then Pilate saith to him: Dost not thou hear how great testimonies they allege against thee?

14 And he answered him to never a word: so that the governor wondered exceedingly.

15 Now upon the solemn day the governor was accustomed to release to the people one prisoner, whom they would.

16 And he had then a notorious prisoner, that was called Barabbas.

17 They therefore being gathered together, Pilate said: Whom will you that I release to you, Barabbas, or JESUS that is called Christ?

---

ᵃ Mark 15. 1. Luke 22. 1. John 18. 28.—ᵇ Acts 1. 18.

CHAP. XXVII. Ver. 6. *Corbona.* A place in the temple where the people put in their gifts or offerings.

ᶜ Acts 1. 19.—ᵈ Zach. 11. 12.—ᵉ Mark 15. 2. Luke 23. 3. John 18 33.

build it; save thy own self: if thou be the Son of God, come down from the cross.

41 In like manner also the chief priests with the scribes and ancients mocking, said:

42 He saved others; himself he cannot save: *if he be the king of Israel, let him now come down from the cross, and we will believe him.

43 *b* He trusted in God; let him now deliver *him* if he will have him: for he said: I am the Son of God.

44 And the self-same thing the thieves also, that were crucified with him, reproached him with.

45 Now from the sixth hour there was darkness over the whole earth, until the ninth hour.

46 And about the ninth hour JESUS cried with a loud voice, saying: *c* Eli, Eli, lamma sabacthani? that is, My God, my God, why hast thou forsaken me?

47 And some that stood there and heard, said: This man calleth Elias.

48 And immediately one of them running, took a sponge, and filled it with vinegar; and put it on a reed, and gave him to drink.

49 And the others said: Let be, let us see whether Elias will come to deliver him.

50 And JESUS again crying with a loud voice, yielded up the ghost.

51 *d* And behold the veil of the temple was rent in two from the top even to the bottom, and the earth quaked, and the rocks were rent.

52 And the graves were opened: and many bodies of the saints that had slept arose.

53 And coming out of the tombs after his resurrection, came into the holy city, and appeared to many.

54 Now the centurion and they that were with him watching JESUS, having seen the earthquake and the things that were done, were sore afraid, saying: Indeed this was the Son of God.

55 And there were there many women afar off, who had followed JESUS from Galilee, ministering unto him.

56 Among whom was Mary Magdalen, and Mary the mother of James and Joseph, and the mother of the sons of Zebedee.

57 *e* And when it was evening, there came a certain rich man of Arimathea, named Joseph, who also himself was a disciple of JESUS.

58 He went to Pilate, and asked the body of JESUS. Then Pilate commanded that the body should be delivered.

59 And Joseph taking the body, wrapt it up in a clean linen cloth.

60 And laid it in his own new monument, which he had hewed out in a rock. And he rolled a great stone to the door of the monument, and went his way.

61 And there was there Mary Magdalen, and the other Mary sitting over against the sepulchre.

62 And the next day, which followed the day of preparation,

---

*e* Mark 15. 42. Luke 23. 50. John 21. 38.

---

Ver. 62. *The day of preparation.* The eve of the Sabbath; so called, because on that day they *prepared* all

---

*a* Wis. 2. 18.—*b* Ps. 21. 9.—*c* Ps. 21. 2.— *d* 2 Par. 3. 14.

the chief priests and the Pharisees came together to Pilate,

63 Saying: Sir, we have remembered, that that seducer said, while he was yet alive: After three days I will rise again.

64 Command therefore the sepulchre to be guarded until the third day: lest perhaps his disciples come, and steal him away, and say to the people, he is risen from the dead: and the last error shall be worse than the first.

65 Pilate said to them: You have a guard: go, guard it as you know.

66 And they departing, made the sepulchre sure, sealing the stone, and setting guards.

## CHAP. XXVIII.

*The resurrection of Christ. His commission to his disciples.*

AND [a] in the end of the Sabbath when it began to dawn towards the first day of the week, came Mary Magdalen and the other Mary to see the sepulchre.

2 And behold there was a great earthquake. For an angel of the Lord descended from heaven: and coming, rolled back the stone, and sat upon it:

3 And his countenance was as lightning, and his raiment as snow.

4 And for fear of him, the guards were struck with terror, and became as dead men.

5 And the angel answering, said to the women: Fear not you: for I know that you seek JESUS who was crucified.

6 He is not here, for he is risen, as he said. Come, and see the place where the Lord was laid.

7 And going quickly, tell ye his disciples that he is risen: and behold he will go before you into Galilee: there you shall see him. Lo, I have foretold it to you.

8 And they went out quickly from the sepulchre with fear and great joy, running to tell his disciples.

9 And behold JESUS met them, saying, All hail. But they came up, and took hold of his feet, and adored him.

10 Then JESUS said to them: Fear not. Go, tell my brethren that they go into Galilee, there they shall see me.

11 Who when they were departed, behold some of the guards came into the city, and told the chief priests all things that had been done.

12 And they being assembled together with the ancients, taking counsel, gave a great sum of money to the soldiers,

13 Saying: Say you, His disciples came by night, and stole him away when we were asleep.

14 And if the governor shall hear of this, we will persuade him, and secure you.

15 So they taking the money, did as they were taught: and this word was spread abroad among the Jews even unto this day.

16 And the eleven disciples went into Galilee, unto the mountain where JESUS had appointed them.

17 And seeing him they adored: but some doubted.

---

[a] Mark 16. 1. John 20. 11.

things necessary; not being allowed so much as to dress their meat on the Sabbath-day.

CHAP. I.  ST. MARK.  CHAP. I.

18 And JESUS coming spoke to them, saying: All power is given to me in heaven and in earth.

19 *a* Going therefore teach ye all nations: baptizing them in the name of the Father, and of the Son, and of the Holy Ghost.

20 Teaching them to observe all things whatsoever I have commanded you: and behold I am with you all days, even to the consummation of the world.

*a* Mark 16. 15.

CHAP. XXVIII. Ver. 18. &c. *All power, &c.* See here the warrant and commission of the apostles and their successors, the bishops and pastors of Christ's church. He received from his Father *all power in heaven and in earth;* and in virtue of *this power, he sends them* (even *as his Father sent him.* St. John xx. 21) *to teach* and *disciple, μαθητεύειν,* not one, but *all nations;* and instruct them in *all truths;* and that he may assist them effectually in the execution of this commission, he promises to be with them (not for three or four hundred years only), but *all days, even to the consummation of the world.* How then could the Catholic Church ever go astray: having always with her pastors, as is here promised. Christ himself, who is *the way, the truth, and the life.* (St. John xiv.)

---

# THE
# HOLY GOSPEL OF JESUS CHRIST,
## ACCORDING TO ST. MARK.

ST. MARK, *the disciple and interpreter of St. Peter* (saith St. Jerome), *according to what he heard from Peter himself, wrote at Rome a brief Gospel at the request of the brethren, about ten years after our Lord's Ascension, which when Peter had heard, he approved of it, and with his authority published it to the Church to be read. Baronius and others say, that the original was written in Latin, but the more general opinion is, that the Evangelist wrote it in Greek.*

## CHAP. I.

*The preaching of John the Baptist. Christ is baptized by him. He calls his disciples, and works many miracles.*

THE beginning of the Gospel of JESUS CHRIST the Son of God.

2 As it is written in Isaias the prophet: *a Behold I send my angel before thy face, who shall prepare the way before thee.*

3 *b A voice of one crying in the desert, Prepare ye the way of the Lord, make straight his paths.*

4 *c* John was in the desert baptizing, and preaching the baptism of penance unto remission of sins.

5 *d* And there went out to him all the country of Judea, and all they of Jerusalem, and were baptized by him in the river of Jordan, confessing their sins.

6 *e* And John was clothed

*a* Malac. 3. 1.—*b* Isaias 40. 3. Matt. 3. 3. Luke 3. 4. John 1. 23.  *c* A.D. 28.—*d* Matt. 3. 5.—*e* Matt. 3. 4.

with camel's hair, and a leathern girdle about his loins: "and he ate locusts and wild honey.

7 And he preached, saying: *b* There cometh after me one mightier than I, the latchet of whose shoes I am not worthy to stoop down and loose.

8 *c* I have baptized you with water; but he shall baptize you with the Holy Ghost.

9 And it came to pass, in those days JESUS came from Nazareth of Galilee; and was baptized by John in the Jordan.

10 And forthwith coming up out of the water, he saw the heavens opened, *d* and the Spirit as a dove descending, and remaining on him.

11 And there came a voice from heaven: Thou art my beloved Son, in thee I am well pleased.

12 *e* And immediately the Spirit drove him out into the desert.

13 And he was in the desert forty days, and forty nights: and was tempted by satan, and he was with beasts, and the angels ministered to him.

14 *f* And after that John was delivered up, JESUS came into Galilee, preaching the gospel of the kingdom of God.

15 And saying: The time is accomplished, and the kingdom of God is at hand: repent, and believe the gospel.

16 *g* And passing by the sea of Galilee, he saw Simon and Andrew his brother, casting nets into the sea (for they were fishermen).

17 And JESUS said to them: Come after me, and I will make you to become fishers of men.

18 And immediately leaving their nets, they followed him.

19 And going on from thence a little farther, he saw James the son of Zebedee, and John his brother, who also were mending their nets in the ship:

20 And forthwith he called them. And leaving their father Zebedee in the ship with his hired men, they followed him.

21 *h* And they entered into Capharnaum, and forthwith upon the Sabbath-days going into the synagogue, he taught them.

22 *i* And they were astonished at his doctrine. For he was teaching them as one having power, and not as the scribes.

23 *k* And there was in their synagogue, a man with an unclean spirit; and he cried out,

24 Saying: What have we to do with thee, JESUS of Nazareth? art thou come to destroy us? I know who thou art, the Holy One of God.

25 And JESUS threatened him, saying: Speak no more and go out of the man.

26 And the unclean spirit tearing him, and crying out with a loud voice, went out of him.

27 And they were all amazed, insomuch that they questioned among themselves, saying: What thing is this? what is this new doctrine? for with power he commandeth even the unclean spirits, and they obey him.

---

*a* Lev. 11. 22.—*b* Matt. 3. 11. Luke 3. 16. John 1. 27.—*c* Acts 1. 5. and 2. 4. and 11. 16. and 19. 4.—*d* Luke 3. 22. John 1. 32.—*e* Matt. 4. 1. Luke 4. 1.— *f* Matt. 4. 12. Luke 4. 14. John 4. 43. —*g* Matt. 4. 18. Luke 5. 2.

*h* Matt. 4. 13. Luke 4. 31.- *i* Matt. 7. 28. Luke 4. 32.—*k* Luke 4. 33.

THE BAPTISM OF JESUS IN THE JORDAN.

CHAP. I. ST. MARK. CHAP. II.

28 And the fame of him was spread forthwith into all the country of Galilee.

29 ᵃ And immediately going out of the synagogue, they came into the house of Simon and Andrew, with James and John.

30 And Simon's wife's mother lay in a fit of a fever: and forthwith they tell him of her.

31 And coming to her he lifted her up, taking her by the hand: and immediately the fever left her, and she ministered unto them.

32 And when it was evening after sunset, they brought to him all that were ill and that were possessed with devils.

33 And all the city was gathered together at the door.

34 And he healed many that were troubled with divers diseases; ᵇ and he cast out many devils, and he suffered them not to speak, because they knew him.

35 And rising very early, going out he went into a desert place: and there he prayed.

36 And Simon and they that were with him followed after him.

37 And when they had found him, they said to him, All seek for thee.

38 And he saith to them: Let us go into the neighbouring towns and cities, that I may preach there also: for to this purpose am I come.

39 And he was preaching in their synagogues, and in all Galilee, and casting out devils.

40 ᶜ And there came a leper to him, beseeching him, and kneeling down, said to him: If thou wilt; thou canst make me clean.

41 And JESUS having compassion on him, stretched forth his hand; and touching him, saith to him: I will. Be thou made clean.

42 And when he had spoken, immediately the leprosy departed from him, and he was made clean.

43 And he strictly charged him, and forthwith sent him away.

44 And he saith to him: See thou tell no one, but go, shew thyself to the high-priest, and offer for thy cleansing ᵈ the things that Moses commanded, for a testimony to them.

45 But he being gone out, began to publish, and to blaze abroad the word; so that he could not openly go into the city, but was without in desert places, and they flocked to him from all sides.

## CHAP. II.

*Christ heals the sick of the palsy: calls Matthew: and excuses his disciples.*

AND ᵉ again he entered into Capharnaum after some days.

2 And it was heard that he was in the house, and many came together, so that there was no room, no not even at the door; and he spoke to them the word.

3 ᶠ And they came to him bringing one sick of the palsy, who was carried by four.

4 And when they could not offer him unto him for the multitude, they uncovered the roof where he was: and opening it

---

ᵃ Matt. 8. 14. Luke 4. 38.—ᵇ Luke 4. 41.—ᶜ Matt. 8. 2. Luke 5. 12.

ᵈ Lev. 14. 2.—ᵉ Matt. 9. 1.—ᶠ Luke 5. 18.

61

they let down the bed wherein the man sick of the palsy lay.

5 And when JESUS had seen their faith, he saith to the sick of the palsy: Son, thy sins are forgiven thee.

6 And there were some of the scribes sitting there, and thinking in their hearts:

7 Why doth this man speak thus? he blasphemeth. *a* Who can forgive sins, but God only?

8 Which JESUS presently knowing in his spirit, that they so thought within themselves, saith to them: Why think you these things in your hearts?

9 Which is easier, to say to the sick of the palsy: Thy sins are forgiven thee; or to say: Arise, take up thy bed, and walk?

10 But that you may know that the son of man hath power on earth to forgive sins (he saith to the sick of the palsy),

11 I say to thee, Arise, take up thy bed, and go into thy house.

12 And immediately he arose; and taking up his bed, went his way in the sight of all, so that all wondered, and glorified God, saying: We never saw the like.

13 And he went forth again to the sea-side: and all the multitude came to him, and he taught them.

14 *b* And when he was passing by, he saw Levi *the son* of Alpheus sitting at the receipt of custom; and he saith to him: Follow me. And rising up he followed him.

15 And it came to pass, that as he sat at meat in his house, many publicans and sinners sat down together with JESUS and his disciples. For they were many, who also followed him.

16 And the scribes and the Pharisees, seeing that he ate with publicans and sinners, said to his disciples: Why doth your master eat and drink with publicans and sinners?

17 *c* JESUS hearing this, saith to them: They that are well have no need of a physician, but they that are sick. For I came not to call the just but sinners.

18 And the disciples of John and the Pharisees used to fast: and they come, and say to him: Why do the disciples of John and of the Pharisees fast: but thy disciples do not fast?

19 And JESUS saith to them: Can the children of the marriage fast, as long as the bridegroom is with them? As long as they have the bridegroom with them, they cannot fast.

20 *d* But the days will come when the bridegroom shall be taken away from them: and then they shall fast in those days.

21 No man seweth a piece of raw cloth to an old garment: otherwise the new piecing taketh away from the old, and there is made a greater rent.

22 And no man putteth new wine into old bottles: otherwise the wine will burst the bottles, and both the wine will be spilled, and the bottles will be lost. But new wine must be put into new bottles.

23 *e* And it came to pass again, as the Lord walked through the corn-fields on the sabbath, that his disciples began

---

*a* Job 14. 4. Isaias 43. 25.—*b* Matt. 9. 9. Luke 5. 27.

*c* 1 Tim. 1. 15.—*d* Matt. 9. 15. Luke 5. 35.—*e* Matt. 12. 1. Luke 6. 1.

to go forward and to pluck the ears of corn.

24 And the Pharisees said to him: Behold, why do they on the sabbath-day that which is not lawful?

25 And he said to them: <sup>a</sup> Have you never read what David did, when he had need, and was hungry himself, and they that were with him?

26 How he went into the house of God under Abiathar the high-priest, and did eat the loaves of proposition <sup>b</sup> which was not lawful to eat but for the priests, and gave to them who were with him?

27 And he said to them: The sabbath was made for man, not man for the sabbath.

28 Therefore the son of man is Lord of the sabbath also.

## CHAP. III.

*Christ heals the withered hand: he chooses the twelve: he confutes the blasphemy of the Pharisees.*

AND <sup>c</sup> he entered again into the synagogue, and there was a man there who had a withered hand.

2 And they watched him whether he would heal on the sabbath-days; that they might accuse him.

3 And he said to the man who had the withered hand: Stand up in the midst.

4 And he saith to them: Is it lawful to do good on the sabbath-days, or to do evil? to save life, or to destroy? But they held their peace.

5 And looking round about on them, with anger, being grieved for the blindness of their hearts, he saith to the man: Stretch forth thy hand. And he stretched it forth: and his hand was restored unto him.

6 <sup>d</sup> And the Pharisees going out immediately made a consultation with the Herodians against him, how they might destroy him.

7 But JESUS retired with his disciples to the sea; and a great multitude followed him, from Galilee and Judea,

8 And from Jerusalem, and from Idumea, and from beyond the Jordan. And they about Tyre and Sidon, a great multitude, hearing the things which he did, came to him.

9 And he spoke to his disciples that a small ship should wait on him because of the multitude, lest they should throng him.

10 For he healed many, so that they pressed upon him for to touch him, as many as had evils.

11 And the unclean spirits, when they saw him, fell down before him: and they cried, saying:

12 Thou art the son of God. And he strictly charged them that they should not make him known.

13 <sup>e</sup> And going up into a mountain, he called unto him whom he would himself: and they came to him.

14 And he made that twelve should be with him, and that he might send them to preach.

15 And he gave them power to heal sicknesses, and to cast out devils.

16 And to Simon he gave the name Peter.

---

<sup>a</sup> 1 Kings 21. 6.—<sup>b</sup> Lev. 24. 9.—<sup>c</sup> Matt. 12. 10. Luke 6. 6. <sup>d</sup> Matt. 12. 14.—<sup>e</sup> Matt. 10. 1. Luke 6. 12. and 9. 1.

17 And James *the son* of Zebedee, and John the brother of James: and he named them Boanerges which is the sons of thunder.

18 And Andrew and Philip, and Bartholomew and Matthew, and Thomas and James of Alpheus, and Thaddeus, and Simon the Cananean,

19 And Judas Iscariot, who also betrayed him.

20 And they come to a house, and the multitude cometh together again, so that they could not so much as eat bread.

21 And when his friends heard of it, they went out to lay hold on him. For they said: He is become mad.

22 And the scribes who were come down from Jerusalem, said: *a* He hath Beelzebub, and by the prince of devils he casteth out devils.

23 And after he had called them together, he said to them in parables: How can satan cast out satan?

24 And if a kingdom be divided against itself, that kingdom cannot stand.

25 And if a house be divided against itself, that house cannot stand.

26 And if satan be risen up against himself, he is divided, and cannot stand, but hath an end.

27 No man can enter into the house of a strong man and rob him of his goods, unless he first bind the strong man, and then shall he plunder his house.

28 *b* Amen I say to you, that all sins shall be forgiven unto the sons of men, and the blasphemies wherewith they shall blaspheme:

29 But he that shall blaspheme against the Holy Ghost, shall never have forgiveness, but shall be guilty of an everlasting sin.

30 Because they said: He hath an unclean spirit.

31 And his mother and his brethren came: and standing without sent unto him calling him.

32 And the multitude sat about him; and they say to him: Behold thy mother and thy brethren without seek for thee.

33 And answering them he said: Who is my mother and my brethren?

34 And looking round about on them who sat about him, he saith: Behold my mother and my brethren.

35 For whosoever shall do the will of God, he is my brother, and my sister and mother.

## CHAP. IV.

*The parable of the sower. Christ stills the tempest at sea.*

AND *c* again he began to teach by the sea-side; and a great multitude was gathered together unto him, so that he went up into a ship and sat in the sea, and all the multitude was upon the land by the sea-side.

2 And he taught them many things in parables, and said unto them in his doctrine:

3 Hear ye; Behold, the sower went out to sow.

4 And whilst he soweth, some fell by the way-side, and the birds of the air came, and ate it up.

5 And other some fell upon stony ground where it had not

---

*a* Matt. 9. 34.—*b* Matt. 12. 31. Luke 12. 10. 1 John 5. 16.

*c* Matt. 13. 2. Luke 8. 5.

THE TEMPTATION OF CHRIST.

much earth: and it shot up immediately because it had no depth of earth:

6 And when the sun was risen, it was scorched, and because it had no root, it withered away.

7 And some fell among thorns: and the thorns grew up, and choked it, and it yielded no fruit.

8 And some fell upon good ground: and brought forth fruit that grew up, and increased, and yielded, one thirty, another sixty, and another a hundred.

9 And he said: He that hath ears to hear, let him hear.

10 And when he was alone, the twelve that were with him asked him the parable.

11 And he said to them: To you it is given to know the mystery of the kingdom of God: but to them that are without, all things are done in parables.

12 *a* That seeing they may see, and not perceive: and hearing they may hear, and not understand: lest at any time they should be converted, and their sins should be forgiven them.

13 And he saith to them: Are you ignorant of this parable? and how shall you know all parables?

14 He that soweth: soweth the word.

15 And these are they by the way-side, where the word is sown, and as soon as they have heard, immediately satan cometh, and taketh away the word that was sown in their hearts.

16 And these likewise are they that are sown on the stony ground: who when they have heard the word, immediately receive it with joy.

17 And they have no root in themselves, but are only for a time: and then when tribulation and persecution ariseth for the word, they are presently scandalized.

18 And others there are who are sown among thorns: these are they that hear the word,

19 And the cares of the world, *b* and the deceitfulness of riches, and the lusts after other things entering in choke the word, and it is made fruitless.

20 And these are they who are sown upon the good ground, who hear the word, and receive it, and yield fruit, the one thirty, another sixty, and another a hundred.

21 *c* And he said to them: Doth a candle come in to be put under a bushel, or under a bed? and not to be set on a candlestick?

22 *d* For there is nothing hid, which shall not be made manifest: neither was it made secret, but that it may come abroad.

23 If any man have ears to hear, let him hear.

24 And he said to them: Take heed what you hear. *e* In what measure you shall mete, it shall be measured to you again, and more shall be given to you.

---

*a* Isaias 6. 9. Matt. 13. 14. John 12. 40. Acts 28. 26. Rom. 11. 8.

CHAP. IV. Ver. 12. *That seeing they may see, &c.* In punishment of their wilfully shutting their eyes (St. Matt. xiii. 15), God justly withdrew those lights, and graces, which otherwise he would have given them, for their effectual conversion.

*b* 1 Tim. 6. 17.—*c* Matt. 5. 15. Luke 8. 16. and 11. 33.—*d* Matt. 10. 26. Luke 8. 17.—*e* Matt. 7. 2. Luke 6. 38.

25 ᵃ For he that hath, to him shall be given: and he that hath not, that also which he hath shall be taken away from him.

26 And he said: So is the kingdom of God, as if a man should cast seed into the earth,

27 And should sleep, and rise, night and day, and the seed should spring and grow up whilst he knoweth not.

28 For the earth of itself bringeth forth fruit, first the blade, then the ear, afterwards the full corn in the ear.

29 And when the fruit is brought forth, immediately he putteth in the sickle, because the harvest is come.

30 And he said: To what shall we liken the kingdom of God, or to what parable shall we compare it?

31 ᵇ It is as a grain of mustard seed; which when it is sown in the earth, is less than all the seeds that are in the earth:

32 And when it is sown, it groweth up, and becometh greater than all herbs, and shooteth out great branches, so that the birds of the air may dwell under the shadow thereof.

33 And with many such parables, he spoke to them the word, according as they were able to hear.

34 And without parable he did not speak unto them; but apart, he explained all things to his disciples.

35 And he saith to them that day, when evening was come: Let us pass over to the other side.

36 ᶜ And sending away the multitude, they take him even as he was in the ship: and there were other ships with him.

37 And there arose a great storm of wind, and the waves beat into the ship, so that the ship was filled.

38 And he was in the hinder part of the ship, sleeping upon a pillow: and they awake him, and say to him: Master, doth it not concern thee that we perish?

39 And rising up he rebuked the wind, and said to the sea: Peace, be still. And the wind ceased; and there was made a great calm.

40 And he said to them: Why are you fearful? have you not faith yet? And they feared exceedingly: and they said one to another: Who is this (thinkest thou) that both wind and sea obey him?

## CHAP. V.

*Christ casts out a legion of devils: he heals the issue of blood, and raises the daughter of Jairus to life.*

AND ᵈ they came over the strait of the sea into the country of the Gerasens.

2 And as he went out of the ship, immediately there met him out of the monuments a man with an unclean spirit,

3 Who had his dwelling in the tombs, and no man now could bind him, not even with chains.

4 For having been often bound with fetters and chains, he had burst the chains, and broken the fetters in pieces, and no one could tame him.

5 And he was always day and night in the monuments and in the mountains, crying and cutting himself with stones.

---

ᵃ Matt. 13. 12. and 25. 29. Luke 8. 18. and 19. 26.—ᵇ Matt. 13. 31. Luke 13. 19.—ᶜ Matt. 8. 23. Luke 8. 22.

ᵈ Matt. 8. 28. Luke 8. 26.

6 And seeing JESUS, afar off, he ran and adored him.

7 And crying with a loud voice, he said: What have I to do with thee, JESUS the Son of the most high God? I adjure thee by God that thou torment me not.

8 For he said unto him: Go out of the man, thou unclean spirit.

9 And he asked him: What is thy name? And he saith to him: My name is Legion, for we are many.

10 And he besought him much, that he would not drive him away out of the country.

11 And there was there near the mountain a great herd of swine, feeding.

12 And the spirits besought him, saying: Send us into the swine, that we may enter into them.

13 And JESUS immediately gave them leave. And the unclean spirits going out, entered into the swine: and the herd with great violence was carried headlong into the sea, being about two thousand, and were stifled in the sea.

14 And they that fed them fled, and told it in the city and in the fields. And they went out to see what was done:

15 And they come to JESUS, and they see him that was troubled with the devil, sitting, clothed, and well in his wits, and they were afraid.

16 And they that had seen it, told them, in what manner he had been dealt with who had the devil; and concerning the swine.

17 And they began to pray him that he would depart from their coasts.

18 And when he went up into the ship, he that had been troubled with the devil, began to beseech him that he might be with him.

19 And he admitted him not, but saith to him: Go into thy house to thy friends, and tell them how great things the Lord hath done for thee, and hath had mercy on thee.

20 And he went his way, and began to publish in Decapolis how great things JESUS had done for him: and all men wondered.

21 And when JESUS had passed again in the ship over the strait, a great multitude assembled together unto him, and he was nigh unto the sea.

22 *a* And there cometh one of the rulers of the synagogue named Jairus: and seeing him falleth down at his feet.

23 And he besought him much, saying: My daughter is at the point of death, come, lay thy hand upon her, that she may be safe, and may live.

24 And he went with him, and a great multitude followed him, and they thronged him.

25 And a woman who was under an issue of blood twelve years,

26 And had suffered many things from many physicians, and had spent all that she had, and was nothing the better, but rather worse,

27 When she had heard of JESUS, came in the crowd behind him, and touched his garment.

28 For she said: If I shall touch but his garment, I shall be whole.

29 And forthwith the fountain

---

*a* Matt. 9. 18. Luke 8. 41.

of her blood was dried up, and she felt in her body that she was healed of the evil.

30 And immediately JESUS knowing in himself the virtue that had proceeded from him, turning to the multitude, said: Who hath touched my garments?

31 And his disciples said to him: Thou seest the multitude thronging thee, and sayest thou who hath touched me?

32 And he looked about to see her who had done this.

33 But the woman fearing and trembling, knowing what was done in her, came and fell down before him, and told him all the truth.

34 And he said to her: *a* Daughter, thy faith hath made thee whole: go in peace, and be thou whole of thy disease.

35 While he was yet speaking, some come from the ruler of the synagogue's house, saying: Thy daughter is dead: why dost thou trouble the master any farther?

36 But JESUS having heard the word that was spoken, saith to the ruler of the synagogue: Fear not, only believe.

37 And he admitted not any man to follow him, but Peter, and James, and John the brother of James.

38 And they come to the house of the ruler of the synagogue; and he seeth a tumult, and people weeping and wailing much.

39 And going in, he saith to them: Why make you this a-do, and weep? the damsel is not dead but sleepeth.

40 And they laughed him to scorn. But he having put them all out, taketh the father and the mother of the damsel, and them that were with him, and entereth in where the damsel was lying.

41 And taking the damsel by the hand, he saith to her: Talitha cumi, which is, being interpreted: damsel (I say to thee) arise.

42 And immediately the damsel rose up, and walked: and she was twelve years old: and they were astonished with a great astonishment.

43 And he charged them strictly that no man should know it: and commanded that something should be given her to eat.

## CHAP. VI.

*Christ teaches at Nazareth: he sends forth the twelve apostles: he feeds five thousand with five loaves; and walks upon the sea.*

AND *b* going out from thence, he went into his own country; and his disciples followed him.

2 And when the sabbath was come he began to teach in the synagogue: and many hearing him were in admiration at his doctrine, saying: How came this man by all these things? and what wisdom is this that is given to him, and such mighty works as are wrought by his hands?

3 *c* Is not this the carpenter, the son of Mary, the brother of James, and Joseph, and Jude, and Simon? are not also his sisters here with us? And they were scandalized in regard of him.

---

*a* Luke 7. 50. and 8. 48.

*b* Matt. 13. 54. Luke 4. 16.—*c* John 6. 42.

ST. JOHN GIVES TESTIMONY OF OUR LORD.

CHAP. VI.        ST. MARK.        CHAP. VI.

4 And JESUS said to them: *A prophet is not without honour, but in his own country, and in his own house, and among his own kindred.

5 And he could not do any miracles there, only that he cured a few that were sick, laying his hands upon them.

6 And he wondered because of their unbelief, and he went through the villages round about teaching.

7 *b* And he called the twelve; and began to send them two and two, and gave them power over unclean spirits.

8 And he commanded them that they should take nothing for the way, but a staff only: no scrip, no bread, nor money in their purse.

9 *c* But to be shod with sandals, and that they should not put on two coats.

10 And he said to them: Wheresoever you shall enter into an house, there abide till you depart from that place.

11 And whosoever shall not receive you, nor hear you; *d* going forth from thence, shake off the dust from your feet for a testimony to them.

12 And going forth they preached that *men* should do penance;

13 And they cast out many devils, *e* and anointed with oil many that were sick, and healed them.

14 *f* And king Herod heard (for his name was made manifest), and he said: John the Baptist is risen again from the dead, and therefore mighty works shew forth themselves in him.

15 And others said: It is Elias. But others said: It is a prophet, as one of the prophets.

16 Which Herod hearing, said: John whom I beheaded, he is risen again from the dead.

17 *g* For Herod himself had sent and apprehended John, and bound him in prison for the sake of Herodias the wife of Philip his brother, because he had married her.

18 For John said to Herod: *h* It is not lawful for thee to have thy brother's wife.

19 Now Herodias laid snares for him: and was desirous to put him to death and could not.

20 For Herod feared John, knowing him to be a just and holy man: and kept him, and when he heard him, did many things: and he heard him willingly.

21 And when a convenient day was come, Herod made a supper for his birth-day, for the princes, and tribunes, and chief men of Galilee.

22 And when the daughter of the same Herodias had come in, and had danced, and pleased Herod, and them that were at table with him, the king said to the damsel: Ask of me what

---

*a* Matt. 18. 57. Luke 4. 22. John 4. 44.—*b* Matt. 10. 1.—Supra, 3. 15. Luke 9. 1.—*c* Acts 12. 8.—*d* Matt. 10. 14. Luke 9. 5. Acts 13. 51. and 18. 6.—*e* Jas. 5. 14.

CHAP. VI. Ver. 5. *He could not.* Not for want of power, but because he would not work miracles in favour of obstinate and incredulous people, who were unworthy of such favours.

*f* Matt. 14. 2. Luke 9. 7.—*g* Luke 3. 19.—*h* Lev. 18. 16.

Ver. 20. *And kept him.* That is, from the designs of Herodias; and for fear of the people, would not put him to death, though she sought it: and through her daughter she effected her wish.

thou wilt, and I will give it thee.

23 And he swore to her: Whatsoever thou shalt ask I will give it thee, though *it be* the half of my kingdom.

24 Who when she was gone out, said to her mother: What shall I ask? But she said: The head of John the Baptist.

25 And when she was come in immediately with haste to the king, she asked, saying: I will that forthwith thou give me in a dish the head of John the Baptist.

26 And the king was struck sad. *Yet* because of his oath, and because of them that were with him at table, he would not displease her:

27 But sending an executioner, he commanded that his head should be brought in a dish.

28 And he beheaded him in the prison, and brought his head in a dish: and gave it to the damsel, and the damsel gave it to her mother.

29 ᵃ Which his disciples hearing, came and took his body; and laid it in a tomb.

30 ᵇ And the apostles coming together unto JESUS, related to him all things that they had done and taught.

31 And he said to them: ᶜ Come apart into a desert place, and rest a little. For there were many coming and going: and they had not so much as time to eat.

32 And going up into a ship, they went into a desert place apart.

33 And they saw them going away, and many knew: and they ran flocking thither on foot from all the cities, and were there before them.

34 ᵈ And JESUS going out saw a great multitude; and he had compassion on them, because they were as sheep not having a shepherd, and he began to teach them many things.

35 And when the day was now far spent, his disciples came to him, saying: This is a desert place, and the hour is now past:

36 ᵉ Send them away, that going into the next villages and towns, they may buy themselves meat to eat.

37 And he answering said to them: Give you them to eat. And they said to him: Let us go and buy bread for two hundred pence, and we will give them to eat.

38 And he saith to them: How many loaves have you? go and see. And when they knew, they say: Five, and two fishes.

39 ᶠ And he commanded them that they should make them all sit down by companies upon the green grass.

40 And they sat down in ranks, by hundreds and by fifties.

41 And when he had taken the five loaves, and the two fishes: looking up to heaven, he blessed, and broke the loaves, and gave to his disciples to set before them: and the two fishes he divided among them all.

42 And they all did eat, and had their fill.

43 And they took up the leavings, twelve full baskets of fragments, and of the fishes.

---

ᵃ Matt. 14. 12.—ᵇ Luke 9. 10.—ᶜ Matt. 14. 13. Luke 9. 10. John 6. 1.     ᵈ Matt. 9. 36. and 14. 14.—ᵉ Luke 9. 12.—ᶠ John 6. 10.

44 And they that did eat, were five thousand men.

45 And immediately he obliged his disciples to go up into the ship, that they might go before him over the water to Bethsaida: whilst he dismissed the people.

46 And when he had dismissed them he went up to the mountain to pray.

47 And when it was late, the ship was in the midst of the sea, and himself alone on the land.

48 <sup>a</sup> And seeing them labouring in rowing (for the wind was against them) and about the fourth watch of the night he cometh to them walking upon the sea, and he would have passed by them.

49 But they seeing him walking upon the sea, thought it was an apparition, and they cried out.

50 For they all saw him, and were troubled. And immediately he spoke with them, and said to them: Have a good heart, it is I, fear ye not.

51 And he went up to them into the ship, and the wind ceased: and they were far more astonished within themselves:

52 For they understood not concerning the loaves; for their heart was blinded.

53 <sup>b</sup> And when they had passed over, they came into the land of Genezareth, and set to the shore.

54 And when they were gone out of the ship, immediately they knew him:

55 And running through that whole country, they began to carry about in beds those that were sick, where they heard he was.

56 And whithersoever he entered, into towns or into villages or cities, they laid the sick in the streets, and besought him that they might touch but the hem of his garment: and as many as touched him were made whole.

## CHAP. VII.

*Christ rebukes the Pharisees. He heals the daughter of the woman of Canaan, and the man that was deaf and dumb.*

AND there assembled together unto him the Pharisees and some of the scribes, coming from Jerusalem.

2 <sup>c</sup> And when they had seen some of his disciples eat bread with common, that is, with unwashed hands, they found fault.

3 For the Pharisees, and all the Jews eat not without often washing their hands, holding the tradition of the ancients:

4 And when they come from the market, unless they be washed, they eat not: and many other things there are that have been delivered to them to observe, the washings of cups and of pots, and of brazen vessels and of beds.

5 And the Pharisees and scribes asked him: Why do not thy disciples walk according to the tradition of the ancients, but they eat bread with common hands?

6 But he answering, said to them: Well did Isaias prophesy of you hypocrites, as it is written: *<sup>d</sup> This people honoureth me with their lips, but their heart is far from me.*

7 *And in vain do they wor-*

---

<sup>a</sup> Matt. 14. 24.—<sup>b</sup> Matt. 14. 34.

<sup>c</sup> Matt. 15. 2.—<sup>d</sup> Isaias 29. 13.

CHAP. VII. Ver. 7. *Doctrines and precepts of men.* See the annotations, Matt. xv. 9. 11.

ship me, teaching doctrines and precepts of men.

8 For leaving the commandment of God, you hold the tradition of men, the washings of pots and of cups: and many other things you do like to these.

9 And he said to them: Well do you make void the commandment of God, that you may keep your own tradition.

10 For Moses said: *a Honour thy father and thy mother; and b He that shall curse father or mother, dying let him die.*

11 But you say: If a man shall say to his father or mother, Corban (which is a gift) whatsoever is from me, shall profit thee:

12 And farther you suffer him not to do anything for his father or mother.

13 Making void the word of God by your own tradition, which you have given forth. And many other such like things you do.

14 c And calling again the multitude unto him, he said to them: Hear ye me all and understand.

15 There is nothing from without a man that entering into him, can defile him. But the things which come from a man, those are they that defile a man.

16 If any man have ears to hear, let him hear.

17 And when he was come into the house from the multitude, his disciples asked him the parable.

18 And he saith to them: So are you also without knowledge? understand you not that everything from without, entering into a man cannot defile him:

19 Because it entereth not into his heart, but goeth into the belly, and goeth out into the privy, purging all meats?

20 But he said that the things which come out from a man, they defile a man.

21 d For from within out of the heart of men proceed evil thoughts, adulteries, fornications, murders,

22 Thefts, covetousness, wickedness, deceit, lasciviousness, an evil eye, blasphemy, pride, foolishness.

23 All these evil things come from within, and defile a man.

24 e And rising from thence he went into the coasts of Tyre and Sidon: and entering into a house, he would that no man should know it, and he could not be hid.

25 For a woman as soon as she heard of him, whose daughter had an unclean spirit, came in, and fell down at his feet.

26 For the woman was a gentile, a Syrophenician born. And she besought him that he would cast forth the devil out of her daughter.

27 Who said to her: Suffer first the children to be filled: for it is not good to take the bread of the children, and cast it to the dogs.

28 But she answered and said to him: Yea, Lord: for the whelps also eat under the table of the crumbs of the children.

29 And he said to her: For this saying go thy way, the devil is gone out of thy daughter.

---

*a* Exod. 20. 12. Deut. 5. 16. Ephes. 6. 2.—*b* Exod. 21. 17. Lev. 20. 9. Prov. 20. 20.—*c* Matt. 15. 10.

*d* Gen. 6. 5.—*e* Matt. 15. 21.

THE FIRST DISCIPLES OF JESUS

30 And when she was come into her house, she found the girl lying upon the bed, and that the devil was gone out.

31 And again going out of the coasts of Tyre, he came by Sidon to the sea of Galilee through the midst of the coasts of Decapolis.

32 ᵃ And they bring to him one deaf and dumb; and they besought him that he would lay his hand upon him.

33 And taking him from the multitude apart, he put his fingers into his ears, and spitting he touched his tongue;

34 And looking up to heaven, he groaned, and said to him: Ephpheta, which is, Be thou opened.

35 And immediately his ears were opened, and the string of his tongue was loosed, and he spoke right.

36 And he charged them that they should tell no man. But the more he charged them, so much the more a great deal did they publish it.

37 And so much the more did they wonder, saying: He hath done all things well; he hath made both the deaf to hear, and the dumb to speak.

## CHAP. VIII.

*Christ feeds four thousand. He gives sight to a blind man. He foretells his passion.*

IN ᵇ those days again when there was a great multitude, and had nothing to eat; calling his disciples together, he saith to them:

2 I have compassion on the multitude, for behold they have now been with me three days, and have nothing to eat.

3 And if I shall send them away fasting to their home, they will faint in the way, for some of them came from afar off.

4 And his disciples answered him: From whence can any one fill them here with bread in the wilderness?

5 And he asked them: How many loaves have ye? Who said: Seven.

6 And taking the seven loaves, giving thanks he broke, and gave to his disciples for to set before them, and they set them before the people.

7 And they had a few little fishes; and he blessed them, and commanded them to be set before them.

8 And they did eat and were filled, and they took up that which was left of the fragments, seven baskets.

9 And they that had eaten were about four thousand: and he sent them away.

10 And immediately going up into a ship with his disciples, he came into the parts of Dalmanutha.

11 ᶜ And the Pharisees came forth, and began to question with him, asking him a sign from heaven, tempting him.

12 And sighing deeply in spirit, he saith, Why doth this generation ask a sign? Amen I say to you, If a sign shall be given to this generation.

13 And leaving them, he went up again into the ship, and passed to the other side of the water.

14 And they forgot to take

---

ᵃ Matt. 9. 32. Luke 11. 14.—ᵇ Matt. 15. 32.

ᶜ Matt. 16. 1. Luke 11. 54.

bread: and they had but one loaf with them in the ship.

15 And he charged them saying: Take heed and beware of the leaven of the Pharisees, and of the leaven of Herod.

16 And they reasoned among themselves, saying: Because we have no bread.

17 Which Jesus knowing, saith to them: Why do you reason, because you have no bread? do you not yet know nor understand? have you still your heart blinded?

18 Having eyes see you not? and having ears hear you not? *a* neither do you remember.

19 When I broke the five loaves among five thousand; how many baskets full of fragments took you up? They say to him, Twelve.

20 When also the seven loaves among four thousand, how many baskets of fragments took you up? And they say to him, Seven.

21 And he said to them: How do you not yet understand?

22 And they came to Bethsaida; and they bring to him a blind man, and they besought him that he would touch him.

23 And taking the blind man by the hand, he led him out of the town: and spitting upon his eyes, laying his hands on him, he asked him if he saw anything.

24 And looking up, he said: I see men as it were trees, walking.

25 After that again he laid his hands upon his eyes, and he began to see, and was restored, so that he saw all things clearly.

26 And he sent him into his house, saying: Go into thy house, and if thou enter into the town, tell nobody.

27 *b* And Jesus went out, and his disciples, into the towns of Cæsarea-Philippi; and in the way he asked his disciples, saying to them: *c* Whom do men say that I am?

28 Who answered him saying: John the Baptist; but some Elias, and others as one of the prophets.

29 Then he saith to them: But whom do you say that I am? Peter answering said to him: Thou art the Christ.

30 And he strictly charged them that they should not tell any man of him.

31 And he began to teach them, that the son of man must suffer many things, and be rejected by the ancients and by the high-priests, and the scribes, and be killed: and after three days rise again.

32 And he spoke the word openly. *d* And Peter taking him, began to rebuke him.

33 Who turning about and seeing his disciples, threatened Peter, saying: Go behind me, satan, because thou savourest not the things that are of God, but that are of men.

34 And calling the multitude together with his disciples, he said to them: *e* If any man will follow me, let him deny himself, and take up his cross, and follow me.

35 *f* For whosoever will save his life, shall lose it; and whosoever shall lose his life for my sake and the gospel shall save it.

---

*a* Supra, 6. 41. John 6. 11.

*b* Matt. 16. 13.—*c* Luke 9. 18.—*d* Matt. 16. 23.—*e* Matt. 10. 38. and 16. 24.—*f* Luke 9. 23. and 14. 27.

36 For what shall it profit a man, if he gain the whole world, and suffer the loss of his soul?

37 Or what shall a man give in exchange for his soul?

38 ᵃ For he that shall be ashamed of me, and of my words in this adulterous and sinful generation: the son of man also will be ashamed of him, when he shall come in the glory of his Father with the holy angels.

39 And he said to them: ᵇ Amen I say to you, that there are some of them that stand here, who shall not taste death, till they see the kingdom of God coming in power.

## CHAP. IX.

*Christ is transfigured. He casts out the dumb spirit. He teaches humility and to avoid scandal.*

AND ᶜ after six days JESUS taketh with him Peter and James and John, and leadeth them up into an high mountain apart by themselves, and was transfigured before them.

2 And his garments became shining and exceeding white as snow, so as no fuller upon earth can make white.

3 And there appeared to them Elias with Moses; and they were talking with JESUS.

4 And Peter answering, said to JESUS: Rabbi, it is good for us to be here; and let us make three tabernacles, one for thee, and one for Moses, and one for Elias.

5 For he knew not what he said; for they were struck with fear:

6 And there was a cloud overshadowing them, and a voice came out of the cloud, saying: This is my most beloved son: hear ye him:

7 And immediately looking about, they saw no man any more but JESUS only with them.

8 ᵈ And as they came down from the mountain, he charged them not to tell any man what things they had seen, till the son of man shall be risen again from the dead.

9 And they kept the word to themselves; questioning together what that should mean, when he shall be risen from the dead.

10 And they asked him, saying: ᵉ Why then do the Pharisees and scribes say that Elias must come first?

11 Who answering said to them: Elias when he shall come first, shall restore all things, and as ᶠ it is written of the son of man, that he must suffer many things and be despised.

12 But I say to you, that Elias also is come (and they have done to him whatsoever they would) as it is written of him.

13 And coming to his disciples, he saw a great multitude about them, and the scribes disputing with them.

14 And presently all the people seeing JESUS, was astonished and struck with fear: and running to him, they saluted him.

15 And he asked them, What do you question about among you?

16 ᵍ And one of the multitude answering, said: Master, I have

---

ᵃ Matt. 10. 33. Luke 9. 26. and 12. 9.—ᵇ Matt. 16. 28. Luke 9. 27.—ᶜ Matt. 17. 1. Luke 9. 28.

ᵈ Matt. 17. 9.—ᵉ Mal. 4. 5.—ᶠ Isaias 53. 3. and 4.—ᵍ Luke 9. 38.

followeth not us, and we forbad him.

38 But JESUS said: Do not forbid him. *a* For there is no man that doth a miracle in my name, and can soon speak ill of me.

39 For he that is not against you, is for you.

40 *b* For whosoever shall give you to drink a cup of water in my name, because you belong to Christ: Amen I say to you, he shall not lose his reward.

41 *c* And whosoever shall scandalize one of these little ones that believe in me: it were better for him that a millstone were hanged about his neck, and he were cast into the sea.

42 *d* And if thy hand scandalize thee, cut it off: it is better for thee to enter into life, maimed, than having two hands to go into hell, into unquenchable fire:

43 Where their worm dieth not, and the fire is not extinguished.

44 And if thy foot scandalize thee, cut it off. It is better for thee to enter lame into life everlasting, than having two feet, to be cast into the hell of unquenchable fire:

45 *e* Where their worm dieth not, and the fire is not extinguished.

46 And if thy eye scandalize thee, pluck it out. It is better for thee with one eye to enter into the kingdom of God, than having two eyes to be cast into the hell of fire:

47 Where their worm dieth not, and the fire is not extinguished.

48 *f* For every one shall be salted with fire: and every victim shall be salted with salt.

49 *g* Salt is good. But if the salt become unsavoury; wherewith will you season it? Have salt in you, and have peace among you.

## CHAP. X.

*Marriage is not to be dissolved. The danger of riches. The ambition of the sons of Zebedee. A blind man is restored to his sight.*

AND *h* rising up from thence, he cometh into the coasts of Judea, beyond the Jordan: and the multitudes flock to him again. And as he was accustomed, he taught them again.

2 And the Pharisees coming to him asked him: Is it lawful for a man to put away his wife? tempting him.

3 But he answering, saith to them: What did Moses command you?

4 Who said: *i* Moses permitted to write a bill of divorce, and to put *her* away.

5 To whom JESUS answering, said: Because of the hardness of your heart he wrote you that precept.

6 But from the beginning of the creation, *k* God made them male and female.

7 For this cause *l* a man shall leave his father and mother; and shall cleave to his wife.

8 *m* And they two shall be in one flesh. Therefore now they are not two, but one flesh.

9 What therefore God hath joined together, let not man put asunder.

---

*a* 1 Cor. 12. 3.—*b* Matt. 10. 42.—*c* Matt. 18. 6. Luke 17. 2.—*d* Matt. 5. 30. and 18. 8.—*e* Isaias 66. 24.

*f* Lev. 2. 13.—*g* Matt. 5. 13. Luke 14. 34.—*h* Matt. 19. 1.—*i* Deut. 24. 1.—*k* Gen. 1. 27.—*l* Gen. 2. 24. Matt. 19. 5. 1 Cor. 7. 10. Ephes. 5. 31.—*m* 1 Cor. 6. 16.

10 And in the house again his disciples asked him concerning the same thing.

11 And he saith to them: Whosoever shall put away his wife and marry another, committeth adultery against her.

12 And if the wife shall put away her husband, and be married to another, she committeth adultery.

13 And they brought to him young children, that he might touch them. And the disciples rebuked those that brought them.

14 Whom when JESUS saw, he was much displeased, and saith to them: Suffer the little children to come unto me, and forbid them not. For of such is the kingdom of God.

15 Amen I say to you, whosoever shall not receive the kingdom of God as a little child, shall not enter into it.

16 And embracing them, and laying his hands upon them, he blessed them.

17 And when he was gone forth into the way, a certain man running up and kneeling before him, asked him, *a* Good Master, what shall I do that I may receive life everlasting?

18 And JESUS said to him, Why callest thou me good? None is good but one, *that is* God.

19 *b* Thou knowest the commandments, *Do not commit adultery, do not kill, do not steal, bear not false witness, do no fraud, honour thy father and mother.*

20 But he answering, said to him: Master, all these things I have observed from my youth.

21 And JESUS looking on him, loved him, and said to him: One thing is wanting unto thee: go, sell whatsoever thou hast, and give to the poor, and thou shalt have treasure in heaven; and come, follow me.

22 Who being struck sad at that saying, went away sorrowful: for he had great possessions.

23 And JESUS looking round about, saith to his disciples: How hardly shall they, that have riches, enter into the kingdom of God!

24 And the disciples were astonished at his words. But JESUS again answering, saith to them: Children, how hard is it for them that trust in riches, to enter into the kingdom of God!

25 It is easier for a camel to pass through the eye of a needle, than for a rich man to enter into the kingdom of God.

26 Who wondered the more, saying among themselves: Who then can be saved?

27 And JESUS looking on them, saith: With men it is impossible; but not with God. For all things are possible with God.

28 *c* And Peter began to say unto him: Behold, we have left all things, and have followed thee.

29 JESUS answering, said: Amen I say to you, there is no man who hath left house, or brethren, or sisters, or **father**, or mother, or children, or lands for my sake and for the gospel,

---

*a* Matt. 19. 10. Luke 18. 18.—*b* Exod. 10. 13.

CHAP. X. Ver. 18. *None is good.* Of himself entirely and essentially, but God alone: men may be good also, but only by participation of God's goodness.

*c* Matt. 19. 37. Luke 18. 28.

30 Who shall not receive an hundred times as much, now in this time; houses, and brethren, and sisters, and mothers, and children, and lands, with persecutions: and in the world to come life everlasting.

31 <sup>a</sup> But many that are first, shall be last: and the last, first.

32 And they were in the way going up to Jerusalem: and JESUS went before them, and they were astonished: and following were afraid. <sup>b</sup> And taking again the twelve, he began to tell them the things that should befall him.

33 *Saying:* Behold we go up to Jerusalem, and the son of man shall be betrayed to the chief priests, and to the scribes and ancients, and they shall condemn him to death, and shall deliver him to the gentiles.

34 And they shall mock him, and spit on him, and scourge him, and kill him: and the third day he shall rise again.

35 <sup>c</sup> And James and John the sons of Zebedee, come to him, saying: Master, we desire that whatsoever we shall ask, thou wouldst do it for us:

36 But he said to them: What would you that I should do for you?

37 And they said: Grant to us, that we may sit, one on thy right hand, and the other on thy left hand, in thy glory.

38 And JESUS said to them: You know not what you ask. Can you drink of the chalice that I drink of: or be baptized with the baptism wherewith I am baptized?

39 But they said to him: We can. And JESUS saith to them: You shall indeed drink of the chalice that I drink of: and with the baptism wherewith I am baptized, you shall be baptized.

40 But to sit on my right hand, or on my left, is not mine to give to you, but to them for whom it is prepared.

41 And the ten hearing it, began to be much displeased at James and John.

42 But JESUS calling them, saith to them: <sup>d</sup> You know that they who seem to rule over the gentiles, lord it over them: and their princes have power over them.

43 But it is not so among you: but whosoever will be greater, shall be your minister.

44 And whosoever will be first among you, shall be the servant of all.

45 For the son of man also is not come to be ministered unto, but to minister, and to give his life a redemption for many.

46 <sup>e</sup> And they come to Jericho: and as he went out of Jericho, with his disciples, and a very great multitude, Bartimeus the blind man, the son of Timeus, sat by the way-side begging.

47 Who when he had heard that it was JESUS of Nazareth, began to cry out, and to say: JESUS, son of David, have mercy on me.

48 And many rebuked him, that he might hold his peace; but he cried a great deal the more: Son of David, have mercy on me.

---

<sup>a</sup> Matt. 19. 30.—<sup>b</sup> Luke 18. 31.—<sup>c</sup> Matt. 20. 20. | <sup>d</sup> Luke 22. 25.—<sup>e</sup> Matt. 20. 29. Luke 18. 35.

49 And JESUS standing still commanded him to be called. And they call the blind man, saying to him: Be of better comfort: arise, he calleth thee.

50 Who casting off his garment leaped up, and came to him.

51 And JESUS answering, said to him: What wilt thou that I should do to thee? And the blind man said to him: Rabboni, that I may see.

52 And JESUS saith to him: Go thy way, thy faith hath made thee whole. And immediately he saw, and followed him in the way.

## CHAP. XI.

*Christ enters into Jerusalem upon an ass: curses the barren fig-tree: and drives t e buyers and sellers out of the temple.*

AND <sup>a</sup> when they were drawing near to Jerusalem and to Bethania at the mount of olives, he sendeth two of his disciples.

2 And saith to them: Go into the village that is over against you, and immediately at your coming in thither, you shall find a colt tied, upon which no man yet hath sat: loose him, and bring *him*.

3 And if any man shall say to you, What are you doing? say ye that the Lord hath need of him: and immediately he will let him come hither.

4 And going their way, they found the colt tied before the gate without in the meeting of two ways: and they loose him.

5 And some of them that stood there, said to them: What do you loosing the colt?

6 Who said to them as JESUS had commanded them: and they let him go with them.

7 <sup>b</sup> And they brought the colt to JESUS: and they lay their garments on him, and he sat upon him.

8 And many spread their garments in the way: and others cut down boughs from the trees, and strewed them in the way.

9 And they that went before and they that followed, cried, saying: *<sup>c</sup> Hosannah, blessed is he that cometh in the name of the Lord:*

10 *Blessed be the kingdom of our father David that cometh: Hosannah in the highest.*

11 <sup>d</sup> And he entered into Jerusalem, into the temple: and having viewed all things round about, when now the eventide was come, he went out to Bethania with the twelve.

12 And the next day when they came out from Bethania, he was hungry.

13 <sup>e</sup> And when he had seen afar off a fig-tree having leaves, he came if perhaps he might find anything on it. And when he was come to it, he found nothing but leaves. For it was not the time for figs.

14 And answering, he said to it: May no man hereafter eat fruit of thee any more for ever. And his disciples heard it.

15 And they come to Jerusalem. And when he was entered into the temple, he began to cast out them that sold and bought in the temple, and overthrew the tables of the moneychangers, and the chairs of them that sold doves.

---

<sup>a</sup> Matt. 21. 1. Luke 19. 29.

<sup>b</sup> John 12. 14.—<sup>c</sup> Ps. 117. 26. Isaias 28. 16. Matt. 21. 9. Luke 19. 38.—<sup>d</sup> Matt. 21. 10.—<sup>e</sup> Matt. 21. 19.

CHRIST PURGING THE TEMPLE.

16 And he suffered not that any man should carry a vessel through the temple:

17 And he taught, saying to them: Is it not written, *ᵃMy house shall be called the house of prayer to all nations? But you have made it a den of thieves.*

18 Which when the chief priests and the scribes had heard, they sought how they might destroy him. For they feared him, because the whole multitude was in admiration at his doctrine.

19 And when evening was come, he went forth out of the city.

20 And when they passed by in the morning, they saw the fig-tree dried up from the roots.

21 And Peter remembering, said to him: Rabbi, behold the fig-tree, which thou didst curse, is withered away.

22 And JESUS answering saith to them: ᵇ Have the faith of God.

23 Amen I say to you, that whosoever shall say to this mountain, Be thou removed and be cast into the sea, and shall not stagger in his heart, but believe, that whatsoever he saith shall be done: it shall be done unto him.

24 ᶜ Therefore I say unto you, all things, whatsoever you ask when ye pray, believe that you shall receive: and they shall come unto you.

25 ᵈ And when you shall stand to pray: forgive, if you have aught against any man; that your Father also, who is in heaven, may forgive you your sins.

26 But if you will not forgive, neither will your Father that is in heaven, forgive you your sins.

27 ᵉ And they come again to Jerusalem. And when he was walking in the temple, there come to him the chief priests and the scribes and the ancients.

28 And they say to him: By what authority dost thou these things? and who hath given thee this authority that thou shouldst do these things?

29 And JESUS answering said to them: I will also ask you one word, and answer you me, and I will tell you by what authority I do these things.

30 The baptism of John was it from heaven, or from men? Answer me.

31 But they thought with themselves saying: If we say from heaven; he will say, Why then did you not believe him?

32 If we say, From men, we fear the people. For all men counted John that he was a prophet indeed.

33 And they answering say to JESUS: We know not. And JESUS answering, saith to them: Neither do I tell you by what authority I do these things.

## CHAP. XII.

*The parable of the vineyard and husbandmen. Cæsar's right to tribute. The Sadducees are confuted. The first commandment. The widow's mite.*

AND ᶠ he began to speak to them in parables: A *certain* man planted a vineyard and made a hedge about it, and dug a place for the wine fat, and built a tower, and let it to hus-

---

ᵃ Isaias 56. 7. Jer. 7. 11.—ᵇ Matt. 21. 21.—ᶜ Matt. 7. 7. and 21. 22.—ᵈ Matt. 6. 14. and 18. 35. Luke 11. 9.

ᵉ Luke 20. 1.—ᶠ Isaias 5. 1. Jer. 2. 21. Matt. 21. 33. Luke 20. 9.

61

bandmen; and went into a far country.

2 And at the season he sent to the husbandmen a servant to receive of the husbandmen, of the fruit of the vineyard.

3 Who having laid hands on him, beat him, and sent him away empty.

4 And again he sent to them another servant; and him they wounded in the head, and used him reproachfully.

5 And again he sent another, and him they killed: and many others, of whom some they beat, and others they killed.

6 Therefore having yet one son most dear to him; he also sent him unto them the last of all, saying: They will reverence my son.

7 But the husbandmen said one to another: This is the heir; come let us kill him; and the inheritance shall be ours.

8 And laying hold on him they killed him, and cast him out of the vineyard.

9 What therefore will the lord of the vineyard do? He will come and destroy *those* husbandmen; and will give the vineyard to others.

10 And have you not read this scripture, *a The stone which the builders rejected, the same is made the head of the corner:*

11 *By the Lord has this been done, and it is wonderful in our eyes?*

12 And they sought to lay hands on him, but they feared the people. For they knew that he spoke this parable to them. And leaving him they went their way.

13 *b* And they send to him some of the Pharisees and of the Herodians; that they should catch him in *his* words.

14 Who coming, say to him: Master, we know that thou art a true speaker, and carest not for any *man*; for thou regardest not the person of men, but teachest the way of God in truth. Is it lawful to give tribute to Cesar; or shall we not give it?

15 Who knowing their willingness, saith to them: Why tempt you me? bring me a penny that I may see *it*.

16 And they brought it him. And he saith to them: Whose is this image and inscription? They say to him, Cesar's.

17 And JESUS answering, said to them: *c* Render therefore to Cesar the things that are Cesar's, and to God the things that are God's. And they marvelled at him.

18 *d* And there came to him the Sadducees, who say there is no resurrection; and they asked him, saying:

19. Master, Moses wrote unto us, *e* that if any man's brother die, and leave his wife behind him, and leave no children, his brother should take his wife and raise up seed to his brother.

20 Now there were seven brethren; and the first took a wife, and died leaving no issue.

21 And the second took her and died: and neither did he leave any issue. And the third in like manner.

22 And the seven *all* took her in like manner; and did not

---

*a* Ps. 117. 22. Isaias 28. 16. Matt. 21. 42. Acts 4. 11. Rom. 9. 33. 1 Pet. 2. 7.
*b* Matt. 22. 15. Luke 20. 20.—*c* Rom. 13. 7.—*d* Matt. 22. 23. Luke 20. 27.—*e* Deut. 20. 5.

leave issue. Last of all the woman also died.

23 In the resurrection therefore, when they shall rise again, whose wife shall she be of them? for the seven had her to wife

24 And JESUS answering saith to them: Do ye not therefore err, because you know not the Scriptures, nor the power of God?

25 For when they shall rise again from the dead, they shall neither marry, nor be married, but are as the angels in heaven.

26 And as concerning the dead that they rise again, have you not read in the book of Moses, how in the bush God spoke to him, saying: *"I am the God of Abraham, and the God of Isaac, and the God of Jacob?*

27 He is not the God of the dead, but of the living. You therefore do greatly err.

28 *b* And there came one of the scribes that had heard them reasoning together, and seeing that he had answered them well, asked him which was the first commandment of all.

29 And JESUS answered him: The first commandment of all is, *c Hear, O Israel: the Lord thy God is one God.*

30 *And thou shalt love the Lord thy God with thy whole heart, and with thy whole soul, and with thy whole mind, and with thy whole strength.* This is the first commandment.

31 *d* And the second is like to it: *Thou shalt love thy neighbour as thyself.* There is no other commandment greater than these.

32 And the scribe said to him: Well, master, thou hast said in truth, that there is one God, and there is no other besides him.

33 And that he should be loved with the whole heart, and with the whole understanding, and with the whole soul, and with the whole strength: and to love one's neighbour as oneself, is a greater thing than all holocausts and sacrifices.

34 And JESUS seeing that he had answered wisely, said to him: Thou art not far from the kingdom of God. And no man after that durst ask him any question.

35 And JESUS answering said, teaching in the temple: How do the scribes say, that Christ is the son of David?

36 For David himself saith by the Holy Ghost: *e The Lord said to my Lord, Sit on my right hand until I make thy enemies thy footstool.*

37 David therefore himself calleth him Lord, and whence is he then his son? And a great multitude heard him gladly.

38 And he said to them in his doctrine: *f* Beware of the scribes, who love to walk in long robes, and to be saluted in the market-place.

39 And to sit in the first chairs in the synagogues, and to have the highest places at suppers:

40 Who devour the houses of widows under the pretence of long prayer: these shall receive greater judgment.

41 *g* And JESUS sitting over

---

*a* Exod. 3. 6. Matt. 22. 32.—*b* Matt. 22. 35.—*c* Deut. 6. 4.—*d* Lev. 19. 18. Matt. 22. 39. Rom. 13. 9. Gal. 5. 14. Jas. 2. 8.

*e* Ps. 109. 1. Matt. 22. 44. Luke 20. 42.—*f* Matt. 23. 6. Luke 11. 43. and 20. 46.—*g* Luke 21. 1.

against the treasury, beheld how the people cast money into the treasury, and many that were rich cast in much.

42 And there came a certain poor widow, and she cast in two mites, which make a farthing.

43 And calling his disciples together, he saith to them: Amen I say to you, this poor widow hath cast in more than all they who have cast into the treasury.

44 For all they did cast in of their abundance; but she of her want cast in all she had, *even* her whole living.

## CHAP. XIII.

*Christ foretells the destruction of the temple, and the signs that shall forerun the day of judgment.*

AND *a* as he was going out of the temple, one of his disciples saith to him: Master, behold what manner of stones, and what buildings *are here.*

2 And JESUS answering, said to him: Seest thou all these great buildings? *b* There shall not be left a stone upon a stone, that shall not be thrown down.

3 And as he sat on the mount of Olivet over against the temple, Peter and James and John and Andrew asked him apart:

4 Tell us, when shall these things be? and what shall be the sign when all these things shall begin to be fulfilled?

5 And JESUS answering, began to say to them: *c* Take heed lest any man deceive you.

6 For many shall come in my name saying, I am he; and they shall deceive many.

7 And when you shall hear of wars and rumours of wars, fear ye not. For such things must needs be, but the end is not yet.

8 For nation shall rise against nation, and kingdom against kingdom, and there shall be earthquakes, in *divers* places, and famines. These things *are* the beginning of sorrows.

9 But look to yourselves. For they shall deliver you up to councils, and in the synagogues you shall be beaten, and you shall stand before governors and kings for my sake, for a testimony unto them.

10 And unto all nations the gospel must first be preached.

11 *d* And when they shall lead you and deliver you up, be not thoughtful beforehand what you shall speak; but whatsoever shall be given you in that hour, that speak ye. For it is not you that speak, but the Holy Ghost.

12 And the brother shall betray his brother unto death, and the father his son; and children shall rise up against the parents, and shall work their death.

13 And you shall be hated by all men for my name's sake. But ye that shall endure unto the end, he shall be saved.

14 *e* And when you shall see the abomination of desolation, standing where it ought not: he that readeth let him understand: then let them that are in Judea, flee unto the mountains:

15 And let him that is on the housetop, not go down into the

---

*a* Matt. 24. 1.—*b* Luke 19. 44. and 21. 6.—*c* Ephes. 5. 6. 2 Thess. 2. 3.

*d* Matt. 10. 19. Luke 12. 11. and 21. 14.—*e* Dan. 9. 27. Matt. 24. 15. Luke 21. 20.

CHRIST'S DISCOURSE WITH NICODEMUS.

house nor enter therein to take anything out of the house:

16 And let him that shall be in the field, not turn back to take up his garment.

17 And wo to them that are with child, and that give suck in those days.

18 But pray ye, that *these things* happen not in winter.

19 For in those days shall be such tribulations as were not from the beginning of the creation which God created until now, neither shall be.

20 And unless the Lord had shortened the days, no flesh should be saved: but for the sake of the elect which he hath chosen, he hath shortened the days.

21 *a* And then if any man shall say to you, Lo, here is Christ; lo, he is here: do not believe.

22 For there will rise up false christs and false prophets, and they shall shew signs and wonders, to seduce (if it were possible) even the elect.

23 Take you heed therefore; behold I have foretold you all things.

24 *b* But in those days, after that tribulation, the sun shall be darkened, and the moon shall not give her light.

25 And the stars of heaven shall be falling down, and the powers, that are in heaven, shall be moved.

26 And then shall they see the son of man coming in the clouds, with great power and glory.

27 *c* And then shall he send his angels, and shall gather together his elect from the four winds, from the uttermost part of the earth to the uttermost part of heaven.

28 Now of the fig-tree learn ye a parable. When the branch thereof is now tender, and the leaves are come forth, you know that summer is very near.

29 So you also when you shall see these things come to pass, know ye that it is very nigh, even at the doors.

30 Amen I say to you, that this generation shall not pass, until all these things be done.

31 Heaven and earth shall pass away, but my word shall not pass away.

32 But of that day or hour no man knoweth, neither the angels in heaven nor the Son, but the Father.

33 *d* Take ye heed, watch and pray. For ye know not when the time is.

34 Even as a man who going into a far country, left his house; and gave authority to his servants over every work, and commanded the porter to watch.

35 Watch ye therefore (for you know not when the lord of the house cometh: at even, or at midnight, or at the cock crowing, or in the morning).

36 Lest coming on a sudden, he find you sleeping.

37 And what I say to you I say to all: Watch.

*d* Matt. 24. 42.

CHAP. XIII. Ver. 32. *Nor the Son.* Not that the Son of God is absolutely ignorant of the day of judgment, but that he knoweth it not, as our teacher; i.e., he knoweth it not so as to teach it to us, as not being expedient.

*a* Matt. 24. 23. Luke 17. 23. and 21. 8. —*b* Isaias 13. 10. Ezech. 32. 7. Joel 2. 10.—*c* Matt. 24. 31.

## CHAP. XIV.

*The first part of the history of the passion of Christ.*

NOW *a* the feast of the pasch, and of the azymes was after two days: and the chief priests and the scribes sought how they might by some wile lay hold on him, and kill him.

2 But they said: Not on the festival day, lest there should be a tumult among the people.

3 *b* And when he was in Bethania in the house of Simon the leper, and was at meat, there came a woman having an alabaster box of ointment of precious spikenard: and breaking the alabaster box she poured it out upon his head.

4 Now there were some that had indignation within themselves, and said: Why was this waste of the ointment made?

5 For this ointment might have been sold for more than three hundred pence, and given to the poor. And they murmured against her.

6 But JESUS said: Let her alone, why do you molest her? She hath wrought a good work upon me.

7 For the poor you have always with you; and whensoever you will, you may do them good; but me you have not always.

8 What she had, she hath done; she is come beforehand to anoint my body for the burial.

9 Amen I say to you, wheresoever this gospel shall be preached in the whole world, that also which she hath done, shall be told for a memorial of her.

10 *c* And Judas Iscariot, one of the twelve, went to the chief priests, to betray him to them.

11 Who hearing it were glad; and they promised him they would give him money. And he sought how he might conveniently betray him.

12 *d* Now on the first day of the unleavened bread when they sacrificed the pasch, the disciples say to him: Whither wilt thou that we go, and prepare for thee to eat the pasch?

13 And he sendeth two of his disciples, and saith to them: Go ye into the city; and there shall meet you a man carrying a pitcher of water, follow him;

14 And whithersoever he shall go in, say to the master of the house, The master saith, Where is my refectory, where I may eat the pasch with my disciples?

15 And he will shew you a large dining-room furnished; and there prepare ye for us.

16 And his disciples went their way, and came into the city; and they found as he had told them, and they prepared the pasch.

17 *e* And when evening was come, he cometh with the twelve.

18 And when they were at table and eating JESUS saith: Amen I say to you, *f* one of you that eateth with me shall betray me.

19 But they began to be sorrowful, and to say to him one by one: Is it I?

20 Who saith to them: One

---

*a* Matt. 26. 2. Luke 22. 1. A.D. 33.—
*b* Matt. 26. 6. John 12. 1.

CHAP. XIV. Ver. 1. *Azymes.* That is, the feast of the unleavened bread.

*c* Matt. 26. 14.—*d* Matt. 26. 17. Luke 22. 7.—*e* Matt. 26. 20. Luke 22. 17.—*f* John 13. 21.

of the twelve, who dippeth with me his hand in the dish.

21 And the son of man indeed goeth, *a* as it is written of him: but wo to that man by whom the son of man shall be betrayed. It were better for him, if that man had not been born.

22 *b* And whilst they were eating, JESUS took bread: and blessing broke, and gave to them, and said: Take ye, This is my body.

23 And having taken the chalice, giving thanks he gave it to them. And they all drank of it.

24 And he said to them: This is my blood of the new testament, which shall be shed for many.

25 Amen I say to you, that I will drink no more of the fruit of the vine, until that day when I shall drink it new in the kingdom of God.

26 And when they had said an hymn, they went forth to the mount of olives.

27 And JESUS saith to them: *c* You will all be scandalized in my regard this night; for it is written, *d* *I will strike the shepherd, and the sheep shall be dispersed.*

28 But after I shall be risen again, I will go before you into Galilee.

29 But Peter saith to him: Although all shall be scandalized in thee, yet not I.

30 And JESUS saith to him: Amen I say to thee, to-day even in this night, before the cock crow twice, thou shalt deny me thrice.

31 But he spoke the more vehemently: Although I should die together with thee, I will not deny thee. And in like manner also said they all.

32 *e* And they come to a farm called Gethsemani. And he saith to his disciples: Sit you here, while I pray.

33 And he taketh Peter and James and John with him; and he began to fear and to be heavy.

34 And he saith to them: My soul is sorrowful even unto death; stay you here, and watch.

35 And when he was gone forward a little he fell flat on the ground; and he prayed that if it might be, the hour might pass from him:

36 And he saith: Abba, Father, all things are possible to thee, remove this chalice from me, but not what I will, but what thou wilt.

37 And he cometh, and findeth them sleeping. And he saith to Peter: Simon, sleepest thou? couldst thou not watch one hour?

38 Watch ye, and pray that you enter not into temptation. The spirit indeed is willing, but the flesh is weak.

39 And going away again, he prayed, saying the same words.

40 And when he returned he

---

*a* Ps. 40. 10. Acts 1. 16.—*b* Matt. 26. 26. 1 Cor. 11. 24.—*c* John 16. 32.— *d* Zach. 13. 7.

*e* Matt. 26. 36. Luke 22. 40.

Ver. 30. *Crow twice.* The cocks crow at two different times of the night; viz., about midnight for the first time; and then about the time commonly called the cock-crowing. And this was the cock-crowing our Saviour spoke of; and therefore the other Evangelists take no notice of the first crowing.

found them again asleep (for their eyes were heavy), and they knew not what to answer him.

41 And he cometh the third time, and saith to them: Sleep ye now, and take *your* rest. It is enough: the hour is come; behold, the son of man shall be betrayed into the hands of sinners.

42 Rise up, let us go. Behold; he that will betray me is at hand.

43 And while he was yet speaking, cometh Judas Iscariot, one of the twelve, *a* and with him a great multitude with swords and staves, from the chief priests and the scribes and the ancients.

44 And he that betrayed him had given them a sign, saying: Whomsoever I shall kiss, that is he, lay hold on him, and lead him away carefully.

45 And when he was come, immediately going up to him, he saith: Hail, Rabbi: and he kissed him.

46 But they laid hands on him, and held him.

47 And one of them that stood by drawing a sword, struck a servant of the chief priest, and cut off his ear.

48 And JESUS answering, said to them: Are you come out as to a robber with swords and staves to apprehend me?

49 I was daily with you in the temple teaching, and you did not lay hands on me. But, that the scriptures may be fulfilled.

50 *b* Then his disciples leaving him, all fled away.

51 And a certain young man followed him having a linen cloth cast about his naked *body;* and they laid hold on him.

52 But he, casting off the linen cloth, fled from them naked.

53 *c* And they brought JESUS to the high-priest; and all the priests and the scribes and the ancients assembled together.

54 And Peter followed him afar off even into the court of the high-priest; and he sat with the servants at the fire, and warmed himself.

55 *d* And the chief priests and all the council sought for evidence against JESUS, that they might put him to death, and found none.

56 For many bore false witness against him, and their evidence were not agreeing.

57 And some rising up, bore false witness against him, saying:

58 We heard him say, *e* I will destroy this temple made with hands, and within three days I will build another not made with hands.

59 And their witness did not agree.

60 And the high-priest rising up in the midst, asked JESUS, saying: Answerest thou nothing to the things that are laid to thy charge by these men?

61 But he held his peace and answered nothing. Again the high-priest asked him, and said to him: Art thou the Christ the Son of the blessed God?

62 And JESUS said to him: I am. *f* And you shall see the son of man sitting on the right hand of the power of God, and

---

*a* Matt. 26. 47. Luke 22. 47. John 18. 3.—*b* Matt. 26. 56. *c* Matt. 26. 57. Luke 22. 54. John 18. 13.—*d* Matt. 26. 59.—*e* John 2. 19.—*f* Matt. 24. 30, and 26. 64.

JESUS AND THE SAMARITAN WOMAN.

coming with the clouds of heaven.

63 Then the high-priest rending his garments, saith: What need we any farther witnesses?

64 You have heard the blasphemy. What think you? Who all condemned him to be guilty of death.

65 And some began to spit on him, and to cover his face, and to buffet him, and to say unto him: Prophesy; and the servants struck him with the palms of their hands.

66 *a* Now when Peter was in the court below, there cometh one of the maid-servants of the high-priest.

67 And when she had seen Peter warming himself, looking on him she saith: Thou also wast with JESUS of Nazareth.

68 But he denied, saying: I neither know nor understand what thou sayest. And he went forth before the court; and the cock crew.

69 *b* And again a maid-servant seeing him, began to say to the standers-by: This is one of them.

70 But he denied again. *c* And after a while they that stood by said again to Peter: Surely thou art one of them; for thou art also a Galilean.

71 But he began to curse and to swear, *saying*, I know not this man of whom you speak.

72 And immediately the cock crew again. *d* And Peter remembered the word that JESUS had said unto him: Before the cock crow twice, thou shalt thrice deny me. And he began to weep.

## CHAP. XV.

*The continuation of the history of the passion.*

AND *e* straightway in the morning the chief priests holding a consultation with the ancients and the scribes and the whole council, binding JESUS, led him away, and delivered him to Pilate.

2 And Pilate asked him: Art thou the king of the Jews? But he answering, saith to him: Thou sayest *it*.

3 *f* And the chief priests accused him in many things.

4 And Pilate again asked him, saying: Answerest thou nothing? behold in how many things they accuse thee.

5 But JESUS still answered nothing; so that Pilate wondered.

6 Now on the festival day he was wont to release unto them one of the prisoners, whomsoever they demanded.

7 And there was one called Barabbas, who was put in prison with some seditious men, who in the sedition had committed murder.

8 And when the multitude was come up, they began to desire *that he would do*, as he had ever done unto them.

9 And Pilate answered them, and said: Will you that I release to you the king of the Jews?

10 For he knew that the chief priests had delivered him up out of envy.

11 But the chief priests moved the people, that he should rather release Barabbas to them.

---

*a* Matt. 26. 69. Luke 22. 56. John 18. 17.—*b* Matt. 26. 1.—*c* Luke 22. 59. John 18. 25.—*d* Matt. 26. 75. John 18. 38. | *e* Matt. 27. 1. Luke 22. 66. John 18. 28.—*f* Matt. 27. 12. Luke 23. 2. John 18. 33.

CHAP. XV. ST. MARK. CHAP. XV.

12 ᵃ And Pilate again answering, saith to them: What will you then that I do to the king of the Jews?

13 ᵇ But they again cried out: Crucify him.

14 And Pilate saith to them: Why, what evil hath he done? But they cried out the more: Crucify him.

15 And so Pilate being willing to satisfy the people, released to them Barabbas, and delivered up JESUS, when he had scourged him, to be crucified.

16 ᶜ And the soldiers led him away into the court of the palace, and they call together the whole band:

17 And they clothe him with purple, and platting a crown of thorns, they put it upon him.

18 And they began to salute him: Hail, king of the Jews.

19 And they struck his head with a reed: And they did spit on him. And bowing their knees, they adored him.

20 And after they had mocked him, they took off the purple from him, and put his own garments on him, and they led him out to crucify him.

21 ᵈ And they forced one Simon a Cyrenian who passed by, coming out of the country, the father of Alexander and of Rufus, to take up his cross.

22 And they bring him into the place *called* Golgotha, which being interpreted is, the place of Calvary.

23 And they gave him to drink wine mingled with myrrh; but he took it not.

24 ᵉ And crucifying him, they divided his garments, casting lots upon them, what every man should take.

25 And it was the third hour, and they crucified him.

26 And the inscription of his cause was written over, THE KING OF THE JEWS.

27 And with him they crucify two thieves, the one on his right hand and the other on his left.

28 ᶠ And the Scripture was fulfilled which saith: *And with the wicked he was reputed.*

29 And they that passed by, blasphemed him, wagging their heads, and saying: ᵍ Vah, thou that destroyest the temple of God, and in three days buildest it up again:

30 Save thyself, coming down from the cross.

31 In like manner also the chief priests mocking said with the scribes one to another: He saved others, himself he cannot save.

32 Let Christ the king of Israel come down now from the cross, that we may see and believe. And they that were crucified with him, reviled him.

33 And when the sixth hour was come, there was darkness over the whole earth until the ninth hour.

34 And at the ninth hour, JESUS cried out with a loud voice, saying: ʰ Eloi, Eloi,

---

ᵃ Matt. 27. 22. Luke 23. 14.—ᵇ John 18. 40.—ᶜ Matt. 27. 27. John 19. 2.—ᵈ Matt. 27. 32. Luke 23. 26.—ᵉ Matt. 27. 35. Luke 23. 34. John 19. 23.

ᶠ Isaias 53. 12.—ᵍ John 2. 19.—ʰ Ps. 21. 2. Matt. 27. 46.

CHAP. XV. Ver. 25. *The third hour.* The ancient account divided the day into four parts, which were named from the hour from which they began: the first, third, sixth and ninth hour. Our Lord was crucified a little before noon; before the *third hour* had quite expired; but when the *sixth hour* was near at hand.

lamma sabacthani? Which is, being interpreted, My God, my God, why hast thou forsaken me?

35 And some of the standers-by hearing, said: Behold he calleth Elias.

36 And one running and filling a sponge with vinegar, and putting it upon a reed, gave him to drink, saying: Stay, let us see if Elias come to take him down.

37 And JESUS having cried out with a loud voice, gave up the ghost.

38 And the veil of the temple was rent in two, from the top to the bottom.

39 And the centurion who stood over against him, seeing that crying out in this manner he had given up the ghost, said: Indeed this man was the Son of God.

40 *a* And there were also women looking on afar off: among whom was Mary Magdalen, and Mary the mother of James the less and of Joseph, and Salome;

41 Who also when he was in Galilee, followed him, *b* and ministered to him, and many other women that came up with him to Jerusalem.

42 *c* And when evening was now come (because it was the Parasceve, that is, the day before the Sabbath),

43 Joseph of Arimathea, a noble counsellor, who was also himself looking for the kingdom of God, came and went in boldly to Pilate, and begged the body of JESUS.

44 But Pilate wondered that he should be already dead. And sending for the centurion, he asked him if he were already dead.

45 And when he had understood it by the centurion, he gave the body to Joseph.

46 And Joseph buying fine linen, and taking him down, wrapped him up in the fine linen, and laid him in a sepulchre, which was hewed out of a rock. And he rolled a stone to the door of the sepulchre.

47 And Mary Magdalen and Mary *the mother* of Joseph beheld where he was laid.

## CHAP. XVI.

*Christ's resurrection and ascension.*

AND *d* when the Sabbath was past, Mary Magdalen and Mary *the mother* of James and Salome brought sweet spices, that coming they might anoint JESUS.

2 And very early in the morning the first day of the week, they come to the sepulchre, the sun being now risen.

3 And they said one to another: Who shall roll us back the stone from the door of the sepulchre?

4 And looking, they saw the stone rolled back. For it was very great.

5 *e* And entering into the sepulchre, they saw a young

---

*a* Matt. 27. 55.—*b* Luke 8. 2.—*c* Matt. 27. 57. Luke 23. 50. John 19. 38.

*d* Matt. 28. 1. Luke 24. 1. John 20. 1.—*e* Matt. 28. 5. Luke 24. 4. John 20. 12.

CHAP. XVI. Ver. 2. *The sun being now risen.* They set out before it was light, to go to the sepulchre; but the sun was risen when they arrived there. Or, figuratively, the sun here spoken of is the *sun of justice,* Christ Jesus our Lord, who was risen before their coming.

CHAP. XVI. ST. MARK. CHAP. XVI.

man sitting on the right side, clothed with a white robe: and they were astonished.

6 Who saith to them: Be not affrighted; you seek JESUS of Nazareth, who was crucified; he is risen, he is not here, behold the place where they laid him.

7 But go, tell his disciples and Peter, that he goeth before you into Galilee; there you shall see him, *a* as he told you.

8 But they going out, fled from the sepulchre. For a trembling and fear had seized them: and they said nothing to any man; for they were afraid.

9 But he rising early *b* the first day of the week, appeared first to Mary Magdalen, out of whom he had cast seven devils.

10 She went and told them that had been with him, who were mourning and weeping.

11 And they hearing that he was alive, and had been seen by her, did not believe.

12 *c* And after that he appeared in another shape to two of them walking, as they were going into the country.

13 And they going told it to the rest: neither did they believe them.

14 At length he appeared to the eleven as they were at table: and he upbraided them with their incredulity and hardness of heart, because they did not believe them who had seen him after he was risen again.

15 And he said to them: Go ye into the whole world and preach the gospel to every creature.

16 He that believeth and is baptized, shall be saved: but he that believeth not shall be condemned.

17 And these signs shall follow them that believe: *d* In my name they shall cast out devils: *e* they shall speak with new tongues;

18 *f* They shall take up serpents; and if they shall drink any deadly thing, it shall not hurt them: *g* they shall lay their hands upon the sick, and they shall recover.

19 And the Lord JESUS, after he had spoken to them, *h* was taken up into heaven, and sitteth on the right hand of God.

20 But they going forth, preached everywhere: the Lord working withal, and confirming the word with signs that followed.

---

*a* Supra, 14. 28.—*b* John 20. 16.—*c* Luke 24. 13. —*d* Acts 16. 18.—*e* Acts 2. 4. and 10. 46. —*f* Acts 28. 5.—*g* Acts 28. 8.—*h* Luke 24. 51.

THE MIRACULOUS DRAUGHT OF FISHES.

# THE
# HOLY GOSPEL OF JESUS CHRIST,
## ACCORDING TO ST. LUKE.

*St. Luke was a native of Antioch, the capital of Syria; he was by profession a physician, and some ancient writers say, that he was very skilful in painting. He was converted by St. Paul, and became his disciple and his companion in his travels, and fellow-labourer in the ministry of the Gospel. He wrote in Greek about twenty-four years after our Lord's ascension.*

## CHAP. I.

*The conception of John the Baptist, and of Christ: the visitation and canticle of the Blessed Virgin: the birth of the Baptist, and the canticle of Zachary.*

FORASMUCH as many have taken in hand to set forth in order a narration of the things that have been accomplished among us;

2 According as they have delivered them unto us, who from the beginning were eye-witnesses and ministers of the word:

3 It seemed good to me also, having diligently attained to all things from the beginning, to write to thee, in order, most excellent Theophilus,

4 That thou mayest know the verity of those words in which thou hast been instructed.

5 There was in the days of Herod the king of Judea, a certain priest named Zachary, *a* of the course of Abia, and his wife was of the daughters of Aaron, and her name Elizabeth.

6 And they were both just before God, walking in all the commandments and justifications of the Lord without blame.

7 And they had no son, for that Elizabeth was barren, and they both were well advanced in years.

8 And it came to pass, when he executed the priestly function in the order of his course before God,

9 According to the custom of the priestly office, it was his lot to offer incense, going into the temple of the Lord;

10 *b* And all the multitude of the people was praying without at the hour of incense.

11 And there appeared to him an Angel of the Lord, standing on the right side of the altar of incense.

12 And Zachary seeing him was troubled, and fear fell upon him;

---

*a* 1 Par. 24. 10.  *b* Exod. 30. 7. Lev. 16. 17.

CHAP. I. Ver. 5. *Of the course of Abia, i.e., of the rank of Abia*, which word in the Greek is commonly put for the employment of *one day*; but here for the functions of a whole week. For, by the appointment of David, 1 Paral. 24, the descendants from Aaron were divided into twenty-four families, of which the eighth was Abia, from whom descended this Zacharias, who at this time was in the week of his priestly functions.

13 But the Angel said to him: Fear not, Zachary, for thy prayer is heard; and thy wife Elizabeth shall bear thee a son, and thou shalt call his name John;

14 And thou shalt have joy and gladness, and many shall rejoice in his nativity.

15 For he shall be great before the Lord: and shall drink no wine nor strong drink; and he shall be filled with the Holy Ghost even from his mother's womb.

16 And he shall convert many of the children of Israel to the Lord their God.

17 And he shall go before him in the spirit and power of Elias; *a*that he may turn the hearts of the fathers unto the children, and the incredulous to the wisdom of the just, to prepare unto the Lord a perfect people.

18 And Zachary said to the Angel: Whereby shall I know this? for I am an old man; and my wife is advanced in years.

19 And the Angel answering, said to him: I am Gabriel who stand before God; and am sent to speak to thee, and to bring thee these good tidings.

20 And behold thou shalt be dumb, and shalt not be able to speak until the day wherein these things shall come to pass; because thou hast not believed my words, which shall be fulfilled in their time.

21 And the people was waiting for Zachary; and they wondered that he tarried so long in the temple.

22 And when he came out he could not speak to them, and they understood that he had seen a vision in the temple. And he made signs to them, and remained dumb.

23 And it came to pass, after the days of his office were accomplished, he departed to his own house.

24 And after those days, Elizabeth his wife conceived; and hid herself five months, saying:

25 Thus hath the Lord dealt with me in the days wherein he hath had regard to take away my reproach among men.

26 And in the sixth month, the Angel Gabriel was sent from God into a city of Galilee, called Nazareth,

27 To a virgin espoused to a man whose name was Joseph, of the house of David; and the virgin's name was Mary.

28 And the Angel being come in, said unto her: Hail, full of grace, the Lord is with thee: Blessed art thou among women.

29 Who having heard, was troubled at his saying, and thought with herself what manner of salutation this should be.

30 And the Angel said to her: Fear not, Mary, for thou hast found grace with God.

31 *b*Behold thou shalt conceive in thy womb, and shalt bring forth a son; *c*and thou shalt call his name JESUS.

32 He shall be great, and shall be called the Son of the most High, and the Lord God shall give unto him the throne of David his father: *d*and he shall reign in the house of Jacob for ever,

33 And of his kingdom there shall be no end.

---

*a* Malac. 4. 6. Matt. 11. 14.
*b* Isaias 7. 14.—*c* Infra. 2. 1.—*d* Dan. 7. 14. and 27. Mich. 4. 7.

34 And Mary said to the Angel: How shall this be done, because I know not man?

35 And the Angel answering, said to her: The Holy Ghost shall come upon thee, and the power of the most High shall overshadow thee. And therefore also the Holy which shall be born of thee shall be called the Son of God.

36 And behold thy cousin Elizabeth, she also hath conceived a son in her old age; and this is the sixth month with her that is called barren;

37 Because no word shall be impossible with God.

38 And Mary said: Behold the handmaid of the Lord, be it done to me according to thy word. And the Angel departed from her.

39 And Mary rising up in those days, went into the hill country with haste into a city of Juda.

40 And she entered into the house of Zachary, and saluted Elizabeth.

41 And it came to pass; that when Elizabeth heard the salutation of Mary, the infant leaped in her womb. And Elizabeth was filled with the Holy Ghost:

42 And she cried out with a loud voice, and said: Blessed art thou among women, and blessed is the fruit of thy womb.

43 And whence is this to me, that the mother of my Lord should come to me?

44 For behold as soon as the voice of thy salutation sounded in my ears, the infant in my womb leaped for joy.

45 And blessed art thou that hast believed, because those things shall be accomplished that were spoken to thee by the Lord.

46 And Mary said: My soul doth magnify the Lord:

47 And my spirit hath rejoiced in God my Saviour.

48 Because he hath regarded the humility of his handmaid: for behold from henceforth all generations shall call me blessed.

49 Because he that is mighty hath done great things to me: and holy is his name.

50 And his mercy is from generation unto generations, to them that fear him.

51 He hath shewed might *a* in his arm: he hath scattered the proud in the conceit of their heart.

52 He hath put down the mighty from their seat, and hath exalted the humble.

53 *b* He hath filled the hungry with good things: and the rich he hath sent empty away.

54 He hath received Israel his servant, being mindful of his mercy.

55 As he spoke to our fathers, *c* to Abraham and to his seed for ever.

56 And Mary abode with her about three months: and she returned to her own house.

57 Now Elizabeth's full time of being delivered was come, and she brought forth a son.

58 And her neighbours and

---

*a* Isaias 51. 9. Ps. 32. 10.—*b* 1 Kings 2. 5. Ps. 33. 11.—*c* Gen. 17. 9. and 22. 16. Ps. 131. 11. Isaias 41. 8.

Ver. 48. *Shall call me blessed.* These words are a prediction of that honour which the church in all ages should pay to the blessed Virgin. Let Protestants examine whether they are any way concerned in this prophecy.

kinsfolks heard that the Lord had shewed his great mercy towards her, and they congratulated with her.

59 And it came to pass, that on the eighth day they came to circumcise the child, and they called him by his father's name Zachary.

60 And his mother answering, said: Not so, but he shall be called John.

61 And they said to her: There is none of thy kindred that is called by this name.

62 And they made signs to his father, how he would have him called.

63 And demanding a writing-table, he wrote, *a*saying: John is his name. And they all wondered.

64 And immediately his mouth was opened, and his tongue *loosed*, and he spoke blessing God.

65 And fear came upon all their neighbours; and all these things were noised abroad over all the hill country of Judea:

66 And all they that had heard them laid them up in their heart, saying: What an one, think ye, shall this child be? For the hand of the Lord was with him.

67 And Zachary his father was filled with the Holy Ghost: and he prophesied, saying:

68 *b* Blessed be the Lord God of Israel: because he hath visited and wrought the redemption of his people:

69 *c* And hath raised up an horn of salvation to us, in the house of David his servant.

70 *d* As he spoke by the mouth of his holy prophets, who are from the beginning.

71 Salvation from our enemies, and from the hand of all that hate us.

72 To perform mercy to our fathers; and to remember his holy testament.

73 *e* The oath which he swore to Abraham our father, that he would grant to us,

74 That being delivered from the hand of our enemies, we may serve him without fear,

75 In holiness and justice before him, all our days.

76 And thou child, shalt be called the prophet of the highest: for thou shalt go before the face of the Lord to prepare his ways.

77 *f* To give knowledge of salvation to his people, unto the remission of their sins.

78 Through the bowels of the mercy of our God, in which *g* the Orient, from on high, hath visited us.

79 To enlighten them that sit in darkness, and in the shadow of death: to direct our feet into the way of peace.

80 And the child grew, and was strengthened in spirit: and was in the deserts until the day of his manifestation to Israel.

---

*d* Jer. 23. 6. and 30. 10.—*e* Gen. 22. 16. Jer. 31. 33. Heb. 6. 13. and 17.—*f* Mal. 4. 5. Supra, 17.—*g* Zach. 3. 9. and 6. 12. Mal. 4. 2.

---

*a* Supra, 13.—*b* Ps. 78. 12—*c* Ps. 131. 7.

---

Ver. 69. *Horn of salvation, i.e., A powerful salvation,* as Dr. Wetham translates it. For in the Scripture, by *horn* is generally understood strength and power.

Ver. 78. *The Orient.* It is one of the titles of the Messias, the true light of the world, and the sun of justice.

CHRIST HEALING THE MAN SICK OF THE PALSY.

## CHAP. II.

*The birth of Christ: his presentation in the temple: Simeon's prophecy. Christ at twelve years of age is found amongst the doctors.*

AND it came to pass that in those days there went out a decree from Cesar Augustus; that the whole world should be enrolled.

2 This enrolling was first made by Cyrinus the governor of Syria.

3 And all went to be enrolled, every one into his own city.

4 And Joseph also went up from Galilee out of the city of Nazareth into Judea, to the city of *a* David, which is called *b* Bethlehem: because he was of the house and family of David,

5 To be enrolled with Mary his espoused wife, who was with child.

6 And it came to pass, that when they were there, her days were accomplished, that she should be delivered.

7 And she brought forth her first-born son, and wrapped him up in swaddling clothes, and laid him in a manger: because there was no room for them in the inn.

8 And there were in the same country shepherds watching, and keeping the night-watches over their flock.

9 And behold an angel of the Lord stood by them, and the brightness of God shone round about them, and they feared with a great fear.

10 And the angel said to them: Fear not; for behold I bring you good tidings of great joy, that shall be to all the people:

11 For this day is born to you a SAVIOUR, who is Christ the Lord, in the city of David.

12 And this shall be a sign unto you. You shall find the infant wrapped in swaddling clothes, and laid in a manger.

13 And suddenly there was with the angel a multitude of the heavenly army, praising God, and saying:

14 Glory to God in the highest: and on earth peace to men of good will.

15 And it came to pass, after the angels departed from them into heaven, the shepherds said one to another, Let us go over to Bethlehem, and let us see this word that is come to pass, which the Lord hath shewed to us.

16 And they came with haste: and they found Mary and Joseph, and the infant lying in the manger.

17 And seeing, they understood of the word that had been spoken to them concerning this child.

18 And all that heard wondered: and at those things that were told them by the shepherds.

19 But Mary kept all these words, pondering *them* in her heart.

20 And the shepherds returned, glorifying and praising God, for all the things they had heard, and seen, as it was told unto them.

21 *c* And after eight days

---

*a* 1 Kings 20. 6.—*b* Mich. 5. 2. Matt. 2. 6.

CHAP. II. Ver. 7. *Her first-born.* The meaning is, not that she had afterward any other child; but it is a way of speech among the *Hebrews*, to call them also the *first-born*, who are the only children. See Annot. *Matt.* 1. 25.

*c* Gen. 17. 12. Lev. 12. 3.

were accomplished that the child should be circumcised; his name was called ᵃ JESUS, which was called by the angel, before he was conceived in the womb.

22 And after the days of her purification ᵇ according to the law of Moses were accomplished, they carried him to Jerusalem, to present him to the Lord.

23 As it is written in the law of the Lord, ᶜ *Every male opening the womb shall be called holy to the Lord.*

24 And to offer a sacrifice according as it is written ᵈ in the law of the Lord, a pair of turtle doves, or two young pigeons.

25 And behold there was a man in Jerusalem named Simeon, and this man was just and devout, waiting for the consolation of Israel: and the Holy Ghost was in him.

26 And he had received an answer from the Holy Ghost, that he should not see death before he had seen the CHRIST of the Lord.

27 And he came by the Spirit into the temple. And when his parents brought in the child JESUS, to do for him according to the custom of the law,

28 He also took him into his arms, and blessed God, and said:

29 Now thou dost dismiss thy servant, O Lord, according to thy word in peace.

30 Because my eyes have seen thy salvation,

31 Which thou hast prepared before the face of all peoples:

32 A light to the revelation of the gentiles, and the glory of thy people Israel.

33 And his father and mother were wondering at those things, which were spoken concerning him.

34 And Simeon blessed them, and said to Mary his mother: ᵉ Behold this *child* is set for the fall, and for the resurrection of many in Israel, and for a sign which shall be contradicted.

35 And thy own soul a sword shall pierce, that out of many hearts thoughts may be revealed.

36 And there was one Anna, a prophetess, the daughter of Phanuel, of the tribe of Aser; she was far advanced in years, and had lived with her husband seven years from her virginity.

37 And she was a widow until fourscore and four years; who departed not from the temple, by fastings and prayers serving night and day.

38 Now she at the same hour coming in, confessed to the Lord; and spoke of him to all that looked for the redemption of Israel.

39 And after they had performed all things according to the law of the Lord, they returned into Galilee, to their city Nazareth.

40 And the child grew, and waxed strong, full of wisdom:

---

ᵉ Isaias 8. 14. Rom. 9. 33. 1 Pet. 2. 7.

Ver. 34. *For the fall,* &c. Christ came for the salvation of all men; but here *Simeon* prophesies what would come to pass, that *many* through their own wilful blindness and obstinacy would not believe in Christ, nor receive his doctrine, which therefore would be *ruin* to them; but to others a *resurrection,* by their believing in him and obeying his commandments.

---

ᵃ Matt. 1. 21. Supra, 1. 31. - ᵇ Lev. 12. 6. - ᶜ Exod. 13. 2. Num. 8. 16. - ᵈ Lev. 12. 8.

and the grace of God was in him.

41 And his parents went every year to Jerusalem *a* at the solemn day of the pasch.

42 And when he was twelve years *b* old, they going up into Jerusalem according to the custom of the feast,

43 And having fulfilled the days, when they returned, the child JESUS remained in Jerusalem; and his parents knew it not.

44 And thinking that he was in the company, they came a day's journey, and sought him among their kinsfolks and acquaintance.

45 And not finding him, they returned into Jerusalem, seeking him.

46 And it came to pass, that after three days they found him in the temple sitting in the midst of the doctors, hearing them and asking them questions.

47 And all that heard him were astonished at his wisdom and his answers.

48 And seeing *him*, they wondered. And his mother said to him: Son, why hast thou done so to us? behold thy father and I have sought thee sorrowing.

49 And he said to them: How is it that you sought me? did you not know that I must be about my father's business?

50 And they understood not the word, that he spoke unto them.

51 And he went down with them, and came to Nazareth: and was subject to them. And his mother kept all these words in her heart.

52 And JESUS advanced in wisdom and age, and grace with God and men.

## CHAP. III.

*John's mission and preaching. Christ is baptized by him.*

NOW in the fifteenth year *c* of the reign of Tiberius Cesar, Pontius Pilate being governor of Judea, and Herod being tetrarch of Galilee, and Philip his brother tetrarch of Iturea and the country of Trachonitis, and Lysanias tetrarch of Abilina,

2 *d* Under the high-priests Annas and Caiphas: the word of the Lord was made unto John the son of Zachary, in the desert.

3 *e* And he came into all the country about the Jordan, preaching the baptism of penance for the remission of sins;

4 As it was written in the book of the sayings of Isaias the prophet: *f A voice of one crying in the wilderness: Prepare ye the way of the Lord, make straight his paths.*

5 *Every valley shall be filled; and every mountain and hill shall be brought low: and the crooked shall be made straight, and the rough ways, plain:*

6 *And all flesh shall see the salvation of God.*

7 He said therefore to the multitudes that went forth to be baptized by him: *g* Ye offspring of vipers, who hath shewed you to flee from the wrath to come?

8 Bring forth therefore fruits worthy of penance, and do not

---

*a* Exod. 23. 15. and 34. 18. Deut. 16. 1.—*b* A.D. 12. Secundum Vul. 8.
*c* A.D. secundum Vul. 26.—*d* Acts 4. 6.—*e* Matt. 3. 1. Mark 1. 4.—*f* Isaias 40. 3. John 1. 23.—*g* Matt. 3. 7. and 23. 33.

begin to say, We have Abraham for our father. For I say unto you, that God is able of these stones to raise up children to Abraham.

9 For now the axe is laid to the root of the trees. Every tree therefore that bringeth not forth good fruit, shall be cut down, and cast into the fire.

10 And the people asked him, saying: What then shall we do?

11 And he answering, said to them: *a* He that hath two coats, let him give to him that hath none; and he that hath meat, let him do in like manner.

12 And the publicans also came to be baptized, and said to him: Master, what shall we do?

13 But he said to them: Do nothing more than that which is appointed you.

14 And the soldiers also asked him, saying: And what shall we do? And he said to them: Do violence to no man, neither calumniate any man: and be content with your pay.

15 And as the people was of opinion, and all were thinking in their hearts of John, that perhaps he might be the Christ:

16 John answered, saying unto all: *b* I indeed baptize you with water; but there shall come one mightier than I, the latchet of whose shoes I am not worthy to loose; *c* he shall baptize you with the Holy Ghost and with fire.

17 Whose fan is in his hand, and he will purge his floor; and will gather the wheat into his barn, but the chaff he will burn with unquenchable fire.

18 And many other things exhorting did he preach to the people.

19 *d* But Herod the tetrarch, when he was reproved by him for Herodias his brother's wife, and for all the evils which Herod had done,

20 He added this also above all, and shut up John in prison.

21 *e* Now it came to pass, when all the people was baptized, that JESUS also being baptized and praying, heaven was opened:

22 And the Holy Ghost descended in a bodily shape as a dove upon him: and a voice came from heaven: *f* Thou art my beloved Son, in thee I am well pleased.

23 And JESUS himself was beginning about the age of thirty years: being (as it was supposed) the son of Joseph, who was of Heli, who was of Mathat,

24 Who was of Levi, who was of Melchi, who was of Janne, who was of Joseph,

25 Who was of Mathathias, who was of Amos, who was of Nahum, who was of Hesli, who was of Nagge,

26 Who was of Mahath, who

---

*a* Jas. 2. 14. 1 John 3. 17.—*b* Matt. 3. 11. Mark 1. 8. John 1. 26.—*c* Matt. 3. 11. Acts. 1. 5. 11. 16 and 19. 4.

*d* Matt. 14. 4. Mark 6. 17.—*e* Matt. 3. 16. Mark 1. 10. John 1. 32.—*f* Matt. 3. 17. and 17. 5. Infra. 9. 35. 2 Pet. 1. 17.

CHAP. III. Ver. 23. *Who was of Heli.* St. *Joseph*, who by nature was the son of *Jacob* (St. *Matt.* L 16). In the account of the law was son of *Heli.* For *Heli* and *Jacob* were brothers, by the same mother: and *Heli*, who was the elder, dying without issue, *Jacob*, as the law directed, married his widow; in consequence of such marriage his son *Joseph* was reputed in the law the son of *Heli.*

THE SERMON ON THE MOUNT.

was of Mathathias, who was of Semei, who was of Joseph, who was of Juda,

27 Who was of Joanna, who was of Reza, who was of Zorobabel, who was of Salathiel, who was of Neri,

28 Who was of Melchi, who was of Addi, who was of Cosan, who was of Helmadan, who was of Her,

29 Who was of Jesus, who was of Eliezer, who was of Jorim, who was of Mathat, who was of Levi,

30 Who was of Simeon, who was of Judas, who was of Joseph, who was of Jona, who was of Eliakim,

31 Who was of Melea, who was of Menna, who was of Mathatha, who was of Nathan, who was of David,

32 Who was of Jesse, who was of Obed, who was of Booz, who was of Salmon, who was of Naasson,

33 Who was of Aminadab, who was of Aram, who was of Esron, who was of Phares, who was of Judas,

34 Who was of Jacob, who was of Isaac, who was of Abraham, who was of Thare, who was of Nachor,

35 Who was of Sarug, who was of Ragau, who was of Phaleg, who was of Heber, who was of Sale,

36 Who was of Cainan, who was of Arphaxad, who was of Sem, who was of Noe, who was of Lamech,

37 Who was of Mathusale, who was of Henoch, who was of Jared, who was of Malaleel, who was of Cainan,

38 Who was of Henos, who was of Seth, who was of Adam, who was of God.

## CHAP. IV.

*Christ's fasting, and temptation. He is persecuted in Nazareth: his miracles in Capharnaum.*

AND <sup>a</sup> JESUS being full of the Holy Ghost, returned from the Jordan, and was led by the Spirit into the desert,

2 For the space of forty days; and was tempted by the devil. And he ate nothing in those days; and when they were ended he was hungry.

3 And the devil said to him: If thou be the Son of God, say to this stone that it be made bread.

4 And JESUS answered him: It is written: <sup>b</sup> that *man liveth not by bread alone, but by every word of God.*

5 And the devil led him into a high mountain, and shewed him all the kingdoms of the world in a moment of time.

6 And he said to him: To thee will I give all this power, and the glory of them; for to me they are delivered, and to whom I will, I give them.

7 If thou therefore wilt adore before me, all shall be thine.

8 And JESUS answering said to him: <sup>c</sup> It is written: *Thou shalt adore the Lord thy God, and him only shalt thou serve.*

9 And he brought him to Jerusalem, and set him on a pinnacle of the temple; and he said to him: If thou be the Son of God, cast thyself from hence.

10 <sup>d</sup> For it is written, that *he hath given his angels charge over thee, that they keep thee:*

11 And that in *their hands they shall bear thee up, lest per-*

---

<sup>a</sup> Matt. 4. 1. Mark 1. 2.—<sup>b</sup> Deut. 8. 3. Matt. 4. 4.—<sup>c</sup> Deut. 6. 13. and 10. 20.—<sup>d</sup> Ps. 90. 11.

haps thou dash thy foot against a stone.

12 And JESUS answering said to him: It is said, "Thou shalt not tempt the Lord thy God."

13 And all the temptation being ended, the devil departed from him for a time.

14 *b* And JESUS returned in the power of the Spirit into Galilee, and the fame of him went out through the whole country.

15 And he taught in their synagogues, and was magnified by all.

16 *c* And he came to Nazareth where he was brought up: and he went into the synagogue according to his custom on the sabbath-day; and he rose up to read,

17 And the book of Isaias the prophet was delivered unto him. And as he unfolded the book, he found the place where it was written:

18 *d The spirit of the Lord is upon me, wherefore he hath anointed me, to preach the gospel to the poor he hath sent me, to heal the contrite of heart:*

19 *To preach deliverance to the captives, and sight to the blind, to set at liberty them that are bruised, to preach the acceptable year of the Lord, and the day of reward.*

20 And when he had folded the book, he restored it to the minister, and sat down. And the eyes of all in the synagogue were fixed on him.

21 And he began to say to them: This day is fulfilled this scripture in your ears.

22 And all gave testimony to him: and they wondered at the words of grace that proceeded from his mouth, and they said: Is not this the son of Joseph?

23 And he said to them: Doubtless you will say to me this similitude: Physician, heal thyself: as great things as we have heard done in Capharnaum, do also here in thy own country.

24 And he said: Amen I say to you, that no prophet is accepted in his own country.

25 In truth I say to you, *e* there were many widows in the days of Elias in Israel, when heaven was shut up three years and six months, when there was a great famine throughout all the earth.

26 And to none of them was Elias sent, but to Sarepta of Sidon, to a widow woman.

27 *f* And there were many lepers in Israel in the time of Eliseus the prophet; and none of them was cleansed but Naaman the Syrian.

28 And all they in the synagogue, hearing these things, were filled with anger.

29 And they rose up and thrust him out of the city: and they brought him to the brow of the hill, whereon their city was built, that they might cast him down headlong.

30 But he passing through the midst of them, went his way.

31 *g* And he went down into Capharnaum, a city of Galilee; and there he taught them on the sabbath-days.

32 *h* And they were astonished

---

*a* Deut 6. 16.—*b* Matt. 4. 12. Mark 1. 14.—*c* Matt. 13. 54. Mark 6. 1. John 4. 45.—*d* Isaias 61. 1.
*e* 3 Kings 17. 9—*f* 4 Kings 5. 14.— *g* Matt. 4. 13. Mark 1. 21.—*h* Matt. 7. 22.

102

at his doctrine: for his speech was with power.

33 ᵃ And in the synagogue there was a man who had an unclean devil, and he cried out with a loud voice,

34 Saying: Let us alone, what have we to do with thee, JESUS of Nazareth? art thou come to destroy us? I know thee who thou art, the Holy One of God.

35 And JESUS rebuked him, saying: Hold thy peace, and go out of him. And when the devil had thrown him into the midst, he went out of him, and hurt him not at all.

36 And there came fear upon all, and they talked among themselves, saying: What word is this, for with authority and power he commandeth the unclean spirits, and they go out?

37 And the fame of him was published into every place of the country.

38 And JESUS rising up out of the synagogue, went into Simon's house. ᵇ And Simon's wife's mother was taken with a great fever, and they besought him for her.

39 And standing over her, he commanded the fever, and it left her. And immediately rising, she ministered to them.

40 And when the sun was down, all they that had any sick with divers diseases, brought them to him. But he laying his hands on every one of them, healed them.

41 ᶜ And devils went out from many, crying out and saying: Thou art the Son of God. And rebuking them, he suffered them not to speak; for they knew that he was Christ.

42 And when it was day, going out he went into a desert place: and the multitudes sought him, and came unto him: and they stayed him that he should not depart from them.

43 To whom he said: To other cities also I must preach the kingdom of God: for therefore am I sent.

44 And he was preaching in the synagogues of Galilee.

## CHAP. V.

*The miraculous draught of fishes. The cure of the leper and of the paralytic. The call of Matthew.*

AND it came to pass that when the multitudes pressed upon him to hear the word of God, he stood by the lake of Genesareth.

2 ᵈ And saw two ships standing by the lake: but the fishermen were gone out of them and were washing their nets

3 And going up into one of the ships that was Simon's, he desired him to draw back a little from the land. And sitting he taught the multitudes out of the ship.

4 Now when he had ceased to speak, he said to Simon: Launch out into the deep, and let down your nets for a draught.

5 And Simon answering, said to him: Master, we have laboured all the night, and have taken nothing; but at thy word I will let down the net.

6 And when they had done this, they enclosed a very great multitude of fishes, and their net broke.

7 And they beckoned to their

---

ᵃ Mark 1. 23.—ᵇ Matt. 8. 14. Mark 1. 31.—ᶜ Mark 1. 34.

ᵈ Matt. 4. 18. Mark 1. 16.

partners that were in the other ship, that they should come and help them. And they came, and filled both the ships, so that they were almost sinking.

8 Which when Simon Peter saw, he fell down at JESUS'S knees, saying: Depart from me, for I am a sinful man, O Lord.

9 For he was wholly astonished, and all that were with him, at the draught of the fishes which they had taken.

10 And so were also James and John the sons of Zebedee, who were Simon's partners. And JESUS saith to Simon: Fear not; from henceforth thou shalt catch men.

11 And having brought their ships to land, leaving all things they followed him.

12 *a* And it came to pass, when he was in a certain city, behold a man full of leprosy, who seeing JESUS, and falling on his face, besought him, saying: Lord, if thou wilt, thou canst make me clean.

13 And stretching forth *his* hand he touched him, saying: I will. Be thou cleansed. And immediately the leprosy departed from him.

14 And he charged him that he should tell no man, but, Go, shew thyself to the priest, *b* and offer for thy cleansing according as Moses commanded, for a testimony to them.

15 But the fame of him went abroad the more, and great multitudes came together to hear, and to be healed *by him* of their infirmities.

16 And he retired into the desert and prayed.

17 And it came to pass on a certain day, as he sat teaching, that there were also Pharisees and doctors of the law sitting by, that were come out of every town of Galilee and Judea and Jerusalem; and the power of the Lord was to heal them.

18 *c* And behold men brought in a bed a man who had the palsy: and they sought means to bring him in, and to lay him before him.

19 And when they could not find by what way they might bring him in, because of the multitude, they went up upon the roof, and let him down through the tiles with his bed into the midst before JESUS.

20 Whose faith when he saw, he said: Man, thy sins are forgiven thee.

21 And the scribes and Pharisees began to think, saying: Who is this who speaketh blasphemies? Who can forgive sins, but God alone?

22 And when JESUS knew their thoughts, answering he said to them: What is it you think in your hearts?

23 Which is easier to say, Thy sins are forgiven thee: or to say, Arise and walk?

24 But that you may know that the son of man hath power on earth to forgive sins (he saith to the sick of the palsy) I say to thee, Arise, take up thy bed, and go into thy house.

25 And immediately rising up before them, he took up the bed on which he lay; and went away to his own house, glorifying God.

26 And all were astonished: and they glorified God. And they were filled with fear, say-

---

*a* Matt. 8. 2. Mark 1. 40.—*b* Lev. 14. 4.

*c* Matt. 9. 2. Mark 2. 3.

JESUS CASTING OUT DEVILS.

ing: We have seen wonderful things to-day.

27 ᵃ And after these things he went forth, and saw a publican named Levi, sitting at the receipt of custom, and he said to him: Follow me.

28 And leaving all things, he rose up and followed him.

29 And Levi made him a great feast in his own house; and there was a great company of publicans, and of others, that were at table with him.

30 ᵇ But the Pharisees and scribes murmured, saying to his disciples: Why do you eat and drink with publicans and sinners?

31 And JESUS answering, said to them: They that are whole, need not the physician: but they that are sick.

32 I came not to call the just, but sinners to penance.

33 And they said to him: ᶜ Why do the disciples of John fast often and make prayers, and the disciples of the Pharisees in like manner; but thine eat and drink?

34 To whom he said: Can you make the children of the bridegroom fast, whilst the bridegroom is with them?

35 But the days will come; when the bridegroom shall be taken away from them, then shall they fast in those days.

36 And he spoke also a similitude to them: That no man putteth a piece from a new garment upon an old garment: otherwise he both rendeth the new, and the piece taken from the new agreeth not with the old.

---

ᵃ Matt. 9. 9. Mark 2. 14.—ᵇ Mark 2. 14.—ᶜ Mark 2. 18.

37 And no man putteth new wine into old bottles: otherwise the new wine will break the bottles, and it will be spilled and the bottles will be lost.

38 But new wine must be put into new bottles; and both are preserved.

39 And no man drinking old, hath presently a mind to new: for he saith, The old is better.

## CHAP. VI.

*Christ excuses his disciples: he cures upon the sabbath-day: chooses the twelve, and makes a sermon to them.*

AND ᵈ it came to pass on the second first sabbath, that as he went through the cornfields his disciples plucked the ears, and did eat, rubbing them in their hands.

2 And some of the Pharisees said to them: Why do you that which is not lawful on the sabbath-days?

3 And JESUS answering them, said: Have you not read so much as this, what David did, when himself was hungry and they that were with him:

4 ᵉ How he went into the house of God, and took and ate the bread of proposition, and gave to them that were with him, which is not lawful to eat, ᶠ but only for the priests?

5 And he said to them: The son of man is Lord also of the sabbath.

6 And it came to pass also on

---

ᵈ Matt. 12. 1. Mark 2. 23.—ᵉ 1 Kings 21. 6.—ᶠ Exod. 29. 32. Lev. 24. 9.

CHAP. VI. Ver. 1. *The second first sabbath.* Some understand this of the sabbath of Pentecost, which was the second in course amongst the great feasts: others, of a sabbath-day that immediately followed any solemn feast.

another sabbath, that he entered into the synagogue, and taught. "And there was a man, whose right hand was withered.

7 And the scribes and Pharisees watched if he would heal on the sabbath; that they might find an accusation against him.

8 But he knew their thoughts; and said to the man who had the withered hand: Arise, and stand forth in the midst. And rising he stood forth.

9 Then JESUS said to them: I ask you, if it be lawful on the sabbath-days to do good or to do evil; to save life, or to destroy?

10 And looking round about on them all, he said to the man: Stretch forth thy hand. And he stretched it forth; and his hand was restored.

11 And they were filled with madness; and they talked one with another, what they might do to JESUS.

12 And it came to pass in those days, that he went out into a mountain to pray, and he passed the whole night in the prayer of God.

13 *b* And when day was come, he called unto him his disciples; and he chose twelve of them (whom also he named Apostles):

14 Simon whom he surnamed Peter, and Andrew his brother, James and John, Philip and Bartholomew,

15 Matthew and Thomas, James *the son* of Alpheus, and Simon who is called Zelotes,

16 And Jude *the brother* of James, and Judas Iscariot who was the traitor.

17 And coming down with them, he stood in a plain place, and the company of his disciples, and a very great multitude of people from all Judea and Jerusalem, and the sea-coast both of Tyre and Sidon:

18 Who were come to hear him, and to be healed of their diseases. And they that were troubled with unclean spirits, were cured.

19 And all the multitude sought to touch him, for virtue went out from him, and healed all.

20 *c* And he, lifting up his eyes on his disciples, said: Blessed are ye poor: for yours is the kingdom of God.

21 *d* Blessed are ye that hunger now: for you shall be filled. Blessed are ye that weep now: for you shall laugh.

22 *e* Blessed shall you be when men shall hate you, and when they shall separate you, and shall reproach you, and cast out your name as evil, for the son of man's sake.

23 Be glad in that day and rejoice; for behold, your reward is great in heaven. For according to these things did their fathers to the prophets.

24 *f* But wo to you that are rich: for you have your consolation.

25 *g* Wo to you that are filled: for you shall hunger. Wo to you that now laugh: for you shall mourn and weep.

26 Wo to you when men shall bless you: For according to these things did their fathers to the false prophets.

---

*a* Matt. 12. 10. Mark 3. 1. *b* Matt. 10. 1. Mark 3. 13.

*c* Matt. 5. 2.—*d* Matt. 5. 6.—*e* Matt. 5. 11.—*f* Eccli. 31. 8. Amos 6. 1.—*g* Isaias 65. 13.

27 But I say to you that hear: *a* Love your enemies, do good to them that hate you.

28 Bless them that curse you, and pray for them that calumniate you.

29 And to him that striketh thee on the *one* cheek, offer also the other. And him that taketh away from thee thy cloak, forbid not to take thy coat also.

30 Give to every one that asketh thee, and of him that taketh away thy goods, ask them not again.

31 And as you would that men should do to you, do you also to them in like manner.

32 And if you love them that love you, what thanks are to you? for sinners also love those that love them.

33 And if you do good to them who do good to you, what thanks are to you? for sinners also do this.

34 *b* And if ye lend to them of whom ye hope to receive, what thanks are to you? for sinners also lend to sinners, for to receive as much.

35 But love ye your enemies; do good, and lend, hoping for nothing thereby: and your reward shall be great, and you shall be the sons of the Highest: for he is kind to the unthankful, and to the evil.

36 Be ye therefore merciful, as your Father also is merciful.

37 *c* Judge not, and you shall not be judged. Condemn not, and you shall not be condemned. Forgive, and you shall be forgiven.

38 Give, and it shall be given to you: good measure and pressed down and shaken together and running over shall they give into your bosom. *d* For with the same measure that you shall mete withal, it shall be measured to you again.

39 And he spoke also to them a similitude: Can the blind lead the blind? do they not both fall into the ditch?

40 *e* The disciple is not above his master: but every one shall be perfect, if he be as his master.

41 *f* And why seest thou the mote in thy brother's eye, but the beam that is in thy own eye thou considerest not?

42 Or how canst thou say to thy brother: Brother, let me pull the mote out of thy eye, when thou thyself seest not the beam in thy own eye? Hypocrite, cast first the beam out of thy own eye; and then shalt thou see clearly to take out the mote from thy brother's eye.

43 *g* For there is no good tree that bringeth forth evil fruit: nor an evil tree that bringeth forth good fruit.

44 For every tree is known by its fruit. For men do not gather figs from thorns; nor from a bramble bush do they gather the grape.

45 A good man out of the good treasure of his heart bringeth forth that which is good: and an evil man out of the evil treasure bringeth forth that which is evil. For out of the abundance of the heart the mouth speaketh.

46 And why call you me

---

*a* Matt. 5. 44.—*b* Deut. 15. 8. Matt. 5. 42.—*c* Matt. 7. 1.
*d* Matt. 7. 2. Mark 4. 24.—*e* Matt. 10. 24. John 18. 16.—*f* Matt. 7. 3.—*g* Matt. 7. 16, and 12. 33.

ᵃ Lord, Lord: and do not the things which I say?

47 Every one that cometh to me, and heareth my words, and doth them, I will shew you to whom he is like.

48 He is like to a man building a house, who digged deep, and laid the foundation upon a rock. And when a flood came, the stream beat vehemently upon that house, and it could not shake it; for it was founded on a rock.

49 But he that heareth, and doth not; is like to a man building his house upon the earth without a foundation: against which the stream beat vehemently, and immediately it fell, and the ruin of that house was great.

## CHAP. VII.

*Christ heals the centurion's servant: raises the widow's son to life: answers the messengers sent by John: and absolves the penitent sinner.*

AND ᵇ when he had finished all his words in the hearing of the people, he entered into Capharnaum.

2 And the servant of a certain centurion, who was dear to him, being sick, was ready to die.

3 And when he had heard of Jesus, he sent unto him the ancients of the Jews, desiring him to come and heal his servant.

4 And when they came to Jesus, they besought him earnestly, saying to him, He is worthy that thou shouldest do this for him.

5 For he loveth our nation: and he hath built us a synagogue.

6 And Jesus went with them. And when he was now not far from the house, the centurion sent his friends to him, saying: ᶜ Lord, trouble not thyself. For I am not worthy that thou shouldest enter under my roof.

7 For which cause neither did I think myself worthy to come to thee; but say the word, and my servant shall be healed.

8 For I also am a man subject to authority, having under me soldiers; and I say to one, Go, and he goeth; and to another, Come, and he cometh; and to my servant, Do this, and he doth it.

9 Which Jesus hearing, marvelled: and turning about to the multitude that followed him, he said: Amen I say to you, I have not found so great faith not even in Israel.

10 And they who were sent being returned to the house, found the servant whole who had been sick.

11 And it came to pass afterwards, that he went into a city that is called Naim; and there went with him his disciples, and a great multitude.

12 And when he came nigh to the gate of the city, behold a dead man was carried out, the only son of his mother; and she was a widow: and a great multitude of the city was with her.

13 Whom when the Lord had seen, being moved with mercy towards her, he said to her: Weep not.

14 And he came near and touched the bier. And they that carried it, stood still. And he said: Young man, I say to thee, arise.

---

ᵃ Matt. 7. 21. Rom. 2. 13. Jas. 1. 22. —ᵇ Matt. 8. 5.

ᶜ Matt. 8. 8.

THE RAISING OF THE WIDOW'S SON.

CHAP. VII.      ST. LUKE.      CHAP. VII.

15 And he that was dead, sat up, and began to speak. And he gave him to his mother.

16 And there came a fear on them all: and they glorified God, saying: "A great prophet is risen up among us: and God hath visited his people.

17 And this rumour of him went forth throughout all Judea, and throughout all the country round about.

18 And John's disciples told him of all these things.

19 ᵇ And John called to him two of his disciples, and sent them to JESUS, saying: Art thou he that art to come; or look we for another?

20 And when the men were come unto him, they said: John the Baptist hath sent us to thee, saying: Art thou he that art to come; or look we for another?

21 (And in that same hour, he cured many of their diseases, and hurts, and evil spirits: and to many that were blind he gave sight.)

22 And answering, he said to them: Go and relate to John what you have heard and seen: ᶜ The blind see, the lame walk, the lepers are made clean, the deaf hear, the dead rise again, to the poor the gospel is preached:

23 And blessed is he whosoever shall not be scandalized in me.

24 And when the messengers of John were departed, he began to speak to the multitudes concerning John. What went you out into the desert to see? a reed shaken with the wind?

25 But what went you out to see? a man clothed in soft garments? Behold they that are in costly apparel and live delicately, are in the houses of kings.

26 But what went you out to see? a prophet? Yea, I say to you, and more than a prophet:

27 ᵈ This is he of whom it is written: *Behold I send my angel before thy face, who shall prepare thy way before thee.*

28 For I say to you: Amongst those that are born of women, there is not a greater prophet than John the Baptist. But he that is the lesser in the kingdom of God, is greater than he.

29 And all the people hearing, and the publicans, justified God, being baptized with John's baptism.

30 But the Pharisees and the lawyers despised the counsel of God against themselves, being not baptized by him.

31 And the Lord said: ᵉ Whereunto then shall I liken the men of this generation? and to what are they like?

32 They are like to children sitting in the market-place, and speaking one to another, and saying: We have piped to you, and you have not danced: we have mourned, and you have not wept.

33 ᶠ For John the Baptist came neither eating bread nor drinking wine; and you say: He hath a devil.

34 The son of man is come eating and drinking; and you

---

ᵃ Infra. 24. 19. John 4. 19.—ᵇ Matt. 11. 2.—ᶜ Isaias 35. 4.

ᵈ Mal. 3. 1. Matt. 11. 10. Mark 1. 2. —ᵉ Matt. 11. 16.—ᶠ Matt. 3. 4. Mark 1. 6.

CHAP. VII. Ver. 29. *Justified God;* i.e., praised the justice of God, feared and worshipped God, as just and merciful.

say: Behold a man that is a glutton and a drinker of wine, a friend of publicans and sinners.

35 And wisdom is justified by all her children.

36 And one of the Pharisees desired him to eat with him. And he went into the house of the Pharisee, and sat down to meat.

37 ᵃAnd behold a woman that was in the city, a sinner, when she knew that he sat at meat in the Pharisee's house, brought an alabaster box of ointment;

38 And standing behind at his feet, she began to wash his feet with tears, and wiped them with the hairs of her head, and kissed his feet, and anointed them with the ointment.

39 And the Pharisee, who had invited him, seeing it, spoke within himself, saying: This man, if he were a prophet, would know surely who and what manner of woman this is that toucheth him, that she is a sinner.

40 And JESUS answering, said to him: Simon, I have somewhat to say to thee. But he said: Master, say it.

41 A certain creditor had two debtors, the one owed five hundred pence, and the other fifty.

42 And whereas they had not wherewith to pay, he forgave them both. Which therefore of the two loveth him most?

43 Simon answering said: I suppose that he to whom he forgave most. And he said to him: Thou hast judged rightly.

44 And turning to the woman, he said unto Simon: Dost thou see this woman? I entered into thy house, thou gavest me no water for my feet; but she with tears hath washed my feet, and with her hairs hath wiped them.

45 Thou gavest me no kiss; but she, since she came in, hath not ceased to kiss my feet.

46 My head with oil thou didst not anoint; but she with ointment hath anointed my feet.

47 Wherefore I say to thee: Many sins are forgiven her, because she hath loved much. But to whom less is forgiven, he loveth less.

48 And he said to her: ᵇ Thy sins are forgiven thee.

49 And they that sat at meat with him began to say within themselves: Who is this that forgiveth sins also?

50 And he said to the woman: Thy faith hath made thee safe, go in peace.

## CHAP. VIII.

*The parable of the seed. Christ stills the storm at sea: casts out the legion: heals the issue of blood: and raises the daughter of Jairus to life.*

AND it came to pass afterwards, that he travelled through the cities and towns,

---

ᵇ Matt. 9. 2.

Ver. 47. *Many sins are forgiven her, because she hath loved much.* In the Scripture an effect sometimes seems attributed to one only cause when there are divers other concurring dispositions; for the sins of this woman, in this verse are said to be forgiven, because *she loved much:* but verse 50. Christ tells her, *thy faith hath made thee safe.* Hence in a true conversion are joined faith, hope, love, sorrow for sin, and other pious dispositions.

---

ᵃ Matt. 26. 7. Mark 14. 3. John 11. 2. and 12. 3.

Ver. 36. *One of the Pharisees;* i.e. Simon.

## CHAP. VIII. ST. LUKE. CHAP. VIII.

preaching and evangelizing the kingdom of God; and the twelve with him.

2 And certain women who had been healed of evil spirits and infirmities; *a* Mary who is called Magdalen, out of whom seven devils were gone forth,

3 And Joanna the wife of Chusa Herod's steward, and Susanna, and many others who ministered unto him of their substance.

4 And when a very great multitude was gathered together and hastened out of the cities unto him, he spoke by a similitude.

5 *b* The sower went out to sow his seed. And as he sowed some fell by the way side, and it was trodden down, and the fowls of the air devoured it.

6 And other some fell upon a rock; and as soon as it was sprung up, it withered away, because it had no moisture.

7 And other some fell among thorns, and the thorns growing up with it, choked it.

8 And other some fell upon good ground; and being sprung up yielded fruit a hundred fold. Saying these things, he cried out: He that hath ears to hear, let him hear.

9 And his disciples asked him what this parable might be.

10 To whom he said: To you it is given to know the mystery of the kingdom of God: but to the rest in parables, *c* that seeing they may not see, and hearing may not understand.

11 Now the parable is this: The seed is the word of God.

12 And they by the way side are they that hear; then the devil cometh, and taketh the word out of their heart, lest believing they should be saved.

13 Now they upon the rock, are they who when they hear, receive the word with joy: and these have no roots: for they believe for awhile, and in time of temptation they fall away.

14 And that which fell among thorns, are they who have heard, and going their way, are choked with the cares and riches and pleasures of this life, and yield no fruit.

15 But that on the good ground, are they who in a good and very good heart, hearing the word, keep it, and bring forth fruit in patience.

16 *d* Now no man lighting a candle covereth it with a vessel, or putteth it under a bed; but setteth it upon a candlestick, that they who come in may see the light.

17 *e* For there is not anything secret, that shall not be made manifest; nor hidden, that shall not be known and come abroad.

18 Take heed therefore how you hear. *f* For whosoever hath, to him shall be given; and whosoever hath not, that also which he thinketh he hath, shall be taken away from him.

19 *g* And his mother and brethren came unto him; and they could not come at him for the crowd.

---

*a* Mark 16. 9.—*b* Matt. 13. 8. Mark 4. 3.—*c* Isaias 6. 9. Matt. 13. 14. Mark 4. 12. John 12. 40. Acts 28. 26. Rom. 11. 8.

CHAP. VIII. Ver. 10. *Seeing they may not see.* See the annotation, Mark iv. 12.

*d* Matt. 5. 15. Mark 4. 21.—*e* Matt. 10. 26. Mark 4. 22.—*f* Matt. 13. 12. and 25. 29.—*g* Matt. 12. 46. Mark 3. 32.

20 And it was told him: Thy mother and thy brethren stand without, desiring to see thee.

21 Who answering said to them: My mother and my brethren, are they who hear the word of God, and do it.

22 ᵃ And it came to pass on a certain day, that he went into a little ship with his disciples, and he said to them: Let us go over to the other side of the lake. And they launched forth.

23 And when they were sailing, he slept; and there came down a storm of wind upon the lake, and they were filled, and were in danger.

24 And they came and awakened him, saying: Master, we perish. But he arising rebuked the wind and the rage of the water; and it ceased, and there was a calm.

25 And he said to them: Where is your faith? Who being afraid, wondered, saying one to another: Who is this (think you) that he commandeth both the winds and the sea, and they obey him?

26 And they sailed to the country of the Gerasens which is over against Galilee.

27 And when he was come forth to the land, there met him a certain man who had a devil now a very long time, and he wore no clothes, neither did he abide in a house, but in the sepulchres.

28 And when he saw JESUS, he fell down before him; and crying out with a loud voice, he said: What have I to do with thee, JESUS, Son of the most high God? I beseech thee, do not torment me.

ᵃ Matt. 8. 28. Mark 4. 36.

29 For he commanded the unclean spirit to go out of the man. For many times it seized him, and he was bound with chains, and kept in fetters; and breaking the bonds he was driven by the devil into the deserts.

30 And JESUS asked him, saying: What is thy name? But he said: Legion; because many devils were entered into him.

31 And they besought him that he would not command them to go into the abyss.

32 And there was there a herd of many swine feeding on the mountain; and they besought him that he would suffer them to enter into them. And he suffered them.

33 The devils therefore went out of the man, and entered into the swine; and the herd ran violently down a steep place into the lake, and was stifled.

34 Which when they that fed them saw done, they fled, and told it in the city and in the villages.

35 And they went out to see what was done; and they came to JESUS, and found the man, out of whom the devils were departed, sitting at his feet, clothed, and in his right mind, and they were afraid.

36 And they also that had seen told them how he had been healed from the legion.

37 And all the multitude of the country of the Gerasens besought him to depart from them; for they were taken with great fear. And he going up into the ship returned back again.

38 Now the man, out of whom the devils were departed, besought him that he might be

THE SINS OF MARY MAGDALEN ARE FORGIVEN.

with him. But JESUS sent him away, saying:

39 Return to thy house, and tell how great things God hath done to thee. And he went through the whole city, publishing how great things JESUS had done to him.

40 And it came to pass, that when JESUS was returned, the multitude received him: for they were all waiting for him.

41 ᵃAnd behold there came a man whose name was Jairus, and he was a ruler of the synagogue: and he fell down at the feet of JESUS, beseeching him that he would come into his house

42 For he had an only daughter almost twelve years old and she was dying. And it happened, as he went, that he was thronged by the multitudes.

43 And there was a certain woman having an issue of blood twelve years, who had bestowed all her substance on physicians, and could not be healed by any:

44 She came behind him, and touched the hem of his garment; and immediately the issue of her blood stopped.

45 And JESUS said: Who is it that touched me? And all denying, Peter and they that were with him said: Master, the multitudes throng and press thee, and dost thou say, Who touched me?

46 And JESUS said: Somebody hath touched me; for I know that virtue is gone out from me.

47 And the woman seeing that she was not hid, came trembling, and fell down before his feet: and declared before all the people for what cause she had touched him, and how she was immediately healed.

48 But he said to her: Daughter, thy faith hath made thee whole; go thy way in peace.

49 As he was yet speaking, there cometh one to the ruler of the synagogue, saying to him: Thy daughter is dead; trouble him not.

50 And JESUS hearing this word, answered the father of the maid: Fear not; believe only, and she shall be safe.

51 And when he was come to the house, he suffered not any man to go in with him, but Peter, and James, and John, and the father and mother of the maiden.

52 And all wept and mourned for her. But he said: Weep not; the maid is not dead, but sleepeth.

53 And they laughed him to scorn, knowing that she was dead.

54 But he taking her by the hand, cried out, saying: Maid, arise.

55 And her spirit returned, and she rose immediately. And he bid them give her to eat.

56 And her parents were astonished, whom he charged to tell no man what was done.

## CHAP IX.

*Christ sends forth his apostles: feeds five thousand with five loaves: is transfigured, and casts out a devil.*

THEN ᵇcalling together the twelve apostles, he gave them power and authority over all devils, and to cure diseases.

---

ᵃ Matt. 9. 18. Mark 5. 22.   ᵇ Matt. 10. 1. Mark 3. 13.

CHAP. IX.  ST. LUKE.  CHAP. IX.

2 And he sent them to preach the kingdom of God, and to heal the sick.

3 "And he said to them: Take nothing for your journey, neither staff, nor scrip, nor bread, nor money, neither have two coats.

4 And whatsoever house you shall enter into, abide there, and depart not from thence.

5 And whosoever will not receive you, *b* when ye go out of that city, shake off even the dust of your feet for a testimony against them

6 And going out they went about through the towns, preaching the gospel and healing everywhere.

7 *c* Now Herod the tetrarch heard of all things that were done by him; and he was in a doubt because it was said

8 By some, that John was risen from the dead: but by other some, that Elias hath appeared; and by others, that one of the old prophets was risen again

9 And Herod said: John I have beheaded; but who is this of whom I hear such things? And he sought to see him.

10 And the apostles, when they were returned, told him all they had done: and taking them he went aside into a desert place apart, which belongeth to Bethsaida.

11 Which when the people knew they followed him, and he received them, and spoke to them of the kingdom of God, and healed them who had need of healing.

12 Now the day began to decline. And the twelve came and said to him: *d* Send away the multitude, that going into the towns and villages round about, they may lodge and get victuals; for we are here in a desert place.

13 But he said to them: Give you them to eat. And they said: *e* We have no more than five loaves and two fishes: unless perhaps we should go and buy food for all this multitude

14 Now there were about five thousand men And he said to his disciples: Make them sit down by fifties in a company.

15 And they did so. And made them all sit down.

16 And taking the five loaves and the two fishes, he looked up to heaven, and blessed them: and he broke, and distributed to his disciples, to set before the multitude.

17 And they did all eat, and were filled And there were taken up of fragments that remained to them, twelve baskets.

18 *f* And it came to pass; as he was alone praying, his disciples also were with him: and he asked them, saying: Whom do the people say that I am?

19 But they answered, and said: John the Baptist; but some say Elias; and others say that one of the former prophets is risen again

20 And he said to them: But whom do you say that I am? Simon Peter answering, said: The Christ of God.

21 But he strictly charging them, commanded they should tell this to no man,

22 Saying: *g* The son of man

---

*a* Matt. 10. 9. Mark 6. 8 —*b* Acts 13. 51.—*c* Matt 14. 1. Mark 6. 14.

*d* Matt. 14. 15. Mark 6 36 —*e* John 6. 9 —*f* Matt. 16 13. Mark 8. 27.—*g* Matt. 17. 21. Mark 8. 31. and 9. 30.

must suffer many things, and be rejected by the ancients and chief priests and scribes, and be killed, and the third day rise again.

23 ᵃ And he said to all: If any man will come after me, let him deny himself and take up his cross daily, and follow me.

24 ᵇ For whosoever will save his life, shall lose it; for he that shall lose his life for my sake, shall save it.

25 For what is a man advantaged, if he gain the whole world, and lose himself, and cast away himself?

26 ᶜ For he that shall be ashamed of me and of my words, of him the son of man shall be ashamed when he shall come in his majesty, and that of his Father, and of the holy Angels.

27 ᵈ But I tell you of a truth: There are some standing here that shall not taste death till they see the kingdom of God.

28 ᵉ And it came to pass about eight days after these words, that he took Peter and James and John, and went up into a mountain to pray

29 And whilst he prayed, the shape of his countenance was altered, and his raiment became white and glittering.

30 And behold two men were talking with him. And they were Moses and Elias,

31 Appearing in majesty. And they spoke of his decease that he should accomplish in Jerusalem.

32 But Peter and they that were with him were heavy with sleep. And waking, they saw his glory, and the two men that stood with him.

33 And it came to pass that as they were departing from him, Peter saith to Jesus: Master, it is good for us to be here; and let us make three tabernacles, one for thee, and one for Moses, and one for Elias: not knowing what he said.

34 And as he spoke these things there came a cloud, and overshadowed them: and they were afraid, when they entered into the cloud.

35 And a voice came out of the cloud, saying: ᶠ This is my beloved Son, hear him.

36 And whilst the voice was uttered, Jesus was found alone And they held their peace, and told no man in those days any of these things which they had seen.

37 And it came to pass the day following, when they came down from the mountain, there met him a great multitude

38 ᵍ And behold a man among the crowd cried out, saying: Master, I beseech thee, look upon my son, because he is my only one.

39 And lo, a spirit seizeth him, and he suddenly crieth out, and he throweth him down and teareth him so that he foameth, and bruising him he hardly departeth from him.

40 And I desired thy disciples to cast him out, and they could not.

41 And Jesus answering said: O faithless and perverse genera-

---

ᵃ Matt. 10. 38. and 16 24. Mark 8. 34. Infra. 14. 27.—ᵇ Infra. 17. 33. John 12. 25.—ᶜ Matt. 10. 33. Mark 8. 38. 2 T III. 2. 12.—ᵈ Matt. 16. 28. Mark 8. 39.— ᵉ Matt. 17. 1. Mark 9. 1.

ᶠ 2 Pet. 1. 17.—ᵍ Matt. 17. 14. Mark 9. 16.

tion, how long shall I be with you and suffer you? Bring hither thy son.

42 And as he was coming to him, the devil threw him down and tore him.

43 And JESUS rebuked the unclean spirit, and cured the boy, and restored him to his father.

44 And all were astonished at the mighty power of God: but while all wondered at all the things he did, he said to his disciples: Lay you up in your hearts these words, for it shall come to pass that the son of man shall be delivered into the hands of men.

45 But they understood not this word, and it was hid from them, so that they perceived it not. And they were afraid to ask him concerning this word.

46 [a] And there entered a thought into them, which of them should be greater.

47 But JESUS seeing the thoughts of their heart, took a child and set him by him.

48 And said to them: Whosoever shall receive this child in my name, receiveth me: and whosoever shall receive me, receiveth him that sent me. For he that is the lesser among you all, he is the greater.

49 And John answering, said: Master, we saw a certain man casting out devils in thy name, and we forbade him, because he followeth not with us.

50 And JESUS said to him: Forbid *him* not: for he that is not against you, is for you.

51 And it came to pass when the days of his assumption were accomplishing, that he steadfastly set his face to go to Jerusalem.

52 And he sent messengers before his face; and going they entered into a city of the Samaritans, to prepare for him.

53 And they received him not, because his face was of one going to Jerusalem.

54 And when his disciples James and John had seen this, they said: Lord, wilt thou that we command fire to come down from heaven and consume them?

55 And turning, he rebuked them, saying: You know not of what spirit you are.

56 [b] The son of man came not to destroy souls, but to save. And they went into another town.

57 And it came to pass as they walked in the way, that a certain man said to him: I will follow thee whithersoever thou goest.

58 [c] JESUS said to him: The foxes have holes, and the birds of the air nests; but the son of man hath not where to lay his head.

59 But he said to another: Follow me. And he said: Lord, suffer me first to go, and to bury my father.

60 And JESUS said to him: Let the dead bury their dead; but go thou, and preach the kingdom of God.

61 And another said: I will follow thee, Lord, but let me first take my leave of them that are at my house.

62 JESUS said to him: No man putting his hand to the plough, and looking back, is fit for the kingdom of God.

---

[a] Matt. 18. 1. Mark 9. 33. [b] John 3. 17, and 12. 47.—[c] Matt. 8. 20.

CURE OF THE MAN SICK THIRTY-EIGHT YEARS.

## CHAP. X.

*Christ sends forth, and instructs his seventy-two disciples. The good Samaritan.*

AND after these things the Lord appointed also other seventy-two: and he sent them two and two before his face into every city and place whither he himself was to come.

2 And he said to them: *a* The harvest indeed is great, but the labourers are few. Pray ye therefore the Lord of the harvest, that he send labourers into his harvest.

3 Go: *b* Behold I send you as lambs among wolves.

4 *c* Carry neither purse, nor scrip, nor shoes; *d* and salute no man by the way.

5 Into whatsoever house you enter, first say; Peace be to this house:

6 And if the son of peace be there, your peace shall rest upon him: but if not, it shall return to you.

7 And in the same house remain, eating and drinking such things as they have. *e* For the labourer is worthy of his hire. Remove not from house to house.

8 And into what city soever you enter, and they receive you, eat such things as are set before you;

9 And heal the sick that are therein, and say to them: The kingdom of God is come nigh unto you.

10 But into whatsoever city you enter, and they receive you not, going forth into the streets thereof, say:

11 *f* Even the very dust of your city that cleaveth to us we wipe off against you. Yet know this that the kingdom of God is at hand.

12 I say to you, it shall be more tolerable at that day for Sodom, than for that city.

13 *g* Wo to thee, Corozain, wo to thee, Bethsaida. For if in Tyre and Sidon had been wrought the mighty works that have been wrought in you, they would have done penance long ago, sitting in sackcloth and ashes.

14 But it shall be more tolerable for Tyre and Sidon at the judgment, than for you.

15 And thou, Capharnaum, which art exalted unto heaven: thou shalt be thrust down to hell.

16 *h* He that heareth you, heareth me: and he that despiseth you, despiseth me. And he that despiseth me, despiseth him that sent me.

17 And the seventy-two returned with joy, saying: Lord, the devils also are subject to us in thy name.

18 And he said to them: I saw satan like lightning falling from heaven

19 Behold, I have given you power to tread upon serpents and scorpions, and upon all the power of the enemy, and nothing shall hurt you

20 But yet rejoice not in this that spirits are subject unto you: but rejoice in this, that your names are written in heaven.

21 *i* In that same hour he

---

*a* Matt. 9. 87.—*b* Matt. 10. 16.—*c* Matt. 10. 10. Mark 6. 8.—*d* 4 Kings 4. 29. —*e* Deut. 24. 14. Matt. 10. 10. 1 Tim. 5. 18.

*f* Acts 13. 51.—*g* Matt. 11. 21.—*h* Matt. 10. 40. John 13. 20.—*i* Matt. 11. 25.

CHAP. X. Ver. 21. *He rejoiced in*

rejoiced in the Holy Ghost, and said: I confess to thee, O Father, Lord of heaven and earth, because thou hast hidden these things from the wise and prudent, and hast revealed them to little ones. Yes, Father, for so it hath seemed good in thy sight.

22 All things are delivered to me by my Father, and no one knoweth who the Son is but the Father; and who the Father is but the Son, and to whom the Son will reveal *him*.

23 And turning to his disciples, he said: *a* Blessed are the eyes that see the things which you see

24 For I say to you that many prophets and kings have desired to see the things that you see, and have not seen them; and to hear the things that you hear, and have not heard them.

25 *b* And behold a certain lawyer stood up, tempting him; and saying: Master, what must I do to possess eternal life?

26 But he said to him: What is written in the law? how readest thou?

27 He answering, said: *c Thou shalt love the Lord thy God with thy whole heart, and with thy whole soul, and with all thy strength, and with all thy mind, and thy neighbour as thyself.*

28 And he said to him: Thou hast answered right: this do, and thou shalt live.

29 But he willing to justify himself, said to JESUS: And who is my neighbour?

---

*a* Matt. 13. 16.—*b* Matt. 22. 35. Mark 12. 28.—*c* Deut. 6. 5.

*the Holy Ghost.* That is, according to his humanity he rejoiced in the Holy Ghost, and gave thanks to his eternal Father.

30 And JESUS answering, said: A certain man went down from Jerusalem to Jericho, and fell among robbers, who also stripped him, and having wounded him, went away leaving him half dead

31 And it chanced that a certain priest went down the same way; and seeing him, passed by

32 In like manner also a Levite, when he was near the place and saw him, passed by.

33 But a certain Samaritan being on his journey, came near him: and seeing him, was moved with compassion.

34 And going up to him, bound up his wounds, pouring in oil and wine: and setting him upon his own beast, brought him to an inn, and took care of him.

35 And the next day he took out two pence, and gave to the host, and said: Take care of him; and whatsoever thou shalt spend over and above, I at my return will repay thee.

36 Which of these three in thy opinion was neighbour to him that fell among the robbers?

37 But he said: He that shewed mercy to him. And JESUS said to him: Go, and do thou in like manner.

38 Now it came to pass as they went, that he entered into a certain town: and a certain woman named Martha received him into her house.

39 And she had a sister called Mary, who sitting also at the Lord's feet, heard his word.

40 But Martha was busy about much serving. Who stood and said: Lord, hast thou no care that my sister hath left

me alone to serve? speak to her therefore, that she help me.

41 And the Lord, answering, said to her: Martha, Martha, thou art careful, and art troubled about many things.

42 But one thing is necessary. Mary hath chosen the best part, which shall not be taken away from her.

## CHAP. XI.

*He teaches his disciples to pray. Casts out a dumb devil. Confutes the Pharisees; and pronounces woes against them for their hypocrisy.*

AND it came to pass, that as he was in a certain place praying, when he ceased, one of his disciples said to him: Lord, teach us to pray, as John also taught his disciples.

2 And he said to them: When you pray, say: ªFather, hallowed be thy name Thy kingdom come.

3 Give us this day our daily bread.

4 And forgive us our sins, for we also forgive every one that is indebted to us. And lead us not into temptation.

5 And he said to them: Which of you shall have a friend, and shall go to him at midnight, and shall say to him: Friend, lend me three loaves,

6 Because a friend of mine is come off his journey to me, and I have not what to set before him.

7 And he from within should answer and say: Trouble me not, the door is now shut, and my children are with me in bed; I cannot rise and give thee.

8 Yet if he shall continue knocking, I say to you, although he will not rise and give him, because he is his friend; yet because of his importunity he will rise, and give him as many as he needeth.

9 ᵇAnd I say to you, Ask, and it shall be given you: seek, and you shall find: knock, and it shall be opened to you.

10 For every one that asketh, receiveth: and he that seeketh, findeth: and to him that knocketh, it shall be opened.

11 ᶜAnd which of you if he ask his father bread, will he give him a stone? or a fish, will he for a fish give him a serpent?

12 Or if he shall ask an egg, will he reach him a scorpion?

13 If you then being evil, know how to give good gifts to your children, how much more will your Father from heaven give the good Spirit to them that ask him?

14 ᵈAnd he was casting out a devil, and the same was dumb; and when he had cast out the devil, the dumb spoke: and the multitudes were in admiration at it.

15 But some of them said: He casteth out devils ᵉ by Beelzebub the prince of devils.

16 And others tempting, asked of him a sign from heaven.

17 But he seeing their thoughts, said to them: Every kingdom divided against itself shall be brought to desolation, and house upon house shall fall.

18 And if satan also be divided against himself, how shall his kingdom stand? be-

---

ª Matt. 6. 9.

ᵇ Matt. 7. 7. and 21. 22. Mark 11. 24. John 14. 13. Jas. 1. 5.—ᶜ Matt. 7. 9.—ᵈ Matt. 9. 32. and 12. 22.—ᵉ Matt. 9. 34. Mark 3. 22.

cause you say, that through Beelzebub I cast out devils.

19 Now if I cast out devils by Beelzebub: by whom do your children cast them out? Therefore they shall be your judges.

20 But if I by the finger of God cast out devils: doubtless the kingdom of God is come upon you.

21 When a strong man armed keepeth his court: those things are in peace which he possesseth.

22 But if a stronger than he come upon him and overcome him: he will take away all his armour wherein he trusted, and will distribute his spoils.

23 He that is not with me, is against me: and he that gathereth not with me, scattereth.

24 When the unclean spirit is gone out of a man, he walketh through places without water, seeking rest: and not finding, he saith: I will return into my house whence I came out.

25 And when he is come, he findeth it swept and garnished.

26 Then he goeth and taketh with him seven other spirits more wicked than himself, and entering in they dwell there. And the last state of that man becomes worse than the first.

27 And it came to pass: as he spoke these things, a certain woman from the crowd lifting up her voice said to him: Blessed is the womb that bore thee, and the paps that gave thee suck.

28 But he said: Yea rather blessed are they who hear the word of God, and keep it.

29 And the multitudes running together, he began to say: <sup>a</sup> This generation is a wicked generation: it asketh a sign, and a sign shall not be given it, but the sign of Jonas the prophet.

30 <sup>b</sup> For as Jonas was a sign to the Ninivites, so shall the son of man also be to this generation.

31 <sup>c</sup> The queen of the south shall rise in the judgment with the men of this generation, and shall condemn them, because she came from the ends of the earth to hear the wisdom of Solomon; and behold more than Solomon here.

32 The men of Ninive shall rise in the judgment with this generation, and shall condemn it, <sup>d</sup> because they did penance at the preaching of Jonas; and behold more than Jonas here.

33 <sup>e</sup> No man lighteth a candle, and putteth it in a hidden place, nor under a bushel: but upon a candlestick, that they that come in may see the light.

34 <sup>f</sup> The light of thy body is thy eye. If thy eye be single, thy whole body will be lightsome: but if it be evil, thy body also will be darksome.

35 Take heed therefore that the light which is in thee be not darkness.

36 If then thy whole body be lightsome, having no part of darkness; the whole shall be lightsome, and as a bright lamp shall enlighten thee.

37 And as he was speaking, a certain Pharisee prayed him that he would dine with him. And he going in, sat down to eat.

---

<sup>a</sup> Matt. 12. 39.

<sup>b</sup> Jonas 2. 1.—<sup>c</sup> 3 Kings 10. 1. 2 Par. 9. 1.—<sup>d</sup> Jonas 3. 5.—<sup>e</sup> Matt. 5. 15. Mark 4. 21.—<sup>f</sup> Matt. 6. 22.

THE APOSTLES ARE SENT OUT TO PREACH.

38 And the Pharisee began to say, thinking within himself, why he was not washed before dinner.

39 And the Lord said to him: *a* Now you Pharisees make clean the outside of the cup and of the platter; but your inside is full of rapine and iniquity.

40 Ye fools, did not he that made that which is without, make also that which is within?

41 But yet that which remaineth, give alms; and behold all things are clean unto you.

42 But wo to you Pharisees, because you tithe mint and rue and every herb, and pass over judgment, and the charity of God. Now these things you ought to have done, and not to leave the other undone.

43 *b* Wo to you Pharisees, because you love the uppermost seats in the synagogues, and salutations in the market-place.

44 Wo to you, because you are as sepulchres that appear not, and men that walk over, are not aware.

45 And one of the lawyers answering, saith to him: Master, in saying these things, thou reproachest us also.

46 But he said: Wo to you lawyers also; *c* because you load men with burdens which they cannot bear, and you yourselves touch not the packs with one of your fingers.

47 Wo to you who build the monuments of the prophets: and your fathers killed them.

48 Truly you bear witness that you consent to the doings of your fathers: for they indeed killed them, and you build their sepulchres.

49 For this cause also the wisdom of God said: I will send to them prophets and apostles, and some of them they will kill and persecute.

50 That the blood of all the prophets which was shed from the foundation of the world, may be required of this generation.

51 *d* From the blood of Abel unto the blood of *e* Zacharias, who was slain between the altar, and the temple. Yea I say to you, it shall be required of this generation.

52 Wo to you lawyers, for you have taken away the key of knowledge: you yourselves have not entered in, and those that were entering in you have hindered.

53 And as he was saying these things to them, the Pharisees and the lawyers began vehemently to urge him, and to *f* oppress his mouth about many things,

54 Lying in wait for him, and seeking to catch something from his mouth that they might accuse him.

---

*a* Matt. 23. 25.—*b* Matt. 23. 6. Mark 12. 39. Infra. 20. 46.—*c* Matt. 23. 4.

CHAP. XI. Ver. 46. *Wo to you lawyers.* He speaks of the doctors of the law of Moses, commonly called the Scribes.

Ver. 47. *Wo to you who build,* &c.

*d* Gen. 4. 8.—*e* 2 Par. 24. 22.—*f* i.e., stop.

Not that the building of the monuments of the prophets was in itself blameworthy, but only the intention of these unhappy men, who made use of this outward shew of religion and piety, as a means to carry on their wicked designs against the prince of the prophets.

121

## CHAP. XII.

*Christ warns us against hypocrisy, the fear of the world, and covetousness: and admonishes all to watch.*

AND when great multitudes stood about him, so that they trod one upon another, he began to say to his disciples: *a* Beware ye of the leaven of the Pharisees, which is hypocrisy.

2 *b* For there is nothing covered, that shall not be revealed: nor hidden, that shall not be known

3 For whatsoever things you have spoken in darkness, shall be published in the light: and that which you have spoken in the ear in the chambers, shall be preached on the house-tops.

4 And I say to you, my friends: Be not afraid of them who kill the body, and after that have no more that they can do.

5 But I will shew you whom ye shall fear: fear ye him, who after he hath killed, hath power to cast into hell. Yea, I say to you, fear him.

6 Are not five sparrows sold for two farthings, and not one of them is forgotten before God?

7 Yea, the very hairs of your head are all numbered. Fear not therefore: you are of more value than many sparrows.

8 And I say to you, *c* whosoever shall confess me before men, him shall the son of man also confess before the Angels of God.

9 But he that shall deny me before men, shall be denied before the Angels of God

10 *d* And whosoever speaketh a word against the son of man, it shall be forgiven him: but to him that shall blaspheme against the Holy Ghost it shall not be forgiven.

11 And when they shall bring you into the synagogues, and to magistrates and powers, be not solicitous how or what you shall answer, or what you shall say

12 For the Holy Ghost shall teach you in the same hour what you must say.

13 And one of the multitude said to him: Master, speak to my brother that he divide the inheritance with me.

14 But he said to him: Man, who hath appointed me judge or divider over you?

15 And he said to them: Take heed and beware of all covetousness: for a man's life doth not consist in the abundance of things which he possesseth.

16 And he spoke a similitude to them, saying: *e* The land of a certain rich man brought forth plenty of fruits.

17 And he thought within himself, saying: What shall I do, because I have no room where to bestow my fruits?

18 And he said: This will I do: I will pull down my barns, and will build greater: and into them will I gather all things that are grown to me, and my goods

19 And I will say to my soul: Soul, thou hast much goods laid up for many years, take thy rest, eat, drink, make good cheer.

20 But God said to him: Thou fool, this night do they require thy soul of thee; and whose shall those things be which thou hast provided?

---

*a* Matt. 16. 6. Mark 8. 15.—*b* Matt. 10. 26. Mark 4. 21.—*c* Matt. 10. 32. Mark 8. 38. 2 Tim. 2. 12.—*d* Matt. 12. 32. Mar'k 3. 29.

*e* Eccli. 11. 19.

21 So is he that layeth up treasure for himself, and is not rich towards God.

22 And he said to his disciples: Therefore I say to you, <sup>a</sup> be not solicitous for your life what you shall eat; nor for your body, what you shall put on

23 The life is more than the meat, and the body is more than the raiment.

24 Consider the ravens, for they sow not, neither do they reap, neither have they storehouse nor barn, and God feedeth them. How much are you more valuable than they?

25 And which of you by taking thought can add to his stature one cubit?

26 If then ye be not able to do so much as the least thing, why are you solicitous for the rest?

27 Consider the lilies how they grow: they labour not, neither do they spin But I say to you, not even Solomon in all his glory was clothed like one of these.

28 Now if God clothe in this manner the grass that is to-day in the field, and to-morrow is cast into the oven; how much more you, O ye of little faith?

29 And seek not you what you shall eat, or what you shall drink: and be not lifted up on high.

30 For all these things do the nations of the world seek. But your Father knoweth that you have need of these things.

31 But seek ye first the kingdom of God and his justice, and all these things shall be added unto you.

32 Fear not, little flock, for it hath pleased your Father to give you a kingdom

33 <sup>b</sup> Sell what you possess, and give alms. Make to yourselves bags which grow not old, <sup>c</sup> a treasure in heaven which faileth not: where no thief approacheth, nor moth corrupteth.

34 For where your treasure is, there will your heart be also.

35 Let your loins be girt. and lamps burning in your hands.

36 And you yourselves like to men who wait for their lord, when he shall return from the wedding: that when he cometh and knocketh, they may open to him immediately.

37 Blessed are those servants, whom the Lord when he cometh, shall find watching. Amen I say to you, that he will gird himself, and make them sit down to meat, and passing will minister unto them.

38 And if he shall come in the second watch, or come in the third watch, and find them so, blessed are those servants.

39 <sup>d</sup> But this know ye, that if the householder did know at what hour the thief would come, he would surely watch, and would not suffer his house to be broken open.

40 Be you then also ready: <sup>e</sup> for at what hour you think not, the son of man will come.

41 And Peter said to him: Lord, dost thou speak this parable to us, or likewise to all?

42 And the Lord said: Who (thinkest thou) is the faithful and wise steward, whom his lord setteth over his family, to give

---

<sup>a</sup> Ps. 54. 22. Matt 6. 25. 1 Pet. 5. 7. <sup>b</sup> Matt. 19. 21.—<sup>c</sup> Matt. 6. 20.—<sup>d</sup> Matt. 24. 43.—<sup>e</sup> Apoc. 16. 15.

them their measure of wheat in due season?

43 Blessed is that servant, whom when his lord shall come he shall find so doing.

44 Verily I say to you, he will set him over all that he possesseth.

45 But if that servant shall say in his heart, My lord is long a coming; and shall begin to strike the men-servants and maid-servants, and to eat and to drink, and be drunk:

46 The lord of that servant will come in the day that he hopeth not, and at the hour that he knoweth not, and shall separate him, and shall appoint him his portion with unbelievers.

47 And that servant who knew the will of his lord, and prepared not *himself*, and did not according to his will, shall be beaten with many stripes.

48 But he that knew not and did things worthy of stripes, shall be beaten with few stripes. And unto whomsoever much is given, of him much shall be required: and to whom they have committed much, of him they will demand the more.

49 I am come to cast fire on the earth; and what will I but that it be kindled?

50 And I have a baptism, wherewith I am to be baptized: and how am I straitened until it be accomplished.

51 ªThink ye that I am come to give peace on earth? I tell you no, but separation.

52 For there shall be from henceforth five in one house divided; three against two, and two against three.

53 The father *shall be divided* against the son, and the son against his father, the mother against the daughter, and the daughter against the mother, the mother-in-law against her daughter-in-law, and the daughter-in-law against her mother-in-law.

54 ᵇAnd he said also to the multitudes: When you see a cloud rising from the west, presently you say: A shower is coming; and so it happeneth:

55 And when *ye see* the south wind blow, you say: There will be heat; and it cometh to pass.

56 You hypocrites, you know how to discern the face of the heaven and of the earth: but how is it that you do not discern this time?

57 And why even of yourselves do you not judge that which is just?

58 ᶜAnd when thou goest with thy adversary to the prince, whilst thou art in the way endeavour to be delivered from him: lest perhaps he draw thee to the judge, and the judge deliver thee to the exacter, and the exacter cast thee into prison.

59 I say to thee, thou shalt not go out thence, until thou pay the very last mite.

CHAP. XIII.

*The necessity of penance. The barren fig-tree. The cure of the infirm woman, &c.*

AND there were present at that very time some that told him of the Galileans, whose blood Pilate had mingled with their sacrifices.

2 And he answering said to them: Think you that these

---

ª Matt. 10. 34.    ᵇ Matt. 16. 2.—ᶜ Matt. 5. 25.

THE PARABLE OF THE COCKLE.

Galileans were sinners above all the men of Galilee, because they suffered such things?

3 No, I say to you: but unless you shall do penance, you shall all likewise perish.

4 Or those eighteen upon whom the tower fell in Siloe, and slew them: think you that they also were debtors above all the men that dwelt in Jerusalem?

5 No, I say to you: but except you do penance, you shall all likewise perish.

6 He spoke also this parable: A certain man had a fig-tree planted in his vineyard, and he came seeking fruit on it, and found none.

7 And he said to the dresser of the vineyard: Behold for these three years I come seeking fruit on this fig-tree, and I find none. Cut it down therefore; why cumbereth it the ground?

8 But he answering said to him: Lord, let it alone this year also, until I dig about it, and dung it.

9 And if happily it bear fruit: but if not, then after that thou shalt cut it down.

10 And he was teaching in their synagogue on their sabbath.

11 And behold there was a woman who had a spirit of infirmity eighteen years: and she was bowed together, neither could she look upwards at all.

12 Whom when JESUS saw, he called her unto him, and said to her: Woman, thou art delivered from thy infirmity.

13 And he laid his hands upon her, and immediately she was made straight, and glorified God.

14 And the ruler of the synagogue, (being angry that JESUS had healed on the sabbath,) answering said to the multitude: Six days there are wherein you ought to work. In them therefore come, and be healed: and not on the sabbath-day.

15 And the Lord answering him, said: Ye hypocrites, doth not every one of you on the sabbath-day loose his ox or his ass from the manger, and lead them to water?

16 And ought not this daughter of Abraham, whom satan hath bound, lo, these eighteen years, be loosed from this bond on the sabbath-day?

17 And when he said these things, all his adversaries were ashamed: and all the people rejoiced for all the things that were gloriously done by him.

18 He said therefore: To what is the kingdom of God like, and whereunto shall I resemble it?

19 *a* It is like to a grain of mustard seed, which a man took and cast into his garden, and it grew, and became a great tree, and the birds of the air lodged in the branches thereof.

20 And again he said: Whereunto shall I esteem the kingdom of God to be like?

21 *b* It is like to leaven, which a woman took and hid in three measures of meal, till the whole was leavened.

22 And he went through the cities and towns teaching, and making his journey to Jerusalem

23 And a certain man said to him: Lord, are they few that are saved? But he said to them:

---

*a* Matt. 13. 31. Mark 4. 31.—*b* Matt. 13. 33.

24 "Strive to enter by the narrow gate: for many, I say to you, shall seek to enter, and shall not be able.

25 ᵇBut when the master of the house shall be gone in, and shall shut to the door, you shall begin to stand without, and knock at the door, saying, Lord, open to us: and he answering shall say to you, I know you not whence you are:

26 Then you shall begin to say: We have eaten and drunk in thy presence, and thou hast taught in our streets.

27 And he shall say to you: ᶜI know you not whence you are: ᵈdepart from me, all ye workers of iniquity.

28 There shall be weeping and gnashing of teeth; when you shall see Abraham and Isaac and Jacob, and all the prophets in the kingdom of God, and you yourselves thrust out

29 And there shall come from the east and the west and the north and the south; and shall sit down in the kingdom of God

30 ᵉAnd behold, they are last that shall be first, and they are first that shall be last.

31 The same day there came some of the Pharisees, saying to him: Depart and get thee hence, for Herod hath a mind to kill thee.

32 And he said to them: Go, and tell that fox, Behold I cast out devils, and do cures to-day and to-morrow, and the third day I am consummated.

33 Nevertheless I must walk to-day and to-morrow, and the day following, because it cannot be that a prophet perish out of Jerusalem.

34 ᶠJerusalem, Jerusalem, that killest the prophets, and stonest them that are sent to thee, how often would I have gathered thy children as the bird doth her brood under her wings, and thou wouldst not?

35 Behold your house shall be left to you desolate. And I say to you, that you shall not see me till the time come, when you shall say: Blessed is he that cometh in the name of the Lord.

## CHAP. XIV.

*Christ heals the dropsical man. The parable of the supper. The necessity of renouncing all to follow Christ.*

AND it came to pass when Jesus went into the house of one of the chief of the Pharisees on the sabbath-day to eat bread, that they watched him.

2 And behold, there was a certain man before him that had the dropsy.

3 And Jesus answering, spoke to the lawyers and Pharisees, saying: Is it lawful to heal on the sabbath-day?

4 But they held their peace. But he taking him, healed him, and sent him away.

5 And answering them, he said: Which of you shall have an ass or an ox fall into a pit; and will not immediately draw him out on the sabbath-day?

---

ᵃ Matt. 7. 13 —ᵇ Matt. 25. 10 —ᶜ Matt. 7. 23.—ᵈ Ps. 6 9. Matt 25 41 —ᵉ Matt. 19, 30. and 20. 16. Mark 10. 31.

CHAP XIII. Ver. 24. *Shall seek, &c.* Shall desire to be saved: but for want of taking sufficient pains, and being thoroughly in earnest, shall not attain to it.

ᶠ Matt. 23. 37.

6 And they could not answer him to these things.

7 And he spoke a parable also to them that were invited, marking how they chose the first seats at the table, saying to them:

8 When thou art invited to a wedding, sit not down in the first place, lest perhaps one more honourable than thou be invited by him;

9 And he that invited thee and him, come and say to thee, Give this man place: and then thou begin with shame to take the lowest place

10 But when thou art invited, go, sit down in the lowest place: that when he who invited thee cometh, he may say to thee: *a* Friend, go up higher Then shalt thou have glory before them that sit at table with thee

11 *b* Because every one that exalteth himself, shall be humbled: and he that humbleth himself, shall be exalted

12 And he said to him also that had invited him: *c* When thou makest a dinner or a supper, call not thy friends, nor thy brethren, nor thy kinsmen, nor thy neighbours who are rich: lest perhaps they also invite thee again, and a recompense be made to thee.

13 But when thou makest a feast, call the poor, the maimed, the lame, and the blind.

14 And thou shalt be blessed, because they have not wherewith to make thee recompense: for recompense shall be made thee at the resurrection of the just.

15 When one of them that sat at table with him, had heard these things, he said to him: Blessed is he that shall eat bread in the kingdom of God.

16 But he said to him: *d* A certain man made a great supper, and invited many.

17 And he sent his servant at the hour of supper to say to them that were invited, that they should come, for now all things are ready.

18 And they began all at once to make excuse. The first said to him, I have bought a farm, and I must needs go out and see it; I pray thee, hold me excused.

19 And another said, I have bought five yoke of oxen, and I go to try them: I pray thee, hold me excused.

20 And another said, I have married a wife, and therefore I cannot come.

21 And the servant returning told these things to his lord. Then the master of the house being angry, said to his servant: Go out quickly into the streets and lanes of the city, and bring in hither the poor and the feeble and the blind and the lame.

22 And the servant said: Lord, it is done as thou hast commanded, and yet there is room.

23 And the lord said to the servant: Go out into the highways and hedges; and compel them to come in, that my house may be filled.

24 But I say unto you, that none of those men that were invited shall taste of my supper.

25 And there went great mul-

---

*a* Prov. 25. 7.—*b* Matt. 23. 12. Infra, 18. 14.—*c* Tobias 4. 7. Prov. 8. 9.

*d* Matt. 22. 2. Apoc. 19. 9.

titudes with him: and turning, he said to them:

26 ᵃIf any man come to me, and hate not his father, and mother, and wife, and children, and brethren, and sisters, yea and his own life also, he cannot be my disciple.

27 ᵇAnd whosoever doth not carry his cross and come after me, cannot be my disciple.

28 For which of you having a mind to build a tower, doth not first sit down and reckon the charges that are necessary, whether he have wherewithal to finish it:

29 Lest after he hath laid the foundation, and is not able to finish it, all that see it begin to mock him,

30 Saying: This man began to build, and was not able to finish.

31 Or what king about to go to make war against another king, doth not first sit down and think whether he be able with ten thousand to meet him that with twenty thousand cometh against him?

32 Or else whilst the other is yet afar off, sending an embassy, he desireth conditions of peace.

33 So likewise every one of you that doth not renounce all that he possesseth, cannot be my disciple.

34 ᶜSalt is good. But if the salt shall lose its savour, wherewith shall it be seasoned?

35 It is neither profitable for the land, nor for the dunghill, but shall be cast out. He that hath ears to hear, let him hear.

## CHAP. XV.

*The parables of the lost sheep, and of the prodigal son.*

NOW the publicans and sinners drew near unto him to hear him.

2 And the Pharisees and the scribes murmured, saying: This man receiveth sinners, and eateth with them.

3 And he spoke to them this parable, saying:

4 ᵈWhat man of you that hath an hundred sheep: and if he shall lose one of them, doth he not leave the ninety-nine in the desert, and go after that which was lost until he find it?

5 And when he hath found it, lay it upon his shoulders, rejoicing:

6 And coming home call together his friends and neighbours, saying to them: Rejoice with me, because I have found my sheep that was lost?

7 I say to you, that even so there shall be joy in heaven upon one sinner that doth penance, more than upon ninety-nine just who need not penance.

8 Or what woman having ten groats: if she lose one groat doth not light a candle and sweep the house and seek diligently, until she find it?

9 And when she hath found it, call together her friends and neighbours, saying: Rejoice

---

ᵃ Matt. 10. 37.—ᵇ Matt. 10. 38. and 16. 24. Mark 8. 34.—ᶜ Matt. 5. 13. Mark 9. 49.

CHAP. XIV. Ver 26. *Hate not.* &c. The law of Christ does not allow us to *hate* even our enemies, much less our parents; but the meaning of the text is, that we must be in that disposition of soul, as to be willing to renounce, and part with everything, how near or dear soever it may be to us, that would keep us from following Christ.

ᵈ Matt. 18. 12.

JESUS SLEEPING DURING THE TEMPEST.

with me, because I have found the groat which I had lost.

10 So I say to you, there shall be joy before the Angels of God upon one sinner doing penance.

11 And he said: A certain man had two sons;

12 And the younger of them said to his father: Father, give me the portion of substance that falleth to me. And he divided unto them his substance.

13 And not many days after, the younger son gathering all together, went abroad into a far country: and there wasted his substance living riotously.

14 And after he had spent all, there came a mighty famine in that country, and he began to be in want.

15 And he went, and cleaved to one of the citizens of that country. And he sent him into his farm to feed swine.

16 And he would fain have filled his belly with the husks the swine did eat: and no man gave unto him.

17 And returning to himself, he said: How many hired servants in my father's house abound with bread, and I here perish with hunger?

18 I will arise, and will go to my father, and say to him: Father, I have sinned against heaven, and before thee:

19 I am not now worthy to be called thy son: make me as one of thy hired servants.

20 And rising up he came to his father. And when he was yet a great way off, his father saw him, and was moved with compassion, and running to him, fell upon his neck and kissed him.

21 And the son said to him: Father, I have sinned against heaven, and before thee, I am not now worthy to be called thy son.

22 And the father said to his servants: Bring forth quickly the first robe, and put it on him, and put a ring on his hand, and shoes on his feet:

23 And bring hither the fatted calf, and kill it, and let us eat and make merry:

24 Because this my son was dead, and is come to life again: was lost, and is found. And they began to be merry.

25 Now his elder son was in the field, and when he came and drew nigh to the house, he heard music and dancing:

26 And he called one of the servants, and asked what these things meant.

27 And he said to him: Thy brother is come, and thy father hath killed the fatted calf, because he hath received him safe.

28 And he was angry, and would not go in. His father therefore coming out began to entreat him.

29 And he answering, said to his father: Behold, for so many years do I serve thee, and I have never transgressed thy commandment, and yet thou hast never given me a kid to make merry with my friends:

30 But as soon as this thy son is come, who hath devoured his substance with harlots, thou hast killed for him the fatted calf.

31 But he said to him: Son,

---

CHAP. XV. Ver. 10. *Before the Angels.* By this it is plain that the spirits in heaven have a concern for us below, and a joy at our repentance, and consequently a knowledge of it.

thou art always with me, and all I have is thine.

32 But it was fit that we should make merry and be glad, for this thy brother was dead, and is come to life again; he was lost, and is found.

## CHAP. XVI.

*The parable of the unjust steward; of the rich man and Lazarus.*

AND he said also to his disciples: There was a certain rich man who had a steward: and the same was accused unto him, that he had wasted his goods.

2 And he called him, and said to him: How is it that I hear this of thee? give an account of thy stewardship: for now thou canst be steward no longer.

3 And the steward said within himself: What shall I do, because my lord taketh away from me the stewardship? To dig I am not able; to beg I am ashamed.

4 I know what I will do, that when I shall be removed from the stewardship, they may receive me into their houses.

5 Therefore calling together every one of his lord's debtors, he said to the first: How much dost thou owe my lord?

6 But he said: An hundred barrels of oil. And he said to him: Take thy bill and sit down quickly, and write fifty.

7 Then he said to another: And how much dost thou owe? Who said: An hundred quarters of wheat. He said to him: Take thy bill, and write eighty.

8 And the lord commended the unjust steward, forasmuch as he had done wisely: for the children of this world are wiser in their generation than the children of light.

9 And I say to you: Make unto you friends of the mammon of iniquity, that when you shall fail they may receive you into everlasting dwellings.

10 He that is faithful in that which is least, is faithful also in that which is greater: and he that is unjust in that which is little, is unjust also in that which is greater.

11 If then you have not been faithful in the unjust mammon; who will trust you with that which is the true?

12 And if you have not been faithful in that which is another's; who will give you that which is your own?

13 *a* No servant can serve two masters, for either he will hate the one, and love the other: or he will hold to the one, and despise the other. You cannot serve God and mammon.

14 Now the Pharisees who were covetous, heard all these things: and they derided him.

15 And he said to them: You are they who justify yourselves before men, but God knoweth your hearts; for that which is high to men is an abomination before God.

16 *b* The law and the prophets *were* until John; from

---

*a* Matt. 6. 24.—*b* Matt. 11. 12.

CHAP. XVI. Ver. 9. *Mammon of iniquity. Mammon* signifies *riches.* They are here called the *mammon of iniquity,* because oftentimes ill gotten, ill bestowed, or an occasion of evil; and at the best are but worldly and false; and not the true riches of a Christian. —Ibid. *They may receive.* By this we see, that the poor servants of God, whom we have relieved by our alms, may hereafter, by their intercession, bring our souls to heaven.

that time the kingdom of God is preached, and every one useth violence towards it.

17 ªAnd it is easier for heaven and earth to pass, than one tittle of the law to fall.

18 ᵇEvery one that putteth away his wife, and marrieth another, committeth adultery: and he that marrieth her that is put away from her husband, committeth adultery.

19 There was a certain rich man, who was clothed in purple and fine linen: and feasted sumptuously every day.

20 And there was a certain beggar named Lazarus, who lay at his gate, full of sores,

21 Desiring to be filled with the crumbs that fell from the rich man's table, and no one did give him; moreover the dogs came and licked his sores.

22 And it came to pass that the beggar died, and was carried by the Angels into Abraham's bosom. And the rich man also died: and he was buried in hell.

23 And lifting up his eyes when he was in torments, he saw Abraham afar off, and Lazarus in his bosom:

24 And he cried, and said: Father Abraham, have mercy on me, and send Lazarus that he may dip the tip of his finger in water, to cool my tongue, for I am tormented in this flame.

25 And Abraham said to him: Son, remember that thou didst receive good things in thy lifetime, and likewise Lazarus evil things: but now he is comforted, and thou art tormented.

26 And besides all this, between us and you there is fixed a great chaos: so that they who would pass from hence to you, cannot, nor from thence come hither.

27 And he said: Then, father, I beseech thee that thou wouldst send him to my father's house, for I have five brethren,

28 That he may testify unto them, lest they also come into this place of torments.

29 And Abraham said to him: They have Moses and the prophets; let them hear them.

30 But he said: No, father Abraham, but if one went to them from the dead, they will do penance.

31 And he said to him: If they hear not Moses and the prophets, neither will they believe if one rise again from the dead.

## CHAP. XVII.

*Lessons of avoiding scandal; of the efficacy of faith, &c. The ten lepers. The manner of the coming of Christ.*

AND ᶜhe said to his disciples: It is impossible that scandals should not come: but wo to him through whom they come.

2 It were better for him, that a millstone were hanged about his neck, and he cast into the sea, than that he should scandalize one of these little ones.

3 Take heed to yourselves. ᵈIf thy brother sin against thee, reprove him: and if he do penance, forgive him.

4 And if he sin against thee seven times in a day, and seven

---

ª Matt. 5. 18.—ᵇ Matt. 5. 32. Mark 10. 11. 1 Cor. 7. 10 and 11.

Ver. 22. *Abraham's bosom.* The place of rest, where the souls of the saints resided, till Christ had opened heaven by his death.

ᶜ Matt. 18. 7. Mark 9. 41.—ᵈ Lev. 19. 17. Eccli. 19. 13. Matt. 18. 15.

times in a day be converted unto thee, saying, I repent: forgive him

5 And the apostles said to the Lord: Increase our faith.

6 <sup>a</sup>And the Lord said: If you had faith like to a grain of mustard-seed, you might say to this mulberry-tree, Be thou rooted up, and be thou transplanted into the sea: and it would obey you.

7 But which of you having a servant plowing or feeding cattle, will say to him when he is come from the field: Immediately go, sit down to meat:

8 And will not *rather* say to him: Make ready my supper, and gird thyself, and serve me whilst I eat and drink, and afterwards thou shalt eat and drink?

9 Doth he thank that servant, for doing the things which he commanded him?

10 I think not. So you also, when you shall have done all these things that are commanded you, say: We are unprofitable servants; we have done that which we ought to do.

11 And it came to pass, as he was going to Jerusalem, he passed through the midst of Samaria and Galilee.

12 And as he entered into a certain town, there met him ten men that were lepers, who stood afar off;

13 And lifted up their voice, saying: JESUS, master, have mercy on us.

14 Whom when he saw, he said: <sup>b</sup>Go, shew yourselves to the priests. And it came to pass, as they went, they were made clean.

15 And one of them when he saw that he was made clean, went back, with a loud voice glorifying God,

16 And he fell on his face before his feet, giving thanks: and this was a Samaritan.

17 And JESUS answering, said: Were not ten made clean? and where are the nine?

18 There is no one found to return and give glory to God, but this stranger.

19 And he said to him: Arise, go thy way; for thy faith hath made thee whole.

20 And being asked by the Pharisees: when the kingdom of God should come? he answered them and said: The kingdom of God cometh not with observation:

21 Neither shall they say: Behold here, or behold there. For lo, the kingdom of God is within you.

22 And he said to his disciples: The days will come when you shall desire to see one day of the son of man; and you shall not see it.

23 <sup>c</sup>And they will say to you: See here, and see there. Go ye not after, nor follow them:

24 For as the lightning that lighteneth from under heaven, shineth unto the parts that are under heaven: so shall the son of man be in his day

---

<sup>a</sup> Matt. 17. 19.

CHAP XVII. Ver. 10. *Unprofitable servants.* Because our service is of *no profit* to our master; and he justly claims it as our bounden duty. But though we are *unprofitable to him,* our serving him is not *unprofitable to us:* for he is pleased to give by his grace a value to our good works, which, in consequence of his promise, entitles them to an eternal reward.

<sup>b</sup> Lev. 14. 2.—<sup>c</sup> Matt. 24. 23. Matt. 13. 21.

THE WOMAN TAKEN IN ADULTERY.

25 But first he must suffer many things, and be rejected by this generation.

26 ᵃAnd as it came to pass in the days of Noe, so shall it be also in the days of the son of man.

27 They did eat and drink, they married wives and were given in marriage, until the day that Noe entered into the ark: and the flood came and destroyed them all.

28 ᵇLikewise as it came to pass in the days of Lot: They did eat and drink, they bought and sold, they planted and built.

29 And in the day that Lot went out of Sodom, it rained fire and brimstone from heaven, and destroyed them all.

30 Even thus shall it be in the day when the son of man shall be revealed.

31 In that hour he that shall be on the house-top, and his goods in the house, let him not go down to take them away: and he that shall be in the field, in like manner let him not return back.

32 Remember Lot's wife.

33 ᶜWhosoever shall seek to save his life, shall lose it: and whosoever shall lose it, shall preserve it.

34 I say to you: ᵈin that night there shall be two men in one bed: the one shall be taken, and the other shall be left.

35 Two women shall be grinding together; the one shall be taken, and the other shall be left: two men shall be in the field; the one shall be taken, and the other shall be left.

36 They answering say to him: Where, Lord?

37 Who said to them: Wheresoever the body shall be, thither will the eagles also be gathered together.

## CHAP. XVIII.

*We must pray always. The Pharisee, and the publican. The danger of riches. The blind man is restored to sight*

AND ᵉ he spoke also a parable to them, that we ought always to pray, and not to faint.

2 Saying: There was a judge in a certain city, who feared not God, nor regarded man.

3 And there was a certain widow in that city, and she came to him, saying: Avenge me of my adversary.

4 And he would not for a long time. But afterwards he said within himself: Although I fear not God, nor regard man,

5 Yet because this widow is troublesome to me, I will avenge her, lest continually coming she weary me.

6 And the Lord said: Hear what the unjust judge saith.

7 And will not God revenge his elect who cry to him day and night: and will he have patience in their regard?

8 I say to you that he will quickly revenge them. But yet the son of man when he cometh, shall he find, think you, faith on earth?

9 And to some who trusted in themselves as just, and despised others, he spoke also this parable:

---

ᵉ Eccli. 18. 22. 1 Thess. 5. 17.

---

ᵃ Gen. 7. 7. Matt. 24. 37.—ᵇ Gen. 19. 25.—ᶜ Matt. 10. 39. Mark 8. 35.—ᵈ Supra. 9. 24. John 12. 25. Matt. 24. 40.

CHAP. XVIII. Ver. 3. *Avenge.* That is, do me justice. It is a *Hebraism.*

10 Two men went up into the temple to pray: the one a Pharisee, and the other a publican.

11 The Pharisee standing prayed thus with himself: O God, I give thee thanks that I am not as the rest of men, extortioners, unjust, adulterers, as also is this publican.

12 I fast twice in a week: I give tithes of all that I possess.

13 And the publican standing afar off would not so much as lift up his eyes towards heaven; but struck his breast, saying: O God, be merciful to me a sinner.

14 I say to you, this man went down into his house justified rather than the other: *a* because every one that exalteth himself, shall be humbled; and he that humbleth himself, shall be exalted.

15 *b* And they brought unto him also infants, that he might touch them. Which when the disciples saw, they rebuked them.

16 But JESUS calling them together, said: Suffer children to come to me, and forbid them not, for of such is the kingdom of God.

17 Amen I say to you: Whosoever shall not receive the kingdom of God as a child, shall not enter into it.

18 *c* And a certain ruler asked him, saying, Good master, what shall I do to possess everlasting life?

19 And JESUS said to him: Why dost thou call me good? None is good but God alone.

20 Thou knowest the commandments: *d* Thou shalt not kill: Thou shalt not commit adultery: Thou shalt not steal: Thou shalt not bear false witness: Honour thy father and mother.

21 Who said: All these things have I kept from my youth.

22 Which when JESUS had heard, he said to him: Yet one thing is wanting to thee: sell all whatever thou hast, and give to the poor, and thou shalt have treasure in heaven: and come, follow me.

23 He having heard these things, became sorrowful: for he was very rich.

24 And JESUS seeing him become sorrowful, said: How hardly shall they that have riches enter into the kingdom of God.

25 For it is easier for a camel to pass through the eye of a needle, than for a rich man to enter into the kingdom of God.

26 And they that heard it said: Who then can be saved?

27 He said to them: The things that are impossible with men, are possible with God.

28 Then Peter said: Behold we have left all things, and have followed thee.

29 Who said to them: Amen I say to you, there is no man that hath left house, or parents, or brethren, or wife, or children, for the kingdom of God's sake,

30 Who shall not receive much more in this present time, and in the world to come life everlasting.

31 *e* Then JESUS took unto him the twelve, and said to them: Behold we go up to Jerusalem, and all things shall be accomplished which were written by

---

*a* Matt. 22. 12. Supra, 14. 11.—*b* Matt. 19. 13. Mark 10. 13.—*c* Matt. 19. 16.—*d* Exod. 20. 13.

*e* Matt. 20. 17. Mark 10. 32.

the prophets concerning the son of man.

32 For he shall be delivered to the Gentiles, and shall be mocked, and scourged, and spit upon:

33 And after they have scourged him, they will put him to death; and the third day he shall rise again.

34 And they understood none of these things, and this word was hid from them, and they understood not the things that were said.

35 *a* Now it came to pass, when he drew nigh to Jericho, that a certain blind man sat by the way-side, begging.

36 And when he heard the multitude passing by, he asked what this meant.

37 And they told him that JESUS of Nazareth was passing by.

38 And he cried out, saying: JESUS son of David, have mercy on me.

39 And they that went before, rebuked him, that he should hold his peace. But he cried out much more: Son of David, have mercy on me.

40 And JESUS standing commanded him to be brought unto him. And when he was come near, he asked him,

41 Saying: What wilt thou that I do to thee? But he said: Lord, that I may see.

42 And JESUS said to him: Receive thy sight; thy faith hath made thee whole.

43 And immediately he saw, and followed him, glorifying God. And all the people when they saw it, gave praise to God.

*a* Matt. 20. 29. Mark 10. 46.

## CHAP. XIX.

*Zacheus entertains Christ. The parable of the pounds. Christ rides upon an ass, and weeps over Jerusalem.*

AND entering in, he walked through Jericho.

2 And behold there was a man named Zacheus: who was the chief of the publicans, and he was rich.

3 And he sought to see JESUS who he was, and he could not for the crowd, because he was low of stature.

4 And running before, he climbed up into a sycamore-tree that he might see him: for he was to pass that way.

5 And when JESUS was come to the place looking up, he saw him, and said to him: Zacheus, make haste and come down: for this day I must abide in thy house.

6 And he made haste and came down, and received him with joy.

7 And when all saw it, they murmured, saying that he was gone to be a guest with a man that was a sinner.

8 But Zacheus standing said to the Lord: Behold, Lord, the half of my goods I give to the poor; and if I have wronged any man of anything, I restore him four-fold.

9 JESUS said to him: This day is salvation come to this house: because he also is a son of Abraham.

10 *b* For the son of man is come to seek and to save that which was lost.

11 As they were hearing these things, he added and spoke a parable because he was nigh to Jerusalem, and because they

*b* Matt. 18 12.

thought that the kingdom of God should immediately be manifested.

12 He said therefore: *a* A certain nobleman went into a far country to receive for himself a kingdom, and to return.

13 And calling his ten servants, he gave them ten pounds, and said to them: Trade till I come.

14 But his citizens hated him: and they sent an embassage after him, saying: We will not have this man to reign over us.

15 And it came to pass that he returned, having received the kingdom: and he commanded his servants to be called, to whom he had given the money; that he might know how much every man had gained by trading.

16 And the first came, saying: Lord, thy pound hath gained ten pounds.

17 And he said to him: Well done, thou good servant; because thou hast been faithful in a little, thou shalt have power over ten cities.

18 And the second came, saying: Lord, thy pound hath gained five pounds.

19 And he said to him: Be thou also over five cities.

20 And another came, saying: Lord, behold here is thy pound, which I have kept laid up in a napkin:

21 For I feared thee, because thou art an austere man: thou takest up what thou didst not lay down, and thou reapest that which thou didst not sow.

22 He saith to him: Out of thy own mouth I judge thee, thou wicked servant. Thou knewest that I was an austere man, taking up what I laid not down, and reaping that which I did not sow:

23 And why then didst thou not give my money into the bank, that at my coming I might have exacted it with usury?

24 And he said to them that stood by: Take the pound away from him, and give it to him that hath the ten pounds.

25 And they said to him: Lord, he hath ten pounds.

26 *b* But I say to you, that to every one that hath shall be given, and he shall abound: and from him that hath not, even that which he hath shall be taken from him.

27 But as for those my enemies, who would not have me reign over them, bring them hither; and kill them before me.

28 And having said these things, he went before, going up to Jerusalem.

29 *c* And it came to pass, when he was come nigh to Bethphage and Bethania unto the mount called Olivet, he sent two of his disciples,

30 Saying: Go into the town which is over against you, at your entering into which, you shall find the colt of an ass tied, on which no man ever hath sitten: loose him; and bring him hither

31 And if any man shall ask

---

*a* Matt. 25. 14.

---

CHAP XIX. Ver 13. *He gave them ten pounds.* In the original, what is here translated a pound, is μνᾶ, or in Latin *mina*, in value of our coin three pounds two shillings and sixpence.

*b* Matt. 13. 12. and 25. 29. Mark 4. 25. Supra, 8. 18.—*c* Matt. 21. 1. Mark 11. 1.

JESUS RESTORES THE DAUGHTER OF JAIRUS.

you: Why do you loose him? you shall say thus unto him: Because the Lord hath need of his service.

32 And they that were sent went their way, and found the colt standing, as he had said unto them.

33 And as they were loosing the colt, the owners thereof said to them: Why loose you the colt?

34 But they said: Because the Lord hath need of him.

35 <sup>a</sup> And they brought him to Jesus. And casting their garments on the colt, they set Jesus thereon.

36 And as he went, they spread their clothes underneath in the way.

37 And when he was now coming near the descent of mount Olivet, the whole multitude of his disciples began with joy to praise God with a loud voice, for all the mighty works they had seen,

38 Saying: Blessed be the king who cometh in the name of the Lord, peace in heaven, and glory on high.

39 And some of the Pharisees from amongst the multitude said to him: Master, rebuke thy disciples

40 To whom he said: I say to you, that if these shall hold their peace, the stones will cry out.

41 And when he drew near, seeing the city, he wept over it, saying:

42 If thou also hadst known, and that in this thy day, the things that are to thy peace: but now they are hidden from thy eyes.

<sup>a</sup> John 12. 14.

43 For the days shall come upon thee: and thy enemies shall cast a trench about thee, and compass thee round, and straiten thee on every side

44 And beat thee flat to the ground, and thy children who are in thee : <sup>b</sup> and they shall not leave in thee a stone upon a stone : because thou hast not known the time of thy visitation.

45 <sup>c</sup> And entering into the temple, he began to cast out them that sold therein and them that bought,

46 Saying to them: It is written : <sup>d</sup> *My house is the house of prayer* But you have made it a den of thieves.

47 And he was teaching daily in the temple. And the chief priests and the scribes and the rulers of the people sought to destroy him :

48 And they found not what to do to him. For all the people were very attentive to hear him.

## CHAP. XX

*The parable of the husbandmen. Of paying tribute to Cæsar; and of the resurrection of the dead.*

AND <sup>a</sup> it came to pass that on one of the days, as he was teaching the people in the temple and preaching the gospel, the chief priests and the scribes with the ancients met together.

2 And spoke to him, saying: Tell us, by what authority dost thou do these things? or, Who is he that hath given thee this authority?

3 And Jesus answering, said

<sup>b</sup> Matt. 24. 2. Mark 13. 2. Infra. 21. 6.—<sup>c</sup> Matt. 21. 12. Mark 11. 15.—<sup>d</sup> Isaias 56. 7. Jer. 7. 11.—<sup>a</sup> Matt. 21. 23. Mark 11. 27.

CHAP. XX.  ST. LUKE.  CHAP. XX.

to them: I will also ask you one thing. Answer me:

4 The baptism of John, was it from heaven, or of men?

5 But they thought within themselves, saying: If we shall say, From heaven; he will say: Why then did you not believe him?

6 But if we say, Of men, the whole people will stone us: for they are persuaded that John was a prophet.

7 And they answered that they knew not whence it was.

8 And JESUS said to them: Neither do I tell you by what authority I do these things.

9 And he began to speak to the people this parable: *a* A certain man planted a vineyard, and let it out to husbandmen: and he was abroad for a long time.

10 And at the season he sent a servant to the husbandmen, that they should give him of the fruit of the vineyard. Who beating him sent him away empty.

11 And again he sent another servant. But they beat him also, and treating him reproachfully, sent him away empty.

12 And again he sent the third: and they wounded him also, and cast him out.

13 Then the lord of the vineyard said: What shall I do? I will send my beloved son: it may be when they see him, they will reverence him.

14 Whom when the husbandmen saw, they thought within themselves, saying: This is the heir, let us kill him, that the inheritance may be ours.

15 So casting him out of the vineyard, they killed him. What therefore will the lord of the vineyard do to them?

16 He will come, and will destroy these husbandmen, and will give the vineyard to others. Which they hearing, said to him: God forbid.

17 But he looking on them, said: What is this then that is written, *b The stone which the builders rejected, the same is become the head of the corner?*

18 Whosoever shall fall upon that stone, shall be bruised: and upon whomsoever it shall fall, it will grind him to powder.

19 And the chief priests and the scribes sought to lay hands on him the same hour; but they feared the people, for they knew that he spoke this parable to them.

20 *c* And being upon the watch, they sent spies, who should feign themselves just, that they might take hold of him in his words, that they might deliver him up to the authority and power of the governor.

21 And they asked him, saying: Master, we know that thou speakest and teachest rightly; and thou dost not respect any person, but teachest the way of God in truth.

22 Is it lawful for us to give tribute to Cesar, or no?

23 But he considering their guile, said to them: Why tempt you me?

24 Shew me a penny. Whose image and inscription hath it? They answering said to him, Cesar's.

25 And he said to them:

---

*a* Isaias 5. 1. Jer. 2. 21. Matt. 21. 33. Mark 12. 1.

*b* Ps. 117. 22. Isaias 28. 16. Matt. 21. 42. Acts 4. 11. Rom. 9. 33. 1 Pet. 2. 7.
—*c* Matt. 2. 15. Mark 12. 13.

*a* Render therefore to Cesar the things that are Cesar's, and to God the things that are God's.

26 And they could not reprehend his word before the people: and wondering at his answer, they held their peace.

27 *b* And there came to him some of the Sadducees, who deny that there is any resurrection, and they asked him,

28 Saying: Master, Moses wrote unto us, *c* If any man's brother die having a wife, and he leave no children, that his brother should take her to wife, and raise up seed unto his brother.

29 There were therefore seven brethren: and the first took a wife, and died without children.

30 And the next took her to wife, and he also died childless.

31 And the third took her. And in like manner all the seven, and they left no children, and died.

32 Last of all the woman died also.

33 In the resurrection therefore, whose wife of them shall she be? For *all* the seven had her to wife.

34 And JESUS said to them: The children of this world marry, and are given in marriage:

35 But they that shall be accounted worthy of that world and of the resurrection from the dead, shall neither be married, nor take wives.

36 Neither can they die any more: for they are equal to the angels, and are the children of God, being the children of the resurrection.

37 Now that the dead rise again, Moses also shewed, at the bush, *d* when he calleth the Lord: *The God of Abraham, and the God of Isaac, and the God of Jacob.*

38 For he is not the God of the dead, but of the living: for all live to him.

39 And some of the scribes answering, said to him: Master, thou hast said well.

40 And after that they durst not ask him any more questions.

41 But he said to them: How say they that Christ is the son of David?

42 And David himself saith in the book of psalms: *e The Lord said to my Lord, sit thou on my right hand,*

43 *Till I make thy enemies, thy footstool.*

44 David then calleth him Lord: and how is he his son?

45 And in the hearing of all the people, he said to his disciples:

46 *f* Beware of the scribes, who desire to walk in long robes, and love salutations in the market-place, and the first chairs in the synagogues, and the chief rooms at feasts:

47 Who devour the houses of widows, feigning long prayer. These shall receive greater damnation.

## CHAP. XXI.

*The widow's mite. The signs that should forerun the destruction of Jerusalem, and the end of the world.*

AND *g* looking on, he saw the rich men cast their gifts into the treasury.

---

*a* Rom. 13. 7.—*b* Matt. 22. 23. Mark 12. 18.—*c* Deut. 25. 5.

*d* Exod. 3. 6.—*e* Ps. 109. 1. Matt. 22. 44. Mark 12. 36.—*f* Matt. 23. 6. Mark 12. 38. Supra, 11. 43.—*g* Mark 12. 41.

2 And he saw also a certain poor widow casting in two brass mites.

3 And he said: Verily I say to you, that this poor widow hath cast in more than they all.

4 For all these have of their abundance cast into the offerings of God: but she of her want, hath cast in all the living that she had.

5 And some saying of the temple, that it was adorned with goodly stones and gifts, he said:

6 These things which you see, <sup>a</sup>the days will come in which there shall not be left a stone upon a stone that shall not be thrown down.

7 And they asked him, saying: Master, when shall these things be: and what shall be the sign when they shall begin to come to pass?

8 Who said: Take heed you be not seduced; for many will come in my name, saying, I am he: and the time is at hand; go ye not therefore after them.

9 And when you shall hear of wars and seditions, be not terrified: these things must first come to pass, but the end is not yet presently.

10 Then he said to them: Nation shall rise against nation, and kingdom against kingdom.

11 And there shall be great earthquakes in divers places, and pestilences and famines, and terrors from heaven, and there shall be great signs.

12 But before all these things they will lay their hands on you and persecute you, delivering you up to the synagogues, and into prisons, dragging you before kings and governors for my name's sake.

13 And it shall happen unto you for a testimony.

14 Lay it up therefore in your hearts, not to meditate before how you shall answer.

15 For I will give you a mouth and wisdom, which all your adversaries shall not be able to resist and gainsay.

16 And you shall be betrayed by your parents and brethren, and kinsmen and friends: and some of you they will put to death.

17 And you shall be hated by all men for my name's sake:

18 But a hair of your head shall not perish.

19 In your patience you shall possess your souls.

20 <sup>b</sup>And when you shall see Jerusalem compassed about with an army: then know that the desolation thereof is at hand.

21 Then let those who are in Judea flee to the mountains: and those who are in the midst thereof, depart out: and those who are in the countries, not enter into it.

22 For these are the days of vengeance, that all things may be fulfilled that are written.

23 But wo to them that are with child, and give suck in those days; for there shall be great distress in the land, and wrath upon this people

24 And they shall fall by the edge of the sword: and shall be led away captives into all nations: and Jerusalem shall be trodden down by the gentiles: till the times of the nations be fulfilled.

---

<sup>a</sup> Matt. 24. 2. Mark 13. 2. Supra, 19. 44.

<sup>b</sup> Dan. 9. 27. Matt. 24. 15. Mark 13. 14.

TWO BLIND MEN ARE RESTORED TO SIGHT.

25 ᵃ And there shall be signs in the sun, and in the moon, and in the stars: and upon the earth distress of nations, by reason of the confusion of the roaring of the sea and of the waves.

26 Men withering away for fear, and expectation of what shall come upon the whole world. For the powers of heaven shall be moved:

27 And then they shall see the son of man coming in a cloud with great power and majesty.

28 But when these things begin to come to pass, look up and lift up your heads: ᵇ because your redemption is at hand.

29 And he spoke to them a similitude. See the fig-tree, and all the trees:

30 When they now shoot forth their fruit, you know that summer is nigh.

31 So you also when you shall see these things come to pass, know that the kingdom of God is at hand.

32 Amen I say to you, this generation shall not pass away, till all things be fulfilled.

33 Heaven and earth shall pass away, but my words shall not pass away.

34 And take heed to yourselves, lest perhaps your hearts be overcharged with surfeiting and drunkenness and the cares of this life: and that day come upon you suddenly.

35 For as a snare shall it come upon all that sit upon the face of the whole earth.

36 Watch ye therefore, praying at all times, that you may be accounted worthy to escape all these things that are to come, and to stand before the son of man.

37 And in the day-time he was teaching in the temple; but at night going out, he abode in the mount that is called Olivet.

38 And all the people came early in the morning to him in the temple to hear him.

## CHAP. XXII.

*The treason of Judas. The last supper. The first part of the history of the passion.*

NOW ᶜ the feast of unleavened bread, which is called the pasch, was at hand.

2 And the chief priests and the scribes sought how they might put JESUS to death: but they feared the people.

3 ᵈ And satan entered into Judas who was surnamed Iscariot, one of the twelve.

4 And he went, and discoursed with the chief priests and the magistrates, how he might betray him to them.

5 And they were glad, and covenanted to give him money.

6 And he promised. And he sought opportunity to betray him in the absence of the multitude.

7 And the day of the unleavened bread came, on which it was necessary that the pasch should be killed.

8 And he sent Peter and John, saying: Go and prepare for us the pasch, that we may eat.

9 But they said: Where wilt thou that we prepare?

10 And he said to them: Behold, as you go into the city, there shall meet you a man car-

---

ᵃ Isaias 13. 10. Ezech. 32. 7. Joel 2. 10. and 3. 7. Matt. 24. 29. Mark 13. 24.—ᵇ Rom. 8. 23.

ᶜ Matt. 26. 2. Mark 14. 1. A.D. 33.—ᵈ Matt. 26. 14. Mark 14. 10.

rying a pitcher of water: follow him into the house where he entereth in:

11 And you shall say to the good man of the house: The master saith to thee: Where is the guest-chamber, where I may eat the pasch with my disciples?

12 And he will shew you a large dining-room furnished: and there prepare.

13 And they going, found as he said to them, and made ready the pasch.

14 ᵃ And when the hour was come, he sat down and the twelve apostles with him.

15 And he said to them: With desire I have desired to eat this pasch with you before I suffer.

16 For I say to you, that from this time I will not eat it till it be fulfilled in the kingdom of God.

17 And having taken the chalice, he gave thanks, and said: Take, and divide it among you.

18 For I say to you, that I will not drink of the fruit of the vine, till the kingdom of God come.

19 ᵇ And taking bread, he gave thanks, and brake; and gave to them, saying: This is my body which is given for you. Do this for a commemoration of me.

20 In like manner the chalice also, after he had supped, saying: This is the chalice, the new testament in my blood, which shall be shed for you.

21 ᶜ But yet behold, the hand of him that betrayeth me is with me on the table.

22 And the son of man indeed goeth, ᵈ according to that which is determined: but yet wo to that man by whom he shall be betrayed.

23 And they began to inquire among themselves which of them it was that should do this thing.

24 And there was also a strife amongst them, which of them should seem to be greater.

25 And he said to them: ᵉ The kings of the gentiles lord it over them; and they that have power over them, are called beneficent.

26 But you not so: but he that is the greater among you, let him become as the younger: and he that is the leader, as he that serveth.

27 For which is greater, he that sitteth at table or he that serveth? Is not he that sitteth at table? but I am in the midst of you as he that serveth:

28 And you are they who have continued with me in my temptations.

29 And I dispose to you, as my Father hath disposed to me, a kingdom:

30 That you may eat and

---

ᵃ Matt. 26. 20. Mark 14. 17.—ᵇ 1 Cor. 11. 24.

---

CHAP. XXII. Ver. 19. *Do this for a commemoration of me.* This sacrifice and sacrament is to be continued in the Church to the end of the world, to shew forth the death of Christ, until he cometh. But this commemoration, or remembrance, is by no means inconsistent with the real presence of his body and blood, under these sacramental veils, which represent his death: on the contrary, it is the manner that he himself hath commanded of commemorating and celebrating his death, by offering in sacrifice, and receiving in the sacrament, that body and blood by which we were redeemed.

ᶜ Matt. 26. 21. Mark 14. 20. John 13. 18.—ᵈ Ps. 40. 9.—ᵉ Matt. 20. 25. Mark 10. 42.

drink at my table in my kingdom: and may sit upon thrones judging the twelve tribes of Israel.

31 And the Lord said: Simon, Simon, behold satan hath desired to have you that he may sift you as wheat.

32 But I have prayed for thee that thy faith fail not: and thou being once converted, confirm thy brethren.

33 Who said to him: Lord, I am ready to go with thee both into prison and to death.

34 *And he said: I say to thee, Peter, the cock shall not crow this day, till thou thrice deniest that thou knowest me. And he said to them:

35 *b* When I sent you without purse and scrip and shoes, did you want anything?

36 But they said: Nothing. Then said he unto them: But now he that hath a purse, let him take it, and likewise a scrip: and he that hath not, let him sell his coat, and buy a sword.

37 For I say to you, that this that is written, must yet be fulfilled in me, *c And with the wicked was he reckoned.* For the things concerning me have an end.

38 But they said: Lord, behold here are two swords. And he said to them: It is enough.

39 *d* And going out he went according to his custom to the mount of Olives. And his disciples also followed him.

40 And when he was come to the place, he said to them: Pray, lest you enter into temptation.

41 *e* And he was withdrawn away from them a stone's cast; and kneeling down he prayed,

42 Saying: Father, if thou wilt, remove this chalice from me: But yet not my will, but thine be done.

43 And there appeared to him an Angel from heaven, strengthening him. And being in an agony, he prayed the longer.

44 And his sweat became as drops of blood trickling down upon the ground.

45 And when he rose up from prayer, and was come to his disciples, he found them sleeping for sorrow.

46 And he said to them: Why sleep you? arise, pray, lest you enter into temptation.

47 *f* As he was yet speaking, behold a multitude: and he that was called Judas, one of the twelve, went before them, and drew near to JESUS for to kiss him.

48 And JESUS said to him: Judas, dost thou betray the son of man with a kiss?

49 And they that were about him, seeing what would follow, said to him: Lord, shall we strike with the sword?

50 And one of them struck the servant of the high-priest, and cut off his right ear.

51 But JESUS answering, said: Suffer ye thus far. And when he had touched his ear, he healed him.

52 And JESUS said to the chief priests, and magistrates of the temple, and the ancients that were come unto him: Are you come out, as it were

---

*a* Matt. 26. 14. Mark 14. 20.—*b* Matt. 10. 9.—*c* Isaias 53. 12.—*d* Matt. 26. 36. Mark 14. 32. John 18. 1.

*e* Matt. 26. 39. Mark 14. 35.—*f* Matt. 26. 47. Mark 14. 43. John 18. 3.

against a thief, with swords and clubs?

53 When I was daily with you in the temple, you did not stretch forth your hands against me: but this is your hour, and the power of darkness.

54 *a* And apprehending him, they led him to the high-priest's house. But Peter followed afar off.

55 *b* And when they had kindled a fire in the midst of the hall, and were sitting about it, Peter was in the midst of them.

56 Whom when a certain servant-maid had seen sitting at the light, and had earnestly beheld him, she said: This man also was with him.

57 But he denied him, saying: Woman, I know him not.

58 And after a little while another seeing him, said: Thou also art one of them. But Peter said: O man, I am not.

59 *c* And after the space as it were of one hour, another certain man affirmed, saying: Of a

*a* Matt. 26. 57. Mark 14. 53. John 18. 24.—*b* Matt. 26. 69. Mark 14. 66. John 18. 25.—*c* John 18. 26.

---

Ver. 58. *Another, &c.* Observe here, in order to reconcile the four Evangelists, that divers persons concurred in charging Peter with being Christ's disciple; till at length they brought him to deny him thrice. 1. The portress that let him in, and afterwards seeing him at the fire, first put the question to him; and then positively affirmed that he was with Christ. 2. Another maid accused him to the standers-by; and gave occasion to the man here mentioned to renew the charge against him, which caused the second denial. 3. Others of the company took notice of his being a Galilean; and were seconded by the kinsman of Malchus, who affirmed he had seen him in the garden. And this drew on the third denial.

144

truth, this man was also with him: for he is also a Galilean.

60 And Peter said: Man, I know not what thou sayest. And immediately as he was yet speaking, the cock crew.

61 And the Lord turning looked on Peter. And Peter remembered the word of the Lord, as he had said: *d* Before the cock crow, thou shalt deny me thrice.

62 And Peter going out wept bitterly.

63 And the men that held him, mocked him, and struck him.

64 And they blindfolded him, and smote his face. And they asked him, saying: Prophesy, who is it that struck thee?

65 And blaspheming, many other things they said against him.

66 *e* And as soon as it was day, the ancients of the people, and the chief priests, and scribes came together, and they brought him into their council, saying: If thou be the Christ, tell us.

67 And he said to them: If I shall tell you, you will not believe me:

68 And if I shall also ask you, you will not answer me, nor let me go.

69 But hereafter the son of man shall be sitting on the right hand of the power of God.

70 Then said they all: Art thou then the Son of God? Who said: You say that I am.

71 And they said: What need we any farther testimony? For we ourselves have heard it from his own mouth.

*d* Matt. 26. 34. Mark 14. 30. John 13. 38.—*e* Matt. 27. 1. Mark 15. 1. John 18. 28.

BEHEADING OF ST. JOHN THE BAPTIST.

## CHAP. XXIII.

*The continuation of the history of the passion.*

AND the whole multitude of them rising up, led him to Pilate.

2 And they began to accuse him, saying: We have found this man perverting our nation, *a* and forbidding to give tribute to Cesar, and saying that he is Christ the king.

3 *b* And Pilate asked him, saying: Art thou the king of the Jews? But he answering, said: Thou sayest it.

4 And Pilate said to the chief priests and to the multitudes: I find no cause in this man.

5 But they were more earnest, saying: He stirreth up the people, teaching throughout all Judea, beginning from Galilee to this place.

6 But Pilate hearing Galilee, asked if the man were of Galilee?

7 And when he understood that he was of Herod's jurisdiction, he sent him away to Herod, who was also himself at Jerusalem in those days.

8 And Herod seeing JESUS, was very glad, for he was desirous of a long time to see him, because he had heard many things of him: and he hoped to see some sign wrought by him.

9 And he questioned him in many words. But he answered him nothing.

10 And the chief priests and the scribes stood by, earnestly accusing him.

11 And Herod with his army set him at nought: and mocked him, putting on him a white garment, and sent him back to Pilate.

12 And Herod and Pilate were made friends that same day: for before they were enemies one to another.

13 And Pilate calling together the chief priests, and the magistrates, and the people,

14 Said to them: You have presented unto me this man, as one that perverteth the people, and behold I, having examined him before you, *c* find no cause in this man in those things wherein you accuse him.

15 No, nor Herod neither. For I sent you to him, and behold nothing worthy of death is done to him.

16 I will chastise him therefore, and release him.

17 Now of necessity he was to release unto them one upon the feast-day.

18 But the whole multitude together cried out, saying: Away with this man, and release unto us Barabbas.

19 Who for a certain sedition made in the city, and for a murder, was cast into prison.

20 And Pilate again spoke to them, desiring to release JESUS.

21 But they cried again, saying: Crucify him, crucify him.

22 And he said to them the third time: *d* Why, what evil hath this man done? I find no cause of death in him: I will chastise him therefore, and let him go.

23 But they were instant with loud voices requiring that he might be crucified: and their voices prevailed.

24 And Pilate gave sentence

---

*a* Matt. 22. 21. Mark 12. 17.—*b* Matt. 27. 11. Mark 15. 2. John 18. 33. | *c* John 18. 38. and 19. 4.—*d* Matt. 27. 23. Mark 15. 14.

that it should be as they required.

25 And he released unto them him who for murder and sedition had been cast into prison, whom they had desired: but JESUS he delivered up to their will.

26 ᵃAnd as they led him away, they laid hold of one Simon of Cyrene, coming from the country; and they laid the cross on him to carry after JESUS.

27 And there followed him a great multitude of people, and of women who bewailed and lamented him.

28 But JESUS turning to them, said: Daughters of Jerusalem, weep not over me, but weep for yourselves, and for your children.

29 For behold the days shall come, wherein they will say: Blessed are the barren, and the wombs that have not borne, and the paps that have not given suck.

30 Then shall they begin to say to the mountains: ᵇFall upon us: and to the hills: Cover us.

31 For if in the green wood they do these things, what shall be done in the dry?

32 And there were also two other malefactors led with him to be put to death.

33 ᶜAnd when they were come to the place which is called Calvary, they crucified him there: and the robbers, one on the right and the other on the left.

34 And JESUS said: Father, forgive them, for they know not what they do. But they dividing his garments, cast lots.

35 And the people stood beholding, and the rulers with them derided him, saying: He saved others, let him save himself, if he be Christ, the elect of God.

36 And the soldiers also mocked him, coming to him, and offering him vinegar.

37 And saying: If thou be the king of the Jews, save thyself.

38 And there was also a superscription written over him in letters of Greek, and Latin, and Hebrew: THIS IS THE KING OF THE JEWS.

39 And one of those robbers who were hanged, blasphemed him, saying: If thou be Christ, save thyself, and us.

40 But the other answering, rebuked him, saying: Neither dost thou fear God, seeing thou art under the same condemnation?

41 And we indeed justly, for we receive the due reward of our deeds: but this man hath done no evil.

42 And he said to JESUS: Lord, remember me when thou shalt come into thy kingdom.

43 And JESUS said to him: Amen I say to thee, this day thou shalt be with me in paradise.

---

CHAP. XXIII. Ver. 43. *In paradise.* That is, in the happy state of rest, joy, and peace everlasting. Christ was pleased, by a special privilege, to reward the faith and confession of the penitent thief, with a full discharge of all his sins, both as to the guilt and punishment; and to introduce him immediately after death into the happy society of the saints, whose *limbo*, that is, the place of their confinement, was now made a *paradise* by our Lord's going thither.

---

ᵃ Matt. 27. 32. Mark 15. 21.—ᵇ Isaias 2. 19. Osee 10. 8. Apoc. 6. 16.—ᶜ Matt. 27. 33. Mark 15. 22. John 19. 17.

CHAP. XXIII.　　ST. LUKE.　　CHAP. XXIV.

44 And it was almost the sixth hour; and there was darkness over all the earth until the ninth hour.

45 And the sun was darkened; and the veil of the temple was rent in the midst.

46 And JESUS crying with a loud voice, said: *a* Father, into thy hands I commend my spirit. And saying this he gave up the ghost.

47 Now the centurion seeing what was done, glorified God, saying: Indeed this was a just man.

48 And all the multitude of them that were come together to that sight, and saw the things that were done, returned striking their breasts.

49 And all his acquaintance, and the women that had followed him from Galilee, stood afar off beholding these things.

50 *b* And behold there was a man named Joseph, who was a counsellor, a good and a just man:

51 (The same had not consented to their counsel and doings,) of Arimathea, a city of Judea, who also himself looked for the kingdom of God.

52 This man went to Pilate, and begged the body of JESUS.

53 And taking him down, he wrapped him in fine linen, and laid him in a sepulchre that was hewed in stone, wherein never yet any man had been laid.

54 And it was the day of the Parasceve, and the sabbath drew on.

55 And the women that were come with him from Galilee, following after, saw the sepulchre, and how his body was laid.

56 And returning, they prepared spices and ointments: and on the sabbath-day they rested according to the commandment.

## CHAP. XXIV.

*Christ's resurrection, and manifestation of himself to his disciples.*

AND *c* on the first *day* of the week very early in the morning they came to the sepulchre, bringing the spices which they had prepared.

2 And they found the stone rolled back from the sepulchre.

3 And going in, they found not the body of the Lord JESUS.

4 And it came to pass, as they were astonished in their mind at this, behold two men stood by them in shining apparel.

5 And as they were afraid and bowed down their countenance towards the ground, they said unto them: Why seek you the living with the dead?

6 He is not here, but is risen. Remember how he spoke unto you, when he was yet in Galilee,

7 Saying: *d* The son of man must be delivered into the hands of sinful men, and be crucified, and the third day rise again.

8 And they remembered his words.

9 And going back from the sepulchre, they told all these

---

*a* Ps. 30. 6.—*b* Matt. 27. 57. Mark 15. 42. John 19. 38.

Ver. 54. *Parasceve.* That is, the eve or day of preparation for the sabbath.

*c* Matt. 28. 1. Mark 16 2. John 20. 1.—*d* Matt. 16. 21. and 17. 21. Mark 8. 31. and 9. 30. Supra, 9. 22.

things to the eleven, and to all the rest.

10 And it was Mary Magdalene, and Joanna, and Mary of James, and the other women that were with them, who told these things to the apostles.

11 And these words seemed to them as idle tales: and they did not believe them.

12 But Peter rising up ran to the sepulchre; and stooping down, he saw the linen cloths laid by themselves, and went away wondering in himself at that which was come to pass.

13 [a] And behold, two of them went the same day to a town which was sixty furlongs from Jerusalem, named Emmaus.

14 And they talked together of all these things which had happened.

15 And it came to pass, that while they talked and reasoned with themselves, JESUS himself also drawing near went with them.

16 But their eyes were held that they should not know him.

17 And he said to them: What are these discourses that you hold one with another as you walk, and are sad?

18 And the one of them, whose name was Cleophas, answering, said to him: Art thou only a stranger in Jerusalem, and hast not known the things that have been done there in these days?

19 To whom he said: What things? And they said: Concerning JESUS of Nazareth, who was a prophet, mighty in work and word before God and all the people.

20 And how our chief priests and princes delivered him to be condemned to death, and crucified him.

21 But we hoped that it was he that should have redeemed Israel: and now besides all this, to-day is the third day since these things were done.

22 Yea, and certain women also of our company affrighted us, who before it was light were at the sepulchre.

23 And not finding his body, came, saying that they had also seen a vision of angels, who say that he is alive.

24 And some of our people went to the sepulchre: and found it so as the women had said, but him they found not.

25 Then he said to them: O foolish, and slow of heart to believe in all things which the prophets have spoken.

26 Ought not Christ to have suffered these things, and so to enter into his glory?

27 And beginning at Moses and all the prophets, he expounded to them in all the scriptures the things that were concerning him.

28 And they drew nigh to the town whither they were going: and he made as though he would go farther.

29 But they constrained him, saying: Stay with us, because it is towards evening, and the day is now far spent. And he went in with them.

30 And it came to pass, whilst he was at table with them, he took bread, and blessed and brake, and gave to them.

31 And their eyes were opened, and they knew him: and he vanished out of their sight.

---

[a] Mark 16. 12.

JESUS SUPPORTING ST. PETER ON THE WATER.

32 And they said one to the other: Was not our heart burning within us, whilst he spoke in the way, and opened to us the scriptures?

33 And rising up the same hour they went back to Jerusalem: and they found the eleven gathered together, and those that were with them,

34 Saying: The Lord is risen indeed, and hath appeared to Simon.

35 And they told what things were done in the way: and how they knew him in the breaking of bread.

36 *a* Now whilst they were speaking these things, JESUS stood in the midst of them, and saith to them: Peace be to you; it is I, fear not.

37 But they being troubled and frighted, supposed that they saw a spirit.

38 And he said to them: Why are you troubled, and why do thoughts arise in your hearts?

39 See my hands and feet, that it is I myself; handle, and see: for a spirit hath not flesh and bones, as you see me to have.

40 And when he had said this, he shewed them his hands and feet.

41 But while they yet believed not and wondered for joy, he said: Have you here anything to eat?

42 And they offered him a piece of a broiled fish, and a honeycomb.

43 And when he had eaten before them, taking the remains he gave to them.

44 And he said to them: These are the words which I spoke to you while I was yet with you, and all things must needs be fulfilled, which are written in the law of Moses, and in the prophets, and in the psalms, concerning me.

45 Then he opened their understanding, that they might understand the scriptures.

46 And he said to them: *b* Thus it is written, and thus it behoved Christ to suffer, and to rise again from the dead the third day:

47 And that penance and the remission of sins should be preached in his name unto all nations, beginning at Jerusalem.

48 *c* And you are witnesses of these things.

49 *d* And I send the promise of my Father upon you: but stay you in the city, till you be endued with power from on high.

50 And he led them out as far as Bethania: and lifting up his hands he blessed them.

51 *e* And it came to pass, whilst he blessed them, he departed from them, and was carried up to heaven.

52 And they adoring went back into Jerusalem with great joy.

53 And they were always in the temple praising and blessing God. Amen.

---

*a* Mark 10. 14. John 20. 19.

*b* Ps. 18. 6.—*c* Acts 1. 8.—*d* John 14. 26.—*e* Mark 16. 19. Acts 1. 9.

---

CHAP. XXIV. Ver. 49. *The promise of my Father,* i.e., the Holy Ghost, whom Christ had promised that his Father and he would send. John xiv. 26, and xvii. 7.

THE

# HOLY GOSPEL OF JESUS CHRIST,

## ACCORDING TO ST. JOHN.

*St. John the Apostle and Evangelist, was the son of Zebedee and Salome, and brother to James the Greater. He was called the* BELOVED DISCIPLE OF CHRIST, *and stood by at his crucifixion. He wrote the Gospel after the other Evangelists, about sixty-three years after our Lord's Ascension. Many things that they had omitted were supplied by him. The original was written in Greek, and by the Greeks he is titled* THE DIVINE. *St.* JEROME *relates that when he was earnestly requested by the brethren to write the Gospel, he answered he would do it, if by ordering a common fast, they would all put up their prayers together to the Almighty God; which being ended, replenished with the clearest and fullest revelation, coming from Heaven, he burst forth into that preface:* In the beginning was the Word, &c.

## CHAP. I.

*The Divinity and Incarnation of Christ. John bears witness of him. He begins to call his disciples.*

IN the beginning was the Word, and the Word was with God, and the Word was God.

2 The same was in the beginning with God.

3 All things were made by him: and without him was made nothing that was made.

4 In him was life, and the life was the light of men:

5 And the light shineth in darkness, and the darkness did not comprehend it.

6 *a* There was a man sent from God, whose name was John.

7 This man came for a witness, to give testimony of the light, that all men might believe through him.

8 He was not the light, but was to give testimony of the light.

9 *b* That was the true light, which enlighteneth every man that cometh into this world.

10 He was in the world, *c* and the world was made by him, and the world knew him not.

11 He came unto his own, and his own received him not.

12 But as many as received him, he gave them power to be made the sons of God, to them that believe in his name.

13 Who are born, not of blood, nor of the will of the flesh, nor of the will of man, but of God.

14 *d* And the Word was made flesh, and dwelt among us (and we saw his glory, the glory as it were of the only-begotten of the Father) full of grace and truth.

15 John beareth witness of him, and crieth out, saying: This was he of whom I spoke: He that shall come after me, is preferred before me: because he was before me.

*a* Matt. 3. 1. Mark 1. 2.

*b* Infra, 3. 19.—*c* Heb. 11. 3.—*d* Matt. 1. 16. Luke 2. 7.

16 *a* And of his fulness we all have received, and grace for grace.

17 For the law was given by Moses, grace and truth came by JESUS CHRIST.

18 *b* No man hath seen God at any time: the only-begotten Son who is in the bosom of the Father, he hath declared him.

19 And this is the testimony of John, when the Jews sent from Jerusalem priests and Levites to him, to ask him: Who art thou?

20 And he confessed, and did not deny: and he confessed: I am not the CHRIST.

21 And they asked him: What then? Art thou Elias? And he said: I am not. Art thou the prophet? And he answered: No.

22 They said therefore unto him: Who art thou, that we may give an answer to them that sent us? what sayest thou of thyself?

23 He said: *e I am the voice of one crying in the wilderness, Make straight the way of the Lord,* as said the prophet Isaias.

24 And they that were sent were of the Pharisees.

25 And they asked him, and said to him: Why then dost thou baptize, if thou be not Christ, nor Elias, nor the prophet?

26 John answered them, saying: *d* I baptize with water; but there hath stood one in the midst of you, whom you know not.

27 *e* The same is he that shall come after me, who is preferred before me: the latchet of whose shoe I am not worthy to loose.

28 These things were done in Bethania beyond the Jordan, where John was baptizing.

29 The next day John saw JESUS coming to him, and he saith: Behold the lamb of God, behold him who taketh away the sin of the world.

30 This is he of whom I said: After me there cometh a man, who is preferred before me: because he was before me.

31 And I knew him not, but that he may be made manifest in Israel, therefore am I come baptizing with water.

32 And John gave testimony, saying: *f* I saw the Spirit coming down as a dove from heaven, and he remained upon him.

33 And I knew him not: but he, who sent me to baptize with water, said to me: He upon whom thou shalt see the Spirit descending and remaining upon him, he it is that baptizeth with the Holy Ghost.

34 And I saw; and I gave testimony, that this is the Son of God.

35 The next day again John stood, and two of his disciples.

36 And beholding JESUS walking, he saith: Behold the lamb of God.

37 And the two disciples heard him speak, and they followed JESUS.

38 And JESUS turning, and seeing them following him, said to them: What seek you? Who said to him: Rabbi (which is to say, being interpreted, Master), where dwellest thou?

39 He saith to them: Come

---

*a* 1 Tim. 6. 17.—*b* 1 Tim. 6. 16. 1 John 4. 12.—*c* Isaias 40. 3. Matt. 3. 3. Mark 1. 3. Luke 3. 4.—*d* Matt. 3. 11.—*e* Mark 1. 7. Luke 3. 16. Acts 1. 5. and 11. 16. and 19. 4.

*f* Matt. 3. 16. Mark 1. 10. Luke 3. 22.

and see. They came, and saw where he abode, and they staid with him that day: now it was about the tenth hour.

40 And Andrew the brother of Simon Peter was one of the two who had heard of John, and followed him.

41 He findeth first his brother Simon, and saith to him: We have found the MESSIAS, which is, being interpreted, the CHRIST.

42 And he brought him to JESUS. And JESUS looking upon him said: Thou art Simon the son of Jona: thou shalt be called Cephas, which is interpreted Peter.

43 On the following day he would go forth into Galilee, and he findeth Philip. And JESUS saith to him: Follow me.

44 Now Philip was of Bethsaida, the city of Andrew and Peter.

45 Philip findeth Nathanael, and saith to him: We have found him of whom *a* Moses in the law, *b* and the prophets did write, JESUS the son of Joseph of Nazareth.

46 And Nathanael said to him: Can anything of good come from Nazareth? Philip saith to him: Come and see.

47 JESUS saw Nathanael coming to him, and he saith of him: Behold an Israelite indeed, in whom there is no guile.

48 Nathanael saith to him: Whence knowest thou me? JESUS answered and said to him: Before that Philip called thee, when thou wast under the fig-tree, I saw thee.

49 Nathanael answered him, and said: Rabbi, thou art the Son of God, thou art the king of Israel.

50 JESUS answered, and said to him: Because I said unto thee, I saw thee under the fig-tree, thou believest: greater things than these shalt thou see.

51 And he saith to him: Amen, amen I say to you, you shall see the heaven opened, and the Angels of God ascending and descending upon the son of man.

## CHAP. II.

*Christ changes water into wine. He casts the sellers out of the temple.*

AND the third day there was a marriage in Cana of Galilee: and the mother of JESUS was there.

2 And JESUS also was invited, and his disciples, to the marriage.

3 And the wine failing, the mother of Jesus saith to him: They have no wine.

4 And JESUS saith to her: Woman, what is it to me and to thee? my hour is not yet come.

5 His mother saith to the waiters: Whatsoever he shall say to you, do ye.

---

CHAP. II. Ver. 4. *What is it to me, &c.* These words of our Saviour spoken to his mother have been understood by some commentators as harsh, they not considering the next following verse: *Whatsoever he shall say to you, do ye,* which plainly shews that his mother knew of the miracle that he was to perform, and that it was at her request he wrought it; besides the manner of speaking the words as to the tone, and the countenance shewn at the same time, which could only be known to those who were present, or from what had followed: for words indicating anger in one tone of voice, would be understood quite the reverse in another.

---

*a* Gen. 49. 10. Deut. 18. 18.—*b* Isaias 40. 10. and 45. 8. Jer. 23. 5. Ezech. 34. 23. and 37. 24. Dan. 9. 24. and 25.

THE MULTIPLICATION OF THE LOAVES AND FISHES.

6 Now there were set there six waterpots of stone, according to the manner of the purifying of the Jews, containing two or three measures a-piece.

7 JESUS saith to them: Fill the waterpots with water. And they filled them up to the brim.

8 And JESUS saith to them: Draw out now, and carry to the chief steward of the feast. And they carried it.

9 And when the chief steward had tasted the water made wine, and knew not whence it was, but the waiters knew who had drawn the water; the chief steward calleth the bridegroom,

10 And saith to him: Every man at first setteth forth good wine, and when men have well drank, then that which is worse. But thou hast kept the good wine until now.

11 This beginning of miracles did JESUS in Cana of Galilee: and manifested his glory, and his disciples believed in him.

12 After this he went down to Capharnaum, he and his mother, and his brethren, and his disciples: and they remained there not many days.

13 And the pasch of the Jews was at hand, and JESUS went up to Jerusalem.

14 And he found in the temple them that sold oxen and sheep and doves, and the changers of money sitting.

15 And when he had made as it were a scourge of little cords, he drove them all out of the temple, the sheep also and the oxen, and the money of the changers he poured out, and the tables he overthrew.

16 And to them that sold doves he said: Take these things hence, and make not the house of my father a house of traffic.

17 And his disciples remembered that it was written: *ª The zeal of thy house hath eaten me up.*

18 The Jews therefore answered, and said to him: What sign dost thou show unto us, seeing thou dost these things?

19 JESUS answered and said to them: *b Destroy this temple, and in three days I will raise it up.*

20 The Jews then said: Six and forty years was this temple in building, and wilt thou raise it up in three days?

21 But he spoke of the temple of his body.

22 When therefore he was risen again from the dead, his disciples remembered that he had said this, *c and they believed the scripture, and the word that JESUS had said.*

23 Now when he was at Jerusalem at the pasch, upon the festival day, many believed in his name, seeing his signs which he did.

24 But JESUS did not trust himself unto them, for that he knew all men,

25 And because he needed not that any should give testimony of man: for he knew what was in man.

## CHAP. III.

*Christ's discourse with Nicodemus. John's testimony.*

AND there was a man of the Pharisees, named Nicodemus, a ruler of the Jews.

2 This man came to JESUS by

---

*ª Ps. 68. 10.—b Mal. 26. 61. and 27. 40. Mark 14. 58. and 15. 29.—c Ps. 3. 6. and 56. 9.*

night, and said to him: Rabbi, we know that thou art come a teacher from God: for no man can do these signs which thou dost, unless God be with him.

3 JESUS answered and said to him: Amen, amen I say to thee, unless a man be born again, he cannot see the kingdom of God.

4 Nicodemus saith to him: How can a man be born when he is old? can he enter a second time into his mother's womb, and be born again?

5 JESUS answered: Amen, amen I say to thee, unless a man be born again of water and the Holy Ghost, he cannot enter into the kingdom of God.

6 That which is born of the flesh, is flesh: and that which is born of the Spirit, is spirit.

7 Wonder not, that I said to thee, you must be born again.

8 The Spirit breatheth where he will: and thou hearest his voice, *a* but thou knowest not whence he cometh and whither he goeth: so is every one that is born of the Spirit.

9 Nicodemus answered, and said to him: How can these things be done?

10 JESUS answered, and said to him: Art thou a master in Israel, and knowest not these things?

11 Amen, amen I say to thee, that we speak what we know, and we testify what we have seen, and you receive not our testimony.

12 If I have spoken to you earthly things, and you believe not: how will you believe if I shall speak to you heavenly things?

13 And no man hath ascended into heaven, but he that descended from heaven, the son of man who is in heaven.

14 *b* And as Moses lifted up the serpent in the desert, so must the son of man be lifted up:

15 That whosoever believeth in him, may not perish, but may have life everlasting.

16 *c* For God so loved the world, as to give his only begotten Son; that whosoever believeth in him, may not perish, but may have life everlasting.

17 For God sent not his Son, into the world, to judge the world, but that the world may be saved by him.

18 He that believeth in him is not judged. But he that doth not believe is already judged: because he believeth not in the name of the only begotten Son of God.

19 And this is the judgment: *d* because the light is come into the world, and men loved darkness rather than the light: for their works were evil.

20 For every one that doth evil hateth the light, and cometh not to the light, that his works may not be reproved.

---

*b* Num. 21. 9.—*c* 1 John 4. 9.—*d* Supra, 1. 9.

Ver. 18. *Is not judged.* He that believeth, viz., by a faith working through charity, is not *judged*, that is, is not *condemned*; but the obstinate *unbeliever* is *judged*, that is, condemned already, by retrenching himself from the society of Christ and his Church.

Ver. 19. *The judgment.* That is, the cause of his condemnation.

---

*a* Ps. 134. 7.

CHAP. III. Ver. 5. *Unless a man be born again,* &c. By these words our Saviour hath declared the necessity of Baptism: and by the word *water,* it is evident that the application of it is necessary with the words, *Matt.* xxviii. 19.

21 But he that doth truth, cometh to the light, that his works may be made manifest, because they are done in God.

22 After these things JESUS and his disciples came into the land of Judea; and there he abode with them *a* and baptized.

23 And John also was baptizing in Ennon near Salim; because there was much water there, and they came, and were baptized.

24 For John was not yet cast into prison.

25 And there arose a question between some of John's disciples and the Jews concerning purification:

26 And they came to John, and said to him: Rabbi, he that was with thee beyond the Jordan, *b* to whom thou gavest testimony, behold he baptizeth, and all men come to him.

27 John answered and said: A man cannot receive anything, unless it be given him from heaven.

28 You yourselves do bear me witness, *c* that I said, I am not CHRIST, but that I am sent before him.

29 He that hath the bride, is the bridegroom: but the friend of the bridegroom, who standeth and heareth him, rejoiceth with joy because of the bridegroom's voice. This my joy therefore is fulfilled.

30 He must increase but I must decrease.

31 He that cometh from above, is above all. He that is of the earth, of the earth he is, and of the earth he speaketh. He that cometh from heaven, is above all.

32 And what he hath seen, and heard, that he testifieth: and no man receiveth his testimony.

33 He that hath received his testimony, hath set to his seal that *d* God is true.

34 For he whom God hath sent, speaketh the words of God: for God doth not give the spirit by measure.

35 The Father loveth the Son: and he hath given all things into his hand.

36 *e* He that believeth in the Son, hath life everlasting: but he that believeth not the Son, shall not see life, but the wrath of God abideth on him.

## CHAP. IV.

*Christ talks with the Samaritan woman. He heals the ruler's son.*

WHEN JESUS therefore understood that the Pharisees had heard that JESUS maketh more disciples, *f* and baptizeth *more* than John,

2 (Though JESUS *himself* did not baptize, but his disciples.)

3 He left Judea, and went again into Galilee.

4 And he was of necessity to pass through Samaria.

5 He cometh therefore to a city of Samaria which is called Sichar; near the land *v* which Jacob gave to his son Joseph.

6 Now Jacob's well was there. JESUS therefore being wearied with his journey, sat thus on

---

*a* Infra, c. 1.—*b* Supra, 1. 19.—*c* Supra, 1. 20.

Ver. 21. *He that doth truth, i.e.,* He that acteth according to truth, which here signifies the law of God. *Thy law is truth.* Ps. cxviii. 142.

*d* Rom. 3. 4.—*e* 1 John 5. 10.—*f* Supra, 3. 22—*g* Gen. 33. 19. and 48. 22. Jos. 24. 32.

the well. It was about the sixth hour.

7 There cometh a woman of Samaria to draw water. JESUS saith to her: Give me to drink.

8 For his disciples were gone into the city to buy meats.

9 Then that Samaritan woman saith to him: How dost thou, being a Jew, ask of me to drink, who am a Samaritan woman? For the Jews do not communicate with the Samaritans.

10 JESUS answered and said to her: If thou didst know the gift of God, and who he is that saith to thee, Give me to drink; thou perhaps wouldst have asked of him, and he would have given thee living water.

11 The woman saith to him: Sir, thou hast nothing wherein to draw, and the well is deep: from whence then hast thou living water?

12 Art thou greater than our father Jacob, who gave us the well, and drank thereof himself, and his children, and his cattle?

13 JESUS answered, and said to her: Whosoever drinketh of this water, shall thirst again: but he that shall drink of the water that I will give him, shall not thirst for ever.

14 But the water that I will give him, shall become in him a fountain of water springing up into life everlasting.

15 The woman saith to him: Sir, give me this water, that I may not thirst, nor come hither to draw.

16 JESUS saith to her: Go, call thy husband, and come hither.

17 The woman answered, and said: I have no husband. JESUS said to her: Thou hast said well, I have no husband:

18 For thou hast had five husbands: and he whom thou now hast, is not thy husband. This thou hast said truly.

19 The woman saith to him: Sir, I perceive that thou art a prophet.

20 Our fathers adored on this mountain, and you say, "that at Jerusalem is the place where men must adore.

21 JESUS saith to her: Woman, believe me, that the hour cometh, when you shall neither on this mountain, nor in Jerusalem adore the Father.

22 $^b$ You adore that which you know not: we adore that which we know; for salvation is of the Jews.

23 But the hour cometh, and now is, when the true adorers shall adore the Father in spirit and in truth. For the Father also seeketh such to adore him.

24 $^c$ God is a spirit, and they that adore him, must adore him in spirit and in truth.

25 The woman saith to him: I know that the MESSIAS cometh (who is called CHRIST), therefore when he is come, he will tell us all things.

26 JESUS saith to her: I am he who am speaking with thee.

27 And immediately his disciples came: and they wondered that he talked with the woman. Yet no man said: What seekest thou, or why talkest thou with her?

28 The woman therefore left her waterpot, and went her way

---

$^a$ Deut. 12. 5.—$^b$ 4 Kings 17. 41.—$^c$ 1 Cor. 3. 17.

CHAP. IV. Ver. 20. *This mountain.* *Garizim,* where the Samaritans had their schismatical temples.

THE PRIMACY CONFERRED ON ST. PETER.

into the city, and saith to the men there:

29 Come, and see a man who has told me all things whatsoever I have done. Is not he the CHRIST?

30 They went therefore out of the city, and came unto him.

31 In the meantime the disciples prayed him, saying: Rabbi, eat.

32 But he said to them: I have meat to eat which you know not.

33 The disciples therefore said one to another: Hath any man brought him to eat?

34 JESUS saith to them: My meat is to do the will of him that sent me, that I may perfect his work.

35 Do not you say, there are yet four months, and then the harvest cometh? Behold I say to you, lift up your eyes, and see the countries, *a* for they are white already to harvest.

36 And he that reapeth receiveth wages, and gathereth fruit unto life everlasting: that both he that soweth, and he that reapeth, may rejoice together.

37 For in this is the saying true: that it is one man that soweth, and it is another that reapeth.

38 I have sent you to reap that in which you did not labour: others have laboured, and you have entered into their labours.

39 Now of that city many of the Samaritans believed in him, for the word of the woman giving testimony: He told me all things whatsoever I have done.

40 So when the Samaritans were come to him, they desired him that he would tarry there. And he abode there two days.

41 And many more believed in him because of his own word.

42 And they said to the woman: We now believe, not for thy saying: for we ourselves have heard him, and know that this is indeed the Saviour of the world.

43 Now after two days he departed thence; and went into Galilee.

44 *b* For JESUS himself gave testimony that a prophet hath no honour in his own country.

45 *c* And when he was come into Galilee, the Galileans received him, having seen all the things he had done at Jerusalem on the festival day: for they also went to the festival day.

46 He came again therefore into Cana of Galilee, *d* where he made the water wine. And there was a certain ruler whose son was sick at Capharnaum.

47 He having heard that JESUS was come from Judea into Galilee, went to him, and prayed him to come down and heal his son: for he was at the point of death.

48 JESUS therefore said to him: Unless you see signs and wonders, you believe not.

49 The ruler saith to him: Lord, come down before that my son die.

50 JESUS saith to him: Go thy way, thy son liveth. The man believed the word which JESUS said to him, and went his way.

---

*a* Matt. 9. 37. Luke 10. 1.
*b* Matt. 13. 57. Mark 6. 4. Luke 4. 24.—*c* Matt. 4. 12. Mark 1. 14. Luke 4. 14.—*d* Supra, 2. 9.

51 And as he was going down, his servants met him: and they brought word, saying, that his son lived.

52 He asked therefore of them the hour, wherein he grew better. And they said to him: Yesterday at the seventh hour the fever left him.

53 The father therefore knew that it was at the same hour, that JESUS said to him, Thy son liveth; and himself believed and his whole house.

54 This is again the second miracle that JESUS did, when he was come out of Judea into Galilee.

## CHAP. V.

*Christ heals on the sabbath the man languishing thirty-eight years; his discourse upon this occasion.*

AFTER *a* these things was a festival day of the Jews, and JESUS went up to Jerusalem.

2 Now there is at Jerusalem a pond, *called* Probatica, which in Hebrew is named Bethsaida, having five porches.

3 In these lay a great multitude of sick, of blind, of lame, of withered, waiting for the moving of the water.

4 And an Angel of the Lord descended at certain times into

---

*a* A.D. 31.

CHAP. V. Ver. 2. *Probatica.* That is, the sheep-pond; either so called, because the sheep were washed therein, that were to be offered up in sacrifice in the temple, or because it was near the sheep-gate. That this was a pond where miracles were wrought is evident from the sacred text: and also that the water had no natural virtue to heal, as one only of those put in after the motion of the water was restored to health; for if the water had the healing quality, the others would have the like benefit, being put into it about the same time.

158

the pond; and the water was moved. And he that went down first into the pond after the motion of the water, was made whole of whatsoever infirmity he lay under.

5 And there was a certain man there, that had been eight and thirty years under his infirmity.

6 Him when JESUS had seen lying, and knew that he had been now a long time, he saith to him: Wilt thou be made whole?

7 The infirm man answered him: Sir, I have no man, when the water is troubled, to put me into the pond. For whilst I am coming, another goeth down before me.

8 JESUS saith to him: Arise, take up thy bed, and walk.

9 And immediately the man was made whole: and he took up his bed and walked. And it was the sabbath that day.

10 The Jews therefore said to him that was healed: *b* It is the sabbath, it is not lawful for thee to take up thy bed.

11 He answered them: He that made me whole, he said to me: Take up thy bed, and walk.

12 They asked him, therefore: Who is that man who said to thee: Take up thy bed, and walk?

13 But he who was healed, knew not who it was. For JESUS went aside from the multitude standing in the place.

14 Afterwards JESUS findeth him in the temple, and saith to him: Behold thou art made whole: sin no more, lest some worse thing happen to thee.

15 And the man went his way,

---

*b* Exod. 20. 11. Jer. 17. 21.

and told the Jews that it was Jesus who had made him whole.

16 Therefore did the Jews persecute Jesus, because he did these things on the sabbath.

17 But Jesus answered them: My Father worketh until now; and I work.

18 Hereupon therefore the Jews sought the more to kill him, because he did not only break the sabbath, but also said God was his Father, making himself equal to God.

19 Then Jesus answered and said to them: Amen, amen, I say unto you: the Son cannot do anything of himself, but what he seeth the Father doing: for what things soever he doth, these the Son also doth in like manner.

20 For the Father loveth the Son, and sheweth him all things which himself doth: and greater works than these will he shew him, that you may wonder.

21 For as the Father raiseth up the dead, and giveth life: so the Son also giveth life to whom he will.

22 For neither doth the Father judge any man: but hath given all judgment to the Son.

23 That all men may honour the Son, as they honour the Father. He who honoureth not the Son, honoureth not the Father who hath sent him.

24 Amen, amen, I say unto you, that he who heareth my word, and believeth him that sent me, hath life everlasting; and cometh not into judgment, but is passed from death to life.

25 Amen, amen, I say unto you, that the hour cometh, and now is, when the dead shall hear the voice of the Son of God, and they that hear shall live.

26 For as the Father hath life in himself; so he hath given to the Son also to have life in himself:

27 And he hath given him power to do judgment, because he is the son of man.

28 Wonder not at this, for the hour cometh wherein all that are in the graves shall hear the voice of the Son of God.

29 *a* And they that have done good things, shall come forth unto the resurrection of life; but they that have done evil, unto the resurrection of judgment.

30 I cannot of myself do anything. As I hear, so I judge: and my judgment is just: because I seek not my own will, but the will of him that sent me.

31 If I bear witness of myself, my witness is not true.

32 *b* There is another that beareth witness of me: and I know that the witness which he witnesseth of me is true.

33 You sent to John: and he gave testimony to the truth.

34 But I receive not testimony from man: but I say these things that you may be saved.

35 He was a burning and a shining light. And you were willing for a time to rejoice in his light.

36 But I have a greater testimony than that of John. For the works which the Father hath given me to perfect: the works themselves, which I do, give testimony of me, that the Father hath sent me.

---

*a* Matt. 25. 46.—*b* Matt. 3. 17. Supra, 1. 15.

---

Ver. 29. *Unto the resurrection of judgment.* That is, condemnation.

37 And the Father himself who hath sent me, <sup>a</sup> hath given testimony of me: neither have you heard his voice at any time, <sup>b</sup> nor seen his shape.

38 And you have not his word abiding in you: for whom he hath sent, him you believe not.

39 Search the scriptures, for you think in them to have life everlasting; and the same are they that give testimony of me:

40 And you will not come to me that you may have life.

41 I receive not glory from men.

42 But I know you, that you have not the love of God in you.

43 I am come in the name of my Father, and you receive me not: if another shall come in his own name, him you will receive.

44 How can you believe, who receive glory one from another: <sup>c</sup> and the glory which is from God alone, you do not seek?

45 Think not that I will accuse you to the Father. There is one that accuseth you, Moses, in whom you trust.

46 For if you did believe Moses, you would perhaps believe me also. <sup>d</sup> For he wrote of me.

47 But if you do not believe his writings: how will you believe my words?

---

<sup>a</sup> Mark 3. 17. and 17. 5.—<sup>b</sup> Deut. 4. 12.—<sup>c</sup> 1 Cor. 4. 3.—<sup>d</sup> Gen. 3. 15. and 22. 18. and 49. 10. Deut. 18. 15.

---

Ver. 39. Or, *You search the scriptures. Scrutamini, ερευνᾶτε.* It is not a command for all to read the scriptures; but a reproach to the Pharisees, that reading the scriptures as they did, and thinking to find everlasting life in them, they would not receive him, to whom all those scriptures gave testimony, and through whom alone they could have that true life.

## CHAP. VI.

*Christ feeds five thousand with five loaves: he walks upon the sea, and discourses of the bread of life.*

AFTER <sup>e</sup> these things, JESUS went over the sea of Galilee, which is that of Tiberias:

2 And a great multitude followed him, because they saw the miracles which he did on them that were diseased.

3 JESUS therefore went up into a mountain, and there he sat with his disciples.

4 Now the Pasch, the festival day <sup>f</sup> of the Jews, was near at hand.

5 When JESUS therefore had lifted up his eyes, and seen that a very great multitude cometh to him, he said to Philip: Whence shall we buy bread that these may eat?

6 And this he said to try him: for he himself knew what he would do.

7 Philip answered him: Two hundred pennyworth of bread is not sufficient for them, that every one may take a little.

8 One of his disciples, Andrew, the brother of Simon Peter, saith to him:

9 There is a boy here that hath five barley loaves and two fishes: but what are these among so many?

10 Then JESUS said: Make the men sit down. Now there was much grass in the place. The men therefore sat down in number about five thousand.

11 And JESUS took the loaves: and when he had given thanks, he distributed to them that were set down. In like manner

---

<sup>e</sup> Matt. 14. 13. Mark 6. 32. Luke 9. 10.—<sup>f</sup> A.D. 32.

THE TRANSFIGURATION OF OUR LORD.

also of the fishes as much as they would.

12 And when they were filled, he said to his disciples: Gather up the fragments that remain, lest they be lost.

13 They gathered up therefore, and filled twelve baskets with the fragments of the five barley loaves, which remained over and above to them that had eaten.

14 Now those men, when they had seen what a miracle JESUS had done, said: This is of a truth the prophet that is to come into the world.

15 JESUS therefore when he knew that they would come to take him by force and make him king, *a* fled again into the mountain himself alone.

16 And when evening was come, his disciples went down to the sea.

17 And when they had gone up into a ship, they went over the sea to Capharnaum: and it was now dark, and JESUS was not come unto them.

18 And the sea arose by reason of a great wind that blew.

19 When they had rowed therefore about five and twenty or thirty furlongs, they see JESUS walking upon the sea, and drawing nigh to the ship, and they were afraid.

20 But he saith to them: It is I: be not afraid.

21 They were willing therefore to take him into the ship: and presently the ship was at the land, to which they were going.

22 The next day, the multitude that stood on the other side of the sea, saw that there was no other ship there but one, and that JESUS had not entered into the ship with his disciples, but that his disciples were gone away alone.

23 But other ships came in from Tiberias, nigh unto the place where they had eaten the bread, the Lord giving thanks.

24 When therefore the multitude saw that JESUS was not there, nor his disciples, they took shipping, and came to Capharnaum seeking for JESUS.

25 And when they had found him on the other side of the sea, they said to him: Rabbi, when camest thou hither?

26 JESUS answered them and said: Amen, amen, I say to you, you seek me, not because you have seen miracles, but because you did eat of the loaves, and were filled.

27 Labour not for the meat which perisheth, but for that which endureth unto life everlasting, which the son of man will give you. *b* For him hath God, the Father, sealed.

28 They said therefore unto him: What shall we do that we may work the works of God?

29 JESUS answered, and said to them: *c* This is the work of God, that you believe in him whom he hath sent.

30 They said therefore to him: What sign therefore dost thou shew that we may see, and may believe thee? what dost thou work?

31 Our fathers did eat manna in the desert as it is written.

---

*a* Matt. 14. 23. Mark 6. 46.
*b* Matt. 8. 17. and 17. 5. Supra, 1. 32.—
*c* 1 John 3. 23.

"*He gave them bread from heaven to eat.*

32 Then JESUS said to them: Amen, amen, I say to you: Moses gave you not bread from heaven, but my Father giveth you the true bread from heaven.

33 For the bread of God is that which cometh down from heaven, and giveth life to the world.

34 They said therefore unto him: Lord, give us always this bread.

35 And JESUS said to them: I am the bread of life: *b* he that cometh to me shall not hunger; and he that believeth in me, shall never thirst.

36 But I said unto you, that you also have seen me, and you believe not.

37 All that the Father giveth me shall come to me; and him that cometh to me, I will not cast out.

38 Because I came down from heaven, not to do my own will, but the will of him that sent me.

39 Now this is the will of the Father who sent me; that of all that he hath given me, I should lose nothing, but should raise it up again in the last day.

40 And this is the will of my Father that sent me; that every one who seeth the Son, and believeth in him, may have life everlasting, and I will raise him up in the last day.

41 The Jews therefore murmured at him, because he had said, I am the living bread which came down from heaven.

42 And they said: 'Is not this JESUS the son of Joseph, whose father and mother we know? How then saith he, I came down from heaven?

43 JESUS therefore answered and said to them: Murmur not among yourselves.

44 No man can come to me, except the Father, who hath sent me, draw him, and I will raise him up in the last day.

45 It is written in the prophets: *d And they shall all be taught of God.* Every one that hath heard of the Father and hath learned, cometh to me.

46 *e* Not that any man hath seen the Father, but he who is of God, he hath seen the Father.

47 Amen, amen, I say unto you: He that believeth in me, hath everlasting life.

48 I am the bread of life.

49 *f* Your fathers did eat manna in the desert, and are dead.

50 This is the bread which cometh down from heaven: that if any man eat of it, he may not die.

51 I am the living bread, which came down from heaven.

52 If any man eat of this bread, he shall live for ever: and the bread that I will give, is my flesh for the life of the world.

53 The Jews therefore strove among themselves, saying: How can this man give us his flesh to eat?

---

*c* Matt. 13. 55. Mark 6. 3.—*d* Isaias 54. 13.—*e* Matt. 11. 27.—*f* Exod. 16. 13.

CHAP. VI. Ver. 44. *Draw him.* Not by compulsion, nor by laying the free will under any necessity, but by the strong and sweet motions of his heavenly grace.

---

*a* Exod. 16. 14. Num. 11. 7. Ps. 77. 14. Wis. 16. 20.—*b* Eccli. 24. 29.

54 Then Jesus said to them: Amen, amen, I say unto you: Except you eat the flesh of the son of man, and drink his blood, you shall not have life in you.

55 He that eateth my flesh, and drinketh my blood, hath everlasting life: and I will raise him up in the last day.

56 *For my flesh is meat indeed: and my blood is drink indeed:

57 He that eateth my flesh, and drinketh my blood, abideth in me, and I in him.

58 As the living Father hath sent me, and I live by the Father: so he that eateth me, the same also shall live by me.

59 This is the bread that came down from heaven. Not as your fathers did eat manna, and are dead. He that eateth this bread shall live for ever.

60 These things he said teaching in the synagogue, in Capharnaum.

61 Many therefore of his disciples hearing it, said: This saying is hard, and who can hear it?

62 But Jesus knowing in himself, that his disciples murmured at this, said to them: Doth this scandalize you?

63 If then you shall see *b* the son of man ascend up where he was before?

64 It is the spirit that quickeneth: the flesh profiteth nothing. The words that I have spoken to you, are spirit and life.

65 But there are some of you that believe not. For Jesus knew from the beginning who they were that did not believe, and who he was that would betray him.

66 And he said: Therefore did I say to you, that no man can come to me, unless it be given him by my Father.

---

*a* 1 Cor. 11. 27.

*b* Supra, 3. 13.

---

Ver. 54. *Except you eat—and drink, &c.* To receive the body and blood of Christ, is a divine precept, insinuated in this text; which the faithful fulfil, though they receive but in one kind; because in one kind they receive both body and blood, which cannot be separated from each other. Hence, life eternal is here promised to the worthy receiving, though but in one kind. Ver. 52. *If any man eat of this bread he shall live for ever: and the bread that I will give, is my flesh for the life of the world.* Ver. 58. *He that eateth me, the same also shall live by me.* Ver. 59. *He that eateth this bread shall live for ever.*

Ver. 63. *If then you shall see, &c.* Christ by mentioning his ascension, by this instance of his power and divinity, would confirm the truth of what he had before asserted; and at the same time correct their gross apprehension of eating his flesh, and drinking his blood, in a vulgar and carnal manner, by letting them know he should take his whole body living with him to heaven; and consequently not suffer it to be, as they supposed, divided, mangled and consumed upon earth.

Ver. 64. *The flesh profiteth nothing.* Dead flesh separated from the spirit, in the gross manner they supposed they were to eat his flesh, would profit nothing. Neither doth man's flesh, that is to say, man's natural and carnal apprehension (which refuses to be subject to the spirit, and words of Christ) profit anything. But it would be the height of blasphemy, to say the living flesh of Christ (which we receive in the blessed sacrament, with his spirit, that is, with his soul and divinity) profiteth nothing. For if Christ's flesh had profited us nothing, he would never have taken flesh for us, nor died in the flesh for us.—Ibid. *Are spirit and life.* By proposing to you a heavenly sacrament, in which you shall receive, in a wonderful manner, spirit, grace and life in its very fountain.

67 After this many of his disciples went back; and walked no more with him.

68 Then JESUS said to the twelve: Will you also go away?

69 And Simon Peter answered him: Lord, to whom shall we go? thou hast the words of eternal life.

70 <sup>a</sup> And we have believed and have known that thou art the Christ the Son of God.

71 JESUS answered them: Have not I chosen you twelve; and one of you is a devil?

72 Now he meant Judas Iscariot, the son of Simon: for this same was about to betray him, whereas he was one of the twelve.

## CHAP. VII.

*Christ goes up to the feast of the tabernacle; he teaches in the temple.*

AFTER these things JESUS walked in Galilee, for he would not walk in Judea, because the Jews sought to kill him.

2 Now the Jews' feast of <sup>b</sup>tabernacles was at hand.

3 And his brethren said to him: Pass from hence and go into Judea: that thy disciples also may see thy works which thou dost.

4 For there is no man that doth anything in secret, and he himself seeketh to be known openly. If thou do these things, manifest thyself to the world.

5 For neither did his brethren believe in him.

6 Then JESUS said to them: My time is not yet come; but your time is always ready.

7 The world cannot hate you; but me it hateth: because I give testimony of it, that the works thereof are evil.

8 Go you up to this festival day, but I go not up to this festival day: because my time is not accomplished.

9 When he had said these things, he himself staid in Galilee.

10 But after his brethren were gone up, then he also went up to the feast, not openly, but as it were in secret.

11 The Jews therefore sought him on the festival day, and said: Where is he?

12 And there was much murmuring among the multitude concerning him. For some said: He is a good man. And others said: No, but he seduceth the people.

13 Yet no man spoke openly of him, for fear of the Jews.

14 Now about the midst of the feast, JESUS went up into the temple, and taught.

15 And the Jews wondered, saying: How doth this man know letters, having never learned?

16 JESUS answered them and said: My doctrine is not mine, but his that sent me.

17 If any man will do the will of him: he shall know of the doctrine, whether it be of God, or whether I speak of myself.

18 He that speaketh of himself, seeketh his own glory: but he that seeketh the glory of him that sent him, he is true, and there is no injustice in him.

19 <sup>c</sup> Did not Moses give you the law, and *yet* none of you keepeth the law?

---

<sup>a</sup> Matt. 16. 16. Mark 8. 29. Luke 9. 20.—<sup>b</sup> Lev. 23. 34.

<sup>c</sup> Exod. 34. 3.

"HE THAT SHALL RECEIVE ONE SUCH LITTLE CHILD IN MY NAME RECEIVETH ME."

20 *Why seek you to kill me? The multitude answered and said: Thou hast a devil; who seeketh to kill thee?

21 Jesus answered and said to them: One work I have done; and you all wonder:

22 Therefore *b* Moses gave you circumcision (not because it is of Moses, *c* but of the fathers;) and on the sabbath-day you circumcise a man.

23 If a man receive circumcision on the sabbath-day, that the law of Moses may not be broken; are you angry at me because I have healed the whole man on the sabbath-day?

24 *d* Judge not according to the appearance, but judge just judgment.

25 Some therefore of Jerusalem said: Is not this he whom they seek to kill?

26 And behold he speaketh openly, and they say nothing to him. Have the rulers known for a truth that this is the Christ?

27 But we know this man whence he is: but when the Christ cometh, no man knoweth whence he is.

28 Jesus therefore cried out in the temple, teaching and saying: You both know me, and you know whence I am, and I am not come of myself; but he that sent me is true, whom you know not.

29 I know him, because I am from him, and he hath sent me.

30 They sought therefore to apprehend him: and no man laid hands on him, because his hour was not yet come.

31 But of the people many believed in him, and said: When the Christ cometh, shall he do more miracles than these which this man doth?

32 The Pharisees heard the people murmuring these things concerning him: and the rulers and Pharisees sent ministers to apprehend him.

33 Jesus therefore said to them: Yet a little while I am with you: and *then* I go to him that sent me.

34 *e* Ye shall seek me, and shall not find me: and where I am, *thither* you cannot come.

35 The Jews therefore said among themselves: Whither will he go, that we shall not find him? will he go unto the dispersed among the gentiles, and teach the gentiles?

36 What is this saying that he hath said: You shall seek me, and shall not find me; and where I am, you cannot come?

37 And on the last *f and* great day of the festivity, Jesus stood and cried, saying: If any man thirst, let him come to me, and drink.

38 *g* He that believeth in me, as the scripture saith, *Out of his belly shall flow rivers of living water.*

39 Now this he said of the spirit which they should receive who believed in him: for as yet the spirit was not given, because Jesus was not yet glorified.

40 Of that multitude therefore, when they had heard these words of his, some said: This is the prophet indeed.

41 Others said: This is the Christ. But some said: Doth the Christ come out of Galilee?

---

*a* Supra, 5. 18.—*b* Lev. 12. 3.—*c* Gen. 17. 10.—*d* Deut. 1. 15. *e* Infra, 13. 83.—*f* Lev. 23. 27.—*g* Deut. 18. 15. Joel 2. 28. Acts 2. 17.

42 ᵃDoth not the scripture say: That Christ cometh out of the seed of David, and from Bethlehem the town where David was?

43 So there arose a dissension among the people because of him.

44 And some of them would have apprehended him: but no man laid hands upon him.

45 The ministers therefore came to the chief priests and the Pharisees. And they said to them: Why have you not brought him?

46 The ministers answered: Never did man speak like this man.

47 The Pharisees therefore answered them: Are you also seduced?

48 Hath any one of the rulers believed in him, or of the Pharisees?

49 But this multitude that knoweth not the law, are accursed.

50 Nicodemus said to them, ᵇhe that came to him by night, who was one of them:

51 Doth our law judge any man, unless it first hear him, ᶜand know what he doth?

52 They answered and said to him: Art thou also a Galilean? Search the scriptures, and see that out of Galilee a prophet riseth not.

53 And every man returned to his own house.

## CHAP. VIII.

*The woman taken in adultery. Christ justifies his doctrine.*

AND JESUS went unto mount Olivet.

2 And early in the morning he came again into the temple, and all the people came to him, and sitting down he taught them.

3 And the scribes and Pharisees bring unto him a woman taken in adultery; and they set her in the midst,

4 And said to him: Master, this woman was even now taken in adultery.

5 ᵈ Now Moses in the law commanded us to stone such a one. But what sayest thou?

6 And this they said, tempting him, that they might accuse him. But JESUS bowing himself down, wrote with his finger on the ground.

7 When therefore they continued asking him, he lifted up himself and said to them: ᵉ He that is without sin among you, let him first cast a stone at her.

8 And again stooping down, he wrote on the ground.

9 But they hearing *this* went out one by one, beginning at the eldest. And JESUS alone remained, and the woman standing in the midst.

10 Then JESUS lifting up himself, said to her: Woman, where are they that accused thee? Hath no man condemned thee?

11 Who said: No man, Lord. And JESUS said: Neither will I condemn thee. Go, and now sin no more.

12 Again therefore JESUS spoke to them, saying: ᶠI am the light of the world: he that followeth me, walketh not in darkness, but shall have the light of life.

13 The Pharisees therefore said to him: Thou givest testi-

---
ᵃ Mich. 5. 2. Matt 2. 6.—ᵇ Supra, 3. 2.—ᶜ Deut. 17. 8. and 19. 15.

ᵈ Lev. 20. 10.—ᵉ Deut. 17. 7.—ᶠ 1 John 1. 3.

mony of thyself: thy testimony is not true.

14 JESUS answered, and said to them: Although I give testimony of myself, my testimony is true: for I know whence I came, and whither I go: but you know not whence I come, or whither I go.

15 You judge according to the flesh: I judge not any man.

16 And if I do judge, my judgment is true: because I am not alone, but I and the Father that sent me.

17 And in your law it is written, *a* that the testimony of two men is true.

18 I am one that give testimony of myself: and the Father that sent me, giveth testimony of me.

19 They said therefore to him: Where is thy Father? JESUS answered: Neither me do you know, nor my Father: if you did know me, perhaps you would know my Father also.

20 These words JESUS spoke in the treasury, teaching in the temple: and no man laid hands on him, because his hour was not yet come.

21 Again therefore JESUS said to them: I go, and you shall seek me, and you shall die in your sin. Whither I go, you cannot come.

22 The Jews therefore said: Will he kill himself, because he said: Whither I go, you cannot come?

23 And he said to them: You are from beneath, I am from above. You are of this world, I am not of this world.

24 Therefore I said to you, that you shall die in your sins. For if you believe not that I am he, you shall die in your sin.

25 They said therefore to him: Who art thou? JESUS said to them: The beginning, who also speak unto you.

26 Many things I have to speak and to judge of you. But he that sent me is *b* true: and the things I have heard of him, these same I speak in the world.

27 And they understood not that he called God his father.

28 JESUS therefore said to them: When you shall have lifted up the son of man, then shall you know that I am he, and that I do nothing of myself, but as the Father hath taught me, these things I speak:

29 And he that sent me is with me, and he hath not left me alone: for I do always the things that please him.

30 When he spoke these things, many believed in him.

31 Then JESUS said to those Jews who believed him: If you continue in my word, you shall be my disciples indeed.

32 And you shall know the truth, and the truth shall make you free.

33 They answered him: We are the seed of Abraham, and we have never been slaves to any man: how sayest thou: You shall be free?

34 JESUS answered them: Amen, amen, I say unto you, *c* that whosoever committeth sin, is the servant of sin.

35 Now the servant abideth not in the house for ever: but the son abideth for ever.

---

*a* Deut. 17. 6. and 19. 15. Matt. 18. 16. 2 Cor. 13. 1. Heb. 10. 28.    *b* Rom. 8. 4.—*c* Rom. 6. 15. and 18. 2 Pet. 2. 19.

36 If therefore the son shall make you free, you shall be free indeed.

37 I know that you are the children of Abraham: but you seek to kill me, because my word hath no place in you.

38 I speak that which I have seen with my Father: and you do the things that you have seen with your father.

39 They answered, and said to him: Abraham is our father. Jesus saith to them: If you be the children of Abraham, do the works of Abraham.

40 But now you seek to kill me, a man who have spoken the truth to you, which I have heard of God. This Abraham did not.

41 You do the works of your father. They said therefore to him: We are not born of fornication: we have one Father *even* God.

42 Jesus therefore said to them: If God were your father, you would indeed love me. For from God I proceeded, and came: for I came not of myself, but he sent me.

43 Why do you not know my speech? Because you cannot hear my word.

44 ᵃ You are of *your* father the devil, and the desires of your father you will do. He was a murderer from the beginning, and he stood not in the truth; because truth is not in him. When he speaketh a lie, he speaketh of his own: for he is a liar, and the father thereof.

45 But if I say the truth, you believe me not.

46 Which of you shall convince me of sin? If I say the truth to you, why do you not believe me?

47 ᵇ He that is of God, heareth the words of God. Therefore you hear them not, because you are not of God.

48 The Jews therefore answered, and said to him: Do not we say well that thou art a Samaritan, and hast a devil?

49 Jesus answered: I have not a devil: but I honour my Father, and you have dishonoured me.

50 But I seek not my own glory: there is one that seeketh and judgeth.

51 Amen, amen, I say to you: If any man keep my word, he shall not see death for ever.

52 The Jews therefore said: Now we know that thou hast a devil. Abraham is dead, and the prophets; and thou sayest: If any man keep my word, he shall not taste death for ever.

53 Art thou greater than our father Abraham, who is dead? and the prophets are dead. Whom dost thou make thyself?

54 Jesus answered: If I glorify myself, my glory is nothing. It is my Father that glorifieth me, of whom you say that he is your God.

55 And you have not known him, but I know him. And if I shall say that I know him not, I shall be like to you, a liar. But I do know him, and do keep his word.

56 Abraham your father rejoiced that he might see my day: he saw it, and was glad.

57 The Jews therefore said to him: Thou art not yet fifty years old, and hast thou seen Abraham?

---

ᵃ 1 John 3. 8.   ᵇ 1 John 4. 6.

THE GOOD SAMARITAN.

58 Jesus said to them: Amen, amen, I say to you, before Abraham was made, I am.

59 They took up stones therefore to cast at him. But Jesus hid himself, and went out of the temple.

## CHAP. IX.

*He gives sight to the man born blind.*

AND Jesus passing by, saw a man who was blind from his birth;

2 And his disciples asked him: Rabbi, who hath sinned, this man, or his parents, that he should be born blind?

3 Jesus answered: Neither hath this man sinned, nor his parents; but that the works of God should be made manifest in him.

4 I must work the works of him that sent me, whilst it is day: the night cometh when no man can work.

5 As long as I am in the world, I am the light of the world.

6 When he had said these things, he spat on the ground, and made clay of the spittle, and spread the clay upon his eyes.

7 And said to him: Go, wash in the pool of Siloe, which is interpreted, Sent. He went therefore, and washed, and he came seeing.

8 The neighbours therefore, and they who had seen him before that he was a beggar, said: Is not this he that sat, and begged? Some said: This is he.

9 But others *said:* No, but he is like him. But he said: I am he.

10 They said therefore to him: How were thy eyes opened?

11 He answered: That man that is called Jesus, made clay, and anointed my eyes, and said to me: Go to the pool of Siloe, and wash. And I went, I washed, and I see.

12 And they said to him: Where is he? He saith: I know not.

13 They bring him that had been blind to the Pharisees.

14 Now it was the sabbath when Jesus made the clay and opened his eyes.

15 Again therefore the Pharisees asked him, how he had received his sight. But he said to them: He put clay upon my eyes, and I washed, and I see.

16 Some therefore of the Pharisees said: This man is not of God, who keepeth not the sabbath. But others said: How can a man that is a sinner do such miracles? And there was a division among them.

17 They say therefore to the blind man again: What sayest thou of him that hath opened thy eyes? And he said: He is a prophet.

18 The Jews then did not believe concerning him, that he had been blind and had received his sight, until they called the parents of him that had received his sight.

19 And asked them, saying: Is this your son, who you say was born blind? How then doth he now see?

20 His parents answered them and said: We know that this is our son, and that he was born blind;

21 But how he now seeth, we know not: or who hath opened his eyes, we know not: ask himself; he is of age, let him speak for himself.

22 These things his parents said, because they feared the Jews: For the Jews had already agreed among themselves, that if any man should confess him to be CHRIST, he should be put out of the synagogue.

23 Therefore did his parents say: He is of age, ask him.

24 They therefore called the man again that had been blind, and said to him: Give glory to God. We know that this man is a sinner.

25 He said therefore to them: If he be a sinner, I know not: one thing I know, that whereas I was blind, now I see.

26 They said then to him: What did he to thee? How did he open thy eyes?

27 He answered them: I have told you already, and you have heard: why would you hear it again? will you also become his disciples?

28 They reviled him therefore, and said: Be thou his disciple; but we are the disciples of Moses.

29 We know that God spoke to Moses: but as to this man, we know not from whence he is.

30 The man answered, and said to them: Why, herein is a wonderful thing that you know not from whence he is, and he hath opened my eyes.

31 Now we know that God doth not hear sinners: but if a man be a server of God, and doth his will, him he heareth.

32 From the beginning of the world it hath not been heard, that any man hath opened the eyes of one born blind.

33 Unless this man were of God, he could not do anything.

34 They answered, and said to him: Thou wast wholly born in sins, and dost thou teach us? And they cast him out.

35 JESUS heard that they had cast him out: and when he had found him, he said to him: Dost thou believe in the Son of God?

36 He answered, and said: Who is he, Lord, that I may believe in him?

37 And JESUS said to him: Thou hast both seen him; and it is he that talketh with thee.

38 And he said: I believe, Lord. And falling down he adored him.

39 And JESUS said: For judgment I am come into this world; that they who see not, may see: and they who see, may become blind.

40 And some of the Pharisees, who were with him, heard; and they said unto him: Are we also blind?

41 JESUS said to them: If you were blind, you should not have sin: but now you say: We see. Your sin remaineth.

## CHAP. X.

*Christ is the door and the good shepherd. He and his Father are one.*

AMEN, amen, I say to you: he that entereth not by the door into the sheepfold, but climbeth up another way, the same is a thief and a robber.

---

CHAP. IX. Ver. 39. *I am come, &c.* Not that Christ came for that end, that any one should be made blind: but that the Jews, by the abuse of his coming, and by their not receiving him, brought upon themselves this judgment of blindness.

Ver. 41. *If you were blind, &c.* If you were invincibly ignorant, and had neither read the scriptures nor seen my miracles, you would not be guilty of the sin of infidelity: but now, as you boast of your knowledge of the scriptures, you are inexcusable.

2 But he that entereth in by the door, is the shepherd of the sheep.

3 To him the porter openeth; and the sheep hear his voice: and he calleth his own sheep by name, and leadeth them out.

4 And when he hath let out his own sheep, he goeth before them: and the sheep follow him, because they know his voice.

5 But a stranger they follow not, but fly from him, because they know not the voice of strangers.

6 This proverb JESUS spoke to them. But they understood not what he spoke to them.

7 JESUS therefore said to them again: Amen, amen, I say to you, I am the door of the sheep.

8 All *others*, as many as have come, are thieves and robbers: and the sheep heard them not.

9 I am the door. By me, if any man enter in, he shall be saved: and he shall go in, and go out, and shall find pastures.

10 The thief cometh not, but for to steal and to kill and to destroy. I am come that they may have life, and may have it more abundantly.

11 I am the good shepherd. *a* The good shepherd giveth his life for his sheep.

12 But the hireling, and he that is not the shepherd, whose own the sheep are not, seeth the wolf coming and leaveth the sheep, and flieth: and the wolf catcheth, and scattereth the sheep:

13 And the hireling flieth, because he is a hireling; and he hath no care for the sheep.

14 I am the good shepherd; and I know mine, and mine know me.

15 *b* As the Father knoweth me, and I know the Father: and I lay down my life for my sheep.

16 And other sheep I have, that are not of this fold; them also I must bring, and they shall hear my voice, and there shall be one fold and one shepherd.

17 Therefore doth the Father love me: *c* because I lay down my life that I may take it again.

18 No man taketh it away from me: but I lay it down of myself, and I have power to lay it down; and I have power to take it up again. This commandment have I received of my Father.

19 A dissension rose again among the Jews for these words.

20 And many of them said: He hath a devil, and is mad: why hear you him?

21 Others said: These are not the words of one that hath a devil: Can a devil open the eyes of the blind?

22 *d* And it was the feast of the dedication at Jerusalem; and it was winter.

23 And JESUS walked in the temple in Solomon's porch.

24 The Jews therefore came round about him, and said to him: How long dost thou hold our souls in suspense? If thou be the CHRIST tell us plainly.

25 JESUS answered them: I speak to you, and you believe not: the works that I do in the name of my Father, they give testimony of me.

26 But you do not believe:

---

*a* Isaias 40. 11. Ezech. 34. 23. and 37. 24.    *b* Matt. 11. 27. Luke 10. 22.—*c* Isaias 53. 7.—*d* 1 Mach. 4. 56. and 59.

because you are not of my sheep.

27 My sheep hear my voice: and I know them, and they follow me.

28 And I give them life everlasting; and they shall not perish for ever, and no man shall pluck them out of my hand.

29 That which my Father hath given me is greater than all: and no one can snatch *them* out of the hand of my Father.

30 I and the Father are one.

31 The Jews then took up stones to stone him.

32 Jesus answered them: Many good works I have shewed you from my Father; for which of those works do you stone me?

33 The Jews answered him: For a good work we stone thee not, but for blasphemy; and because that thou, being a man, makest thyself God?

34 Jesus answered them: Is it not written in your law: *a I said, you are gods?*

35 If he called them gods, to whom the word of God was spoken, and the scripture cannot be broken;

36 Do you say of him, whom the Father hath sanctified and sent into the world: Thou blasphemest, because I said, I am the Son of God?

37 If I do not the works of my Father, believe me not.

38 But if I do, though you will not believe me, believe the works: that you may know and believe that the Father is in me, and I in the Father.

---

*a* Ps. 81. 6.

CHAP. X. Ver. 30. *I and the Father are one.* That is, one divine nature, but two distinct persons.

39 They sought therefore to take him: and he escaped out of their hands.

40 And he went again beyond the Jordan into that place where John was baptizing first: and there he abode.

41 And many resorted to him, and they said: John indeed did no sign:

42 But all things whatsoever John said of this man were true. And many believed in him.

## CHAP. XI.

*Christ raises Lazarus to life. The rulers resolve to put him to death.*

NOW there was a certain man sick, named Lazarus, of Bethania, of the town of Mary and of Martha her sister.

2 (And Mary was she *b* that anointed the Lord with ointment and wiped his feet with her hair: whose brother Lazarus was sick.)

3 His sisters therefore sent to him, saying: Lord, behold, he whom thou lovest is sick.

4 And Jesus hearing it, said to them: This sickness is not unto death, but for the glory of God: that the Son of God may be glorified by it.

5 Now Jesus loved Martha, and her sister Mary, and Lazarus.

6 When he had heard therefore that he was sick, he still remained in the same place two days:

7 Then after that he said to his disciples: Let us go into Judea again.

8 The disciples say to him: Rabbi, the Jews but now sought to stone thee: and goest thou thither again?

---

*b* Matt. 26. 7. Luke 7. 37. Infra, 12. 3.

"MARY HATH CHOSEN THE BETTER PART."

9 JESUS answered: Are there not twelve hours of the day? If a man walk in the day, he stumbleth not, because he seeth the light of this world:

10 But if he walk in the night he stumbleth, because the light is not in him.

11 These things he said: and after that he said to them: Lazarus our friend sleepeth; but I go that I may awake him out of sleep.

12 His disciples therefore said: Lord, if he sleep, he shall do well.

13 But JESUS spoke of his death; and they thought that he spoke of the repose of sleep.

14 Then therefore JESUS said to them plainly: Lazarus is dead;

15 And I am glad for your sakes, that I was not there, that you may believe: but let us go to him.

16 Thomas therefore, who is called Didymus, said to his fellow-disciples: Let us also go, that we may die with him.

17 JESUS therefore came and found that he had been four days already in the grave.

18 (Now Bethania was near Jerusalem, about fifteen furlongs off.)

19 And many of the Jews were come to Martha and Mary, to comfort them concerning their brother.

20 Martha therefore, as soon as she heard that JESUS was come, went out to meet him; but Mary sat at home.

21 Martha therefore said to JESUS: Lord, if thou hadst been here, my brother had not died.

22 But now also I know that whatsoever thou wilt ask of God, God will give it thee.

23 JESUS saith to her: Thy brother shall rise again.

24 Martha saith to him: I know that he shall rise again *a* in the resurrection at the last day.

25 JESUS said to her: I am the resurrection and the life: *b* he that believeth in me although he be dead, shall live:

26 And every one that liveth, and believeth in me, shall not die for ever. Believest thou this?

27 She saith to him: Yea, Lord, I have believed that thou art CHRIST the Son of the living God, who art come into this world.

28 And when she had said these things, she went, and called her sister Mary secretly, saying: The master is come and calleth for thee.

29 She, as soon as she heard *this*, riseth quickly and cometh to him.

30 For JESUS was not yet come into the town; but he was still in that place where Martha had met him.

31 The Jews therefore who were with her in the house and comforted her, when they saw Mary that she rose up speedily and went out, followed her, saying: She goeth to the grave, to weep there.

32 When Mary therefore was come where JESUS was, seeing him, she fell down at his feet, and saith to him: Lord, if thou hadst been here, my brother had not died.

33 JESUS therefore, when he saw her weeping, and the Jews that were come with her, weep-

---

*a* Luke 14. 14. Supra, 5. 29. *b* Supra, c. 40.

ing, groaned in the spirit, and troubled himself,

34 And said: Where have you laid him? They say to him: Lord, come and see.

35 And JESUS wept.

36 The Jews therefore said: Behold how he loved him.

37 But some of them said: ᵃ Could not he that opened the eyes of the man born blind, have caused that this man should not die?

38 JESUS therefore again groaning in himself, cometh to the sepulchre: Now it was a cave; and a stone was laid over it.

39 JESUS said: Take away the stone. Martha, the sister of him that was dead, saith to him: Lord, by this time he stinketh, for he is now of four days.

40 JESUS saith to her: Did not I say to thee, that if thou believe, thou shalt see the glory of God?

41 They took therefore the stone away. And JESUS lifting up his eyes said: Father, I give thee thanks that thou hast heard me.

42 And I knew that thou hearest me always, but because of the people who stand about have I said it; that they may believe that thou hast sent me.

43 When he had said these things, he cried with a loud voice: Lazarus, come forth.

44 And presently he that had been dead came forth, bound feet and hands with winding-bands, and his face was bound about with a napkin. JESUS said to them: Loose him and let him go.

45 Many therefore of the Jews who were come to Mary and Martha, and had seen the things that JESUS did, believed in him.

46 But some of them went to the Pharisees, and told them the things that JESUS had done.

47 The chief priests therefore and the Pharisees gathered a council, and said: What do we, for this man doth many miracles?

48 If we let him alone so, all will believe in him, and the Romans will come, and take away our place and nation.

49 ᵇ But one of them named Caiphas, being the high-priest that year, said to them: You know nothing:

50 Neither do you consider that it is expedient for you that one man should die for the people, and that the whole nation perish not.

51 And this he spoke not of himself: but being the high-priest of that year, he prophesied that JESUS should die for the nation.

52 And not only for the nation, but to gather together in one the children of God, that were dispersed.

53 From that day therefore they devised to put him to death.

54 Wherefore JESUS walked no more openly among the Jews, but he went into a country near the desert, unto a city that is called Ephrem, and there he abode with his disciples.

55 And the pasch of the Jews was at hand: and many from the country went up to Jerusalem before the pasch, to purify themselves.

56 They sought therefore for JESUS; and they discoursed one with another, standing in the

---

ᵃ Supra, 9. 6.  ᵇ Infra, 18. 14.

temple: What think you, that he is not come to the festival day? And the chief priests and the Pharisees had given a commandment, that if any man knew where he was, he should tell, that they might apprehend him.

## CHAP. XII.

*The anointing of Christ's feet. His riding into Jerusalem upon an ass. A voice from heaven.*

JESUS *a* therefore six days before the pasch came to Bethania, where Lazarus had been dead, whom JESUS raised to life.

2 And they made him a supper there: and Martha served, but Lazarus was one of them that were at table with him.

3 Mary therefore took a pound of ointment of right spikenard, of great price, and anointed the feet of JESUS, and wiped his feet with her hair: and the house was filled with the odour of the ointment.

4 Then one of his disciples, Judas Iscariot, he that was about to betray him, said:

5 Why was not this ointment sold for three hundred pence, and given to the poor?

6 Now he said this, not because he cared for the poor; but because he was a thief, and having the purse, carried the things that were put therein.

7 JESUS therefore said: Let her alone, that she may keep it against the day of my burial.

8 For the poor you have always with you; but me you have not always.

---

*a* Matt. 26. 6. Mark 14. 3.

9 A great multitude therefore of the Jews knew that he was there: and they came, not for JESUS'S sake only, but that they might see Lazarus, whom he had raised from the dead.

10 But the chief priests thought to kill Lazarus also:

11 Because many of the Jews by reason of him went away, and believed in JESUS.

12 And on the next day a great multitude, that was come to the festival day, when they had heard that JESUS was coming to Jerusalem,

13 Took branches of palm-trees, and went forth to meet him, and cried: Hosanna, blessed is he that cometh in the name of the Lord, the king of Israel.

14 *b* And JESUS found a young ass, and sat upon it, as it is written:

15 *Fear not, daughter of Sion: behold, thy king cometh, sitting on an ass's colt.*

16 These things his disciples did not know at the first: but when JESUS was glorified, then they remembered that these things were written of him, and that they had done these things to him.

17 The multitude therefore gave testimony, which was with him when he called Lazarus out of the grave, and raised him from the dead.

18 For which reason also the people came to meet him: because they heard that he had done this miracle.

19 The Pharisees therefore said among themselves: Do you see that we prevail nothing?

---

CHAP. XII. Ver. 8. See the annotations on St. Matt. xxvi. 11.

*b* Zach. 9. 9. Mark 11. 7. Luke 19. 35.

behold, the whole world is gone after him.

20 Now there were certain gentiles among them who came up to adore on the festival day.

21 These therefore came to Philip, who was of Bethsaida of Galilee, and desired him, saying: Sir, we would see JESUS.

22 Philip cometh and telleth Andrew. Again Andrew and Philip told JESUS.

23 But JESUS answered them saying: The hour is come, that the son of man should be glorified.

24 Amen, amen, I say to you, unless the grain of wheat falling into the ground die;

25 Itself remaineth alone. But if it die, it bringeth forth much fruit. ᵃ He that loveth his life shall lose it: and he that hateth his life in this world, keepeth it unto life eternal.

26 If any man minister to me, let him follow me: and where I am, there also shall my minister be. If any man minister to me, him will my Father honour.

27 Now is my soul troubled. And what shall I say? Father, save me from this hour. But for this cause I came unto this hour.

28 Father, glorify thy name. A voice therefore came from heaven: I have both glorified it, and will glorify it again.

29 The multitude therefore that stood and heard, said that it thundered. Others said, An Angel spoke to him.

30 JESUS answered and said: This voice came not because of me, but for your sakes.

31 Now is the judgment of the world: now shall the prince of this world be cast out.

32 And I, if I be lifted up from the earth, will draw all things to myself.

33 (Now this he said, signifying what death he should die.)

34 The multitude answered him: We have heard ᵇ out of the law, that CHRIST abideth for ever; and how sayest thou: The son of man must be lifted up? Who is this son of man?

35 JESUS therefore said to them: Yet a little while, the light is among you. Walk whilst you have the light, that the darkness overtake you not. And he that walketh in darkness knoweth not whither he goeth.

36 Whilst you have the light, believe in the light, that you may be the children of light. These things JESUS spoke, and he went away, and hid himself from them.

37 And whereas he had done so many miracles before them, they believed not in him:

38 That the saying of Isaias the prophet might be fulfilled, which he said: ᶜ *Lord, who hath believed our hearing? and to whom hath the arm of the Lord been revealed?*

39 Therefore they could not believe, because Isaias said again:

40 ᵈ *He hath blinded their*

---

ᵃ Matt. 10. 39. and 16. 25. Mark 8. 35. Luke 9. 24. and 17. 33.

ᵇ Ps. 109. 4. and 116. 2. Isaias 40. 8. Ezech. 37. 25.—ᶜ Isaias 53. 1. Rom. 10. 16.—ᵈ Isaias 6. 9. Matt. 13. 14. Mark 4. 12. Luke 8. 10. Acts 28. 26. Rom. 11. 8.

Ver. 39. *They could not believe.* Because they would not, saith St. *August. Tr. 53 in Joan.* See the annotation, St. *Mark* iv. 12.

THE GOOD SHEPHERD.

eyes, and hardened their heart, that they should not see with their eyes, nor understand with their heart, and be converted, and I should heal them:

41 These things said Isaias, when he saw his glory and spoke of him.

42 However many of the chief men also believed in him: but because of the Pharisees they did not confess him, that they might not be cast out of the synagogue.

43 For they loved the glory of men, more than the glory of God.

44 But JESUS cried, and said: He that believeth in me, doth not believe in me, but in him that sent me.

45 And he that seeth me, seeth him that sent me.

46 I am come a light into the world ; that whosoever believeth in me, may not remain in darkness.

47 And if any man hear my words, and keep them not: I do not judge him : for I came not to judge the world, but to save the world.

48 He that despiseth me, and receiveth not my words, hath one that judgeth him : *the word that I have spoken, the same shall judge him in the last day.

49 For I have not spoken of myself, but the Father who sent me, he gave me commandment what I should say, and what I should speak.

50 And I know that his commandment is life everlasting. The things therefore that I speak ; even as the Father said unto me, so do I speak.

---

*Matt. 16. 16.

## CHAP. XIII.

*Christ washes his disciples' feet: the treason of Judas: the new commandment of love.*

BEFORE *b* the festival day of the pasch, JESUS knowing that his hour was come, that he should pass out of this world to the Father : having loved his own who were in the world, he loved them unto the end.

2 And when supper was done, (the devil having now put into the heart of Judas Iscariot the son of Simon, to betray him,)

3 Knowing that the Father had given him all things into his hands, and that he came from God, and goeth to God.

4 He riseth from supper, and layeth aside his garments, and having taken a towel, girded himself.

5 After that, he putteth water into a basin, and began to wash the feet of his disciples, and to wipe them with the towel, wherewith he was girded.

6 He cometh therefore to Simon Peter. And Peter said to him : Lord, dost thou wash my feet ?

7 JESUS answered, and said to him : What I do, thou knowest not now, but thou shalt know hereafter.

8 Peter said to him : Thou shalt never wash my feet. JESUS

---

*b* A.D. 33. Matt. 26. 2. Mark 14. 1. Luke 22. 1.

CHAP. XIII. Ver. 1. *Before the festival day of the pasch.* This was the fourth and last pasch of the ministry of Christ, and according to the common computation was in the 33d year of our Lord : and in the year of the world 4036. Some chronologers are of opinion that our Saviour suffered in the 37th year of his age: but these different opinions on the subject are of no consequence.

177

answered him: If I wash thee not, thou shalt have no part with me.

9 Simon Peter saith to him: Lord, not only my feet, but also my hands and my head.

10 Jesus saith to him: He that is washed, needeth not but to wash his feet, but is clean wholly. And you are clean, but not all.

11 For he knew who he was that would betray him; therefore he said: You are not all clean.

12 Then after he had washed their feet, and taken his garments, being sat down again, he said to them: Know you what I have done to you?

13 You call me Master, and Lord: and you say well, for so I am.

14 If then I, being *your* Lord and Master, have washed your feet; you also ought to wash one another's feet.

15 For I have given you an example, that as I have done to you, so you do also.

16 *a* Amen, amen, I say to you: The servant is not greater than his lord: neither is the apostle greater than he that sent him.

17 If you know these things, you shall be blessed if you do them.

18 I speak not of you all: I know whom I have chosen: but that the scripture may be fulfilled, *b He that eateth bread with me, shall lift up his heel against me.*

19 At present I tell you, before it come to pass: that when it shall come to pass, you may believe that I am he.

*a* Matt. 10. 24. Luke 6. 40. Infra, 15. 20.—*b* Ps. 40. 10.

178

20 *c* Amen, amen, I say to you, he that receiveth whomsoever I send, receiveth me: and he that receiveth me, receiveth him that sent me.

21 When Jesus had said these things, he was troubled in spirit: and he testified, and said: *d* Amen, amen, I say to you, one of you shall betray me.

22 The disciples therefore looked one upon another, doubting of whom he spoke.

23 Now there was leaning on Jesus's bosom one of his disciples whom Jesus loved.

24 Simon Peter therefore beckoned to him, and said to him: Who is it of whom he speaketh?

25 He therefore leaning on the breast of Jesus saith to him: Lord, who is it?

26 Jesus answered: He it is to whom I shall reach bread dipped. And when he had dipped the bread, he gave it to Judas Iscariot, *the son* of Simon.

27 And after the morsel, satan entered into him. And Jesus said to him: That which thou dost, do quickly.

28 Now no man at the table knew to what purpose he said this unto him.

29 For some thought, because Judas had the purse, that Jesus had said to him: Buy those things which we have need of for the festival day: or that he

*c* Matt. 10. 40. Luke 10. 16.—*d* Matt. 26. 21. Mark 14. 18. Luke 22. 21.

Ver. 27. *That which thou dost, do quickly.* It is not a license, much less a command, to go about his treason; but a signification to him that Christ would not hinder, or resist what he was about, do it as soon as he pleased: but was both ready, and desirous to suffer for our redemption.

should give something to the poor.

30 He therefore having received the morsel, went out immediately. And it was night.

31 When he therefore was gone out JESUS said: Now is the son of man glorified, and God is glorified in him.

32 If God be glorified in him, God also will glorify him in himself: and immediately will he glorify him.

33 Little children, yet a little while I am with you. ᵃ You shall seek me, and as I said to the Jews: Whither I go, you cannot come: so I say to you now.

34 ᵇ A new commandment I give unto you: That you love one another, as I have loved you, that you also love one another.

35 By this shall all men know that you are my disciples, if you have love one for another.

36 Simon Peter saith to him: Lord, whither goest thou? JESUS answered: Whither I go, thou canst not follow me now, but thou shalt follow hereafter.

37 Peter saith to him: Why cannot I follow thee now? ᶜ I will lay down my life for thee.

38 JESUS answered him: Wilt thou lay down thy life for me? Amen, amen, I say to thee, the cock shall not crow, till thou deny me thrice.

## CHAP. XIV.

*Christ's discourse after his last supper.*

LET not your heart be troubled. You believe in God, believe also in me.

ᵃ Supra, 7. 34.—ᵇ Lev. 19. 18. Matt. 22. 39. Infra. 15. 12.—ᶜ Matt. 26. 35. Mark 14. 29. Luke 22. 33.

2 In my Father's house there are many mansions. If not, I would have told you, that I go to prepare a place for you.

3 And if I shall go, and prepare a place for you: I will come again, and will take you to myself, that where I am, you also may be.

4 And whither I go you know, and the way you know.

5 Thomas saith to him: Lord, we know not whither thou goest, and how can we know the way?

6 JESUS saith to him: I am the way, and the truth, and the life. No man cometh to the Father but by me.

7 If you had known me, you would without doubt have known my Father also; and from henceforth you shall know him, and you have seen him.

8 Philip saith to him: Lord, shew us the Father, and it is enough for us.

9 JESUS saith to him: So long a time have I been with you: and have you not known me? Philip, he that seeth me, seeth the Father also. How sayest thou, shew us the Father?

10 Do you not believe, that I am in the Father, and the Father in me? The words that I speak to you, I speak not of myself. But the Father who abideth in me, he doth the works.

11 Believe you not that I am in the Father, and the Father in me?

12 Otherwise believe for the very works' sake. Amen, amen, I say to you, he that believeth in me, the works that I do, he also shall do, and greater than these shall he do.

13 Because I go to the Father:

179

*a* and whatsoever you shall ask the Father in my name, that will I do: that the Father may be glorified in the Son.

14 If you shall ask me anything in my name, that I will do.

15 If you love me keep my commandments.

16 And I will ask the Father, and he shall give you another Paraclete, that he may abide with you for ever.

17 The Spirit of truth, whom the world cannot receive, because it seeth him not, nor knoweth him: but you shall know him; because he shall abide with you, and shall be in you.

18 I will not leave you orphans: I will come to you.

19 Yet a little while: and the world seeth me no more. But you see me: because I live, and you shall live.

20 In that day you shall know that I am in my Father, and you in me, and I in you.

21 He that hath my commandments, and keepeth them: he it is that loveth me. And he that loveth me, shall be loved of my Father: and I will love him, and will manifest myself to him.

22 Judas saith to him, not the Iscariot: Lord, how is it, that thou wilt manifest thyself to us, and not to the world?

23 JESUS answered, and said to him: If any one love me, he will keep my word, and my Father will love him, and we will come to him, and will make our abode with him:

24 He that loveth me not, keepeth not my words. And the word which you have heard is not mine; but the Father's who sent me.

25 These things have I spoken to you, abiding with you.

26 But the Paraclete, the Holy Ghost, whom the Father will send in my name, he will teach you all things, and bring all things to your mind, whatsoever I shall have said to you.

27 Peace I leave with you, my peace I give unto you: not as the world giveth, do I give unto you. Let not your heart be troubled, nor let it be afraid.

28 You have heard that I said to you: I go away and I come unto you. If you loved me, you would indeed be glad, because I go to the Father: for the Father is greater than I.

---

*a* Matt. 7. 7. and 21. 22. Mark 11. 24. Infra. 16. 23.

CHAP. XIV. Ver. 16. *Paraclete.* That is, a comforter; or also an advocate: inasmuch as by inspiring prayer, he prays, as it were, in us, and pleads for us.—Ibid. *For ever.* Hence it is evident that this Spirit of truth was not only promised to the persons of the apostles, but also to their successors through all generations.

Ver. 24. *Teach you all things.* Here the Holy Ghost is promised to the apostles and their successors, particularly, in order to teach them all truth, and to preserve them from error.

Ver. 28. *For the Father is greater than I.* It is evident that Christ our Lord speaks here of himself, as he is made man: for as God he is equal to the Father: (See Philippians ii.) Any difficulty of understanding the meaning of these words will vanish, when the relative circumstances of the text here are considered; for Christ being at this time shortly to suffer death, signified to his apostles his human nature by these very words: for as God he could not die. And therefore as he was both God and man, it must follow that according to his humanity he was to die, which the apostles were soon to see and believe, as he expresses, ver. 29. *And now I have told you before it come to pass: that when it shall come to pass, you may believe.*

THE PRODIGAL SON.

29 And now I have told you before it come to pass: that when it shall come to pass you may believe.

30 I will not now speak many things with you. For the prince of this world cometh, and in me he hath not anything.

31 But that the world may know that I love the Father: *a* and as the Father hath given me commandment, so do I: Arise, let us go hence.

## CHAP. XV.

*A continuation of Christ's discourse to his disciples.*

I AM the true vine; and my Father is the husbandman.

2 Every branch in me, that beareth not fruit, he will take away: and every one that beareth fruit he will purge it, that it may bring forth more fruit.

3 *b* Now you are clean by reason of the word which I have spoken to you.

4 Abide in me: and I in you. As the branch cannot bear fruit of itself, unless it abide in the vine, so neither can you, unless you abide in me.

5 I am the vine; you the branches: he that abideth in me, and I in him, the same beareth much fruit: for without me you can do nothing.

6 If any one abide not in me: he shall be cast forth as a branch, and shall wither, and they shall gather him up, and cast him into the fire, and he burneth.

7 If you abide in me, and my words abide in you, you shall ask whatever you will, and it shall be done unto you.

8 In this is my Father glorified; that you bring forth very much fruit, and become my disciples.

9 As the Father hath loved me, I also have loved you. Abide in my love.

10 If you keep my commandments, you shall abide in my love; as I also have kept my Father's commandments, and do abide in his love.

11 These things I have spoken to you, that my joy may be in you, and your joy may be filled.

12 *c* This is my commandment, that you love one another, as I have loved you.

13 Greater love than this no man hath, that a man lay down his life for his friends.

14 You are my friends, if you do the things that I command you.

15 I will not now call you servants: for the servant knoweth not what his lord doth. But I have called you friends: because all things whatsoever I have heard of my Father, I have made known to you.

16 You have not chosen me: but I have chosen you; and have appointed you, *d* that you should go, and should bring forth fruit, and your fruit should remain: that whatsoever you shall ask of the Father in my name, he may give it you.

17 *e* These things I command you, that you love one another.

18 If the world hate you, know you that it hath hated me before you.

19 If you had been of the

---

*a* Acts 2. 22.—*b* Supra, 13. 10.

*c* Supra, 13. 34. Ephes. 5. 2. 1 Thess. 4. 9.—*d* Matt. 28. 19.—*e* 1 John 3. 11. and 4. 7.

world; the world would love its own: but because you are not of the world, but I have chosen you out of the world, therefore the world hateth you.

20 Remember my word that I said to you: *a* The servant is not greater than his master. If they have persecuted me, *b* they will also persecute you: if they have kept my word, they will keep yours also.

21 But all these things they will do to you for my name's sake: because they know not him that sent me.

22 If I had not come, and spoken to them, they would not have sin: but now they have no excuse for their sin.

23 He that hateth me, hateth my Father also.

24 If I had not done among them the works that no other man hath done, they would not have sin: but now they have both seen and hated both me and my Father.

25 But that the word may be fulfilled which is written in their law: *c* They have hated me without cause.

26 *d* But when the Paraclete cometh, whom I will send you from the Father, the Spirit of truth, who proceedeth from the Father, he shall give testimony of me:

27 And you shall give testimony, because you are with me from the beginning.

## CHAP. XVI.

*The conclusion of Christ's last discourse to his disciples.*

THESE things have I spoken to you, that you may not be scandalized.

2 They will put you out of the synagogues: yea, the hour cometh, that whosoever killeth you, will think that he doth a service to God.

3 And these things will they do to you, because they have not known the Father, nor me.

4 But these things I have told you, that when the hour shall come, you may remember that I told you of them.

5 But I told you not these things from the beginning, because I was with you. And now I go to him that sent me, and none of you asketh me: Whither goest thou?

6 But because I have spoken these things to you sorrow hath filled your heart.

7 But I tell you the truth: it is expedient to you that I go: for if I go not, the Paraclete will not come to you: but if I go, I will send him to you.

8 And when he is come, he will convince the world of sin, and of justice, and of judgment.

9 Of sin: because they believed not in me.

10 And of justice: because I

---

*a* Supra, 13. 16. Matt. 10. 24.—*b* Matt. 24. 9.—*c* Ps. 24. 19.—*d* Luke 24. 49.

CHAP. XV. Ver. 26. *Whom I will send.* This proves, against the modern Greeks, that the Holy Ghost proceedeth from the Son, as well as from the Father: otherwise he could not be sent by the Son.

CHAP. XVI. Ver. 8. *He will convince the world of sin, &c.* The Holy Ghost, by his coming, brought over many thousands, 1st, to a sense of their sin in not believing in Christ. 2ndly, to a conviction of the justice of Christ, now sitting at the right hand of his Father. And, 3rdly, to a right apprehension of the judgment prepared for them that choose to follow satan, who is already judged and condemned.

go to the Father; and you shall see me no longer.

11 And of judgment: because the prince of this world is already judged.

12 I have yet many things to say to you: but you cannot bear them now.

13 But when he, the Spirit of truth, is come, he will teach you all truth. For he shall not speak of himself: but what things soever he shall hear, he shall speak: and the things that are to come he shall shew you.

14 He shall glorify me; because he shall receive of mine, and shall shew it to you.

15 All things whatsoever the Father hath, are mine. Therefore I said, he shall receive of mine, and shew it to you.

16 A little while, and now you shall not see me: and again a little while, and you shall see me: because I go to the Father.

17 Then some of his disciples said one to another: What is this that he saith to us: A little while, and you shall not see me: and again a little while, and you shall see me, and because I go to the Father?

18 They said therefore: What is this that he saith, A little while? we know not what he speaketh.

19 And Jesus knew that they had a mind to ask him: and he said to them: Of this do you inquire among yourselves, because I said: A little while, and you shall not see me: and again a little while, and you shall see me?

20 Amen, amen, I say to you, that you shall lament and weep, but the world shall rejoice: and you shall be made sorrowful, but your sorrow shall be turned into joy.

21 A woman, when she is in labour, hath sorrow, because her hour is come: but when she hath brought forth the child, she remembereth no more the anguish, for joy that a man is born into the world.

22 So also you now indeed have sorrow, but I will see you again, and your heart shall rejoice; and your joy no man shall take from you.

23 And in that day you shall not ask me anything. *a* Amen, amen, I say to you: if you ask the Father anything in my name, he will give it you.

24 Hitherto you have not asked anything in my name. Ask, and you shall receive: that your joy may be full.

25 These things I have spoken to you in proverbs. The hour cometh when I will no more speak to you in proverbs, but will shew you plainly of the Father.

26 In that day you shall ask in my name: and I say not to you, that I will ask the Father for you:

27 For the Father himself loveth you, because you have loved me, and have believed that I came out from God.

28 I came forth from the Father, and am come into the world: again I leave the world, and I go to the Father.

29 His disciples say to him: Behold now thou speakest plainly, and speakest no proverb.

---

Ver. 13. *Will teach you all truth.* See the annotation on chap. xiv. 26.

*a* Matt. 7. 7. and 21. 22. Mark 11. 24. Luke 11. 9. Supra, 14. 13. Jas. 1. 5.

30 Now we know that thou knowest all things, and thou needest not that any man should ask thee. By this we believe that thou comest forth from God.

31 Jesus answered them: Do you now believe?

32 ªBehold the hour cometh, and it is now come, that you shall be scattered every man to his own, and shall leave me alone: and yet I am not alone, because the Father is with me.

33 These things I have spoken to you, that in me you may have peace. In the world you shall have distress: but have confidence, I have overcome the world.

## CHAP. XVII.

*Christ's prayer for his disciples.*

THESE things Jesus spoke, and lifting up his eyes to heaven, he said: Father, the hour is come, glorify thy Son, that thy Son may glorify thee.

2 ᵇAs thou hast given him power over all flesh, that he may give eternal life to all whom thou hast given him.

3 Now this is eternal life: that they may know thee, the only true God, and Jesus Christ, whom thou hast sent.

4 I have glorified thee on the earth: I have finished the work which thou gavest me to do;

5 And now glorify thou me, O Father, with thyself, with the glory which I had, before the world was, with thee.

---
ª Matt. 26. 31. Mark 14. 27.—ᵇ Matt. 15. 18.

6 I have manifested thy name to the men whom thou hast given me out of the world. Thine they were, and to me thou gavest them: and they have kept thy word.

7 Now they have known that all things which thou hast given me are from thee:

8 Because the words which thou gavest me, I have given to them: and they have received them, and have known in very deed that I came out from thee, and they have believed that thou didst send me.

9 I pray for them: I pray not for the world, but for them whom thou hast given me: because they are thine:

10 And all my things are thine, and thine are mine: and I am glorified in them.

11 And now I am not in the world, and these are in the world, and I come to thee. Holy Father, keep them in thy name, whom thou hast given me: that they may be one, as we also are.

12 While I was with them, I kept them in thy name. ᶜThose whom thou gavest me have I kept: and none of them is lost, but the son of perdition, ᵈthat the scripture may be fulfilled.

13 And now I come to thee: and these things I speak in the world, that they may have my joy filled in themselves.

14 I have given them thy word, and the world hath hated them, because they are not of the world; as I also am not of the world.

15 I pray not that thou shouldst take them out of the

---
ᶜ Infra, 18. 9.—ᵈ Ps. 108. 8.

LAZARUS AND DIVES.

world, but that thou shouldst keep them from evil.

16 They are not of the world: as I also am not of the world.

17 Sanctify them in truth. Thy word is truth.

18 As thou hast sent me into the world, I also have sent them into the world.

19 And for them do I sanctify myself: that they also may be sanctified in truth.

20 And not for them only do I pray, but for them also who through their word shall believe in me:

21 That they all may be one, as thou, Father, in me, and I in thee: that they also may be one in us: that the world may believe that thou hast sent me.

22 And the glory which thou hast given me, I have given to them: that they may be one, as we also are one.

23 I in them, and thou in me: that they may be made perfect in one; and the world may know that thou hast sent me, and hast loved them, as thou hast also loved me.

24 Father, I will that where I am, they also whom thou hast given me may be with me: that they may see my glory which thou hast given me, because thou hast loved me before the creation of the world.

25 Just Father, the world hath not known thee: but I have known thee: and these have known, that thou hast sent me.

26 And I have made known thy name to them, and will make it known; that the love, wherewith thou hast loved me, may be in them, and I in them.

## CHAP. XVIII.

*The history of the passion of Christ.*

WHEN *a* JESUS had said these things, he went forth with his disciples over the brook Cedron, where there was a garden, into which he entered with his disciples.

2 And Judas also, who betrayed him, knew the place: because JESUS had often resorted thither together with his disciples.

3 *b* Judas therefore having received a band of soldiers, and servants from the chief priests and the Pharisees, cometh thither with lanterns and torches and weapons.

4 JESUS therefore knowing all things that should come upon him, went forth, and said to them: Whom seek ye?

5 They answered him: JESUS of Nazareth. JESUS saith to them: I am he. And Judas also, who betrayed him, stood with them.

6 As soon therefore as he had said to them: I am he: they went backward, and fell to the ground.

7 Again therefore he asked them: Whom seek ye? And they said: JESUS of Nazareth.

8 JESUS answered, I have told you, that I am he. If therefore you seek me, let these go their way.

9 That the word might be fulfilled, which he said: *c* Of them whom thou hast given me, I have not lost any one.

10 Then Simon Peter having a sword, drew it; and struck

---

*a* 2 Kings 15. 22. Matt. 26. 36. Mark 14. 32. Luke 22. 39.—*b* Matt. 26. 47. Mark 14. 43. Luke 22. 47.—*c* Supra. 17. 12

the servant of the high-priest, and cut off his right ear. And the name of the servant was Malchus.

11 JESUS therefore said to Peter: Put up thy sword into the scabbard. The chalice which my Father hath given me, shall I not drink it?

12 Then the band and the tribune, and the servants of the Jews, took JESUS, and bound him:

13 And they led him away to *a* Annas first, for he was father-in-law to Caiphas, who was the high-priest of that year.

14 Now Caiphas was he *b* who had given the counsel to the Jews, that it was expedient, that one man should die for the people.

15 And Simon Peter followed JESUS, and so did another disciple. And that disciple was known to the high-priest, and went in with JESUS into the court of the high-priest.

16 But Peter stood at the door without. *c* The other disciple therefore who was known to the high-priest, went out, and spoke to the portress, and brought in Peter.

17 The maid therefore that was portress, saith to Peter: Art not thou also one of this man's disciples? He saith: I am not.

18 Now the servants and ministers stood at a fire of coals, because it was cold, and warmed themselves. And with them was Peter also standing, warming himself.

19 The high-priest therefore asked JESUS of his disciples, and of his doctrine.

20 JESUS answered him: I have spoken openly to the world: I have always taught in the synagogue, and in the temple, whither all the Jews resort; and in secret I have spoken nothing.

21 Why askest thou me? ask them who have heard what I have spoken unto them: behold they know what things I have said.

22 And when he had said these things, one of the servants standing by gave JESUS a blow, saying: Answerest thou the high-priest so?

23 JESUS answered him: If I have spoken evil, give testimony of the evil: but if well, why strikest thou me?

24 *d* And Annas sent him bound to Caiphas the high-priest.

25 And Simon Peter was standing, and warming himself. *e* They said therefore to him: Art not thou also one of his disciples? He denied it, and said: I am not.

26 One of the servants of the high-priest (a kinsman to him whose ear Peter cut off) saith to him: Did I not see thee in the garden with him?

27 Again therefore Peter denied: and immediately the cock crew.

28 *f* Then they led JESUS from Caiphas to the governor's hall. And it was morning: and they went not into the hall, *g* that they might not be defiled, but that they might eat the pasch.

29 Pilate therefore went out

---

*a* Luke 23.—*b* Supra, 11. 49.—*c* Matt. 26. 59. Mark 14. 54. Luke 22. 54.

*d* Matt. 26. 57. Mark 14. 53. Luke 22. 54.—*e* Matt. 26. 69. Mark 14. 67. Luke 22. 56.—*f* Matt. 27. 2. Mark 15. 1. Luke 23. 1.—*g* Acts 10. 28. and 11. 3.

CHAP. XVIII. ST. JOHN. CHAP. XIX.

to them, and said: What accusation bring you against this man?

30 They answered and said to him: If he were not a malefactor, we would not have delivered him up to thee.

31 Pilate therefore said to them: Take him you, and judge him according to your law. The Jews therefore said to him: It is not lawful for us to put any man to death.

32 ª That the word of JESUS might be fulfilled which he said, signifying what death he should die.

33 ᵇ Pilate therefore went into the hall again, and called JESUS, and said to him: Art thou the king of the Jews?

34 JESUS answered: Sayest thou this thing of thyself, or have others told it thee of me?

35 Pilate answered: Am I a Jew? Thy own nation and the chief priests have delivered thee up to me: what hast thou done?

36 JESUS answered: My kingdom is not of this world. If my kingdom were of this world, my servants would certainly strive that I should not be delivered to the Jews: but now my kingdom is not from hence.

37 Pilate therefore said to him: Art thou a king then? JESUS answered: Thou sayest, that I am a king. For this was I born, and for this came I into the world: that I should give testimony to the truth. Every one that is of the truth, heareth my voice.

38 Pilate saith to him: What is truth? And when he said this he went out again to the Jews, and saith to them: I find no cause in him.

39 ᶜ But you have a custom that I should release one unto you at the pasch: will you therefore that I release unto you the king of the Jews?

40 Then cried they all again, saying: Not this man, but Barabbas. Now Barabbas was a robber.

## CHAP. XIX.

*The continuation of the history of the passion of Christ.*

THEN ᵈ therefore Pilate took JESUS, and scourged him.

2 And the soldiers platting a crown of thorns, put it upon his head: and they put on him a purple garment.

3 And they came to him, and said: Hail, king of the Jews: and they gave him blows.

4 Pilate therefore went forth again, and saith to them: Behold I bring him forth unto you, that you may know that I find no cause in him.

5 (JESUS therefore came forth bearing the crown of thorns, and the purple garment.) And he saith to them: Behold the Man.

6 When the chief priests therefore and the servants had seen him, they cried out, saying: Crucify him, crucify him. Pilate saith to them: Take him you, and crucify him; for I find no cause in him.

7 The Jews answered him: We have a law; and according to the law he ought to die, because he made himself the Son of God.

---

ª Matt. 20. 19.—ᵇ Matt. 27. 11. Mark 15. 2. Luke 23. 3.

ᶜ Matt. 27. 15. Mark 15. 6. Luke 23. 17.—ᵈ Matt. 27. 26. Mark 15. 15.

8 When Pilate therefore had heard this saying, he feared the more.

9 And he entered into the hall again, and he said to Jesus: Whence art thou? But Jesus gave him no answer.

10 Pilate therefore saith to him: Speakest thou not to me? knowest thou not that I have power to crucify thee, and I have power to release thee?

11 Jesus answered: Thou shouldest not have any power against me, unless it were given thee from above. Therefore he that hath delivered me to thee, hath the greater sin.

12 And from thenceforth Pilate sought to release him. But the Jews cried out, saying: If thou release this man, thou art not Cesar's friend. For whosoever maketh himself a king, speaketh against Cesar.

13 Now when Pilate had heard these words, he brought Jesus forth; and sat down in the judgment-seat, in the place that is called Lithostrotos, and in Hebrew Gabbatha.

14 And it was the parasceve of the pasch, about the sixth hour, and he saith to the Jews: Behold your king.

15 But they cried out: Away with him, away with him, crucify him. Pilate saith to them: Shall I crucify your king? The chief priests answered: We have no king but Cesar.

16 Then therefore he delivered him to them to be crucified.

And they took Jesus, and led him forth.

17 ᵃAnd bearing his own cross he went forth to that place which is called Calvary, but in Hebrew Golgotha.

18 Where they crucified him, and with him two others, one on each side, and Jesus in the midst.

19 And Pilate wrote a title also: and he put it upon the cross. And the writing was, JESUS OF NAZARETH THE KING OF THE JEWS.

20 This title therefore many of the Jews did read: because the place where Jesus was crucified was nigh to the city: and it was written in Hebrew, in Greek, and in Latin.

21 Then the chief priests of the Jews said to Pilate: Write not, the king of the Jews; but that he said: I am the king of the Jews.

22 Pilate answered: What I have written, I have written.

23 The soldiers therefore when they had crucified him, ᵇtook his garments (and they made four parts, to every soldier a part) and also his coat. Now the coat was without seam, woven from the top throughout.

24 They said then one to another: Let us not cut it, but let us cast lots for it whose it shall be; that the scripture might be fulfilled, saying: ᶜ*They have parted my garments among them: and upon my vesture they have cast lot.* And the soldiers indeed did these things.

25 Now there stood by the

---

CHAP. XIX. Ver. 14. *The parasceve of the pasch.* That is, the day before the paschal sabbath. The eve of every sabbath was called the parasceve, or day of preparation. But this was the eve of a high sabbath, viz., that which fell in the paschal week.

ᵃ Matt. 27. 33. Mark 15. 22. Luke 23. 33.—ᵇ Matt. 27. 35. Mark 15. 24. Luke 23. 34.—ᶜ Ps. 21. 19.

JESUS CURES THE MAN BORN BLIND.

cross of JESUS, his mother, and his mother's sister, Mary of Cleophas, and Mary Magdalen.

26 When JESUS therefore had seen his mother and the disciple standing, whom he loved, he saith to his mother: Woman, behold thy son.

27 After that, he saith to the disciple: Behold thy mother. And from that hour the disciple took her to his own.

28 Afterwards JESUS knowing that all things were now accomplished, *a* that the scripture might be fulfilled, said: I thirst.

29 Now there was a vessel set there full of vinegar. And they putting a sponge full of vinegar about hyssop, put it to his mouth.

30 JESUS therefore when he had taken the vinegar, said: It is consummated. And bowing his head, he gave up the ghost.

31 Then the Jews (because it was the parasceve) that the bodies might not remain upon the cross on the sabbath-day (for that was a great sabbath-day) besought Pilate that their legs might be broken, and that they might be taken away.

32 The soldiers therefore came: and they broke the legs of the first, and of the other that was crucified with him.

33 But after they were come to JESUS, when they saw that he was already dead, they did not break his legs.

34 But one of the soldiers with a spear opened his side, and immediately there came out blood and water.

35 And he that saw it hath given testimony: and his testimony is true. And he knoweth that he saith true; that you also may believe.

36 For these things were done that the scripture might be fulfilled: *b* *You shall not break a bone of him.*

37 And again another scripture saith: *c They shall look on him whom they pierced.*

38 *d* After these things Joseph of Arimathea (because he was a disciple of JESUS, but secretly for fear of the Jews) besought Pilate that he might take away the body of JESUS. And Pilate gave leave. He came therefore and took away the body of JESUS.

39 And Nicodemus also came, *e* he who at first came to JESUS by night, bringing a mixture of myrrh and aloes, about an hundred pound *weight.*

40 They took therefore the body of JESUS, and bound it in linen cloths with the spices, as the manner of the Jews is to bury.

41 Now there was in the place, where he was crucified, a garden; and in the garden, a new sepulchre, wherein no man yet had been laid.

42 There therefore because of the parasceve of the Jews, they laid JESUS, because the sepulchre was nigh at hand.

## CHAP. XX.

*Christ's resurrection, and manifestation to his disciples.*

AND *f* on the first day of the week, Mary Magdalen cometh early, when it was yet dark unto the sepulchre: and she

---

*a* Ps. 68. 22.

*b* Exod. 12. 46. Num. 9. 12.—*c* Zach. 12. 10.—*d* Matt. 27. 57. Mark 15. 42. Luke 23. 50.—*e* Supra, 3. 2.—*f* Matt. 28. 1. Mark 16. 1. Luke 24. 1.

saw the stone taken away from the sepulchre.

2 She ran therefore, and cometh to Simon Peter, and to the other disciple whom JESUS loved, and saith to them: They have taken away the Lord out of the sepulchre, and we know not where they have laid him.

3 Peter therefore went out, and that other disciple, and they came to the sepulchre.

4 And they both ran together, and that other disciple did outrun Peter, and came first to the sepulchre.

5 And when he stooped down, he saw the linen cloths lying: but yet he went not in.

6 Then cometh Simon Peter, following him, and went into the sepulchre, and saw the linen cloths lying.

7 And the napkin that had been about his head, not lying with the linen cloths, but apart, wrapt up into one place.

8 Then that other disciple also went in, who came first to the sepulchre: and he saw and believed.

9 For as yet they knew not the scripture, that he must rise again from the dead.

10 The disciples therefore departed again to their home.

11 a But Mary stood at the sepulchre without, weeping. Now as she was weeping, she stooped down, and looked into the sepulchre:

12 And she saw two angels in white, sitting, one at the head, and one at the feet, where the body of JESUS had been laid.

13 They say to her: Woman, why weepest thou? She saith to them: Because they have taken away my Lord: and I know not where they have laid him.

14 When she had thus said, she turned herself back, and saw JESUS standing; and she knew not that it was JESUS.

15 JESUS saith to her: Woman, why weepest thou? whom seekest thou? She thinking that it was the gardener, saith to him: Sir, if thou hast taken him hence, tell me where thou hast laid him: and I will take him away.

16 JESUS saith to her: Mary. She turning, saith to him: Rabboni (which is to say, Master).

17 JESUS saith to her: Do not touch me, for I am not yet ascended to my Father: but go to my brethren, and say to them: I ascend to my Father and to your Father, to my God and your God.

18 Mary Magdalen cometh and telleth the disciples: I have seen the Lord, and these things he said to me.

19 b Now when it was late that same day, the first of the week, and the doors were shut, where the disciples were gathered together for fear of the Jews, JESUS came and stood in the midst, and said to them: Peace be to you.

20 And when he had said this, he shewed them his hands,

---

b Mark 16. 14. Luke 24. 36. 1 Cor. 15. 5.

---

CHAP. XX. Ver. 19. *The doors were shut.* The same power which could bring Christ's whole body, entire in all its dimensions, through the doors, can without the least question make the same body really present in the sacrament; though both the one and the other be above our comprehension.

---

a Matt. 28. 1. Mark 16. 5. Luke 24. 4.

and his side. The disciples therefore were glad, when they saw the Lord.

21 He said therefore to them again: Peace be to you. As the Father hath sent me, I also send you.

22 When he had said this, he breathed on them; and he said to them: Receive ye the Holy Ghost:

23 *a* Whose sins you shall forgive, they are forgiven them: and whose *sins* you shall retain, they are retained.

24 Now Thomas, one of the twelve, who is called Didymus, was not with them when JESUS came.

25 The other disciples therefore said to him: We have seen the Lord. But he said to them: Except I shall see in his hands the print of the nails, and put my finger into the place of the nails, and put my hand into his side, I will not believe.

26 And after eight days, again his disciples were within, and Thomas with them. JESUS cometh, the doors being shut, and stood in the midst, and said: Peace be to you.

27 Then he saith to Thomas: Put in thy finger hither, and see my hands, and bring hither thy hand and put it into my side; and be not faithless, but believing.

28 Thomas answered, and said to him: My Lord, and my God.

---

*a* Matt. 18. 18.

---

Ver. 23. *Whose sins, &c.* See here the commission, stamped by the broad seal of Heaven, by virtue of which the pastors of Christ's Church absolve repenting sinners upon their confession.

29 Jesus saith to him: Because thou hast seen me, Thomas, thou hast believed: blessed are they that have not seen, and have believed.

30 *b* Many other signs also did JESUS in the sight of his disciples, which are not written in this book.

31 But these are written that you may believe that JESUS is the CHRIST the Son of God; and that believing you may have life in his name.

## CHAP. XXI.

*Christ manifests himself to his disciples by the seaside, and gives Peter the charge of his sheep.*

AFTER this JESUS shewed himself again to the disciples at the sea of Tiberias. And he shewed *himself* after this manner.

2 There were together Simon Peter, and Thomas who is called Didymus, and Nathanael who was of Cana in Galilee, and the sons of Zebedee, and two others of his disciples.

3 Simon Peter saith to them: I go a fishing. They say to him: We also come with thee. And they went forth and entered into the ship: and that night they caught nothing.

4 But when the morning was come, JESUS stood on the shore: yet the disciples knew not that it was JESUS.

5 JESUS therefore said to them: Children, have you any meat? They answered him: No.

6 He saith to them: Cast the net on the right side of the ship; and you shall find. They cast therefore: and now they

---

*b* Infra, 21. 25.

were not able to draw it for the multitude of fishes.

7 That disciple therefore whom JESUS loved, said to Peter: It is the Lord. Simon Peter, when he heard that it was the Lord, girt his coat about him (for he was naked) and cast himself into the sea.

8 But the other disciples came in the ship (for they were not far from the land, but as it were two hundred cubits) dragging the net with fishes.

9 As soon then as they came to land, they saw hot coals lying, and a fish laid thereon, and bread.

10 JESUS saith to them: Bring hither of the fishes which you have now caught.

11 Simon Peter went up, and drew the net to land, full of great fishes, one hundred fifty three. And although there were so many, the net was not broken.

12 JESUS saith to them: Come, and dine. And none of them who were at meat, durst ask him: Who art thou? knowing that it was the Lord.

13 And JESUS cometh and taketh bread, and giveth them, and fish in like manner.

14 This is now the third time that JESUS was manifested to his disciples, after he was risen from the dead.

15 When therefore they had dined, JESUS saith to Simon Peter: Simon son of John, lovest thou me more than these? He saith to him: Yea, Lord, thou knowest that I love thee. He saith to him: Feed my lambs.

16 He saith to him again: Simon son of John, lovest thou me? He saith to him: Yea, Lord, thou knowest that I love thee. He saith to him: Feed my lambs.

17 He said to him the third time: Simon son of John, lovest thou me? Peter was grieved, because he had said to him the third time, Lovest thou me? And he said to him: Lord, thou knowest all things: thou knowest that I love thee. He said to him: Feed my sheep.

18 Amen, amen, I say to thee: *a* when thou wast younger, thou didst gird thyself, and didst walk where thou wouldst. But when thou shalt be old, thou shalt stretch forth thy hands, and another shall gird thee, and lead thee whither thou wouldst not.

19 And this he said, signifying by what death he should glorify God. And when he had said this, he saith to him: Follow me.

20 Peter turning about, saw that disciple whom JESUS loved following, *b* who also leaned on his breast at supper, and said: Lord, who is he that shall betray thee?

21 Him therefore when Peter had seen, he saith to JESUS: Lord, and what *shall* this man *do?*

22 JESUS saith to him: So I will have him to remain till I come, what is it to thee? follow thou me.

---

*a* 2 Pet. 1. 14.—*b* Supra, 13. 23.

CHAP. XXI. Ver. 17. *Feed my sheep.* Our Lord had promised the spiritual supremacy to St. Peter; St. Matt. xvi. 19; and here he fulfils that promise, by charging him with the superintendency of all his sheep, without exception; and consequently of his whole flock, that is, of his whole Church.

ONE OF THE TEN LEPERS RETURNS TO GIVE THANKS.

23 This saying therefore went abroad among the brethren, that that disciple should not die. And JESUS did not say to him: He should not die; but, So I will have him to remain till I come, what is it to thee?

24 This is that disciple who giveth testimony of these things, and hath written these things: and we know that his testimony is true.

25 ᵃ But there are also many other things which JESUS did: which if they were written every one, the world itself, I think, would not be able to contain the books that should be written.

ᵃ Supra, 20. 30.

# THE
# ACTS OF THE APOSTLES.

*This book, which from the first ages hath been called* THE ACTS OF THE APOSTLES, *is not to be considered as a history of what was done by all the Apostles, who were dispersed into different nations; but only a short view of the first establishment of the Christian Church. A part of the preaching and actions of St. Peter are related in the twelve first chapters; and a particular account of St. Paul's apostolical labours in the subsequent chapters. It was written by St. Luke the Evangelist, and the original in Greek. Its history commences from the Ascension of Christ our Lord, and ends in the year sixty-three, being a brief account of the Church for the space of about thirty years.*

## CHAP. I.

*The Ascension of Christ. Matthias is chosen in place of Judas.*

THE former treatise I made, O Theophilus, of all things, which JESUS began to do and to teach.

2 Until the day ᵃ on which, giving commandments by the Holy Ghost to the apostles whom he had chosen, he was taken up.

3 To whom also he shewed himself alive after his passion, by many proofs, for forty days appearing to them, and speaking of the kingdom of God,

4 And eating together with them, ᵇ he commanded them, that they should not depart from Jerusalem, but should wait for the promise of the Father, ᶜ which you have heard (saith he) by my mouth:

5 For John indeed baptized with water, but you shall be baptized with the Holy Ghost not many days hence.

6 They therefore who were come together, asked him, saying: Lord, wilt thou at this time restore again the kingdom to Israel?

7 But he said to them: It is

ᵃ A.D. 33.

ᵇ Luke 24. 49. John 14. 26.—ᶜ Matt. 3. 11. Mark 1. 8. Luke 3. 16. John 1. 20.

not for you to know the times or moments, which the Father hath put in his own power:

8 <sup>a</sup> But you shall receive the power of the Holy Ghost coming upon you, <sup>b</sup> and you shall be witnesses unto me in Jerusalem, and in all Judea and Samaria, and even to the uttermost part of the earth.

9 And when he had said these things, while they looked on, he was raised up: and a cloud received him out of their sight.

10 And while they were beholding him going up to heaven, behold two men stood by them in white garments.

11 Who also said: Ye men of Galilee, why stand you looking up to heaven? This JESUS who is taken up from you into heaven, shall so come as you have seen him going into heaven.

12 Then they returned to Jerusalem, from the mount that is called Olivet, which is nigh Jerusalem, within a sabbath-day's journey.

13 And when they were come in, they went up into an upper room, where abode Peter and John, James and Andrew, Philip and Thomas, Bartholomew and Matthew, James of Alpheus and Simon Zelotes, and Jude *the brother* of James.

14 All these were persevering with one mind in prayer with the women, and Mary the mother of JESUS, and with his brethren.

15 In those days Peter rising up in the midst of the brethren, said: (now the number of persons together was about an hundred and twenty,)

16 Men brethren, the scripture must needs be fulfilled, <sup>c</sup> which the Holy Ghost spoke before by the mouth of David concerning Judas, who was the leader of them that apprehended JESUS:

17 Who was numbered with us, and had obtained part of this ministry.

18 <sup>d</sup> And he indeed hath possessed a field of the reward of iniquity, and being hanged, burst asunder in the midst: and all his bowels gushed out.

19 And it became known to all the inhabitants of Jerusalem: so that the same field was called in their tongue Haceldama, that is to say, The field of blood.

20 For it is written in the book of Psalms: *<sup>e</sup> Let their habitation become desolate, and let there be none to dwell therein. <sup>f</sup> And his bishoprick let another take.*

21 Wherefore of these men who have companied with us, all the time that the Lord JESUS came in and went out among us,

22 Beginning from the baptism of John until the day wherein he was taken up from us, one of these must be made a witness with us of his resurrection.

23 And they appointed two, Joseph, called Barsabas, who was surnamed Justus, and Matthias.

24 And praying they said: Thou, Lord, who knowest the hearts of all men, shew whether of these two thou hast chosen,

25 To take the place of this ministry and apostleship, from which Judas hath by transgres-

---

<sup>a</sup> Infra, 2. 2.—<sup>b</sup> Luke 24. 48.

<sup>c</sup> Ps. 40. 10. John 13. 18.—<sup>d</sup> Matt. 27. 7.—<sup>e</sup> Ps. 68. 26.—<sup>f</sup> Ps. 108. 8.

sion fallen, that he might go to his own place.

26 And they gave them lots, and the lot fell upon Matthias, and he was numbered with the eleven apostles.

## CHAP. II.

*The disciples receive the Holy Ghost. Peter's sermon to the people. The piety of the first converts.*

AND when the days of the pentecost were accomplished, they were altogether in one place:

2 And suddenly there came a sound from heaven, as of a mighty wind coming, and it filled the whole house where they were sitting.

3 And there appeared to them parted tongues as it were of fire, and it sat upon every one of them:

4 a And they were all filled with the Holy Ghost, and they began to speak with divers tongues, according as the Holy Ghost gave them to speak.

5 Now there were dwelling at Jerusalem Jews, devout men out of every nation under heaven.

6 And when this was noised abroad, the multitude came together, and were confounded in mind, because that every man heard them speak in his own tongue.

7 And they were all amazed and wondered, saying: Behold are not all these, that speak, Galileans?

8 And how have we heard, every man our own tongue wherein we were born?

---

a Matt. 8. 11. Mark 1. 8. Luke 3. 16. John 7. 39. Supra, 1. 5. Infra, 11. 16. and 9. 4.

9 Parthians, and Medes, and Elamites, and inhabitants of Mesopotamia, Judea, and Cappadocia, Pontus and Asia,

10 Phrygia, and Pamphilia, Egypt, and the parts of Libya about Cyrene, and strangers of Rome,

11 Jews also, and proselytes, Cretes and Arabians: we have heard them speak in our own tongues the wonderful works of God.

12 And they were all astonished, and wondered, saying one to another: What meaneth this?

13 But others mocking said: These men are full of new wine.

14 But Peter standing up with the eleven, lifted up his voice, and spoke to them: Ye men of Judea, and all you that dwell in Jerusalem, be this known to you, and with your ears receive my words.

15 For these are not drunk, as you suppose, seeing it is but the third hour of the day.

16 But this is that which was spoken of by the prophet Joel:

17 b *And it shall come to pass, in the last days, (saith the Lord) I will pour out of my Spirit upon all flesh: and your sons and your daughters shall prophesy, and your young men shall see visions, and your old men shall dream dreams.*

18 *And upon my servants indeed, and upon my handmaids will I pour out in those days of my Spirit, and they shall prophesy.*

19 *And I will shew wonders in the heaven above, and signs on the earth beneath; blood and fire, and vapour of smoke.*

---

b Isaias 44. 3. Joel 2. 28.

20 *The sun shall be turned into darkness, and the moon into blood, before the great and manifest day of the Lord come.*

21 <sup>a</sup> *And it shall come to pass, that whosoever shall call upon the name of the Lord, shall be saved.*

22 Ye men of Israel, hear these words: JESUS of Nazareth, a man approved of God among you, by miracles and wonders and signs, which God did by him in the midst of you, as you also know:

23 This same being delivered up, by the determinate counsel and foreknowledge of God, you by the hands of wicked men have crucified and slain.

24 Whom God hath raised up, having loosed the sorrows of hell, as it was impossible that he should be holden by it.

25 For David saith concerning him: <sup>b</sup> *I foresaw the Lord before my face: because he is at my right hand that I may not be moved.*

26 *For this my heart hath been glad, and my tongue hath rejoiced: moreover my flesh also shall rest in hope.*

---

<sup>a</sup> Joel 2. 32.   Rom. 10. 13.—<sup>b</sup> Ps. 15. 8.

CHAP. II. Ver. 23. *By the determinate, &c.* God delivered up his Son; and his Son delivered up himself, for the love of us, and for the sake of our salvation: and so Christ's being delivered up was holy, and was God's own determination. But they who betrayed and crucified him did wickedly, following therein their own malice and the instigation of the devil; not the will and determination of God, who was by no means the author of their wickedness; though he permitted it; because he could, and did draw out of it so great a good, viz. the salvation of man.

Ver. 24. *Having loosed the sorrows, &c.* Having overcome the grievous pains of death, and all the power of hell.

27 *Because thou wilt not leave my soul in hell, nor suffer thy Holy One to see corruption.*

28 *Thou hast made known to me the ways of life: thou shalt make me full of joy with thy countenance.*

29 Ye men brethren, let me freely speak to you of the patriarch David; <sup>c</sup> that he died and was buried; and his sepulchre is with us to this present day.

30 Whereas therefore he was a prophet, and knew <sup>d</sup> that *God had sworn to him with an oath that of the fruit of his loins one should sit upon his throne;*

31 Foreseeing this, he spoke of the resurrection of Christ. <sup>e</sup> For neither was he left in hell, neither did his flesh see corruption.

32 This JESUS hath God raised again, whereof all we are witnesses.

33 Being exalted therefore by the right hand of God, and having received of the Father the promise of the Holy Ghost, he hath poured forth this which you see and hear.

34 For David ascended not into heaven; but he himself said: <sup>f</sup> *The Lord said to my Lord, sit thou on my right hand,*

35 *Until I make thy enemies thy footstool.*

36 Therefore let all the house of Israel know most certainly that God hath made both Lord, and CHRIST, this same JESUS, whom you have crucified.

37 Now when they had heard these things they had compunction in their heart, and

---

<sup>c</sup> 3 Kings 2. 10.—<sup>d</sup> Ps. 131. 11.—<sup>e</sup> Ps. 15. 10. Infra, 13. 35.—<sup>f</sup> Ps. 109. 1.

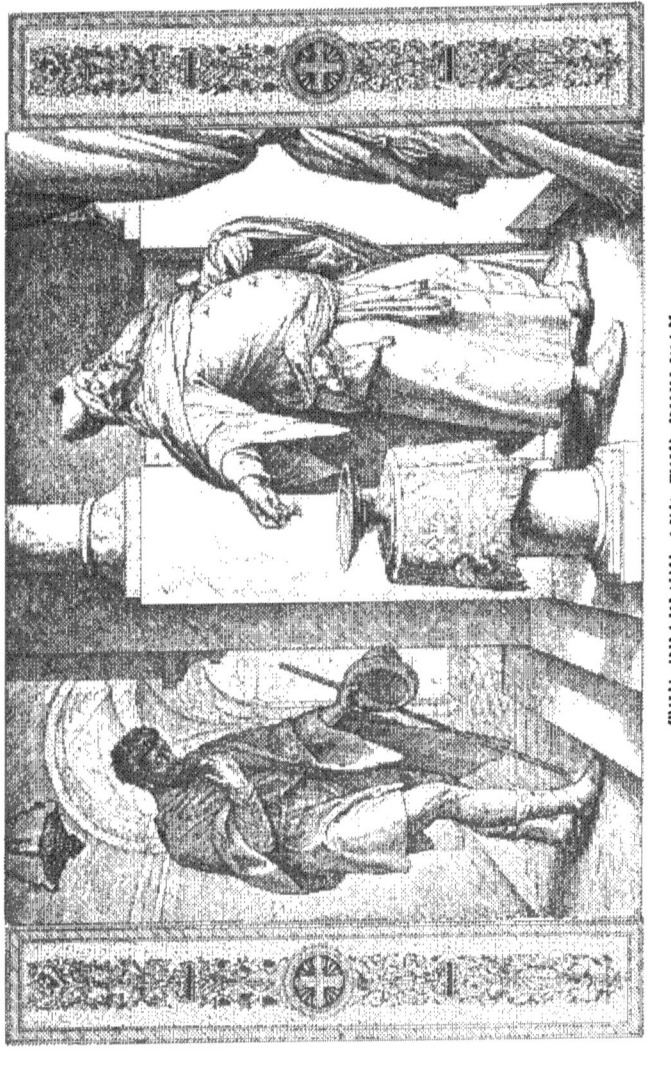

THE PHARISEE AND THE PUBLICAN.

said to Peter and to the rest of the apostles: What shall we do, men *and* brethren?

38 But Peter *said* to them: Do penance, and be baptized every one of you in the name of JESUS CHRIST, for the remission of your sins: and you shall receive the gift of the Holy Ghost.

39 For the promise is to you, and to your children, and to all that are far off, whomsoever the Lord our God shall call.

40 And with very many other words did he testify and exhort them, saying: Save yourselves from this perverse generation.

41 They therefore that received his word were baptized: and there were added in that day about three thousand souls.

42 And they were persevering in the doctrine of the apostles, and in the communication of the breaking of bread, and in prayers.

43 And fear came upon every soul: many wonders also and signs were done by the apostles in Jerusalem, and there was great fear in all.

44 And all they that believed were together, and had all things common.

45 Their possessions and goods they sold, and divided them to all, according as every one had need.

46 And continuing daily with one accord in the temple, and breaking bread from house to house, they took their meat with gladness and simplicity of heart:

47 Praising God and having favour with all the people. And the Lord increased daily together such as should be saved.

## CHAP. III.

*The miracle upon the lame man, followed by the conversion of many.*

NOW Peter and John went up into the temple, at the ninth hour of prayer.

2 And a certain man who was lame from his mother's womb, was carried; whom they laid every day at the gate of the temple, which is called Beautiful, that he might ask alms of them that went into the temple.

3 He, *a* when he had seen Peter and John about to go into the temple, asked to receive an alms.

4 But Peter with John fastening his eyes upon him, said: Look upon us.

5 But he looked earnestly upon them, hoping that he should receive something of them.

6 But Peter said: Silver and gold I have none; but what I have, I give thee: in the name of JESUS CHRIST of Nazareth, arise, and walk.

7 And taking him by the right hand, he lifted him up, and forthwith his feet and soles received strength.

8 And he leaping up stood, and walked and went in with them into the temple, walking, and leaping, and praising God.

9 And all the people saw him walking and praising God.

10 And they knew him, that it was he who sat begging alms at the Beautiful gate of the temple: and they were filled with wonder and amazement at that which had happened to him.

11 And as he held Peter and John, all the people ran to them to the porch which is called Solomon's, greatly wondering.

*a* A.D. 33.

CHAP. III.  THE ACTS.  CHAP. IV.

12 But Peter seeing, made answer to the people: Ye men of Israel, why wonder you at this? or why look you upon us, as if by our strength or power we had made this man to walk?

13 The God of Abraham, and the God of Isaac, and the God of Jacob, the God of our fathers, hath glorified his Son JESUS, whom you indeed delivered up and denied before the face of Pilate, when he judged he should be released.

14 *a* But you denied the Holy One and the Just, and desired a murderer to be granted unto you.

15 But the author of life you killed, whom God hath raised from the dead, of which we are witnesses.

16 And in the faith of his name, this man whom you have seen and known, hath his name strengthened; and the faith which is by him, hath given this perfect soundness in the sight of you all.

17 And now, brethren, I know that you did it through ignorance, as *did* also your rulers.

18 But those things which God before had shewed by the mouth of all the prophets, that his CHRIST should suffer, he hath so fulfilled.

19 Be penitent, therefore, and be converted, that your sins may be blotted out.

20 That when the times of refreshment shall come from the presence of the Lord, and he shall send him who hath been preached unto you, JESUS CHRIST,

21 Whom heaven indeed must receive until the times of the restitution of all things, which God hath spoken by the mouth of his holy prophets from the beginning of the world.

22 For Moses said: *b A prophet shall the Lord your God raise up unto you of your brethren, like unto me: him you shall hear according to all things whatsoever he shall speak to you.*

23 *And it shall be, that every soul which will not hear that prophet, shall be destroyed from among the people.*

24 And all the prophets from Samuel and afterwards, who have spoken, have told of these days.

25 You are the children of the prophets and of the testament which God made to our fathers, saying to Abraham: *c And in thy seed shall all the kindreds of the earth be blessed.*

26 To you first God raising up his Son, hath sent him to bless you: that every one may convert himself from his wickedness.

CHAP. IV.

*Peter and John are apprehended. Their constancy. The Church is increased.*

AND *d* as they were speaking to the people, the priests and the officer of the temple and the Sadducees came upon them,

2 Being grieved that they taught the people, and preached in JESUS the resurrection from the dead:

3 And they laid hands upon them, and put them in hold, till the next day; for it was now evening.

---

*a* Matt. 27. 20. Mark 15. 11. Luke 23. 18. John 18. 40.

*b* Deut. 18. 15.—*c* Gen. 12. 3.—*d* A.D. 33.

4 But many of them, who had heard the word, believed: and the number of the men was made five thousand.

5 And it came to pass on the morrow, that their princes, and ancients, and scribes were gathered together in Jerusalem;

6 And Annas the high-priest, and Caiphas, and John, and Alexander, and as many as were of the kindred of the high-priest.

7 And setting them in the midst, they asked: By what power, or by what name have you done this?

8 Then Peter, filled with the Holy Ghost, said to them: Ye princes of the people and ancients, hear:

9 If we this day are examined concerning the good deed done to the infirm man, by what means he hath been made whole,

10 Be it known to you all, and to all the people of Israel, that by the name of our Lord JESUS CHRIST of Nazareth, whom you crucified, whom God hath raised from the dead, even by him this man standeth here before you whole.

11 ᵃThis is *the stone which was rejected by* you *the builders: which is become the head of the corner:*

12 Neither is there salvation in any other. For there is no other name under heaven given to men, whereby we must be saved.

13 Now seeing the constancy of Peter and of John, understanding that they were illiterate and ignorant men, they wondered; and they knew them that they had been with JESUS:

14 Seeing the man also who had been healed, standing with them, they could say nothing against it.

15 But they commanded them to go aside out of the council: and they conferred among themselves,

16 Saying: What shall we do to these men? for indeed a known miracle hath been done by them to all the inhabitants of Jerusalem: it is manifest, and we cannot deny it.

17 But that it may be no farther spread among the people, let us threaten them, that they speak no more in this name to any man.

18 And calling them, they charged them not to speak at all, nor teach in the name of JESUS.

19 But Peter and John answering, said to them: If it be just in the sight of God, to hear you rather than God, judge ye.

20 For we cannot but speak the things which we have seen and heard.

21 But they threatening, sent them away: not finding how they might punish them, because of the people: for all men glorified what had been done, in that which had come to pass.

22 For the man was above forty years old, in whom that miraculous cure had been wrought.

23 And being let go, they came to their own company, and related all that the chief priests and ancients had said to them.

24 Who having heard it, with one accord lifted up their voice to God, and said: Lord, thou

---

ᵃ Ps. 117. 22. Isaias 28. 16. Matt. 21. 42. Mark 12. 10. Luke 20. 17. Rom. 9. 33. 1 Pet. 2. 7.

art he that didst make heaven and earth, the sea, and all things that are in them.

25 Who by the Holy Ghost, by the mouth of our father David thy servant hast said, *Why did the gentiles rage, and the people meditate vain things?*

26 *The kings of the earth stood up, and the princes assembled together against the Lord, and against his* CHRIST.

27 For of a truth there assembled together in this city, against thy holy child JESUS whom thou hast anointed, Herod, and Pontius Pilate, with the gentiles and the people of Israel.

28 To do what thy hand and thy counsel decreed to be done.

29 And now, Lord, behold their threatenings, and grant unto thy servants, that with all confidence they may speak thy word,

30 By stretching forth thy hand to cures and signs and wonders, to be done by the name of thy holy Son JESUS.

31 And when they had prayed, the place was moved wherein they were assembled: and they were all filled with the Holy Ghost, and they spoke the word of God with confidence.

32 And the multitude of believers had but one heart and one soul: neither did any one say that aught of the things which he possessed was his own, but all things were common unto them.

33 And with great power did the apostles give testimony of the resurrection of JESUS CHRIST our Lord: and great grace was in them all.

34 For neither was there any one needy among them. For as many as were owners of lands or houses sold them, and brought the price of the things they sold.

35 And laid it down before the feet of the apostles. And distribution was made to every one according as he had need.

36 And Joseph, who by the apostles was surnamed Barnabas (which is by interpretation, the son of consolation), a Levite, a Cyprian born,

37 Having land, sold it, and brought the price, and laid it at the feet of the apostles.

CHAP. V.

*The judgment of God upon Ananias and Saphira. The apostles are cast into prison.*

BUT ᵇ a certain man named Ananias, with Saphira his wife, sold a piece of land,

2 And by fraud kept back part of the price of the land, his wife being privy thereunto: and bringing a certain part of it, laid it at the feet of the apostles.

3 But Peter said: Ananias, why hath satan tempted thy heart, that thou shouldst lie to the Holy Ghost, and by fraud keep part of the price of the land?

4 Whilst it remained, did it not remain to thee? and after it was sold, was it not in thy power? Why hast thou conceived this thing in thy heart? Thou hast not lied to men, but to God.

5 And Ananias hearing these words, fell down, and gave up the ghost. And there came

THE RICH YOUNG MAN.

great fear upon all that heard it.

6 And the young men rising up, removed him, and carrying him out buried him.

7 And it was about the space of three hours after, when his wife, not knowing what had happened, came in.

8 And Peter said to her: Tell me, woman, whether you sold the land for so much? And she said: Yes, for so much.

9 And Peter *said* unto her: Why have you agreed together to tempt the Spirit of the Lord? Behold the feet of them who have buried thy husband are at the door, and they shall carry thee out.

10 Immediately she fell down before his feet, and gave up the ghost. And the young men coming in, found her dead: and carried her out, and buried her by her husband.

11 And there came great fear upon the whole church, and upon all that heard these things.

12 And by the hands of the apostles were many signs and wonders wrought among the people. And they were all with one accord in Solomon's porch.

13 But of the rest no man durst join himself unto them; but the people magnified them.

14 And the multitude of men and women who believed in the Lord was more increased:

15 Insomuch that they brought forth the sick into the streets, and laid them on beds and couches, that when Peter came, his shadow at the least might overshadow any of them, and they might be delivered from their infirmities.

16 And there came also together to Jerusalem a multitude out of the neighbouring cities, bringing sick persons, and such as were troubled with unclean spirits; who were all healed.

17 Then the high-priest rising up, and all they that were with him (which is the heresy of the Sadducees), were filled with envy.

18 And they laid hands on the apostles, and put them in the common prison.

19 But an Angel of the Lord by night opening the doors of the prison, and leading them out, said:

20 Go, and standing speak in the temple to the people all the words of this life.

21 Who having heard *this*, early in the morning entered into the temple, and taught. And the high-priest coming, and they that were with him, called together the council, and all the ancients of the children of Israel: and they sent to the prison to have them brought.

22 But when the ministers came, and opening the prison, found them not there; they returned and told,

23 Saying: The prison indeed we found shut with all diligence, and the keepers standing before the doors: but opening it, we found no man within.

24 Now when the officer of the temple, and the chief priests heard these words, they were in doubt concerning them, what would come to pass.

25 But one came and told them: Behold the men whom you put in prison, are in the temple standing, and teaching the people.

26 Then went the officer with the ministers, and brought

them without violence: for they feared the people, lest they should be stoned.

27 And when they had brought them, they set them before the council. And the high-priest asked them,

28 Saying: Commanding we commanded you that you should not teach in this name: and behold you have filled Jerusalem with your doctrine, and you have a mind to bring the blood of this man upon us.

29 But Peter and the apostles answering, said: We ought to obey God rather than men.

30 The God of our fathers hath raised up JESUS, whom you put to death, hanging him upon a tree.

31 Him hath God exalted with his right hand, *to be* prince and saviour, to give repentance to Israel, and remission of sins.

32 And we are witnesses of these things, and the Holy Ghost, whom God hath given to all that obey him.

33 When they had heard these things, they were *cut to the heart*, and they thought to put them to death.

34 But one in the council rising up, a Pharisee, named Gamaliel, a doctor of the law, respected by all the people, commanded the men to be put forth a little while.

35 And he said to them: Ye men of Israel, take heed to yourselves what you intend to do, as touching these men.

36 For before these days rose up Theodas, affirming himself to be somebody, to whom a number of men, about four hundred, joined themselves: who was slain; and all that believed him were scattered and brought to nothing.

37 After this man rose up Judas of Galilee in the days of the enrolling, and drew away the people after him: he also perished; and all, even as many as consented to him, were dispersed.

38 And now therefore I say to you, refrain from these men, and let them alone: for if this counsel or this work be of men, it will come to nought.

39 But if it be of God, you cannot overthrow it: lest perhaps you be found even to fight against God. And they consented to him.

40 And calling in the apostles, after they had scourged them, they charged them that they should not speak at all in the name of JESUS, and they dismissed them.

41 And they indeed went from the presence of the council rejoicing, that they were accounted worthy to suffer reproach for the name of JESUS.

42 And every day they ceased not, in the temple, and from house to house, to teach and preach CHRIST JESUS.

## CHAP VI.

*The ordaining of the seven deacons. The zeal of Stephen.*

AND ᵃ in those days, the number of the disciples increasing, there arose a murmuring of the Greeks against the Hebrews, for that their widows were neglected in the daily ministration.

ᵃ A.D. 33.

CHAP. VI. Ver. 1. *Greeks.* So they called the Jews that were born and brought up in Greece.

2 Then the twelve calling together the multitude of the disciples said: It is not reason that we should leave the word of God and serve tables.

3 Wherefore, brethren, look ye out among you seven men of good reputation, full of the Holy Ghost and wisdom, whom we may appoint over this business.

4 But we will give ourselves continually to prayer, and to the ministry of the word.

5 And the saying was liked by all the multitude. And they chose Stephen, a man full of faith and of the Holy Ghost, and Philip, and Prochorus, and Nicanor, and Timon, and Parmenas, and Nicolas a proselyte of Antioch.

6 These they set before the apostles: and they praying imposed hands upon them.

7 And the word of the Lord increased, and the number of the disciples was multiplied in Jerusalem exceedingly: a great multitude also of the priests obeyed the faith.

8 And Stephen full of grace and fortitude did great wonders and signs among the people.

9 Now there arose some of that which is called the synagogue of the Libertines, and of the Cyrenians, and of the Alexandrians, and of them that were of Cilicia and Asia, disputing with Stephen.

10 And they were not able to resist the wisdom and the spirit that spoke.

11 Then they suborned men to say they had heard him speak words of blasphemy against Moses and against God.

12 And they stirred up the people, and the ancients, and the scribes: and running together they took him, and brought him to the council.

13 And they set up false witnesses, who said: This man ceaseth not to speak words against the holy place and the law.

14 For we have heard him say, that this JESUS of Nazareth shall destroy this place, and shall change the traditions which Moses delivered unto us.

15 And all that sat in the council looking on him, saw his face as if it had been the face of an Angel.

## CHAP. VII.

*Stephen's speech before the council: his martyrdom.*

THEN ᵃ the high-priest said: Are these things so?

2 Who said: Ye men, brethren and fathers, hear. The God of glory appeared to our father Abraham, when he was in Mesopotamia, before he dwelt in Charan.

3 And said to him: ᵇ *Go forth out of thy country and from thy kindred, and come into the land which I shall shew thee.*

4 Then he went out of the land of the Chaldeans, and dwelt in Charan. And from thence, after his father was dead, he removed him into this land wherein you now dwell.

5 And he gave him no inheritance in it, no not the pace of a foot: but he promised to give it him in possession, and to his seed after him, when as yet he had no child.

6 And God said to him, ᶜ *That his seed should sojourn in a strange country, and that they*

---
ᵃ A.D. 33.—ᵇ Gen. 12. 1. — ᶜ Gen. 15. 13.

should bring them under bondage, and treat them evil four hundred years:

7 And the nation which they shall serve, will I judge, saith the Lord: and after these things they shall go out, and shall serve me in this place.

8 ªAnd he gave him the covenant of circumcision, ᵇand so he begot Isaac, and circumcised him the eighth day: and ᶜIsaac begot Jacob: ᵈand Jacob the twelve patriarchs.

9 And the patriarchs, through envy, ᵉsold Joseph in Egypt; and God was with him,

10 And delivered him out of all his tribulations: ᶠand he gave him favour and wisdom in the sight of Pharao king of Egypt, and he appointed him governor over Egypt, and over all his house.

11 Now there came a famine upon all Egypt, and Canaan, and great tribulation: and our fathers found no food.

12 ᵍBut when Jacob had heard that there was corn in Egypt, he sent our fathers first:

13 ʰAnd at the second time Joseph was known by his brethren, and his kindred was made known to Pharao.

14 And Joseph sending, called thither his father Jacob and all his kindred in seventy-five souls.

15 ⁱSo Jacob went down into Egypt, and ᵏhe died, and our fathers.

16 And they were translated into Sichem, and were laid in the sepulchre ˡthat Abraham bought for a sum of money of the sons of Hemor, the son of Sichem.

17 And when the time of the promise drew near, which God had promised to Abraham, ᵐthe people increased and was multiplied in Egypt.

18 Till another king arose in Egypt who knew not Joseph.

19 This same dealing craftily with our race, afflicted our fathers, that they should expose their children to the end they might not be kept alive.

20 ⁿAt the same time was Moses born, and he was acceptable to God; who was nourished three months in his father's house.

21 And when he was exposed, Pharao's daughter took him up, and nourished him for her own son.

22 And Moses was instructed in all the wisdom of the Egyptians: and he was mighty in his words and in his deeds.

23 And when he was full forty years old, it came into his heart to visit his brethren the children of Israel.

24 ᵒAnd when he had seen one of them suffering wrong, he defended him: and striking the Egyptian, he avenged him who suffered the injury.

25 And he thought that his brethren understood that God by his hand would save them: but they understood it not.

26 ᵖAnd the day following he shewed himself to them when they were at strife; and would have reconciled them in peace, saying; Men, ye are brethren, why hurt you one another?

---

ªGen. 17. 10.—ᵇGen. 21, 2.—ᶜGen. 25. 25.—ᵈGen. 29. 32. and 35. 22.—ᵉGen. 37. 28.—ᶠGen. 41. 37.—ᵍGen. 42. 2.—ʰGen. 45. 3.—ⁱGen. 46. 5.—ᵏGen. 49. 32.—ˡGen. 23. 16. and 50. 5. and 13. Jos. 24. 32.

ᵐExod. 1. 7.—ⁿExod. 2. 2. Heb. 11. 23.—ᵒExod. 2. 12.—ᵖExod. 2. 13.

THE LABORERS IN THE VINEYARD.

27 But he that did the injury to his neighbour, thrust him away, saying: *Who hath appointed thee prince and judge over us?*

28 *What, wilt thou kill me, as thou didst yesterday kill the Egyptian?*

29 And Moses fled upon this word: and was a stranger in the land of Madian, where he begot two sons.

30 And when forty years were expired, *a* there appeared to him in the desert of Mount Sina an Angel in a flame of fire in a bush.

31 And Moses seeing it, wondered at the sight. And as he drew near to view it, the voice of the Lord came unto him, saying:

32 *I am the God of thy fathers; the God of Abraham, the God of Isaac, and the God of Jacob.* And Moses being terrified, durst not behold.

33 And the Lord said to him: *Loose the shoes from thy feet; for the place wherein thou standest, is holy ground.*

34 *Seeing I have seen the affliction of my people, which is in Egypt, and I have heard their groaning, and am come down to deliver them. And now come, and I will send thee into Egypt.*

35 This Moses, whom they refused, saying: *Who hath appointed thee prince and judge?* him God sent to be prince and redeemer by the hand of the Angel who appeared to him in the bush.

36 *b* He brought them out, doing wonders and signs in the land of Egypt, and in the Red Sea, and in the desert forty years.

37 This is that Moses who said to the children of Israel: *c A prophet shall God raise up to you of your own brethren, as myself: him shall you hear.*

38 *d* This is he that was in the church in the wilderness, with the Angel who spoke to him on mount Sina, and with our fathers: who received the words of life to give unto us.

39 Whom our fathers would not obey; but thrust him away, and in their hearts turned back into Egypt.

40 Saying to Aaron: *e Make us gods to go before us. For as for this Moses, who brought us out of the land of Egypt, we know not what is become of him.*

41 And they made a calf in those days, and offered sacrifice to the idol, and rejoiced in the works of their own hands.

42 And God turned, and gave them up to serve the host of heaven, as it is written in the book of the prophets: *f Did you offer victims and sacrifices to me for forty years in the desert, O house of Israel?*

43 *And you took unto you the tabernacle of Moloch, and the star of your god Rempham, figures which you made, to adore them. And I will carry you away beyond Babylon.*

44 The tabernacle of the testimony was with our fathers in the desert, as God ordained for them, *g* speaking to Moses *that he should make it according to the form which he had seen.*

---

*a* Exod. 3. 2.—*b* Exod. 7. 8. and 8. 10. and 11. 1.

*c* Deut. 18. 15.—*d* Exod. 19. 3.—*e* Exod. 32. 1.—*f* Amos 5. 25.—*g* Exod. 25. 40.

45 ᵃ Which also our fathers receiving, brought in with Jesus, into the possession of the gentiles, whom God drove out before the face of our fathers: unto the days of David.

46 ᵇ Who found grace before God, ᶜ and desired to find a tabernacle for the God of Jacob.

47 ᵈ But Solomon built him a house.

48 ᵉ Yet the Most High dwelleth not in houses made by hand, as the prophet saith:

49 ᶠ *Heaven is my throne: and the earth my footstool. What house will you build me, saith the Lord, or what is the place of my resting?*

50 *Hath not my hand made all these things?*

51 You stiff-necked and uncircumcised in hearts and ears, you always resist the Holy Ghost: as your fathers *did*, so do you also.

52 Which of the prophets have not your fathers persecuted? And they have slain them who foretold of the coming of the Just One; of whom you have been now the betrayers and murderers:

53 Who have received the law by the disposition of Angels, and have not kept it.

ᵃ Jos. 3. 14. Heb. 8. 9.—ᵇ 1 Kings 16. 13.—ᶜ Ps. 131. 5.—ᵈ 3 Kings 6. 1. 1 Par. 17. 12.—ᵉ Infra, 17. 24.—ᶠ Isaias 66. 1.

CHAP. VII. Ver. 45. *Jesus.* That is, Josue, so called in Greek.
Ver. 48. *Dwelleth not in houses,* &c. That is, so as to stand in need of earthly dwellings, or to be contained, or circumscribed by them. Though, otherwise by his immense divinity, he is in our houses, and everywhere else; and Christ in his humanity dwelt in houses, and is now on our altars.

54 Now hearing these things they were cut to the heart, and they gnashed with their teeth at him.

55 But he being full of the Holy Ghost, looking up steadfastly to heaven, saw the glory of God, and JESUS standing on the right hand of God. And he said: Behold I see the heavens opened, and the son of man standing on the right hand of God.

56 And they crying out with a loud voice, stopped their ears, and with one accord ran violently upon him.

57 And casting him forth without the city, they stoned him: and the witnesses laid down their garments at the feet of a young man whose name was Saul.

58 And they stoned Stephen, invoking, and saying: Lord JESUS, receive my spirit.

59 And falling on his knees, he cried with a loud voice, saying: Lord, lay not this sin to their charge. And when he had said this, he fell asleep in the Lord And Saul was consenting to his death.

## CHAP. VIII.

*Philip converts the Samaritans, and baptizes the eunuch.*

AND ᵍ at that time there was raised a great persecution against the church, which was at Jerusalem, and they were all dispersed through the countries of Judea and Samaria, except the apostles

2 And devout men took orders for Stephen's funeral, and made great mourning over him.

3 But Saul made havoc of the

ᵍ A.D. 33.

church, entering in from house to house, and dragging away men and women, committed them to prison.

4 They therefore that were dispersed, went about preaching the word of God.

5 And Philip, going down to the city of Samaria, preached CHRIST unto them.

6 And the people with one accord were attentive to those things which were said by Philip, hearing, and seeing the miracles which he did.

7 For many of them who had unclean spirits, crying with a loud voice, went out.

8 And many taken with the palsy and that were lame, were healed.

9 There was therefore great joy in that city. Now *there was* a certain man named Simon, who before had been a magician in that city, seducing the people of Samaria, giving out that he was some great one:

10 To whom they all gave ear, from the least to the greatest, saying: This man is the power of God, which is called great.

11 And they were attentive to him, because for a long time he had bewitched them with his magical practices.

12 But when they had believed Philip preaching of the kingdom of God, in the name of JESUS CHRIST, they were baptized *both* men and women.

13 Then Simon himself believed also: and being baptized, he stuck close to Philip. And being astonished, wondered to see the signs and exceeding great miracles which were done.

14 Now when the apostles, who were in Jerusalem, had heard that Samaria had received the word of God; they sent unto them Peter and John.

15 Who when they were come, prayed for them, that they might receive the Holy Ghost.

16 For he was not as yet come upon any of them: but they were only baptized in the name of the Lord JESUS.

17 Then they laid their hands upon them, and they received the Holy Ghost.

18 And when Simon saw that by the imposition of the hands of the apostles the Holy Ghost was given, he offered them money,

19 Saying: Give me also this power, that on whomsoever I shall lay *my* hands, he may receive the Holy Ghost. But Peter said to him:

20 Keep thy money to thyself, to perish with thee, because thou hast thought that the gift of God may be purchased with money.

21 Thou hast no part nor lot in this matter. For thy heart is not right in the sight of God.

22 Do penance therefore for this thy wickedness: and pray to God, if perhaps this thought of thy heart may be forgiven thee.

23 For I see thou art in the gall of bitterness, and in the bonds of iniquity.

24 Then Simon answering,

---

CHAP. VIII. Ver. 17. *They laid their hands upon them*, &c. The apostles administered the sacrament of confirmation, by imposition of hands, and prayer: and the faithful thereby received the Holy Ghost. Not but they had received the grace of the Holy Ghost at their baptism: yet not that plenitude of grace and those spiritual gifts which they afterwards received from Bishops in the sacrament of confirmation, which strengthened them to profess their faith publicly.

said: Pray you for me to the Lord, that none of these things which you have spoken, may come upon me.

25 And they indeed having testified and preached the word of the Lord: returned to Jerusalem, and preached the gospel to many countries of the Samaritans.

26 Now an Angel of the Lord spoke to Philip, saying: Arise, go towards the south, to the way that goeth down from Jerusalem into Gaza: this is desert.

27 And rising up he went. And behold a man of Ethiopia, an eunuch, of great authority under Candace the queen of the Ethiopians, who had charge over all her treasures, had come to Jerusalem to adore.

28 And he was returning sitting in his chariot, and reading Isaias the prophet.

29 And the Spirit said to Philip: Go near, and join thyself to this chariot.

30 And Philip running thither, heard him reading the prophet Isaias, and he said: Thinkest thou that thou understandest what thou readest?

31 Who said: And how can I, unless some man shew me? And he desired Philip that he would come up and sit with him.

32 And the place of the scripture which he was reading was this: *a He was led as a sheep to the slaughter: and like a lamb without voice before his shearer, so openeth he not his mouth.*

33 *In humility his judgment was taken away. His generation who shall declare, for his life shall be taken from the earth?*

34 And the eunuch answering Philip, said: I beseech thee, of whom doth the prophet speak this? of himself, or some other man?

35 Then Philip opening his mouth, and beginning at this scripture, preached unto him JESUS.

36 And as they went on their way, they came to a certain water: and the eunuch said: See here is water, what doth hinder me from being baptized?

37 And Philip said: If thou believest with all thy heart, thou mayest. And he answering said: I believe that JESUS CHRIST is the Son of God.

38 And he commanded the chariot to stand still: and they went down into the water, both Philip and the eunuch, and he baptized him.

39 And when they were come up out of the water, the Spirit of the Lord took away Philip, and the eunuch saw him no more. And he went on his way rejoicing.

40 But Philip was found in Azotus, and passing through he preached the gospel to all the cities, till he came to Cesarea.

## CHAP. IX.

*Paul's conversion and zeal. Peter heals Eneas, and raises Tabitha to life.*

AND *b Saul* as yet breathing out threatenings and slaughter against the disciples

---

*a* Isaias 53. 7.

*b* A.D. 34. Gal. 1. 13.

Ver. 37. *If thou believest with all thy heart.* The Scripture many times mentions only one disposition, as here belief, when others equally necessary are not expressed, viz., a sorrow for sins, a firm hope, and the love of God. Moreover, believing with the whole heart signifies a belief of everything necessary for salvation.

CHRIST BLESSING LITTLE CHILDREN.

of the Lord, went to the high-priest,

2 And asked of him letters to Damascus, to the synagogues: that if he found any men and women of this way, he might bring them bound to Jerusalem.

3 ᵃAnd as he went on his journey, it came to pass that he drew nigh to Damascus: and suddenly a light from heaven shined round about him.

4 And falling on the ground, he heard a voice saying to him: Saul, Saul, why persecutest thou me?

5 Who said: Who art thou, Lord? And he: I am JESUS whom thou persecutest. It is hard for thee to kick against the goad.

6 And he trembling and astonished, said: Lord, what wilt thou have me to do?

7 And the Lord said to him: Arise, and go into the city, and there it shall be told thee what thou must do. Now the men who went in company with him stood amazed, hearing indeed a voice, but seeing no man.

8 And Saul arose from the ground, and when his eyes were opened, he saw nothing. But they leading him by the hands, brought him to Damascus.

9 And he was there three days without sight, and he did neither eat nor drink.

10 Now there was a certain disciple at Damascus, named Ananias: ᵇand the Lord said to him in a vision: Ananias. And he said: Behold I am here, Lord.

11 And the Lord said to him: Arise, and go into the street

ᵃ Infra. 22. 6. and 26. 10. and 26. 12. 1 Cor. 15. 8. 2 Cor. 12. 2.—ᵇ Infra. 22. 12.

that is called Strait, and seek in the house of Judas, one named Saul of Tarsus. For behold he prayeth.

12 (And he saw a man named Ananias, coming in and putting his hands upon him, that he might receive his sight.)

13 But Ananias answered: Lord, I have heard by many of this man, how much evil he hath done to thy saints in Jerusalem:

14 And here he hath authority from the chief priests to bind all that invoke thy name.

15 And the Lord said to him: Go thy way, for this man is to me a vessel of election, to carry my name before the gentiles, and kings, and the children of Israel.

16 For I will shew him how great things he must suffer for my name's sake.

17 And Ananias went his way, and entered into the house: and laying his hands upon him, he said: Brother Saul, the Lord JESUS hath sent me, he that appeared to thee in the way as thou camest: that thou mayest receive thy sight, and be filled with the Holy Ghost.

18 And immediately there fell from his eyes as it were scales, and he received his sight; and rising up he was baptized.

19 And when he had taken meat he was strengthened. And he was with the disciples, that were at Damascus, for some days.

20 And immediately he preached JESUS in the synagogues, that he is the Son of God.

21 And all that heard him were astonished, and said: Is not this he who persecuted in

209

Jerusalem those that called upon this name; and came hither for that intent, that he might carry them bound to the chief priests?

22 But Saul increased much more in strength, and confounded the Jews who dwelt at Damascus, affirming that this is the CHRIST.

23 And when many days were passed, the Jews consulted together to kill him.

24 But their laying in wait was made known to Saul. *a* And they watched the gates also day and night, that they might kill him.

25 But the disciples taking him in the night, conveyed him away by the wall, letting him down in a basket.

26 And when he was come into Jerusalem, he essayed to join himself to the disciples, and they were all afraid of him, not believing that he was a disciple.

27 But Barnabas took him and brought him to the apostles, and told them how he had seen the Lord, and that he had spoken to him, and how in Damascus he had dealt confidently in the name of JESUS.

28 And he was with them coming in and going out in Jerusalem, and dealing confidently in the name of the Lord.

29 He spoke also to the gentiles, and disputed with the Greeks: but they sought to kill him.

30 Which when the brethren had known, they brought him down to Cesarea, and sent him away to Tarsus.

31 Now the church had peace throughout all Judea and Galilee and Samaria, and was edified, walking in the fear of the Lord, and was filled with the consolation of the Holy Ghost.

32 And it came to pass, that Peter, as he passed through visiting all, came to the saints who dwelt at Lydda.

33 And he found there a certain man named Eneas, who had kept his bed for eight years, who was ill of the palsy.

34 And Peter said to him: Eneas, the Lord JESUS CHRIST healeth thee: arise, and make thy bed. And immediately he arose.

35 And all that dwelt at Lydda and Saron saw him: who were converted to the Lord.

36 And in Joppe there was a certain disciple named Tabitha, which by interpretation is called Dorcas. This woman was full of good works and alms-deeds which she did.

37 And it came to pass in those days, that she was sick and died. Whom when they had washed, they laid her in an upper chamber.

38 And forasmuch as Lydda was nigh to Joppe, the disciples hearing that Peter was there, sent unto him two men, desiring him that he would not be slack to come unto them.

39 And Peter rising up went with them. And when he was come, they brought him into the upper chamber: and all the widows stood about him weeping, and shewing him the coats and garments which Dorcas made them.

40 And they all being put forth: Peter kneeling down prayed, and turning to the body he said: Tabitha, arise. And

---

*a* 2 Cor. 11. 32.

she opened her eyes; and seeing Peter, she sat up.

41 And giving her his hand, he lifted her up. And when he had called the saints and the widows, he presented her alive.

42 And it was made known throughout all Joppe; and many believed in the Lord.

43 And it came to pass that he abode many days in Joppe, with one Simon a tanner.

## CHAP. X.
*Cornelius is received into the church. Peter's vision.*

AND *a* there was a certain man in Cesarea, named Cornelius, a centurion of that which is called the Italian band,

2 A religious man, and fearing God with all his house, giving much alms to the people, and always praying to God.

3 This man saw in a vision manifestly, about the ninth hour of the day, an Angel of God coming in unto him, and saying to him: Cornelius.

4 And he beholding him, being seized with fear, said: What is it, Lord? And he said to him: Thy prayers and thy alms are ascended for a memorial in the sight of God.

5 And now send men to Joppe, and call hither one Simon, who is surnamed Peter:

6 He lodgeth with one Simon a tanner, whose house is by the seaside: he will tell thee what thou must do.

7 And when the Angel who spoke to him was departed, he called two of his household servants, and a soldier who feared the Lord, of them that were under him:

---
*a* A.D. 39.

8 To whom when he had related all, he sent them to Joppe.

9 And on the next day whilst they were going on their journey, and drawing nigh to the city, Peter went up to the higher parts of the house, to pray about the sixth hour.

10 And being hungry, he was desirous to taste *somewhat*. And as they were preparing, there came upon him an ecstasy of mind:

11. And he saw the heaven opened, and a certain vessel descending, as it were a great linen sheet let down by the four corners from heaven to the earth.

12 Wherein were all manner of four-footed beasts, and creeping things of the earth, and fowls of the air.

13 And there came a voice to him: Arise, Peter, kill, and eat.

14 But Peter said: Far be it from me; for I never did eat anything that is common and unclean.

15 And the voice spoke to him again the second time: That which God hath cleansed do not thou call common.

16 And this was done thrice: and presently the vessel was taken up into heaven.

17 Now whilst Peter was doubting within himself, what the vision that he had seen should mean: behold the men who were sent from Cornelius, inquiring for Simon's house, stood at the gate.

18 And when they had called, they asked, if Simon, who is surnamed Peter, were lodged there?

19 And as Peter was thinking of the vision, the Spirit said to

him: Behold three men seek thee.

20 Arise, therefore, get thee down, and go with them, doubting nothing: for I have sent them.

21 Then Peter going down to the men, said: Behold I am he whom you seek; what is the cause for which you are come?

22 Who said: Cornelius, a centurion, a just man and one that feareth God, and having good testimony from all the nation of the Jews, received an answer of an holy Angel, to send for thee into his house, and to hear words of thee.

23 Then bringing them in, he lodged them. And the day following he arose and went with them: and some of the brethren from Joppe accompanied him.

24 And the morrow after he entered into Cesarea. And Cornelius waited for them, having called together his kinsmen, and special friends.

25 And it came to pass, that when Peter was come in, Cornelius came to meet him, and falling at his feet adored.

26 But Peter lifted him up, saying: Arise, I myself also am a man.

27 And talking with him, he went in, and found many that were come together.

28 And he said to them: You know how abominable it is for a man that is a Jew, to keep company or to come unto one of another nation: but God hath shewed to me, to call no man common or unclean.

29 For which cause, making no doubt, I came when I was sent for. I ask therefore, for what cause you have sent for me?

30 And Cornelius said: Four days ago, unto this hour, I was praying in my house, at the ninth hour, and behold a man stood before me in white apparel, and said:

31 Cornelius, thy prayer is heard, and thy alms are had in remembrance in the sight of God.

32 Send therefore to Joppe, and call hither Simon, who is surnamed Peter: he lodgeth in the house of Simon a tanner by the seaside.

33 Immediately therefore I sent to thee: and thou hast done well in coming. Now therefore all we are present in thy sight, to hear all things whatsoever are commanded thee by the Lord.

34 And Peter opening his mouth, said: In very deed I perceive *that God is not a respecter of persons.

35 But in every nation, he that feareth him, and worketh justice, is acceptable to him.

36 God sent the word to the children of Israel, preaching peace by JESUS CHRIST: (he is Lord of all.)

*Deut. 10. 17. 2 Par. 19. 7. Job 34. 9. Wis. 6. 8. Eccli. 35. 15. Rom. 2. 11. Gal. 2. 6. Ephes. 6. 9. Col. 3. 25. 1 Pet. 1. 17.

CHAP. X. Ver. 35. *In every nation, &c.* That is to say, not only Jews, but gentiles also, of what nation soever, are acceptable to God, if they fear him and work justice. But then true faith is always to be presupposed, *without which (saith St. Paul. Heb. xi. 6) it is impossible to please God.* Beware than of the error of those, who would infer from this passage, that men of all religions may be pleasing to God. For since none but the true religion can be from God, all other religions must be from the father of lies, and therefore highly displeasing to the God of truth.

THE RAISING OF LAZARUS.

37 You know the word which hath been published through all Judea: *for it began from Galilee, after the baptism which John preached,

38 JESUS of Nazareth: how God anointed him with the Holy Ghost, and with power, who went about doing good, and healing all that were oppressed by the devil, for God was with him.

39 And we are witnesses of all things that he did in the land of the Jews and in Jerusalem, whom they killed, hanging him upon a tree.

40 Him God raised up the third day, and gave him to be made manifest,

41 Not to all the people, but to witnesses pre-ordained by God, even to us, who did eat and drink with him after he arose again from the dead.

42 And he commanded us to preach to the people, and to testify that it is he who was appointed by God to be judge of the living and of the dead.

43 *b* To him all the prophets give testimony, that by his name all receive remission of sins, who believe in him.

44 While Peter was yet speaking these words, the Holy Ghost fell on all them that heard the word.

45 And the faithful of the circumcision, who came with Peter, were astonished, for that the grace of the Holy Ghost was poured out upon the gentiles also.

46 For they heard them speaking with tongues, and magnifying God.

---

*a* Luke 4. 14.—*b* Jer. 31. 64. Mich. 7. 18.

47 Then Peter answered: Can any man forbid water, that these should not be baptized, who have received the Holy Ghost as well as we?

48 And he commanded them to be baptized in the name of the Lord JESUS CHRIST. Then they desired him to tarry with them some days.

## CHAP. XI.

*Peter defends his having received the gentiles into the Church. Many are converted at Antioch.*

AND the apostles and brethren who were in Judea, heard that the gentiles also had received the word of God.

2 And when Peter was come up to Jerusalem, they that were of the circumcision contended with him,

3 Saying: Why didst thou go in to men uncircumcised, and didst eat with them?

4 But Peter began and declared to them the *matter in* order, saying:

5 I was in the city of Joppe praying, and I saw in an ecstasy of mind a vision, a certain vessel descending, as it were a great sheet let down from heaven by four corners, and it came even unto me.

6 Into which looking I considered, and saw four-footed creatures of the earth, and beasts, and creeping things, and fowls of the air:

7 And I heard also a voice saying to me: Arise, Peter, kill, and eat.

8 And I said: Not so, Lord; for nothing common or unclean hath ever entered into my mouth.

9 And the voice answered again from heaven: What God

hath made clean, do not thou call common.

10 And this was done three times: and all were taken up again into heaven.

11 And behold, immediately there were three men come to the house wherein I was, sent to me from Cesarea.

12 And the Spirit said to me, that I should go with them, nothing doubting. And these six brethren went with me also: and we entered into the man's house.

13 And he told us, how he had seen an angel in his house, standing and saying to him: Send to Joppe, and call hither Simon, who is surnamed Peter,

14 Who shall speak to thee words whereby thou shalt be saved, and all thy house.

15 And when I had begun to speak, the Holy Ghost fell upon them, as upon us also in the beginning.

16 And I remembered the word of the Lord, how that he said: *John indeed baptized with water, but you shall be baptized with the Holy Ghost.*

17 If then God gave them the same grace, as to us also who believed in the Lord JESUS CHRIST: who was I, that could withstand God?

18 Having heard these things, they held their peace, and glorified God, saying: God then hath also to the gentiles given repentance unto life.

19 Now they who had been dispersed, by the persecution that arose on occasion of Stephen, went about as far as Phenice and Cyprus and Antioch, speaking the word to none, but to the Jews only.

20 But some of them were men of Cyprus and Cyrene, who when they were entered into Antioch, spoke also to the Greeks, preaching the Lord JESUS.

21 And the hand of the Lord was with them: and a great number believing was converted to the Lord.

22 And the tidings came to the ears of the church that was at Jerusalem, touching these things: and they sent Barnabas as far as Antioch.

23 Who when he was come, and had seen the grace of God, rejoiced: and he exhorted them all with purpose of heart to continue in the Lord.

24 For he was a good man and full of the Holy Ghost, and of faith. And a great multitude was added to the Lord.

25 And Barnabas went to Tarsus, to seek Saul: whom when he had found he brought to Antioch.*b*

26 And they conversed there in the church a whole year: and they taught a great multitude, so that at Antioch the disciples were first named CHRISTIANS.

27 And in these days there came prophets from Jerusalem to Antioch.

28 And one of them named Agabus, rising up signified by the Spirit that there should be a great famine over the whole world, which came to pass under Claudius.

---

*a* Matt. 3. 11. Mark 1. 8. Luke 3. 16. John 1. 26. Supra, 1. 5. Infra, 19. 4.

*b* A.D. 41.

29 And the disciples, every man according to his ability, proposed to send relief to the brethren who dwelt in Judea: 30 Which also they did, sending it to the ancients, by the hands of Barnabas and Saul.*a*

## CHAP. XII.

*Herod's persecution. Peter's deliverance by an Angel. Herod's punishment.*

AND *b* at the same time Herod the king stretched forth his hands, to afflict some of the church.

2 And he killed James the brother of John with the sword.

3 And seeing that it pleased the Jews, he proceeded to take up Peter also. Now it was in the days of the azymes.

4 And when he had apprehended him, he cast him into prison, delivering him to four files of soldiers to be kept, intending after the pasch to bring him forth to the people.

5 Peter therefore was kept in prison. But prayer was made without ceasing by the church unto God for him.

6 And when Herod would have brought him forth, the same night Peter was sleeping between two soldiers, bound with two chains: and the keepers before the door kept the prison.

7 And behold an Angel of the Lord stood by him: and a light shined in the room: and he striking Peter on the side raised him up, saying: Arise quickly. And the chains fell off from his hands.

8 And the Angel said to him: Gird thyself, and put on thy sandals. And he did so. And he said to him: Cast thy garment about thee, and follow me.

9 And going out he followed him, and he knew not that it was true which was done by the Angel: but thought he saw a vision.

10 And passing through the first and the second ward, they came to the iron gate that leadeth to the city, which of itself opened to them. And going out, they passed on through one street: and immediately the Angel departed from him.

11 And Peter coming to himself, said: Now I know in very deed that the Lord hath sent his Angel, and hath delivered me out of the hand of Herod, and from all the expectation of the people of the Jews.

12 And considering, he came to the house of Mary the mother of John, who was surnamed Mark, where many were gathered together and praying.

13 And when he knocked at the door of the gate, a damsel came to hearken, whose name was Rhode.

14 And as soon as she knew Peter's voice, she opened not the gate for joy, but running in she told that Peter stood before the gate.

15 But they said to her: Thou art mad. But she affirmed that it was so. Then said they: It is his Angel.

16 But Peter continued knocking. And when they had opened, they saw him, and were astonished.

---

*a* A.D. 42 — *b* A.D. 42.

CHAP. XII. Ver. 3. *Azymes.* The festival of the unleavened bread, or the pasch, which answers to our Easter.

17 But he beckoning to them with his hand to hold their peace, told how the Lord had brought him out of prison, and he said: Tell these things to James and to the brethren. And going out he went into another place.

18 Now when day was come, there was no small stir among the soldiers, what was become of Peter.

19 And when Herod had sought for him, and found him not; having examined the keepers, he commanded they should be put to death: and going down from Judea to Cesarea, he abode there.

20 And he was angry with the Tyrians and the Sidonians. But they with one accord came to him, and having gained Blastus, who was the king's chamberlain, they desired peace, because their countries were nourished by him.

21 And upon a day appointed, Herod being arrayed in kingly apparel, sat in the judgment-seat, and made an oration to them.

22 And the people made acclamation, saying: It is the voice of a god, and not of a man.

23 And forthwith an Angel of the Lord struck him, because he had not given the honour to God: and being eaten up by worms, he gave up the ghost.*a*

24 But the word of the Lord increased and multiplied.

25 And Barnabas and Saul returned from Jerusalem, *b* having fulfilled their ministry, taking with them John, who was surnamed Mark.

## CHAP. XIII.

*Saul and Barnabas are sent forth by the Holy Ghost. They preach in Cyprus and in Antioch of Pisidia.*

NOW *c* there were in the church which was at Antioch, prophets and doctors, among whom was Barnabas, and Simon who was called Niger, and Lucius of Cyrene, and Manahen, who was the foster-brother of Herod the tetrarch, and Saul.

2 And as they were ministering to the Lord, and fasting, the Holy Ghost said to them: Separate me Saul and Barnabas, for the work whereunto I have taken them.

3 Then they fasting and praying, and imposing their hands upon them, sent them away.

4 So they being sent by the Holy Ghost, went to Seleucia: and from thence they sailed to Cyprus.

5 And when they were come to Salamina, they preached the word of God in the synagogues of the Jews. And they had John also in their ministry.

6 And when they had gone through the whole island as far as Paphos, they found a certain man a magician, a false prophet, a Jew, whose name was Bar-jesu,

7 Who was with the proconsul Sergius Paulus, a prudent man. He, sending for Barnabas and Saul, desired to hear the word of God.

8 But Elymas the magician (for so his name is interpreted) withstood them, seeking to turn away the proconsul from the faith.

9 Then Saul, otherwise Paul, filled with the Holy Ghost, looking upon him,

---

*a* A.D. 42.—*b* Supra, 11. 30.

*c* A.D. 42.

MARY MAGDALEN ANOINTING THE HEAD OF JESUS.

10 Said: O full of all guile, and of all deceit, child of the devil, enemy of all justice, thou ceasest not to pervert the right ways of the Lord.

11 And now behold the hand of the Lord is upon thee, and thou shalt be blind, not seeing the sun for a time. And immediately there fell a mist and a darkness upon him, and going about, he sought some one to lead him by the hand.

12 Then the proconsul, when he had seen what was done, believed, admiring at the doctrine of the Lord.

13 Now when Paul and they that were with him had sailed from Paphos, they came to Perge in Pamphylia. *a* And John departing from them, returned to Jerusalem.

14 But they passing through Perge, came to Antioch in Pisidia: and entering into the synagogue on the sabbath-day, they sat down.

15 And after the reading of the law and the prophets, the rulers of the synagogue sent to them, saying: Ye men brethren, if you have any word of exhortation to make to the people, speak.

16 Then Paul rising up, and with his hand bespeaking silence, said: Ye men of Israel, and you that fear God, give ear.

17 The God of the people of Israel chose our fathers, and exalted the people when they were sojourners *b* in the land of Egypt, *c* and with an high arm brought them out from thence.

18 *d* And for the space of forty years endured their manners in the desert.

19 And destroying seven nations in the land of Chanaan, *e* divided their land among them, by lot,

20 As it were after four hundred and fifty years: *f* and after these things he gave *unto them* judges, until Samuel the prophet.

21 And after that *g* they desired a king: and God gave them Saul the son of Cis, a man of the tribe of Benjamin, forty years.

22 *h* And when he had removed him, he raised them up David to be king: to whom giving testimony, he said: *i I have found David the son of Jesse, a man according to my own heart, who shall do all my wills.*

23 Of this man's seed God, *k* according to his promise, hath raised up to Israel a saviour, JESUS.

24 *l* John first preaching before his coming the baptism of penance to all the people of Israel.

25 And when John was fulfilling his course, he said: *m* I am not he whom you think me to be: but behold there cometh one after me, whose shoes of his feet I am not worthy to loose.

26 Men brethren, children of the stock of Abraham, and whosoever among you fear God, to you the word of this salvation is sent.

---

*a* A.D. 42.—*b* Exod. 1. 1.—*c* Exod. 13. 21. and 22.—*d* Exod. 16. 1.

*e* Jos. 14. 2.—*f* Judges 2. 9.—*g* 1 Kings 8. 5. and 9. 16. and 10. 1.—*h* 1 Kings 13. 14. and 16. 2.—*i* Ps. 88. 21.— *k* Isaias 11. 1.—*l* Matt. 3. 1. Mark 1. 4. Luke 3. 3.—*m* Matt. 3. 11. Mark 1. 7. John 1. 27.

27 For they that inhabited Jerusalem, and the rulers thereof, not knowing him, nor the voices of the prophets, which are read every sabbath, judging him have fulfilled them.

28 And finding no cause of death in him, *a* they desired of Pilate that they might kill him.

29 And when they had fulfilled all things that were written of him, taking him down from the tree they laid him in a sepulchre.

30 *b* But God raised him up from the dead the third day:

31 Who was seen for many days, by them who came up with him from Galilee to Jerusalem, who to this present are his witnesses to the people.

32 And we declare unto you that the promise which was made to our fathers,

33 This same God hath fulfilled to our children, raising up JESUS, as in the second Psalm also is written: *c Thou art my Son, this day have I begotten thee.*

34 And to shew that he raised him up from the dead, not to return now any more to corruption, he said thus: *d I will give you the holy things of David faithful.*

35 And therefore in another place also he saith: *e Thou shalt not suffer thy Holy One to see corruption.*

36 For David when he had served in his generation according to the will of God *f* slept: and was laid unto his fathers, and saw corruption.

37 But he whom God hath raised from the dead, saw no corruption.

38 Be it known therefore to you, men brethren, that through him forgiveness of sins is preached to you: And from all the things, from which you could not be justified by the law of Moses.

39 In him every one that believeth, is justified.

40 Beware therefore lest that come upon you which is spoken in the prophets:

41 *g Behold, ye despisers, and wonder, and perish: for I work a work in your days, a work which you will not believe, if any men shall tell it you.*

42 And as they went out, they desired them that on the next sabbath they would speak unto them these words.

43 And when the synagogue was broken up, many of the Jews, and of the strangers who served God, followed Paul and Barnabas: who speaking to them persuaded them to continue in the grace of God.

44 But the next sabbath-day the whole city almost came together to hear the word of God.

45 And the Jews seeing the multitudes, were filled with envy, and contradicted those things which were said by Paul, blaspheming.

46 Then Paul and Barnabas said boldly: To you it behoved us first to speak the word of God; but because you reject it,

---

*a* Matt. 27. 20. and 22. Mark 15. 18. Luke 23. 21. and 23. John 19. 15.—*b* Matt. 28. Mark 16. Luke 24. John 20.—*c* Ps. 2. 7.—*d* Isaias 55. 3.—*e* Ps. 15. 10.

CHAP. XIII. Ver. 34. *I will give you the holy, &c.* These are the words of the prophet Isaias, chap. lv. 3. According to the Septuagint, the sense is: *I will faithfully fulfil the promises I made to David.*

*f* 3 Kings 2. 10.—*g* Habac. 1. 5.

and judge yourselves unworthy of eternal life, behold we turn to the gentiles.

47 For so the Lord hath commanded us : *a I have set thee to be the light of the gentiles; that thou mayest be for salvation unto the utmost part of the earth.*

48 And the gentiles hearing it, were glad, and glorified the word of the Lord; and as many as were ordained to life everlasting, believed.

49 And the word of the Lord was published throughout the whole country.

50 But the Jews stirred up religious and honourable women, and the chief men of the city, and raised persecution against Paul and Barnabas; and cast them out of their coasts.

51 *b* But they, shaking off the dust of their feet against them, came to Iconium.*c*

52 And the disciples were filled with joy and with the Holy Ghost.

## CHAP. XIV.

*Paul and Barnabas preach in Iconium and Lystra: Paul heals a cripple: they are taken for gods. Paul is stoned. They preach in Derbe and Perga.*

AND it came to pass in Iconium, that they entered together into the synagogue of the Jews, and so spoke that a very great multitude both of the Jews and of the Greeks did believe.

2 But the unbelieving Jews stirred up and incensed the minds of the gentiles against the brethren.

3 A long time therefore they abode there, dealing confidently in the Lord, who gave testimony to the word of his grace, granting signs and wonders to be done by their hands.

4 And the multitude of the city was divided: and some of them indeed held with the Jews, but some with the apostles.

5 And when there was an assault made by the gentiles and the Jews with their rulers, to use them contumeliously, and to stone them:

6 *d* They understanding it, fled to Lystra and Derbe, cities of Lycaonia, and to the whole country round about, and were there preaching the gospel.

7 And there sat a certain man at Lystra, impotent in his feet, a cripple from his mother's womb, who never had walked.

8 This same heard Paul speaking. Who looking upon him, and seeing that he had faith to be healed,

9 Said with a loud voice: Stand upright on thy feet. And he leaped up and walked.

10 And when the multitude had seen what Paul had done, they lifted up their voice in the Lycaonian tongue, saying: The gods are come down to us, in the likeness of men;

11 And they called Barnabas, Jupiter: but Paul, Mercury; because he was chief speaker.

12 The priest also of Jupiter that was before the city, bringing oxen and garlands before the gate, would have offered sacrifice with the people.

13 Which when the apostles Barnabas and Paul had heard, rending their clothes, they leaped out among the people crying,

---
*a* Isaias 49. 6.—*b* Matt. 10. 14. Mark 6. 11. Luke 9. 5.—*c* A.D. 42.

*d* A.D. 43.

14 And saying: Ye men, why do ye these things? We also are mortals, men like unto you, preaching to you to be converted from these vain things, to the living God, *a* who made the heaven, and the earth, and the sea, and all things that are in them:

15 Who in times past suffered all nations to walk in their own ways.

16 Nevertheless he left not himself without testimony, doing good from heaven, giving rains, and fruitful seasons, filling our hearts with good and gladness.

17 And speaking these things, they scarce restrained the people from sacrificing to them.

18 Now there came thither certain Jews from Antioch and Iconium; and persuading the multitude, and stoning Paul, drew him out of the city, thinking him to be dead.

19 But as the disciples stood round about him, he rose up and entered into the city, and the next day he departed with Barnabas to Derbe.

20 And when they had preached the gospel to that city, and had taught many, they returned again to Lystra and to Iconium, and to Antioch:

21 Confirming the souls of the disciples, and exhorting them to continue in the faith; and that through many tribulations we must enter into the kingdom of God.

22 And when they had ordained to them priests in every church, and had prayed with fasting, they commended them to the Lord, in whom they believed.

23 And passing through Pisidia, they came into Pamphylia,

24 And having spoken the word of the Lord in Perge, they went down into Attalia:

25 *b* And thence they sailed to Antioch, from whence they had been delivered to the grace of God, unto the work which they accomplished.

26 And when they were come, and had assembled the church, they related what great things God had done with them, and how he had opened the door of faith to the gentiles.

27 And they abode no small time with the disciples.

## CHAP. XV.

*A dissension about circumcision. The decision and letter of the council of Jerusalem.*

AND *c* some coming down from Judea, taught the brethren: That except you be circumcised after the manner of Moses, you cannot be saved.

2 And when Paul and Barnabas had no small contest with them, they determined that Paul and Barnabas, and certain others of the other side, should go up to the apostles and priests to Jerusalem, about this question.

3 They therefore being brought on their way by the church, passed through Phenice and Samaria, relating the conversion of the gentiles: and they caused great joy to all the brethren.

4 And when they were come to Jerusalem, they were received by the church and by the apos-

---

*a* Gen. 1. 1. Ps. 145. 6. Apoc. 14. 7.  *b* Supra, 13. 1.— *c* A. D. 49. Gal. 5. 2.

CHRIST'S ENTRY INTO JERUSALEM.

tles and ancients, declaring how great things God had done with them.

5 But there arose some of the sect of the Pharisees that believed, saying: They must be circumcised, and be commanded to observe the law of Moses.

6 And the apostles and ancients assembled to consider this matter.

7 And when there had been much disputing, Peter rising up said to them: *a* Men brethren, you know that in former days God made choice among us, that by my mouth the gentiles should hear the word of the gospel, and believe.

8 And God, who knoweth the hearts, gave testimony, *b* giving unto them the Holy Ghost as well as to us,

9 And put no difference between us and them, purifying their hearts by faith.

10 Now therefore why tempt you God, to put a yoke upon the necks of the disciples, which neither our fathers nor we have been able to bear?

11 But by the grace of the Lord JESUS CHRIST we believe to be saved, in like manner as they also.

12 And all the multitude held their peace: and they heard Barnabas and Paul telling what great signs and wonders God had wrought among the gentiles by them.

13 And after they had held their peace, James answered, saying: Men brethren, hear me.

14 Simon hath related how God first visited to take of the gentiles a people to his name.

15 And to this agree the words of the prophets, as it is written:

16 *c After these things I will return, and will rebuild the tabernacle of David, which is fallen down, and the ruins thereof I will rebuild, and I will set it up:*

17 *That the residue of men may seek after the Lord, and all nations upon whom my name is invoked, saith the Lord who doth these things.*

18 To the Lord was his own work known from the beginning of the world.

19 For which cause I judge that they, who from among the gentiles are converted to God, are not to be disquieted.

20 But that we write unto them that they refrain themselves from the pollutions of idols, and from fornication, and from things strangled, and from blood.

21 For Moses of old time hath in every city them that preach him in the synagogues, where *d* he is read every sabbath.

22 Then it pleased the apostles and ancients with the whole church, to choose men of their own company, and to send to Antioch with Paul and Barnabas, *namely*, Judas, who was surnamed Barsabas, and Silas, chief men among the brethren,

23 Writing by their hands, The apostles and ancients brethren, to the brethren of the gentiles that are at Antioch and in Syria and Cilicia greeting.

---

*a* Supra, 10. 20.—*b* Supra, 10. 45.    *c* Amos 9. 11.—*d* Supra, 13. 27.

24 Forasmuch as we have heard that some going out from us have troubled you with words: subverting your souls, to whom we gave no commandment:

25 It hath seemed good to us, being assembled together, to choose out men, and to send them unto you with our well-beloved Barnabas and Paul,

26 Men that have given their lives for the name of our Lord JESUS CHRIST.

27 We have sent therefore Judas and Silas, who themselves also will by word of mouth tell you the same things.

28 For it hath seemed good to the Holy Ghost and to us, to lay no farther burden upon you than these necessary things:

29 That you abstain from things sacrificed to idols, and from blood, and from things strangled, and from fornication: from which things keeping yourselves, you shall do well. Fare ye well.

30 They therefore being dismissed went down to Antioch: and gathering together the multitude, delivered the epistle.

31 Which when they had read, they rejoiced for the consolation:

32 But Judas and Silas being prophets also themselves, with many words comforted the brethren, and confirmed them.

33 And after they had spent some time there, they were let go with peace by the brethren, unto them that had sent them.

34 But it seemed good unto Silas to remain there, and Judas alone departed to Jerusalem.

35 And Paul and Barnabas continued at Antioch, teaching and preaching with many others the word of the Lord.

36 ᵃAnd after some days, Paul said to Barnabas: Let us return and visit our brethren in all the cities, wherein we have preached the word of the Lord, to see how they do.

37 And Barnabas would have taken with them John also, that was surnamed Mark:

38 But Paul desired that he (as having departed from them out of Pamphylia, ᵇand not gone with them to the work) might not be received.

39 And there arose a dissension, so that they departed one from another, and Barnabas indeed taking Mark, sailed to Cyprus.

40 But Paul choosing Silas departed, being delivered by the brethren to the grace of God.

41 And he went through Syria and Cilicia, confirming the churches: commanding them to keep the precepts of the apostles and the ancients.

## CHAP. XVI.

*Paul visits the churches. He is called to preach in Macedonia. He is scourged at Philippi.*

AND ᶜhe came to Derbe and Lystra. And behold there was a certain disciple there

---

CHAP. XV. Ver. 29. *From blood, and from things strangled.* The use of these things, though of their own nature indifferent, was here prohibited, to bring the *Jews* more easily to admit of the society of the *gentiles;* and to exercise the latter in obedience. But this prohibition was but temporary, and has long since ceased to oblige; more especially in the Western Churches.

ᵃ A.D. 51. — ᵇ Supra, 13. 13. — ᶜ A.D. 51.

named Timothy, the son of a Jewish woman that believed, but his father was a gentile.

2 To this man the brethren that were in Lystra and Iconium gave a good testimony.

3 Him Paul would have to go along with him: and taking him he circumcised him, because of the Jews who were in those places. For they all knew that his father was a gentile.

4 And as they passed through the cities, they delivered unto them the decrees for to keep, that were decreed by the apostles and ancients who were at Jerusalem.

5 And the churches were confirmed in faith, and increased in number daily.

6 And when they had passed through Phrygia and the country of Galatia, they were forbidden by the Holy Ghost to preach the word in Asia.

7 And when they were come into Mysia, they attempted to go into Bithynia, and the Spirit of JESUS suffered them not.

8 And when they had passed through Mysia, they went down to Troas:

9 And a vision was shewed to Paul in the night, which was a man of Macedonia standing and beseeching him, and saying: Pass over into Macedonia, and help us.

10 And as soon as he had seen the vision, immediately we sought to go into Macedonia, being assured that God had called us to preach the gospel to them.

11 And sailing from Troas, we came with a straight course to Samothracia, and the day following to Neapolis:

12 And from thence to Philippi, which is the chief city of part of Macedonia, a colony. And we were in this city some days conferring together.

13 And upon the sabbath-day we went forth without the gate by a river-side, where it seemed that there was prayer; and sitting down we spoke to the women that were assembled.

14 And a certain woman named Lydia, a seller of purple of the city of Thyatira, one that worshipped God, did hear: whose heart the Lord opened to attend to those things which were said by Paul.

15 And when she was baptized, and her household, she besought us, saying: If you have judged me to be faithful to the Lord, come into my house and abide there. And she constrained us.

16 And it came to pass as we went to prayer, a certain girl, having a pythonical spirit, met us, who brought to her masters much gain by divining.

17 This same following Paul and us, cried out, saying: These men are the servants of the most high God, who preach unto you the way of salvation.

18 And this she did many days. But Paul being grieved, turned and said to the spirit: I command thee, in the name of JESUS CHRIST, to go out from her. And he went out the same hour.

19 But her masters seeing that the hope of their gain was gone, apprehending Paul and

---

CHAP. XVI. Ver. 16. *A pythonical spirit.* That is, a spirit pretending to divine, and tell fortunes.

Silas, brought them into the market-place to the rulers.

20 And presenting them to the magistrates, they said: These men disturb our city, being Jews:

21 And preach a fashion which it is not lawful for us to receive, nor observe, being Romans.

22 And the people ran together against them: and <sup>a</sup> the magistrates rending off their clothes, commanded them to be beaten with rods.

23 And when they had laid many stripes upon them, they cast them into prison, charging the gaoler to keep them diligently.

24 Who having received such a charge, thrust them into the inner prison, and made their feet fast in the stocks.

25 And at midnight, Paul and Silas praying, praised God. And they that were in prison heard them.

26 And suddenly there was a great earthquake, so that the foundations of the prison were shaken. And immediately all the doors were opened, and the bands of all were loosed.

27 And the keeper of the prison awaking out of his sleep, and seeing the doors of the prison open, drawing his sword, would have killed himself, supposing that the prisoners had been fled.

28 But Paul cried with a loud voice, saying: Do thyself no harm, for we all are here.

29 Then calling for a light, he went in, and trembling fell down at the feet of Paul and Silas.

---

*a* 2 Cor. 11. 25. Phil. 1. 15. 1 Thess. 2. 2.

30 And bringing them out, he said: Masters, what must I do, that I may be saved?

31 But they said: Believe in the Lord JESUS: and thou shalt be saved, and thy house.

32 And they preached the word of the Lord to him and to all that were in his house.

33 And he taking them the same hour of the night, washed their stripes: and himself was baptized, and all his house immediately.

34 And when he had brought them into his own house, he laid the table for them, and rejoiced with all his house, believing God.

35 And when the day was come, the magistrates sent the serjeants, saying: Let those men go.

36 And the keeper of the prison told these words to Paul: The magistrates have sent to let you go: now therefore depart, and go in peace.

37 But Paul said to them: They have beaten us publicly, uncondemned, men that are Romans, and have cast us into prison: and now do they thrust us out privately? Not so, but let them come,

38 And let us out themselves. And the serjeants told these words to the magistrates. And they were afraid, hearing that they were Romans.

39 And coming they besought them; and bringing them out they desired them to depart out of the city.

40 And they went out of the prison, and entered into the house of Lydia: and having seen the brethren, they comforted them, and departed.

THE COIN OF TRIBUTE.

## CHAP. XVII.

*Paul preaches to the Thessalonians and Bereans. His discourse to the Athenians.*

AND [a] when they had passed through Amphipolis and Apollonia, they came to Thessalonica, where there was a synagogue of the Jews.

2 And Paul according to his custom went in unto them; and for three sabbath-days he reasoned with them out of the scriptures,

3 Declaring and insinuating that the CHRIST was to suffer, and to rise again from the dead: and that this is JESUS CHRIST, whom I preach to you.

4 And some of them believed, and were associated to Paul and Silas, and of those that served God and of the gentiles a great multitude, and of noble women not a few.

5 But the Jews moved with envy, and taking unto them some wicked men of the vulgar sort, and making a tumult, set the city in an uproar; and besetting Jason's house, sought to bring them out unto the people.

6 And not finding them, they drew Jason and certain brethren to the rulers of the city, crying: They that set the city in an uproar are come hither also,

7 Whom Jason hath received, and these all do contrary to the decrees of Cesar, saying that there is another king, JESUS.

8 And they stirred up the people, and the rulers of the city hearing these things.

9 And having taken satisfaction of Jason, and of the rest, they let them go.

10 But the brethren immediately sent away Paul and Silas by night unto Berea. Who when they were come thither went into the synagogue of the Jews.

11 Now these were more noble than those in Thessalonica, who received the word with all eagerness, daily searching the scriptures, whether these things were so.

12 And many indeed of them believed, and of honourable women that were gentiles, and of men not a few.

13 And when the Jews of Thessalonica had knowledge that the word of God was also preached by Paul at Berea, they came thither also, stirring up and troubling the multitude.

14 And then immediately the brethren sent away Paul, to go unto the sea: but Silas and Timothy remained there.

15 And they that conducted Paul brought him as far as Athens, and receiving a commandment from him to Silas and Timothy, that they should come to him with all speed, they departed.

16 [b] Now whilst Paul waited for them at Athens, his spirit was stirred within him, seeing

---

[a] A.D. 51.

CHAP. XVII. Ver. 6. *City.* Urhem. In the Greek *oikoumenen,* the world

[b] A.D. 52.

Ver. 11. *More noble.* The Jews of *Berea* are justly commended for their eagerly embracing the truth, and searching the Scriptures to find out the texts alleged by the apostle: which was a far more generous proceeding than that of their countrymen at *Thessalonica,* who persecuted the preachers of the gospel, without examining the grounds they alleged for what they taught.

the city wholly given to idolatry.

17 He disputed therefore in the synagogue with the Jews, and with them that served God, and in the market-place, every day with them that were there.

18 And certain philosophers of the Epicureans and of the Stoics disputed with him, and some said: What is it that this word-sower would say? But others: He seemeth to be a setter forth of new gods; because he preached to them JESUS and the resurrection.

19 And taking him they brought him to Areopagus, saying: May we know what this new doctrine is which thou speakest of?

20 For thou bringest in certain new things to our ears. We would know therefore what these things mean.

21 (Now all the Athenians, and strangers that were there, employed themselves in nothing else but either in telling or in hearing some new thing.)

22 But Paul standing in the midst of Areopagus, said: Ye men of Athens, I perceive that in all things you are too superstitious.

23 For passing by and seeing your idols, I found an altar also on which was written: *To the unknown God.* What therefore you worship, without knowing it, that I preach to you,

24 ᵃ God, who made the world and all things therein, He being Lord of heaven and earth, dwelleth ᵇ not in temples made with hands.

25 Neither is he served with men's hands as though he needed anything, seeing it is he who giveth to all life, and breath, and all things:

26 And hath made of one, all mankind, to dwell upon the whole face of the earth, determining appointed times, and the limits of their habitation.

27 That they should seek God, if happily they may feel after him or find him: although he be not far from every one of us:

28 For in him we live and move and be: as some also of your own poets said, *For we are also his offspring.*

29 Being therefore the offspring of God, we must not suppose the divinity to be like unto gold or silver, or stone, the graving of art and device of man.

30 And God indeed having winked at the times of this ignorance, now declareth unto men that all should everywhere do penance.

31 Because he hath appointed a day wherein he will judge the world in equity, by the man whom he hath appointed, giving faith to all, by raising him up from the dead.

32 And when they had heard of the resurrection of the dead, some indeed mocked; but others said: We will hear thee again concerning this matter.

33 So Paul went out from among them.

34 But certain men adhering

---

ᵃ Gen. 1. 1.

---

Ver. 24. *Dwelleth not in temples.* God is not contained in temples, so as to need them for his dwelling, or any other uses, as the heathens imagined. Yet by his omnipresence he is both there and everywhere.

ᵇ Supra, 7. 48.

to him, did believe: among whom was also Dionysius the Areopagite, and a woman named Damaris, and others with them.

## CHAP. XVIII.

*Paul founds the Church of Corinth, and preaches at Ephesus, &c. Apollo goes to Corinth.*

AFTER *a* these things, departing from Athens, he came to Corinth.

2 And finding a certain Jew, named Aquila, born in Pontus, lately come from Italy, with Priscilla his wife (because that Claudius had commanded all Jews to depart from Rome), he came to them.

3 And because he was of the same trade, he remained with them and wrought: (now they were tent-makers by trade.)

4 And he reasoned in the synagogue every sabbath, bringing in the name of the Lord JESUS, and he persuaded the Jews and the Greeks.

5 And when Silas and Timothy were come from Macedonia, Paul was earnest in preaching, testifying to the Jews that JESUS is the CHRIST.

6 But they gainsaying and blaspheming, he shook his garments, and said to them: Your blood be upon your own heads: I am clean; from henceforth I will go unto the gentiles.

7 And departing thence, he entered into the house of a certain man, named Titus Justus, one that worshipped God, whose house was adjoining to the synagogue.

8 And Crispus the ruler of the synagogue believed in the Lord with all his house: and many of the Corinthians hearing believed, and were baptized.

9 And the Lord said to Paul in the night by a vision: Do not fear, but speak, and hold not thy peace.

10 Because I am with thee: and no man shall set upon thee to hurt thee; for I have much people in this city.

11 And he stayed there a year and six months, teaching among them the word of God.

12 But when Gallio was proconsul of Achaia, the Jews with one accord rose up against Paul, and brought him to the judgment-seat,

13 Saying: This man persuadeth men to worship God contrary to the law.

14 And when Paul was beginning to open his mouth, Gallio said to the Jews: If it were some matter of injustice, or an heinous deed, O you Jews, I should with reason bear with you.

15 But if they be questions of word and names, and of your law, look you to it: I will not be judge of such things.

16 And he drove them from the judgment-seat.

17 And all laying hold on Sosthenes the ruler of the synagogue, beat him before the judgment-seat: and Gallio cared for none of those things.

18 But Paul when he had stayed yet many days, taking his leave of the brethren, sailed thence into *b* Syria, (and with him Priscilla and Aquila,) *c* having shorn his head in Cenchra. For he had a vow.

---

*a* A.D. 54.

*b* A.D. 54.—*c* Num. 6. 18. Infra, 21. 24.

## CHAP. XIX.

*Paul comes to the Church at Ephesus. The miracle of the discriples.*

1 And it came to pass while Apollo was at Corinth, that Paul having passed through the upper coasts, came to Ephesus, and found certain disciples;

2 And he said to them: Have you received the Holy Ghost since ye believed? But they said to him: We have not so much as heard whether there be a Holy Ghost.

3 And he said: In what then were you baptized? Who said: In John's baptism.

4 Then Paul said: John baptized the people with the baptism of penance, saying: That they should believe in him who was to come after him, that is to say, in Jesus.

5 Having heard these things, they were baptized in the name of the Lord Jesus.

6 And when Paul had imposed his hands on them, the Holy Ghost came upon them, and they spoke with tongues and prophesied.

7 And all the men were about twelve.

8 And entering into the synagogue, he spoke boldly for the space of three months, disputing and exhorting concerning the kingdom of God.

9 But when some were hardened, and believed not, speaking evil of the way of the Lord before the multitude, departing from them, he separated the disciples, disputing daily in the school of one Tyrannus.

10 And this continued for the

THE PARABLE OF THE MAN WITHOUT A WEDDING GARMENT.

19 And he came to Ephesus, and left them there. But he himself entering into the synagogue, disputed with the Jews.
20 And when they desired him, that he would tarry a longer time, he consented not.
21 But taking his leave and saying: I will return to you again, God willing, he departed from Ephesus.
22 And going down to Cesarea, he went up *to Jerusalem*, and saluted the church, and so came down to Antioch.
23 And after he had spent some time there, he departed, and went through the country of Galatia and Phrygia, in order, confirming all the disciples.
24 Now a certain Jew named Apollo, born at Alexandria, an eloquent man, came to Ephesus, one mighty in the scriptures.
25 This man was instructed in the way of the Lord: and being fervent in spirit spoke, and taught diligently the things that are of JESUS, knowing only the baptism of John.
26 This man therefore began to speak boldly in the synagogue. Whom when Priscilla and Aquila had heard, they took him to them, and expounded to him the way of the Lord more diligently.
27 And whereas he was desirous to go to Achaia, the brethren exhorting, wrote to the disciples to receive him. Who, when he was come, helped them much who had believed.
28 For with much vigour he convinced the Jews openly, shewing by the scriptures that JESUS is the CHRIST.

## CHAP. XIX.

*Paul establishes the Church at Ephesus. The tumult of the silversmiths.*

AND *a* it came to pass while Apollo was at Corinth, that Paul having passed through the upper coasts, came to Ephesus, and found certain disciples:
2 And he said to them: Have you received the Holy Ghost since ye believed? But they said to him: We have not so much as heard whether there be a Holy Ghost.
3 And he said: In what then were you baptized? Who said: In John's baptism.
4 Then Paul said: *b* John baptized the people with the baptism of penance, saying: That they should believe in him who was to come after him, that is to say, in JESUS.
5 Having heard these things, they were baptized in the name of the Lord JESUS.
6 And when Paul had imposed his hands on them, the Holy Ghost came upon them, and they spoke with tongues and prophesied.
7 And all the men were about twelve.
8 And entering into the synagogue, he spoke boldly for the space of three months, disputing and exhorting concerning the kingdom of God.
9 But when some were hardened, and believed not, speaking evil of the way of the Lord before the multitude, departing from them, he separated the disciples, disputing daily in the school of one Tyrannus.*c*
10 And this continued for the

*a* A.D. 54.—*b* Matt. 3. 11. Mark 1. 8. Luke 3. 16. John 1. 26. Supra, 1. 5. and 11. 16.—*c* A.D. 55.

THE PARABLE OF THE MAN WITHOUT A WEDDING GARMENT.

space of two years, so that all they who dwelt in Asia heard the word of the Lord, both Jews and gentiles.

11 And God wrought by the hand of Paul more than common miracles:

12 So that even there were brought from his body to the sick handkerchiefs and aprons, and the diseases departed from them, and the wicked spirits went out of them.

13 ªNow some also of the Jewish exorcists, who went about, attempted to invoke, over them that had evil spirits, the name of the Lord JESUS, saying: I conjure you by JESUS whom Paul preacheth.

14 And there were certain men, seven sons of Sceva, a Jew, a chief priest, that did this.

15 But the wicked spirit answering, said to them: JESUS I know, and Paul I know: but who are you?

16 And the man in whom the wicked spirit was, leaping upon them and mastering them both, prevailed against them, so that they fled out of that house naked and wounded.

17 And this became known to all the Jews and the gentiles that dwelt at Ephesus: and fear fell on them all, and the name of the Lord JESUS was magnified.

18 And many of them that believed came confessing and declaring their deeds.

19 And many of them who had followed curious arts, brought together their books and burnt them before all: and counting the price of them, they found the money to be fifty thousand pieces of silver.

20 So mightily grew the word of God and was confirmed.

21 And when these things were ended, Paul purposed in the spirit, when he had passed through Macedonia and Achaia, to go to Jerusalem, saying: After I have been there I must see Rome also.

22 And sending into Macedonia two of them that ministered to him, Timothy and Erastus, he himself remained for a time in Asia.

23 Now at that time there arose no small disturbance about the way of the Lord.ᵇ

24 For a certain man named Demetrius, a silversmith, who made silver temples for Diana, brought no small gain to the craftsmen.

25 Whom he calling together, with the workmen of like occupation, said: Sirs, you know that our gain is by this trade;

26 And you see and hear that this Paul by persuasion hath drawn away a great multitude, not only of Ephesus, but almost of all Asia, saying: They are not gods which are made by hands.

27 So that not only this our craft is in danger to be set at nought, but also the temple of great Diana shall be reputed for nothing, yea and her majesty shall begin to be destroyed, whom all Asia and the world worshippeth.

28 Having heard these things, they were full of anger, and cried out, saying: Great is Diana of the Ephesians.

29 And the whole city was

ª A.D. 56.   ᵇ A.D. 57.

filled with confusion, and having caught Gaius and Aristarchus, men of Macedonia, Paul's companions, they rushed with one accord into the theatre.

30 And when Paul would have entered in unto the people, the disciples suffered him not.

31 And some also of the rulers of Asia, who were his friends, sent unto him, desiring that he would not venture himself into the theatre.

32 Now some cried one thing, some another. For the assembly was confused, and the greater part knew not for what cause they were come together.

33 And they drew forth Alexander out of the multitude, the Jews thrusting him forward. And Alexander beckoning with his hand for silence would have given the people satisfaction.

34 But as soon as they perceived him to be a Jew, all with one voice, for the space of about two hours, cried out: Great is Diana of the Ephesians.

35 And when the town-clerk had appeased the multitudes, he said: Ye men of Ephesus, what man is there that knoweth not that the city of the Ephesians is a worshipper of the great Diana, and of Jupiter's offspring?

36 Forasmuch therefore as these things cannot be gainsayed, you ought to be quiet, and to do nothing rashly.

37 For you have brought hither these men, who are neither guilty of sacrilege, nor of blasphemy against your goddess.

38 But if Demetrius and the craftsmen that are with him have a matter against any man, the courts of justice are open, and there are proconsuls; let them accuse one another.

39 And if you inquire after any other matter, it may be decided in a lawful assembly.

40 For we are even in danger to be called in question for this day's uproar: there being no man guilty (of whom we may give account) of this concourse. And when he had said these things, he dismissed the assembly.

## CHAP. XX.

*Paul passes through Macedonia and Greece; he raises a dead man to life at Troas: his discourse to the clergy of Ephesus.*

AND after the tumult was ceased, Paul calling to him the disciples, and exhorting them, took his leave, and set forward to go into Macedonia.

2 And when he had gone over those parts, and had exhorted them with many words, he came into Greece.

3 Where when he had spent three months, the Jews laid wait for him, as he was about to sail into Syria: ª so he took a resolution to return through Macedonia.

4 And there accompanied him Sopater the son of Pyrrhus, of Berea; and of the Thessalonians, Aristarchus, and Secundus, and Gaius of Derbe, and Timothy: and of Asia, Tychicus and Trophimus,

5 These going before, stayed for us at Troas.

6 But we sailed from Philippi after the days of the azymes, and came to them to Troas in five days, where we abode seven days.

---

ª A.D. 58.

CHAP. XX.   THE ACTS.   CHAP. XX.

7 And on the first day of the week, when we were assembled to break bread, Paul discoursed with them, being to depart on the morrow: and he continued his speech until midnight.

8 And there were a great number of lamps in the upper chamber where we were assembled.

9 And a certain young man named Eutychus, sitting on the window, being oppressed with a deep sleep, (as Paul was long preaching,) by occasion of his sleep fell from the third loft down, and was taken up dead.

10 To whom when Paul had gone down, he laid himself upon him; and embracing him, said: Be not troubled, for his soul is in him.

11 Then going up, and breaking bread and tasting, and having talked a long time to them until daylight, so he departed.

12 And they brought the youth alive, and were not a little comforted.

13 But we going aboard the ship, sailed to Assos, being there to take in Paul; for so he had appointed, himself purposing to travel by land.

14 And when he had met with us at Assos, we took him in and came to Mitylene.

15 And sailing thence, the day following we came over against Chios: and the next day we arrived at Samos: and the day following we came to Miletus.

16 For Paul had determined to sail by Ephesus, lest he should be stayed any time in Asia. For he hasted, if it were possible for him, to keep the day of Pentecost at Jerusalem.

17 And sending from Miletus to Ephesus, he called the ancients of the church.

18 And when they were come to him, and were together, he said to them: You know from the first day that I came into Asia, in what manner I have been with you for all the time,

19 Serving the Lord with all humility, and with tears, and temptations which befell me by the conspiracies of the Jews;

20 How I have kept back nothing that was profitable to you, but have preached it to you, and taught you publicly, and from house to house,

21 Testifying both to Jews and gentiles penance towards God, and faith in our Lord JESUS CHRIST.

22 And now behold, being bound in the Spirit, I go to Jerusalem: not knowing the things which shall befall me there:

23 Save that the Holy Ghost in every city witnesseth to me, saying: that bands and afflictions wait for me at Jerusalem.

24 But I fear none of these things, neither do I count my life more precious than myself, so that I may consummate my course and the ministry of the word which I received from the Lord JESUS, to testify the gospel of the grace of God.

25 And now behold I know

---

CHAP. XX. Ver. 7. *And on the first day of the week.* Here St. Chrysostom, with many other interpreters of the Scripture explain, that the Christians, even at this time, must have changed the Sabbath into the first day of the week (the Lord's day), as all Christians now keep it: This change was undoubtedly made by the authority of the Church: Hence the exercise of the power which Christ had given to her; for he is Lord of the sabbath.

CHAP. XX. THE ACTS. CHAP. XXI.

that all you, among whom I have gone preaching the kingdom of God, shall see my face no more.

26 Wherefore I take you to witness this day, that I am clear from the blood of all men.

27 For I have not spared to declare unto you all the counsel of God.

28 Take heed to yourselves, and to the whole flock, wherein the Holy Ghost hath placed you bishops, to rule the church of God, which he hath purchased with his own blood.

29 I know that after my departure ravening wolves will enter in among you, not sparing the flock.

30 And of your own selves shall arise men speaking perverse things, to draw away disciples after them.

31 Therefore watch, keeping in memory, that for three years I ceased not with tears to admonish every one of you night and day.

32 And now I commend you to God and to the word of his grace, who is able to build up, and to give an inheritance among all the sanctified.

33 I have not coveted any man's silver, gold, or apparel, as

34 You yourselves know: *a* for such things as were needful for me and them that are with me, these hands have furnished.

35 I have shewed you all things, how that so labouring you ought to support the weak, and to remember the word of the Lord JESUS, how he said: It is a more blessed thing to give, rather than to receive.

36 And when he had said these things, kneeling down he prayed with them all.

37 And there was much weeping among them all; and falling on the neck of Paul, they kissed him.

38 Being grieved most of all for the word which he had said, that they should see his face no more. And they brought him on his way to the ship.

CHAP. XXI.

*Paul goes up to Jerusalem. He is apprehended by the Jews in the temple.*

AND *b* when it came to pass that being parted from them we set sail, we came with a straight course to Coos, and the day following to Rhodes, and from thence to Patara.

2 And when we had found a ship sailing over to Phenice, we went aboard and set forth.

3 And when we had discovered Cyprus, leaving it on the left hand, we sailed into Syria, and came to Tyre; for there the ship was to unlade her burden.

4 And finding disciples, we tarried there seven days: who said to Paul through the Spirit, that he should not go up to Jerusalem.

5 And the days being expired, departing we went forward, they all bringing us on our way, with their wives and children, till we were out of the city: and we kneeled down on the shore, and we prayed.

6 And when we had bid one another farewell, we took ship; and they returned home.

7 But we having finished the voyage by sea, from Tyre came down to Ptolemais: and saluting

*a* 1 Cor. 4. 12. 2 Thess. 3. 8.

*b* A. D. 58.

THE WISE AND THE FOOLISH VIRGINS.

the brethren we abode one day with them.

8 And the next day departing, we came to Cesarea. And entering into the house of Philip the evangelist, *a* who was one of the seven, we abode with him.

9 And he had four daughters virgins, who did prophesy.

10 And as we tarried there for some days, there came from Judea a certain prophet, named Agabus.

11 Who when he was come to us, took Paul's girdle, and binding his own feet and hands, he said: Thus saith the Holy Ghost: The man whose girdle this is, the Jews shall bind in this manner in Jerusalem, and shall deliver him into the hands of the gentiles.

12 Which when we had heard, both we and they that are of that place, desired him that he would not go up to Jerusalem.

13 Then Paul answered, and said: What do you mean weeping and afflicting my heart? For I am ready not only to be bound, but to die also in Jerusalem, for the name of the Lord JESUS.

14 And when we could not persuade him, we ceased, saying: The will of the Lord be done.

15 And after those days, being prepared, we went up to Jerusalem.

16 And there went also with us some of the disciples from Cesarea, bringing with them one Mnason, a Cyprian, an old disciple, with whom we should lodge.

17 And when we were come to Jerusalem, the brethren received us gladly.

18 And the day following Paul went in with us unto James; and all the ancients were assembled.

19 Whom when he had saluted, he related particularly what things God had wrought among the gentiles by his ministry.

20 But they hearing it, glorified God and said to him: Thou seest, brother, how many thousands there are among the Jews that have believed: and they are all zealots for the law.

21 Now they have heard of thee that thou teachest those Jews who are among the gentiles to depart from Moses: saying that they ought not to circumcise their children, nor walk according to the custom.

22 What is it therefore? the multitude must needs come together: for they will hear that thou art come.

23 Do therefore this that we say to thee. We have four men, who have a vow on them.

24 Take these and sanctify thyself with them: and bestow on them, *b* that they may shave their heads: and all will know

---

*a* Supra, 6. 5. and 8. 5.     *b* Num. 6. 18. Supra, 18. 18.

CHAP. XXI. Ver. 8. *The evangelist.* That is, the preacher of the gospel: the same that before converted the Samaritans and baptised the eunuch, chap. viii., being one of the seven first deacons.

Ver. 24. *Keeping the law.* The law, though now no longer obligatory, was for a time observed by the Christian Jews; to bury, as it were, the synagogue with honour.

that the things which they have heard of thee are false: but that thou thyself also walkest keeping the law.

25 But as touching the gentiles that believe, *a* we have written decreeing that they should only refrain themselves from that which has been offered to idols, and from blood, and from things strangled, and from fornication.

26 Then Paul took the men, and the next day being purified with them, entered into the temple, giving notice of the accomplishment of the days of purification, until an oblation should be offered for every one of them.

27 But when the seven days were drawing to an end, those Jews that were of Asia, when they saw him in the temple, stirred up all the people, and laid hands upon them, crying out:

28 Men of Israel, help: This is the man that teacheth all men everywhere against the people, and the law, and this place: and moreover hath brought in gentiles into the temple, and hath violated this holy place.

29 (For they had seen Trophimus the Ephesian in the city with him, whom they supposed that Paul had brought into the temple.)

30 And the whole city was in an uproar: and the people ran together. And taking Paul, they drew him out of the temple, and immediately the doors were shut.

31 And as they went about to kill him, it was told the tribune of the band, that all Jerusalem was in confusion.

32 Who forthwith taking with him soldiers and centurions, ran down to them. And when they saw the tribune and the soldiers, they left off beating Paul.

33 Then the tribune coming near took him, and commanded him to be bound with two chains: and demanded who he was, and what he had done.

34 And some cried one thing, some another, among the multitude. And when he could not know the certainty for the tumult, he commanded him to be carried into the castle.

35 And when he was come to the stairs, it fell out that he was carried by the soldiers, because of the violence of the people.

36 For the multitude of the people followed after, crying: Away with him.

37 And as Paul was about to be brought into the castle, he said to the tribune: May I speak something to thee? Who said: Canst thou speak Greek?

38 Art not thou that Egyptian who before these days didst raise a tumult, *b* and didst lead forth into the desert four thousand men that were murderers?

39 But Paul said to him: I am a Jew of Tarsus in Cilicia, a citizen of no mean city. And I beseech thee, suffer me to speak to the people.

40 And when he had given him leave, Paul standing on the stairs, beckoned with his hand to the people. And a great silence being made, he spoke unto them in the Hebrew tongue, saying:

---

*a* Supra, 15. 20. and 29.   *b* A.D. 55.

## CHAP. XXII.

*Paul declares to the people the history of his conversion. He escapes scourging by claiming the privilege of a Roman.*

MEN *a* brethren, and fathers, hear ye the account which I now give unto you.

2 (And when they heard that he spoke to them in the Hebrew tongue, they kept the more silence.)

3 And he saith: I am a Jew, born at Tarsus in Cilicia, but brought up in this city, at the feet of Gamaliel, taught according to the truth of the law of the fathers, zealous for the law, as also all you are this day:

4 *b* Who persecuted this way unto death, binding and delivering into prisons both men and women.

5 As the high-priest doth bear me witness, and all the ancients: *c* from whom also receiving letters to the brethren, I went to Damascus, that I might bring them bound from thence to Jerusalem to be punished.

6 And it came to pass, as I was going, and drawing nigh to Damascus at mid-day, that suddenly from heaven there shone round about me a great light:

7 And falling on the ground, I heard a voice saying to me: Saul, Saul, why persecutest thou me?

8 And I answered: Who art thou, Lord? And he said to me: I am JESUS of Nazareth, whom thou persecutest.

9 And they that were with me, saw indeed the light, but they heard not the voice of him that spoke with me.

10 And I said: What shall I do, Lord? And the Lord said to me: Arise, and go to Damascus; and there it shall be told thee of all things that thou must do.

11 And whereas I did not see for the brightness of that light, being led by the hand by my companions, I came to Damascus.

12 And one Ananias, a man according to the law, having testimony of all the Jews who dwelt there,

13 Coming to me, and standing by me, said to me: Brother Saul, look up. And I the same hour looked upon him.

14 But he said: The God of our fathers hath pre-ordained thee that thou shouldst know his will, and see the Just One, and shouldst hear the voice from his mouth.

15 For thou shalt be his witness to all men, of those things which thou hast seen and heard.

16 And now why tarriest thou? Rise up, and be baptized, and wash away thy sins, invoking his name.

17 And it came to pass when I was come again to Jerusalem, *d* and was praying in the temple, that I was in a trance.

18 And saw him saying unto me: Make haste, and get thee quickly out of Jerusalem: because they will not receive thy testimony concerning me.

---

*a* A.D. 58.—*b* Supra, 8. 3.—*c* Supra, 9. 2.

*d* A.D. 57.

CHAP. XXII. Ver. 9. *Heard not the voice.* That is, they distinguished not the words, though they heard the voice. Acts ix. 7.

Ver. 14. *Just One.* Our Saviour, who appeared to St. Paul. Acts ix. 17.

19 And I said: Lord, they know that I cast into prison, and beat in every synagogue, them that believed in thee.

20 And when the blood of Stephen thy witness was shed, ᵇI stood by and consented, and kept the garments of them that killed him.

21 And he said to me: Go, for unto the gentiles afar off will I send thee.

22 And they heard him until this word, and then lifted up their voice, saying: Away with such an one from the earth: for it is not fit that he should live.

23 And as they cried out, and threw off their garments, and cast dust into the air,

24 The tribune ᶜ commanded him to be brought into the castle, and that he should be scourged and tortured: to know for what cause they did so cry out against him.

25 And when they had bound him with thongs, Paul saith to the centurion that stood by him: Is it lawful for you to scourge a man that is a Roman, and uncondemned?

26 Which the centurion hearing, went to the tribune, and told him, saying: What art thou about to do? For this man is a Roman citizen.

27 And the tribune, coming, said to him: Tell me, art thou a Roman? But he said: Yes.

28 And the tribune answered: I obtained the being free of this city with a great sum. And Paul said: But I was born so.

29 Immediately therefore they departed from him that were about to torture him. The tribune also was afraid after he understood that he was a Roman citizen, and because he had bound him.

30 But on the next day meaning to know more diligently for what cause he was accused by the Jews, he loosed him, and commanded the priests to come together and all the council: and bringing forth Paul, he set him before them.

## CHAP. XXIII.

*Paul stands before the council. The Jews conspire his death. He is sent away to Cesarea.*

AND ᵈ Paul looking upon the council, said: Men brethren, I have conversed with all good conscience before God, until this present day.

2 And the high-priest Ananias commanded them that stood by him to strike him on the mouth.

3 Then Paul said to him: God shall strike thee, thou whited wall. For sittest thou to judge me according to the law, and contrary to the law commandest me to be struck?

4 And they that stood by said: Dost thou revile the high-priest of God?

5 And Paul said: I knew not, brethren, that he is the high-priest. For it is written: *ᵉThou shalt not speak evil of the prince of thy people.*

6 And Paul knowing that the one part were Sadducees, and the other Pharisees, cried out in the council: Men brethren, ᶠI am a Pharisee, the son of Pharisees: concerning the hope and

ᵃ Supra, 8. a.—ᵇ Supra, 7. 57.—ᶜ i.e. Lysias.

ᵈ A.D. 55.—ᵉ Exod. 22. 22.—ᶠ Phil. 3. 5.

JESUS WASHES HIS DISCIPLES' FEET.

resurrection of the dead I am called in question.

7 And when he had so said, there arose a dissension between the Pharisees and the Sadducees; and the multitude was divided.

8 ᵃ For the Sadducees say that there is no resurrection, neither angel, nor spirit: but the Pharisees confess both.

9 And there arose a great cry. And some of the Pharisees rising up, strove, saying: We find no evil in this man. What if a spirit hath spoken to him, or an Angel?

10 And when there arose a great dissension, the tribune fearing lest Paul should be pulled in pieces by them, commanded the soldiers to go down, and to take him by force from among them, and to bring him into the castle.

11 And the night following the Lord standing by him, said: Be constant; for as thou hast testified of me in Jerusalem, so must thou bear witness also at Rome.

12 And when day was come, some of the Jews gathered together, and bound themselves under a curse, saying, that they would neither eat nor drink till they killed Paul.

13 And they were more than forty men that had made this conspiracy.

14 Who came to the chief priests and the ancients, and said: We have bound ourselves under a great curse that we will eat nothing till we have slain Paul.

15 Now therefore do you with the council signify to the tribune, that he bring him forth to you, as if you meant to know something more certain touching him. And we, before he come near, are ready to kill him.

16 Which when Paul's sister's son had heard of their lying in wait, he came, and entered into the castle and told Paul.

17 And Paul calling to him one of the centurions, said: Bring this young man to the tribune, for he hath something to tell him.

18 And he taking him, brought him to the tribune, and said: Paul the prisoner desired me to bring this young man unto thee, who hath something to say to thee.

19 And the tribune taking him by the hand, went aside with him privately and asked him: What is it that thou hast to tell me?

20 And he said: The Jews have agreed to desire thee, that thou wouldst bring forth Paul to-morrow into the council, as if they meant to inquire something more certain touching him.

21 But do not thou give credit to them; for there lie in wait for him more than forty men of them, who have bound themselves by oath, neither to eat nor to drink till they have killed him: and they are now ready, looking for a promise from thee.

22 The tribune therefore dismissed the young man, charging him that he should tell no man that he had made known these things unto him.

23 Then having called two centurions, he said to them: Make ready two hundred sol-

---
ᵃ Matt. 22. 22.

diers to go as far as Cesarea, and seventy horsemen, and two hundred spearmen for the third hour of the night.

24 And provide beasts, that they may set Paul on, and bring him safe to Felix the governor.

25 (For he feared lest perhaps the Jews might take him away by force and kill him, and he should afterwards be slandered as if he was to take money.) And he wrote a letter after this manner:

26 Claudius Lysias to the most excellent governor Felix, greeting.

27 This man being taken by the Jews, and ready to be killed by them, I rescued coming in with an army, understanding that he is a Roman:

28 And meaning to know the cause which they objected unto him, I brought him forth into their council.

29 Whom I found to be accused concerning questions of their law; but having nothing laid to his charge worthy of death or of bands.

30 And when I was told of ambushes that they had prepared for him, I sent him to thee, signifying also to his accusers to plead before thee. Farewell.

31 Then the soldiers, according as it was commanded them, taking Paul, brought him by night to Antipatris.

32 And the next day leaving the horsemen to go with him, they returned to the castle.

33 Who when they were come to Cesarea, and had delivered the letter to the governor, did also present Paul before him.

34 And when he had read it, and had asked of what province he was: and understood that he was of Cilicia:

35 I will hear thee, said he, when thy accusers come. And he commanded him to be kept in Herod's judgment-hall.

## CHAP. XXIV.

*Paul defends his innocence before Felix the governor. He preaches the faith to him.*

AND after five days the high-priest Ananias came down, with some of the ancients, and one Tertullus an orator, who went to the governor against Paul.

2 And Paul being called for, Tertullus began to accuse him saying: Whereas through thee we live in much peace, and many things are rectified by thy providence,

3 We accept it always and in all places, most excellent Felix, with all thanksgiving.

4 But that I be no further tedious to thee, I desire thee of thy clemency to hear us in few words.

5 We have found this to be a pestilent man, and raising seditions among all the Jews throughout the world, and author of the sedition of the sect of the Nazarenes.

6 Who also hath gone about to profane the temple: whom we having apprehended would also have judged according to our law.

7 But Lysias the tribune coming upon us, with great violence took him away out of our hands,

8 Commanding his accusers to come to thee: of whom thou mayest thyself, by examination,

have knowledge of all these things, whereof we accuse him.

9 And the Jews also added, and said that these things were so.

10 Then Paul answered, (the governor making a sign to him to speak:) Knowing that for many years thou hast been judge over this nation, I will with good courage answer for myself:

11 That thou mayest understand that there are yet but twelve days since I went up to adore in Jerusalem:

12 And neither in the temple did they find me disputing with any man, or causing any concourse of the people, neither in the synagogues, nor in the city:

13 Neither can they prove unto thee the things whereof they now accuse me.

14 But this I confess to thee, that according to the sect which they call heresy, so I serve the Father and my God, believing all things which are written in the law and the prophets:

15 Having hope in God, which these also themselves look for, that there shall be a resurrection of the just and unjust.

16 And herein do I endeavour to have always a conscience without offence towards God and towards men.

17 Now after many years I came to bring alms to my nation and offerings and vows:

18 ᵃIn which I was found purified in the temple: neither with multitude nor with tumult:

19 By certain Jews of Asia, who ought to have been here before thee, and to accuse, if they had anything against me:

20 Or let these men themselves say, if they found in me any iniquity, when standing before their council,

21 Except it be for this one voice only, that I cried standing among them, ᵇConcerning the resurrection of the dead am I judged this day by you.

22 And Felix put them off, having most certain knowledge of this way, saying: When Lysias the tribune shall come down, I will hear you.

23 And he commanded a centurion to keep him, and that he should be easy, and that he should not prohibit any of his friends to minister unto him.

24 And after some days, Felix coming with Drusilla his wife, who was a Jew, sent for Paul, and heard of him the faith that is in CHRIST JESUS.

25 And as he treated of justice and chastity, and of the judgment to come, Felix being terrified, answered: For this time go thy way; but when I have a convenient time I will send for thee.

26 Hoping also withal, that money should be given him by Paul; for which cause also oftentimes sending for him, he spoke with him.

27 ᶜBut when two years were ended, Felix had for successor Portius Festus. And Felix being willing to shew the Jews a pleasure, left Paul bound.

## CHAP. XXV.

*Paul appeals to Cæsar. King Agrippa desires to hear him.*

NOW ᵈwhen Festus was come into the province, after

---

ᵃ Supra, 21. 26.

ᵇ Supra, 23. 6. — ᶜ A.D. 60. — ᵈ A.D. 60.

three days he went up to Jerusalem from Cesarea.

2 And the chief priests and principal men of the Jews went unto him against Paul; and they besought him,

3 Requesting favour against him, that he would command him to be brought to Jerusalem, laying wait to kill him in the way.

4 But Festus answered: That Paul was kept in Cesarea; and that he himself would very shortly depart thither.

5 Let them therefore, saith he, among you that are able, go down with me, and accuse him, if there be any crime in the man.

6 And having tarried among them no more than eight or ten days, he went down to Cesarea, and the next day he sat in the judgment-seat, and commanded Paul to be brought.

7 Who being brought, the Jews stood about him, who were come down from Jerusalem, objecting many and grievous causes which they could not prove;

8 Paul making answer for himself: Neither against the law of the Jews, nor against the temple, nor against Cesar, have I offended in anything.

9 But Festus willing to shew the Jews a pleasure, answering Paul, said: Wilt thou go up to Jerusalem, and there be judged of these things before me?

10 Then Paul said: I stand at Cesar's judgment-seat where I ought to be judged. To the Jews I have done no injury, as thou very well knowest.

11 For if I have injured them, or have committed anything worthy of death, I refuse not to die. But if there be none of these things whereof they accuse me, no man may deliver me to them: I appeal to Cesar.

12 Then Festus having conferred with the council, answered: Hast thou appealed to Cesar? To Cesar shalt thou go.

13 And after some days king Agrippa and Bernice came down to Cesarea to salute Festus.

14 And as they tarried there many days, Festus told the king of Paul, saying: A certain man was left prisoner by Felix.

15 About whom, when I was at Jerusalem, the chief priests and the ancients of the Jews came unto me, desiring condemnation against him.

16 To whom I answered: It is not the custom of the Romans to condemn any man before that he who is accused have his accusers present, and have liberty to make his answer, to clear himself of the things laid to his charge

17 When therefore they were come hither, without any delay, on the day following, sitting in the judgment-seat, I commanded the man to be brought.

18 Against whom, when the accusers stood up, they brought no accusation of things which I thought ill of:

19 But had certain questions of their own superstition against him, and of one JESUS deceased, whom Paul affirmed to be alive.

20 I therefore being in doubt of this manner of question, asked him whether he would go to Jerusalem, and there be judged of these things.

21 But Paul appealing to be reserved unto the hearing of Augustus, I commanded him to

THE LAST SUPPER.

be kept, till I might send him to Cesar.

22 And Agrippa said to Festus: I would also hear the man myself. To-morrow, said he, thou shalt hear him.

23 And on the next day, when Agrippa and Bernice were come with great pomp, and had entered into the hall of audience, with the tribunes and principal men of the city, at Festus's commandment, Paul was brought forth.

24 And Festus saith: King Agrippa, and all ye men who are here present with us, you see this man, about whom all the multitude of the Jews dealt with me at Jerusalem, requesting and crying out that he ought not to live any longer.

25 Yet have I found nothing that he hath committed worthy of death. But forasmuch as he himself hath appealed to Augustus, I have determined to send him.

26 Of whom I have nothing certain to write to my lord. For which cause I have brought him forth before you, and especially before thee, O king Agrippa, that examination being made, I may have what to write.

27 For it seemeth to me unreasonable to send a prisoner, and not to signify the things laid to his charge.

## CHAP. XXVI. *

*Paul gives an account to Agrippa of his life, conversion, and calling.*

THEN *a* Agrippa said to Paul: Thou art permitted to speak for thyself. Then Paul stretching forth his hand, began to make his answer.

2 I think myself happy, O king Agrippa, that I am to answer for myself this day before thee, touching all the things whereof I am accused by the Jews.

3 Especially as thou knowest all, both customs and questions, that are among the Jews: Wherefore I beseech thee to hear me patiently.

4 And my life indeed from my youth, which was from the beginning among my own nation in Jerusalem, all the Jews do know:

5 Having known me from the beginning (if they will give testimony) that according to the most sure sect of our religion I lived a Pharisee.

6 And now for the hope of the promise that was made by God to the fathers do I stand subject to judgment.

7 Unto which, our twelve tribes, serving night and day, hope to come, for which hope, O king, I am accused by the Jews.

8 Why should it be thought a thing incredible, that God should raise the dead?

9 And I indeed did formerly think that I ought to do many things contrary to the name of JESUS of Nazareth.

10 *b* Which also I did at Jerusalem, and many of the saints did I shut up in prison, having received authority of the chief priests; and when they were put to death, I brought the sentence.

11 And oftentimes punishing them, in every synagogue, I

---

*a* A.D. 60.   *b* Supra, 8. 3.

compelled them to blaspheme: and being yet more mad against them, I persecuted them even unto foreign cities.

12 "Whereupon when I was going to Damascus with authority and permission of the chief priests,

13 At mid-day, O king, I saw in the way a light from heaven above the brightness of the sun, shining round about me and them that were in company with me.

14 And when we were all fallen down on the ground, I heard a voice speaking to me in the Hebrew tongue: Saul, Saul, why persecutest thou me? It is hard for thee to kick against the goad.

15 And I said: Who art thou, Lord? And the Lord answered: I am JESUS whom thou persecutest.

16 But rise up and stand upon thy feet; for to this end have I appeared to thee, that I may make thee a minister and a witness of those things which thou hast seen, and of those things wherein I will appear to thee,

17 Delivering thee from the people, and from the nations unto which now I send thee:

18 To open their eyes, that they may be converted from darkness to light, and from the power of satan to God, that they may receive forgiveness of sins, and a lot among the saints by the faith that is in me.

19 Whereupon, O king Agrippa, I was not incredulous to the heavenly vision:

20 ᵇ But to them first that are at Damascus, and at Jerusalem, and unto all the country of Judea, and to the gentiles did I preach, that they should do penance, and turn to God, doing works worthy of penance.

21 For this cause the Jews, when I was in the temple, ᶜ having apprehended me, went about to kill me.

22 But being aided by the help of God, I stand unto this day, witnessing both to small and great, saying no other thing than those which the prophets and Moses did say should come to pass:

23 That CHRIST should suffer, and that he should be the first that should rise from the dead, and should shew light to the people and to the gentiles

24 As he spoke these things and made his answer, Festus said with a loud voice: Paul, thou art beside thyself: much learning doth make thee mad.

25 And Paul said: I am not mad, most excellent Festus, but I speak words of truth and soberness.

26 For the king knoweth of these things, to whom also I speak with confidence. For I am persuaded that none of these things are hidden from him. For neither was any of these things done in a corner.

27 Believest thou the prophets, O king Agrippa? I know that thou believest.

28 And Agrippa said to Paul: In a little thou persuadest me to become a Christian.

29 And Paul said: I would to God, that both in a little and in much, not only thou, but also all that hear me this day, should become such as I also am, except these bands.

ᵃ Supra, 9. 2.—ᵇ Supra, 9. 20.   ᶜ Supra, 21. 31.

30 And the king rose up, and the governor, and Bernice, and they that sat with them.

31 And when they were gone aside, they spoke among themselves, saying: This man hath done nothing worthy of death or of bands.

32 And Agrippa said to Festus: This man might have been set at liberty, if he had not appealed to Cesar.

### CHAP. XXVII.

*Paul is shipped for Rome. His voyage and shipwreck.*

AND[a] when it was determined that he should sail into Italy, and that Paul with the other prisoners should be delivered to a centurion, named Julius, of the band Augusta,

2 [b] Going on board a ship of Adrumetum, we launched, meaning to sail by the coasts of Asia, Aristarchus the Macedonian of Thessalonica continuing with us.

3 And the day following we came to Sidon. And Julius treating Paul courteously, permitted him to go to his friends, and to take care of himself.

4 And when we had launched from thence we sailed under Cyprus, because the winds were contrary.

5 And sailing over the sea of Cilicia and Pamphylia, we came to Lystra, which is in Lycia :

6 And there the centurion finding a ship of Alexandria sailing into Italy, removed us into it.

7 And when for many days we had sailed slowly, and were scarce come over against Gnidus, the wind not suffering us,

———

[a] A.D 60.—[b] 2 Cor. 11. 25.

we sailed near Crete by Salmone:

8 And with much ado sailing by it, we came into a certain place which is called Goodhavens, nigh to which was the city of Thalassa.

9 And when much time was spent, and when sailing now was dangerous, because the fast was now past, Paul comforted them,

10 Saying to them: Ye men, I see that the voyage beginneth to be with injury and much damage, not only of the lading and ship, but also of our lives.

11 But the centurion believed the pilot and the master of the ship, more than those things which were said by Paul.

12 And whereas it was not a commodious haven to winter in, the greatest part gave counsel to sail thence, if by any means they might reach Phenice to winter there, which is a haven of Crete looking towards the south-west and north-west.

13 And the south wind gently blowing, thinking that they had obtained their purpose, when they had loosed from Asson, they sailed close by Crete.

14 But not long after there arose against it a tempestuous wind called Euro-aquilo.

15 And when the ship was caught, and could not bear up against the wind, giving up the ship to the winds, we were driven.

16 And running under a certain island that is called Cauda, we had much work to come by the boat.

17 Which being taken up, they used helps, under-girding the ship; and fearing lest they should fall into the quicksands,

they let down the sail yard, and so were driven.

18 And we being mightily tossed with the tempest, the next day they lightened the ship.

19 And the third day they cast out with their own hands the tackling of the ship.

20 And when neither sun nor stars appeared for many days, and no small storm lay on us, all hope of our being saved was now taken away.

21 And after they had fasted a long time, Paul standing forth in the midst of them, said: You should indeed, O ye men, have hearkened unto me, and not have loosed from Crete, and have gained this harm and loss.

22 And now I exhort you to be of good cheer. For there shall be no loss of any man's life among you, but only of the ship.

23 For an Angel of God, whose I am, and whom I serve, stood by me this night,

24 Saying: Fear not, Paul; thou must be brought before Cesar: and behold God hath given thee all them that sail with thee.

25 Wherefore, sirs, be of good cheer: for I believe God, that it shall be so, as it hath been told me.

26 And we must come unto a certain island.

27 But after the fourteenth night was come, as we were sailing in Adria, about midnight the ship-men deemed that they discovered some country:

28 Who also sounding, found twenty fathoms; and going on a little farther they found fifteen fathoms.

29 Then fearing lest we should fall upon rough places, they cast four anchors out of the stern, and wished for the day.

30 But as the ship-men sought to fly out of the ship, having let down the boat into the sea, under colour as though they would have cast anchors out of the fore-part of the ship,

31 Paul said to the centurion and to the soldiers: Except these stay in the ship, you cannot be saved.

32 Then the soldiers cut off the ropes of the boat, and let her fall off.

33 And when it began to be light, Paul besought them all to take meat, saying: This day is the fourteenth day that you expect and remain fasting, taking nothing.

34 Wherefore I pray you to take some meat for your health's sake: for there shall not an hair of the head of any of you perish.

35 And when he had said these things, taking bread, he gave thanks to God in the sight of them all; and when he had broken it, he began to eat.

36 Then were they all of better cheer, and they also took some meat.

37 And we were in all in the ship, two hundred threescore and sixteen souls.

38 And when they had eaten enough, they lightened the ship, casting the wheat into the sea.

39 And when it was day, they knew not the land: but they discovered a certain creek that had a shore, into which they minded, if they could, to thrust in the ship.

40 And when they had taken up the anchors, they committed themselves to the sea, loosing

THE AGONY IN THE GARDEN.

withal the rudder-bands; and hoisting up the main-sail to the wind, they made towards shore.

41 And when we were fallen into a place where two seas met, they run the ship aground: and the fore-part indeed, sticking fast, remained unmoveable; but the hinder part was broken with the violence of the sea.

42 And the soldiers' counsel was, that they should kill the prisoners; lest any of them, swimming out, should escape.

43 But the centurion, willing to save Paul, forbade it to be done: and he commanded that they who could swim, should cast themselves first into the sea, and save themselves and get to land:

44 And the rest, some they carried on boards, and some on those things that belonged to the ship. And so it came to pass, that every soul got safe to land.

## CHAP. XXVIII.

*Paul, after three months' stay in Melita, continues his voyage, and arrives at Rome. His conference there with the Jews.*

AND when we had escaped, then we knew that the island was called Melita. But the barbarians shewed us no small courtesy.

2 For, kindling a fire they refreshed us all, because of the present rain and of the cold.

3 And when Paul had gathered together a bundle of sticks, and had laid them on the fire, a viper coming out of the heat, fastened on his hand.

4 And when the barbarians saw the beast hanging on his hand, they said one to another:

Undoubtedly this man is a murderer, who though he hath escaped the sea, yet vengeance doth not suffer him to live.

5 And he indeed shaking off the beast into the fire, suffered no harm.

6 But they supposed that he would begin to swell up, and that he would suddenly fall down and die. But expecting long, and seeing that there came no harm to him, changing their minds, they said that he was a god.

7 Now in these places were possessions of the chief man of the island named Publius, who receiving us, for three days entertained us courteously.

8 And it happened that the father of Publius lay sick of a fever, and of a bloody flux. To whom Paul entered in: and when he had prayed, and laid his hands on him, he healed him.

9 Which being done, all that had diseases in the island came, and were healed:

10 Who also honoured us with many honours, and when we were to sail, they laded us with such things as were necessary.

11 [a] And after three months, we sailed in a ship of Alexandria, that had wintered in the island, whose sign was the Castors.

12 And when we were come to Syracuse, we tarried there three days.

13 From thence compassing by the shore, we came to Rhegium: and after one day the south wind blowing, we came the second day to Puteoli:

14 Where finding brethren,

---

[a] A.D. 61.

we were desired to tarry with them seven days: and so we went to Rome.

15 And from thence when the brethren had heard of us, they came to meet us as far as Appii Forum and the Three Taverns, whom when Paul saw, he gave thanks to God, and took courage.

16 And when we were come to Rome, Paul was suffered to dwell by himself with a soldier that kept him.

17 And after the third day he called together the chief of the Jews. And when they were assembled, he said to them: Men brethren, I having done nothing against the people, or the custom of our fathers, was delivered prisoner from Jerusalem into the hands of the Romans,

18 Who when they had examined me, would have released me, for that there was no cause of death in me:

19 But the Jews contradicting it, I was constrained to appeal unto Cesar; not that I had anything to accuse my nation of.

20 For this cause therefore I desired to see you and to speak to you. Because that for the hope of Israel, I am bound with this chain.

21 But they said to him: We neither received letters concerning thee from Judea, neither did any of the brethren that came hither, relate or speak any evil of thee.

22 But we desire to hear of thee what thou thinkest: for as concerning this sect, we know that it is gainsayed everywhere.

23 And when they had appointed him a day, there came very many to him unto his lodgings; to whom he expounded, testifying the kingdom of God, and persuading them concerning JESUS, out of the law of Moses and the prophets, from morning until evening.

24 And some believed the things that were said: but some believed not.

25 And when they agreed not among themselves, they departed, Paul speaking this one word: Well did the Holy Ghost speak to our fathers by Isaias the prophet,

26 Saying: "*Go to this people, and say to them: With the ear you shall hear, and shall not understand: and seeing you shall see, and shall not perceive.*

27 *For the heart of this people is grown gross, and with their ears have they heard heavily, and their eyes they have shut: lest perhaps they should see with their eyes, and hear with their ears, and understand with their heart, and should be converted, and I should heal them.*

28 Be it known therefore to you that this salvation of God is sent to the gentiles, and they will hear it.

29 And when he had said these things, the Jews went out from him, having much reasoning among themselves

30 And he remained two whole years *b* in his own hired lodging: and he received all that came in to him,

31 Preaching the kingdom of God, and teaching the things which concern the Lord JESUS CHRIST with all confidence, without prohibition.

*a* Isaias 6. 9. Matt. 13, 14. Mark 4, 12. Luke 8. 10. John 12. 40. Rom. 11. 8.—
*b* Until A.D. 63.

# THE
# EPISTLE OF ST. PAUL THE APOSTLE TO THE ROMANS.

*St. Paul wrote this Epistle at Corinth, when he was preparing to go to Jerusalem with the charitable contributions collected in Achaia and Macedonia for the relief of the Christians in Judea; which was about twenty-four years after our Lord's Ascension. It was written in Greek, but at the same time translated into Latin for the benefit of those who did not understand that language. And though it is not the first of his Epistles in the order of time, yet it is first placed on account of the sublimity of the matter contained in it, of the pre-eminence of the place to which it was sent, and in veneration of the Church.*

## CHAP. I.

*He commends the faith of the Romans, whom he longs to see. The philosophy of the heathens, being void of faith and humility, betrayed them into shameful sins.*

PAUL a servant of JESUS CHRIST, called to be an apostle, separated unto the gospel of God,

2 Which he had promised before by his prophets in the holy scriptures,

3 Concerning his Son, who was made to him of the seed of David according to the flesh,

4 Who was predestinated the Son of God in power according to the spirit of sanctification, by the resurrection of our Lord JESUS CHRIST from the dead,

5 By whom we have received grace and apostleship for obedience to the faith in all nations for his name,

6 Among whom are you also the called of JESUS CHRIST:

7 To all that are at Rome the beloved of God, called *to be* saints. Grace to you and peace from God our Father, and from the Lord JESUS CHRIST.

8 First I give thanks to my God through JESUS CHRIST for you all, because your faith is spoken of in the whole world.

9 For God is my witness, whom I serve in my spirit in the gospel of his Son, that without ceasing I make a commemoration of you:

10 Always in my prayers, making request, if by any means now at length I may have a prosperous journey by the will of God to come unto you.

11 For I long to see you, that I may impart unto you some spiritual grace, to strengthen you:

12 That is to say, that I may be comforted together in you, by that which is common to us both, your faith and mine.

---

CHAP. I. Ver. 4. *Predestinated, &c.* Christ, as man, was predestinated to be the Son of God: and declared to be so (as the apostle here signifies) *first*, by *power*, that is, by his working stupendous miracles; *secondly*, by the *spirit of sanctification*, that is, by his infinite sanctity; *thirdly*, by his *resurrection*, or raising himself from the dead.

13 And I would not have you ignorant, brethren, that I have often purposed to come unto you, (and have been hindered hitherto,) that I might have some fruit among you also, even as among other gentiles.

14 To the Greeks and to the barbarians, to the wise and to the unwise, I am a debtor.

15 So (as much as is in me) I am ready to preach the gospel to you also that are at Rome.

16 For I am not ashamed of the gospel. For it is the power of God unto salvation to every one that believeth, to the Jew first and to the Greek.

17 For the justice of God is revealed therein from faith unto faith: as it is written: *a The just man liveth by faith.*

18 For the wrath of God is revealed from heaven, against all ungodliness and injustice of those men that detain the truth of God in injustice:

19 Because that which is known of God is manifest in them. For God hath manifested it unto them.

20 For the invisible things of him, from the creation of the world, are clearly seen, being understood by the things that are made: his eternal power also and divinity: so that they are inexcusable.

21 *b* Because that, when they knew God, they have not glorified him as God, or given thanks: but became vain in their thoughts, and their foolish heart was darkened.

22 For professing themselves to be wise they became fools.

23 *c* And they changed the glory of the incorruptible God into the likeness of the image of a corruptible man, and of birds and of four-footed beasts and of creeping things.

24 Wherefore God gave them up to the desires of their heart, *d* unto uncleanness, to dishonour their own bodies among themselves:

25 Who changed the truth of God into a lie : and worshipped and served the creature rather than the Creator, who is blessed for ever. Amen.

26 For this cause God delivered them up to shameful affections. For their women have changed the natural use into that use which is against nature.

27 And in like manner the men also, leaving the natural use of the women, have burned in their lusts one towards another, men with men working that which is filthy, and receiving in themselves the recompense which was due to their error.

28 And as they liked not to have God in their knowledge; God delivered them up to a reprobate sense, to do those things which are not convenient.

29 Being filled with all iniquity, malice, fornication, avarice, wickedness, full of envy, murder, contention, deceit, malignity, whisperers,

30 Detractors, hateful to God,

---

*a* Habac. 2. 4. Gal. 3. 11. Heb. 10. 38.
*b* Ephes. 4. 17.

*c* Ps. 105. 20. Jer. 11. 10.—*d* Gal. 5. 19. Ephes. 4. 19. and 5. 3. Col. 3. 5. 1 Thess. 2. 3. and 4. 7.

Ver. 28. *God delivered them up.* Not by being author of their sins, but by withdrawing his grace, and so permitting them, in punishment of their pride, to fall into those shameful sins.

JUDAS BETRAYS HIS MASTER.

contumelious, proud, haughty, inventors of evil things, disobedient to parents,

31 Foolish, dissolute, without affection, without fidelity, without mercy.

32 Who, having known the justice of God, did not understand that they, who do such things, are worthy of death: and not only they that do them, but they also that consent to them that do them.

## CHAP. II.

*The Jews are censured, who make their boast of the law, and keep it not. He declares who are the true Jews.*

WHEREFORE thou art inexcusable, O man, whosoever thou art that judgest. [a] For wherein thou judgest another, thou condemnest thyself. For thou dost the same things which thou judgest.

2 For we know that the judgment of God is according to truth against them that do such things.

3 And thinkest thou this, O man, that judgest them who do such things, and dost the same, that thou shalt escape the judgment of God?

4 Or despisest thou the riches of his goodness, and patience, and long-suffering? [b] knowest thou not that the benignity of God leadeth thee to penance?

5 But according to thy hardness and impenitent heart, thou treasurest up to thyself wrath, against the day of wrath and revelation of the just judgment of God,

6 [c] Who will render to every man according to his works.

7 To them indeed, who, according to patience in good work, seek glory and honour and incorruption, eternal life:

8 But to them that are contentious, and who obey not the truth, but give credit to iniquity, wrath and indignation.

9 Tribulation and anguish upon every soul of man that worketh evil, of the Jew first and also of the Greek:

10 But glory and honour and peace to every one that worketh good, to the Jew first and also the Greek.

11 [d] For there is no respect of persons with God.

12 For whosoever have sinned without the law, shall perish without the law: and whosoever have sinned in the law, shall be judged by the law.

13 [e] For not the hearers of the law are just before God; but the doers of the law shall be justified.

14 For when the gentiles who have not the law, do by nature those things that are of the law; these having not the law, are a law to themselves:

15 Who shew the work of the law written in their hearts, their conscience bearing witness to them, and their thoughts between themselves accusing, or also defending one another,

16 In the day when God shall judge the secrets of men by JESUS CHRIST, according to my gospel.

17 [f] But if thou art called a Jew, and restest in the law, and makest thy boast of God,

---

[a] Matt. 7. 2.—[b] Wis. 9. 24. 2 Pet. 3. 2.—[c] Matt. 16. 27.

[d] Deut. 10. 17. 2 Par. 19. 7. Job 34. 19. Wis. 6. 8. Eccli. 35. 15. Acts 10. 34. Ephes. 6. 9. Col. 3. 25. 1 Pet. 1. 17.—[e] Matt. 7. 21. Jas. 1. 22.—[f] Apoc. 11. 9.

18 And knowest his will, ᵃ and approvest the more profitable things, being instructed by the law,

19 Art confident that thou thyself art a guide of the blind, a light of them that are in darkness,

20 An instructor of the foolish, a teacher of infants, having the form of knowledge and of truth in the law.

21 Thou therefore that teachest another, teachest not thyself: thou that preachest that men should not steal, stealest:

22 Thou that sayest, men should not commit adultery, committest adultery: thou that abhorrest idols, committest sacrilege:

23 Thou that makest thy boast of the law, by transgression of the law dishonourest God.

24 ᵇ (*For the name of God through you is blasphemed among the gentiles, as it is written.*)

25 Circumcision profiteth indeed if thou keep the law; but if thou be a transgressor of the law, thy circumcision is made uncircumcision.

26 If then the uncircumcised keep the justice of the law, shall not this uncircumcision be counted for circumcision?

27 ᶜ And shall not that which by nature is uncircumcision, if it fulfil the law, judge thee who by the letter and circumcision art a transgressor of the law?

28 ᵈ For it is not he is a Jew, that is so outwardly: nor is that circumcision which is outward in the flesh,

29 But he is a Jew that is one inwardly; and the circumcision is that of the heart, in the spirit, not in the letter: whose praise is not of men, but of God.

## CHAP. III.

*The advantages of the Jews. All men are sinners, and none can be justified by the works of the law; but only by the grace of Christ.*

WHAT advantage then hath the Jew, or what is the profit of circumcision?

2 Much every way. First indeed, ᵉ because the words of God were committed to them.

3 For what if some of them have not believed? / shall their unbelief make the faith of God without effect? God forbid.

4 ᵍ But God is true: and every man a liar, as it is written: ʰ *That thou mayest be justified in thy words, and mayest overcome when thou art judged.*

5 But if our injustice commend the justice of God, what shall we say? Is God unjust, who executeth wrath?

6 (I speak according to man.) God forbid; otherwise how shall God judge this world?

7 For if the truth of God hath more abounded through my lie unto his glory, why am I also yet judged as a sinner?

8 And not rather (as we are slandered, and as some affirm that we say) let us do evil, that there may come good? whose damnation is just.

---

ᵃ Phil. 1. 10.—ᵇ Isaias 52. 5. Ezech. 36. 20.—ᶜ Matt. 12. 42.—ᵈ Isaias 48.

ᵉ Infra, 9. 4.—/ 2 Tim. 2. 13.—ᵍ John 3. 33. Ps. 115. 11.—ʰ Ps. 50. 6.

CHAP. III. Ver. 4. *God only is essentially true.* All men in their own capacity are liable to lies and errors: nevertheless God, who is the *truth*, will make good his promise of keeping his Church in all *truth.* See St. John xvi. 17.

9 What then? Do we excel them? No, not so. *a* For we have charged both Jews, and Greeks, that they are all under sin;

10 As it is written: *b There is not any man just,*

11 *There is none that understandeth, there is none that seeketh after God.*

12 *All have turned out of the way, they are become unprofitable together: there is none that doth good, there is not so much as one.*

13 *c Their throat is an open sepulchre, with their tongues they have dealt deceitfully. d The venom of asps is under their lips.*

14 *e Whose mouth is full of cursing and bitterness:*

15 *f Their feet swift to shed blood.*

16 *Destruction and misery in their ways.*

17 *And the way of peace they have not known.*

18 *g There is no fear of God before their eyes.*

19 *h* Now we know that what things soever the law speaketh, it speaketh to them that are in the law; that every mouth may be stopped, and all the world may be made subject to God.

20 Because by the works of the law no flesh shall be justified before him. For by the law is the knowledge of sin.

21 But now without the law the justice of God is made manifest; being witnessed by the law and the prophets.

22 Even the justice of God by faith of JESUS CHRIST, unto all and upon all them that believe in him: for there is no distinction.

23 For all have sinned; and do need the glory of God.

24 Being justified freely by his grace, through the redemption that is in CHRIST JESUS.

25 Whom God hath proposed to be a propitiation, through faith in his blood, to the shewing of his justice, for the remission of former sins.

26 Through the forbearance of God, for the shewing of his justice in this time: that he himself may be just, and the justifier of him who is of the faith of JESUS CHRIST.

27 Where is then thy boasting? It is excluded. By what law? Of works? No, but by the law of faith.

28 For we account a man to be justified by faith without the works of the law.

29 Is he the God of the Jews only? Is he not also of the gentiles? Yes, of the gentiles also.

30 For it is one God that justifieth circumcision by faith and uncircumcision through faith.

---

*a* Gal. 3. 22. Supra, 1. 17. Infra, 11. 9.—*b* Ps. 13. 3.—*c* Ps. 5. 11. Jas. 3. 8.—*d* Ps. 139. 4.—*e* Ps. 9. 7.—*f* Isaias 59. 7. Prov. 1. 16.—*g* Ps. 35. 2.—*h* Gal. 2. 16.

Ver. 10. *There is not any man just,* viz., by virtue either of the law of nature, or of the law of *Moses;* but only by faith and grace.

Ver. 22. *By faith,* &c. The faith to which the apostle here attributes man's justification, is not a presumptuous *assurance* of our being justified; but a firm and lively *belief* of all that God has revealed or promised: *Heb.* xi. *A faith working through charity* in Jesus Christ, *Gal.* v. 6. In short, *a faith* which takes in hope, love, repentance, and the use of the Sacraments. And *the works* which he here excludes are only the *works of the law;* that is, such as are done by the law of nature, or that of *Moses,* antecedent to the faith of Christ: but by no means such as follow faith and proceed from it.

CHAP. IV. TO THE ROMANS. CHAP. IV.

31 Do we then destroy the law through faith? God forbid: but we establish the law.

## CHAP. IV.

*Abraham was not justified by works done, as of himself: but by grace, and by faith; and that before he was circumcised. Gentiles by faith are his children.*

WHAT shall we say then that Abraham hath found, who is our father according to the flesh?

2 For if Abraham were justified by works, he hath whereof to glory, but not before God.

3 For what saith the Scripture? *ᵃAbraham believed God, and it was reputed to him unto justice.*

4 Now to him that worketh, the reward is not reckoned according to grace, but according to debt.

5 But to him that worketh not, yet believeth in him that justifieth the ungodly, his faith is reputed to justice according to the purpose of the grace of God.

6 As David also termed the blessedness of a man, to whom God reputeth justice without works:

7 *Blessed are they whose ᵇiniquities are forgiven, and whose sins are covered.*

8 *Blessed is the man to whom the Lord hath not imputed sin.*

9 This blessedness then doth it remain in the circumcision only, or in the uncircumcision also? For we say that unto Abraham faith was reputed to justice.

10 How then was it reputed? When he was in circumcision, or in uncircumcision? Not in circumcision, but in uncircumcision.

11 ᶜ And he received the sign of circumcision, a seal of the

---

ᵃ Gen. 15. 6. Gal. 3. 6. Jas. 2. 23. Mac. 11. 62.

ᵇ Ps. 31. 1.—ᶜ Gen. 17. 10. and 11.

CHAP. IV. Ver. 2. *By works.* Done by his own strength, without the grace of God, and faith in him. — Ibid. *Not before God.* Whatever glory or applause such works might procure from men, they would be of no value in the sight of God.

Ver. 3. *Reputed*, &c. By God, who *reputeth* nothing otherwise than it is. However, we may gather from this word, that when we are justified, our justification proceedeth from God's free grace and bounty; and not from any efficacy which any act of ours could have of its own nature, abstracting from God's grace.

Ver. 4. *To him that worketh.* Viz., as of his own fund, or by his own strength.. Such a man, says the apostle, challenges his reward as a *debt*, due to his own performances; whereas he who *worketh not*, that is, who presumeth not upon any works done by his own strength; but seeketh justice through faith and grace, is freely justified by God's grace.

Ver. 7. *Blessed are they whose iniquities are forgiven, and whose sins are covered.* That is, blessed are those who, by doing penance, have obtained pardon and remission of their sins, and also are *covered*; that is, newly clothed with the habit of grace, and vested with the stole of charity.

Ver. 8. *Blessed is the man to whom the Lord hath not imputed sin.* That is, blessed is the man who hath retained his baptismal innocence, that no grievous sin can be imputed to him. And likewise, blessed is the man who, after falling into sin, hath done penance and leads a virtuous life by frequenting the sacraments necessary for obtaining the grace to prevent a relapse, that sin is no more imputed to him.

Ver. 9. *In the circumcision, &c.* That is, is it only for the Jews that are circumcised? No, says the apostle, but also for the uncircumcised gentiles; who by faith and grace may come to justice; as Abraham did before he was circumcised.

CHRIST BEFORE THE HIGH PRIEST ANNAS.

justice of the faith which he had being uncircumcised: that he might be the father of all them that believe being uncircumcised, that unto them also it may be reputed to justice.

12 And might be the father of circumcision, not to them only that are of the circumcision, but to them also that follow the steps of the faith that is in the uncircumcision of our father Abraham.

13 *a* For not through the law was the promise to Abraham, or to his seed, that he should be heir of the world; but through the justice of faith.

14 For if they who are of the law be heirs; faith is made void, the promise is made of no effect.

15 For the law worketh wrath. For where there is no law; neither is there transgression.

16 Therefore is it of faith, that according to grace the promise might be firm to all the seed, not to that only which is of the law, but to that also which is of the faith of Abraham, who is the father of us all,

17 (As it is written: *b I have made thee a father of many nations,*) before God, whom he believed, who quickeneth the dead; and calleth those things that are not, as those that are.

18 Who against hope believed in hope; that he might be made the father of many nations according to that which was said to him: *c So shall thy seed be.*

19 And he was not weak in faith; neither did he consider his own body now dead, whereas he was almost an hundred years old, nor the dead womb of Sara.

20 In the promise also of God he staggered not by distrust: but was strengthened in faith, giving glory to God:

21 Most fully knowing that whatsoever he has promised, he is able also to perform.

22 And therefore it was reputed to him unto justice.

23 Now it is not written only for him, that it was reputed to him unto justice,

24 But also for us, to whom it shall be reputed, if we believe in him, *d* that raised up JESUS CHRIST our Lord from the dead,

25 *e* Who was delivered up for our sins, and rose again for our justification.

## CHAP. V.

*The grounds we have for hope in Christ. Sin and death came by Adam; grace and life by Christ.*

BEING justified therefore by faith, let us have peace with God through our Lord JESUS CHRIST.

2 *f* By whom also we have access through faith into this grace wherein we stand, and glory in the hope of the glory of the sons of God.

3 And not only so; but we

---

*a* Gal. 3. 16. Heb. 11. 9.—*b* Gen. 17. 4.

Ver. 14. *Be heirs.* That is, if they alone, who follow the ceremonies of the law, be heirs of the blessings promised to Abraham; then that faith which was so much praised in him, will be found to be of little value. And the very promise will be made void, by which he was promised to be the father, not of the Jews only, but of all nations of believers.

Ver. 15. *The law worketh wrath.* The law, abstracting from faith and grace, worketh wrath occasionally, by being an occasion of many transgressions which provoke God's wrath.

*c* Gen. 15. 5.—*d* 1 Pet. 1. 21.—*e* Isaias 53. 6. 1 Pet. 1. 3.—*f* Ephes. 2. 18.

glory also in tribulations, <sup>a</sup> knowing that tribulation worketh patience:

4 And patience trial; and trial hope.

5 <sup>b</sup> And hope confoundeth not: because the charity of God is poured forth in our hearts, by the Holy Ghost who is given to us.

6 For why did Christ, when as yet we were weak, according to the time, <sup>c</sup> die for the ungodly?

7 For scarce for a just man will one die: yet perhaps for a good man some one would dare to die.

8 But God commendeth his charity towards us: because when as yet we were sinners, according to the time,

9 Christ died for us: much more therefore being now justified by his blood, shall we be saved from wrath through him.

10 For if, when we were enemies, we were reconciled to God by the death of his Son: much more being reconciled, shall we be saved by his life.

11 And not only so; but also we glory in God through our Lord JESUS CHRIST, by whom we have now received reconciliation.

12 Wherefore as by one man sin entered into this world, and by sin death; and so death passed upon all men in whom all have sinned.

13 For until the law sin was in the world; but sin was not imputed when the law was not.

14 But death reigned from Adam unto Moses, even over them also who have not sinned after the similitude of the transgression of Adam, who is a figure of him who was to come.

15 But not as the offence, so also the gift. For if by the offence of one many died: much more the grace of God and the gift, by the grace of one man JESUS CHRIST, hath abounded unto many.

16 And not as it was by one sin, so also is the gift. For judgment indeed was by one unto condemnation; but grace is of many offences, unto justification.

17 For if by one man's offence death reigned through one: much more they who receive abundance of grace, and of the gift, and of justice, shall reign in life through one JESUS CHRIST.

18 Therefore as by the offence of one, unto all men to condemnation: so also by the justice of one, unto all men to justification of life.

19 <sup>d</sup> For as by the disobedience of one man, many were made sinners: so also by the obedience of one, many shall be made just.

20 Now the law entered in that sin might abound. And

---

<sup>d</sup> Phil. 2. 8. and 9.

<sup>a</sup> Jas. 1. 3.—<sup>b</sup> Ps. 22. 6.—<sup>c</sup> Heb. 9. 14. 1 Pet. 3. 18.

in the manner it was afterwards, when they transgressed the known written law of God.

CHAP. V. Ver. 12. *By one man.* Adam, from whom we all contracted original sin.

Ver. 13. *Not imputed.* That is, men knew not, or made no account of sin; neither was it *imputed* to them.

Ver. 20. *That sin might abound.* Not as if the law were given on purpose for sin to abound: but that it so happened through man's perversity, taking occasion of sinning more, from the prohibition of sin.

where sin abounded, grace did more abound.

21 That as sin hath reigned to death: so also grace might reign by justice unto life everlasting, through JESUS CHRIST our Lord.

## CHAP. VI.

*The Christian must die to sin, and live to God.*

WHAT shall we say then? shall we continue in sin that grace may abound?

2 God forbid. For we that are dead to sin, *a* how shall we live any longer therein?

3 Know ye not that all we, who are baptized in CHRIST JESUS, are baptized in his death?

4 *b* For we are buried together with him by baptism into death: that as Christ is risen from the dead by the glory of the Father, *c* so we also may walk in newness of life.

5 For if we have been planted together in the likeness of his death, we shall be also in the likeness of his resurrection.

6 Knowing this, that our old man is crucified with him, that the body of sin may be destroyed, to the end that we may serve sin no longer.

7 For he that is dead is justified from sin.

8 Now if we be dead with Christ, we believe that we shall live also together with Christ:

9 Knowing that Christ rising again from the dead, dieth now no more, death shall no more have dominion over him.

10 For in that he died to sin, he dieth once; but in that he liveth, he liveth unto God:

11 So do you also reckon that you are dead to sin, but alive unto God in CHRIST JESUS our Lord.

12 Let not sin therefore reign in your mortal body, so as to obey the lusts thereof.

13 *d* Neither yield ye your members as instruments of iniquity unto sin: but present yourselves to God as those that are alive from the dead, and your members as instruments of justice unto God.

14 For sin shall not have dominion over you: for you are not under the law, but under grace.

15 What then? Shall we sin, because we are not under the law, but under grace? God forbid.

16 *e* Know you not, that to whom you yield yourselves servants to obey, his servants you are whom you obey, whether it be of sin, unto death, or of obedience, unto justice.

17 But thanks be to God, that you were the servants of sin, but have obeyed from the heart, unto that form of doctrine, into which you have been delivered.

18 Being then free from sin, we have been made servants of justice.

19 I speak an human thing

---

*a* 2 Pet. 2. 22.—*b* Gal. 3. 27. Col. 2. 12.—*c* Ephes. 4. 13. Heb. 12. 1. 1 Pet. 2. 1. and 4. 2.

---

CHAP. VI. Ver. 6. *Old man—body of sin.* Our corrupt state, subject to sin and concupiscence, coming to us from Adam, is called our *old man*, as our state, reformed in and by Christ, is called the *new man*. And the vices and sins which then ruled in us are named *the body of sin*.

*d* Col. 3. 5.—*e* John 8. 34. 2 Pet. 2. 19.

because of the infirmity of your flesh. For as you have yielded your members to serve uncleanness and iniquity, unto iniquity; so now yield your members to serve justice, unto sanctification.

20. For when you were the servants of sin, you were free men to justice.

21 What fruit therefore had you then in those things, of which you are now ashamed? For the end of them is death.

22 But now being made free from sin, and become servants to God, you have your fruit unto sanctification, and the end life everlasting.

23 For the wages of sin is death. But the grace of God, life everlasting, in CHRIST JESUS our Lord.

## CHAP. VII.

*We are released by Christ from the law, and from the guilt of sin: though the inclination to it still tempt us.*

KNOW you not, brethren, (for I speak to them that know the law,) that the law hath dominion over a man, as long as it liveth?

2 *a* For the woman that hath an husband, whilst her husband liveth is bound to the law. But if her husband be dead, she is loosed from the law of her husband.

3 Therefore, whilst her husband liveth, she shall be called an adulteress, if she be with another man: but if her husband be dead, she is delivered from the law of her husband:

so that she is not an adulteress if she be with another man.

4 Therefore, my brethren, you also are become dead to the law by the body of Christ; that you may belong to another, who is risen again from the dead, that we may bring forth fruit to God.

5 For when we were in the flesh, the passions of sin which were by the law did work in our members, to bring forth fruit unto death.

6 But now we are loosed from the law of death, wherein we were detained: so that we should serve in newness of spirit, and not in the oldness of the letter.

7 What shall we say then? Is the law sin? God forbid. But I did not know sin, but by the law: for I had not known concupiscence, if the law did not say: *b Thou shalt not covet.*

8 But sin taking occasion by the commandment wrought in me all manner of concupiscence. For without the law sin was dead.

9 And I lived some time without the law. But when the commandment came, sin revived,

10 And I died. And the commandment that was ordained to life, the same was found to be unto death to me.

11 For sin, taking occasion by the commandment, seduced me, and by it killed *me*.

---

*b* Exod. 20. 17. Deut. 5. 21.

Ver. 8. *Sin taking occasion.* Sin, or concupiscence, which is called *sin*, because it is from sin, and leads to sin, which was asleep before, was wakened by the prohibition: the law not being the cause thereof, nor properly *giving occasion* to it: but *occasion being taken* by our corrupt nature to resist the commandment laid upon us.

---

*a* 1 Cor. 7. 39.

CHAP. VII. Ver. 1. *As long as it liveth;* or, as long as he liveth.

ST. PETER DENIES OUR LORD.

12 ᵃ Wherefore the law indeed is holy, and the commandment holy, and just, and good.

13 Was that then which is good made death unto me? God forbid. But sin, that it may appear sin, by that which is good, wrought death in me: that sin by the commandment might become sinful above measure.

14 For we know that the law is spiritual, but I am carnal, sold under sin.

15 For that which I work, I understand not. For I do not that good which I will, but the evil which I hate, that I do.

16 If then I do that which I will not, I consent to the law, that it is good.

17 Now then it is no more I that do it; but sin that dwelleth in me.

18 For I know that there dwelleth not in me, that is to say, in my flesh, that which is good. For to will is present with me, but to accomplish that which is good, I find not.

19 For the good which I will, I do not; but the evil which I will not, that I do.

20 Now if I do that which I will not, it is no more I that do it, but sin that dwelleth in me.

21 I find then a law, that when I have a will to do good, evil is present with me.

22 For I am delighted with the law of God, ᵇ according to the inward man:

23 But I see another law in my members, fighting against the law of my mind, and captivating me in the law of sin, that is in my members.

24 Unhappy man that I am, who shall deliver me from the body of this death?

25 The grace of God by JESUS CHRIST our Lord. Therefore I myself, with the mind, serve the law of God; but, with the flesh, the law of sin.

## CHAP. VIII.

*There is no condemnation to them that, being justified by Christ, walk not according to the flesh, but according to the spirit. Their strong hope and love of God.*

THERE is now therefore no condemnation to them that are in CHRIST JESUS, who walk not according to the flesh.

2 For the law of the spirit of life, in CHRIST JESUS, hath delivered me from the law of sin and of death.

3 ᶜ For what the law could not do, in that it was weak through the flesh; God sending his own Son, in the likeness of sinful flesh, and of sin hath condemned sin in the flesh.

4 That the justification of the law might be fulfilled in us, who

---

ᵃ 1 Tim. 1. 8.

---

Ver. 13. *That it may appear sin,* or *that sin may appear,* viz, to be the monster it is, which is even capable to take occasion from that which is good to work death.

Ver. 15. *I do not that good which I will,* &c. The apostle here describes the disorderly motions of passion and concupiscence: which oftentimes in us get the start of reason: and by means of which even good men suffer in the inferior appetite what their will abhors: and are much hindered in the accomplishment of the desires of their spirit and mind. But these evil motions (though they are called the *law of sin,* because they come from original sin, and violently tempt and incline to sin) as long as the will does not consent to them, are not sins, because they are not voluntary.

ᵇ 1 Pet. 3. 4.—ᶜ Acts 15. 10. Heb. 9. 15.

walk not according to the flesh, but according to the spirit.

5 For they that are according to the flesh, mind the things that are of the flesh; but they that are according to the spirit, mind the things that are of the spirit.

6 For the wisdom of the flesh is death; but the wisdom of the spirit is life and peace.

7 Because the wisdom of the flesh is an enemy to God: for it is not subject to the law of God, neither can it be.

8 And they who are in the flesh cannot please God.

9 But you are not in the flesh, but in the spirit, if so be that the Spirit of God dwell in you. Now if any man have not the Spirit of Christ, he is none of his.

10 And if Christ be in you, the body indeed is dead because of sin, but the spirit liveth because of justification.

11 <sup>a</sup> And if the Spirit of him, that raised up JESUS from the dead, dwell in you; he that raised up JESUS CHRIST from the dead shall quicken also your mortal bodies, because of his Spirit that dwelleth in you.

12 Therefore, brethren, we are debtors, not to the flesh, to live according to the flesh.

13 For if you live according to the flesh, you shall die. But if by the Spirit you mortify the deeds of the flesh, you shall live.

14 For whosoever are led by the Spirit of God, they are the sons of God.

15 <sup>b</sup> For you have not received the spirit of bondage again in fear: but you have received the spirit of <sup>c</sup> adoption of sons, whereby we cry: Abba, (Father).

16 For the Spirit himself giveth testimony to our spirit, that we are the sons of God.

17 And if sons, heirs also: heirs indeed of God, and joint-heirs with Christ: yet so if we suffer with him, that we may be also glorified with him.

18 For I reckon that the sufferings of this time are not worthy to be compared with the glory to come, that shall be revealed in us.

19 For the expectation of the creature waiteth for the revelation of the sons of God.

20 For the creature was made subject to vanity, not willingly,

---

<sup>c</sup> Gal. 4. 5.

CHAP. VIII. Ver. 16. *The Spirit himself*, &c. By the inward motions of divine love, and the peace of conscience, which the children of God experience, they have a kind of testimony of God's favour; by which they are much strengthened in their hope of their justification and salvation: but yet not so as to pretend to an absolute assurance; which is not usually granted in this mortal life: during which we are taught to *work out our salvation with fear and trembling*, Phil. ii. 12. And *that he who thinketh himself to stand must take heed lest he fall*, 1 Cor. x. 12. See also Rom. xi. 20, 21, 22.

Ver. 19. *The expectation of the creature*, &c. He speaks of the corporeal creation, made for the use and service of man; and, by occasion of his sin, made subject to vanity, that is, to a perpetual instability, tending to corruption and other defects: so that by a figure of speech it is here said to groan and be in labour, and to long for its deliverance, which is then to come, when sin shall reign no more; and God shall raise the bodies and unite them to their souls never more to separate, and to be in everlasting happiness in heaven.

---

<sup>a</sup> Acts 3. 15. and 4. 18. and 5. 30. and 13. 33. Supra, 4. 24. 1 Cor. 6. 14. — <sup>b</sup> 2 Tim. 1. 7.

but by reason of him that made it subject, in hope:

21 Because the creature also itself shall be delivered from the servitude of corruption, into the liberty of the glory of the children of God.

22 For we know that every creature groaneth, and travaileth in pain even till now.

23 And not only it, but ourselves also, who have the firstfruits of the Spirit, even we ourselves groan within ourselves, waiting for the adoption of the sons of God, the redemption of our body.

24 For we are saved by hope. But hope that is seen, is not hope. For what a man seeth, why doth he hope for?

25 But if we hope for that which we see not: we wait for it with patience.

26 Likewise the Spirit also helpeth our infirmity. For we know not what we should pray for as we ought: but the Spirit himself asketh for us with unspeakable groanings.

27 And he that searcheth the hearts, knoweth what the Spirit desireth; because he asketh for the saints according to God.

28 And we know that to them that love God, all things work together unto good, to such as according to *his* purpose are called *to be* saints.

29 For whom he foreknew, he also predestinated to be made conformable to the image of his Son: that he might be the firstborn amongst many brethren.

30 And whom he predestinated; them he also called. And whom he called; them he also justified. And whom he justified; them he also glorified.

31 What shall we then say to these things? If God be for us, who is against us?

32 ᵃ He that spared not even his own Son: but delivered him up for us all, how hath he not also, with him, given us all things?

33 Who shall accuse against the elect of God? God that justifieth.

34 Who is he that shall condemn? CHRIST JESUS that died, yea that is risen also again, who is at the right hand of God, who also maketh intercession for us.

35 Who then shall separate us from the love of Christ? shall tribulation? or distress? or famine? or nakedness? or danger? or persecution? or the sword?

36 (As it is written: ᵇ *For thy sake we are put to death all the day long. We are accounted as sheep for the slaughter.*)

37 But in all these things we overcome because of him that hath loved us.

38 For I am sure that neither death, nor life, nor Angels, nor

---

ᵃ Gen. 22. 12.—ᵇ Ps. 43. 22.

---

Ver. 26. *Asketh for us.* The Spirit is said to ask, and desire for the saints, and to pray in us; inasmuch as he inspireth prayer, and teacheth us to pray.

Ver. 29. *He also predestinated, &c.* That is, God hath preordained that all his elect should be conformable to the image of his Son. We must not here offer to dive into the secrets of God's eternal election: only firmly believe that all our *good*, in time and eternity, flows *originally* from God's free *goodness*; and all our *evil* from man's free-will.

Ver. 38. *I am sure.* That is, I am *persuaded:* as it is in the Greek, πεπεισμαι.

principalities, nor powers, nor things present, nor things to come, nor might,

39 Nor height, nor depth, nor any other creature shall be able to separate us from the love of God, which is in CHRIST JESUS our Lord.

## CHAP. IX.

*The apostle's concern for the Jews. God's election is free, and not confined to their nation.*

I SPEAK the truth in Christ, I lie not, my conscience bearing me witness in the Holy Ghost.

2 That I have great sadness, and continual sorrow in my heart.

3 <sup>a</sup> For I wished myself to be an anathema from Christ, for my brethren, who are my kinsmen according to the flesh,

4 Who are Israelites, to whom belongeth the adoption *as of* children, and the glory, and the testament, and the giving of the law, and the service *of God*, and the promises:

5 Whose are the fathers, and of whom is Christ according to the flesh, who is over all things, God blessed for ever, Amen.

6 Not as though the word of God hath miscarried. For all are not Israelites that are of Israel:

---

<sup>a</sup> Acts 9. 2. 1 Cor. 15. 9.

---

CHAP. IX. Ver. 3. *Anathema*; a curse. The apostle's concern and love for his countrymen the Jews was so great that he was willing to suffer even an *anathema*, or curse, for their sake; or any evil that could come upon him, without his offending God.

Ver. 6. *All are not Israelites*, &c. Not all who are the carnal seed of *Israel*, are true *Israelites* in God's account: who, as by his free grace he heretofore preferred Isaac before Ismael, and Jacob

260

7 Neither are all they, that are the seed of Abraham, children: <sup>b</sup> *but in Isaac shall thy seed be called:*

8 That is to say, not they that are the children of the flesh, are the children of God: but they <sup>c</sup> that are the children of the promise, are accounted for the seed.

9 For this is the word of promise: <sup>d</sup> *According to this time will I come; and Sara shall have a son.*

10 And not only she. <sup>e</sup> But when Rebecca also had conceived at once, of Isaac our father.

11 For when the *children* were not yet born, nor had done any good or evil (that the purpose of God according to election might stand),

12 Not of works, but of him that calleth, it was said to

---

<sup>b</sup> Gen. 21. 12.—<sup>c</sup> Gal. 4. 28.—<sup>d</sup> Gen. 18. 10.—<sup>e</sup> Gen. 25. 24.

---

before Esau, so he could, and did by the like free grace, election and mercy, raise up spiritual children by faith to Abraham and Israel, from among the gentiles, and prefer them before the carnal Jews.

Ver. 11. *Not yet born*, &c. By this example of these twins, and the preference of the younger to the elder, the drift of the apostle is, to shew that God, in his election, mercy, and grace, is not tied to any particular nation, as the Jews imagined, nor to any prerogative of birth, or any foregoing merits. For us, antecedently to his grace, he sees no merits in any, but finds all involved in sin. In the common mass of condemnation; and all children of wrath: there is no one whom he might not justly leave in that mass; so that whomsoever he delivers from it, he delivers in his mercy; and whomsoever he leaves in it, he leaves in his justice. As when, of two equally criminal, the king is pleased out of pure mercy to pardon one, whilst he suffers justice to take place in the execution of the other.

JESUS BEFORE CAIPHAS.

her: *"The elder shall serve the younger.*

13 As it is written: *ᵇJacob I have loved, but Esau I have hated.*

14 What shall we say then? Is there injustice with God? God forbid.

15 For he saith to Moses: *ᶜI will have mercy on whom I will have mercy; and I will shew mercy to whom I will shew mercy.*

16 So then it is not of him that willeth, nor of him that runneth, but of God that sheweth mercy.

17 For the scripture saith to Pharao: *ᵈTo this purpose have I raised thee, that I may shew my power in thee; and that my name may be declared throughout all the earth.*

18 Therefore he hath mercy on whom he will; and, whom he will he hardeneth.

19 Thou wilt say therefore to me: Why doth he then find fault? for who resisteth his will?

20 O man, who art thou that repliest against God? *ᵉShall the thing formed say to him that formed it, why hast thou made me thus?*

21 Or hath not the potter power over the clay, of the same lump, to make one vessel unto honour, and another unto dishonour?

22 What if God, willing to shew his wrath, and to make his power known, endured with much patience vessels of wrath, fitted for destruction,

23 That he might shew the riches of his glory on the vessels of mercy, which he hath prepared unto glory?

24 Even us, whom also he hath called, not only of the Jews, but also of the gentiles.

25 As in Osee he saith: *ƒI will call that which was not my people, my people; and her that was not beloved, beloved; and her, that had not obtained mercy, one that hath obtained mercy.*

26 *ᵍAnd it shall be, in the place where it was said unto them, you are not my people: there they shall be called the sons of the living God.*

27 And Isaias crieth out con-

---

ᵃ Gen. 25. 23.—ᵇ Mal. 1. 2.—ᶜ Exod. 33. 19.—ᵈ Exod. 9. 16.—ᵉ Wis. 15. 7. Isaias 45. 9. Jer. 18. 6.

ƒ Osee 2. 24.  1 Pet. 2. 10.—ᵍ Osee 1. 10.

Ver. 16. *Not of him that willeth, &c.* That is, by any power or strength of his own, abstracting from the grace of God.

Ver. 17. *To this purpose, &c.* Not that God made him on purpose that he should sin, and so be damned: but foreseeing his obstinacy in sin, and the abuse of his own free-will, he raised him up to be a mighty king, to make a more remarkable example of him: and that his power might be better known: and his justice, in punishing him, published throughout the earth.

Ver. 18. *He hardeneth.* Not by being the cause, or author of his sin, but by withholding his grace, and so leaving him in his sin, in punishment of his past demerits.

Ver. 21. *The potter.* This similitude is used, only to shew that we are not to dispute with our Maker: nor to reason with him why he does not give as much grace to one as to another: for since the whole lump of our clay is vitiated by sin, it is owing to his goodness and mercy that he makes out of it so many vessels of honour: and it is no more than just that others, in punishment of their unrepented of sins, should be given up to be vessels of dishonour.

Ver. 27. *A remnant.* That is, a small number only of the *children of Israel* shall be converted and saved. How perversely is this text quoted for the salvation of men of all religions, when it speaks only of the converts of the children of Israel!

cerning Israel : *If the number of the children of Israel be as the sand of the sea ; a remnant shall be saved.*

28 *For he shall finish his word, and cut it short in justice : because a short word shall the Lord make upon the earth.*

29 And as Isaias foretold : *Unless the Lord of Sabaoth had left us a seed, we had been made as Sodom, and we had been like unto Gomorrha.*

30 What then shall we say? That the gentiles, who followed not after justice, have attained to justice, even the justice that is of faith.

31 But Israel, by following after the law of justice, is not come unto the law of justice.

32 Why so? because *they* sought *it* not by faith, but as it were of works. For they stumbled at the stumbling-stone.

33 As it is written : *Behold I lay in Sion a stumbling-stone and a rock of scandal: and whosoever believeth in him shall not be confounded.*

## CHAP. X.

*The end of the law is faith in Christ: which the Jews, refusing to submit to, cannot be justified.*

BRETHREN, the will of my heart, indeed, and my prayer to God, is for them unto salvation.

2 For I bear them witness, that they have a zeal of God, but not according to knowledge.

3 For they not knowing the justice of God, and seeking to establish their own, have not submitted themselves to the justice of God.

4 For the end of the law is Christ, unto justice to every one that believeth.

5 For Moses wrote, that the justice which is of the law, *the man that shall do it, shall live by it.*

6 But the justice which is of faith, speaketh thus : *Say not in thy heart, Who shall ascend into heaven?* that is, to bring Christ down :

7 *Or who shall descend into the deep?* that is, to bring up Christ again from the dead.

8 But what saith the scripture? *The word is nigh thee, even in thy mouth, and in thy heart.* This is the word of faith, which we preach.

9 For if thou confess with thy mouth the Lord JESUS, and believe in thy heart that God hath raised him up from the dead, thou shalt be saved.

10 For, with the heart, we believe unto justice ; but, with the mouth, confession is made unto salvation.

11 For the scripture saith : *Whosoever believeth in him, shall not be confounded.*

12 For there is no distinction

---

*Isaias 10. 22.—Isaias 1. 9.—Isaias 8. 14. and 28. 16. 1 Pet. 2. 6.

CHAP. X. Ver. 3. *The justice of God.* That is, the justice which God giveth us through Christ: as, on the other hand, the Jews' own *justice* is, that which they pretended to by their own strength, or by the observance of the law without faith in Christ.

Ver. 9. *Thou shalt be saved.* To confess the Lord Jesus, and to call upon the name of the Lord (ver. 13), is not barely professing a belief in the person of Christ; but moreover implies a belief of his whole doctrine, and an obedience to his law; without which the calling him Lord will save no man. St. *Matt.* vii. 21.

*Lev. 18. 5. Ezech. 20. 11.—*Deut. 30. 12.—*Deut. 30. 14.—*Isaias 28. 16.

of the Jew and the Greek: for the same is Lord over all, rich unto all that call upon him.

13 *a* For *whosoever shall call upon the name of the Lord, shall be saved.*

14 How then, shall they call on him, in whom they have not believed? Or how shall they believe him, of whom they have not heard? And how shall they hear without a preacher?

15 And how shall they preach unless they be sent? as it is written: *b How beautiful are the feet of them that preach the gospel of peace, of them that bring glad tidings of good things!*

16 But all do not obey the gospel. For Isaias saith: *c Lord, who hath believed our report?*

17 Faith then cometh by hearing: and hearing by the word of Christ.

18 But I say: Have they not heard? *d* Yes, verily, *their sound hath gone forth into all the earth, and their words unto the ends of the whole world.*

19 But I say: Hath not Israel known? First Moses saith: *e I will provoke you to jealousy by that which is not a nation; by a foolish nation I will anger you.*

20 But Isaias is bold, and saith: *f I was found by them that did not seek me: I ap-* peared *openly to them that asked not after me.*

21 But to Israel he saith: *g All the day long have I spread my hands to a people that believeth not, and contradicteth me.*

## CHAP. XI.

*God hath not cast off all Israel. The gentiles must not be proud; but stand in faith, and fear.*

I SAY then: Hath God cast away his people? God forbid. For I also am an Israelite of the seed of Abraham, of the tribe of Benjamin.

2 God hath not cast away his people, which he foreknew. Know you not what the scripture saith of Elias; how he calleth on God against Israel?

3 *h Lord, they have slain thy prophets, they have dug down thy altars: and I am left alone, and they seek my life.*

4 But what saith the divine answer to him? *i I have left me seven thousand men, that have not bowed their knees to Baal.*

5 Even so then at this present time also, there is a remnant saved according to the election of grace.

6 And if by grace, it is not

---

*a* Joel 2. 32. Acts 2. 21.—*b* Isaias 52. 7. Nahum 1. 15.—*c* Isaias 53. 1. John 12. 38.—*d* Ps. 18. 5.—*e* Deut. 32. 21.—*f* Isaias 65. 1.

*g* Isaias 65. 2.—*h* 3 Kings 19. 10.—*i* 3 Kings 19. 18.

---

Ver. 15. *Unless they be sent.* Here is an evident proof against all new teachers, who have all usurped to themselves the ministry without any lawful mission, derived by succession from the apostles, to whom Christ said, John xx. 21. *As my Father hath sent me, I also send you.*

CHAP. XI. Ver. 4. *Seven thousand,* &c. This is very ill alleged by some against the perpetual visibility of the Church of Christ: the more because however the number of the faithful might be abridged by the persecution of Jezebel in the kingdom of the ten tribes, the Church was at the same time in a most flourishing condition (under *Asa* and *Josaphat*) in the kingdom of Judah.

Ver. 6. *It is not now by works,* &c. If salvation were to come by *works,* done by nature, without faith and grace, salvation would not be a grace now by works, otherwise grace is no more grace.

7 What then? That which Israel sought, he hath not obtained: but the election hath obtained it, and the rest have been blinded.

8 As it is written: *ᵃGod hath given them the spirit of insensibility; eyes that they should not see, and ears that they should not hear; until this present day.*

9 And David saith: *ᵇLet their table be made a snare and a trap, and a stumbling-block, and a recompense unto them.*

10 *Let their eyes be darkened, that they may not see: and bow down their back always.*

11 I say then, have they so stumbled, that they should fall? God forbid. But by their offence, salvation is come to the gentiles, that they may be emulous of them.

12 Now if the offence of them be the riches of the world, and the diminution of them, the riches of the gentiles; how much more the fulness of them.

ᵃ Isaias 6. 9. and 10. 29. 10. Matt. 13. 14. John 12. 40. Acts 28. 26.—ᵇ Ps. 68. 23.

or favour, but a debt; but such *dead works* are indeed of no value in the sight of God towards salvation. It is not the same with regard to *works done with and by God's grace,* for to such works as these he has promised eternal salvation.

Ver. 8. *God hath given them, &c.* Not by his working or acting in them; but by his permission, and by withdrawing his grace in punishment of their obstinacy.

Ver. 11. *That they should fall.* The nation of the Jews is not absolutely and without remedy cast off for ever; but in part only (many thousands of them having been at first converted) and for a time; which fall of theirs God has been pleased to turn to the good of the gentiles.

13 For I say to you gentiles: *ᶜas* long indeed as I am the apostle of the gentiles, I will honour my ministry,

14 If by any means I may provoke to emulation them who are my flesh, and may save some of them.

15 For if the loss of them be the reconciliation of the world; what shall the receiving of them be, but life from the dead?

16 For if the first-fruit be holy, so is the lump also: and if the root be holy, so are the branches.

17 And if some of the branches be broken, and thou being a wild olive, art ingrafted in them, and art made partaker of the root and of the fatness of the olive-tree,

18 Boast not against the branches. But if thou boast: thou bearest not the root, but the root thee.

19 Thou wilt say then: The branches were broken off that I might be grafted in.

20 Well: because of unbelief they were broken off. But thou standest by faith: be not high-minded; but fear.

21 For if God hath not spared the natural branches: lest perhaps he also spare not thee.

22 See then the goodness and the severity of God; towards

ᶜ Acts 9. 15. Gal. 2. 7.

Ver. 20. *Thou standest by faith: be not high-minded; but fear.* We see here that he who standeth by faith may fall from it; and therefore must live in fear, and not in the vain presumption and security of modern sectaries.

Ver. 22. *Otherwise thou also shalt be cut off.* The gentiles are here admonished not to be proud, nor to glory against the Jews; but to take

JESUS BEFORE HEROD.

them indeed that are fallen, the severity; but towards thee, the goodness of God, if thou abide in goodness, otherwise thou also shalt be cut off.

23 And they also, if they abide not still in unbelief, shall be grafted in: for God is able to graft them in again.

24 For if thou wert cut out of the wild olive-tree, which is natural to thee: and contrary to nature were grafted into the good olive-tree; how much more shall they, that are the natural branches, be grafted into their own olive-tree?

25 For I would not have you ignorant, brethren, of this mystery, *a* (lest you should be wise in your own conceits) that blindness in part has happened in Israel, until the fulness of the gentiles should come in.

26 And so all Israel should be saved, as it is written: *b There shall come out of Sion, he that shall deliver, and shall turn away ungodliness from Jacob.*

27 *And this is to them my covenant:* when I shall take away their sins.

28 As concerning the gospel, indeed, they are enemies for your sake: but as touching the election, they are most dear for the sake of the fathers.

29 For the gifts and the calling of God are without repentance.

30 For as you also in times past did not believe God, but now have obtained mercy, through their unbelief;

31 So these also now have not believed, for your mercy, that they also may obtain mercy.

32 For God hath concluded all in unbelief, that he may have mercy on all.

33 O the depth of the riches of the wisdom and of the knowledge of God! How incomprehensible are his judgments, and how unsearchable his ways!

34 *c For who hath known the mind of the Lord? Or who hath been his counsellor?*

35 Or who hath first given to him, and recompense shall be made him?

36 For of him, and by him, and in him, are all things: to him be glory for ever. Amen.

## CHAP. XII.

*Lessons of Christian virtue.*

I BESEECH you therefore, brethren, by the mercy of God, *d that you present your bodies a living sacrifice, holy, pleasing unto God, your reasonable service.

2 And be not conformed to this world: but be reformed in

---

*a* Prov. 3. 7. Isaias 5. 21.—*b* Isa. as 59. 20. *c* Wis. 9. 13. Isaias 40. 13. 1 Cor. 2. 16.—*d* Phil. 4. 18.

---

occasion rather from their fall to fear and to be humble, lest they be cast off. Not that the whole Church of Christ can ever fail from him; having been secured by so many divine promises in holy writ; but that each one in particular may fall; and therefore all in general are to be admonished to beware of that, which may happen to any one in particular.

Ver. 29. *For the gifts and the calling of God are without* his repenting himself of them; for the promises of God are unchangeable, nor can he repent of conferring his *gifts.*

Ver. 32. *Concluded all in unbelief* He hath found all nations, both Jews and gentiles, in unbelief and sin; not by his causing, but by the abuse of their own free-will; so that their calling and election is purely owing to his mercy.

the newness of your mind, *a* that you may prove what is the good, and the acceptable, and the perfect will of God.

3 For I say, by the grace that is given me, to all that are among you, not to be more wise than it behoveth to be wise, but to be wise unto sobriety, *b* and according as God hath divided to every one the measure of faith.

4 For as in one body we have many members, but all the members have not the same office:

5 So we being many, are one body in Christ, and every one members one of another.

6 And having different gifts, according to the grace that is given us, either prophecy, *to be used* according to the rule of faith;

7 Or ministry, in ministering; or he that teacheth, in doctrine,

8 He that exhorteth in exhorting, he that giveth with simplicity, he that ruleth with carefulness, he that sheweth mercy with cheerfulness.

9 Let love be without dissimulation. *c* Hating that which is evil, cleaving to that which is good.

10 *d* Loving one another with the charity of brotherhood, with honour preventing one another.

11 In carefulness not slothful. In spirit fervent. Serving the Lord.

12 Rejoicing in hope. Patient in tribulation. Instant in prayer.

13 Communicating to the necessities of the saints. *e* Pursuing hospitality.

14 Bless them that persecute you; bless, and curse not.

15 Rejoice with them that rejoice, weep with them that weep.

16 Being of one mind one towards another. Not minding high things, but consenting to the humble. Be not wise in your own conceits.

17 To no man rendering evil for evil. *f* Providing good things not only in the sight of God, but also in the sight of all men.

18 *g* If it be possible as much as is in you, having peace with all men.

19 *h* Not revenging yourselves, my dearly beloved; but give place unto wrath, for it is written: *Revenge to me; I will repay,* saith the Lord.

20 *k* But if thy enemy be hungry, give him to eat: if he thirst, give him to drink. For, doing this, thou shalt heap coals of fire upon his head.

21 Be not overcome by evil, but overcome evil by good.

## CHAP. XIII.

*Lessons of obedience to superiors, and mutual charity.*

LET *i* every soul be subject to higher powers: for there is no power but from God: and those that are, are ordained of God.

2 Therefore he that resisteth the power, resisteth the ordinance of God. And they that resist, purchase to themselves damnation.

3 For princes are not a terror to the good work, but to the

---

*a* Ephes. 5. 17. 1 Thess. 4. 3.—*b* 1 Cor. 12. 11. Ephes. 4. 7.—*c* Amos 5. 15.—*d* Ephes. 4. 3. 1 Pet. 2. 17.—*e* Heb. 13. 2. 1 Pet. 4. 9.

*f* 2 Cor. 8. 21.—*g* Heb. 12 14.—*h* Eccli. 28. 1. and 2. 8.—*i* Matt. 5. 39. Deut. 32. 35. Heb. 10. 30.—*k* Prov. 25. 21.—*l* Wis. 6. 4. 1 Pet. 2. 13.

evil. Wilt thou then not be afraid of the power? Do that which is good: and thou shalt have praise from the same.

4 For he is God's minister to thee, for good. But if thou do that which is evil, fear: for he beareth not the sword in vain. For he is God's minister: an avenger to execute wrath upon him that doth evil.

5 Wherefore be subject of necessity, not only for wrath, but also for conscience-sake.

6 For therefore also you pay tribute. For they are the ministers of God, serving unto this purpose.

7 <sup>a</sup> Render therefore to all men their dues. Tribute, to whom tribute is due: custom to whom custom: fear to whom fear: honour to whom honour.

8 Owe no man anything, but to love one another. For he that loveth his neighbour, hath fulfilled the law.

9 <sup>b</sup> For *Thou shalt not commit adultery, Thou shalt not kill, Thou shalt not steal, Thou shalt not bear false witness, Thou shalt not covet:* and if there be any other commandment, it is comprised in this word, <sup>c</sup> *Thou shalt love thy neighbour as thyself.*

10 The love of our neighbour worketh no evil. Love therefore is the fulfilling of the law.

11 And that knowing the season: that it is now the hour for us to rise from sleep. For now our salvation is nearer than when we believed.

12 The night is past, and the day is at hand. Let us therefore cast off the works of dark-

---

<sup>a</sup> Matt. 22. 21.—<sup>b</sup> Exod. 20. 14. Deut. 5. 18.—<sup>c</sup> Lev. 19. 18. Matt. 22. 39. Mark 12. 31. Gal. 5. 14. Jas. 2. 8.

ness, and put on the armour of light.

13 Let us walk honestly as in the day: <sup>d</sup> not in rioting and drunkenness, not in chambering and impurities, not in contention and envy:

14 <sup>e</sup> But put ye on the Lord JESUS CHRIST, and make not provision for the flesh in its concupiscences.

## CHAP. XIV.

*The strong must bear with the weak. Cautions against judging; and giving scandal.*

NOW him that is weak in faith take unto you; not in disputes about thoughts.

2 For one believeth that he may eat all things: but he that is weak let him eat herbs.

3 Let not him that eateth, despise him that eateth not: and he that eateth not, let him not judge him that eateth. For God hath taken him to him.

4 <sup>f</sup> Who art thou that judgest another man's servant? To his

---

<sup>d</sup> Luke 21. 34.—<sup>e</sup> Gal. 5. 16. 1 Pet. 2. 11.—<sup>f</sup> Jas. 4. 12.

CHAP. XIV. Ver. 2. *Eat all things.* Viz., without observing the distinction of clean and unclean meats, prescribed by the law of *Moses;* which was now no longer obligatory. Some weak Christians, converted from among the Jews, as we here gather from the apostle, made a scruple of eating such meats as were deemed unclean by the law; such as swine's flesh, &c., which the stronger sort of Christians did eat without scruple. Now the apostle, to reconcile them together, exhorts the former not to judge or condemn the latter, using their Christian liberty: and the latter, to take care not to despise or scandalize their weaker brethren, either by bringing them to eat what in their conscience they think they should not: or by giving them such offence, as to endanger the driving them thereby from the Christian religion.

own lord he standeth or falleth. And he shall stand: for God is able to make him stand.

5 For one judgeth between day and day; and another judgeth every day: let every man abound in his own sense.

6 He that regardeth the day, regardeth it unto the Lord. And he that eateth, eateth to the Lord: for he giveth thanks to God. And he that eateth not, to the Lord he eateth not, and giveth thanks to God.

7 For none of us liveth to himself; and no man dieth to himself.

8 For whether we live, we live unto the Lord; or whether we die, we die unto the Lord. Therefore whether we live or whether we die, we are the Lord's.

9 For to this end Christ died and rose again; that he might be Lord both of the dead and of the living.

10 But thou, why judgest thou thy brother? or thou, why dost thou despise thy brother? *a* For we shall all stand before the judgment-seat of Christ.

11 For it is written: *b* As I live, saith the Lord, *every knee shall bow to me; and every tongue shall confess to God.*

12 Therefore every one of us shall render account to God for himself.

13 Let us not therefore judge one another any more. But judge this rather, that you put not a stumbling-block or a scandal in your brother's way.

14 I know, and am confident, in the Lord JESUS, that nothing is unclean of itself; but to him that esteemeth anything to be unclean, to him it is unclean.

15 For if, because of thy meat, thy brother be grieved, thou walkest not now according to charity. *c* Destroy not him with thy meat, for whom Christ died.

16 Let not then our good be evil spoken of.

17 For the kingdom of God is not meat and drink; but justice, and peace, and joy in the Holy Ghost.

18 For he, that in this serveth Christ, pleaseth God, and is approved of men.

19 Therefore let us follow after the things that are of peace: and keep the things that are of edification one towards another.

20 Destroy not the work of God for meat. *d* All things indeed are clean: but it is evil for that man who eateth with offence.

21 *e* It is good not to eat flesh, and not to drink wine, nor any thing whereby thy brother is offended, or scandalized, or made weak.

22 Hast thou faith? Have it to thyself before God. Blessed is he that condemneth not himself in that which he alloweth.

23 But he that discerneth, if he eat, is condemned; because not of faith. For all that is not of faith is sin.

---

*a* 2 Cor. 5. 10.—*b* Isaias 45. 24. Phil. 2. 10.

Ver. 5. *Between day, &c.* Still observing the sabbaths and festivals of the law.

*c* 1 Cor. 8. 11.—*d* Titus 1. 15.—*e* 1 Cor. 8. 13.

Ver. 23. *Discerneth.* That is, distinguisheth between meats, and eateth against his conscience, what he deems unclean.—Ibid. *Of faith.* By *faith* is here understood judgment and conscience: to act against which is always a sin.

JESUS IS CROWNED WITH THORNS.

## CHAP. XV.

*He exhorts them to be all of one mind: and promises to come and see them.*

NOW we that are stronger, ought to bear the infirmities of the weak, and not to please ourselves.

2 Let every one of you please his neighbour unto good, to edification.

3 For Christ did not please himself, but as it is written: <sup>a</sup> *The reproaches of them that reproached thee, fell upon me.*

4 For what things soever were written, were written for our learning: that through patience and the comfort of the scriptures, we might have hope.

5 Now the God of patience and of comfort <sup>b</sup> grant you to be of one mind one towards another, according to JESUS CHRIST:

6 That with one mind, and with one mouth, you may glorify God and the Father of our Lord JESUS CHRIST.

7 Wherefore receive one another, as Christ also hath received you unto the honour of God.

8 For I say that CHRIST JESUS was minister of the circumcision for the truth of God, to confirm the promises made unto the fathers.

9 But that the gentiles are to glorify God for his mercy, as it is written: <sup>c</sup> *Therefore will I confess to thee, O Lord, among the gentiles, and will sing to thy name.*

10 And again he saith: *Rejoice, ye gentiles, with his people.*

11 And again: <sup>d</sup> *Praise the Lord, all ye gentiles; and magnify him, all ye people.*

12 And again Isaias saith: <sup>e</sup> *There shall be a root of Jesse; and he that shall rise up to rule the gentiles, in him the gentiles shall hope.*

13 Now the God of hope fill you with all joy and peace in believing; that you may abound in hope, and in the power of the Holy Ghost.

14 And I myself also, my brethren, am assured of you, that you also are full of love, replenished with all knowledge, so that you are able to admonish one another.

15 But I have written to you, brethren, more boldly in some sort, as it were putting you in mind: because of the grace which is given me from God.

16 That I should be the minister of CHRIST JESUS among the gentiles: sanctifying the gospel of God, that the oblation of the gentiles may be made acceptable and sanctified in the Holy Ghost.

17 I have therefore glory in CHRIST JESUS towards God.

18 For I dare not to speak of any of those things which Christ worketh not by me, for the obedience of the gentiles, by word and deed:

19 By the virtue of signs and wonders, in the power of the Holy Ghost: so that from Jerusalem round about as far as unto Illyricum, I have replenished the gospel of Christ.

20 And I have so preached this gospel, not where Christ

---

<sup>a</sup> Ps. 68. 10.—<sup>b</sup> 1 Cor. 1. 10.—<sup>c</sup> 2 Kings 22. 50. Ps. 17. 50.

CHAP. XV. Ver. 8. *Minister of the circumcision.* That is, executed his office and *ministry* towards the Jews, the people of the *circumcision.*

<sup>d</sup> Ps. 116. 1.—<sup>e</sup> Isaias 11. 10.

was named, lest I should build upon another man's foundation.

21 But as it is written: "*They to whom he was not spoken of, shall see, and they that have not heard shall understand.*

22 For which cause also I was hindered very much from coming to you, and have been kept away till now.

23 But now having no more place in these countries, and having a great desire these many years past to come unto you:

24 When I shall begin to take my journey into Spain, I hope that as I pass, I shall see you, and be brought on my way thither by you, if first, in part, I shall have enjoyed you.

25 But now I shall go to Jerusalem, to minister unto the saints.

26 For it hath pleased them of Macedonia and Achaia to make a contribution for the poor of the saints that are in Jerusalem.

27 For it hath pleased them; and they are their debtors. *b* For if the gentiles have been made partakers of their spiritual things; they ought also in carnal things to minister to them.

28 When therefore I shall have accomplished this, and consigned to them this fruit, I will come by you into Spain.

29 And I know, that when I come to you, I shall come in the abundance of the blessing of the gospel of Christ.

30 I beseech you, therefore, brethren, through our Lord JESUS CHRIST, and by the charity of the Holy Ghost, that you help me in your prayers for me to God.

31 That I may be delivered from the unbelievers that are in Judea, and that the oblation of my service may be acceptable in Jerusalem to the saints.

32 That I may come to you with joy, by the will of God, and may be refreshed with you.

33 Now the God of peace be with you all. Amen.

## CHAP. XVI.

*He concludes with salutations, bidding them beware of all that should oppose the doctrine they had learnt.*

AND I commend to you Phebe, our sister, who is in the ministry of the church that is in Cenchre:

2 That you receive her in the Lord as becometh saints: and that you assist her in whatsoever business she shall have need of you. For she also hath assisted many, and myself also.

3 Salute *c* Prisca and Aquila, my helpers in CHRIST JESUS,

4 (Who have for my life laid down their own necks: to whom not I only give thanks, but also all the churches of the gentiles,)

5 And the church which is in their house. Salute Epenetus my beloved, who is the first-fruits of Asia in Christ.

6 Salute Mary, who hath laboured much among you.

7 Salute Andronicus and Junias, my kinsmen and fellow-prisoners, who are of note among the apostles, who also were in Christ before me.

8 Salute Ampliatus, most beloved to me in the Lord.

---

*a* Isaias 52. 15.—*b* 1 Cor. 9. 11.

*c* Acts 18. 2. and 26.

9 Salute Urbanus, our helper in CHRIST JESUS, and Stachys my beloved.

10 Salute Apelles, approved in Christ.

11 Salute them that are of Aristobulus's household. Salute Herodian my kinsman. Salute them that are of Narcissus's household who are in the Lord.

12 Salute Tryphena and Tryphosa, who labour in the Lord. Salute Persis the dearly beloved, who hath much laboured in the Lord.

13 Salute Rufus, elect in the Lord, and his mother and mine.

14 Salute Asyncritus, Phlegon, Hermas, Patrobas, Hermes, and the brethren that are with them.

15 Salute Philologus, and Julia, Nereus, and his sister, and Olympias; and all the saints that are with them.

16 Salute one another with an holy kiss. All the churches of Christ salute you.

17 Now I beseech you, brethren, to mark them who make dissensions and offences contrary to the doctrines which you have learnt, and to avoid them.

18 For they that are such serve not Christ our Lord, but their own belly: and by pleasing speeches, and good words, seduce the hearts of the innocent.

19 For your obedience is published in every place. I rejoice therefore in you. But I would have you to be wise in good, and simple in evil.

20 And the God of peace crush satan under your feet speedily. The grace of our Lord JESUS CHRIST be with you.

21 ᵃTimothy my fellow-labourer saluteth you, and Lucius, and Jason, and Sosipater, my kinsmen.

22 I Tertius, who wrote this epistle, salute you in the Lord.

23 Caius, my host, and the whole church, saluteth you. Erastus, the treasurer of the city, saluteth you, and Quartus, a brother.

24 The grace of our Lord JESUS CHRIST be with you all. Amen.

25 Now to him that is able to establish you, according to my gospel and the preaching of JESUS CHRIST, according to the revelation of the mystery, which was kept secret from eternity,

26 (Which now is made manifest by the scriptures of the prophets, according to the precept of the eternal God, for the obedience of faith,) known among all nations,

27 To God the only wise through JESUS CHRIST, to whom be honour and glory for ever and ever. Amen.

---

ᵃ Acts 16. 1.

# THE FIRST EPISTLE OF ST. PAUL TO THE CORINTHIANS.

*St. Paul having planted the faith in Corinth, where he had preached a year and a half, and converted a great many, went to Ephesus. After being there three years, he wrote this first Epistle to the Corinthians, and sent it by the same persons, Stephanas, Fortunatus, and Achaicus, who had brought their letter to him. It was written about twenty-four years after our Lord's Ascension, and contains several matters appertaining to faith and morals, and also to ecclesiastical discipline.*

## CHAP. I.

*He reproveth their dissensions about their teachers; the world was to be saved by preaching of the cross, and not by human wisdom or eloquence.*

PAUL called *to be* an apostle of JESUS CHRIST, by the will of God, and Sosthenes a brother,

2 To the church of God that is at Corinth, to them that are sanctified in CHRIST JESUS, called *to be* saints, with all that invoke the name of our Lord JESUS CHRIST in every place of theirs and ours.

3 Grace to you, and peace from God our Father, and from the Lord JESUS CHRIST.

4 I give thanks to my God always for you for the grace of God that is given you in CHRIST JESUS.

5 That in all things you are made rich in him, in all utterance, and in all knowledge;

6 As the testimony of Christ was confirmed in you.

7 So that nothing is wanting to you in any grace, waiting for the manifestation of our Lord JESUS CHRIST.

8 Who also will confirm you unto the end without crime, in the day of the coming of our Lord JESUS CHRIST.

9 <sup>a</sup> God is faithful: by whom you are called unto the fellowship of his son JESUS CHRIST our Lord.

10 Now I beseech you, brethren, by the name of our Lord JESUS CHRIST, that you all speak the same thing, and that there be no schisms among you: but that you be perfect in the same mind and in the same judgment.

11 For it hath been signified unto me, my brethren, of you, by them that are of *the house of* Chloe, that there are contentions among you.

12 Now this I say that every one of you saith: I indeed am of Paul: and I am <sup>b</sup> of Apollo: and I of Cephas; and I of Christ.

13 Is Christ divided? Was Paul then crucified for you? or were you baptized in the name of Paul?

14 I give God thanks, that I

---

<sup>a</sup> 1 Thess. 5. 24.—<sup>b</sup> Acts 18. 24.

JESUS IS GIVEN TO BE CRUCIFIED.

baptized none of you, *a but* Crispus and Caius:

15 Lest any should say that you were baptized in my name.

16 And I baptized also the household of Stephanas: besides, I know not whether I baptized any other.

17 For Christ sent me not to baptize, but to preach the gospel: *b* not in the wisdom of speech, lest the cross of Christ should be made void.

18 For the word of the cross, to them indeed that perish, is foolishness; but to them that are saved, that is, to us, *c* it is the power of God.

19 For it is written: *d I will destroy the wisdom of the wise; and the prudence of the prudent I will reject.*

20 *e Where is the wise? Where is the scribe? Where is the disputer of this world?* Hath not God made foolish the wisdom of this world?

21 For seeing that in the wisdom of God the world by wisdom knew not God; it pleased God by the foolishness of our preaching to save them that believe.

22 For both the Jews require signs, and the Greeks seek after wisdom:

23 But we preach Christ crucified, unto the Jews indeed a stumbling-block, and unto the gentiles, foolishness.

24 But unto them that are called, both Jews and Greeks, Christ the power of God and the wisdom of God.

25 For the foolishness of God is wiser than men: and the weakness of God is stronger than men.

26 For see your vocation, brethren, that *there are* not many wise according to the flesh, not many mighty, not many noble:

27 But the foolish things of the world hath God chosen, that he may confound the wise: and the weak things of the world hath God chosen, that he may confound the strong:

28 And the base things of the world, and the things that are contemptible hath God chosen, and things that are not, that he might bring to nought things that are:

29 That no flesh should glory in his sight.

30 But of him are you in CHRIST JESUS, who of God is made unto us wisdom, *f* and justice, and sanctification, and redemption:

31 That, as it is written, *g He that glorieth, may glory in the Lord.*

## CHAP. II.

*His preaching was not in loftiness of words; but in spirit and power. And the wisdom he taught was not to be understood by the worldly wise or sensual man, but only by the spiritual man.*

AND I, brethren, when I came to you, *h* came not in loftiness of speech or of wisdom; declaring unto you the testimony of Christ.

2 For I judged not myself to

---

*a* Acts 18. 8.—*b* 2 Pet. 1. 16. Infra. 2. 1, 4, and 13.—*c* Rom. 1. 16.—*d* Isaias 29. 14.—*e* Isaias 33. 18.

CHAP. I. Ver. 25. *The foolishness, &c.*

*f* Jer. 23. 5.—*g* Jer. 9. 23, and 24. 2 Cor. 10. 17.—*h* Supra, 1. 17.

That is to say, what appears foolish to the world in the ways of God, is indeed most wise: and what appears weak, is indeed above all the strength and comprehension of man.

CHAP. II.    I. TO THE CORINTHIANS.    CHAP. III.

know anything among you, but JESUS CHRIST; and him crucified.

3 ᵃAnd I was with you in weakness, and in fear, and in much trembling:

4 ᵇAnd my speech and my preaching was not in the persuasive words of human wisdom, but in shewing of the spirit and power:

5 That your faith might not stand on the wisdom of men, but on the power of God.

6 Howbeit we speak wisdom among the perfect: yet not the wisdom of this world, neither of the princes of this world, that come to nought:

7 But we speak the wisdom of God in a mystery, *a wisdom* which is hidden, which God ordained before the world, unto our glory:

8 Which none of the princes of this world knew: for if they had known it, they would never have crucified the Lord of glory.

9 But, as it is written: ᶜ*That eye hath not seen, nor ear heard, neither hath it entered into the heart of man, what things God hath prepared for them that love him.*

10 But to us God hath revealed them, by his Spirit. For the Spirit searcheth all things, yea the deep things of God.

11 For what man knoweth the things of a man, but the spirit of a man that is in him? So the things also that are of God no man knoweth, but the Spirit of God.

12 Now we have received not the spirit of this world, but the Spirit that is of God: that we may know the things that are given us from God.

13 ᵈWhich things also we speak, not in the learned words of human wisdom; but in the doctrine of the Spirit, comparing spiritual things with spiritual.

14 But the sensual man perceiveth not these things that are of the Spirit of God: for it is foolishness to him, and he cannot understand: because it is spiritually examined.

15 But the spiritual man judgeth all things: and he himself is judged of no man.

16 ᵉFor who hath known the mind of the Lord, that he may instruct him? But we have the mind of Christ.

## CHAP. III.

*They must not contend about their teachers, who are but God's ministers: and accountable to him. Their works shall be tried by fire.*

AND I, brethren, could not speak to you as unto spiritual, but as unto carnal. As unto little ones in Christ.

2 I gave you milk to drink,

---

ᵈ Supra, 1. 17. and 2. 1 and 4.  2 Pet. 1. 16.—ᵉ Wis. 9. 13.  Isaias 40. 13.  Rom. 11. 34.

---

CHAP. II. Ver. 14, 15. *The sensual man—the spiritual man.* The sensual man is either he who is taken up with sensual pleasures, with carnal and worldly affections; or he who measureth divine mysteries by natural reason, sense, and human wisdom only. Now such a man has little or no notion of the things of God. Whereas the *spiritual man,* who, in the mysteries of religion, takes not human sense for his guide, but submits his judgment to the decisions of the Church, which he is commanded to hear and obey. For Christ hath promised to remain to the end of the world with his Church, and to direct her in all things by the spirit of truth.

---

ᵃ Acts 18. 3.—ᵇ 2 Pet. 1. 16.—ᶜ Isaias 64. 4.

not meat: for you were not able as yet. But neither indeed are you now able; for you are yet carnal.

3 For whereas there is among you envying and contention, are you not carnal, and walk according to man?

4 For while one saith, I indeed am of Paul; and another, I am of Apollo; are you not men? What then is Apollo, and what is Paul?

5 The ministers of him whom you have believed: and to every one as the Lord hath given.

6 I have planted, Apollo watered, but God gave the increase.

7 Therefore neither he that planteth is anything, nor he that watereth; but God that giveth the increase.

8 Now he that planteth, and he that watereth, are one. *And every man shall receive his own reward according to his own labour.

9 For we are God's coadjutors: you are God's husbandry, you are God's building.

10 According to the grace of God, that is given to me, as a wise architect, I have laid the foundation: and another buildeth thereon. But let every man take heed how he buildeth thereupon.

11 For other foundation no man can lay, but that which is laid; which is CHRIST JESUS.

12 Now if any man build upon this foundation, gold, silver, precious stones, wood, hay, stubble:

13 Every man's work shall be manifest: for the day of the Lord shall declare it, because it shall be revealed in fire: and the fire shall try every man's work, of what sort it is.

14 If any man's work abide, which he hath built thereupon: he shall receive a reward.

15 If any man's work burn, he shall suffer loss: but he himself shall be saved, yet so as by fire.

16 Know you not that you are the temple of God, and that the Spirit of God dwelleth in you?

17 But if any man violate the temple of God; him shall God destroy. *For the temple of God is holy: which you are.

18 Let no man deceive himself: if any man among you

---

*Ps. 61. 13. Matt. 16. 27. Rom. 2. 6. Gal. 6. 5.

CHAP. III. Ver. 12. *Upon this foundation.* The foundation is Christ and his doctrine: or the true faith in him, working through charity. The

*Infra, 6. 19. 2 Cor. 6. 16.

building upon this foundation, *gold, silver, and precious stones,* signifies the more perfect preaching and practice of the gospel: the *wood, hay, and stubble,* such preaching as that of the Corinthian teachers, (who affected the pomp of words and human eloquence,) and such practice as is mixed with much imperfection, and many lesser sins. Now the *day of the Lord,* and his *fiery* trial (in the particular judgment immediately after death) shall make manifest of what sort every man's work has been; of which, during this life, it is hard to make a judgment. For then *the fire* of God's judgment *shall try every man's work.* And they, whose *works,* like *wood, hay, and stubble,* cannot abide the fire, *shall suffer loss;* these works being found to be of no value; yet they themselves, having built upon the right *foundation,* (by living and dying in the true faith, and in the state of grace, though with some imperfection,) *shall be saved,* yet so as by *fire;* being liable to this punishment, by reason of the *wood, hay, and stubble,* which was mixed with their building.

seem to be wise in this world, let him become a fool that he may be wise.

19 For the wisdom of this world is foolishness with God. For it is written: *a I will catch the wise in their own craftiness.*

20 And again: *b The Lord knoweth the thoughts of the wise, that they are vain.*

21 Let no man therefore glory in men.

22 For all things are yours, whether it be Paul, or Apollo, or Cephas, or the world, or life, or death, or things present, or things to come: for all are yours:

23 And you are Christ's: and Christ is God's.

## CHAP. IV.

*God's ministers are not to be judged. He reprehends their boasting of their preachers; and describes the treatment the apostles everywhere met with.*

LET *c* a man so account of us as of the ministers of Christ, and the dispensers of the mysteries of God.

2 Here now it is required among the dispensers, that a man be found faithful.

3 But to me it is a very small thing to be judged by you, or by man's day: but neither do I judge my own self.

4 For I am not conscious to myself of anything, yet am I not hereby justified: but he that judgeth me, is the Lord.

5 Therefore judge not before the time: until the Lord come, who both will bring to light the hidden things of darkness, and will make manifest the counsels of the hearts: and then shall every man have praise from God.

6 But these things, brethren, I have in a figure transferred to myself and to Apollo, for your sakes; that in us you may learn, that one be not puffed up against the other for another, above that which is written.

7 For who distinguisheth thee? Or what hast thou that thou hast not received? and if thou hast received, why dost thou glory, as if thou hadst not received it?

8 You are now full: you are now become rich: you reign without us; and I would to God you did reign, that we also might reign with you.

9 For I think that God hath set forth us apostles, the last, as it were men appointed to death: we are made a spectacle to the world, and to Angels, and to men.

10 We are fools for Christ's sake, but you are wise in Christ: we are weak, but you are strong: you are honourable, but we without honour.

11 Even unto this hour we both hunger, and thirst, and are naked, and are buffeted, and have no fixed abode,

12 *d* And we labour working with our own hands: we are reviled, and we bless: we are persecuted, and we suffer it.

13 We are blasphemed, and we entreat: we are made as the refuse of this world, the offscouring of all even until now.

14 I write not these things to confound you; but I admonish you as my dearest children:

15 For if you have ten thou-

---

*a* Job 5. 12.—*b* Ps. 93. 11.—*c* 2 Cor. 6. 4.   *d* Acts 20. 34. 1 Thess. 2. 9. 2 Thess. 3. 8.

THE DEATH OF JUDAS.

sand instructors in Christ, yet not many fathers. For in CHRIST JESUS by the gospel I have begotten you:

16 Wherefore I beseech you, be ye followers of me, as I also am of Christ.

17 For this cause have I sent to you Timothy, who is my dearest son and faithful in the Lord; who will put you in mind of my ways, which are in CHRIST JESUS; as I teach everywhere in every church.

18 As if I would not come to you, so some are puffed up.

19 But I will come to you shortly, if the Lord will, and will know, not the speech of them that are puffed up, but the power.

20 For the kingdom of God is not in speech but in power.

21 What will you? shall I come to you with a rod; or in charity, and in the spirit of meekness?

## CHAP. V.

*He excommunicates the incestuous adulterers, and admonishes them to purge out the old leaven.*

IT *a* is absolutely heard that there is fornication among you, and such fornication as the like is not among the heathens; that one should have his father's wife.

2 And you are puffed up; and have not rather mourned, that he might be taken away from among you, that have done this deed.

3 *b* I indeed absent in body, but present in spirit, have already judged, as though I were present, him that hath so done,

4 In the name of our Lord JESUS CHRIST, you being gathered together and my spirit, with the power of our Lord JESUS;

5 To deliver such a one to satan for the destruction of the flesh, that the spirit may be saved in the day of our Lord JESUS CHRIST.

6 Your glorying is not good. *c* Know you not that a little leaven corrupteth the whole lump?

7 Purge out the old leaven, that you may be a new paste, as you are unleavened. For Christ our pasch is sacrificed.

8 Therefore let us feast, not with the old leaven, nor with the leaven of malice and wickedness, but with the unleavened bread of sincerity and truth.

9 I wrote to you in an epistle, not to keep company with fornicators.

10 I mean not with the fornicators of this world, or with the covetous, or the extortioners, or the servers of idols: otherwise you must needs go out of this world.

11 But now I have written to you, not to keep company, if any man that is named a brother, be a fornicator, or covetous, or a server of idols, or a railer, a drunkard, or an extortioner: with such an one not so much as to eat.

12 For what have I to do to judge them that are without? Do not you judge them that are within?

13 For them that are without, God will judge. Put away the evil one from among yourselves.

---

*a* Lev. 18. 7. 8. and 20. 11. — *b* Col. 2. 5.

*c* Gal. 5. 9.

## CHAP. VI.

*He blames them for going to law before unbelievers. Of sins that exclude from the kingdom of heaven. The evil of fornication.*

DARE any of you, having a matter against another, go to be judged before the unjust, and not before the saints?

2 Know you not that the saints shall judge this world? And if the world shall be judged by you, are you unworthy to judge the smallest matters?

3 Know you not that we shall judge angels? how much more things of this world.

4 If therefore you have judgments of things pertaining to this world, set them to judge who are the most despised in the church.

5 I speak to your shame. Is it so that there is not among you any one wise man, that is able to judge between his brethren?

6 But brother goeth to law with brother, and that before unbelievers.

7 *a* Already indeed there is plainly a fault among you, that you have lawsuits one with another. Why do you not rather take wrong? why do you not rather suffer yourselves to be defrauded?

8 But you do wrong and defraud and that to *your* brethren.

9 Know you not that the unjust shall not possess the kingdom of God? Do not err: Neither fornicators, nor idolaters, nor adulterers,

10 Nor the effeminate, nor liers with mankind, nor thieves, nor covetous, nor drunkards, nor railers, nor extortioners shall possess the kingdom of God.

11 And such some of you were: but you are washed, but you are sanctified, but you are justified in the name of our Lord JESUS CHRIST, and the Spirit of our God.

12 All things are lawful to me, but all things are not expedient. All things are lawful to me, but I will not be brought under the power of any.

13 Meat for the belly, and the belly for the meats: but God shall destroy both it and them: but the body is not for fornication, but for the Lord, and the Lord for the body.

14 Now God hath both raised up the Lord, and will raise us up also by his power.

15 Know you not that your bodies are the members of Christ? Shall I then take the members of Christ, and make them the members of an harlot? God forbid.

16 Or know you not that he who is joined to a harlot is made one body? *b For they shall be,* saith he, *two in one flesh.*

17 But he who is joined to the Lord is one spirit.

18 Fly fornication. Every

---

*a* Matt. 5. 39. Luke 6. 29. Rom. 12. 17. 1 Thess. 4. 6.

*b* Gen. 2. 24. Matt. 19. 5. Mark 10. 8. Ephes. 5. 31.

---

CHAP. VI. Ver. 7. *A fault.* Lawsuits can hardly ever be without a fault, on one side or the other; and oftentimes on both sides.

Ver. 12. *All things are lawful, &c.* That is, all *indifferent things* are indeed lawful, inasmuch as they are not prohibited; but oftentimes they are not expedient: as in the case of lawsuits, &c. And much less would it be expedient to be enslaved by an irregular affection to anything, how indifferent soever.

sin that a man doth is without the body: but he that committeth fornication, sinneth against his own body.

19 Or know you not *a*that your members are the temple of the Holy Ghost, who is in you, whom you have from God; and you are not your own?

20 *b*For you are bought with a great price. Glorify and bear God in your body.

## CHAP. VII.

*Lessons relating to marriage and celibacy. Virginity is preferable to a married state.*

NOW concerning the things whereof you wrote to me: It is good for a man not to touch a woman.

2 But for fear of fornication, let every man have his own wife, and let every woman have her own husband.

3 *c*Let the husband render the debt to his wife: and the wife also in like manner to the husband.

4 The wife hath not power of her own body; but the husband. And in like manner the husband also hath not power of his own body; but the wife.

5 Defraud not one another, except, perhaps by consent, for a time, that you may give yourselves to prayer: and return together again, lest satan tempt you for your incontinency.

6 But I speak this by indulgence, not by commandment.

7 For I would that all men were even as myself: but every one hath his proper gift from God; one after this manner, and another after that.

8 But I say to the unmarried, and to the widows: it is good for them if they so continue, even as I.

9 But if they do not contain themselves, let them marry. For it is better to marry than to be burnt.

10 But to them that are married, not I, but the Lord commandeth, *d*that the wife depart not from her husband.

11 And if she depart, that she remain unmarried, or be reconciled to her husband. And let not the husband put away his wife.

12 For to the rest I speak, not the Lord. If any brother have a wife that believeth not, and she consent to dwell with him; let him not put her away.

13 And if any woman have a husband that believeth not, and he consent to dwell with her;

---

*a* Supra, R. 17. 2 Cor. 6. 16.—*b* Infra, 7. 23. 1 Pet. 1. 18.—*c* 1 Pet. 3. 7.

*d* Matt. 5. 32. and 19. 9. Mark 10. 9. Luke 16. 18.

---

CHAP. VII. Ver. 2. *Have his own wife.* That is, keep to his wife, which he hath. His meaning is not to exhort the unmarried to marry; on the contrary, he would have them rather continue as they are. Ver. 8. But he speaks here to them that are already married; who must not depart from one another, but live together as they ought to do in the marriage state.

Ver. 6. *By indulgence.* That is, by a condescension to your weakness.

Ver. 9. *If they do not contain, &c.* This is spoken of such as are free; and not of such as, by vow, have given their first faith to God: to whom, if they will use proper means to obtain it, God will never refuse the gift of continency. Some translators have corrupted this text, by rendering it, *if they cannot contain.*

Ver. 12. *I speak, not the Lord.* Viz., by any express commandment or ordinance.

let her not put away her husband.

14 For the unbelieving husband is sanctified by the believing wife; and the unbelieving wife is sanctified by the believing husband: otherwise your children should be unclean; but now they are holy.

15 But if the unbeliever depart, let him depart. For a brother or sister is not under servitude in such *cases*. But God hath called us in peace.

16 For now knowest thou, O wife, whether thou shalt save thy husband? Or how knowest thou, O man, whether thou shalt save thy wife?

17 But as the Lord hath distributed to every one, as God hath called every one, so let him walk: and so in all churches I teach.

18 Is any man called being circumcised? let him not procure uncircumcision. Is any man called in uncircumcision? let him not be circumcised.

19 Circumcision is nothing, and uncircumcision is nothing: but the observation of the commandments of God.

20 *a* Let every man abide in the same calling in which he was called.

21 Wast thou called, being a bond-man? care not for it: but if thou mayest be made free, use it rather.

---

*a* Ephes. 4. 1.

---

Ver. 14. *Is sanctified.* The meaning is not, that the faith of the husband or the wife is of itself sufficient to put the unbelieving party, or their children, in the state of grace and salvation: but that it is very often an occasion of their sanctification, by bringing them to the true faith.

22 For he that is called in the Lord, being a bond-man, is the freeman of the Lord. Likewise he that is called, being free, is the bond-man of Christ.

23 *b* You are bought with a price, be not made the bond-slaves of men.

24 Brethren, let every man wherein he was called, therein abide with God.

25 Now concerning virgins, I have no commandment of the Lord: but I give counsel, as having obtained mercy of the Lord, to be faithful.

26 I think therefore that this is good for the present necessity, that it is good for a man so to be.

27 Art thou bound to a wife? seek not to be loosed. Art thou loosed from a wife? seek not a wife.

28 But if thou take a wife, thou hast not sinned. And if a virgin marry, she hath not sinned: nevertheless, such shall have tribulation of the flesh. But I spare you.

29 This therefore I say, brethren: the time is short: it remaineth, that they also who have wives, be as if they had none:

30 And they that weep, as though they wept not; and they that rejoice, as if they rejoiced not; and they that buy, as though they possessed not;

31 And they that use this world, as if they used it not: for the fashion of this world passeth away.

32 But I would have you to be without solicitude. He that is without a wife, is solicitous for the things that belong to

---

*b* Supra, 6. 20. 1 Pet. 1. 18.

JESUS IS LED AWAY TO BE CRUCIFIED.

CHAP. VII.　　I. TO THE CORINTHIANS.　　CHAP. VIII.

the Lord, how he may please God.

33 But he that is with a wife, is solicitous for the things of the world, how he may please his wife: and he is divided.

34 And the unmarried woman and the virgin thinketh on the things of the Lord: that she may be holy both in body and in spirit. But she that is married thinketh on the things of the world, how she may please her husband.

35 And this I speak for your profit: not to cast a snare upon you, but for that which is decent, and which may give you power, to attend upon the Lord, without impediment.

36 But if any man think that he seemeth dishonoured with regard to his virgin, for that she is above the age, and it must so be: let him do what he will: he sinneth not, if she marry.

37 For he that hath determined being steadfast in his heart, having no necessity, but having power of his own will; and hath judged this in his heart to keep his virgin, doth well.

38 Therefore both he that giveth his virgin in marriage doth well: and he that giveth her not, doth better.

39 ᵃ A woman is bound by the law as long as her husband liveth: but if her husband die, she is at liberty: let her marry to whom she will: only in the Lord.

40 But more blessed shall she be, if she so remain, according to my counsel: and I think that I also have the Spirit of God.

## CHAP. VIII.

*Though an idol be nothing, yet things offered up to idols are not to be eaten, for fear of scandal.*

NOW concerning those things that are sacrificed to idols, we know that we all have knowledge. Knowledge puffeth up: but charity edifieth.

2 And if any man think that he knoweth anything, he hath not yet known, as he ought to know.

3 But if any man love God, the same is known by him.

4 But as for the meats that are sacrificed to idols, we know that an idol is nothing in the world, and that there is no God, but one.

5 For although there be that are called gods either in heaven, or on earth (for there be gods many, and lords many;)

6 Yet to us there is but one God, the Father, of whom are all things, and we unto him: and one Lord JESUS CHRIST, by whom are all things, and we by him.

7 But there is not knowledge in every one. For some until this present with conscience of the idol, eat as a thing sacri-

---

ᵃ Rom. 7. 2.

Ver. 36. *Let him do what he will: he sinneth not,* &c. The meaning is not, as libertines would have it, that persons may do what they will, and not sin: provided they afterwards marry; but that the father with regard to the giving his virgin in marriage, may do as he pleaseth: and that it will be no sin to him if she marry.

CHAP. VIII. Ver. 1. *Knowledge puffeth up,* &c. Knowledge without charity and humility, serveth only to puff persons up.
Ver. 5. *Gods many,* &c. Reputed for such among the heathens.

ficed to an idol: and their conscience, being weak, is defiled.

8 But meat doth not commend us to God. For neither, if we eat, shall we have the more: nor, if we eat not, shall we have the less.

9 But take heed lest perhaps this your liberty become a stumbling-block to the weak.

10 For if a man see him that hath knowledge sit at meat in the idol's temple; shall not his conscience, being weak, be emboldened to eat those things which are sacrificed to idols?

11 "And through thy knowledge shall the weak brother perish, for whom Christ hath died?

12 Now when you sin thus against the brethren, and wound their weak conscience, you sin against Christ.

13 *b* Wherefore if meat scandalize my brother, I will never eat flesh, lest I should scandalize my brother.

## CHAP. IX.

*The apostle did not make use of his power, of being maintained at the charges of those to whom he preached, that he might give no hindrance to the gospel. Of running in the race, and striving for the mastery*

AM not I free? Am not I an apostle? Have not I seen CHRIST JESUS our Lord? Are not you my work in the Lord?

2 And if unto others I be not an apostle, but yet to you I am. For you are the seal of my apostleship in the Lord.

3 My defence with them that do examine me is this.

4 Have not we power to eat and to drink?

5 Have we not power to carry about a woman a sister, as well as the rest of the apostles, and the brethren of the Lord, and Cephas?

6 Or I only and Barnabas have not we power to do this?

7 Who serveth as a soldier at any time, at his own charges? Who planteth a vineyard, and eateth not of the fruit thereof? Who feedeth a flock, and eateth not of the milk of the flock?

8 Speak I these things according to man? Or doth not the law also say these things?

9 For it is written in the Law of Moses: *c Thou shalt not muzzle the mouth of the ox that treadeth out the corn.* Doth God take care for oxen?

10 Or doth he say this indeed for our sakes? For *these things* are written for our sakes; that he that ploweth should plow in hope: and he that thrasheth, in hope to receive fruit.

11 "If we have sown unto you spiritual things, is it a great matter if we reap your carnal things?

12 If others be partakers of this power over you; why not we rather? Nevertheless we

---

*a* Rom. 14. 15.—*b* Rom. 14. 21.

Ver. 13. *If meat scandalize.* That is, if my eating cause my brother to sin.

*c* Deut. 25. 4. 1 Tim. 5. 18.—*d* Rom. 15. 27.

CHAP. IX. Ver. 5. *A woman a sister.* Some erroneous translators have corrupted this text by rendering it, *a sister, a wife;* whereas it is certain St. Paul had no wife [Chap. vii. 7, 8], and that he only speaks of such devout women, as, according to the custom of the Jewish nation, waited upon the preachers of the gospel, and supplied them with necessaries.

have not used this power: but we bear all things, lest we should give any hindrance to the gospel of Christ.

13 "Know you not that they who work in the holy place eat the things that are of the holy place; and they that serve the altar partake with the altar?

14 So also the Lord ordained that they who preach the gospel should live by the gospel.

15 But I have used none of these things. Neither have I written these things, that they should be so done unto me: for it is good for me to die, rather than that any man should make my glory void.

16 For if I preach the gospel, it is no glory to me: for a necessity lieth upon me: for wo is unto me if I preach not the gospel.

17 For if I do this thing willingly, I have a reward: but if against my will, a dispensation is committed to me.

18 What is my reward then? That preaching the gospel, I may deliver the gospel without charge, that I abuse not my power in the gospel.

19 For whereas I was free as to all, I made myself the servant of all, that I might gain the more.

20 And I became to the Jews a Jew, that I might gain the Jews:

21 To them that are under the law, as if I were under the law, (whereas myself was not under the law,) that I might gain them that were under the law. To them that were without the law, as if I were without the law, (whereas I was not without the law of God, but was in the law of Christ,) that I might gain them that were without the law.

22 To the weak I became weak, that I might gain the weak. I became all things to all men that I might save all.

23 And I do all things for the gospel's sake: that I may be made partaker thereof.

24 Know you not that they that run in the race, all run indeed, but one receiveth the prize? So run that you may obtain.

25 And every one that striveth for the mastery refraineth himself from all things: and they indeed that they may receive a corruptible crown: but we an incorruptible one.

26 I therefore so run, not as at an uncertainty: I so fight, not as one beating the air:

27 But I chastise my body, and bring it into subjection: lest perhaps, when I have preached to others, I myself should become a cast-away.

## CHAP. X.

*By the example of the Israelites he shews that we are not to build too much upon favours received; but avoid their sins; and fly from the service of idols, and from things offered to devils.*

FOR I would not have you ignorant, brethren, that our fathers were all *b* under the

---

*a* Deut. 18. 1.

*b* Exod. 13. 21. Num. 9. 21.

Ver. 16. *It is no glory.* That is, I have nothing to glory of.

Ver. 27. *I chastise, &c.* Here St. Paul shews the necessity of self-denial and mortification to subdue the flesh, and its inordinate desires.

cloud, and all passed through *the sea.

2 And all in Moses were baptized, in the cloud, and in the sea:

3 ᵇAnd did all eat the same spiritual food,

4 ᶜAnd all drank the same spiritual drink, (and they drank of the spiritual rock that followed them, and the rock was Christ.)

5 But with the most of them God was not well pleased: ᵈfor they were overthrown in the desert.

6 Now these things were done in a figure of us, that we should not covet evil things, ᵉas they also coveted.

7 Neither become ye idolaters, as some of them: as it is written: *The people sat down to eat and drink, and rose up to play.*

8 Neither let us commit fornication, ᵍas some of them committed fornication, and there fell in one day three and twenty thousand.

9 Neither let us tempt Christ, as some of them tempted, and perished by the serpents.

10 ʰNeither do you murmur, as some of them murmured, and were destroyed by the destroyer.

11 Now all these things happened to them in figure: and they are written for our correction, upon whom the ends of the world are come.

12 Wherefore he that thinketh himself to stand, let him take heed lest he fall.

13 Let no temptation take hold on you, but such as is human. And God is faithful, who will not suffer you to be tempted above that which you are able: but will make also with temptation issue, that you may be able to bear it.

14 Wherefore, my dearly beloved, fly from the service of idols.

15 I speak as to wise men: judge ye yourselves what I say.

16 The chalice of benediction, which we bless, is it not the communion of the blood of Christ? And the bread, which we break, is it not the partaking of the body of the Lord?

17 For we, being many, are one bread, one body, all that partake of one bread.

---

ᵃ Exod. 14. 22.—ᵇ Exod. 16. 15.—ᶜ Exod. 17. 6. Num. 20. 11.—ᵈ Num. 26. 64. and 65.—ᵉ Ps. 105. 14.—ᶠ Exod. 32. 6.—ᵍ Num. 21. 5. and 6.—ʰ Num. 11. 1. and 14. 1.

Ver. 11. *The ends of the world.* That is, the last ages.

Ver. 13. Or, *no temptation hath taken hold of you,* or come upon you as yet, but what is human, or incident to man.—Ibid. *Issue,* or a way to escape.

Ver. 16. *Which we bless.* Here the apostle puts them in mind of their partaking of the body and blood of Christ in the sacred mysteries, and becoming thereby one mystical body with Christ. From whence he infers, ver. 21, that they who are made partakers with Christ, by the eucharistic sacrifice and sacrament, must not be made partakers with devils by eating of the meats sacrificed to them.

Ver. 17. *One bread;* or, as it may be rendered, agreeably both to the Latin and Greek, *because the bread is*

---

CHAP. X. Ver. 2. *In Moses.* Under the conduct of Moses, they received baptism in figure, by passing under the cloud, and through the sea: and they partook of the body and blood of Christ in figure, by eating of the manna, (called here a *spiritual food,* because it was a figure of the true bread which comes down from heaven,) and drinking the water, miraculously brought out of the rock, called here a *spiritual rock;* because it was also a figure of Christ.

THE CRUCIFIXION.

18 Behold Israel according to the flesh: are not they that eat of the sacrifices partakers of the altar?

19 What then? Do I say that what is offered in sacrifice to idols is anything? or that the idol is anything?

20 But the things which the heathens sacrifice, they sacrifice to devils, and not to God. And I would not that you should be made partakers with devils.

21 You cannot drink the chalice of the Lord, and the chalice of devils: you cannot be partakers of the table of the Lord, and of the table of devils.

22 Do we provoke the Lord to jealousy? Are we stronger than he? <sup>a</sup> All things are lawful for me, but all things are not expedient.

23 All things are lawful for me, but all things do not edify.

24 Let no man seek his own, but that which is another's.

25 Whatsoever is sold in the shambles, eat: asking no question for conscience-sake.

26 <sup>b</sup> *The earth is the Lord's, and the fulness thereof.*

27 If any of them that believe not, invite you, and you be willing to go: eat of anything that is set before you, asking no question for conscience-sake.

28 But if any man say: This has been sacrificed to idols; do not eat of it for his sake that told it, and for conscience-sake.

29 Conscience, I say, not thy own, but the other's. For why is my liberty judged by another man's conscience?

30 If I partake with thanksgiving, why am I evil-spoken of for that for which I give thanks?

31 <sup>c</sup> Therefore, whether you eat or drink, or whatsoever else you do, do all to the glory of God.

32 Be without offence to the Jews and to the gentiles, and to the church of God:

33 As I also in all things please all men, not seeking that which is profitable to myself, but to many; that they may be saved.

## CHAP. XI.

*Women must have a covering over their heads. He blameth the abuses of their love feasts; and upon that occasion, treats of the blessed sacrament.*

BE ye followers of me, as I also am of Christ.

2 Now I praise you, brethren, that in all things you are mindful of me: and keep my ordinances as I have delivered them to you.

3 But I would have you know, <sup>d</sup> that the head of every man is Christ: and the head of the woman is the man: and the head of Christ is God.

4 Every man praying or prophesying with his head covered, disgraceth his head.

5 But every woman praying or prophesying with her head not covered, disgraceth her head: for it is all one as if she were shaven.

---

<sup>a</sup> Supra, 6. 12. — <sup>b</sup> Ps. 23. 1. Eccli. 17. 51.

one, all we, being many, are one body, who partake of that one bread. For it is by our communicating with Christ, and with one another, in this blessed sacrament, that we are formed into one mystical body; and made, as it were, one bread, compounded of many grains of corn, closely united together.

<sup>c</sup> Col. 3. 17.— <sup>d</sup> Ephes. 5. 23.

6 For if a woman be not covered, let her be shorn. But if it be a shame to a woman to be shorn or made bald, let her cover her head.

7 The man indeed ought not to cover his head, because he is the ᵃimage and glory of God; but the woman is the glory of the man.

8 For the man is not of the woman, but the woman of the man.

9 ᵇFor the man was not created for the woman, but the woman for the man.

10 Therefore ought the woman to have a power over her head, because of the Angels.

11 But yet neither is the man without the woman, nor the woman without the man, in the Lord.

12 For as the woman is of the man, so also is the man by the woman; but all things of God.

13 You yourselves judge: doth it become a woman to pray unto God, uncovered?

14 Doth not even nature itself teach you, that a man indeed, if he nourish his hair, it is a shame unto him:

15 But if a woman nourish her hair, it is a glory to her, for her hair is given to her for a covering.

16 But if any man seem to be contentious, we have no such custom, nor the church of God.

17 Now this I ordain: not praising you, that you come together not for the better, but for the worse.

18 For first of all I hear that when you come together in the church, there are schisms among you, and in part I believe it.

19 For there must be also heresies: that they also, who are reproved, may be made manifest among you.

20 When you come therefore together into one place, it is not now to eat the Lord's supper.

21 For every one taketh before his own supper to eat. And one indeed is hungry, and another is drunk.

22 What, have you not houses to eat and to drink in? Or despise ye the church of God, and put them to shame that have not? What shall I say to you? Do I praise you? In this I praise you not.

23 For I have received of the Lord that which also I delivered unto you, that the Lord JESUS, the same night in which he was betrayed, took bread,

24 And giving thanks, broke, and said: ᶜTake ye and eat: this is my body which shall be

---

ᵃ Gen. 1. 26.—ᵇ Gen. 2. 22.

---

CHAP. XI. Ver. 10. *A power.* That is, a veil or covering, as a sign that she is under the *power* of her husband; and this, the apostle adds, *because of the Angels,* who are present in the assemblies of the faithful.

ᶜ Matt. 26. 26. Mark 14. 22. Luke 22. 17.

---

Ver. 19. *There must be also heresies.* By reason of the pride and perversity of man's heart; not by God's will or appointment; who nevertheless draws good out of this evil, manifesting, by that occasion, who are the good and firm Christians, and making their faith more remarkable.

Ver. 20. *The Lord's supper.* So the apostle here calls the *charity feasts* observed by the primitive Christians; and reprehends the abuses of the Corinthians, on these occasions; which were the more criminal, because these feasts were accompanied with the celebrating the eucharistic sacrifice and sacrament.

CHAP. XI. I. TO THE CORINTHIANS. CHAP. XII.

delivered for you: this do for the commemoration of me.

25 In like manner also the chalice, after he had supped, saying: This chalice is the new testament in my blood: this do ye, as often as you shall drink, for the commemoration of me.

26 For as often as you shall eat this bread, and drink the chalice, you shall shew the death of the Lord, until he come.

27 ᵃ Therefore whosoever shall eat this bread, or drink the chalice of the Lord unworthily, shall be guilty of the body and of the blood of the Lord.

28 ᵇ But let a man prove himself: and so let him eat of that bread, and drink of the chalice.

29 For he that eateth and drinketh unworthily, eateth and drinketh judgment to himself, not discerning the body of the Lord.

30 Therefore are there many infirm and weak among you, and many sleep.

31 But if we would judge ourselves, we should not be judged.

32 But whilst we are judged, we are chastised by the Lord; that we be not condemned with this world.

33 Wherefore, my brethren, when you come together to eat, wait for one another.

34 If any man be hungry, let him eat at home; that you come not together unto judgment. And the rest I will set in order, when I come.

## CHAP. XII.

*Of the diversity of spiritual gifts. The members of the mystical body, like those of the natural body, must mutually cherish one another.*

NOW concerning spiritual things, my brethren, I would not have you ignorant.

2 You know that, when you were heathens, you went to dumb idols, according as you were led.

3 Wherefore I give you to understand, ᶜ that no man speaking by the spirit of God, saith Anathema to JESUS. And no man can say, the Lord JESUS, but by the Holy Ghost.

4 Now there are diversities of graces, but the same Spirit;

5 And there are diversities of ministries, but the same Lord.

6 And there are diversities of operations, but the same God, who worketh all in all.

7 And the manifestation of the Spirit is given to every man unto profit.

8 To one indeed, by the Spirit, is given the word of wisdom: and to another, the word of knowledge, according to the same Spirit.

9 To another, faith in the same Spirit: to another, the grace of healing in one Spirit:

---

ᵃ John 6. 59.—ᵇ 2 Cor. 13. 5.

---

Ver. 27. *Or drink.* Here erroneous translators corrupted the text, by putting *and drink* (contrary to the original, ἤ πίῃ) instead of *or drink*.

Ver. 27. 29. *Guilty of the body, &c. not discerning the body, &c.* This demonstrates the real presence of the body and blood of Christ, even to the unworthy communicant; who otherwise could not be *guilty of the body and blood* of Christ, or justly condemned for *not discerning the Lord's body.*

Ver. 28. *Drink of the chalice.* This is not said by way of command, but by way of allowance, viz., where and when it is agreeable to the practice and discipline of the Church.

---

ᶜ Mark 9. 38.

10 To another, the working of miracles: to another, prophecy: to another, the discerning of spirits: to another, *diverse* kinds of tongues: to another, interpretation of speeches.

11 <sup>a</sup> But all these things one and the same Spirit worketh, dividing to every one according as he will.

12 For as the body is one, and hath many members; and all the members of the body, whereas they are many, yet are one body; so also is Christ.

13 For in one Spirit were we all baptized into one body, whether Jews, or gentiles, whether bond, or free: and in one Spirit we have all been made to drink.

14 For the body also is not one member, but many.

15 If the foot should say, because I am not the hand, I am not of the body: is it therefore not of the body?

16 And if the ear should say, because I am not the eye, I am not of the body: is it therefore not of the body?

17 If the whole body were the eye: where would be the hearing? If the whole were hearing: where would be the smelling?

18 But now God hath set the members every one of them in the body as it hath pleased him.

19 And if they all were one member, where would be the body?

20 But now *there are* many members indeed, yet one body.

21 And the eye cannot say to the hand: I need not thy help; nor again the head to the feet: I have no need of you.

22 Yea, much more those that seem to be the more feeble members of the body, are more necessary:

23 And such as we think to be the less honourable members of the body, about these we put more abundant honour: and those that are our uncomely parts, have more abundant comeliness.

24 But our comely parts have no need: but God hath tempered the body together, giving to that which wanted the more abundant honour.

25 That there might be no schism in the body, but the members might be mutually careful one for another.

26 And if one member suffer anything, all the members suffer with it: or if one member glory, all the members rejoice with it.

27 Now you are the body of Christ, and members of member.

28 <sup>b</sup> And God indeed hath set some in the church, first apostles, secondly prophets, thirdly doctors, after that miracles, then the graces of healings, helps, governments, kinds of tongues, interpretations of speeches.

29 Are all apostles? Are all prophets? Are all doctors?

30 Are all *workers of* miracles? Have all the grace of healing? Do all speak with tongues? Do all interpret?

31 But be zealous for the better gifts. And I shew unto you yet a more excellent way.

## CHAP. XIII.

*Charity is to be preferred before all other gifts.*

IF I speak with the tongues of men, and of angels, and

---

<sup>a</sup> Rom. 12. a. and 4. Ephes. 4. 7.

<sup>b</sup> Ephes. 4. 11.

THE BURIAL OF CHRIST.

have not charity, I am become as sounding brass or a tinkling cymbal.

2 And if I should have prophecy, and should know all mysteries, and all knowledge, and if I should have all faith, so that I could remove mountains, and have not charity, I am nothing.

3 And if I should distribute all my goods to feed the poor, and if I should deliver my body to be burned, and have not charity, it profiteth me nothing.

4 Charity is patient, is kind: charity envieth not, dealeth not perversely: is not puffed up.

5 Is not ambitious, seeketh not her own, is not provoked to anger, thinketh no evil.

6 Rejoiceth not in iniquity, but rejoiceth with the truth:

7 Beareth all things, believeth all things, hopeth all things, endureth all things.

8 Charity never falleth away: whether prophecies shall be made void, or tongues shall cease, or knowledge shall be destroyed.

9 For we know in part, and prophesy in part.

10 But when that which is perfect is come, that which is in part shall be done away.

11 When I was a child, I spoke as a child, I understood as a child, I thought as a child. But when I became a man, I put away the things of a child.

12 We see now through a glass in a dark manner: but then face to face. Now I know in part; but then I shall know even as I am known.

13 And now there remain faith, hope, charity, these three: but the greater of these is charity.

## CHAP. XIV.

*The gift of prophesying is to be preferred before that of speaking strange tongues.*

FOLLOW after charity, be zealous for spiritual gifts: but rather that you may prophesy.

2 For he that speaketh in a tongue, speaketh not unto men, but unto God: for no man heareth. Yet by the Spirit he speaketh mysteries.

3 But he that prophesieth, speaketh to men unto edification and exhortation and comfort.

4 He that speaketh in a tongue, edifieth himself; but he that prophesieth, edifieth the church.

5 And I would have you all to speak with tongues, but rather to prophesy. For greater is he that prophesieth, than he that speaketh with tongues: unless perhaps he interpret, that the church may receive edification.

6 But now, brethren, if I come to you, speaking with tongues, what shall I profit you unless I speak to you either in revelation, or in knowledge, or in prophecy, or in doctrine?

7 Even things without life that give sound, whether pipe or harp, except they give a distinction of sounds, how shall it be known what is piped or harped?

8 For if the trumpet give an uncertain sound, who shall prepare himself to the battle?

9 So likewise you, except you utter by the tongue plain

CHAP. XIV. Ver. 1 *Prophesy.* That is, declare or expound the mysteries of faith.
Ver. 2. *Not unto men.* Viz., so as to be heard, that is, so as to be understood by them.

speech, how shall it be known what is said? For you shall be speaking into the air.

10 There are, for example, so many kinds of tongues in this world: and none is without voice.

11 If then I know not the power of the voice, I shall be to him, to whom I speak, a barbarian, and he, that speaketh, a barbarian to me.

12 So you also, forasmuch as you are zealous of spirits, seek to abound unto the edifying of the church.

13 And therefore he that speaketh by a tongue, let him pray that he may interpret.

14 For if I pray in a tongue, my spirit prayeth, but my understanding is without fruit.

15 What is it then? I will pray with the spirit, I will pray also with the understanding: I will sing with the spirit, I will sing also with the understanding.

16 Else if thou shalt bless with the spirit, how shall he that holdeth the place of the unlearned say, Amen, to thy blessing? because he knoweth not what thou sayest.

17 For thou indeed givest thanks well, but the other is not edified.

18 I thank my God I speak with all your tongues.

19 But in the church I had rather speak five words with my understanding, that I may instruct others also, than ten thousand words in a tongue.

20 Brethren, do not become children in sense, but in malice be children, and in sense be perfect.

21 In the law it is written: *In other tongues and other lips, I will speak to this people: and neither so will they hear me, saith the Lord.*

22 Wherefore tongues are for a sign, not to believers, but to unbelievers: but prophecies, not to unbelievers, but to believers.

23 If therefore the whole church come together into one place, and all speak with tongues, and there come in unlearned persons or infidels, will they not say that you are mad?

24 But if all prophesy, and there come in one that believeth not, or an unlearned person, he is convinced of all, he is judged of all.

25 The secrets of his heart are made manifest, and so, falling down on his face, he will adore God, affirming that God is among you indeed.

26 How is it then, brethren? When you come together, every one of you hath a psalm, hath a doctrine, hath a revelation, hath a tongue, hath an interpretation: let all things be done to edification.

---

Ver. 12. *Of spirits.* Of spiritual gifts.

Ver. 16. *Amen.* The unlearned, not knowing that you are then blessing, will not be qualified to join with you by saying Amen to your blessing. The use or abuse of strange tongues, of which the apostle here speaks, does not regard the public liturgy of the Church, (in which strange tongues were never used,) but certain conferences of the faithful, ver. 26, &c., in which, meeting together, they discovered to one another their various miraculous gifts of the Spirit, common in those primitive times; amongst which the apostle prefers that of prophesying before that of speaking strange tongues, because it was more to the public edification. Where also note, that the Latin, used in our liturgy, is so far from being a strange or unknown tongue, that it is perhaps the best known tongue in the world.

*a* Isaias 28. 11.

27 If any speak with a tongue, let it be by two, or at the most by three, and in course, and let one interpret.

28 But if there be no interpreter, let him hold his peace in the church, and speak to himself and to God.

29 And let the prophets speak, two or three: and let the rest judge.

30 But if anything be revealed to another sitting, let the first hold his peace.

31 For you may all prophesy one by one; that all may learn, and all may be exhorted:

32 And the spirits of the prophets are subject to the prophets.

33 For God is not the God of dissension, but of peace: as also I teach in all the churches of the saints.

34 Let women keep silence in the churches: for it is not permitted them to speak, but to be subject, *a* as also the law saith.

35 But if they would learn anything, let them ask their husbands at home. For it is a shame for a woman to speak in the church.

36 Or did the word of God come out from you? or came it only unto you?

37 If any seem to be a prophet, or spiritual, let him know the things that I write to you, that they are the commandments of the Lord.

38 But if any man know not, he shall not be known.

39 Wherefore, brethren, be zealous to prophesy: and forbid not to speak with tongues.

40 But let all things be done decently and according to order.

---

*a* Gen. 3. 16.

## CHAP. XV.

*Christ's resurrection and ours: the manner of our resurrection.*

NOW *b* I make known unto you, brethren, the gospel which I preached to you, which also you have received, and wherein you stand;

2 By which also you are saved, if you hold fast after what manner I preached unto you, unless you have believed in vain.

3 For I delivered unto you first of all, which I also received: How that Christ died for our sins *c* according to the scriptures:

4 *d* And that he was buried, and that he rose again the third day according to the scriptures:

5 And that he was seen by Cephas; *e* and after that by the eleven.

6 Then was he seen by more than five hundred brethren at once: of whom many remain until this present, and some are fallen asleep.

7 After that, he was seen by James, then by all the apostles.

8 And last of all, he was seen also by me, as by one born out of due time.

9 *f* For I am the least of the apostles, who am not worthy to be called an apostle, because I persecuted the church of God.

10 But by the grace of God, I am what I am; and his grace in me hath not been void, but I have laboured more abundantly than all they: yet not I, but the grace of God with me:

11 For whether I, or they, so

---

*b* Gal. 1. 11.— *c* Isaias 53. 5.— *d* Jonas 2. 1.— *e* John 20. 19.— *f* Acts 9. 6. Ephes. 3. 8.

we preach, and so you have believed.

12 Now if Christ be preached that he arose again from the dead, how do some among you say, that there is no resurrection of the dead?

13 But if there be no resurrection of the dead, then Christ is not risen again.

14 And if Christ be not risen again, then is our preaching vain, and your faith is also vain.

15 Yea, and we are found false witnesses of God, because we have given testimony against God, that he hath raised up Christ; whom he hath not raised up if the dead rise not again.

16 For if the dead rise not again, neither is Christ risen again.

17 And if Christ be not risen again, your faith is vain, for you are yet in your sins.

18 Then they also that are fallen asleep in Christ, are perished.

19 If in this life only we have hope in Christ, we are of all men most miserable.

20 But now Christ is risen from the dead, the first-fruits of them that sleep.

21 *a* For by a man *came* death, and by a man the resurrection of the dead.

22 And as in Adam all die, so also in Christ all shall be made alive.

23 *b* But every one in his own order: the first-fruits Christ, then they that are of Christ, who have believed in his coming.

24 Afterwards the end, when he shall have delivered up the kingdom to God and the Father, when he shall have brought to nought all principality, and power, and virtue.

25 For he must reign, *c Until he hath put all his enemies under his feet.*

26 And the enemy death shall be destroyed last, *d For he hath put all things under his feet.* And whereas he saith,

27 *All things are put under him;* undoubtedly, he is excepted who put all things under him.

28 And when all things shall be subdued unto him, then the Son also himself shall be subject unto him that put all things under him, that God may be all in all.

29 Otherwise what shall they do that are baptized for the dead, if the dead rise not again at all? why are they then baptized for them?

30 Why also are we in danger every hour?

31 I die daily, I protest by your glory, brethren, which I have in CHRIST JESUS our Lord.

---

*c* Ps. 109. L Heb. 1. 13. and 10. 13.—
*d* Ps. 8. 8. Heb. 2. 8.

---

CHAP. XV. Ver. 28. *The Son also himself shall be subject unto him.* That is, the Son will be subject to the Father, according to his human nature, even after the general resurrection, and also the whole mystical body of Christ will be entirely subject to God, obeying him in everything.

Ver. 29. *That are baptized for the dead.* Some think the apostle here alludes to a ceremony then in use: but others, more probably, to the prayers and penitential labours performed by the primitive Christians for the souls of the faithful departed: or to the baptism of afflictions and sufferings undergone for sinners spiritually dead.

---

*a* Col. 1. 18. Apoc. 1. 5.—*b* 1 Thess. 4. 15.

THE RESURRECTION OF CHRIST.

CHAP. XV.  I. TO THE CORINTHIANS.  CHAP. XV.

32 If (according to man) I fought with beasts at Ephesus, what doth it profit me, if the dead rise not again? *a Let us eat and drink, for to-morrow we shall die.*

33 Be not seduced: *Evil communications corrupt good manners.*

34 Awake, ye just, and sin not. For some have not the knowledge of God, I speak it to your shame.

35 But some man will say: How do the dead rise again? or with what manner of body shall they come?

36 Senseless man, that which thou sowest is not quickened, except it die first.

37 And that which thou sowest, thou sowest not the body that shall be; but bare grain, as of wheat, or of some of the rest.

38 But God giveth it a body as he will: and to every seed its proper body.

39 All flesh is not the same flesh: but one *is the flesh* of men, another of beasts, another of birds, another of fishes.

40 And *there are* bodies celestial, and bodies terrestrial: but, one *is the* glory of the celestial, and another of the terrestrial.

41 One *is the* glory of the sun, another the glory of the moon, and another the glory of the stars. For star differeth from star in glory:

42 So also is the resurrection of the dead. It is sown in corruption, it shall rise in incorruption.

43 It is sown in dishonour, it shall rise in glory. It is sown in weakness, it shall rise in power.

44 It is sown a natural body, it shall rise a spiritual body. If there be a natural body, there is also a spiritual body, as it is written:

45 *b The first man Adam was made into a living soul:* the last Adam into a quickening spirit.

46 Yet that was not first which is spiritual, but that which is natural: afterwards that which is spiritual.

47 The first man *was* of the earth, earthly: the second man, from heaven, heavenly.

48 Such as *is* the earthly, such also *are* the earthly: and such as *is* the heavenly, such also *are* they that are heavenly.

49 Therefore as we have borne the image of the earthly, let us bear also the image of the heavenly.

50 Now this I say, brethren, that flesh and blood cannot possess the kingdom of God: neither shall corruption possess incorruption.

51 Behold I tell you a mystery. We shall all indeed rise again: but we shall not all be changed.

52 In a moment, in the twinkling of an eye, at the last trumpet: for the trumpet shall sound, and the dead shall rise again incorruptible: and we shall be changed.

53 For this corruptible must put on incorruption; and this mortal must put on immortality.

54 And when this mortal hath put on immortality, then shall

---

*a* Wis. 2. 6.  Isaias 22. 13. and 56. 12.

Ver. 32. *Let us eat and drink,* &c. That is, if we did not believe that we are to rise again from the dead, we might live like the impious and wicked, who have no belief in the resurrection.

*b* Gen. 2. 7.

come to pass the saying that is written: *a Death is swallowed up in victory.*

55 O death, where is thy victory? O death, where is thy sting?

56 Now the sting of death is sin: and the strength of sin is the law.

57 *b* But thanks be to God, who hath given us the victory through our Lord JESUS CHRIST.

58 Therefore, my beloved brethren, be ye steadfast and unmoveable; always abounding in the work of the Lord, knowing that your labour is not vain in the Lord.

## CHAP. XVI.

*Of collection of alms, admonitions, and salutations.*

NOW concerning the collections that are made for the saints, as I have given order to the churches of Galatia, so do ye also.

2 On the first day of the week let every one of you put apart with himself, laying up what it shall well please him; that when I come, the collections be not then to be made.

3 And when I shall be with you; whomsoever you shall approve by letters, them will I send to carry your grace to Jerusalem.

4 And if it be meet that I also go, they shall go with me.

5 Now I will come to you, when I shall have passed through Macedonia. For I shall pass through Macedonia.

6 And with you perhaps I shall abide, or even spend the winter: that you may bring me on my way whithersoever I shall go.

7 For I will not see you now by the way, for I trust that I shall abide with you some time, if the Lord permit.

8 But I will tarry at Ephesus until pentecost.

9 For, a great door and evident is opened unto me: and many adversaries.

10 Now if Timothy come, see that he be with you without fear, for he worketh the work of the Lord, as I also do.

11 Let no man therefore despise him, but conduct ye him on his way in peace: that he may come to me. For I look for him with the brethren.

12 And touching *our* brother Apollo, I give you to understand, that I much entreated him to come unto you with the brethren: and indeed it was not his will at all to come at this time. But he will come when he shall have leisure.

13 Watch ye, stand fast in the faith, do manfully, and be strengthened.

14 Let all your things be done in charity.

15 And I beseech you, brethren, you know the house of Stephanus, and of Fortunatus, and of Achaicus, that they are the first-fruits of Achaia, and have dedicated themselves to the ministry of the saints:

16 That you also be subject to such, and to every one that worketh with us, and laboureth.

17 And I rejoice in the presence of Stephanus, and Fortunatus, and Achaicus, because that which was wanting on your part, they have supplied.

18 For they have refreshed

---

*a* Osee 13. 14.  Heb. 2. 14.—*b* 1 John 5. 5.

both my spirit and yours. Know them therefore that are such.

19 The churches of Asia salute you. Aquila and Priscilla salute you much in the Lord, with the church that is in their house, with whom I also lodge.

20 All the brethren salute you. Salute one another in a holy kiss.

21 The salutation of *me* Paul, with my own hand.

22 If any man love not our Lord JESUS CHRIST, let him be anathema, maran-atha.

23 The grace of our Lord JESUS CHRIST be with you.

24 My charity be with you all in CHRIST JESUS. Amen.

CHAP. XVI. Ver. 22. *Let him be anathema, maran-atha.* Anathema signifies here a thing accursed. *Maran-atha*, which, according to St. Jerome and St. Chrysostom, signify, *The Lord is come already*, and therefore is to be taken as an admonition to those who doubted of the resurrection, and to put them in mind that Christ, the judge of the living and the dead, is come already. Others explain *Maran-atha: May our Lord come*, that is, to judge and punish those with exemplary judgments and punishments that do not love the Lord Jesus Christ.

# THE SECOND EPISTLE OF ST. PAUL TO THE CORINTHIANS.

*In this Epistle St. PAUL comforts those who are now reformed by his admonitions to them in the former, and absolves the incestuous man on doing penance, whom he had before excommunicated for his crime. Hence he treats of true penance and of the dignity of the ministers of the New Testament. He cautions the faithful against false teachers and the society of infidels. He gives an account of his sufferings, and also of the favours and graces which God hath bestowed on him. This second Epistle was written in the same year with the first, and sent by TITUS from some place in Macedonia.*

## CHAP. I.

*He speaks of his troubles in Asia. His not coming to them was not out of levity. The constancy and sincerity of his doctrine.*

PAUL an apostle of JESUS CHRIST by the will of God, and Timothy *our* brother: to the Church of God that is at Corinth, with all the saints that are in all Achaia:

2 Grace unto you and peace from God our father, and from the Lord JESUS CHRIST.

3 ᵃ Blessed be the God and Father of our Lord JESUS CHRIST, the Father of mercies, and the God of all comfort.

4 Who comforteth us in all our tribulation; that we also

ᵃ Ephes. 1. 3.  1 Pet. 1. 3.

may be able to comfort them who are in all distress, by the exhortation wherewith we also are exhorted by God.

5 For as the sufferings of Christ abound in us: so also by Christ doth our comfort abound.

6 Now whether we be in tribulation, *it is* for your exhortation and salvation: or whether we be comforted, *it is* for your consolation: or whether we be exhorted, *it is* for your exhortation and salvation, which worketh the enduring of the same sufferings which we also suffer.

7 That our hope for you may be steadfast: knowing that as you are partakers of the sufferings, so shall you be also of the consolation.

8 For we would not have you ignorant, brethren, of our tribulation, which came to us in Asia, that we were pressed out of measure above *our* strength, so that we were weary even of life.

9 But we had in ourselves the answer of death, that we should not trust in ourselves, but in God who raiseth the dead,

10 Who hath delivered and doth deliver us out of so great dangers: in whom we trust that he will yet also deliver us.

11 You helping withal in prayer for us: that for this gift obtained for us, by the means of many persons, thanks may be given by many in our behalf.

12 For our glory is this, the testimony of our conscience, that in simplicity of heart and sincerity of God, and not in carnal wisdom, but in the grace of God, we have conversed in this world: and more abundantly towards you.

13 For we write no other things to you, than what you have read and known. And I hope that you shall know unto the end:

14 As also you have known us in part, that we are your glory, as you also are ours in the day of our Lord JESUS CHRIST.

15 And in this confidence I had a mind to come to you before, that you might have a second grace:

16 And to pass by you into Macedonia, and again from Macedonia to come to you, and by you to be brought on my way towards Judea.

17 Whereas then I was thus minded, did I use lightness? Or the things that I purpose, do I purpose according to the flesh, that there should be with me, *It is*, and *It is not*.

18 But God is faithful, for our preaching which was to you, was not, *It is*, and *It is not*.

19 For the Son of God, JESUS CHRIST, who was preached among you by us, by me, and Sylvanus, and Timothy, was not, *It is*, and *It is not*, but *It is*, was in him.

20 For all the promises of God are in him, *It is*: therefore also by him, amen to God, unto our glory.

21 Now he that confirmeth us with you in Christ, and that hath anointed us, is God:

22 Who also hath sealed us, and given the pledge of the Spirit in our hearts.

---

CHAP. I. Ver. 19 *It was* in him. There was no inconstancy in the doctrine of the apostles, sometimes, like modern sectaries, saying, *It is*, and at other times saying, *It is not*. But their doctrine was ever the same, one uniform yea, in Jesus Christ, one *Amen*, that is, one *truth* in him.

THE ANGEL DECLARING THE RESURRECTION OF CHRIST.

23 But I call God to witness upon my soul, that to spare you, I came not any more to Corinth, not because we exercise dominion over your faith: but we are helpers of your joy: for in faith you stand.

## CHAP. II.

*He grants a pardon to the incestuous man, upon his doing penance.*

BUT I determined this with myself, not to come to you again in sorrow.

2 For if I make you sorrowful; who is he then that can make me glad, but the same who is made sorrowful by me?

3 And I wrote this same to you; that I may not, when I come, have sorrow upon sorrow, from them of whom I ought to rejoice; having confidence in you all that my joy is the joy of you all.

4 For out of much affliction, and anguish of heart I wrote to you with many tears; not that you should be made sorrowful; but that you might know the charity I have more abundantly towards you.

5 And if any one have caused grief, he hath not grieved me; but in part, that I may not burden you all.

6 To him that is such a one this rebuke is sufficient, that is given by many:

7 So that contrariwise you should rather pardon and comfort him, lest perhaps such an one be swallowed up with overmuch sorrow.

8 For which cause I beseech you, that you would confirm your charity towards him.

9 For to this end also did I write, that I may know the experiment of you, whether you be obedient in all things.

10 And to whom you have pardoned anything, I also. For, what I have pardoned, if I have pardoned anything, for your sakes have I done it in the person of Christ,

11 That we be not overreached by satan. For we are not ignorant of his devices.

12 And when I was come to Troas for the gospel of Christ, and a door was opened unto me in the Lord,

13 I had no rest in my spirit, because I found not Titus my brother, but bidding them farewell, I went into Macedonia.

14 Now thanks be to God, who always maketh us to triumph in CHRIST JESUS, and manifesteth the odour of his knowledge by us in every place.

15 For we are the good odour of Christ unto God, in them that are saved, and in them that perish.

16 To the one indeed the odour of death unto death; but to the others the odour of life unto life. And for these things who is so sufficient?

17 For we are not as many adulterating the word of God, but with sincerity, but as from God, before God in Christ we speak.

CHAP. II. Ver. 10. *I also.* The apostle here granted an indulgence or pardon, *in the person* and by the authority of Christ, to the incestuous Corinthian, whom before he had put under penance: which pardon consisted in a releasing of part of the temporal punishment due to his sin.

Ver. 16. *The odour of death, &c.* The preaching of the apostle, which by its fragrant odour brought many to life, was to others, through their own fault, the occasion of death, by their wilfully opposing and resisting that divine call.

## CHAP. III.

*He needs no commendatory letters. The glory of the ministry of the New Testament.*

DO we begin again to commend ourselves? Or do we need (as some do) epistles of commendation to you, or from you?

2 You are our epistle, written in our hearts, which is known and read by all men:

3 Being manifested, that you are the epistle of Christ, ministered by us, and written not with ink, but with the Spirit of the living God: not in tables of stone, but in the fleshy tables of the heart.

4 And such confidence we have, through Christ towards God.

5 Not that we are sufficient to think anything of ourselves, as of ourselves; but our sufficiency is from God.

6 Who also hath made us fit ministers of the new testament, not in the letter, but in the spirit. For the letter killeth: but the spirit quickeneth.

7 Now if the ministration of death, engraven with letters upon stones, was glorious: so that the children of Israel could not steadfastly behold the face of Moses, for the glory of his countenance, which is made void:

8 How shall not the ministration of the Spirit be rather in glory?

9 For if the ministration of condemnation be glory, much more the ministration of justice aboundeth in glory.

10 For even that which was glorious in this part was not glorified, by reason of the glory that excelleth.

11 For if that which is done away was glorious, much more that which remaineth is in glory.

12 Having therefore such hope, we use much confidence:

13 *a* And not as Moses put a veil upon his face that the children of Israel might not steadfastly look on the face of that which is made void.

14 But their senses were made dull. For until this present day, the self-same veil, in the reading of the old testament, remaineth not taken away (because in Christ it is made void).

15 But even until this day when Moses is read, the veil is upon their heart.

16 But when they shall be converted to the Lord, the veil shall be taken away.

17 *b* Now the Lord is a Spirit. And where the Spirit of the Lord is, there is liberty.

18 But we all beholding the glory of the Lord with open face, are transformed into the same image from glory to glory, as by the Spirit of the Lord.

## CHAP. IV.

*The sincerity of his preaching: his comfort in his afflictions.*

THEREFORE seeing we have this ministration, according as we have obtained mercy, we faint not.

2 But we renounce the hidden things of dishonesty, not walking in craftiness, nor adulterating the word of God, but by manifestation of the truth commending ourselves to every man's conscience, in the sight of God.

*a* Exod. 34. 33.—*b* John 4. 24.

---

CHAP. III. Ver. 6. *The letter.* Not rightly understood, and taken without the spirit.

3 And if our gospel be also hid; it is hid to them that are lost,

4 In whom the god of this world hath blinded the minds of unbelievers, that the light of the gospel of the glory of Christ, who is the image of God, should not shine unto them.

5 For we preach not ourselves, but JESUS CHRIST our Lord: and ourselves your servants through JESUS.

6 For God, who commanded the light to shine out of darkness, hath shined in our hearts, to give the light of the knowledge of the glory of God in the face of CHRIST JESUS.

7 But we have this treasure in earthen vessels, that the excellency may be of the power of God, and not of us.

8 In all things we suffer tribulation, but are not distressed: we are straitened, but are not destitute:

9 We suffer persecution, but are not forsaken: we are cast down, but we perish not:

10 Always bearing about in our body the mortification of JESUS, that the life also of JESUS may be made manifest in our bodies.

11 For we who live are always delivered unto death for JESUS' sake: that the life also of JESUS may be made manifest in our mortal flesh.

12 So then death worketh in us, but life in you.

13 But having the same spirit of faith, as it is written: "*I believed, for which cause I have spoken*:" we also believe, for which cause we speak also:

14 Knowing that he who raised up JESUS will raise up us also with JESUS, and place us with you.

15 For all things *are* for your sakes: that the grace abounding through many may abound in thanksgiving unto the glory of God.

16 For which cause we faint not: but though our outward man is corrupted, yet the inward man is renewed day by day.

17 For that which is at present momentary and light of our tribulation, worketh for us above measure exceedingly an eternal weight of glory.

18 While we look not at the things which are seen, but at the things which are not seen. For the things which are seen are temporal: but the things which are not seen are eternal.

## CHAP. V.

*He is willing to leave his earthly mansion to be with the Lord. His charity for the Corinthians.*

FOR we know, if our earthly house of this habitation be dissolved, that we have a building of God, a house not made with hands, eternal in heaven.

2 For in this also we groan, desiring to be clothed upon with our habitation that is from heaven:

3 *b* Yet so, that we be found clothed, not naked.

4 For we also, who are in this tabernacle, do groan being burthened: because we would not be unclothed, but clothed upon, that that which is mortal may be swallowed up by life.

5 Now he that maketh us for this very thing is God, who

---

*a* Ps. 115. 10.   *b* Apoc. 16. 15.

hath given us the pledge of the Spirit.

6 Therefore having always confidence, knowing that, while we are in the body, we are absent from the Lord.

7 (For we walk by faith and not by sight.)

8 But we are confident, and have a good will to be absent rather from the body, and to be present with the Lord.

9 And therefore we labour, whether absent or present, to please him.

10 <sup>a</sup> For we must all be manifested before the judgment-seat of Christ, that every one may receive the proper things of the body, according as he hath done, whether it be good or evil.

11 Knowing therefore the fear of the Lord, we use persuasion to men: but to God we are manifest. And I trust also that in your consciences we are manifest.

12 We commend not ourselves again to you, but give you occasion to glory in our behalf: that you may have *somewhat to answer* them who glory in face, and not in heart.

13 For whether we be transported in mind, *it is* to God: or whether we be sober, *it is* for you.

14 For the charity of Christ presseth us: judging this, that if one die for all, then all were dead.

15 And Christ died for all: that they also, who live, may not now live to themselves, but unto him who died for them and rose again.

16 Wherefore henceforth we know no man according to the flesh. And if we have known Christ according to the flesh: but now we know him so no longer.

17 If then any be in Christ a new creature, the old things are passed away, <sup>b</sup> behold all things are made new.

18 But all things *are* of God, who hath reconciled us to himself by Christ. and hath given to us the ministry of reconciliation.

19 For God indeed was in Christ reconciling the world to himself, not imputing to them their sins, and he hath placed in us the word of reconciliation.

20 For Christ therefore we are ambassadors, God as it were exhorting by us. For Christ, we beseech you be reconciled to God.

21 Him, that knew no sin. for us he hath made sin, that we might be made the justice of God in him.

---

<sup>b</sup> Isaias 43. 19. Apoc. 21. 5.

Ver. 16. *We know no man according to the flesh.* That is, we consider not any man with regard to his nation, family, kindred, or other natural qualities or advantages, but only with relation to Christ, and according to the order of divine charity, in God, and for God. The apostle adds, that even with respect to Christ himself, he now no longer considers him according to the flesh, by taking a satisfaction in his being his countryman; his affection being now purified from all such earthly considerations.

Ver. 21. *Sin for us.* That is, to be a *sin-offering*, a victim for sin.

---

<sup>a</sup> Rom. 14. 10.

---

CHAP. V. Ver. 10. *The proper things of the body.* In the particular judgment, immediately after death, the soul is rewarded or punished according to what it has done in the body.

MARY MAGDALEN AT THE SEPULCHRE.

## CHAP. VI.

*He exhorts them to a correspondence with God's grace, and not to associate with unbelievers.*

AND we helping do exhort you, that you receive not the grace of God in vain.

2 For he saith: *a In an accepted time have I heard thee; and in the day of salvation have I helped thee.* Behold, now is the acceptable time: behold now is the day of salvation.

3 *b* Giving no offence to any man, that our ministry be not blamed:

4 But in all things let us exhibit ourselves *c* as the ministers of God, in much patience, in tribulation, in necessities, in distresses,

5 In stripes, in prisons, in seditions, in labours, in watchings, in fastings,

6 In chastity, in knowledge, in long-suffering, in sweetness, in the Holy Ghost, in charity unfeigned,

7 In the word of truth, in the power of God; by the armour of justice on the right hand and on the left,

8 By honour and dishonour, by evil report and good report: as deceivers, and yet true: as unknown, and yet known:

9 As dying, and behold we live: as chastised, and not killed:

10 As sorrowful, yet always rejoicing: as needy, yet enriching many: as having nothing, and possessing all things.

11 Our mouth is open to you, O ye Corinthians, our heart is enlarged.

12 You are not straitened in us: but in your own bowels you are straitened.

13 But having the same recompense (I speak as to my children) be you also enlarged.

14 Bear not the yoke with unbelievers. For what participation hath justice with injustice? or what fellowship hath light with darkness?

15 And what concord hath Christ with Belial? or what part hath the faithful with the unbeliever?

16 And what agreement hath the temple of God with idols? *d* For you are the temple of the living God: as God saith: *e I will dwell in them, and walk among them, and I will be their God, and they shall be my people.*

17 *f* Wherefore, *Go out from among them, and be ye separate,* saith the Lord, *and touch not the unclean thing.*

18 *And I will receive you: g and I will be a Father to you: and you shall be my sons and daughters, saith the Lord almighty.*

## CHAP. VII.

*The apostle's affection for the Corinthians; his comfort and joy on their account.*

HAVING therefore these promises, dearly beloved, let us cleanse ourselves from all defilement of the flesh and of the spirit, perfecting sanctification in the fear of God.

2 Receive us. We have injured no man, we have corrupted no man, we have overreached no man.

3 I speak not this to your

---

*a* Isaias 49. 8.—*b* 1 Cor. 10. 32.—*c* 1 Cor. 4. 1.  *d* 1 Cor. 3. 16. 17. and 6. 19.—*e* Lev. 26. 12.—*f* Isaias 52. 11.—*g* Jer. 31. 9.

condemnation. For we have said before, that you are in our hearts, to die together, and to live together.

4 Great is my confidence with you, great is my glorying for you. I am filled with comfort: I exceedingly abound with joy in all our tribulation.

5 For also when we were come into Macedonia, our flesh had no rest, but we suffered all tribulation: combats without, fears within.

6 But God, who comforteth the humble, comforted us by the coming of Titus.

7 And not by his coming only, but also by the consolation, wherewith he was comforted in you, relating to us your desire, your mourning, your zeal for me, so that I rejoiced the more.

8 For although I made you sorrowful by my epistle, I do not repent: and if I did repent, seeing that the same epistle (although but for a time) did make you sorrowful:

9 Now I am glad: not because you were made sorrowful; but because you were made sorrowful unto penance. For you were made sorrowful according to God, that you might suffer damage by us in nothing.

10 <sup>a</sup> For the sorrow that is according to God worketh penance steadfast unto salvation: but the sorrow of the world worketh death.

11 For behold this self-same thing, that you were made sorrowful according to God, how great carefulness it worketh in you: yea defence, yea indignation, yea fear, yea desire, yea zeal, yea revenge: in all things you have shewed yourselves to be undefiled in the matter.

12 Wherefore although I wrote to you, it was not for his sake that did the wrong, not for him that suffered it: but to manifest our carefulness that we have for you,

13 Before God: therefore we were comforted. But in our consolation we did the more abundantly rejoice for the joy of Titus, because his spirit was refreshed by you all.

14 And if I have boasted anything to him of you, I have not been put to shame, but as we have spoken all things to you in truth, so also our boasting that was made to Titus, is found truth.

15 And his <sup>b</sup> bowels are more abundantly towards you; remembering the obedience of you all, how with fear and trembling you received him.

16 I rejoice that in all things I have confidence in you.

## CHAP. VIII.

*He exhorts them to contribute bountifully to relieve the poor of Jerusalem.*

NOW we make known unto you, brethren, the grace of God, that hath been given in the churches of Macedonia;

2 That in much experience of tribulation they have had abundance of joy, and their very deep poverty hath abounded unto the riches of their simplicity.

3 For according to their power, (I bear them witness,)

---

<sup>a</sup> 1 Pet. 2. 19.

<sup>b</sup> i.e., affection.

CHAP. VIII. Ver. 2. *Simplicity.* That is, sincere bounty and charity.

and beyond their power, they were willing;

4 With much entreaty begging of us the grace and communication of the ministry that is done toward the saints.

5 And not as we hoped, but they gave their own selves first to the Lord, then to us by the will of God:

6 Insomuch, that we desired Titus, that as he had begun, so also he would finish among you this same grace:

7 That as in all things you abound in faith, and word, and knowledge, and all carefulness; moreover also in your charity towards us, so in this grace also you may abound.

8 I speak not as commanding: but by the carefulness of others, approving also the good disposition of your charity.

9 For you know the grace of our Lord JESUS CHRIST, that being rich he became poor, for your sakes; that through his poverty you might be rich.

10 And herein I give my advice: for this is profitable for you, who have begun not only to do, but also to be willing, a year ago:

11 Now therefore perform ye it also in deed; that, as your mind is forward to be willing, so it may be also to perform, out of that which you have.

12 For if the will be forward, it is accepted according to that which *a man* hath, not according to that which he hath not.

13 For *I mean* not that others should be eased, and you burthened: but by an equality.

14 In this present time let your abundance supply their want: that their abundance also may supply your want, that there may be an equality.

15 As it is written: *ᵃHe that had much, had nothing over: and he that had little, had no want.*

16 And thanks be to God, who hath given the same carefulness for you in the heart of Titus.

17 For indeed he accepteth the exhortation: but being more careful, of his own will he went unto you.

18 We have sent also with him the brother, whose praise is in the gospel through all the churches:

19 And not that only, but he was also ordained by the churches companion of our travels, for this grace, which is administered by us to the glory of the Lord, and our determined will:

20 Avoiding this lest any man should blame us in this abundance which is administered by us.

21 ᵇFor we forecast what may be good not only before God, but also before men.

22 And we have sent with them our brother also, whom we have often proved diligent in many things: but now much more diligent, with much confidence in you.

23 Either for Titus, who is my companion and fellowlabourer towards you, or our brethren, the apostles of the churches the glory of Christ.

24 Wherefore shew ye to them, in the sight of the churches, the evidence of your charity, and of our boasting on your behalf.

---

ᵃ Exod. 16. 18.—ᵇ Rom. 12. 17.

## CHAP. IX.

*A further exhortation to almsgiving: the fruits of it.*

FOR concerning the ministry, that is done towards the saints, it is superfluous for me to write unto you.

2 For I know your forward mind: for which I boast of you to the Macedonians. That Achaia also is ready from the year past, and your emulation hath provoked very many.

3 Now I have sent the brethren, that the thing which we boast of concerning you be not made void in this behalf, that (as I have said) you may be ready:

4 Lest when the Macedonians shall come with me, and find you unprepared, we (not to say ye) should be ashamed in this matter.

5 Therefore I thought it necessary to desire the brethren that they would go to you before, and prepare this blessing before promised, to be ready, so as a blessing, not as covetousness.

6 Now this I say: He who soweth sparingly, shall also reap sparingly: and he who soweth in blessings, shall also reap of blessings.

7 Every one as he hath determined in his heart, not with sadness or of necessity: *a For God loveth a cheerful giver.*

8 And God is able to make all grace abound in you: that ye always having all sufficiency in all things may abound to every good work.

9 As it is written: *b He hath dispersed abroad, he hath given to the poor; his justice remaineth for ever.*

---
*a* Eccli. xx. 11.—*b* Ps. 111. 9.

10 And he that ministereth seed to the sower, will both give you bread to eat, and will multiply your seed, and increase the growth of the fruits of your justice:

11 That being enriched in all things, you may abound unto all simplicity, which worketh through us thanksgiving to God.

12 Because the administration of this office doth not only supply the want of the saints, but aboundeth also by many thanksgivings in the Lord,

13 By the proof of this ministry, glorifying God for the obedience of your confession unto the gospel of Christ, and for the simplicity of *your* communicating unto them, and unto all,

14 And in their praying for you, being desirous of you because of the excellent grace of God in you.

15 Thanks be to God for his unspeakable gift.

## CHAP. X.

*To stop the calumny and boasting of false apostles, he sets forth the power of his apostleship.*

NOW I Paul myself beseech you, by the mildness and modesty of Christ, who in presence indeed am lowly among you, but being absent am bold toward you.

2 But I beseech you, that I may not be bold when I am present, with that confidence wherewith I am thought to be bold, against some, who reckon us as if we walked according to the flesh.

3 For though we walk in the flesh, we do not war according to the flesh.

4 For the weapons of our

CHRIST APPEARS TO MARY MAGDALEN.

warfare are not carnal, but mighty to God unto the pulling down of fortifications, destroying counsels,

5 And every height that exalteth itself against the knowledge of God, and bringeth into captivity every understanding unto the obedience of Christ,

6 And having in readiness to revenge all disobedience, when your obedience shall be fulfilled,

7 See the things that are according to outward appearance. If any man trust to himself, that he is Christ's, let him think this again with himself, that as he is Christ's so are we also.

8 For if also I should boast somewhat more of our power, which the Lord hath given us unto edification, and not for your destruction; I should not be ashamed.

9 But that I may not be thought as it were to terrify you by epistles,

10 (For his epistles indeed, say they, are weighty and strong; but his bodily presence is weak, and his speech contemptible,)

11 Let such a one think this, that such as we are in word by epistles, when absent; such also *we will be* indeed when present.

12 For we dare not match, or compare ourselves with some, that commend themselves: but we measure ourselves by ourselves, and compare ourselves with ourselves.

13 *a* But we will not glory beyond our measure; but according to the measure of the rule, which God hath measured to us, a measure to reach even unto you.

14 For we stretch not out ourselves beyond our measure, as if we reached not unto you. For we are come as far as to you in the gospel of Christ.

15 Not glorying beyond measure in other men's labours; but having hope of your increasing faith, to be magnified in you according to our rule abundantly.

16 Yea, unto those places that are beyond you, to preach the gospel, not to glory in another man's rule, in those things that are made ready to our hand.

17 *b* But he that glorieth, let him glory in the Lord.

18 For not he who commendeth himself is approved, but he whom God commendeth.

## CHAP. XI.

*He is forced to commend himself and his labours, lest the Corinthians should be imposed upon by the false apostles.*

WOULD to God you could bear with some little of my folly: but do bear with me.

2 For I am jealous of you with the jealousy of God. For I have espoused you to one husband, that I may present you as a chaste virgin to Christ.

3 But I fear lest, *c* as the serpent seduced Eve by his subtilty, so your minds should be corrupted, and fall from the simplicity that is in Christ.

4 For if he that cometh preacheth another Christ, whom we have not preached; or if you

---

*a* Ephes. 4. 7. — *b* Jer. 9. 23. 1 Cor. 1. 31. — *c* Gen. 3. 4.

CHAP. XI. Ver. 1. *My folly.* So he calls his reciting his own praises, which, commonly speaking, is looked upon as a piece of folly and vanity; though the apostle was constrained to do it, for the good of the souls committed to his charge.

receive another Spirit, whom you have not received; or another gospel, which you have not received: you might well bear *with him.*

5 For I suppose that I have done nothing less than the great apostles.

6 For although I be rude in speech, yet not in knowledge: but in all things we have been made manifest to you.

7 Or did I commit a fault, humbling myself, that you might be exalted? Because I preached unto you the gospel of God freely?

8 I have taken from other churches, receiving wages of them for your ministry.

9 And, when I was present with you, and wanted, I was chargeable to no man: for that which was wanting to me, the brethren supplied who came from Macedonia: and in all things I have kept myself from being burthensome to you, and so I will keep myself.

10 The truth of Christ is in me, that this glorying shall not be broken off in me in the regions of Achaia.

11 Wherefore? Because I love you not? God knoweth it.

12 But what I do, that I will do, that I may cut off the occasion from them that desire occasion, that wherein they glory, they may be found even as we.

13 For such false apostles are deceitful workmen, transforming themselves into the apostles of Christ.

14 And no wonder: for satan himself transformeth himself into an angel of light.

15 Therefore it is no great thing if his ministers be trans- formed as the ministers of justice: whose end shall be according to their works.

16 Again I say, (let no man think me to be foolish, otherwise take me as foolish, that I also may glory a little,)

17 That which I speak, I speak not according to God, but as it were in foolishness, in this matter of glorying

18 Seeing that many glory according to the flesh, I will glory also.

19 For you gladly suffer the foolish: whereas yourselves are wise.

20 For you suffer if a man bring you into bondage, if a man devour *you,* if a man take *from you,* if a man be lifted up, if a man strike you on the face.

21 I speak according to dishonour, as if we had been weak in this part. Wherein if any man dare (I speak foolishly) I dare also.

22 They are Hebrews: so am I. They are Israelites: so am I. They are the seed of Abraham: so am I.

23 They are the ministers of Christ: (I speak as one less wise,) I am more: in many more labours, in prisons more frequently, in stripes above measure, in deaths often.

24 Of the Jews *a* five times did I receive forty *stripes*, save one.

25 *b* Thrice was I beaten with rods. *c* once I was stoned, *d* thrice I suffered shipwreck; a night and a day I was in the depth of the sea.

26 In journeying often, in perils of waters, in perils of rob-

*a* Deut. 25. 3.—*b* Acts 16. 22.—*c* Acts 14. 19.—*d* Acts 27. 41.

bers, in perils from my own nation, in perils from the gentiles, in perils in the city, in perils in the wilderness, in perils in the sea, in perils from false brethren:

27 In labour and painfulness, in much watchings, in hunger and thirst, in fastings often, in cold and nakedness,

28 Besides those things which are without: my daily instance, the solicitude for all the churches.

29 Who is weak, and I am not weak? Who is scandalized, and I am not on fire?

30 If I must needs glory, I will glory of the things that concern my infirmity.

31 The God and Father of our Lord JESUS CHRIST, who is blessed for ever, knoweth that I lie not.

32 *a* At Damascus the governor of the nation under Aretas the king, guarded the city of the Damascenes to apprehend me:

33 And through a window in a basket was I let down by the wall, and so escaped his hands.

## CHAP. XII.

*His raptures and revelations. His being buffeted by satan. His fear for the Corinthians.*

IF I must glory (it is not expedient indeed:) but I will come to the visions and revelations of the Lord.

2 *b* I know a man in Christ above fourteen years ago, (whether in the body, I know not, or out of the body, I know not, God knoweth,) such an one rapt even to the third heaven.

3 And I know such a man (whether in the body, or out of the body, I cannot tell: God knoweth:)

4 That he was caught up into paradise; and heard secret words, which it is not granted to man to utter.

5 For such an one I will glory; but for myself I will glory nothing, but in my infirmities.

6 For though I should have a mind to glory, I shall not be foolish: for I will say the truth. But I forbear, lest any man should think of me above that which he seeth in me, or anything he heareth from me.

7 And lest the greatness of the revelations should exalt me, there was given me a sting of my flesh, an angel of satan to buffet me.

8 For which thing thrice I besought the Lord, that it might depart from me:

9 And he said to me: My grace is sufficient for thee: for power is made perfect in infirmity. Gladly therefore will I glory in my infirmities, that the power of Christ may dwell in me.

10 For which cause I please myself in my infirmities, in reproaches, in necessities, in persecutions, in distresses, for Christ. For when I am weak, then am I powerful.

11 I am become foolish: you

---

*a* Acts 9. 24.—*b* Acts 9. 3.

Ver. 28. *My daily instance.* The labours that come in, and press upon me every day.

CHAP. XII. Ver. 9. *Power is made perfect.* The strength and power of God more perfectly shines forth in our weakness and infirmity; as the more weak we are of ourselves, the more illustrious is his grace in supporting us, and giving us the victory under all trials and conflicts.

have compelled me. For I ought to have been commended by you: for I have no way come short of them that are above measure apostles: although I be nothing.

12 Yet the signs of my apostleship have been wrought on you, in all patience, in signs, and wonders, and mighty deeds.

13 For what is there that you have had less than the other churches; but that I myself was not burthensome to you? Pardon me this injury.

14 Behold, now the third time I am ready to come to you; and I will not be burthensome unto you. For I seek not the things that are yours, but you. For neither ought the children to lay up for the parents, but the parents for the children.

15 But I most gladly will spend and be spent myself for your souls: although, loving you more, I be loved less.

16 But be it so: I did not burthen you: but being crafty, I caught you by guile.

17 Did I overreach you by any of them whom I sent to you?

18 I desired Titus, and I sent with him a brother. Did Titus overreach you? Did we not walk with the same spirit? did we not in the same steps?

19 Of old, think you that we excuse ourselves to you? We speak before God in Christ: but all things (my dearly beloved) for your edification.

20 For I fear lest perhaps when I come, I shall not find you such as I would, and that I shall be found by you such as you would not. Lest perhaps contentions, envyings, animosities, dissensions, detractions, whisperings, swellings, seditions, be among you.

21 Lest again, when I come, God humble me among you: and I mourn many of them that sinned before, and have not done penance for the uncleanness and fornication and lasciviousness, that they have committed.

## CHAP. XIII.

*He threatens the impenitent, to provoke them to penance.*

BEHOLD, this is the third time I am coming to you. <sup>a</sup> In the mouth of two or three witnesses shall every word stand.

2 I have told before, and foretell, as present and now absent, to them that sinned before and to all the rest, that if I come again, I will not spare.

3 Do you seek a proof of Christ that speaketh in me, who towards you is not weak, but is mighty in you?

4 For although he was crucified through weakness; yet he liveth by the power of God. For we also are weak in him; but we shall live with him by the power of God towards you.

5 Try your own selves if you be in the faith: prove ye yourselves. Know you not your own selves, that CHRIST JESUS is in you, unless perhaps you be reprobates?

6 But I trust that you shall know that we are not reprobates.

7 Now we pray God that you may do no evil, not that we may

---

<sup>a</sup> Deut. 19. 15. Matt. 18. 16. John 8. 17. Heb. 10. 28.

CHAP. XIII. Ver. 7. *Reprobates:* that is, without proof, by having no occasion of shewing our power in punishing you.

JESUS AND THE TWO DISCIPLES OF EMMAUS.

appear approved, but that you may do that which is good, and that we may be as reprobates.

8 For we can do nothing against the truth, but for the truth.

9 For we rejoice that we are weak, and you are strong. This also we pray for, your perfection.

10 Therefore I write these things being absent, that, being present, I may not deal more severely, according to the power which the Lord hath given me unto edification, and not unto destruction.

11 For the rest, brethren, rejoice, be perfect, take exhortation, be of one mind, have peace: and the God of peace and of love shall be with you.

12 Salute one another in a holy kiss. All the saints salute you.

13 The grace of our Lord JESUS CHRIST, and the charity of God, and the communication of the Holy Ghost be with you all. Amen.

# THE EPISTLE OF ST. PAUL TO THE GALATIANS.

*The Galatians, soon after ST. PAUL had preached the gospel to them, were seduced by some false teachers, who had been Jews, and who were for obliging all Christians, even those who had been gentiles, to observe circumcision, and the other ceremonies of the Mosaical law. In this Epistle he refutes the pernicious doctrine of those teachers, and also their calumny against his mission and apostleship. The subject-matter of this Epistle is much the same as in that to the Romans. It was written at Ephesus about twenty-three years after our Lord's Ascension.*

## CHAP. I.

*He blames the Galatians for suffering themselves to be imposed upon by new teachers. The apostle's calling.*

PAUL, an apostle, not of men, neither by man, but by JESUS CHRIST, and God the Father, who raised him from the dead,

2 And all the brethren who are with me, to the churches of Galatia.

3 Grace be to you and peace from God the Father, and from our Lord JESUS CHRIST.

4 Who gave himself for our sins, that he might deliver us from this present wicked world, according to the will of God and our Father:

5 To whom is glory for ever and ever. Amen.

6 I wonder that you are so soon removed from him that

called you into the grace of Christ, unto another gospel.

7 Which is not another, only there are some that trouble you, and would pervert the gospel of Christ.

8 But though we, or an angel from heaven, preach a gospel to you besides that which we have preached to you, let him be anathema.

9 As we said before, so now I say again: If any one preach to you a gospel, besides that which you have received, let him be anathema.

10 For do I now persuade men, or God? Or do I seek to please men? If I yet pleased men, I should not be the servant of Christ.

11 ᵃ For I give you to understand, brethren, that the gospel which was preached by me is not according to man.

12 ᵇ For neither did I receive it of man, nor did I learn it; but by the revelation of JESUS CHRIST.

13 For you have heard of my conversation in time past in the Jews' religion: how that beyond measure I persecuted the church of God, and wasted it.

14 And I made progress in the Jews' religion: above many of my equals in my own nation, being more abundantly zealous for the traditions of my fathers:

15 But when it pleased him, who separated me from my mother's womb, and called me by his grace,

16 To reveal his Son in me, that I might preach him among the gentiles, immediately I condescended not to flesh and blood.

17 Neither went I to Jerusalem to the apostles who were before me; but I went into Arabia, and again I returned to Damascus.

18 Then, ᶜ after three years, I went to Jerusalem to see Peter, and I tarried with him fifteen days.

19 But other of the apostles I saw none; saving James the brother of the Lord.

20 Now the things which I write to you; behold before God, I lie not.

21 Afterwards I came into the regions of Syria and Cilicia.

22 And I was unknown by face to the churches of Judea, which were in Christ:

23 But they had heard only: He, who persecuted us in times past, doth now preach the faith which once he impugned:

24 And they glorified God in me.

## CHAP. II.

*The apostle's preaching was approved of by the other apostles. The gentiles were not to be constrained to the observation of law.*

THEN ᵈ after fourteen years, I went up again to Jerusalem with Barnabas, taking Titus also with me.

2 And I went up according to revelation, and conferred with them the gospel which I preach among the gentiles, but apart with them who seemed to be something: lest perhaps I should run, or had run in vain.

3 But neither Titus, who was with me, being a gentile, was compelled to be circumcised.

4 But because of false brethren unawares brought in, who

---

ᵃ 1 Cor. 15. 1.—ᵇ Ephes. 3. 3.

ᶜ A.D. 37.—ᵈ A.D. 51.

CHAP. II. TO THE GALATIANS. CHAP. II.

came in privately to spy our liberty, which we have in CHRIST JESUS, that they might bring us into servitude.

5 To whom we yielded not by subjection, no not for an hour, that the truth of the gospel might continue with you.

6 But of them who seemed to be something, (what they were some time, it is nothing to me. *a* God accepteth not the person of man,) for to me they that seemed to be something added nothing.

7 But contrariwise, when they had seen that to me was committed the gospel of the uncircumcision, as to Peter was that of the circumcision:

8 (For he who wrought in Peter to the apostleship of the circumcision wrought in me also among the gentiles.)

9 And when they had known the grace that was given to me, James and Cephas and John, who seemed to be pillars, gave to me and Barnabas the right hands of fellowship: that we should go unto the gentiles, and they unto the circumcision:

10 Only that we should be mindful of the poor: which same thing also I was careful to do.

11 But when Cephas was come to Antioch, I withstood him to the face, because he was to be blamed.

12 For before that some came from James, he did eat with the gentiles: but when they were come, he withdrew and separated himself, fearing them who were of the circumcision.

13 And to his dissimulation the rest of the Jews consented, so that Barnabas also was led by them into that dissimulation.

14 But when I saw that they walked not uprightly unto the truth of the gospel, I said to Cephas before them all: If thou, being a Jew, livest after the manner of the gentiles, and not as the Jews do, how dost thou compel the gentiles to live as do the Jews?

15 We by nature are Jews, and not of the gentiles sinners.

16 But knowing that man is not justified by the works of the law, but by the faith of JESUS CHRIST; we also believe in CHRIST JESUS, that we may be justified by the faith of Christ, and not by the works of the law: *b* because by the works of the law no flesh shall be justified.

---

*b* Rom. 3. 20.

---

*a* Deut. 10. 17. Job. 34. 19. Wis. 6. 8. Eccli. 35. 15. Acts 10. 34. Rom. 2. 11. Ephes. 6. 9. Col. 3. 25. 1 Pet. 1. 17.

---

CHAP. II. Ver. 7. *The gospel of the uncircumcision.* The preaching of the gospel to the uncircumcised, that is, to the gentiles. St. *Paul* was called in an extraordinary manner to be the apostle of the gentiles: St. *Peter,* besides his general commission over the whole flock (*John* xxi. 15, &c.), had a peculiar charge of the people of the circumcision, that is, of the Jews.

Ver. 11. *I withstood, &c.* The fault that is here noted in the conduct of St. Peter was only a certain imprudence, in withdrawing himself from the table of the gentiles, for fear of giving offence to the Jewish converts: but this, in such circumstances, when his so doing might be of ill consequence to the gentiles; who might be induced thereby to think themselves obliged to conform to the Jewish way of living, to the prejudice of their Christian liberty. Neither was St. Paul's reprehending him any argument against his supremacy; for in such cases an inferior may, and sometimes ought, with respect to admonish his superior.

17 But if while we seek to be justified in Christ, we ourselves also are found sinners; is Christ then the minister of sin? God forbid.

18 For if I build up again the things which I have destroyed, I make myself a prevaricator.

19 For I, through the law, am dead to the law, that I may live to God: with Christ I am nailed to the cross.

20 And I live, now not I; but Christ liveth in me. And that I live now in the flesh: I live in the faith of the Son of God, who loved me, and delivered himself for me.

21 I cast not away the grace of God. For if justice be by the law, then Christ died in vain.

## CHAP. III.

*The Spirit, and the blessing promised to Abraham, cometh not by the law, but by faith.*

O SENSELESS Galatians, who hath bewitched you, that you should not obey the truth, before whose eyes JESUS CHRIST hath been set forth, crucified among you?

2 This only would I learn of you: Did you receive the Spirit by the works of the law, or by the hearing of faith?

3 Are you so foolish, that, whereas you began in the Spirit, you would now be made perfect by the flesh?

4 Have you suffered so great things in vain? If *it be* yet in vain.

5 He therefore who giveth to you the Spirit, and worketh miracles among you; doth he do it by the works of the law, or by the hearing of the faith?

6 As it is written: *ªAbraham believed God, and it was reputed to him unto justice.*

7 Know ye therefore, that they who are of faith, the same are the children of Abraham.

8 And the scripture foreseeing that God justifieth the gentiles by faith, told unto Abraham before: *ᵇIn thee shall all nations be blessed.*

9 Therefore they that are of faith shall be blessed with faithful Abraham.

10 For as many as are of the works of the law are under a curse. For it is written: *ᶜCursed is every one that abideth not in all things which are written in the book of the law, to do them.*

11 But that in the law no man is justified with God, it is manifest: ᵈbecause *the just man liveth by faith.*

12 But the law is not of faith: but, *ᵉHe that doth those things shall live in them.*

13 Christ hath redeemed us from the curse of the law, being made a curse for us: for it is written: *ƒCursed is every one that hangeth on a tree:*

14 That the blessing of Abraham might come on the gentiles through CHRIST JESUS: that we may receive the promise of the Spirit by faith.

15 Brethren, (I speak after the manner of man,) ᵍyet a man's testament, if it be confirmed, no man despiseth, nor addeth to it.

16 To Abraham were the promises made and to his seed. He saith not, *And to his seeds,* as of

---

ª Gen. 15 6. Rom. 4. 3. Jas. 2. 23.— ᵇ Gen. 12. 3. Eccli. 44. 20.—ᶜ Deut. 27. 26.—ᵈ Habac. 2. 4. Rom. 1. 17.— ᵉ Lev. 18. 5.—ƒ Deut. 21. 23.—ᵍ Heb. 9. 17.

312

CHRIST APPEARS TO HIS DISCIPLES AT THE SEA OF TIBERIAS.

CHAP. III. TO THE GALATIANS. CHAP. IV.

many: but as of one, *And to thy seed*, which is Christ.

17 Now this I say, that the testament which was confirmed by God, the law which was made after four hundred and thirty years, doth not disannul, to make the promise of no effect.

18 For if the inheritance be of the law, it is no more of promise. But God gave it to Abraham by promise.

19 Why then was the law? It was set because of transgressions, until the seed should come, to whom he made the promise, being ordained by angels in the hand of a mediator.

20 Now a mediator is not of one: but God is one.

21 Was the law then against the promises of God? God forbid. For if there had been a law given which could give life, verily justice should have been by the law.

22 ᵃ But the scripture hath concluded all under sin, that the promise by the faith of JESUS CHRIST might be given to them that believe.

23 But before the faith came, we were kept under the law, shut up, unto that faith which was to be revealed.

24 Wherefore the law was our pedagogue in Christ; that we might be justified by faith.

25 But after the faith is come, we are no longer under a pedagogue.

26 For you are all the children of God by faith in CHRIST JESUS.

27 ᵇ For as many of you as have been baptized in Christ have put on Christ.

28 There is neither Jew, nor Greek: there is neither bond, nor free: there is neither male, nor female. For you are all one in CHRIST JESUS.

29 And if you be Christ's, then are you the seed of Abraham, heirs according to the promise.

CHAP. IV.

*Christ has freed us from the servitude of the law: we are the free-born sons of Abraham.*

NOW I say: As long as the heir is a child, he differeth nothing from a servant, though he be lord of all:

2 But is under tutors and governors until the time appointed by the father:

3 So we also, when we were children, were serving under the elements of the world.

4 But when the fulness of the time was come, God sent his Son, made of a woman, made under the law:

5 That he might redeem them who were under the law; that

---

ᵃ Rom. 3. 9.

CHAP. III. Ver. 19. *Because of transgressions.* To restrain them from sin, by fear and threats.—Ibid. *Ordained by angels.* The law was delivered by angels, speaking in the name and person of God to Moses, who was the *mediator*, on this occasion, between God and the people.

Ver. 22. *Ha'h concluded all under sin*, i.e., hath declared all to be under sin, from which they could not be delivered but by faith in Jesus Christ, the promised seed.

Ver. 24. *Pedagogue*, i.e., schoolmaster, conductor, or instructor.

ᵇ Rom. 6. 3.

Ver. 28. *Neither Jew*, &c. That is, no distinction of Jew, &c.

CHAP. IV. Ver. 3. *Under the elements*, &c. That is, under the first rudiments of religion, in which the carnal Jews were trained up: or under those corporal creatures, used in their manifold rites, sacrifices, and sacraments.

313

we might receive the adoption of sons.

6 And because you are sons, God hath sent the Spirit of his Son into your hearts, crying: Abba, Father.

7 Therefore now he is not a servant, but a son. And if a son, an heir also through God.

8 But then indeed, not knowing God, you serve them who by nature are not gods.

9 But now, after that you have known God, or rather are known by God: how turn you again to the weak and needy elements, which you desire to serve again?

10 You observe days, and months, and times, and years.

11 I am afraid of you, lest perhaps, I have laboured in vain among you.

12 Be ye as I, because I also am as you: brethren, I beseech you: you have not injured me at all.

13 And you know how through infirmity of the flesh I preached the gospel to you heretofore: and your temptation in my flesh.

14 You despised not, nor rejected; but received me as an angel of God, *even* as CHRIST JESUS.

15 Where is then your blessedness? For I bear you witness, that, if it could be done, you would have plucked out your own eyes, and would have given them to me.

16 Am I then become your enemy, because I tell you the truth?

17 They are zealous in your regard not well: but they would exclude you, that you might be zealous for them.

18 But be zealous for that which is good in a good thing always: and not only when I am present with you.

19 My little children, of whom I am in labour again, until Christ be formed in you.

20 And I would willingly be present with you now, and change my voice: because I am ashamed for you.

21 Tell me, you that desire to be under the law, have you not read the law?

22 For it is written that Abraham had two sons: *a*the one by a bond-woman, *b*and the other by a free-woman.

23 But he who *was* of the bond-woman was born according to the flesh: but he of the free-woman *was* by promise.

24 Which things are said by an allegory. For these are the two testaments. The one from Mount Sina, engendering unto bondage; which is Agar:

25 For Sina is a mountain in Arabia, which hath affinity to that Jerusalem which now is, and is in bondage with her children.

26 But that Jerusalem which is above is free; which is our mother.

27 For it is written: *c Rejoice, thou barren, that bearest not: break forth and cry, thou that travailest not: for many are the children of the desolate, more*

---

Ver. 10. *You observe days,* &c. He speaks not of the observation of the Lord's day, or other Christian festivals; but either of the superstitious observation of days lucky and unlucky; or else of the Jewish festivals, to the observance of which certain Jewish teachers sought to induce the Galatians.

*a* Gen. 16. 15.—*b* Gen. 21. 2.—*c* Isaias 54. 1.

## TO THE GALATIANS.

than of her that hath a husband:

28 ᵃ Now we, brethren, as Isaac was, are the children of promise.

29 But as then he that was born according to the flesh persecuted him that was after the spirit: so also it is now.

30 But what saith the scripture? *Cast out the bond-woman and her son: for the son of the bond-woman shall not be heir with the son of the free-woman.*

31 So then, brethren, we are not the children of the bondwoman, but of the free: by the freedom wherewith Christ has made us free.

### CHAP. V.

*He exhorts them to stand to their Christian liberty. Of the fruits of the flesh, and of the spirit.*

STAND fast, and be not held again under the yoke of bondage.

2 ᵇ Behold, I Paul tell you, that if you be circumcised, Christ shall profit you nothing.

3 And I testify again to every man circumcising himself, that he is a debtor to do the whole law.

4 You are made void of Christ, you who are justified in the law; you are fallen from grace.

5 For we in spirit by faith wait for the hope of justice.

6 For in CHRIST JESUS neither circumcision availeth anything, nor uncircumcision; but faith that worketh by charity.

7 You did run well; who hath hindered you, that you should not obey the truth?

8 This persuasion is not from him that calleth you.

9 ᶜ A little leaven corrupteth the whole lump.

10 I have confidence in you in the Lord: that you will not be of another mind: but he that troubleth you shall bear the judgment, whosoever he be.

11 And I, brethren, if I yet preach circumcision, why do I yet suffer persecution? Then is the scandal of the cross made void.

12 I would they were even cut off who trouble you.

13 For you, brethren, have been called unto liberty: only make not liberty an occasion to the flesh, but by charity of the spirit serve one another.

14 For all the law is fulfilled in one word, ᵈ *Thou shalt love thy neighbour as thyself.*

15 But if you bite and devour one another: take heed you be not consumed one of another.

16 I say then, ᵉ walk in the spirit, and you shall not fulfil the lusts of the flesh.

17 For the flesh lusteth against the spirit: and the spirit against the flesh; for these are contrary one to another: so that you do not the things that you would.

18 But if you are led by the spirit, you are not under the law.

19 Now the works of the flesh are manifest, which are, fornication, uncleanness, immodesty, luxury,

20 Idolatry, witchcrafts, enmities, contentions, emulations, wraths, quarrels, dissensions, sects,

21 Envies, murders, drunkenness, revellings, and such like.

---

ᵃ Rom. 9. 8.—ᵇ Acts 15. 1.

ᶜ 1 Cor. 5. 6.—ᵈ Lev. 19. 18. Matt. 22. 39. Rom. 13. 8.—ᵉ 1 Pet. 2. 11.

Of the which I foretell you, as I have foretold to you, that they who do such things shall not obtain the kingdom of God.

22 But the fruit of the spirit is charity, joy, peace, patience, benignity, goodness, longanimity,

23 Mildness, faith, modesty, continency, chastity. Against such there is no law.

24 And they that are Christ's have crucified their flesh, with the vices and concupiscences.

25 If we live in the Spirit, let us also walk in the Spirit.

26 Let us not be made desirous of vainglory, provoking one another, envying one another.

## CHAP. VI.

*He exhorts to charity, humility, &c. He glories in nothing but in the cross of Christ.*

BRETHREN, and if a man be overtaken in any fault, you, who are spiritual, instruct such a one in the spirit of meekness, considering thyself, lest thou also be tempted.

2 Bear ye one another's burdens: and so you shall fulfil the law of Christ.

3 For if any man think himself to be something, whereas he is nothing, he deceiveth himself.

4 But let every one prove his own work, and so he shall have glory in himself only, and not in another.

5 ᵃ For every one shall bear his own burden.

6 And let him that is instructed in the word, communicate to him, that instructeth him, in all good things.

7 Be not deceived, God is not mocked.

8 For what things a man shall sow, those also shall he reap. For he that soweth in his flesh, of the flesh also shall reap corruption. But he, that soweth in the spirit, of the spirit shall reap life everlasting.

9 ᵇ And in doing good, let us not fail. For in due time we shall reap, not failing.

10 Therefore, whilst we have time, let us work good to all men, but especially to those who are of the household of the faith.

11 See what a letter I have written to you with my own hand.

12 For as many as desire to please in the flesh, they constrain you to be circumcised, only that they may not suffer the persecution of the cross of Christ.

13 For neither they themselves who are circumcised keep the law: but they will have you to be circumcised, that they may glory in your flesh.

14 But God forbid that I should glory, save in the cross of our Lord JESUS CHRIST; by whom the world is crucified to me, and I to the world.

15 For in CHRIST JESUS neither circumcision availeth anything, nor uncircumcision, but a new creature.

16 And whosoever shall follow this rule, peace on them, and mercy, and upon the Israel of God.

17 From henceforth let no man be troublesome to me: for I bear the marks of the Lord JESUS in my body.

18 The grace of our Lord JESUS CHRIST be with your spirit, brethren. Amen.

---

ᵃ 1 Cor. 3. 8.   ᵇ 2 Thess. 3. 13.

JESUS APPEARS TO ST. THOMAS AND THE OTHER DISCIPLES

# THE EPISTLE OF ST. PAUL TO THE EPHESIANS.

*Ephesus was the capital of Lesser Asia, and celebrated for the temple of Diana, to which the most part of the people of the East went frequently to worship. But St. Paul having preached the gospel there for two years the first time, and afterwards for about a year, converted many. He wrote this Epistle to them when he was a prisoner in Rome, and sent it by Tychicus. He admonishes them to hold firmly the faith which they had received, and warns them, and also those of the neighbouring cities, against the sophistry of philosophers and the doctrine of false teachers, who were come among them. The matters of faith contained in this Epistle are exceedingly sublime, and consequently very difficult to be understood. It was written about twenty-nine years after our Lord's Ascension.*

## CHAP. I.

*The great blessings we have received through Christ. He is head of all the Church.*

PAUL, an apostle of JESUS CHRIST by the will of God, to all the saints who are at Ephesus, and to the faithful in CHRIST JESUS.

2 Grace be to you and peace from God the Father, and from the Lord JESUS CHRIST.

3 "Blessed be the God and Father of our Lord JESUS CHRIST, who hath blessed us with spiritual blessings in heavenly *places*, in Christ.

4 As he chose us in him before the foundation of the world, that we should be holy and unspotted in his sight in charity.

5 Who hath predestinated us unto the adoption of children through JESUS CHRIST unto himself; according to the purpose of his will:

6 Unto the praise of the glory of his grace, in which he hath graced us in his beloved Son.

7 In whom we have redemption through his blood, the remission of sins, according to the riches of his grace.

8 Which hath super-abounded in us in all wisdom and prudence.

9 That he might make known unto us the mystery of his will, according to his good pleasure, which he hath purposed in him,

10 In the dispensation of the fulness of times, to re-establish all things in Christ, that are in heaven and on earth, in him.

11 In whom we also are called by lot, being predestinated according to the purpose of him who worketh all things according to the counsel of his will:

12 That we may be unto the praise of his glory, we who before hoped in Christ:

13 In whom you also, after

---

*a* 2 Cor. 1. 3. 1 Pet. 1. 3.

CHAP. I. Ver. 3. *In heavenly places:* or, in heavenly *things*. *In coelestibus.*

CHAP. I. TO THE EPHESIANS. CHAP. II.

you had heard the word of truth (the gospel of your salvation:) in whom also believing you were signed with the holy spirit of promise,

14 Who is the pledge of our inheritance, unto the redemption of acquisition, unto the praise of his glory.

15 Wherefore I also hearing of your faith that is in the Lord JESUS, and of your love towards all the saints,

16 Cease not to give thanks for you, making commemoration of you in my prayers,

17 That the God of our Lord JESUS CHRIST, the Father of glory, may give unto you the spirit of wisdom and of revelation, in the knowledge of him,

18 The eyes of your heart enlightened, that you may know what the hope is of his calling, and what are the riches of the glory of his inheritance in the saints,

19 And what is the exceeding greatness of his power towards us, who believe ᵃ according to the operation of the might of his power,

20 Which he wrought in Christ, raising him up from the dead, and setting him on his right hand in the heavenly *places*,

21 Above all principality, and power, and virtue, and dominion, and every name that is named, not only in this world, but also in that which is to come:

22 ᵇ And he hath subjected all things under his feet, and hath made him head over all the church,

23 Which is his body, and the fulness of him who is filled all in all.

## CHAP. II.

*All our good comes through Christ. He is our peace.*

AND ᶜ you, when you were dead in your offences and sins,

2 Wherein in time past you walked according to the course of this world, according to the prince of the power of this air, of the spirit that now worketh on the children of unbelief,

3 In which also we all conversed in time past, in the desires of our flesh, fulfilling the will of the flesh and of *our* thoughts, and were by nature children of wrath, even as the rest:

4 But God, (who is rich in mercy,) for his exceeding charity wherewith he loved us,

5 Even when we were dead in sins, hath quickened us together in Christ, (by whose grace you are saved,)

6 And hath raised us up together, and hath made us sit together in the heavenly *places* through CHRIST JESUS.

7 That he might shew in the ages to come the abundant riches of his grace, in his bounty towards us in CHRIST JESUS.

8 For by grace you are saved through faith, and that not of yourselves, for it is the gift of God;

9 Not of works, that no man may glory

---

ᵃ Isaia, 3 7.—ᵇ Ps. 8. 6.   ᶜ Col. 2. 13.

Ver. 14. *Acquisition*, i.e., a purchased possession.

CHAP. II. Ver 9. *Not of works*, as of our own growth, or from ourselves, but as from the grace of God.

318

## TO THE EPHESIANS.

10 For we are his workmanship, created in CHRIST JESUS in good works, which God hath prepared that we should walk in them.

11 For which cause be mindful that you being heretofore gentiles in the flesh, who are called uncircumcision by that which is called circumcision in the flesh, made by hands:

12 That you were at that time without Christ, being aliens from the conversation of Israel, and strangers to the testament, having no hope of the promise, and without God in this world.

13 But now in CHRIST JESUS, you, who some time were afar off, are made nigh by the blood of Christ.

14 For he is our peace, who hath made both one, and breaking down the middle wall of partition, the enmities in his flesh:

15 Making void the law of commandments *contained* in decrees: that he might make the two in himself into one new man, making peace,

16 And might reconcile both to God in one body by the cross, killing the enmities in himself.

17 And coming, he preached peace to you that were afar off, and peace to them that were nigh.

18 *a* For by him we have access both in one Spirit to the Father.

19 Now therefore you are no more strangers and foreigners; but you are fellow-citizens with the saints, and the domestics of God,

20 Built upon the foundation of the apostles and prophets, JESUS CHRIST himself being the chief corner-stone:

21 In whom all the building, being framed together, groweth up into an holy temple in the Lord.

22 In whom you also are built together into an habitation of God in the Spirit.

### CHAP. III.

*The mystery hidden from former ages was discovered to the apostle, to be imparted to the gentiles. He prays that they may be strengthened in God.*

FOR this cause, I Paul, the prisoner of JESUS CHRIST, for you gentiles:

2 If yet you have heard of the dispensation of the grace of God, which is given me towards you:

3 How that according to revelation, the mystery has been made known to me, as I have written above in a few words:

4 As you reading may understand my knowledge in the mystery of Christ.

5 Which in other generations was not known to the sons of men, as it is now revealed to his holy apostles, and prophets in the Spirit.

6 That the gentiles should be fellow-heirs, and of the same body and copartners of his promise in CHRIST JESUS by the gospel:

7 Of which I am made a minister according to the gift of the grace of God, which is given to me *b* according to the operation of his power.

8 *c* To me, the least of all the

---

*a* Rom. 5. 2.     *b* Supra, 1. 19.—*c* 1 Cor. 15. 9.

saints, is given this grace, to preach among the gentiles the unsearchable riches of Christ.

9 And to enlighten all men, that they may see what is the dispensation of the mystery which hath been hidden from eternity in God who created all things:

10 That the manifold wisdom of God may be made known to the principalities and powers in the heavenly *places* through the church,

11 According to the eternal purpose, which he made in CHRIST JESUS our Lord.

12 In whom we have boldness and access with confidence by the faith of him.

13 Wherefore I pray you not to faint at my tribulations for you, which is your glory.

14 For this cause I bow my knees to the Father of our Lord JESUS CHRIST,

15 Of whom all paternity in heaven and earth is named,

16 That he would grant you, according to the riches of his glory, to be strengthened by his Spirit with might unto the inward man.

17 That Christ may dwell by faith in your hearts: that being rooted and founded in charity,

18 You may be able to comprehend, with all the saints, what is the breadth, and length, and height, and depth.

19 To know also the charity of Christ, which surpasseth all knowledge, that you may be filled unto all the fulness of God.

20 Now to him who is able to do all things more abundantly than we desire or understand, according to the power that worketh in us:

21 To him be glory in the church, and in CHRIST JESUS, unto all generations, world without end. Amen.

## CHAP. IV.

*He exhorts them to unity; to put on the new man; and to fly sin.*

I THEREFORE, a prisoner in the Lord, beseech you *a* that you walk worthy of the vocation in which you are called,

2 With all humility and mildness, with patience, supporting one another in charity,

3 *b* Careful to keep the unity of the Spirit in the bond of peace.

4 One body and one Spirit: as you are called in one hope of your calling.

5 One Lord, one faith, one baptism.

6 *c* One God and Father of all, who is above all, and through all, and in us all.

7 *d* But to every one of us is given grace according to the measure of the giving of Christ.

8 Wherefore he saith: *Ascending on high he led captivity captive: he gave gifts to men.*

9 Now that he ascended, what is it, but because he also descended first into the lower parts of the earth?

10 He that descended is the same also that ascended above all the heavens, that he might fill all things.

---

CHAP. III. Ver. 15. *All paternity.* Or, *the whole family,* πατρια. God is the Father both of angels and men: whosoever besides is named father, is so named with subordination to him.

*a* 1 Cor. 7. 17. Phil. 1. 27.—*b* Rom. 12. 10.—*c* Mal. 2. 10.—*d* Rom. 12. 3. 1 Cor. 12. 11. 2 Cor. 10. 13.—*e* Ps. 67. 19.

## TO THE EPHESIANS.

11 And he gave some *apostles, and some prophets, and other some evangelists, and other some pastors and doctors.

12 For the perfecting of the saints, for the work of the ministry, for the edifying of the body of Christ:

13 Until we all meet into the unity of faith, and of the knowledge of the Son of God, unto a perfect man, unto the measure of the age of the fulness of Christ:

14 That henceforth we be no more children tossed to and fro, and carried about with every wind of doctrine by the wickedness of men, by cunning craftiness by which they lie in wait to deceive.

15 But doing the truth in charity, we may in all things grow up in him who is the head, even Christ:

16 From whom the whole body, being compacted and fitly joined together, by what every joint supplieth, according to the operation in the measure of every part, maketh increase of the body unto the edifying of itself in charity.

17 *b* This then I say and testify in the Lord: that henceforward you walk not as also the gentiles walk in the vanity of their mind,

18 Having their understanding darkened, being alienated from the life of God through the ignorance that is in them, because of the blindness of their hearts,

19 Who despairing, have given themselves up to lasciviousness, unto the working of all uncleanness, unto covetousness.

20 But you have not so learned Christ:

21 If so be that you have heard him, and have been taught in him, as the truth is in Jesus.

22 *c* To put off, according to former conversation, the old man, who is corrupted according to the desire of error.

23 *d* And be renewed in the spirit of your mind:

24 *e* And put on the new man, who according to God, is created in justice and holiness of truth.

25 *f* Wherefore putting away lying, *g* speak ye the truth every man with his neighbour: for we are members one of another.

26 *h* Be angry, and sin not. Let not the sun go down upon your anger.

27 'Give not place to the devil.

28 He that stole, let him now steal no more: but rather let him labour, working with his hands the thing which is good, that he may have something to give to him that suffereth need.

29 Let no evil speech proceed from your mouth: but that which is good to the edification of faith, that it may administer grace to the hearers.

30 And grieve not the holy

---

*a* 1 Cor. 12. 28.—*b* Rom. 1. 21.

CHAP. IV. Ver. 11, 12. *Gave some apostles—Until we all meet, &c.* Here it is plainly expressed, that Christ has left in his Church a *perpetual* succession of orthodox pastors and teachers, to preserve the faithful in unity and truth.

*c* Col. 3. 8.—*d* Rom. 6. 4.—*e* Col. 3. 12.—*f* 1 Pet. 2. 1.—*g* Zach. 8. 16.—*h* Ps. 4. 5.—*i* Jas. 4. 7.

Spirit of God: whereby you are sealed unto the day of redemption.

31 Let all bitterness and anger, and indignation and clamour, and blasphemy be put away from you, with all malice.

32 ᵃ And be ye kind one to another, merciful, forgiving one another, even as God hath forgiven you in Christ.

## CHAP. V.

*Exhortations to a virtuous life. The mutual duties of man and wife, by the example of Christ, and of the church.*

BE ye therefore followers of God, as most dear children.:

2 ᵇ And walk in love, as Christ also hath loved us, and hath delivered himself for us, an oblation and a sacrifice to God for an odour of sweetness.

3 ᶜ But fornication and all uncleanness, or covetousness, let it not so much as be named among you, as becometh saints:

4 Or obscenity, or foolish talking, or scurrility, which is to no purpose: but rather giving of thanks.

5 For know ye this and understand that no fornicator, or unclean, or covetous person, (which is a serving of idols,) hath inheritance in the kingdom of Christ and of God.

6 ᵈ Let no man deceive you with vain words. For because of these things cometh the anger of God upon the children of unbelief.

7 Be ye not therefore partakers with them.

8 For you were heretofore darkness, but now light in the Lord. Walk then as children of the light:

9 For the fruit of the light is in all goodness, and justice, and truth:

10 Proving what is well-pleasing to God.

11 And have no fellowship with the unfruitful works of darkness, but rather reprove them.

12 For the things that are done by them in secret, it is a shame even to speak of:

13 But all things that are reproved are made manifest by the light: for all that is made manifest is light.

14 Wherefore he saith: *Rise thou that sleepest, and arise from the dead: and Christ shall enlighten thee.*

15 See therefore, brethren, now you walk circumspectly: ᵉ not as unwise,

16 But as wise: redeeming the time, because the days are evil.

17 ᶠ Wherefore become not unwise, but understanding what is the will of God.

18 And be not drunk with wine, wherein is luxury, but be ye filled with the Holy Spirit,

19 Speaking to yourselves in psalms and hymns, and spiritual canticles, singing and making melody in your hearts to the Lord:

20 Giving thanks always for all things, in the name of our Lord JESUS CHRIST, to God and the Father.

21 But subject one to another in the fear of Christ.

---

ᵃ Col. 3. 13.—ᵇ John 13. 34. and 15. 12. 1 John 4. 21.—ᶜ Col. 3. 5.—ᵈ Matt. 24. 4. Mark 13. 5. Luke 21. 8. 2 Thess. 2. 3.

ᵉ Col. 4. 5.—ᶠ Rom. 12. 2. 1 Thess. 4. 3.

ST. PETER IS APPOINTED CHIEF PASTOR.

22 ᵃ Let women be subject to their husbands, as to the Lord:

23 ᵇ Because the husband is the head of the wife: as Christ is the head of the church. He *is* the saviour of his body.

24 Therefore as the church is subject to Christ, so also let the wives be to their husbands in all things.

25 ᶜ Husbands, love your wives, as Christ also loved the church, and delivered himself up for it:

26 That he might sanctify it, cleansing it by the laver of water in the word of life.

27 That he might present it to himself a glorious church, not having spot or wrinkle, or any such thing, but that it should be holy and without blemish.

28 So also ought men to love their wives as their own bodies. He that loveth his wife loveth himself.

29 For no man ever hated his own flesh: but nourisheth and cherisheth it, as also Christ doth the church.

30 Because we are members of his body, of his flesh, and of his bones.

31 ᵈ *For this cause shall a man leave his father and mother: and shall cleave to his wife, ᵉ and they shall be two in one flesh.*

32 This is a great sacrament: but I speak in Christ and in the church.

33 Nevertheless let every one of you in particular love his wife as himself: and let the wife fear her husband.

## CHAP. VI.

*Duties of children and servants. The Christian's armour.*

CHILDREN, obey your parents in the Lord: for this is just.

2 ᶠ *Honour thy father and thy mother*, which is the first commandment with a promise.

3 *That it may be well with thee, and thou mayest be long-lived upon the earth.*

4 And you, fathers, provoke not your children to anger: but bring them up in the discipline and correction of the Lord.

5 ᵍ Servants, be obedient to them that are your lords according to the flesh, with fear and trembling, in the simplicity of your heart, as to Christ.

6 Not serving to the eye, as it were pleasing men, but, as the servants of Christ, doing the will of God from the heart,

7 With a good will serving, as to the Lord, and not to men.

8 Knowing that whatsoever good thing any man shall do, the same shall he receive from the Lord, whether he be bond or free.

9 And you masters, do the same things to them, forbearing threatenings: knowing that the Lord both of them and you is

---

ᵃ Gen. 3. 16. Col. 3. 18. 1 Pet. 3. 1.—ᵇ 1 Cor. 11. 3.—ᶜ Col. 3. 19.—ᵈ Gen. 2. 24. Matt. 19. 5. Mark 10. 7.—ᵉ 1 Cor. 6. 16.

CHAP. V. Ver. 24. *As the church is subject to Christ.* The Church then, according to St. Paul, is ever obedient to Christ; and can never fall from him, but remain faithful to him, unspotted and unchanged to the end of the world.

ᶠ Exod. 20. 12. Deut. 5. 16. Eccli. 3. 9. Matt. 15. 4. Mark 7. 10. Col. 3. 20.—ᵍ Col. 3. 22. Titus 2. 9. 1 Pet. 2. 18.

## TO THE EPHESIANS.

in heaven: *a* and there is no respect of persons with him.

10 Finally, brethren, be strengthened in the Lord, and in the might of his power.

11 Put you on the armour of God, that you may be able to stand against the deceits of the devil.

12 For our wrestling is not against flesh and blood: but against principalities and powers, against the rulers of the world of this darkness, against the spirits of wickedness in the high places.

13 Therefore take unto you the armour of God, that you may be able to resist in the evil day, and to stand in all things perfect.

14 Stand therefore, having your loins girt about with truth, and having on the breastplate of justice,

15 And your feet shod with the preparation of the gospel of peace:

16 In all things taking the shield of faith, wherewith you may be able to extinguish all the fiery darts of the most wicked one.

17 *b* And take unto you the helmet of salvation; and the sword of the spirit, (which is the word of God,)

18 By all prayer and supplication, praying at all times in the spirit: *c* and in the same watching with all instance and supplication for all the saints:

19 *d* And for me, that speech may be given me, that I may open my mouth with confidence, to make known the mystery of the gospel.

20 For which I am an ambassador in a chain, so that therein I may be bold to speak according as I ought.

21 But that you also may know the things that concern me, *and* what I am doing, Tychicus, my dearest brother and faithful minister in the Lord, will make known to you all things:

22 Whom I have sent to you for this same purpose, that you may know the things concerning us, and that he may comfort your hearts.

23 Peace be to the brethren and charity with faith, from God the Father, and the Lord JESUS CHRIST.

24 Grace *be* with all them that love our Lord JESUS CHRIST in incorruption. Amen.

---

*a* Deut. 10. 17. 2 Par. 19. 7. Job 34. 19. Wis. 6. 8. Eccli. 35. 15. Acts 10. 34. Rom. 2. 11. Col. 3. 25. 1 Pet. 1. 17.

---

CHAP. VI. Ver. 12. *High places,* or *heavenly places.* That is to say, in the air, the lowest of the celestial regions; in which God permits these wicked spirits or fallen angels to wander.

*b* Isaias 59. 17. 1 Thess. 5. 8.—*c* Col. 4. 2.—*d* Col. 4. 8. 2 Thess. 3. 1.

---

Ver. 24. *In incorruption;* that is with a pure and perfect love.

# THE EPISTLE OF ST. PAUL TO THE PHILIPPIANS.

*The PHILIPPIANS were the first among the Macedonians converted to the faith. They had a great veneration for ST. PAUL, and supplied his wants when he was a prisoner in Rome, sending to him by Epaphroditus, by whom he sent this epistle; in which he recommends charity, unity, and humility, and warns them against false teachers, which he calls dogs and enemies of the cross of Christ. He also returns thanks for their benefactions. It was written about twenty-nine years after our Lord's Ascension.*

## CHAP. I.

*The apostle's affection for the Philippians.*

PAUL and Timothy, the servants of JESUS CHRIST: to all the saints in CHRIST JESUS, who are at Philippi, with the bishops and deacons.

2 Grace be unto you and peace from God our Father, and from the Lord JESUS CHRIST.

3 I give thanks to my God in every remembrance of you.

4 Always in all my prayers making supplication for you all, with joy:

5 For your communication in the gospel of Christ from the first day until now.

6 Being confident of this very thing, that he who hath begun a good work in you, will perfect it unto the day of CHRIST JESUS.

7 As it is meet for me to think this for you all: for that I have you in my heart; and that in my bands, and in the defence, and confirmation of the gospel, you all are partakers of my joy.

8 For God is my witness, how I long after you all in the bowels of JESUS CHRIST.

9 And this I pray, that your charity may more and more abound in knowledge and in all understanding:

10 That you may approve the better things, that you may be sincere and without offence unto the day of Christ,

11 Filled with the fruit of justice through JESUS CHRIST, unto the glory and praise of God.

12 Now, brethren, I desire you should know that the things which have happened to me have fallen out rather to the furtherance of the gospel.

13 So that my bonds are made manifest, in Christ, in all the court, and in all other places:

14 And many of the brethren in the Lord, *growing* confident by my bands, are much more bold to speak the word of God without fear.

15 Some indeed even out of envy and contention: but some also for good-will preach Christ:

16 Some out of charity: knowing that I am set for the defence of the gospel.

17 And some out of contention

preach Christ not sincerely: supposing that they raise affliction to my bands.

18 But what then? So that by all means, whether by occasion, or by truth, Christ be preached: in this also I rejoice, yea, and will rejoice.

19 For I know that this shall fall out to me unto salvation, through your prayer, and the supply of the Spirit of JESUS CHRIST.

20 According to my expectation and hope; that in nothing I shall be confounded, but with all confidence, as always, so now also shall Christ be magnified in my body, whether *it be* by life, or by death.

21 For to me, to live is Christ: and to die is gain.

22 And if to live in the flesh, this is to me the fruit of labour, and what I shall choose I know not.

23 But I am straitened between two; having a desire to be dissolved and to be with Christ, a thing by far the better.

24 But to abide still in the flesh, is needful for you.

25 And having this confidence, I know that I shall abide, and continue with you all, for your furtherance and joy of faith:

26 That your rejoicing may abound in CHRIST JESUS for me, by my coming to you again.

27 ª Only let your conversation be worthy of the gospel of Christ: that, whether I come and see you, or being absent may hear of you, that you stand f st in one spirit, with one mind, labouring together for the faith of the gospel.

28 And in nothing be ye terrified by the adversaries: which to them is a cause of perdition, but to you of salvation, and this from God.

29 For unto you it is given for Christ, not only to believe in him, but also to suffer for him,

30 Having the same conflict as that which you have seen in me, and now have heard of me.

## CHAP. II.

*He recommends to them unity and humility; and t work out their salvation with fear and trembling.*

IF there be therefore any consolation in Christ, if any comfort of charity, if any society of the Spirit, if any bowels of commiseration;

2 Fulfil ye my joy, that you be of one mind, having the same charity, being of one accord, agreeing in sentiment.

3 Let nothing be done through contention, neither by vainglory: but in humility, let each esteem others better than themselves:

4 Each one not considering the things that are his own, but those that are other men's.

5 For let this mind be in you, which was also in CHRIST JESUS:

6 Who being in the form of God, thought it not robbery to be equal with God:

7 But emptied himself, taking

---

ª Ephes. 4. 1. Col. L 10. 1 Thess. 2. 13.

CHAP. L Ver. 22. *This is to me, &c.* His meaning is, that although his dying immediately for Christ would be his gain, by putting him presently in possession of heaven, yet he is doubtful what he should choose, because by staying longer in the flesh, he should be more beneficial to the souls of his neighbours.

CHAP. II. Ver. 7. *Emptied himself, exinanisit,* made himself as of no account.

CHAP. II. TO THE PHILIPPIANS. CHAP. II.

the form of a servant, being made in the likeness of men, and in habit found as a man.

8 [a] He humbled himself, becoming obedient unto death: even to the death of the cross.

9 For which cause God also hath exalted him, and hath given him a name which is above all names:

10 [b] That in the name of JESUS every knee should bow, of those that are in heaven, on earth, and under the earth:

11 And that every tongue should confess that the Lord JESUS CHRIST is in the glory of God the Father.

12 Wherefore my dearly beloved, (as you have always obeyed,) not as in my presence only, but much more now in my absence with fear and trembling work out your salvation.

13 For it is God who worketh in you both to will and to accomplish, according to *his* good will.

14 [c] And do ye all things without murmurings and hesitations:

15 That you may be blameless, and sincere children of God, without reproof, in the midst of a crooked and perverse generation: among whom you shine as lights in the world.

16 Holding forth the word of life to my glory in the day of Christ, because I have not run in vain, nor laboured in vain.

17 Yea, and if I be made a victim upon the sacrifice and service of your faith, I rejoice and congratulate with you all.

18 And for the self same thing do you also rejoice, and congratulate with me.

19 And I hope in the Lord JESUS, [d] to send Timothy unto you shortly, that I also may be of good comfort, when I know the things concerning you.

20 For I have no man so of the same mind, who with sincere affection is solicitous for you.

21 [e] For all seek the things that are their own: not the things that are JESUS CHRIST'S.

22 Now know ye the proof of him, that as a son with the father, so hath he served with me in the gospel.

23 Him therefore I hope to send unto you immediately, so soon as I shall see how it will go with me.

24 And I trust in the Lord, that I myself also shall come to you shortly.

25 But I have thought it necessary to send to you Epaphroditus, my brother and fellow-labourer and fellow-soldier, but your apostle, and he that hath ministered to my wants.

26 For indeed he longed after you all: and was sad, for that you had heard, that he was sick.

27 For indeed he was sick nigh unto death: but God had mercy on him: and not only on him, but on me also, lest I should have sorrow upon sorrow.

28 Therefore I send him the more speedily: that, seeing him again, you may rejoice, and I may be without sorrow.

---

[a] Heb. 2. 9.—[b] Isaias 45. 24. Rom. 14. 11.—[c] 1 Pet. 5. 6.

Ver. 12. *With fear, &c.* This is against the false faith and presumptuous security of modern sectaries.

[d] Acts 16. 1.—[e] 1 Cor. 13. 5.

29 Receive him therefore with all joy in the Lord: and treat with honour such as he is.

30 Because for the work of Christ, he came to the point of death: delivering his life, that he might fulfil that which on your part was wanting towards my service.

## CHAP. III.

*He warneth them against false teachers: he counts all other things loss that he may gain Christ.*

AS to the rest, my brethren, rejoice in the Lord. To write the same things to you, to me indeed *is* not wearisome, but to you *is* necessary.

2 Beware of dogs, *a* beware of evil workers, beware of the concision.

3 For we are the circumcision, who in spirit serve God: and glory in CHRIST JESUS, not having confidence in the flesh.

4 Though I might also have confidence in the flesh. If any other thinketh he may have confidence in the flesh, I more,

5 Being circumcised the eighth day, of the stock of Israel, of the tribe of Benjamin, an Hebrew of the Hebrews: *b* according to the law, a Pharisee:

6 According to zeal, persecuting the church of God: according to the justice that is in the law, conversing without blame.

7 But the things that were gain to me, the same I have counted loss for Christ.

8 Furthermore I count all things to be but loss, for the excellent knowledge of JESUS CHRIST my Lord: for whom I have suffered the loss of all things, and count them but as dung, that I may gain Christ:

9 And may be found in him not having my justice, which is of the law, but that which is of the faith of CHRIST JESUS, which is of God, justice in faith:

10 That I may know him, and the power of his resurrection, and the fellowship of his sufferings, being made conformable to his death,

11 If by any means I may attain to the resurrection which is from the dead.

12 Not as though I had already attained, or were already perfect: but I follow after, if I may by any means apprehend, wherein I am also apprehended by CHRIST JESUS.

13 Brethren, I do not count myself to have apprehended. But one thing *I do:* forgetting the things that are behind, and stretching forth myself to those that are before,

14 I press towards the mark, to the prize of the supernal vocation of God in CHRIST JESUS.

15 Let us therefore, as many as are perfect, be thus minded: and if in anything you be otherwise minded: this also God will reveal to you.

16 Nevertheless whereunto we are come, that we be of the same mind, let us also continue in the same rule.

17 Be followers of me, brethren, and observe them who walk so as you have our model.

18 *c* For many walk, of whom I have told you often, (and now tell you weeping,) that they are enemies of the cross of Christ;

19 Whose end is destruction: whose God is their belly: and

---

*i.e.*, false teachers.—*b* Acts 22. 6.   *c* Rom. 16. 17.

THE ASCENSION OF CHRIST

CHAP. IV. TO THE PHILIPPIANS. CHAP. IV.

*whose* glory is in their shame: who mind earthly things.

20 But our conversation is in heaven: from whence also we look for the Saviour, our Lord JESUS CHRIST.

21 Who will reform the body of our lowness, made like to the body of his glory, according to the operation whereby also he is able to subdue all things unto himself.

## CHAP. IV.

*He exhorts them to perseverance in all good; and acknowledges their charitable contributions to him.*

THEREFORE, my dearly beloved brethren, and most desired, my joy and my crown: so stand fast in the Lord, my dearly beloved.

2 I beg of Evodia, and I beseech Syntyche to be of one mind in the Lord.

3 And I entreat thee also, my sincere companion, help those women that have laboured with me in the gospel with Clement and the rest of my fellow-labourers, whose names are in the book of life.

4 Rejoice in the Lord always; again, I say, rejoice.

5 Let your modesty be known to all men. The Lord is nigh.

6 Be nothing solicitous; but in everything by prayer and supplication with thanksgiving let your petitions be made known to God.

7 And the peace of God, which surpasseth all understanding, keep your hearts and minds in CHRIST JESUS.

8 For the rest, brethren, whatsoever things are true,

whatsoever modest, whatsoever just, whatsoever holy, whatsoever lovely, whatsoever of good fame, if there be any virtue, if any praise of discipline, think on these things.

9 The things which you have both learned, and received, and heard, and seen in me, these do ye, and the God of peace shall be with you.

10 Now I rejoice in the Lord exceedingly, that now at length your thought for me hath flourished again, as you did also think: but you were busied.

11 I speak not as it were for want. For I have learned, in whatsoever state I am, to be content therewith.

12 I know both how to be

---

CHAP. IV. Ver. 8. *For the rest, brethren, whatsoever things are true,* &c. Here the apostle enumerates general precepts of morality which they ought to practise. *Whatsoever things are true:* in words, in promises, in lawful oaths, &c., he commands rectitude of mind and sincerity of heart. *Whatsoever modest:* by these words he prescribes gravity of manners, modesty in dress, and decency in conversation. *Whatsoever just:* that is, in dealing with others, in buying or selling, in trade or business, to be fair and honest. *Whatsoever holy:* by these words may be understood that those who are in a religious state professed, or in holy orders, should lead a life of *sanctity* and *chastity* according to the vows they make; but these words being also applied to those in the world, indicate the virtuous life they are bound by the divine commandments to follow. *Whatsoever lovely:* that is, to practise those good offices in society that procure us the esteem and good-will of our neighbours. *Whatsoever of good fame:* that is, that by our conduct and behaviour we should edify our neighbours and give them good example by our actions. *If there be any virtue, if any praise of discipline:* that those in error, by seeing the morality and good discipline of the true religion, may be converted. And finally, the apostle commands, not only the Philippians, but all Christians, *to think on these things;* that is, to make it their study and concern, that the *peace of God might be with them.*

brought low, and I know how to abound: (everywhere and in all things I am instructed,) both to be full and to be hungry; both to abound, and to suffer need.

13 I can do all things in him who strengtheneth me.

14 Nevertheless you have done well, in communicating to my tribulation.

15 And you also know, O Philippians, that in the beginning of the gospel, when I departed from Macedonia, no church communicated with me as concerning giving and receiving, but you only:

16 For unto Thessalonica also, you sent once and again for my use.

17 Not that I seek the gift, but I seek the fruit that may abound to your account.

18 But I have all, and abound: I am filled, having received from Epaphroditus the things you sent, an odour of sweetness, <sup>a</sup> an acceptable sacrifice, pleasing God.

19 And may my God supply all your wants, according to his riches in glory in CHRIST JESUS.

20 Now to God and our Father be glory world without end. Amen.

21 Salute ye every saint in CHRIST JESUS.

22 The brethren, who are with me, salute you. All the saints salute you: especially they that are of Cesar's household.

23 The grace of our Lord JESUS CHRIST be with your spirit. Amen.

<sup>a</sup> ROM. 12. 1.

# THE EPISTLE OF ST. PAUL TO THE COLOSSIANS.

*COLOSSA was a city of Phrygia, near Laodicea. It does not appear that ST. PAUL had preached there himself, but that the Colossians were converted by Epaphras, a disciple of the Apostles. However, as ST. PAUL was the great Apostle of the Gentiles, he wrote this Epistle to the COLOSSIANS when he was in prison, and about the same time that he wrote to the Ephesians and Philippians. The exhortations and doctrine it contains are similar to that which is set forth in his Epistle to the Ephesians.*

## CHAP. I.

*He gives thanks for the grace bestowed upon the Colossians; and prays for them: Christ is the head of the church and the peace-maker through his blood. Paul is his minister.*

PAUL, an apostle of JESUS CHRIST, by the will of God, and Timothy a brother:

2 To the saints and faithful brethren in CHRIST JESUS who are at Colossa.

3 Grace be to you and peace from God our Father, and from the Lord JESUS CHRIST. We give thanks to God, and the Father of our Lord JESUS

CHAP. I. TO THE COLOSSIANS. CHAP. I.

Christ, praying always for you:

4 Hearing your faith in Christ Jesus, and the love which you have towards all the saints,

5. For the hope that is laid up for you in heaven, which you have heard in the word of the truth of the gospel,

6 Which is come unto you, as also it is in the whole world, and bringeth forth fruit and groweth, even as it doth in you, since the day you heard and knew the grace of God in truth,

7 As you learned of Epaphras, our most beloved fellow-servant, who is for you a faithful minister of Christ Jesus,

8 Who also hath manifested to us your love in the spirit.

9 Therefore we also, from the day that we heard it, cease not to pray for you and to beg that you may be filled with the knowledge of his will, in all wisdom, and spiritual understanding:

10 That you may walk worthy of God, in all things pleasing: being fruitful in every good work, and increasing in the knowledge of God:

11 Strengthened with all might according to the power of his glory, in all patience and long-suffering with joy,

12 Giving thanks to God the Father, who hath made us worthy to be partakers of the lot of the saints in light.

13 Who hath delivered us from the power of darkness, and hath translated us into the kingdom of the Son of his love,

14 In whom we have redemption through his blood, the remission of sins:

15 Who is the image of the invisible God, the first-born of every creature:

16 [a] For in him were all things created in heaven, and on earth, visible, and invisible, whether thrones, or dominations, or principalities, or powers: all things were created by him and in him:

17 And he is before all, and by him all things consist.

18 And he is the head of the body, the church, [b] who is the beginning, the first-born from the dead: that in all things he may hold the primacy:

19 Because in him, it hath well pleased the Father, that all fulness should dwell:

20 And through him to reconcile all things unto himself, making peace through the blood of his cross, both as to the things on earth, and the things that are in heaven.

21 And you, whereas you were some time alienated and enemies in mind, in evil works:

22 Yet now he hath reconciled in the body of his flesh through death to present you holy and unspotted, and blameless before him:

23 If so ye continue in the faith, grounded and settled, and immoveable from the hope of the gospel which you have heard, which is preached in all the creation that is under heaven, whereof I Paul am made a minister.

---

[a] John 1. 3.—[b] 1 Cor. 15. 20. Apoc. 1. 5.

CHAP. I. Ver. 15. *The first-born.* That is, first begotten; as the Evangelist declares, *the only begotten* of his Father: hence, St. Chrysostom explains *first-born*, not first created, as he was not created at all, but born of his Father before all ages; that is, coeval with the Father and with the Holy Ghost.

24 Who now rejoice in my sufferings for you, and fill up those things that are wanting of the sufferings of Christ, in my flesh for his body, which is the church:

25 Whereof I am made a minister according to the dispensation of God, which is given me towards you, that I may fulfil the word of God.

26 The mystery which had been hidden from ages and generations, but now is manifested to his saints,

27 To whom God would make known the riches of the glory of this mystery among the gentiles, which is Christ, in you the hope of glory,

28 Whom we preach, admonishing every man, and teaching every man in all wisdom, that we may present every man perfect in CHRIST JESUS.

29 Wherein also I labour, striving according to his working which he worketh in me in power.

## CHAP. II.

*He warns them against the impostures of the philosophers and the Jewish teachers, that would withdraw them from Christ.*

FOR I would have you know, what manner of care I have for you and for them that are at Laodicea, and whosoever have not seen my face in the flesh;

2 That their hearts may be comforted, being instructed in charity, and unto all riches of fulness of understanding, unto the knowledge of the mystery of God the Father and of CHRIST JESUS:

3 In whom are hid all the treasures of wisdom and knowledge.

4 Now this I say, that no man may deceive you by loftiness of words.

5 ª For though I be absent in body, yet in spirit I am with you; rejoicing and beholding your order, and the steadfastness of your faith which is in Christ.

6 As therefore you have received JESUS CHRIST the Lord, walk ye in him,

7 Rooted and built up in him, and confirmed in the faith, as also you have learned, abounding in him in thanksgiving.

8 Beware lest any man cheat you by philosophy and vain deceit; according to the tradition of men, according to the elements of the world, and not according to Christ.

9 For in him dwelleth all the fulness of the Godhead corporally;

10 And you are filled in him, who is the head of all principality and power:

11 In whom also you are circumcised with circumcision not made by hand in despoiling of the body of the flesh, but in the circumcision of Christ:

12 Buried with him in baptism, in whom also you are risen again by the faith of the operation of God, who hath raised him up from the dead.

13 ᵇ And you, when you were dead in your sins and the uncircumcision of your flesh, he hath quickened together with him; forgiving you all offences.

---

Ver. 24. *Wanting.* There is no want in the sufferings of Christ in himself as head; but many sufferings are still wanting, or are still to come, in his body the Church, and his members the faithful.

ª 1 Cor. 5. 3.— ᵇ Ephes. 2. 1.

14 Blotting out the handwriting of the decree that was against us, which was contrary to us. And he hath taken the same out of the way, fastening it to the cross:

15 And despoiling the principalities and powers, he hath exposed them confidently in open shew, triumphing over them in himself.

16 Let no man therefore judge you in meat or in drink, or in respect of a festival day, or of the new moon, or of the sabbaths,

17 Which are a shadow of things to come, but the body is Christ's.

18 [a] Let no man seduce you, willing in humility, and religion of angels, walking in the things which he hath not seen, in vain puffed up by the sense of his flesh.

19 And not holding the head, from which the whole body, by joints and bands being supplied with nourishment and compacted, groweth unto the increase of God.

20 If then you be dead with Christ from the elements of this world; why do you yet decree as living in the world?

21 Touch not, taste not, handle not:

22 Which all are unto destruction by the very use, according to the precepts and doctrines of men.

23 Which things have indeed a shew of wisdom in superstition and humility, and not sparing the body, not in any honour to the filling of the flesh.

---

[a] Matt. 24. 4.

---

CHAP. II. Ver. 16. *In meat, &c.* He means with regard to the Jewish observations of the distinction of clean and unclean meats; and of their festivals, new moons, and *sabbaths*; as being no longer obligatory.

Ver. 18. *Willing, &c.* That is, by a self-willed, self-invented, superstitious worship, falsely pretending *humility*, but really proceeding from pride. Such was the worship, that many of the philosophers (against whom St. Paul speaks, ver. 8) paid to angels or demons, by sacrificing to them, as carriers of intelligence betwixt God and men; pretending *humility* in so doing, as if God was too great to be addressed to by men; and setting aside the mediatorship of Jesus Christ, who is the head both of angels and men. Such also was the worship paid by the ancient heretics, disciples of Simon and Menander, to the angels, whom they believed to b the makers and lords of this lower world. This is certain, that they whom the apostle here condemns did not *hold the head*, (ver. 19,) that is, Jesus Christ, and his mediatorship: and therefore what he writes here no ways touches the Catholic doctrine and practice of desiring our good angels to pray to God for us, through Jesus Christ. St. Jerome (*Epist. ad Alyas*)

## CHAP. III.

*He exhorts them to put off the old man, and to put on the new. The duties of wives and husbands, children and servants.*

THEREFORE, if you be risen with Christ, seek the things that are above, where Christ is sitting at the right hand of God:

2 Mind the things that are above, not the things that are upon the earth.

---

understands by the *religion* or service of *angels* the Jewish religion given by angels; and shows all that is here said to be directed against the Jewish teachers, who sought to subject the new Christians to the observances of the Mosaic law.

Ver. 21. *Touch not, &c.* The meaning is, that Christians should not subject themselves, either to the ordinances of the old law, forbidding touching or tasting things unclean: or to the superstitious inventions of heretics, imposing such restraints, under pretence of wisdom, humility, or mortification.

3 For you are dead; and your life is hid with Christ in God.

4 When Christ shall appear, who is your life; then you also shall appear with him in glory.

5 Mortify therefore your members which are upon the earth, *fornication, uncleanness, lust, evil concupiscence, and covetousness, which is the service of idols.

6 For which things the wrath of God cometh upon the children of unbelief.

7 In which you also walked some time, when you lived in them.

8 ᵇ But now lay you also all away: anger, indignation, malice, blasphemy, filthy speech out of your mouth.

9 Lie not one to another: stripping yourselves of the old man with his deeds,

10 And putting on the new, him who is renewed unto knowledge, ᶜ according to the image of him that created him.

11 Where there is neither gentile nor Jew, circumcision nor uncircumcision, Barbarian nor Scythian, bond nor free. But Christ is all, and in all.

12 Put ye on therefore, as the elect of God, holy, and beloved, the bowels of mercy, benignity, humility, modesty, patience:

13 Bearing with one another, and forgiving one another, if any have a complaint against another. Even as the Lord hath forgiven you, so you also.

14 But above all these things have charity, which is the bond of perfection:

15 And let the peace of Christ rejoice in your hearts, wherein also you are called in one body: and be ye thankful.

16 Let the word of Christ dwell in you abundantly, in all wisdom: teaching and admonishing one another ᵈ in psalms, hymns, and spiritual canticles, singing in grace in your hearts to God.

17 ᵉ All whatsoever you do in word or in work, all things do ye in the name of the Lord Jesus Christ, giving thanks to God and the Father by him.

18 ᶠ Wives, be subject to your husbands, as it behoveth in the Lord.

19 Husbands, love your wives, and be not bitter towards them.

20 ᵍ Children, obey your parents in all things: for this is well pleasing to the Lord.

21 ʰ Fathers, provoke not your children to indignation: lest they be discouraged.

22 ⁱ Servants, obey in all things your masters according to the flesh, not serving to the eye, as pleasing men, but in simplicity of heart, fearing God.

23 Whatsoever you do, do it from the heart as to the Lord, and not to men.

24 Knowing that you shall receive of the Lord the reward of inheritance. Serve ye the Lord Christ.

25 ᵏ For he that doeth wrong, shall receive *for* that which he hath done wrongfully: and there is no respect of persons with God.

---

ᵃ Ephes. 5. 3.—ᵇ Rom. 6. 4. Ephes. 4. 22. Heb. 12. 1. 1 Pet. 2. 1. and 4. 2.—ᶜ Gen. 1. 26.

ᵈ Ephes. 5. 19.—ᵉ 1 Cor. 10. 31.—ᶠ Ephes. 5. 22. 1 Pet. 3. 1.—ᵍ Ephes. 6. 1.—ʰ Ephes. 6. 4.—ⁱ Titus 2. 9. 1 Pet. 2. 18.—ᵏ Rom. 2. 6.

THE DESCENT OF THE HOLY GHOST.

## CHAP. IV.

*He recommends constant prayer and wisdom. Various salutations.*

MASTERS, do to your servants that which is just and equal, knowing that you also have a master in heaven.

2 *a* Be instant in prayer: watching in it in thanksgiving:

3 *b* Praying withal for us also, that God may open unto us a door of speech to speak the mystery of Christ, (for which also I am bound).

4 That I may make it manifest as I ought to speak.

5 *c* Walk with wisdom towards them that are without, redeeming the time.

6 Let your speech be always in grace seasoned with salt, that you may know how you ought to answer every man.

7 All the things that concern me, Tychicus, our dearest brother, and faithful minister, and fellow-servant in the Lord, will make known to you;

8 Whom I have sent to you for this same purpose, that he may know the things that concern you, and comfort your hearts;

9 With Onesimus, a most beloved and faithful brother, who is one of you. All things that are done here, they shall make known to you.

10 Aristarchus my fellow-prisoner saluteth you, and Mark, the cousin-german of Barnabas, touching whom you have received commandments: if he come unto you, receive him:

11 And Jesus that is called Justus: who are of the circumcision: these only are my helpers in the kingdom of God: who have been a comfort to me.

12 Epaphras saluteth you, who is one of you, a servant of CHRIST JESUS, who is always solicitous for you in prayers, that you may stand perfect and full in all the will of God.

13 For I bear him testimony that he hath much labour for you, and for them that are at Laodicea, and them at Hierapolis.

14 *d* Luke, the most dear physician, saluteth you; and Demas.

15 Salute the brethren who are at Laodicea: and Nymphas, and the church that is in his house.

16 And when this epistle shall have been read with you, cause that it be read also in the church of the Laodiceans: and that you

---

*a* Luke 18. 1. 1 Thess. 5. 17.—*b* Ephes. 6. 19. 2 Thess. 3. 1. Col. 4. 3.—*c* Ephes. 5. 15.

*d* 2 Tim. 4. 11.

CHAP. IV. Ver. 16. *And that you read that which is of the Laodiceans.* What this epistle was is uncertain, and annotators have given different opinions concerning it. Some expound these words of an epistle which St. Paul wrote to the Laodiceans, and is since lost, for that now extant is no more than a collection of sentences out of the other epistles of St. Paul; therefore it cannot be considered even as a part of that epistle. Others explain that the text means a letter sent to St. Paul by the Laodiceans, which he sends to the Colossians to be read by them. However, this opinion does not seem well founded. Hence it is more probable that St. Paul wrote an epistle from Rome to the Laodiceans about the same time that he wrote to the Colossians, as he had them both equally at heart, and that he ordered that epistle to be read by the Colossians for their instructions; and, being neighbouring cities, they might communicate to each other what they had received from him: as one epistle might contain some matters not related in the other, and would be

CHAP. I. I. TO THE THESSALONIANS. CHAP. I

read that which is of the Laodiceans.

equally useful for their concern; and more particularly as they were equally disturbed by intruders and false teachers, against which the apostle was anxious to warn them, lest they should be infected by their pernicious doctrine.

17 And say to Archippus: Take heed to the ministry which thou hast received in the Lord, that thou fulfil it.
18 The salutation of Paul with my own hand. Be mindful of my bands. Grace be with you. Amen.

# THE FIRST EPISTLE OF ST. PAUL TO THE THESSALONIANS.

*Thessalonica was the capital of Macedonia, in which St. Paul having preached the gospel, converted some Jews and a great number of the gentiles: but the unbelieving Jews, envying his success, raised such a commotion against him, that he and his companion Sylvanus were obliged to quit the city. Afterwards he went to Athens, where he heard that the converts in Thessalonica were under a severe persecution ever since his departure, and lest they should lose their fortitude he sent Timothy to strengthen and comfort them in their sufferings. In the meantime St. Paul came to Corinth, where he wrote this first Epistle, and also the second to the Thessalonians, both in the same year, being the nineteenth after our Lord's Ascension. These are the first of his Epistles in the order of time.*

## CHAP. I.

*He gives thanks for the graces bestowed on the Thessalonians.*

PAUL and Sylvanus and Timothy: to the church of the Thessalonians, in God the Father, and in the Lord JESUS CHRIST.

2 Grace be to you and peace. We give thanks to God always for you all: making remembrance of you in our prayers without ceasing.

3 Being mindful of the work of your faith, and labour, and charity, and of the enduring of the hope of our Lord JESUS CHRIST before God and our Father;

4 Knowing, brethren beloved of God, your election:

5 For our gospel hath not been unto you in word only, but in power also, and in the Holy Ghost, and in much fulness, as you know what manner of men we have been among you for your sakes.

6 And you became followers of us, and of the Lord; receiving the word in much tribulation, with joy of the Holy Ghost.

## I. TO THE THESSALONIANS.

### CHAP. II.

7 So that you were made a pattern to all that believe in Macedonia and in Achaia.

8 For from you was spread abroad the word of the Lord, not only in Macedonia and in Achaia, but also in every place, your faith which is towards God, is gone forth, so that we need not to speak anything.

9 For they themselves relate of us, what manner of entering in we had unto you: and how you turned to God from idols, to serve the living and true God.

10 And to wait for his Son from heaven, (whom he raised up from the dead,) JESUS, who hath delivered us from the wrath to come.

### CHAP. II.

*The sincerity of the apostle's preaching the gospel to them: and of their receiving it.*

FOR yourselves know, brethren, our entrance in unto you, that it was not in vain:

2 But having suffered many things before, and been shamefully treated (as you know) at Philippi, *a* we had confidence in our God to speak unto you the gospel of God in much carefulness.

3 For our exhortation was not of error, nor of uncleanness, nor in deceit.

4 But as we were approved by God that the gospel should be committed to us: even so we speak, not as pleasing men, but God, who proveth our hearts.

5 For neither have we used, at any time, the speech of flattery, as you know; nor taken an occasion of covetousness, God is witness.

6 Nor sought we glory of men, neither of you, nor of others.

7 Whereas we might have been burthensome to you, as the apostles of Christ: but we became little ones in the midst of you, as if a nurse should cherish her children:

8 So desirous of you, we would gladly impart unto you not only the gospel of God, but also our own souls: because you were become most dear unto us.

9 For you remember, brethren, our labour and toil: *b* working night and day lest we should be chargeable to any of you, we preached among you the gospel of God.

10 You are witnesses, and God *also*, how holily, and justly, and without blame, we have been to you that have believed:

11 As you know in what manner, entreating and comforting you, (as a father doth his children,)

12 We testified to every one of you that you would walk worthy of God, who hath called you unto his kingdom and glory.

13 Therefore we also give thanks to God without ceasing, because that when you had received of us the word of the hearing of God, you received it not as the word of men, but (as it is indeed) the word of God, who worketh in you that have believed.

14 For you, brethren, are become followers of the churches of God which are in Judea, in CHRIST JESUS: for you also have suffered the same things from

---
*a* Acts 16. 19.  *b* Acts 20. 34. 1 Cor. 4. 12.

your own countrymen, even as they have from the Jews,

15 Who both killed the Lord Jesus, and the prophets, and have persecuted us, and please not God, and are adversaries to all men,

16 Prohibiting us to speak to the gentiles that they may be saved, to fill up their sins always: for the wrath of God is come upon them to the end.

17 But we, brethren, being taken away from you for a short time, in sight, not in heart, have hastened the more abundantly to see your face with great desire.

18 For we would have come unto you, I Paul indeed, once and again: but satan hath hindered us.

19 For what is our hope, or joy, or crown of glory? Are not you, in the presence of our Lord JESUS CHRIST at his coming?

20 For you are our glory and joy.

## CHAP. III.

*The apostle's concern and love for the Thessalonians.*

FOR which cause forbearing no longer, we thought it good to remain at Athens, alone.

2 *a* And we sent Timothy our brother, and the minister of God in the gospel of Christ, to confirm you and exhort you concerning your faith.

---

*a* Acts 16. 1.

CHAP. II. Ver. 16. *To fill up their sins.* That is, to fill up the measure of their sins, after which God's justice would punish them.—Ibid. *For the wrath of God is come upon them to the end.* That is, to continue on them to the end.

3 That no man should be moved in these tribulations: for yourselves know that we are appointed thereunto.

4 For even when we were with you, we foretold you that we should suffer tribulations, as also it is come to pass, and you know.

5 For this cause also I, forbearing no longer, sent to know your faith: lest perhaps he that tempteth should have tempted you, and our labour should be made vain.

6 But now when Timothy came to us from you, and related to us your faith and charity, and that you have a good remembrance of us always, desiring to see us, as we also to see you:

7 Therefore we were comforted, brethren, in you, in all our necessity, and tribulation, by your faith.

8 Because now we live, if you stand in the Lord.

9 For what thanks can we return to God for you, in all the joy wherewith we rejoice for you before our God,

10 Night and day more abundantly praying that we may see your face, and may accomplish those things that are wanting to your faith?

11 Now God himself and our Father, and our Lord JESUS CHRIST direct our way unto you.

12 And may the Lord multiply you, and make you abound in charity towards one another, and towards all men: as we do also towards you.

13 To confirm your hearts without blame, in holiness, before God and our Father, at the coming of our Lord JESUS CHRIST with all his saints. Amen.

## CHAP. IV.

*He exhorts them to purity and mutual charity: he treats of the resurrection of the dead*

FOR the rest therefore, brethren, we pray and beseech you in the Lord JESUS, that as you have received of us, how you ought to walk, and to please God, so also you would walk, that you may abound the more.

2 For you know what precepts I have given to you by the Lord JESUS.

3 ᵃ For this is the will of God, your sanctification: that you should abstain from fornication,

4 That every one of you should know how to possess his vessel in sanctification and honour:

5 Not in the passion of lust, like the gentiles that know not God:

6 And that no man overreach, nor circumvent his brother in business: because the Lord is the avenger of all these things, as we have told you before, and have testified.

7 For God hath not called us unto uncleanness, but unto sanctification.

8 Therefore he that despiseth these things, despiseth not man but God: who also hath given his holy Spirit in us.

9 But as touching the charity of brotherhood, we have no need to write to you: ᵇ for yourselves have learned of God to love one another.

10 For indeed you do it towards all the brethren in all Macedonia. But we entreat you, brethren, that you abound more:

11 And that you use your endeavour to be quiet, and that you do your own business, and work with your own hands, as we commanded you: and that you walk honestly towards them that are without; and that you want nothing of any man's.

12 And we will not have you ignorant, brethren, concerning them that are asleep, that you be not sorrowful, even as others who have no hope

13 For if we believe that JESUS died and rose again, even so them who have slept through JESUS will God bring with him.

14 For this we say unto you in the word of the Lord, ᶜ that we who are alive, who remain unto the coming of the Lord, shall not prevent them who have slept.

15 For the Lord himself shall come down from heaven with commandment, and with the voice of an Archangel, and with the trumpet of God: and the dead who are in Christ shall rise first.

16 Then we who are alive, who are left, shall be taken up together with them in the clouds to meet Christ, into the air, and so shall we be always with the Lord.

17 Wherefore comfort ye one another with these words.

## CHAP. V.

*The day of the Lord shall come when least expected. Exhortations to several duties.*

BUT of the times and moments, brethren, you need not that we should write to you.

---

ᵃ Rom. 12. 2. Ephes. 5. 17.—ᵇ John 13. 34. and 15. 12. and 17. 1 John 2. 10. and 4. 12.

ᶜ 1 Cor. 15. 23.

## I. TO THE THESSALONIANS.

2 *For yourselves know perfectly, that the day of the Lord shall so come, as a thief in the night.

3 For when they shall say, peace and security; then shall sudden destruction come upon them, as the pains upon her that is with child, and they shall not escape.

4 But you, brethren, are not in darkness; that that day should overtake you as a thief.

5 For all you are the children of light, and children of the day: we are not of the night nor of darkness.

6 Therefore let us not sleep as others do; but let us watch and be sober.

7 For they that sleep, sleep in the night; and they that are drunk, are drunk in the night.

8 But let us, who are of the day, be sober, *b* having on the breastplate of faith and charity, and for a helmet, the hope of salvation.

9 For God hath not appointed us unto wrath, but unto the purchasing of salvation by our Lord JESUS CHRIST.

10 Who died for us: that, whether we watch or sleep, we may live together with him.

11 For which cause comfort one another: and edify one another, as you also do.

12 And we beseech you, brethren, to know them who labour among you, and are over you in the Lord, and admonish you:

13 That you esteem them more abundantly in charity for their work's sake. Have peace with them.

14 And we beseech you, brethren, rebuke the unquiet, comfort the feeble-minded, support the weak, be patient towards all men.

15 *c* See that none render evil for evil to any man: but ever follow that which is good towards each other, and towards all men.

16 Always rejoice.

17 *d* Pray without ceasing.

18 In all things give thanks; for this is the will of God in CHRIST JESUS concerning you all.

19 Extinguish not the spirit.

20 Despise not prophecies.

21 But prove all things: hold fast that which is good.

22 From all appearance of evil refrain yourselves.

23 And may the God of peace himself sanctify you in all things: that your whole spirit, and soul, and body, may be preserved blameless in the coming of our Lord JESUS CHRIST.

24 *e* He is faithful, who hath called you, who also will do it.

25 Brethren, pray for us.

26 Salute all the brethren in a holy kiss.

27 I charge you by the Lord that this epistle be read to all the holy brethren.

28 The grace of our Lord JESUS CHRIST be with you. Amen.

---

*e* Prov. 17. 13. and 20. 22. Rom. 12. 17. 1 Pet. 3. 9.—*d* Eccli. 18. 22. Luke 18. 1. Col. 4. 2.—*f* 1 Cor. 1. 9.

---

*a* 2 Pet. 3. 10. Apoc. 3. 3. and 16. 15.—*b* Isaias 59. 17. Ephes. 6. 14. and 17.

CHAP. V. Ver. 14. *The unquiet.* That is, such as are irregular and disorderly.

ST. PETER CURING THE LAME MAN.

# THE SECOND EPISTLE OF ST. PAUL TO THE THESSALONIANS.

*In this Epistle St. Paul admonishes the Thessalonians to be constant in the faith of Christ, and not to be terrified by the insinuations of false teachers telling them that the day of judgment was near at hand, as there must come many signs and wonders before it. He bids them to hold firm the traditions received from him, whether by word, or by epistle; and shews them how they may be certain of his letters by the manner he writes.*

## CHAP. I.

*He gives thanks to God for their faith and constancy; and prays for their advancement in all good.*

PAUL and Sylvanus and Timothy, to the church of the Thessalonians in God our Father, and the Lord JESUS CHRIST.

2 Grace unto you and peace from God our Father and from the Lord JESUS CHRIST.

3 We are bound to give thanks always to God for you, brethren, as it is fitting, because your faith groweth exceedingly, and the charity of every one of you towards each other aboundeth:

4 So that we ourselves also glory in you in the churches of God, for your patience, and faith, and in all your persecutions, and tribulations, which you endure.

5 For an example of the just judgment of God, that you may be counted worthy of the kingdom of God, for which also you suffer.

6 Seeing it is a just thing with God to repay tribulation to them that trouble you:

7 And to you who are troubled, rest with us when the Lord JESUS shall be revealed from heaven with the angels of his power:

8 In a flame of fire yielding vengeance to them who know not God, and who obey not the gospel of our Lord JESUS CHRIST.

9 Who shall suffer eternal punishment in destruction, from the face of the Lord and from the glory of his power:

10 When he shall come to be glorified in his saints, and to be made wonderful in all them who have believed: because our testimony was believed upon you in that day.

11 Wherefore also we pray always for you: that our God would make you worthy of his vocation, and fulfil all the good pleasure of his goodness and the work of faith in power.

12 That the name of our Lord JESUS may be glorified in you, and you in him, according to the grace of our God, and of the Lord JESUS CHRIST.

## CHAP. II.

*The day of the Lord is not to come till the man of sin be revealed. The apostles' traditions are to be observed.*

AND we beseech you, brethren, by the coming of our Lord JESUS CHRIST, and of our gathering together unto him:

2 That you be not easily moved from your mind, nor be frighted. neither by spirit, nor by word, nor by epistle, as sent from us, as if the day of the Lord were at hand.

3 ᵃ Let no man deceive you by any means: for unless there come a revolt first, and the man of sin be revealed, the son of perdition,

4 Who opposeth, and is lifted up above all that is called God, or that is worshipped, so that he sitteth in the temple of God, shewing himself as if he were God.

5 Remember you not, that when I was yet with you, I told you these things?

6 And now you know what withholdeth, that he may be revealed in his time.

7 For the mystery of iniquity already worketh: only that he who now holdeth, do hold, until he be taken out of the way.

8 And then that wicked one shall be revealed, ᵇ whom the Lord JESUS shall kill with the spirit of his mouth: and shall destroy with the brightness of his coming: him,

9 Whose coming is according to the working of satan, in all power, and signs, and lying wonders,

10 And in all seduction of iniquity to them that perish: because they received not the love of the truth that they might be saved. Therefore God shall send them the operation of error, to believe lying:

11 That all may be judged who have not believed the truth, but have consented to iniquity.

12 But we ought to give thanks to God always for you, brethren beloved of God, for that God hath chosen you firstfruits unto salvation, in sanctification of the spirit, and faith of the truth:

13 Whereunto also he hath called you by our gospel, unto the purchasing of the glory of our Lord JESUS CHRIST.

14 Therefore, brethren, stand

---

ᵃ Ephes. 5. 6.

CHAP. II. Ver. 3. *A revolt.* This revolt, or *falling off,* is generally understood, by the ancient fathers, of a revolt from the Roman empire, which was first to be destroyed, before the coming of Antichrist. It may, perhaps, be understood also of a *revolt* of many nations from the Catholic Church; which has, in part, happened already, by the means of Mahomet, Luther, &c., and it may be supposed, will be more general in the days of Antichrist.—Ibid. *The man of sin.* Here must be in-sinuated some particular man, as is evident from the frequent repetition of the Greek article ὁ, *the man of sin, the son of perdition, the adversary or opposer,* ὁ ἀντικείμενος. It agrees to the wicked and great Antichrist, who will come before the end of the world.

Ver. 4. *In the temple.* Either that of Jerusalem, which some think he will rebuild; or in some Christian church, which he will pervert to his own worship: as Mahomet has done by the churches of the East.

---

ᵇ Isaias 11. 4.

Ver. 10. *God shall send.* That is, God shall suffer them to be deceived by lying wonders and false miracles, in punishment of their not entertaining the love of truth.

Ver. 14. *Traditions.* See here that

fast; and hold the traditions which you have learned, whether by word, or by our epistle.

15 Now our Lord JESUS CHRIST himself, and God our Father, who hath loved us, and hath given us everlasting consolation, and good hope in grace,

16 Exhort your hearts, and confirm you in every good work and word.

## CHAP. III.

*He begs their prayers, and warns them against idleness.*

FOR *a* the rest, brethren, pray for us, that the word of God may run and may be glorified even as among you:

2 And that we may be delivered from importunate and evil men: for all men have not faith.

3 But God is faithful, who will strengthen and keep you from evil.

4 And we have confidence concerning you in the Lord, that the things which we command, you both do, and will do.

5 And the Lord direct your hearts in the charity of God, and the patience of Christ.

6 And we charge you, brethren, in the name of our Lord JESUS CHRIST, that you withdraw yourselves from every brother walking disorderly, and not according to the tradition which they have received of us.

7 For yourselves know how you ought to imitate us: for we were not disorderly among you:

8 *b* Neither did we eat any man's bread for nothing, but in labour and in toil we worked night and day, lest we should be chargeable to any of you.

9 Not as if we had not power: but that we might give ourselves a pattern unto you, to imitate us.

10 For also when we were with you, this we declared to you: that if any man will not work neither let him eat.

11 For we have heard there are some among you who walk disorderly, working not at all, but curiously meddling.

12 Now we charge them that are such, and beseech them by the Lord JESUS CHRIST, that, working with silence, they would eat their own bread.

13 *c* But you, brethren, be not weary in well-doing.

14 And if any man obey not our word by this epistle, note that man, and do not keep company with him, that he may be ashamed.

15 Yet do not esteem him as an enemy, but admonish him as a brother.

16 Now the Lord of peace himself give you everlasting peace in every place. The Lord be with you all.

17 The salutation of Paul with my own hand: which is the sign in every epistle. So I write.

18 The grace of our Lord JESUS CHRIST be with you all. Amen.

---

*a* Ephes. 4. 19. Col. 4. 2.

the unwritten *traditions* of the apostles are no less to be received than their epistles.

CHAP. III. Ver. 1. *May run*, that is, may spread itself, and have free course.

*b* Acts 20. 34. 1 Cor. 4. 12. 1 Thess. 2. 9. — *c* Gal. 6. 9.

# THE FIRST EPISTLE OF ST. PAUL TO TIMOTHY.

*St. Paul writes this Epistle to his beloved Timothy, being then Bishop of Ephesus, to instruct him in the duties of a bishop, both in respect to himself and to his charge; and that he ought to be well informed of the good morals of those on whom he was to impose hands: Impose not hands lightly upon any man. He tells him also how he should behave towards his clergy. This Epistle was written about thirty-three years after our Lord's Ascension, but where it was written is uncertain: the more general opinion is, that it was in Macedonia.*

## CHAP. I.

*He puts Timothy in mind of his charge: and blesses God for the mercy he himself had received.*

PAUL, an apostle of JESUS CHRIST, according to the commandment of God our Saviour, and of CHRIST JESUS our hope:

2 <sup>a</sup> To Timothy his beloved son in faith. Grace, mercy, and peace from God the Father, and from CHRIST JESUS our Lord.

3 As I desired thee to remain at Ephesus when I went into Macedonia, that thou mightest charge some not to teach otherwise,

4 <sup>b</sup> Nor to give heed to fables and genealogies without end: which minister questions rather than the edification of God which is in faith.

5 Now the end of the commandment is charity from a pure heart, and a good conscience, and an unfeigned faith.

6 From which things some going astray, are turned aside unto vain babbling:

7 Desiring to be teachers of the law, understanding neither the things they say, nor whereof they affirm.

8 <sup>c</sup> But we know that the law is good, if a man use it lawfully:

9 Knowing this, that the law was not made for the just man, but for the unjust and disobedient, for the ungodly, and for sinners, for the wicked and defiled, for murderers of fathers, and murderers of mothers, for man-slayers,

10 For fornicators, for them who defile themselves with mankind, for men-stealers, for liars, for perjured persons, and

---

<sup>c</sup> Rom. 7. 12.

CHAP. I. Ver. 9. *The law is not,* &c. He means, that the just man doth good, and avoideth evil, not as *compelled* by the law, and merely for fear of the punishment appointed for transgressors; but voluntarily, and out of the love of God and virtue; and would do so though there were no law.

---

<sup>a</sup> Acts 16. 1.—<sup>b</sup> Infra, 4. 7. 2 Tim. 2. 16. Titus 3. 9.

whatever other thing is contrary to sound doctrine,

11 Which is according to the gospel of the glory of the blessed God, which hath been committed to my trust.

12 I give him thanks, who hath strengthened me, *even* to CHRIST JESUS our Lord, for that he hath counted me faithful, putting me in the ministry.

13 Who before was a blasphemer and a persecutor and contumelious. But I obtained the mercy of God, because I did it ignorantly in unbelief.

14 Now the grace of our Lord hath abounded exceedingly with faith and love which is in CHRIST JESUS.

15 A faithful saying, and worthy of all acceptation, *a* that CHRIST JESUS came into this world to save sinners, of whom I am the chief.

16 But for this cause have I obtained mercy: that in me first CHRIST JESUS might shew forth all patience, for the information of them that shall believe in him unto life everlasting.

17 Now to the king of ages, immortal, invisible, the only God, be honour and glory for ever and ever. Amen.

18 This precept I commend to thee, O son Timothy: according to the prophecies going before on thee, that thou war in them a good warfare.

19 Having faith and a good conscience, which some rejecting have made shipwreck concerning the faith.

20 Of whom is Hymeneus and Alexander, whom I have delivered up to satan, that they may learn not to blaspheme.

*a* Matt. 9. 13. Mark 2. 17.

## CHAP. II.

*Prayers are to be said for all men: because God wills the salvation of all. Women are not to teach.*

I DESIRE therefore first of all that supplications, prayers, intercessions and thanksgivings be made by men,

2 For kings, and for all that are in high stations: that we may lead a quiet and a peaceable life in all piety and chastity.

3 For this is good and acceptable in the sight of God our Saviour,

4 Who will have all men to be saved, and to come to the knowledge of the truth.

5 For there is one God, and one mediator of God and men, the man CHRIST JESUS:

6 Who gave himself a redemption for all, a testimony in due times.

7 Whereunto I am appointed a preacher and an apostle, (I say the truth, I lie not,) a doctor of the gentiles in faith and truth.

8 I will therefore that men pray in every place, lifting up pure hands without anger and contention.

9 *b* In like manner women also in decent apparel: adorning

*b* 1 Pet. 3. 3.

CHAP. II. Ver. 5. *One mediator.* Christ is the one and *only mediator* of *redemption;* who gave himself, as the apostle writes in the following verse, *redemption for all.* He is also the *only mediator* who stands in need of no other to recommend his petitions to the Father. But this is not against our seeking the prayers and intercession, as well of the faithful upon earth as of the saints and angels in heaven, for obtaining mercy, grace, and salvation through Jesus Christ. And St. Paul himself often desired the help of the prayers of the faithful, without any injury to the mediatorship of Jesus Christ.

themselves with modesty and sobriety, not with plaited hair, or gold, or pearls, or costly attire.

10 But as it becometh women professing godliness, with good works.

11 Let the women learn in silence, with all subjection.

12 ᵃ But I suffer not a woman to teach, nor to use authority over the man: but to be in silence.

13 ᵇ For Adam was first formed; then Eve.

14 ᶜ And Adam was not seduced; but the woman being seduced, was in the transgression.

15 Yet she shall be saved through child-bearing: if she continue in faith and love and sanctification with sobriety.

## CHAP. III.

*What sort of men to be admitted into the clergy: the church is the pillar of truth.*

A FAITHFUL saying: If a man desire the office of a bishop, he desireth a good work.

2 ᵈ It behoveth therefore a bishop to be blameless, the husband of one wife, sober, prudent, of good behaviour, chaste, given to hospitality, a teacher.

3 Not given to wine, no striker, but modest, not quarrelsome, not covetous, but

4 One that ruleth well his own house, having his children in subjection with all chastity.

5 But if a man know not how to rule his own house, how shall he take care of the church of God?

6 Not a neophyte: lest being puffed up with pride, he fall into the judgment of the devil.

7 Moreover he must have a good testimony of them who are without: lest he fall into reproach and the snare of the devil.

8 Deacons in like manner chaste, not double-tongued, not given to much wine, not greedy of filthy lucre:

9 Holding the mystery of faith in a pure conscience.

10 And let these also first be proved: and so let them minister, having no crime.

11 The women in like manner chaste, not slanderers, but sober, faithful in all things.

12 Let deacons be the husbands of one wife: who rule well their children, and their own houses.

13 For they that have ministered well shall purchase to themselves a good degree, and much confidence in the faith which is in CHRIST JESUS.

14 These things I write to thee, hoping that I shall come to thee shortly.

15 But if I tarry long, that thou mayest know how thou oughtest to behave thyself in the house of God, which is the

---

ᵃ 1 Cor. 14. 34.—ᵇ Gen. 1. 24.—ᶜ Gen. 3. 6.—ᵈ Titus 1. 7.

---

CHAP. III. Ver. 2. *Of one wife.* The meaning is not that every bishop should have a wife, (for St. Paul himself had none,) but that no one should be admitted to the holy orders of bishop, priest, or deacon, who had been married more than once.

Ver. 6. *A neophyte.* That is, one lately baptized, a young convert.

Ver. 15. *The pillar and ground of the truth.* Therefore the Church of the living God can never uphold error, nor bring in corruption, superstition, or idolatry.

THE MARTYRDOM OF ST. STEPHEN.

church of the living God, the pillar and ground of the truth.

16 And evidently great is the mystery of godliness, which was manifested in the flesh, was justified in the spirit, appeared unto Angels, hath been preached unto the gentiles, is believed in the world, is taken up in glory.

## CHAP. IV.

*He warns him against heretics: and exhorts him to the exercise of piety.*

NOW the Spirit manifestly saith, *a* that in the last times some shall depart from the faith, giving heed to spirits of error, and doctrines of devils,

2 Speaking lies in hypocrisy, and having their conscience seared,

3 Forbidding to marry, to abstain from meats, which God hath created to be received with thanksgiving by the faithful, and by them that have known the truth.

4 For every creature of God is good, and nothing to be rejected that is received with thanksgiving:

5 For it is sanctified by the word of God and prayer.

6 These things proposing to the brethren, thou shalt be a good minister of CHRIST JESUS, nourished up in the words of faith and of the good doctrine which thou hast attained unto.

7 *b* But avoid foolish and old wives' fables: and exercise thyself unto godliness.

8 For bodily exercise is profitable to little: but godliness is profitable to all things, having promise of the life that now is, and of that which is to come.

9 A faithful saying and worthy of all acceptation.

10 For therefore we labour and are reviled because we hope in the living God, who is the Saviour of all men, especially of the faithful.

11 These things command and teach.

12 Let no man despise thy youth: but be thou an example of the faithful, in word, in conversation, in charity, in faith, in chastity.

13 Till I come, attend unto reading, to exhortation, and to doctrine.

14 Neglect not the grace that is in thee, which was given thee by prophecy, with imposition of the hands of the priesthood.

15 Meditate upon these things, be wholly in these things; that thy profiting may be manifest to all.

16 Take heed to thyself, and to doctrine: be earnest in them. For in doing this thou shalt both save thyself and them that hear thee.

---

*a* 2 Tim. 3. 1. 2 Pet. 3. 3. Jude 18.

---

CHAP. IV. Ver. 3. *Forbidding to marry, to abstain from meats, &c.* He speaks of the Gnostics, the Marcionites, the Encratites, the Manichæans, and other ancient heretics, who absolutely condemned marriage, and the use of all kind of meat: because they pretended that all flesh was from an evil principle. Whereas the Church of God, so far from condemning marriage, holds it a holy sacrament; and forbids it to none but such as by vow have chosen the better part; and prohibits not the use of any meats whatsoever in proper times and seasons; though she does not judge all kind of diet proper for days of fasting and penance.

*b* Supra, 1. 4. 2 Tim. 2. 23. Titus 3. 9.

## CHAP. V.

*He gives him lessons concerning widows, and how he is to behave to his clergy.*

AN ancient man rebuke not, but entreat him as a father: young men, as brethren:

2 Old women, as mothers: young women, as sisters, in all chastity.

3 Honour widows, that are widows indeed.

4 But if any widow have children, or grandchildren; let her learn first to govern her own house, and to make a return of duty to her parents: for this is acceptable before God.

5 But she that is a widow indeed and desolate, let her trust in God, and continue in supplications and prayers night and day.

6 For she that liveth in pleasures is dead while she is living.

7 And this give in charge, that they may be blameless.

8 But if any man have not care of his own, and especially of those of his house, he hath denied the faith, and is worse than an infidel.

9 Let a widow be chosen of no less than threescore years of age, who hath been the wife of one husband,

10 Having testimony for her good works, if she have brought up children, if she have received to harbour, if she have washed the saints' feet, if she have ministered to them that suffer tribulation, if she have diligently followed every good work.

11 But the younger widows avoid. For when they have grown wanton in Christ, they will marry:

12 Having damnation, because they have made void their first faith.

13 And withal being idle, they learn to go about from house to house: and are not only idle, but tattlers also, and busy-bodies, speaking things which they ought not.

14 I will therefore that the younger should marry, bear children, be mistresses of families, give no occasion to the adversary to speak evil.

15 For some are already turned aside after satan.

16 If any of the faithful have widows, let him minister to them, and let not the church be charged: that there may be sufficient for them that are widows indeed.

17 Let the priests that rule well be esteemed worthy of double honour: especially they who labour in the word and doctrine:

18 For the scripture saith: *" Thou shalt not muzzle the ox that treadeth out the corn:* and *b the labourer is worthy of his reward.*

19 Against a priest receive not an accusation, but under two or three witnesses.

20 Them that sin reprove before all: that the rest also may have fear.

21 I charge thee before God, and CHRIST JESUS, and the elect angels, that thou observe these things without prejudice, doing nothing by declining to either side.

---

*a* Deut. 25. 4.  1 Cor. 9. 9.—*b* Matt. 10. 10.  Luke 10. 7.

CHAP. V. Ver. 12. *Their first faith.* Their vow, by which they had engaged themselves to Christ.

22 Impose not hands lightly upon any man, neither be partaker of other men's sins. Keep thyself chaste.

23 Do not still drink water: but use a little wine for thy stomach's sake, and thy frequent infirmities.

24 Some men's sins are manifest, going before to judgment: and some men they follow after.

25 In like manner also good deeds are manifest: and they that are otherwise cannot be hid.

## CHAP. VI.

*Duties of servants: the danger of covetousness. Lessons for the rich.*

WHOSOEVER are servants under the yoke, let them count their masters worthy of all honour; lest the name of the Lord and *his* doctrine be blasphemed.

2 But they that have believing masters, let them not despise them, because they are brethren, but serve them the rather, because they are faithful and beloved, who are partakers of the benefit. These things teach and exhort.

3 If any man teach otherwise, and consent not to the sound words of our Lord JESUS CHRIST, and to that doctrine which is according to godliness,

4 He is proud, knowing nothing, but sick about questions and strifes of words: from which arise envies, contentions, blasphemies, evil suspicions.

5 Conflicts of men corrupted in mind, and who are destitute of the truth, supposing gain to be godliness.

6 But godliness with contentment is great gain.

7 *a* For we brought nothing into this world: and certainly we can carry nothing out.

8 *b* But having food, and wherewith to be covered, with these we are content.

9 For they that will become rich, fall into temptation, and into the snare of the devil, and into many unprofitable and hurtful desires, which drown men into destruction and perdition.

10 For the desire of money is the root of all evils; which some coveting have erred from the faith, and have entangled themselves in many sorrows.

11 But thou, O man of God, fly these things: and pursue justice, godliness, faith, charity, patience, mildness.

12 Fight the good fight of faith: lay hold on eternal life whereunto thou art called, and hast confessed a good confession before many witnesses.

13 I charge thee before God, who quickeneth all things, and before CHRIST JESUS who gave testimony *c* under Pontius Pilate, a good confession,

14 That thou keep the commandment without spot, blameless, until the coming of our Lord JESUS CHRIST.

15 Which in his times he shall shew, *d* who is the Blessed and only Mighty, the King of kings, and Lord of lords.

16 Who only hath immortality, and inhabiteth light inaccessible, *e* whom no man hath seen nor can see, to whom be honour and empire everlasting. Amen.

---

*a* Job 1. 21. Eccli. 5. 14.—*b* Prov. 27. 26.—*c* Matt. 27. 11. John 18. 33. 37.—*d* Apoc. 17. 14. and 19. 16.—*e* John 1. 18. 1 John 4. 12.

17 Charge the rich of this world not to be high-minded, *a* nor to trust in the uncertainty of riches, but in the living God (who giveth us abundantly all things to enjoy);

18 To do good, to be rich in good works, to give easily, to communicate to others.

19 To lay up in store for themselves a good foundation against the time to come, that they may lay hold on the true life.

20 O Timothy, keep that which is committed to thy trust, avoiding the profane novelties of words and oppositions of knowledge falsely so called.

21 Which some promising, have erred concerning the faith. Grace be with thee. Amen.

*a* Luke 12.

# THE SECOND EPISTLE OF ST. PAUL TO TIMOTHY.

*In this Epistle the Apostle again instructs and admonishes* TIMOTHY *in what belonged to his office, as in the former; and also warns him to shun the conversation of those who had erred from the truth, describing at the same time their character. He tells him of his approaching death, and desires him to come speedily to him. It appears from this circumstance, that he wrote this second Epistle in the time of his last imprisonment at Rome, and not long before his martyrdom.*

## CHAP. I.

*He admonishes him to stir up the grace he received by his ordination, and not to be discouraged at his sufferings, but to hold firm the sound doctrine of the gospel.*

PAUL, an apostle of JESUS CHRIST, by the will of God, according to the promise of life, which is in CHRIST JESUS:

2 To Timothy, my dearly beloved son, grace, mercy, *and* peace from God the Father, and from CHRIST JESUS our Lord.

3 I give thanks to God, whom I serve from my forefathers with a pure conscience, that without ceasing I have a remembrance of thee in my prayers night and day.

4 Desiring to see thee, being mindful of thy tears, that I may be filled with joy.

5 Calling to mind that faith which is in thee unfeigned, which also dwelt first in thy grandmother Lois, and in thy mother Eunice, and I am certain that in thee also.

6 For which cause I admonish thee, that thou stir up the grace

of God, which is in thee by the imposition of my hands.

7 *a* For God hath not given us the spirit of fear: but of power, and of love, and of sobriety.

8 Be not thou therefore ashamed of the testimony of our Lord, nor of me his prisoner: but labour with the gospel according to the power of God:

9 Who hath delivered us and called us by his holy calling, *b* not according to our works, but according to his own purpose and grace which was given us in CHRIST JESUS before the times *c* of the world:

10 But is now made manifest by the illumination of our Saviour JESUS CHRIST, who hath destroyed death, and hath brought to light life and incorruption by the gospel:

11 Wherein *d* I am appointed a preacher, and an apostle, and teacher of the gentiles.

12 For which cause I also suffer these things: but I am not ashamed. For I know whom I have believed, and I am certain that he is able to keep that which I have committed unto him, against that day.

13 Hold the form of sound words, which thou hast heard of me in faith, and in the love which is in CHRIST JESUS.

14 Keep the good thing committed to thy trust by the Holy Ghost, who dwelleth in us.

15 Thou knowest this, that all they who are in Asia are turned away from me: of whom are Phigellus and Hermogenes.

16 The Lord give mercy to the *e* house of Onesiphorus: because he hath often refreshed me, and hath not been ashamed of my chain:

17 But when he was come to Rome, he carefully sought me, and found me.

18 The Lord grant unto him to find mercy of the Lord in that day. And in how many things he ministered unto me at Ephesus, thou very well knowest.

## CHAP II.

*He exhorts him to diligence in his office, and patience in sufferings. The danger of the delusions of heretics.*

THOU therefore, my son, be strong in the grace which is in CHRIST JESUS.

2 And the things which thou hast heard of me by many witnesses, the same commend to faithful men, who shall be fit to teach others also.

3 Labour as a good soldier of CHRIST JESUS.

4 No man being a soldier to God, entangleth himself with secular business; that he may please him to whom he hath engaged himself.

5 For he also, that striveth for the mastery, is not crowned except he strive lawfully.

6 The husbandman, that laboureth, must first partake of the fruits.

7 Understand what I say: for the Lord will give thee in all things understanding.

8 Be mindful that the Lord

---

*a* Rom. 8. 15.— *b* Titus 3. 5.— *c* That is, the beginning.— *d* 1 Tim. 2. 7.

CHAP. I. Ver. 10. *By the illumination.* That is, by the bright coming and appearing of our Saviour.

*e* Infra, 4. 19.

JESUS CHRIST is risen again from the dead, of the seed of David, according to my gospel.

9 Wherein I labour even unto bands, as an evil-doer: but the word of God is not bound.

10 Therefore I endure all things for the sake of the elect, that they also may obtain the salvation which is in CHRIST JESUS, with heavenly glory.

11 A faithful saying. For if we be dead with him, we shall live also with him.

12 If we suffer, we shall also reign with him. *a* If we deny him, he will also deny us.

13 *b* If we believe not, he continueth faithful: he cannot deny himself.

14 Of these things put them in mind, charging them before the Lord. Contend not in words, for it is to no profit, but to the subverting of the hearers.

15 Carefully study to present thyself approved unto God, a workman that needeth not to be ashamed, rightly handling the word of truth.

16 But shun profane and vain babblings: for they grow much towards ungodliness.

17 And their speech spreadeth like a canker: of whom are Hymeneus and Philetus:

18 Who have erred from the truth, saying that the resurrection is past already, and have subverted the faith of some.

19 But the sure foundation of God standeth firm, having this seal: the Lord knoweth who are his; and let every one depart from iniquity who nameth the name of the Lord.

20 But in a great house there are not only vessels of gold and of silver, but also of wood and of earth: and some indeed unto honour, but some unto dishonour.

21 If any man therefore shall cleanse himself from these, he shall be a vessel unto honour, sanctified and profitable to the Lord, prepared unto every good work.

22 But flee thou youthful desires, and pursue justice, faith, charity, and peace with them that call on the Lord out of a pure heart.

23 *c* And avoid foolish and unlearned questions, knowing that they beget strifes.

24 But the servant of the Lord must not wrangle: but be mild towards all men, apt to teach, patient,

25 With modesty admonishing them that resist the truth: if peradventure God may give them repentance to know the truth,

26 And they may recover themselves from the snares of the devil, by whom they are held captive at his will.

## CHAP. III.

*The character of heretics of latter days: he exhorts Timothy to constancy. Of the great profit of the knowledge of the Scriptures.*

KNOW also this, that, *d* in the last days, shall come on dangerous times.

2 Men shall be lovers of themselves, covetous, haughty, proud, blasphemers, disobedient to parents, ungrateful, wicked.

---

*a* Matt. 10. 32. Mark 8. 38.—*b* Rom. 3. 3.

*c* 1 Tim. 1. 4. and 7. Titus 3. 9.—*d* 1 Tim. 4. 1. 2 Pet. 3. 3. Jude 18.

THE CONVERSION OF THE EUNUCH.

3 Without affection, without peace, slanderers, incontinent, unmerciful, without kindness,

4 Traitors, stubborn, puffed up, and lovers of pleasures more than of God:

5 Having an appearance indeed of godliness, but denying the power thereof. Now these avoid.

6 For of these sort are they who creep into houses, and lead captive silly women loaden with sins, who are led away with divers desires:

7 Ever learning, and never attaining to the knowledge of the truth.

8 Now as *a* Jannes and Mambres resisted Moses, so these also resist the truth, men corrupted in mind, reprobate concerning the faith.

9 But they shall proceed no farther: for their folly shall be manifest to all men, as theirs also was.

10 But thou hast fully known my doctrine, manner of life, purpose, faith, long-suffering, love, patience,

11 Persecutions, afflictions: *b* such as came upon me at Antioch, at Iconium, and at Lystra: what persecutions I endured, and out of them all the Lord delivered me.

12 And all that will live godly in CHRIST JESUS shall suffer persecution.

13 But evil men and seducers shall grow worse and worse: erring, and driving into error.

14 But continue thou in those things which thou hast learned, and which have been committed to thee: knowing of whom thou hast learned *them;*

15 And because from thy infancy thou hast known the holy scriptures, which can instruct thee to salvation, by the faith which is in CHRIST JESUS.

16 *c* All scripture, inspired of God, is profitable to teach, to reprove, to correct, to instruct in justice,

17 That the man of God may be perfect, furnished to every good work.

## CHAP. IV.

*His charge to Timothy: he tells him of his approaching death, and desires him to come to him.*

I CHARGE thee before God and JESUS CHRIST, who shall judge the living and the dead, by his coming, and his kingdom:

2 Preach the word: be instant in season, out of season: reprove, entreat, rebuke in all patience and doctrine.

3 For there shall be a time, when they will not endure sound doctrine: but according to their own desires they will heap to themselves teachers, having itching ears,

---

*c* 2 Pet. 1. 20.

---

Ver. 16. *All scripture, &c.* Every part of divine Scripture is certainly *profitable* for all these ends. But, if we would have the *whole* rule of Christian faith and practice, we must not be content with those Scriptures which Timothy *knew from his infancy,* that is, with the Old Testament alone; nor yet with the New Testament, without taking along with it the traditions of the apostles, and the interpretation of the Church, to which the apostles delivered both the book and the true meaning of it.

---

*a* Exod. 7. 11.—*b* Acts 14. 1. et seq.

CHAP. III. Ver. 8. *Jannes and Mambres.* The magicians of king Pharao.

4 And will indeed turn away their hearing from the truth, but will be turned unto fables.

5 But be thou vigilant, labour in all things, do the work of an evangelist, fulfil thy ministry. Be sober.

6 For I am even now ready to be sacrificed: and the time of my dissolution is at hand.

7 I have fought a good fight, I have finished my course, I have kept the faith.

8 As to the rest, there is laid up for me a crown of justice, which the Lord the just judge will render to me in that day: and not only to me, but to them also that love his coming. Make haste to come to me quickly.

9 For Demas hath left me, loving this world, and is gone to Thessalonica:

10 Crescens into Galatia, Titus into Dalmatia.

11 *Only Luke is with me. Take Mark, and bring him with thee: for he is profitable to me for the ministry.

12 But Tychicus I have sent to Ephesus.

13 The cloak that I left at Troas with Carpus, when thou comest, bring with thee, and the books, especially the parchments.

14 Alexander the coppersmith hath done me much evil: the Lord will reward him according to his works:

15 Whom do thou also avoid, for he hath greatly withstood our words.

16 At my first answer no man stood with me, but all forsook me: may it not be laid to their charge.

17 But the Lord stood by me, and strengthened me, that by me the preaching may be accomplished, and that all the gentiles may hear: and I was delivered out of the mouth of the lion.

18 The Lord hath delivered me from every evil work: and will preserve me unto his heavenly kingdom, to whom be glory for ever and ever. Amen.

19 Salute Prisca and Aquila, *b* and the household of Onesiphorus.

20 Erastus remained at Corinth. And Trophimus I left sick at Miletus.

21 Make haste to come before winter. Eubulus and Pudens and Linus and Claudia, and all the brethren salute thee.

22 The Lord JESUS CHRIST be with thy spirit. Grace be with you. Amen.

---

*a* Col. 4. 14.

---

CHAP. IV. Ver. 5. *An evangelist*, a diligent preacher of the gospel.

*b* Supra, 1. 16.

# THE
# EPISTLE OF ST. PAUL TO TITUS.

*St. Paul having preached the faith in the Island of Crete, he ordained his beloved disciple and companion Titus bishop, and left him there to finish the work which he had begun. Afterwards the Apostle, on a journey to Nicopolis, a city of Macedonia, wrote this Epistle to Titus; in which he directs him to ordain bishops and priests for the different cities, shewing him the principal qualities necessary for a bishop, also gives him particular advice for his own conduct to his flock, exhorting him to hold in strictness of discipline, but seasoned with lenity. It was written about thirty-three years after our Lord's Ascension.*

## CHAP. I.

*What kind of men he is to ordain priests. Some men are to be sharply rebuked.*

PAUL, a servant of God, and an apostle of JESUS CHRIST, according to the faith of the elect of God and the acknowledging of the truth, which is according to godliness,

2 Unto the hope of life everlasting, which God, who lieth not, hath promised before the times of the world:

3 But hath in due times manifested his word in preaching, which is committed to me according to the commandment of God our Saviour:

4 To Titus my beloved son, according to the common faith, grace, and peace from God the Father, and from CHRIST JESUS our Saviour.

5 For this cause I left thee in Crete, that thou shouldest set in order the things that are wanting, and shouldest ordain priests in every city, as I also appointed thee:

6 ᵃ If any be without crime, the husband of one wife, having faithful children, not accused of riot or unruly.

7 For a bishop must be without crime, as the steward of God: not proud, not subject to anger, not given to wine, no striker, nor greedy of filthy lucre:

8 But given to hospitality, gentle, sober, just, holy, continent:

9 Embracing that faithful word which is according to doctrine, that he may be able to exhort in sound doctrine, and to convince the gainsayers

10 For there are many disobedient, vain talkers, and seducers, especially they of the circumcision.

11 Who must be reproved: who subvert whole houses, teaching the things which they

---
ᵃ 1 Tim. 3. 2.

---

CHAP. I. Ver. 6. *Of one wife.* See the note upon 1 Tim. iii. 2.

ought not, for filthy lucre's sake.

12 One of them said, a prophet of their own, *The Cretians are always liars, evil beasts, slothful bellies.*

13 This testimony is true. Wherefore rebuke them sharply, that they may be sound in the faith.

14 Not giving heed to Jewish fables and commandments of men, who turn themselves away from the truth.

15 *a* All things are clean to the clean: but to them that are defiled, and to unbelievers, nothing is clean: but both their mind and their conscience are defiled.

16 They profess that they know God: but in their works they deny *him;* being abominable, and incredulous, and to every good work reprobate.

### CHAP. II.
*How he is to instruct both old and young. The duty of servants. The Christian's rule of life.*

BUT speak thou the things that become sound doctrine:

2 That the aged men be sober, chaste, prudent, sound in faith, in love, in patience.

3 The aged women, in like manner, in holy attire, not false accusers, not given to much wine: teaching well;

4 That they may teach the young women to be wise, to love their husbands, to love their children,

5 To be discreet, chaste, sober, having a care of the house, gentle, obedient to their hus-

bands, that the word of God be not blasphemed.

6 Young men in like manner exhort that they be sober.

7 In all things shew thyself an example of good works, in doctrine, in integrity, in gravity,

8 The sound word that cannot be blamed: that he, who is on the contrary part, may be afraid, having no evil to say of us.

9 *b Exhort* servants to be obedient to their masters, in all things pleasing, not gainsaying:

10 Not defrauding, but in all things shewing good fidelity, that they may adorn the doctrine of God our Saviour in all things.

11 *c* For the grace of God our Saviour hath appeared to all men,

12 Instructing us that, denying ungodliness and worldly desires, we should live soberly, and justly, and godly in this world,

13 Looking for the blessed hope and coming of the glory of the great God and our Saviour JESUS CHRIST,

14 Who gave himself for us, that he might redeem us from all iniquity, and might cleanse to himself a people acceptable, a pursuer of good works.

15 These things speak and exhort, and rebuke with all authority. Let no man despise thee.

### CHAP. III.
*Other instructions and directions for life and doctrine.*

ADMONISH them to be subject to princes and powers,

---
*a* Rom. 14. 20.

*b* Ephes. 6. 5. Col. 3. 22. 1 Pet. 2. 18. —*c* Infra, 3. 4.

to obey at a word, to be ready to every good work,

2 To speak evil of no man, not to be litigious, but gentle: shewing all mildness towards all men.

3 For we ourselves also were some time unwise, incredulous, erring, slaves to divers desires and pleasures, living in malice and envy, hateful, hating one another.

4 But when the goodness and kindness of God our Saviour appeared,

5 ª Not by the works of justice, which we have done, but according to his mercy he saved us, by the laver of regeneration, and renovation of the Holy Ghost,

6 Whom he hath poured forth upon us abundantly through JESUS CHRIST our Saviour:

7 That, being justified by his grace, we may be heirs, according to hope of life everlasting.

8 It is a faithful saying: and these things I will have thee affirm constantly: that they, who believe in God, may be careful to excel in good works. These things are good and profitable unto men.

ª 2 Tim. 1. 9.

9 ᵇ But avoid foolish questions, and genealogies, and contentions, and strivings about the law. For they are unprofitable and vain.

10 A man that is a heretic, after the first and second admonition avoid:

11 Knowing that he, that is such a one, is subverted, and sinneth, being condemned by his own judgment.

12 When I shall send to thee Artemius or Tychicus, make haste to come unto me to Nicopolis. For there I have determined to winter.

13 Send forward Zenas the lawyer and Apollo with care, that nothing be wanting to them.

14 And let our men also learn to excel in good works for necessary uses: that they be not unfruitful.

15 All that are with me salute thee; salute them that love us in the faith. The grace of God be with you all. Amen.

ᵇ 1 Tim. 1. 4. and 4. 7. 2 Tim. 2. 23.

CHAP. III. Ver. 11. *By his own judgment.* Other offenders are judged, and cast out of the Church, by the sentence of the pastors of the same Church. Heretics, more unhappy, run out of the Church of their own accord: and, by so doing, give judgment and sentence against their own souls.

# THE
# EPISTLE OF ST. PAUL TO PHILEMON.

*Philemon, a noble citizen of Colossa, had a servant named Onesimus, who robbed him, and fled to Rome, where he met St. Paul, who was then a prisoner there the first time. The Apostle took compassion on him, and received him with tenderness and converted him to the faith; for he was a gentile before. St. Paul sends him back to his master with this Epistle in his favour; and though he beseeches Philemon to pardon him, yet the Apostle writes with becoming dignity and authority. It contains divers profitable instructions, and points out the charity and humanity that masters should have for their servants.*

## CHAP. I.

*He commends the faith and charity of Philemon; and sends back to him his fugitive servant, whom he converted in prison.*

PAUL, a prisoner of CHRIST JESUS, and Timothy a brother: to Philemon our beloved and fellow-labourer,

2 And to Appia our dearest sister, and to Archippus our fellow-soldier, and to the church which is in thy house.

3 Grace to you and peace from God our Father, and from the Lord JESUS CHRIST.

4 I give thanks to my God, always making a remembrance of thee in my prayers.

5 Hearing of thy charity and faith which thou hast in the Lord JESUS, and towards all the saints:

6 That the communication of thy faith may be made evident in the acknowledgment of every good work, that is in you in CHRIST JESUS.

7 For I have had great joy and consolation in thy charity, because the bowels of the saints have been refreshed by thee, brother.

8 Wherefore though I have much confidence in CHRIST JESUS, to command thee that which is to the purpose:

9 For charity sake I rather beseech, whereas thou art such an one, as Paul an old man, and now a prisoner also of JESUS CHRIST:

10 I beseech thee for my son, whom I have begotten in my bands, Onesimus,

11 Who hath been heretofore unprofitable to thee, but now is profitable both to me and thee,

12 Whom I have sent back to thee. And do thou receive him as my own bowels:

13 Whom I would have retained with me, that in thy stead he might have ministered to me in the bands of the gospel:

14 But without thy counsel I would do nothing: that thy good deed might not be as it were of necessity, but voluntary.

15 For perhaps he therefore departed for a season from thee, that thou mightest receive him again for ever:

16 Not now as a servant, but instead of a servant, a most

THE CONVERSION OF ST. PAUL.

dear brother, especially to me: but how much more to thee both in the flesh and in the Lord?

17 If therefore thou count me a partner; receive him as myself.

18 And if he hath wronged thee in anything, or is in thy debt, put that to my account.

19 I Paul have written it with my own hand: I will repay it: not to say to thee, that thou owest me thy ownself also.

20 Yea, brother. May I enjoy thee in the Lord. Refresh my bowels in the Lord.

21 Trusting in thy obedience, I have written to thee: knowing that thou wilt also do more than I say.

22 But withal prepare me also a lodging. For I hope that through your prayers I shall be given unto you.

23 There salute thee Epaphras, my fellow-prisoner in CHRIST JESUS.

24 Mark, Aristarchus, Demas, and Luke, my. fellow-labourers.

25 The grace of our Lord JESUS CHRIST be with your spirit. Amen.

# THE
# EPISTLE OF ST. PAUL TO THE HEBREWS.

ST. PAUL *wrote this Epistle to the Christians in Palestine, the most part of whom being Jews before their conversion, they were called Hebrews. He exhorts them to be thoroughly converted and confirmed in the faith of Christ, clearly shewing them the pre-eminence of Christ's priesthood above the Levitical, and also the excellence of the new law above the old. He commends faith by the example of the ancient fathers: and exhorts them to patience and perseverance, and to remain in fraternal charity. It appears, from chap. xiii. that this Epistle was written in Italy, and probably at Rome, about twenty-nine years after our Lord's Ascension.*

## CHAP. I.

*God spoke of old by the prophets, but now by his Son, who is incomparably greater than the angels.*

GOD, who at sundry times and in divers manners spoke in times past to the fathers by the prophets, last of all,

2 In these days hath spoken to us by his Son, whom he hath appointed heir of all things, by whom also he made the world.

3 ᵃ Who being the brightness

ᵃ Wis. 7. 26.

CHAP. I. Ver. 3. *The figure,* χαρακτηρ. That is, the express image of his glory, and the figure of his substance, and upholding all things by the word of his power, making purgation of sins, sitteth on the right hand of the majesty on high;

4 Being made so much better than the angels, as he hath inherited a more excellent name than they.

5 For to which of the angels hath he said at any time: *a Thou art my son; to-day have I begotten thee?* And again, *b I will be to him a father, and he shall be to me a son?*

6 And again, when he bringeth in the first begotten into the world he saith: *c And let all the angels of God adore him.*

7 And to the angels indeed he saith: *d He that maketh his angels, spirits; and his ministers, a flame of fire.*

8 But to the Son: *e Thy throne, O God, is for ever and ever: a sceptre of justice is the sceptre of thy kingdom.*

9 *Thou hast loved justice, and hated iniquity: therefore God, thy God, hath anointed thee with the oil of gladness above thy fellows.*

10 And: *f Thou in the beginning, O Lord, didst found the earth: and the works of thy hands are the heavens.*

11 *They shall perish, but thou shalt continue: and they shall all grow old as a garment.*

12 *And as a vesture shalt thou change them, and they shall be changed: but thou art the self-same, and thy years shall not fail.*

13 But to which of the angels said he at any time: *g Sit on my right hand, until I make thy enemies thy footstool?*

14 Are they not all ministering spirits, sent to minister for them, who shall receive the inheritance of salvation?

## CHAP. II.

*The transgression of the precepts of the Son of God is far more condemnable, than those of the Old Testament given by angels.*

THEREFORE ought we more diligently to observe the things which we have heard, lest perhaps we should let them slip.

2 For if the word, spoken by angels, became steadfast, and every transgression and disobedience received a just recompense of reward:

3 How shall we escape if we neglect so great salvation? which having begun to be declared by the Lord, was confirmed unto us by them that heard him.

4 *h* God also bearing them witness by signs and wonders, and divers miracles, and distributions of the Holy Ghost according to his own will.

5 For God hath not subjected unto angels the world to come, whereof we speak.

6 But one in a certain place hath testified, saying: *i What is man, that thou art mindful of him: or the son of man, that thou visitest him?*

7 *Thou hast made him a little lower than the angels: thou hast*

---

*a* Ps. 2. 7.—*b* 2 Kings 7. 14.—*c* Ps. 96. 7.—*d* Ps. 103. 4.—*e* Ps. 44. 7.—*f* Ps. 110. 26.

and most perfect resemblance.—Ibid. *Making purgation.* That is, having purged away our sins by his passion.

*g* Ps. 109. 1. 1 Cor. 1. 25.—*h* Mark 16. 20.—*i* Ps. 8. 5.

crowned him with glory and honour, and hast set him over the works of thy hands.

8 <sup>a</sup>Thou hast subjected all things under his feet. For in that he hath subjected all things to him, he left nothing not subject to him. But now we see not as yet all things subject to him.

9 <sup>b</sup>But we see JESUS, who was made a little lower than the angels, for the suffering of death, crowned with glory and honour: that through the grace of God he might taste death for all.

10 For it became him, for whom *are* all things, and by whom *are* all things, who had brought many children into glory, to perfect the author of their salvation, by *his* passion.

11 For both he that sanctifieth, and they who are sanctified, *are* all of one. For which cause he is not ashamed to call them brethren, saying:

12 <sup>c</sup>*I will declare thy name to my brethren: in the midst of the church will I praise thee.*

13 And again: <sup>d</sup>*I will put my trust in him.* And again: *<sup>e</sup>Behold I and my children, whom God hath given me.*

14 Therefore because the children are partakers of flesh and blood, he also himself in like manner hath been partaker of the same: that <sup>f</sup>through death he might destroy him who had the empire of death, that is to say, the devil:

15 And might deliver them, who through the fear of death were all their lifetime subject to servitude.

16 For nowhere doth he take hold of the angels: but of the seed of Abraham he taketh hold.

17 Wherefore it behoved him in all things to be made like unto his brethren, that he might become a merciful and faithful high-priest before God, that he might be a propitiation for the sins of the people.

18 For in that, wherein he himself hath suffered and been tempted, he is able to succour them also that are tempted.

## CHAP. III.

*Christ is more excellent than Moses: and therefore we must adhere to him by faith and obedience.*

WHEREFORE, holy brethren, partakers of the heavenly vocation, consider the apostle and high-priest of our confession, JESUS:

2 Who is faithful to him that made him, as was also <sup>g</sup>Moses in all his house.

3 For this man was counted worthy of greater glory than Moses, by so much as he that hath built the house, hath greater honour than the house.

4 For every house is built by some man; but he that created all things is God.

5 And Moses indeed was faithful in all his house as a

---

<sup>a</sup> Matt. 28. 18. 1 Cor. 15. 26.—<sup>b</sup> Phil. 2. 6.—<sup>c</sup> Ps. 21. 23.—<sup>d</sup> Ps. 17. 3.—<sup>e</sup> Isaias 8. 18.—<sup>f</sup> Osee. 13. 14. 1 Cor. 15. 54.

<sup>g</sup> Num. 12. 7.

---

CHAP. II. Ver. 10. *Perfect by his passion.* By suffering Christ was to enter into his glory, Luke xxiv. 26, which the apostle here calls being made perfect.

Ver. 16. *Nowhere doth he, &c.* That is, he never took upon him the nature of angels, but that of the seed of Abraham.

servant, for a testimony of those things which were to be said:

6 But Christ as the Son in his own house: which house are we, if we hold fast the confidence and glory of hope unto the end.

7 Wherefore, as the Holy Ghost saith: *ᵃTo-day if you shall hear his voice,*

8 *Harden not your hearts, as in the provocation; in the day of temptation in the desert,*

9 *Where your fathers tempted me, proved and saw my works,*

10 *Forty years: For which cause I was offended with this generation, and said: They always err in heart. And they have not known my ways,*

11 *As I have sworn in my wrath: If they shall enter into my rest.*

12 Take heed, brethren, lest perhaps there be in any of you an evil heart of unbelief, to depart from the living God.

13 But exhort one another every day, whilst it is called to-day, that none of you be hardened through the deceitfulness of sin.

14 For we are made partakers of Christ: yet so if we hold the beginning of his substance firm unto the end.

15 While it is said: *To-day if you shall hear his voice, harden not your hearts as in that provocation.*

16 For some who heard did provoke: but not all that came out of Egypt by Moses.

17 And with whom was he offended forty years? Was it not with them that sinned, ᵇ whose carcasses were overthrown in the desert?

18 And to whom did he swear that they should not enter into his rest: but to them that were incredulous?

19 And we see that they could not enter in, because of unbelief.

## CHAP. IV.

*The Christian's rest: we are to enter into it, through Jesus Christ.*

LET us fear therefore lest the promise being left of entering into his rest, any of you should be thought to be wanting.

2 For unto us also it hath been declared, in like manner as unto them. But the word of hearing did not profit them, not being mixed with faith of those things they heard.

3 For we who have believed, shall enter into rest: as he said: ᶜ *As I have sworn in my wrath: If they shall enter into my rest;* and this indeed when the works from the foundation of the world were finished.

4 For in a certain place he spoke of the seventh day thus: ᵈ *And God rested the seventh day from all his works.*

5 And in this *place* again: *If they shall enter into my rest.*

6 Seeing then it remaineth that some are to enter into it, and they, to whom it was first preached, did not enter because of unbelief:

7 Again he limiteth a certain day, saying in David: *To-day,* after so long a time, as it is above said: *ᵉTo-day if you shall hear his voice; harden not your hearts.*

8 For if JESUS had given

---
ᶜ Ps. 94. 11.—ᵈ Gen. 2. 2.—ᵉ Supra, 3. 7.

CHAP. IV. Ver. 8. *Jesus,* Josue, who in the Greek is called Jesus.

---
ᵃ Ps. 94. 8. Infra, 4. 7.—ᵇ Num. 14. 17.

them rest: he would never have afterwards spoken of another day.

9 There remaineth therefore a day of rest for the people of God.

10 For he that is entered into his rest, the same also hath rested from his works, as God did from his.

11 Let us hasten therefore to enter into that rest: lest any man fall into the same example of unbelief.

12 For the word of God is living and effectual, and more piercing than any two-edged sword: and reaching unto the division of the soul and the spirit, of the joints also and the marrow, and is a discerner of the thoughts and intents of the heart.

13 *a* Neither is there any creature invisible in his sight: but all things are naked and open to his eyes, to whom our speech is.

14 Having therefore a great high-priest that hath passed into the heavens, JESUS the Son of God: let us hold fast our confession.

15 For we have not a high-priest, who cannot have compassion on our infirmities: but one tempted in all things like as we are, without sin.

16 Let us go therefore with confidence to the throne of grace; that we may obtain mercy, and find grace in seasonable aid.

## CHAP. V.

*The office of a high-priest. Christ is our high-priest.*

FOR every high-priest taken from among men, is ordained for men in the things that appertain to God, that he may offer up gifts and sacrifices for sins:

2 Who can have compassion on them that are ignorant and that err: because he himself also is compassed with infirmity:

3 And therefore he ought, as for the people, so also for himself, to offer for sins.

4 *b* Neither doth any man take the honour to himself, but he that is called by God, as Aaron was.

5 So Christ also did not glorify himself that he might be made a high-priest: but he that said unto him, *c Thou art my Son; this day have I begotten thee.*

6 As he saith also in another place: *d Thou art a priest for ever, according to the order of Melchisedech.*

7 Who in the days of his flesh with a strong cry and tears offering up prayers and supplications to him that was able to save him from death, was heard for his reverence.

8 And whereas indeed he was the Son of God, he learned obedience by the things which he suffered:

9 And being consummated, he became, to all that obey him, the cause of eternal salvation,

10 Called by God a high-priest according to the order of Melchisedech.

11 Of whom we have much to say, and hard to be intelligibly uttered: because you are become weak to hear.

12 For whereas for the time you ought to be masters, you

---

*a* Ps. 33. 16. Eccli. 15. 20.    *b* Exod. 29. 1. 2 Par. 26. 18.—*c* Ps. 2. 7. —*d* Ps. 109. 4.

have need to be taught again what are the first elements of the words of God: and you are become such as have need of milk, and not of strong meat.

13 For every one, that is a partaker of milk, is unskilful in the word of justice: for he is a little child.

14 But strong meat is for the perfect: for them who by custom have their senses exercised to the discerning of good and evil.

## CHAP. VI.

*He warns them of the danger of falling by apostacy; and exhorts them to patience and perseverance.*

WHEREFORE leaving the word of the beginning of Christ, let us go on to things more perfect, not laying again the foundation of penance from dead works, and of faith towards God,

2 Of the doctrine of baptisms, and imposition of hands, and of the resurrection of the dead, and of eternal judgment.

3 And this will we do, if God permit.

4 *a* For it is impossible for those, who were once illuminated, have tasted also the heavenly gift, and were made partakers of the Holy Ghost,

5 Have moreover tasted the good word of God, and the powers of the world to come,

6 And are fallen away; to be renewed again to penance, crucifying again to themselves the Son of God, and making him a mockery.

7 For the earth that drinketh in the rain which cometh often upon it, and bringeth forth herbs meet for them by whom it is tilled, receiveth blessing from God.

8 But that which bringeth forth thorns and briars is reprobate, and very near unto a curse, whose end is to be burnt.

9 But, my dearly beloved, we trust better things of you, and nearer to salvation; though we speak thus.

10 For God is not unjust, that he should forget your work and the love which you have shewn in his name, you who have ministered, and do minister to the saints.

11 And we desire that every one of you shew forth the same carefulness to the accomplishing of hope unto the end:

12 That you become not slothful, but followers of them who through faith and patience shall inherit the promises.

13 For God making promise to Abraham, because he had no one greater by whom he might swear, swore by himself,

14 Saying: *b Unless blessing I shall bless thee, and multiplying I shall multiply thee.*

15 And so patiently enduring he obtained the promise.

16 For men swear by one greater than themselves: and an oath for confirmation is the end of all their controversy.

---

*a* Matt. 12. 45. Infra, 10. 26. 2 Pet. 2. 20.

CHAP. VI. Ver. 1. *The word of the beginning.* The first rudiments of the Christian doctrine.

Ver. 4. *It is impossible, &c.* The meaning is, that it is *impossible* for such as have fallen after baptism to be again baptized; and very hard for such as have apostatized from the faith, after having received many graces, to return again to the happy state from which they fell.

*b* Gen. 22. 16.

"THAT WHICH GOD HATH CLEANSED, DO NOT THOU CALL COMMON."—ACTS X. 15.

17 Wherein God, meaning more abundantly to shew to the heirs of the promise the immutability of his counsel, interposed an oath:

18 That by two immutable things, in which it is impossible for God to lie, we may have the strongest comfort, who have fled for refuge to hold fast the hope set before us.

19 Which we have as an anchor of the soul, sure and firm, and which entereth in even within the veil:

20 Where the forerunner Jesus is entered for us, made a high-priest for ever according to the order of Melchisedech.

## CHAP. VII.

*The priesthood of Christ, according to the order of Melchisedech, excels the Levitical priesthood, and puts an end both to that, and to the law.*

FOR *a* this Melchisedech was king of Salem, priest of the most high God, who met Abraham returning from the slaughter of the kings, and blessed him:

2 To whom also Abraham divided the tithes of all: who first indeed by interpretation, is king of justice: and then also king of Salem, that is, king of peace.

3 Without father, without mother, without genealogy, having neither beginning of days nor end of life, but likened unto the Son of God, continueth a priest for ever.

4 Now consider how great this man is, to whom also Abraham the patriarch gave tithes out of the principal things.

5 And indeed they that are of the sons of Levi, who receive the priesthood, *b* have a commandment to take tithes of the people according to the law, that is to say, of their brethren: though they themselves also came out of the loins of Abraham.

6 But he, whose pedigree is not numbered among them, received tithes of Abraham, and blessed him that had the promises.

7 And without all contradiction, that which is less is blessed by the better.

8 And here indeed men that die, receive tithes: but there he hath witness, that he liveth.

9 And (as it may be said) even Levi who received tithes, paid tithes in Abraham:

10 For he was yet in the loins of his father, when Melchisedech met him:

11 If then perfection was by the Levitical priesthood, (for under it the people received the law,) what further need was there that another priest should rise according to the order of Melchisedech, and not be called according to the order of Aaron?

12 For the priesthood being translated, it is necessary that a translation also be made of the law.

13 For he, of whom these things are spoken, is of another tribe, of which no one attended on the altar.

14 For it is evident that our Lord sprung out of Juda: in

---

*a* Gen. 14. 18.

CHAP. VII. Ver. 3. *Without father, &c.* Not that he had no father, &c., but that neither his father, nor his pedigree, nor his birth, nor his death, are set down in Scripture.

*b* Deut. 18. 3. Jos. 14. 4.

which tribe Moses spoke nothing concerning priests.

15 And it is yet far more evident: if according to the similitude of Melchisedech there ariseth another priest,

16 Who is made not according to the law of a carnal commandment, but according to the power of an indissoluble life:

17 For he testifieth: *a Thou art a priest for ever, according to the order of Melchisedech.*

18 There is indeed a setting aside of the former commandment, because of the weakness and unprofitableness thereof:

19 (For the law brought nothing to perfection) but the bringing in of a better hope, by which we draw nigh to God.

20 And inasmuch as it is not without an oath, (for the others indeed were made priests without an oath;

21 But this with an oath, by him that said unto him: *b The Lord hath sworn, and he will not repent, thou art a priest for ever:*)

22 By so much is JESUS made a surety of a better testament.

23 And the others indeed were made many priests, because by reason of death they were not suffered to continue:

24 But this, for that he continueth for ever, hath an everlasting priesthood,

25 Whereby he is able also to save for ever them that come to God by him: always living to make intercession for us.

26 For it was fitting that we should have such a high-priest, holy, innocent, undefiled, separated from sinners, and made higher than the heavens:

27 Who needeth not daily (as the *other* priests) *c to offer sacrifices first for his own sins, and then for the people's: for this he did once in offering himself.

28 For the law maketh men priests, who have infirmity: but the word of the oath, which was since the law, the Son who is perfected for evermore.

## CHAP. VIII.

*More of the excellence of the priesthood of Christ, and of the New Testament.*

NOW of the things which we have spoken, this is the sum: We have such an high-priest, who is set on the right hand of the throne of majesty in the heavens,

2 A minister of the Holies, and of the true tabernacle, which the Lord hath pitched, and not man.

3 For every high-priest is appointed to offer gifts and sacrifices: wherefore it is necessary

---

*a* Ps. 109. 4.—*b* Ps. 109. 4.

*c* Lev. 16. 6.

Ver. 23. *Many priests, &c.* The apostle notes this difference between the high-priests of the law and our high-priest Jesus Christ: that they being removed by death, made way for their successors; whereas our Lord Jesus is a priest for ever, and hath no successor; but liveth and concurreth for ever with his ministers, the priests of the New Testament, in all their functions. 2ndly, That no one priest of the law, nor all of them together, could offer that absolute sacrifice of everlasting redemption which our one high-priest Jesus Christ, has offered once and for ever.

Ver. 25. *Make intercession.* Christ, as man, continually maketh intercession for us, by representing his passion to his Father.

CHAP. VIII. Ver. 2. *The Holies,* that is, the sanctuary.

that he also should have something to offer.

4 If then he were on earth, he would not be a priest: seeing that there would be *others* to offer gifts according to the law,

5 Who serve unto the example and shadow of heavenly things. As it was answered to Moses, when he was to finish the tabernacle: *a See (says he) that thou make all things according to the pattern which was shewn thee on the mount.*

6 But now he hath obtained a better ministry, by how much also he is mediator of a better testament, which is established on better promises.

7 For if that former had been faultless, there should not indeed a place have been sought for a second.

8 For finding fault with them, he saith: *b Behold, the days shall come, saith the Lord: and I will perfect unto the house of Israel, and unto the house of Juda, a new testament.*

9 *Not according to the testament, which I made to their fathers on the day when I took them by the hand to lead them out of the land of Egypt: because they continued not in my testament:*

―――
*a* Exod. 25. 40. Acts 7. 44.―*b* Jer. 31. 31.

―――
Ver. 4. *If then he were on earth, &c.* That is, If he were not of a higher condition than the Levitical order of earthly priests, and had not another kind of sacrifice to offer, he should be excluded by them from the priesthood and its functions, which by the law were appropriated to their tribe.

Ver. 5. *Who serve unto, &c.* The priesthood of the law and its functions were a kind of an example and shadow of what is done by Christ in his Church militant and triumphant, of which the tabernacle was a pattern.

*and I regarded them not, saith the Lord:*

10 *For this is the testament which I will make to the house of Israel after those days, saith the Lord: I will give my laws into their mind, and in their heart will I write them: and I will be their God, and they shall be my people.*

11 *And they shall not teach every man his neighbour, and every man his brother, saying: Know the Lord: for all shall know me from the least to the greatest of them.*

12 *Because I will be merciful to their iniquities, and their sins I will remember no more.*

13 Now in saying a new, he hath made the former old. And that, which decayeth and groweth old, is near its end.

## CHAP. IX.

*The sacrifices of the law were far inferior to that of Christ.*

THE former indeed had also justifications of *divine* service, and a worldly sanctuary.

2 *c* For there was a tabernacle made the first, wherein were the candlesticks, and the table, and the setting forth of loaves, which is called the Holy.

3 And after the second veil, the tabernacle, which is called the Holy of Holies:

4 Having a golden *d* censer,

―――
*c* Exod. 26. 1. and 36. 8.―*d* Lev. 16. Num. 16.

―――
Ver. 11. *They shall not teach, &c.* So great shall be the light and grace of the New Testament, that it shall not be necessary to inculcate to the faithful the belief and knowledge of the true God, for they shall all know him.

Ver. 13. *A new:* supply covenant.

and the ark of the testament covered about on every part with gold, in which was a golden pot that had manna, and the rod of Aaron that had blossomed, and the ᵃ tables of the testament.

5 And over it were the Cherubims of glory overshadowing the propitiatory: of which it is not needful to speak now particularly.

6 Now these things being thus ordered, into the first tabernacle the priests indeed always entered, accomplishing the offices of sacrifices.

7 But into the second, the high-priest alone, ᵇ once a year: not without blood, which he offereth for his own, and the people's ignorance.

8 The Holy Ghost signifying this, that the way into the Holies was not yet made manifest, whilst the former tabernacle was yet standing.

9 Which is a parable of the time present: according to which gifts and sacrifices are offered, which cannot, as to the conscience, make him perfect that serveth, only in meats and in drinks,

10 And divers washings, and justices of the flesh laid on them until the time of correction.

11 But Christ, being come an high-priest of the good things to come, by a greater and more perfect tabernacle not made with hand, that is, not of this creation:

12 Neither by the blood of goats, or of calves, but by his own blood, entered once into the Holies, having obtained eternal redemption.

13 ᶜ For if the blood of goats and of oxen, and the ashes of an heifer being sprinkled, sanctify such as are defiled, to the cleansing of the flesh:

14 ᵈ How much more shall the blood of Christ, who by the Holy Ghost offered himself unspotted unto God, cleanse our conscience from dead works, to serve the living God?

15 And therefore he is the mediator of the new testament: ᵉ that by means of his death, for the redemption of those transgressions, which were under the former testament, they that are called may receive the promise of eternal inheritance.

16 For where there is a testament; the death of the testator must of necessity come in.

17 For a testament is of force, after men are dead: otherwise it is as yet of no strength, whilst the testator liveth.

18 Whereupon neither was the first indeed dedicated without blood.

19 For when every commandment of the law had been read by Moses to all the people, he took the blood of calves and goats with water and scarlet wool and hyssop, and sprinkled

---

ᶜ Lev. 16. 15.—ᵈ 1 Pet. 1. 19. 1 John 1. 7. Apoc. 1. 5.—ᵉ Gal. 3. 15.

ᵃ 3 Kings 8. 9. 2 Par. 5. 10.—ᵇ Exod. 30. 10. Lev. 16. 2.

---

CHAP. IX. Ver. 10. *Of correction.* Viz., when Christ should correct and settle all things.

Ver. 12. *Eternal redemption.* By that one sacrifice of his blood, once offered on the cross, Christ our Lord paid and exhibited, once for all, the general price and ransom of all mankind, which no other priest could do.

both the book itself and all the people,

20 Saying: *ᵃThis is the blood of the testament, which God hath enjoined unto you.*

21 The tabernacle also and all the vessels of the ministry, in like manner he sprinkled with blood:

22 And almost all things, according to the law, are cleansed with blood: and without shedding of blood there is no remission.

23 It is necessary therefore that the patterns of heavenly things should be cleansed with these: but the heavenly things themselves with better sacrifices than these.

24 For JESUS is not entered into the Holies made with hands, the patterns of the true: but into heaven itself, that he may appear now in the presence of God for us.

25 Nor yet that he should offer himself often, as the high-priest entereth into the Holies every year with the blood of others:

26 For then he ought to have suffered often from the beginning of the world: but now once at the end of ages he hath appeared for the destruction of sin by the sacrifice of himself.

27 And as it is appointed unto men once to die, and, after this, the judgment:

28 ᵇ So also Christ was offered once to exhaust the sins of many; the second time he shall appear without sin, to them that expect him, unto salvation.

## CHAP. X.

*Because of the insufficiency of the sacrifices of the law, Christ our high-priest shed his own blood for us, offering up once for all the sacrifice of our redemption. He exhorts them to perseverance.*

FOR the law having a shadow of the good things to come, not the very image of the things: by the self-same sacrifices which they offer continually every year, can never make the comers thereunto perfect:

2 For then they would have ceased to be offered: because the worshippers once cleansed should have no conscience of sin any longer:

3 But in them there is made a commemoration of sins every year.

4 For it is impossible that with the blood of oxen and goats sins should be taken away.

5 Wherefore when he cometh into the world, he saith: *ᶜ Sacri-*

---

ᵃ Exod. 24. 8.

ᵇ Rom. 5. 9. 1 Pet. 2. 18. — ᶜ Ps. 39. 7.

Ver. 25. *Offer himself often.* Christ shall never more offer himself in sacrifice, in that violent, painful, and bloody manner, nor can there be any occasion for it; since by that one sacrifice upon the cross, he has furnished the full ransom, redemption, and remedy for all the sins of the world. But this hinders not that he may offer himself daily in the sacred mysteries in an unbloody manner, for the daily application of that one sacrifice of redemption to our souls.

Ver. 28. *To exhaust.* That is, to empty or draw out to the very bottom, by a plentiful and perfect redemption.

CHAP. X. Ver. 2. *They would have ceased.* If they had been of themselves perfect to all the intents of redemption and remission, as Christ's death is; there would have been no occasion of so often repeating them: as there is no occasion for Christ's dying any more for our sins.

fice and oblation thou wouldest not: but a body thou hast fitted to me:

6 Holocausts for sin did not please thee.

7 *Then said I: Behold I come: ᵃ in the head of the book it is written of me: that I should do thy will, O God.*

8 In saying before, *Sacrifices, and oblations, and holocausts, for sin thou wouldest not, neither are they pleasing to thee,* which are offered according to the law.

9 *Then said I, Behold, I come to do thy will, O God:* he taketh away the first, that he may establish that which followeth.

10 In the which will we are sanctified by the oblation of the body of JESUS CHRIST once.

11 And every priest indeed standeth daily ministering, and often offering the same sacrifices, which can never take away sins.

12 But this man offering one sacrifice for sins, for ever sitteth on the right hand of God,

13 From henceforth expecting, ᵇ until his enemies be made his footstool.

14 For by one oblation he hath perfected for ever them that are sanctified.

15 And the Holy Ghost also doth testify *this* to us. For after that he said:

16 ᶜ *And this is the testament which I will make unto them after those days, saith the Lord. I will give my laws in their hearts, and on their minds will I write them:*

17 *And their sins and iniquities I will remember no more.*

ᵃ Ps. 39. 8.—ᵇ Ps. 109. 1. 1 Cor. 15. 25. —ᶜ Jer. 31. 33. Supra, c. 8.

570

18 Now where there *is* a remission of these, there is no more an oblation for sin.

19 Having therefore, brethren, a confidence in the entering into the Holies by the blood of Christ:

20 A new and living way which he hath dedicated for us through the veil, that is to say, his flesh,

21 And a high-priest over the house of God:

22 Let us draw near with a true heart in fulness of faith, having our hearts sprinkled from an evil conscience, and our bodies washed with clean water.

23 Let us hold fast the confession of our hope without wavering, (for he is faithful that hath promised,)

24 And let us consider one another to provoke unto charity and to good works;

25 Not forsaking our assembly, as some are accustomed, but comforting *one another*, and so much the more as you see the day approaching.

26 ᵈ For if we sin wilfully

ᵈ Supra, c. 4.

Ver. 18. *There is no more an oblation for sin:* where there is a full remission of sins, as in baptism; there is no more occasion for a *sin-offering* to be made for such sins already remitted: and as for sins committed afterwards, they can only be remitted in virtue of the one oblation of Christ's death.

Ver. 26. *If we sin wilfully.* He speaks of the sin of wilful apostacy from the known truth; after which, as we cannot be baptized again, we cannot expect to have that abundant remission of sins, which Christ purchased by his death, applied to our souls in that ample manner as it is in baptism: but we have rather all manner of reason to look for a dreadful judgment; the more because apostates from the known truth seldom or never have the grace to return to it.

PETER SPEAKING OF JESUS CHRIST TO THE CENTURION.

after having the knowledge of the truth, there is now left no sacrifice for sins,

27 But a certain dreadful expectation of judgment, and the rage of a fire which shall consume the adversaries.

28 A man making void the law of Moses dieth without any mercy under *a* two or three witnesses:

29 How much more, do you think he deserveth worse punishments, who had trodden under foot the Son of God, and hath esteemed the blood of the testament unclean, by which he was sanctified, and hath offered an affront to the Spirit of grace?

30 For we know him that hath said: *b Vengeance belongeth to me, and I will repay.* And again: *The Lord shall judge his people.*

31 It is a fearful thing to fall into the hands of the living God.

32 But call to mind the former days, wherein being illuminated, you endured a great fight of afflictions.

33 And on the one hand indeed, by reproaches and tribulations were made a gazing stock; and on the other, became companions of them that were used in such sort.

34 For you both had compassion on them that were in bands, and took with joy the being stripped of your own goods, knowing that you have a better and a lasting substance.

35 Do not therefore lose your confidence, which hath a great reward.

36 For patience is necessary for you: that doing the will of God, you may receive the promise.

37 For yet a little and a very little while, and he that is to come, will come, and will not delay.

38 *c* But my just man liveth by faith: but if he withdraw himself, he shall not please my soul.

39 But we are not the children of withdrawing unto perdition, but of faith to the saving of the soul.

## CHAP. XI.

*What faith is: its wonderful fruits and efficacy, demonstrated in the fathers.*

NOW faith is the substance of things to be hoped for, the evidence of things that appear not.

2 For by this the ancients obtained a testimony.

3 *d* By faith we understand that the world was framed by the word of God; that from invisible things visible things might be made.

4 *e* By faith Abel offered to God a sacrifice exceeding that of Cain, *f* by which he obtained a testimony that he was just, God giving testimony to his gifts, and by it he being dead yet speaketh.

5 *g* By faith Henoch was translated, that he should not see death, and he was not found because God had translated him: For before his translation he had testimony that he pleased God.

---

*a* Deut. 17. 6. Matt. 18. 16. John 8. 17. 2 Cor. 13. 1.—*b* Deut. 32. 35. Rom. 12. 19.

*c* Habac. 2. 4. Rom. 1. 17. Gal. 3. 11.—*d* Gen. 1. 4.—*e* Gen. 4. 4.—*f* Matt. 23. 35.—*g* Gen. 5. 24. Eccli. 44. 16.

6 But without faith it is impossible to please God. For he that cometh to God, must believe that he is, and is a rewarder to them that seek him.

7 *a* By faith Noe having received an answer concerning those things which as yet were not seen, moved with fear framed the ark for the saving of his house, by the which he condemned the world: and was instituted heir of the justice which is by faith.

8 *b* By faith he that is called Abraham, obeyed to go out into a place which he was to receive for an inheritance: and he went out, not knowing whither he went.

9 By faith he abode in the land, dwelling in cottages, with Isaac and Jacob, the co-heirs of the same promise.

10 For he looked for a city that hath foundations: whose builder and maker is God.

11 *c* By faith Sara also herself, being barren, received strength to conceive seed, even past the time of age: because she believed that he was faithful who had promised.

12 For which cause there sprung even from one (and him as good as dead) as the stars of heaven in multitude, and as the sand which is by the sea-shore innumerable.

13 All these died according to faith, not having received the promises, but beholding them afar off, and saluting them, and confessing that they are pilgrims and strangers on the earth.

14 For they that say these things do signify that they seek a country.

15 And truly if they had been mindful of that from whence they came out, they had doubtless time to return.

16 But now they desire a better, that is to say, a heavenly country. Therefore God is not ashamed to be called their God: for he hath prepared for them a city.

17 *d* By faith Abraham, when he was tried, offered Isaac; and he that had received the promises, offered up his only begotten son:

18 (To whom it was said: *e In Isaac shall thy seed be called.*)

19 Accounting that God is able to raise up even from the dead. Whereupon also he received him for a parable.

20 *f* By faith also of things to come Isaac blessed Jacob and Esau.

21 *g* By faith Jacob dying blessed each of the sons of Joseph, *h* and adored the top of his rod.

---

*d* Gen. 22. 1. Eccli. 44. 21 —*e* Gen. 21. 12. Rom. 9. 7.—*f* Gen. 27. 27. 39.—*g* Gen. 48. 15.—*h* Gen. 47. 31.

Ver. 19. *For a parable.* That is, as a figure of Christ, slain and coming to life again.

Ver. 21. *Adored the top of his rod.* The apostle here follows the ancient Greek Bible of the seventy interpreters, (which translates in this manner Gen. xlvii. 31,) and alleges this fact of Jacob, in paying a relative honour and veneration to the top of the rod or sceptre of Joseph, as to a figure of Christ's sceptre and kingdom, as an instance and argument of his faith. But some translators, who are no friends to this relative honour, have corrupted

---

*a* Gen. 6. 14. Eccli. 44. 17.—*b* Gen. 12. 1.—*c* Gen. 17. 19.

CHAP. XI. Ver. 8. *He that is called Abraham:* or, Abraham being called.

22 ᵃBy faith Joseph, when he was dying, made mention of the going out of the children of Israel; and gave commandment concerning his bones.

23 ᵇBy faith Moses, when he was born, was hid three months by his parents: because they saw he was a comely babe, ᶜand they feared not the king's edict.

24 ᵈBy faith Moses, when he was grown up, denied himself to be the son of Pharao's daughter;

25 Rather choosing to be afflicted with the people of God, than to have the pleasure of sin for a time,

26 Esteeming the reproach of Christ, greater riches than the treasure of the Egyptians. For he looked unto the reward.

27 By faith he left Egypt, not fearing the fierceness of the king: for he endured as seeing him that is invisible.

28 ᵉBy faith he celebrated the pasch, and the shedding of the blood: that he, who destroyed the first-born, might not touch them.

29 ᶠBy faith they passed through the Red Sea, as by dry land: which the Egyptians attempting were swallowed up.

30 ᵍBy faith the walls of Jericho fell down, by the going round them seven days.

31 ʰBy faith Rahab the har-

---

ᵃ Gen. 50. 28.—ᵇ Exod. 2 2.—ᶜ Exod. 1, 1:—ᵈ Exod. 2. 11.—ᵉ Exod. 12 21.—ᶠ Exod. 14. 22.—ᵍ Jos. 6. 20.—ʰ Jos. 2. 3. Jas. 2. 25.

the text, by translating it, *he worshipped, leaning upon the top of his staff;* as if this circumstance of leaning upon his staff were an argument of Jacob's faith, or worthy the being thus particularly taken notice of by the Holy Ghost.

---

lot perished not with the unbelievers, receiving the spies with peace.

32 And what shall I yet say? For the time would fail me to tell of Gedeon, Barac, Samson, Jephte, David, Samuel, and the prophets:

33 Who by faith conquered kingdoms, wrought justice, obtained promises, stopped the mouths of lions,

34 Quenched the violence of fire, escaped the edge of the sword, recovered strength from weakness, became valiant in battle, put to flight the armies of foreigners:

35 Women received their dead raised to life again. But others were racked, not accepting deliverance, that they might find a better resurrection.

36 And others had trial of mockeries and stripes, moreover also of bands and prisons:

37 They were stoned, they were cut asunder, they were tempted, they were put to death by the sword, they wandered about in sheep-skins, in goat-skins, being in want, distressed, afflicted:

38 Of whom the world was not worthy; wandering in deserts, in mountains, and in dens, and in caves of the earth.

39 And all these being approved by the testimony of faith, received not the promise,

40 God providing some better thing for us, that they should not be perfected without us.

## CHAP. XII.

*Exhortation to constancy under their crosses. The danger of abusing the grace of the New Testament.*

AND therefore we also having so great a cloud of witnesses

over our head, *laying aside every weight and sin which surrounds us, let us run by patience to the fight proposed to us:

2 Looking on Jesus the author and finisher of faith, who having joy set before him, endured the cross, despising the shame, and now sitteth on the right hand of the throne of God.

3 For think diligently upon him that endured such opposition from sinners against himself: that you be not wearied, fainting in your minds.

4 For you have not yet resisted unto blood, striving against sin:

5 And you have forgotten the consolation, which speaketh to you, as unto children, saying: *b My son, neglect not the discipline of the Lord: neither be thou wearied whilst thou art rebuked by him.*

6 *For whom the Lord loveth he chastiseth: and he scourgeth every son whom he receiveth.*

7 Persevere under discipline. God dealeth with you as with his sons: for what son is there, whom the father doth not correct?

8 But if you be without chastisement, whereof all are made partakers; then are you bastards, and not sons.

9 Moreover we have had fathers of our flesh, for instructors, and we reverenced them: shall we not much more obey the Father of spirits, and live?

10 And they indeed for a few days according to their own pleasure instructed us: but he,

for our profit, that we might receive his sanctification.

11 Now all chastisement for the present indeed seemeth not to bring with it joy, but sorrow: but afterwards it will yield, to them that are exercised by it, the most peaceable fruit of justice.

12 Wherefore lift up the hands which hang down, and the feeble knees:

13 And make straight steps with your feet: that no one, halting, may go out of the way; but rather be healed.

14 *c* Follow peace with all men, and holiness: without which no man shall see God:

15 Looking diligently lest any man be wanting to the grace of God: lest any root of bitterness springing up do hinder, and by it many be defiled.

16 Lest there be any fornicator, or profane person, *d* as Esau: who for one mess sold his first birth-right.

17 For know ye that *e* afterwards when he desired to inherit the benediction, he was rejected: for he found no place of repentance, although with tears he had sought it.

18 *f* For you are not come to a mountain that might be touched, and a burning fire, and a whirlwind, and darkness, and storm,

19 And the sound of a trumpet, and the voice of words,

---

*c* Rom. 12. 18.—*d* Gen. 25. 31.—*e* Gen. 27. 38.—*f* Exod. 19. 12. and 20. 21.

CHAP. XII. Ver. 17. *He found, &c.* That is, he found no way to bring his father to repent, or change his mind, with relation to his having given the blessing to his younger brother Jacob.

---

*a* Rom. 6. 4. Ephes. 4. 22. Col. 3. 8. 1 Pet. 2. 1. and 4. 2.—*b* Prov. 3. 11. Apoc. 3. 19.

374

which they that heard excused themselves, that the word might not be spoken to them:

20 For they did not endure that which was said: *a And if so much as a beast shall touch the mount, it shall be stoned.*

21 And so terrible was that which was seen, Moses said: *I am frighted and tremble.*

22 But you are come to Mount Sion, and to the city of the living God, the heavenly Jerusalem, and to the company of many thousands of angels,

23 And to the church of the first-born, who are written in the heavens, and to God the Judge of all, and to the spirits of the just made perfect,

24 And to JESUS the mediator of the new testament, and to the sprinkling of blood which speaketh better than that of Abel.

25 See that you refuse him not that speaketh. For if they escaped not who refused him that spoke upon earth, much more *shall not* we, that turn away from him that speaketh to us from heaven.

26 Whose voice then moved the earth: but now he promiseth, saying: *b Yet once more, and I will move not only the earth, but heaven also.*

27 And in that he saith, *Yet once more*, he signifieth the translation of the moveable things as made, that those things may remain which are immoveable.

28 Therefore receiving an immoveable kingdom, we have grace: whereby let us serve, pleasing God, with fear and reverence.

*a* Exod. 19. 18.—*b* Aggeus 2. 7.

29 *c* For our God is a consuming fire.

## CHAP. XIII.

*Divers admonitions and exhortations.*

LET the charity of the brotherhood abide in you.

2 *d* And hospitality do not forget, for by this some, *e* being not aware of it, have entertained angels.

3 Remember them that are in bands, as if you were bound with them; and them that labour, as being yourselves also in the body.

4 Marriage honourable in all, and the bed undefiled. For fornicators and adulterers God will judge.

5 Let your manners be without covetousness, contented with such things as you have: For he hath said: *f I will not leave thee, neither will I forsake thee.*

6 So that we may confidently say: *g The Lord is my helper: I will not fear what man shall do to me.*

7 Remember your prelates who have spoken the word of

*c* Deut. 4. 24.—*d* Rom. 12. 13. 1 Pet. 4. 9.—*e* Gen. 18. 3. and 19. 2.—*f* Jos. 1. 5. —*g* Ps. 117. 6.

CHAP. XIII. Ver. 4. Or, *let marriage be honourable in all.* That is, in *all things* belonging to the marriage state. This is a warning to married people not to abuse the sanctity of their state by any liberties or irregularities contrary thereunto. Now it does not follow from this text that all persons are obliged to marry, even if the word *omnibus* were rendered *in all persons*, instead of *in all things*: for if it was a precept, St. Paul himself would have transgressed it, as he never married. Moreover, those who have already made a vow to God to lead a single life, should they attempt to marry, they would incur their own damnation. 1 Tim. v. 12.

God to you: whose faith follow, considering the end of their conversation,

8 JESUS CHRIST, yesterday, and to-day, and the same for ever.

9 Be not led away with various and strange doctrines. For it is best that the heart be established with grace, not with meats: which have not profited those that walk in them.

10 We have an altar, whereof they have no power to eat who serve the tabernacle.

11 ᵃ For the bodies of those beasts, whose blood is brought into the Holies by the high-priest for sin, are burned without the camp.

12 Wherefore JESUS also, that he might sanctify the people by his own blood, suffered without the gate.

13 Let us go forth therefore to him without the camp; bearing his reproach.

14 ᵇ For we have not here a lasting city; but we seek one that is to come.

15 By him therefore let us offer the sacrifice of praise always to God, that is to say, the fruit of lips confessing to his name.

---

ᵃ Lev. 16. 27.—ᵇ Mich. 2. 10.

---

Ver. 13. *Let us go forth therefore to him without the camp, bearing his reproach.* That is, bearing his cross. It is an exhortation to them to be willing to suffer with Christ, reproaches, persecutions, and even death, if they desire to partake of the benefit of his suffering for man's redemption.

16 And do not forget to do good and to impart; for by such sacrifices God's favour is obtained.

17 Obey your prelates, and be subject to them. For they watch as being to render an account of your souls: that they may do this with joy, and not with grief. For this is not expedient for you.

18 Pray for us. For we trust we have a good conscience, being willing to behave ourselves well in all things.

19 And I beseech you the more to do this, that I may be restored to you the sooner.

20 And may the God of peace, who brought again from the dead the great pastor of the sheep, our Lord JESUS CHRIST, in the blood of the everlasting testament,

21 Fit you in all goodness, that you may do his will: doing in you that which is well pleasing in his sight, through JESUS CHRIST: to whom is glory for ever and ever. Amen.

22 And I beseech you, brethren, that you suffer *this* word of consolation. For I have written to you in a few words.

23 Know ye that our brother Timothy is set at liberty: with whom (if he come shortly) I will see you.

24 Salute all your prelates, and all the saints. The brethren from Italy salute you.

25 Grace be with you all. Amen.

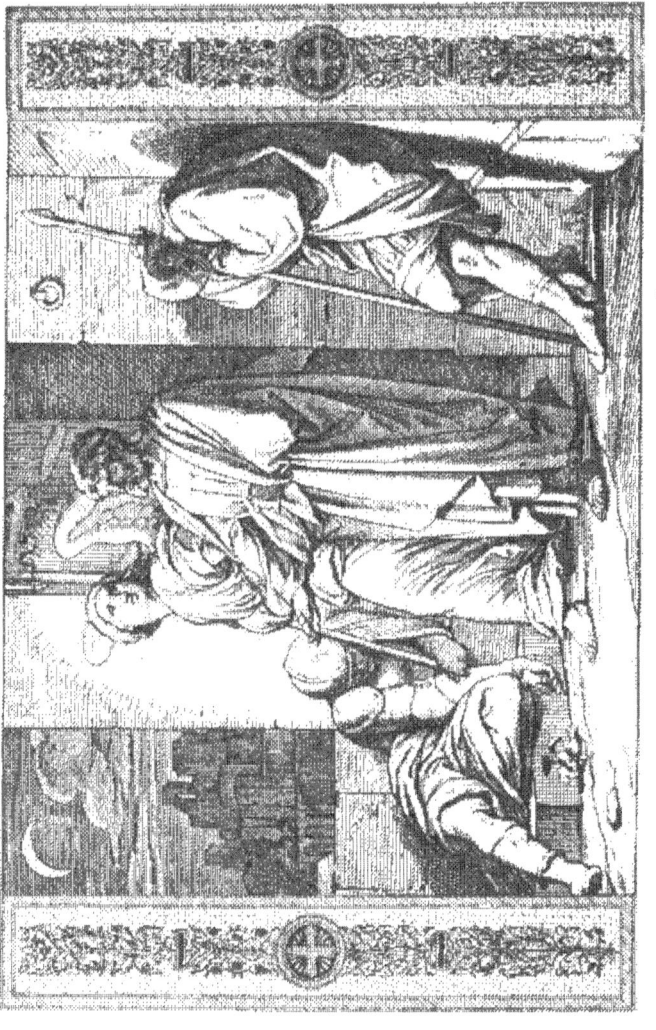

ST. PETER IS DELIVERED FROM PRISON.

THE
# CATHOLIC EPISTLE OF ST. JAMES THE APOSTLE.

*This Epistle is called CATHOLIC or UNIVERSAL, as formerly were also the two Epistles of ST. PETER, the first of ST. JOHN, and the one of ST. JUDE, because they were not written to any peculiar people or particular person, but to the faithful in general. It was written by the Apostle ST. JAMES, called THE LESS, who was also called THE BROTHER OF OUR LORD, being his kinsman (for cousin-germans with the Hebrews were called brothers). He was the first bishop of Jerusalem. In this Epistle are set forth many precepts appertaining to faith and morals; and particularly, that faith without good works will not save a man, that true wisdom is given only from above. In the fifth chapter he publishes the Sacrament of anointing the sick. It was written a short time before his martyrdom, about twenty-eight years after our Lord's Ascension.*

## CHAP. I.

*The benefit of tribulations. Prayer with faith. God is the author of all good, but not of evil. We must be slow to anger: and not hearers only, but doers of the word. Of bridling the tongue; and of pure religion.*

JAMES, the servant of God and of our Lord JESUS CHRIST, to the twelve tribes which are scattered abroad, greeting.

2 My brethren, count it all joy, when you shall fall into divers temptations:

3 *a* Knowing that the trying of your faith worketh patience.

4 And patience hath a perfect work: that you may be perfect and entire, failing in nothing.

5 But if any of you want wisdom, let him ask of God, who giveth to all men abundantly, and upbraideth not: and it shall be given him.

6 *b* But let him ask in faith, nothing wavering. For he that wavereth is like a wave of the sea, which is moved and carried about by the wind.

7 Therefore let not that man think that he shall receive anything of the Lord.

8 A double-minded man is inconstant in all his ways.

9 But let the brother of low condition glory in his exaltation:

10 And the rich, in his being low, *c* because as the flower of the grass shall he pass away.

11 For the sun rose with a burning heat, and parched the grass, and the flower thereof fell off, and the beauty of the shape thereof perished: so also

---

*a* Rom. 5. 3.

CHAP. I. Ver. 2. *Into divers temptations.* The word *temptation*, in this Epistle, is sometimes taken for trials by afflictions or persecutions, as in this place; at other times, it is to be understood; tempting, enticing or drawing others into sin.

*b* Matt. 7. 7. and 21. 22. Mark 11. 24. Luke 11. 9. John 14. 13. and 16.— *c* Eccli. 14. 18. Isaias 40. 6. 1 Pet. 1. 24.

shall the rich man fade away in his ways.

12 ᵃ Blessed is the man that endureth temptation: for when he hath been proved, he shall receive the crown of life, which God hath promised to them that love him.

13 Let no man when he is tempted, say that he is tempted by God. For God is not a tempter of evils, and he tempteth no man.

14 But every man is tempted by his own concupiscence, being drawn away and allured.

15 Then when concupiscence hath conceived, it bringeth forth sin. But sin, when it is completed, begetteth death.

16 Do not err therefore, my dearest brethren.

17 Every best gift, and every perfect gift, is from above, coming down from the Father of lights, with whom there is no change, nor shadow of alteration.

18 For of his own will hath he begotten us by the word of truth, that we might be some beginning of his creature.

19 You know, my dearest brethren. ᵇ And let every man be swift to hear, but slow to speak, and slow to anger.

20 For the anger of man worketh not the justice of God.

21 Wherefore casting away all uncleanness, and abundance of naughtiness, with meekness receive the ingrafted word which is able to save your souls.

22 ᶜ But be ye doers of the word, and not hearers only, deceiving your own selves.

23 For if a man be a hearer of the word and not a doer; he shall be compared to a man beholding his own countenance in a glass.

24 For he beheld himself, and went his way, and presently forgot what manner of man he was.

25 But he that hath looked into the perfect law of liberty, and hath continued therein, not becoming a forgetful hearer, but a doer of the work; this man shall be blessed in his deed.

26 And if any man think himself to be religious, not bridling his tongue, but deceiving his own heart, this man's religion is vain.

27 Religion clean and undefiled before God and the Father, is this: to visit the fatherless and widows in their tribulation: and to keep one's self unspotted from this world.

## CHAP. II.

*Against respect of persons. The danger of transgressing one point of the law. Faith is dead without works.*

MY ᵈ brethren, have not the faith of our Lord JESUS CHRIST of glory with respect of persons.

2 For if there shall come into your assembly a man having a golden ring, in fine apparel, and

---

ᵃ Job 5. 17.—ᵇ Prov. 17. 27.—ᶜ Matt. 7. 21. and 24. Rom. 2. 13.

Ver. 18. *Some beginning:* that is, kind of first-fruits of his creatures.

ᵈ Lev. 19. 15. Deut. 1. 17. and 16. 19. Prov. 24. 23. Eccli. 42. 1.

CHAP. II. Ver. 1. *With respect of persons.* The meaning is, that in matters relating to faith, the administering of the sacraments, and other spiritual functions in God's Church, there should be no *respect of persons;* but that the souls of the poor should be as much regarded as those of the rich. See *Deut.* I. 17.

there shall come in also a poor man in mean attire,

3 And you have respect to him that is clothed with the fine apparel, and shall say to him: Sit thou here well: but say to the poor man: Stand thou there, or sit under my footstool:

4 Do you not judge within yourselves, and are become judges of unjust thoughts?

5 Hearken, my dearest brethren: hath not God chosen the poor in this world, rich in faith, and heirs of the kingdom which God hath promised to them that love him?

6 But you have dishonoured the poor man. Do not the rich oppress you by might; and do not they draw you before the judgment-seats?

7 Do not they blaspheme the good name that is invoked upon you?

8 If then you fulfil the royal law, according to the scriptures, *Thou shalt love thy neighbour as thyself:* you do well.

9 *b* But if you have respect to persons, you commit sin, being reproved by the law as transgressors.

10 *c* And whosoever shall keep the whole law, but offend in one *point*, is become guilty of all.

11 For he that said, Thou shalt not commit adultery, said also, Thou shalt not kill. Now if thou do not commit adultery, but shalt kill, thou art become a transgressor of the law.

12 So speak ye, and so do, as being to be judged by the law of liberty.

13 For judgment without mercy to him that hath not done mercy. And mercy exalteth itself above judgment.

14 What shall it profit, my brethren, if a man say he hath faith, but hath not works? Shall faith be able to save him?

15 *d* And if a brother or sister be naked, and want daily food:

16 And one of you say to them: Go in peace, be you warmed and filled; yet give them not those things that are necessary for the body, what shall it profit?

17 So faith also, if it have not works, is dead in itself.

18 But some man will say: Thou hast faith, and I have works: shew me thy faith without works, and I will shew thee, by works, my faith.

19 Thou believest that there is one God. Thou dost well: the devils also believe and tremble.

20 But wilt thou know, O

---

*a* Lev. 19. 18. Matt. 22. 39. Mark 12. 31. Rom. 13. 9. Gal. 5. 14.—*b* Supra, 1. Lev. 19. 15.—*c* Deut. 1. 16. Matt. 5. 19.

*d* 1 John 3. 17.

---

Ver. 10. *Guilty of all;* that is, becomes a transgressor of the law in such a manner, that the observing of all other points will not avail him to salvation: for he despises the lawgiver, and breaks through the great and general commandment of charity, even by one mortal sin. For all the precepts of the law are to be considered as one total and entire law, and as it were a chain of precepts whereby breaking one link of this chain, the whole chain is broken, or the integrity of the law consisting of a collection of precepts. A sinner, therefore, by a grievous offence against any one precept, incurs eternal punishment: yet the punishments in hell shall be greater for those who have been greater sinners, as a greater reward small be for those in heaven who have lived with greater sanctity and perfection.

vain man, that faith without works is dead?

21 "Was not Abraham our father justified by works, offering up Isaac his son upon the altar?

22 Seest thou that faith did co-operate with his works: and by works faith was made perfect.

23 And the scripture was fulfilled, saying: *b Abraham believed God, and it was reputed to him to justice, and he was called the friend of God.*

24 Do you see that by works a man is justified, and not by faith only?

25 *c* And in like manner also Rahab the harlot, was not she justified by works, receiving the messengers, and sending them out another way?

26 For even as the body without the spirit is dead, so also faith without works is dead.

## CHAP. III.

*Of the evils of the tongue. Of the difference between the earthly and heavenly wisdom.*

BE *d* ye not many masters, my brethren, knowing that you receive the greater judgment.

2 For in many things we all offend. If any man offend not in word, the same is a perfect man. He is able also with a bridle to lead about the whole body.

3 For if we put bits into the mouths of horses that they may obey us, and we turn about their whole body.

4 Behold also ships, whereas they are great, and are driven by strong winds, yet are they turned about with a small helm, whithersoever the force of the governor willeth.

5 So the tongue also is indeed a little member, and boasteth great things. Behold how small a fire what a great wood it kindleth!

6 And the tongue is a fire, a world of iniquity. The tongue is placed among our members, which defileth the whole body, and inflameth the wheel of our nativity, being set on fire by hell.

7 For every nature of beasts, and of birds, and of serpents, and of the rest, is tamed and hath been tamed by the nature of man:.

8 But the tongue no man can tame, an unquiet evil, full of deadly poison.

9 By it we bless God and the Father: and by it we curse men, who are made after the likeness of God.

10 Out of the same mouth proceedeth blessing and cursing. My brethren, these things ought not so to be.

11 Doth a fountain send forth, out of the same hole, sweet and bitter water?

12 Can the fig-tree, my brethren, bear grapes; or the vine, figs? So neither can the salt water yield sweet.

13 Who is a wise man and endued with knowledge among you? Let him shew, by a good conversation, his work in the meekness of wisdom.

14 But if you have bitter zeal, and there be contentions in your hearts; glory not, and be not liars against the truth.

15 For this is not wisdom,

---

*a* Gen. 22. 9.—*b* Gen. 15. 6. Rom. 4. 3. Gal. 3. 6.—*c* Jos. 2. 4. Heb. 11. 31.—*d* Matt. 23. 8.

descending from above: but earthly, sensual, devilish.

16 For where envying and contention is, there is inconstancy, and every evil work.

17 But the wisdom that is from above, first indeed is chaste, then peaceable, modest, easy to be persuaded, consenting to the good, full of mercy and good fruits, without judging, without dissimulation.

18 And the fruit of justice is sown in peace, to them that make peace.

## CHAP. IV.

*The evils that flow from yielding to concupiscence, and being friends to this world. Admonitions against pride, detraction, &c.*

FROM whence are wars and contentions among you? Are they not hence, from your concupiscences, which war in your members?

2 You covet, and have not: you kill, and envy, and cannot obtain. You contend and war, and you have not, because you ask not.

3 You ask, and receive not: because you ask amiss: that you may consume it on your concupiscences.

4 Adulterers, know you not that the friendship of this world is the enemy of God? Whosoever therefore will be a friend of this world, becometh an enemy of God.

5 Or do you think that the scripture saith in vain: *To envy doth the spirit covet which dwelleth in you?*

6 But he giveth greater grace. Wherefore he saith: *ᵃGod resisteth the proud, and giveth grace to the humble.*

7 Be subject therefore to God, but resist the devil and he will fly from you.

8 Draw nigh to God, and he will draw nigh to you. Cleanse your hands, ye sinners: and purify your hearts, ye doubleminded.

9 Be afflicted, and mourn, and weep: let your laughter be turned into mourning, and your joy into sorrow.

10 Be humbled in the sight of the Lord, and he will exalt you.

11 Detract not one another, my brethren. He that detracteth his brother, or he that judgeth his brother, detracteth the law, and judgeth the law. But if thou judge the law, thou art not a doer of the law, but a judge.

12 There is one lawgiver, and judge, that is able to destroy and to deliver.

13 ᵇBut who art thou that judgest thy neighbour? Behold, now you that say: To-day or tomorrow we will go into such a city, and there we will spend a year, and will traffic, and make our gain.

14 Whereas you know not what shall be on the morrow.

15 For what is your life? It is a vapour which appeareth for a little while, and afterwards shall vanish away. For that you should say: If the Lord will, and, if we shall live, we will do this or that.

16 But now you rejoice in your arrogancies. All such rejoicing is wicked.

17 To him therefore who knoweth to do good, and doth it not, to him it is sin.

---

ᵃ Prov. 3. 34. 1 Pet. 5. 5.   ᵇ Rom. 14. 4.

## CHAP. V.

*A wo to the rich that oppress the poor. Exhortations to patience, and to avoid swearing. Of the anointing the sick, confession of sins, and fervour in prayer.*

GO to now, ye rich men, weep and howl in your miseries, which shall come upon you.

2 Your riches are corrupted: and your garments are moth-eaten.

3 Your gold and silver is cankered: and the rust of them shall be for a testimony against you, and shall eat your flesh like fire. You have stored up to yourselves wrath against the last days.

4 Behold the hire of the labourers, who have reaped down your fields, which by fraud has been kept back by you, crieth: and the cry of them hath entered into the ears of the Lord of sabaoth.

5 You have feasted upon earth: and in riotousness you have nourished your hearts, in the day of slaughter.

6 You have condemned and put to death the just one, and he resisted you not.

7 Be patient therefore, brethren, until the coming of the Lord. Behold, the husbandman waiteth for the precious fruit of the earth: patiently bearing till he receive the early and the latter *rain*.

8 Be you therefore also patient, and strengthen your hearts: for the coming of the Lord is at hand.

9 Grudge not, brethren, one against another, that you may not be judged. Behold the judge standeth before the door.

10 Take, my brethren, for an example of suffering evil, of labour and patience, the prophets, who spoke in the name of the Lord.

11 Behold we account them blessed who have endured. You have heard of the patience of Job, and you have seen the end of the Lord, that the Lord is merciful and compassionate.

12 But above all things, my brethren, *a* swear not, neither by heaven nor by the earth, nor by any other oath. But let your speech be, yea, yea: no, no: that you fall not under judgment.

13 Is any of you sad? Let him pray. Is he cheerful in mind? Let him sing.

14 Is any man sick among you? Let him bring in the priests of the church, and let them pray over him, anointing him with oil in the name of the Lord.

15 And the prayer of faith shall save the sick man: and the Lord shall raise him up: and if he be in sins, they shall be forgiven him.

16 Confess therefore your sins one to another: and pray one for another, that you may be

---

*a* Matt. 5. 34.

CHAP. V. Ver. 14. *Let him bring in, &c.* See here a plain warrant of scripture for the sacrament of extreme unction, that any controversy against its institution would be against the express words of the sacred text in the plainest terms.

Ver. 16. *Confess your sins one to another.* That is, to the priests of the Church, whom, ver. 14, he had ordered to be called for, and brought in to the sick; moreover, to confess to persons who had no power to forgive sins, would be useless. Hence the precept here means, that we must confess to men whom God hath appointed, and who, by their ordination and jurisdiction, have received the power of remitting sins in his name.

ST. PETER ADDRESSING THE COUNCIL OF JERUSALEM.

saved. For the continual prayer of a just man availeth much.

17 ᵃ Elias was a man passible like unto us: and with prayer he prayed that it might not rain upon the earth, and it rained not for three years and six months.

18 And he prayed again: and the heaven gave rain, and the earth brought forth her fruit.

19 My brethren, if any of you err from the truth, and one convert him:

20 He must know, that he who causeth a sinner to be converted from the error of his way, shall save his soul from death, and shall cover a multitude of sins.

---

ᵃ 3 Kings 17. 1. Luke 4. 25.

# THE FIRST EPISTLE OF ST. PETER THE APOSTLE.

*This first Epistle of St. Peter, though brief, contains much doctrine concerning Faith, Hope, and Charity, with divers instructions to all persons of what state or condition soever. The Apostle commands submission to rulers and superiors, and exhorts all to the practice of a virtuous life in imitation of Christ. This Epistle is written with such apostolical dignity as to manifest the supreme authority with which its writer, the prince of the Apostles, had been vested by his lord and master Jesus Christ. He wrote it at Rome, which figuratively he calls Babylon, about fifteen years after our Lord's Ascension.*

## CHAP. I.

*He gives thanks to God for the benefit of our being called to the true faith, and to eternal life: into which we are to enter by many tribulations. He exhorts to holiness of life: considering the holiness of God, and our redemption by the blood of Christ.*

PETER, an apostle of JESUS CHRIST, to the strangers dispersed through Pontus, Galatia, Cappadocia, Asia, and Bithynia, elect,

2 According to the foreknowledge of God the Father, unto the sanctification of the Spirit, unto obedience and sprinkling of the blood of JESUS CHRIST: Grace unto you and peace be multiplied.

3 ᵃ Blessed be the God and Father of our Lord JESUS CHRIST, who according to his great mercy hath regenerated us unto a lively hope, by the resurrection of JESUS CHRIST from the dead.

4 Unto an inheritance incorruptible, and undefiled, and that cannot fade, reserved in heaven for you.

---

ᵃ 2 Cor. 1. 3. Ephes. 1. 3.

5 Who, by the power of God, are kept by faith unto salvation ready to be revealed in the last time.

6 Wherein you shall greatly rejoice, if now you must be for a little time made sorrowful in divers temptations:

7 That the trial of your faith (much more precious than gold which is tried by the fire) may be found unto praise and glory and honour at the appearing of JESUS CHRIST:

8 Whom having not seen, you love: in whom also now, though you see him not, you believe: and believing shall rejoice with joy unspeakable and glorified.

9 Receiving the end of your faith, even the salvation of your souls.

10 Of which salvation the prophets have inquired and diligently searched, who prophesied of the grace to come in you,

11 Searching what or what manner of time the Spirit of Christ in them did signify: when it foretold those sufferings that are in Christ, and the glories that should follow:

12 To whom it was revealed, that not to themselves, but to you they ministered those things which are now declared to you by them that have preached the gospel to you, the Holy Ghost being sent down from heaven, on whom the angels desire to look.

13 Wherefore having the loins of your mind girt up, being sober, trust perfectly in the grace which is offered to you in the revelation of JESUS CHRIST,

14 As children of obedience, not fashioned according to the former desires of your ignorance:

15 But according to him that hath called you, who is Holy, be you also in all manner of conversation holy:

16 Because it is written: *a You shall be holy, for I am holy.*

17 And if you invoke as Father him who, *b* without respect of persons, judgeth according to every one's work: converse in fear during the time of your sojourning here.

18 Knowing that you were not redeemed with corruptible things as gold or silver, from your vain conversation of the tradition of your fathers:

19 *c* But with the precious blood of Christ, as of a lamb unspotted and undefiled;

20 Foreknown indeed before the foundation of the world, but manifested in the last times for you,

21 Who through him are faithful in God, who raised him up from the dead, and hath given him glory, that your faith and hope might be in God.

22 Purifying your souls in the obedience of charity, with a brotherly love, from a sincere heart love one another earnestly:

23 Being born again not of corruptible seed, but incorruptible, by the word of God who liveth and remaineth for ever.

24 *d For all flesh is as grass: and all the glory thereof as the flower of grass. The grass is*

---

*a* Lev. 11. 44. and 19. 2. and 20. 7.— *b* Deut. 10. 17. Rom. 2. 11. Gal. 2. 6.— *c* 1 Cor. 6. 20. and 7. 23. Heb. 9. 14. 1 John 1. 7. Apoc. 1. 5.—*d* Eccli. 14. 18. Isaias 40. 6. Jas. 1. 10.

withered, and the flower thereof is fallen away.

25 But the word of the Lord endureth for ever, and this is the word which by the gospel hath been preached unto you.

## CHAP. II.

*We are to lay aside all guile, and go to Christ the living stone: and as being now his people, walk worthily of him, with submission to superiors, and patience under sufferings.*

WHEREFORE ᵃ laying away all malice, and all guile, and dissimulations, and envies, and all detractions,

2 As new-born babes, desire the rational milk without guile, that thereby you may grow unto salvation.

3 If so be you have tasted that the Lord is sweet.

4 Unto whom coming, as to a living stone, rejected indeed by men, but chosen and made honourable by God:

5 Be you also as living stones built up, a spiritual house, a holy priesthood, to offer up spiritual sacrifices, acceptable to God by JESUS CHRIST.

6 Wherefore it is said in the scripture: ᵇ *Behold I lay in Sion a chief corner-stone, elect, precious. And he that shall believe in him, shall not be confounded.*

7 To you therefore, that believe, he is honour; but to them that believe not, ᶜ *the stone which the builders rejected, the same is made the head of the corner:*

8 And a stone of stumbling, and a rock of scandal, to them who stumble at the word, neither do believe, whereunto also they are set.

9 But you are a chosen generation, a kingly priesthood, a holy nation, a purchased people: that you may declare his virtues, who hath called you out of darkness into his marvellous light,

10 ᵈ *Who in time past were not a people: but are now the people of God. Who had not obtained mercy: but now have obtained mercy.*

11 ᵉ Dearly beloved, I beseech you as strangers and pilgrims, to refrain yourselves from carnal desires which war against the soul,

12 Having your conversation good among the gentiles: that whereas they speak against you as evil-doers, they may by the good works, which they shall behold in you, glorify God in the day of visitation.

13 ᶠ Be ye subject therefore to every human creature for God's sake: whether it be to the king as excelling:

14 Or to governors as sent by him for the punishment of evil-doers, and for the praise of the good:

15 For so is the will of God, that by doing well, you may put to silence the ignorance of foolish men:

16 As free, and not as making liberty a cloak for malice, but as the servants of God.

17 Honour all men. ᵍ Love the brotherhood. Fear God. Honour the king.

18 ʰ Servants, be subject to

---

ᵃ Rom. 6. 4. Ephes. 4. 22. Col. 3. 8. Heb. 12. 1.—ᵇ Isaias 28. 16. Rom. 9. 33. —ᶜ Ps. 117. 22. Is. 8. 14. Matt. 21. 42. Acts 4. 11. ᵈ Osee 2. 24. Rom. 9. 25.—ᵉ Rom. 12. 14. Gal. 5. 16.—ᶠ Rom. 13. 1.—ᵍ Rom. 12. 10.—ʰ Ephes. 6. 5. Col. 3. 22. Titus 2. 9.

your masters with all fear, not only to the good and gentle, but also to the froward.

19 For this is thanks-worthy, if for conscience towards God, a man endure sorrows, suffering wrongfully.

20 For what glory is it, if committing sin and being buffeted *for it* you endure? But if doing well you suffer patiently; this is thanks-worthy before God.

21 For unto this are you called: because Christ also suffered for us, leaving you an example that you should follow his steps.

22 *a Who did no sin, neither was guile found in his mouth.*

23 Who, when he was reviled, did not revile: when he suffered, he threatened not: but delivered himself to him that judged him unjustly.

24 *b* Who his own self bore our sins in his body upon the tree; that we being dead to sins, should live to justice: by whose stripes you were healed.

25 For you were as sheep going astray; but you are now converted to the shepherd and bishop of your souls.

## CHAP. III.

*How wives are to behave to their husbands; what ornaments they are to seek. Exhortations to divers virtues.*

IN *c* like manner also let wives be subject to their husbands: that if any believe not the word, they may be won without the word, by the conversation of the wives,

2 Considering your chaste conversation with fear.

3 *d* Whose adorning let it not be the outward plaiting of the hair, or the wearing of gold, or the putting on of apparel:

4 But the hidden man of the heart in the incorruptibility of a quiet and meek spirit, which is rich in the sight of God.

5 For after this manner heretofore the holy women also, who trusted in God, adorned themselves, being in subjection to their own husbands.

6 *e* As Sara obeyed Abraham, calling him Lord: whose daughters you are, doing well, and not fearing any disturbance.

7 *f* Ye husbands, likewise dwelling with them according to knowledge, giving honour to the female as to the weaker vessel, and as to the co-heirs of the grace of life: that your prayers be not hindered.

8 And in fine be ye all of one mind, having compassion one of another, being lovers of the brotherhood, merciful, modest, humble:

9 *g* Not rendering evil for evil, nor railing for railing, but contrariwise, blessing: for unto this are you called, that you may inherit a blessing.

10 *h For he that will love life, and see good days, let him refrain his tongue from evil, and his lips that they speak no guile.*

11 *i Let him decline from evil, and do good: let him seek after peace, and pursue it:*

12 *Because the eyes of the Lord are upon the just, and his ears unto their prayers: but the coun-*

---

*a* Isaias 53. 9.—*b* Isaias 53. 5. *c* 1 John 3. 5.—*e* Ephes. 5. 22. Col. 3. 18.

*d* 1 Tim. 2. 9.—*e* Gen. 18. 12.—*f* 1 Cor. 7. 3.—*g* Prov. 17. 13. Rom. 12. 17. 1 Thess. 5. 15.—*h* Ps. 33. 12.—*i* Isaias 1. 16.

tenance of the Lord upon them that do evil things.

13 And who is he that can hurt you, if you be zealous of good?

14 ᵃ But if also you suffer any thing for justice sake, blessed are ye. And be not afraid of their fear, and be not troubled.

15 But sanctify the Lord Christ in your hearts, being ready always to satisfy every one that asketh you a reason of that hope which is in you.

16 ᵇ But with modesty and fear, having a good conscience: that whereas they speak evil of you, they may be ashamed who falsely accuse your good conversation in Christ.

17 For it is better doing well (if such be the will of God) to suffer than doing ill.

18 ᶜ Because Christ also died once for our sins, the just for the unjust: that he might offer us to God, being put to death indeed in the flesh, but enlivened in the spirit.

19 In which also coming he preached to those spirits that were in prison:

20 Which had been some time incredulous, ᵈ when they waited for the patience of God in the days of Noe, when the ark was a building: wherein a few, that is, eight souls, were saved by water.

21 Whereunto baptism being of the like form, now saveth you also: not the putting away of the filth of the flesh, but the examination of a good conscience towards God by the resurrection of JESUS CHRIST.

22 Who is on the right hand of God, swallowing down death, that we might be made heirs of life everlasting: being gone into heaven, the angels and powers and virtues being made subject to him.

## CHAP. IV.

*Exhortations to cease from sin; to mutual charity; to do all for the glory of God; to be willing to suffer for Christ.*

CHRIST therefore having suffered in the flesh, be you also armed with the same thought: for he that hath suffered in the flesh hath ceased from sins:

2 ᵉ That now he may live the rest of his time in the flesh, not after the desires of men, but according to the will of God.

3 For the time past is sufficient to have fulfilled the will of the gentiles, for them who have walked in riotousness, lusts, excess of wine, revellings, banquetings, and unlawful worshipping of idols.

---

ᵉ Ephes. 4, 22.

---

ᵃ Matt. 5. 10.—ᵇ Supra, 2. 12.—ᶜ Rom. 5. 6. Heb. 9. 28.—ᵈ Gen. 7. 7. Matt. 24. 37. Luke 17. 26.

CHAP. III. Ver. 19. *Spirits that were in prison.* See here a proof of a third place, or middle state of souls: for these spirits in prison, to whom Christ went to preach, after his death, were not in heaven: nor yet in the hell of the damned; because heaven is no prison: and Christ did not go to preach to the damned.

Ver. 21. *Whereunto baptism, &c.* Baptism is said to be *of the like form* with the *water* by which Noe was saved, because the one was a figure of the other.—Ibid. *Not the putting away, &c.* As much as to say that baptism has not its efficacy, in order to salvation, from its washing away any bodily filth or dirt; but from its purging the conscience from sin: when accompanied with suitable dispositions in the party, to answer the interrogations made at that time, with relation to faith, the renouncing of satan with all his works, and the obedience to God's commandments.

I. OF ST. PETER.   CHAP. V.

14 If you be reproached for the name of Christ, you shall be blessed: for that which is of the honour, glory and power of God, and that which is his Spirit, resteth upon you.

15 But let none of you suffer as a murderer, or a thief, or a railer, or a coveter of other men's things.

16 But if as a Christian, let him not be ashamed, but let him glorify God in this name.

17 For the time is that judgment should begin at the house of God. And if first at us, what shall be the end of them that believe not the gospel of God!

18 And if the just man shall scarcely be saved, where shall the ungodly and the sinner appear?

19 Wherefore let them also that suffer according to the will of God, commend their souls in good deeds to the faithful Creator.

## CHAP. V.

THE ancients therefore that are among you, I beseech, who am myself also an ancient and a witness of the sufferings of Christ: as also a partaker of that glory which is to be revealed in times to come:

2 Feed the flock of God which is among you, taking care of it not by constraint, but willingly

SS. PAUL AND BARNABAS TAKEN FOR GODS BY THE PEOPLE OF LYSTRA.

4 Wherein they think it strange that you run not with them into the same confusion of riotousness, speaking evil *of you.*

5 Who shall render account to him who is ready to judge the living and the dead.

6 For, for this cause was the gospel preached also to the dead: that they might be judged indeed, according to men in the flesh: but may live according to God in the Spirit.

7 But the end of all is at hand. Be prudent therefore and watch in prayers.

8 But before all things have a constant mutual charity among yourselves: *a* for charity covereth a multitude of sins.

9 *b* Using hospitality one towards another *c* without murmuring.

10 *d* As every man hath received grace, ministering the same one to another: *e* as good stewards of the manifold grace of God.

11 If any man speak, *let him speak* as the words of God. If any man minister, *let him do it* as of the power, which God administereth: that in all things God may be honoured through JESUS CHRIST: to whom is glory and empire for ever and ever. Amen.

12 Dearly beloved, think not strange the burning heat which is to try you, as if some new thing happened to you.

13 But if you partake of the suffering of Christ, rejoice that when his glory shall be revealed you may also be glad with exceeding joy.

14 If you be reproached for the name of Christ, you shall be blessed: for that which is of the honour, glory and power of God, and that which is his Spirit, resteth upon you.

15 But let none of you suffer as a murderer, or a thief, or a railer, or a coveter of other men's things.

16 But if as a Christian, let him not be ashamed, but let him glorify God in this name.

17 For the time is that judgment should begin at the house of God. And if first at us, what shall be the end of them that believe not the gospel of God?

18 *f* And if the just man shall scarcely be saved, where shall the ungodly and the sinner appear?

19 Wherefore let them also that suffer according to the will of God, commend their souls in good deeds to the faithful Creator.

## CHAP. V.

*He exhorts both priests and laity, to their respective duties, and recommends to all humility and watchfulness.*

THE ancients *g* therefore that are among you, I beseech, who am myself also an ancient and a witness of the sufferings of Christ: as also a partaker of that glory which is to be revealed in time to come:

2 Feed the flock of God which is among you, taking care *of it* not by constraint, but willingly

---

*f* Prov. 11. 31.—*g i.e.*, senior priests.

CHAP. IV. Ver. 18. *Scarcely.* That is, not without much labour and difficulty, and because of the dangers which constantly surround, the temptations of the world, of the devil, and of our own corrupt nature.

---

*a* Prov. 10. 12.—*b* Rom. 2. 12. Heb. 13. 2.—*c* Phil. 2. 14.—*d* Rom. 2. 6.—*e* 1 Cor. 4. 2.

88. PAUL AND BARNABAS TAKEN FOR GODS BY THE PEOPLE OF LYSTRA.

according to God: not for filthy lucre's sake, but voluntarily:

3 Neither as lording it over the clergy, but being made a pattern of the flock from the heart.

4 And when the prince of pastors shall appear, you shall receive a never-fading crown of glory.

5 In like manner, ye young men, be subject to the ancients. *a* And do ye all insinuate humility one to another, *b for God resisteth the proud, but to the humble he giveth grace.*

6 *c* Be you humbled therefore under the mighty hand of God, that he may exalt you in the time of visitation:

7 *d* Casting all your care upon him, for he hath care of you.

8 Be sober and watch: because your adversary the devil, as a roaring lion, goeth about seeking whom he may devour.

9 Whom resist ye, strong in faith: knowing that the same affliction befalls your brethren who are in the world.

10 But the God of all grace, who hath called us unto his eternal glory in CHRIST JESUS, after you have suffered a little, will himself perfect you, and confirm you, and establish you.

11 To him be glory and empire for ever and ever. Amen.

12 By Sylvanus, a faithful brother unto you, as I think I have written briefly: beseeching and testifying that this is the true grace of God wherein you stand.

13 The church that is in *e* Babylon, elected together with you, saluteth you: and so doth my son Mark.

14 Salute one another with a holy kiss. Grace be to all you who are in CHRIST JESUS. Amen.

*a* Rom. 12. 10.—*b* Jas. 4. 6.—*c* Jas. 4. 10.—*d* Ps. 54. 23. Matt. 6. 25. Luke 12. 22.

*e* Figuratively, Rome.

---

# THE
# SECOND EPISTLE OF ST. PETER THE APOSTLE.

*In this Epistle St. Peter says (chap. III.), Behold this second Epistle I write to you: and before (chap. i. 14), Being assured that the laying away of this my tabernacle is at hand. This shews that it was written a very short time before his martyrdom, which was about thirty-five years after our Lord's Ascension. In this Epistle he admonishes the faithful to be mindful of the great gifts they received from God, and to join all other virtues with their faith. He warns them against false teachers, by describing their practices and foretelling their punishments. He describes the dissolution of this world by fire, and the day of judgment.*

---

## CHAP. I.

*He exhorts them to join all other virtues with their faith, in order to secure their salvation.*

SIMON PETER, servant and apostle of JESUS CHRIST, to them that have obtained equal faith with us in the justice of our God and Saviour JESUS CHRIST.

2 Grace to you and peace be accomplished in the knowledge

of God, and of CHRIST JESUS our Lord.

3 As all things of his divine power, which appertain to life and godliness, are given us, through the knowledge of him who hath called us by his own proper glory and virtue.

4 By whom he hath given us most great and precious promises: that by these you may be made partakers of the divine nature: flying the corruption of that concupiscence which is in the world.

5 And you, employing all care, minister in your faith, virtue: and in virtue, knowledge:

6 And in knowledge, abstinence: and in abstinence, patience: and in patience, godliness:

7 And in godliness, love of brotherhood: and in love of brotherhood, charity.

8 For if these things be with you, and abound, they will make you to be neither empty nor unfruitful in the knowledge of our Lord JESUS CHRIST.

9 For he that hath not these things with him is blind, and groping, having forgotten that he was purged from his old sins.

10 Wherefore, brethren, labour the more, that by good works you may make sure your calling and election. For doing these things, you shall not sin at any time.

11 For so an entrance shall be ministered to you abundantly into the everlasting kingdom of our Lord and Saviour JESUS CHRIST.

12 For which cause I will begin to put you always in remembrance of these things: though indeed you know them, and are confirmed in the present truth.

13 But I think it meet as long as I am in this tabernacle, to stir you up by putting you in remembrance.

14 Being assured that the laying away of *this* my tabernacle is at hand, according as our Lord JESUS CHRIST also hath *a* signified to me.

15 And I will do my endeavour, that after my decease also, you may often have whereby you may keep a memory of these things.

16 *b* For we have not followed cunningly devised fables, when we made known to you the power and presence of our Lord JESUS CHRIST: but having been made eye-witnesses of his majesty.

17 For, he received from God the Father, honour and glory; this voice coming down to him from the excellent glory, *c This is my beloved Son in whom I have pleased myself, hear ye him.*

18 And this voice we heard brought from heaven, when we were with him in the holy mount.

19 And we have the more firm prophetic l word, whereunto you do well to attend, as to a light that shineth in a dark place, until the day dawn, and the day-star arise in your hearts:

20 *d* Understanding this first, that no prophecy of scripture is made by private interpretation.

---

*a* John 21. 19.—*b* 1 Cor. 1. 17.—*c* Matt. 17. 5.—*d* 2 Tim. 3. 16.

CHAP. I. Ver. 20. *No prophecy of scripture is made by private interpretation.* This shews plainly that the

21 For prophecy came not by the will of man at any time: but the holy men of God spoke, inspired by the Holy Ghost.

## CHAP II.

*He warns them against false teachers, and foretells their punishment.*

BUT there were also false prophets among the people, even as there shall be among you lying teachers, who shall bring in sects of perdition, and deny the Lord who bought them: bringing upon themselves swift destruction.

2 And many shall follow their riotousnesses, through whom the way of truth shall be evil spoken of.

3 And through covetousness shall they with feigned words make merchandise of you. Whose judgment now of a long time lingereth not, and their perdition slumbereth not.

4 [a] For if God spared not the angels that sinned: but delivered them, drawn down by infernal ropes to the lower hell, unto torments, to be reserved unto judgment:

5 And spared not the original world, [b] but preserved Noe the eighth person, the preacher of justice, bringing in the flood upon the world of the ungodly.

6 [c] And reducing the cities of the Sodomites and of the Gomorrhites into ashes, condemned them to be overthrown, making them an example to those that should after act wickedly.

7 And delivered just Lot, oppressed by the injustice and lewd conversation of the wicked.

8 For in sight and hearing he was just: dwelling among them, who from day to day vexed the just soul with unjust works.

9 The Lord knoweth how to deliver the godly from temptation, but to reserve the unjust unto the day of judgment to be tormented:

10 And especially them who walk after the flesh in the lust of uncleanness, and despise government, audacious, self-willed, they fear not to bring in sects, blaspheming.

11 Whereas angels, who are greater in strength and power, bring not against themselves a railing judgment.

12 But these men, as irrational beasts, naturally tending to the snare and to destruction, blaspheming those things which they know not, shall perish in their corruption,

13 Receiving the reward of

---

[a] Job 4. 18. Jude 1. 6.

Scriptures are not to be expounded by any one's private judgment or private spirit, because every part of the holy scriptures were written by men inspired by the Holy Ghost, and declared as such by the Church; therefore they are not to be interpreted but by the Spirit of God, which he hath left, and promised to remain with his Church to guide her in all truth to the end of the world. Some may tell us that many of our divines interpret the Scriptures: they may do so, but they do it always with a submission to the judgment of the Church, and not otherwise.

CHAP. II. Ver. 1. *Sects of perdition;* that is, heresies destructive of salvation.

[b] Gen. 7. 1.—[c] Gen. 19. 25.

Ver. 11. *Bring not a railing judgment, &c.* That is, they use no railing nor cursing sentence: not even in their conflicts with the evil angels. See St. Jude, ver. 9.

Ver. 13. *The delights of a day,*

391

*their* injustice, counting for a pleasure the delights of a day: stains and spots, sporting themselves to excess, rioting in their feasts with you,

14 Having eyes full of adultery and of sin that ceaseth not: alluring unstable souls, having their heart exercised with covetousness, children of malediction:

15 Leaving the right way they have gone astray, *a* having followed the way of Balaam of Bosor, who loved the wages of iniquity,

16 But had a check of his madness, the dumb beast used to the yoke, which *b* speaking with man's voice, forbade the folly of the prophet.

17 *c* These are fountains without water and clouds tossed with whirlwinds, to whom the mist of darkness is reserved.

18 For, speaking proud words of vanity, they allure by the desires of fleshly riotousness, those who for a little while escape, such as converse in error:

19 Promising them liberty, whereas they themselves are the slaves of corruption. *d* For by whom a man is overcome, of the same also he is the slave.

20 For if, flying from the pollutions of the world through the knowledge of our Lord and Saviour JESUS CHRIST, *e* they *be* again entangled in them and overcome: *f* their latter state is become unto them worse than the former.

21 For it had been better for them not to have known the way of justice, than after they have known it, to turn back from that holy commandment which was delivered to them.

22 For that of the true proverb has happened to them: *g* The dog is returned to his vomit: and, The sow that was washed to her wallowing in the mire.

## CHAP. III.

*Against scoffers, denying the second coming of Christ, he declares the sudden dissolution of this world; and exhorts to holiness of life.*

BEHOLD this second epistle I write to you, my dearly beloved, in which I stir up by way of admonition your sincere mind:

2 That you may be mindful of those words which I told you before from the holy prophets, and of your apostles, of the precepts of the Lord and Saviour.

3 Knowing this first, *h* that in the last days there shall come deceitful scoffers, walking after their own lusts,

4 Saying: 'Where is his promise or his coming? for since the time that the fathers slept, all things continue as they were from the beginning of the creation.

5 For this they are wilfully ignorant of, that the heavens were before, and the earth, out of water, and through water, consisting by the word of God.

6 Whereby the world that

---

*a* Jude 11.—*b* Num. 22. 28.—*c* Jude 12.—*d* John 8. 34. Rom. 6. 16. and 20.—*e* Heb. 6. 4.—*f* Matt. 12. 45.

that is, the short delights of this world, in which they place all their happiness.

*g* Prov. 26. 11.—*h* 1 Tim. 4. 1. 2 Tim. 3. 1. Jude 18.—*i* Eccch. 12. 27.

men was, being overflowed with water, perished.

7 But the heavens and the earth, which are now, by the same word are kept in store, reserved unto fire against the day of judgment and perdition of the ungodly men.

8 But of this one thing be not ignorant, my beloved, that one day with the Lord is as a thousand years, and a thousand years as one day.

9 The Lord delayeth not his promise, as some imagine: but dealeth patiently for your sake, not willing that any should perish, but that all should return to penance.

10 ᵃ But the day of the Lord shall come as a thief, in which the heavens shall pass away with great violence, and the elements shall be melted with heat, and the earth and the works which are in it shall be burnt up.

11 Seeing then that all these things are to be dissolved, what manner of people ought you to be in holy conversation and godliness.

12 Looking for and hasting unto the coming of the day of the Lord, by which the heavens being on fire shall be dissolved, and the elements shall melt with the burning heat.

13 ᵇ But we look for new heavens and a new earth according to his promises, in which justice dwelleth.

14 Wherefore, dearly beloved, seeing that you look for these things, be diligent that ye may be found undefiled and unspotted to him in peace.

15 ᶜ And account the longsuffering of our Lord salvation, as also our most dear brother Paul, according to the wisdom given him, hath written to you:

16 As also in all *his* epistles, speaking in them of these things; in which are certain things hard to be understood, which the unlearned and unstable wrest, as they do also the other scriptures, to their own destruction.

17 You therefore, brethren, knowing these things before, take heed, lest being led aside by the error of the unwise, you fall from your own steadfastness.

18 But grow in grace, and in the knowledge of our Lord and Saviour JESUS CHRIST. To him be glory both now and unto the day of eternity. Amen.

---

ᵃ 1 Thess. 5. 2. Apoc. 3. 3. and 16. 15.

ᵇ Isaias 65. 17. and 66. 22. Apoc. 21. 1.—ᶜ Rom. 2. 4.

## THE
# FIRST EPISTLE OF ST. JOHN THE APOSTLE.

---

*The same vein of divine love and charity towards our neighbour, which runs throughout the Gospel written by the beloved disciple and evangelist, St. John, is found also in his Epistles. He confirms the two principal mysteries of our faith: the mystery of the Trinity, and the mystery of the incarnation of Jesus Christ the Son of God. The sublimity and excellence of the evangelical doctrine he declares: And this commandment we have from God, that he, who loveth God, love also his brother (chap. iv. 21); and again: For this is the charity of God, that we keep his commandments; and his commandments are not heavy (chap. v. 3). He shews how to distinguish the children of God from those of the devil: marks out those who should be called Antichrists: describes the turpitude and gravity of sin. Finally, he shews how the sinner may hope for pardon. It was written, according to Baronius' account, sixty-six years after our Lord's Ascension.*

---

## CHAP. I.

*He declares what he has seen and heard of Christ, (who is the life eternal,) to the end that we may have fellowship with God, and all good through him, yet so if we confess our sins.*

THAT which was from the beginning, which we have heard, which we have seen with our eyes, which we have looked upon, and our hands have handled, of the word of life:

2 For the life was manifested: and we have seen, and do bear witness, and declare unto you the life eternal, which was with the Father, and hath appeared to us:

3 That which we have seen and have heard, we declare unto you, that you also may have fellowship with us, and our fellowship may be with the Father, and with his Son JESUS CHRIST.

4 And these things we write to you, that you may rejoice, and your joy may be full.

5 And this is the declaration which we have heard from him, and declare unto you: *a* That God is light, and in him there is no darkness.

6 If we say that we have fellowship with him, and walk in darkness, we lie, and do not the truth.

7 But if we walk in the light, as he also is in the light, we have fellowship one with another, *b* and the blood of JESUS CHRIST his Son cleanseth us from all sin.

8 *c* If we say that we have no sin, we deceive ourselves, and the truth is not in us.

9 If we confess our sins, he is faithful and just, to forgive us our sins, and to cleanse us from all iniquity.

10 If we say that we have not sinned, we make him a liar, and his word is not in us.

---

*a* John 8. 12.—*b* Heb. 9. 14. 1 Pet. 1. 19. Apoc. 1. 5.—*c* 3 Kings 8. 46. 2 Par. 6. 36. Prov. 20. 9. Eccl. 7. 21.

ST. PAUL PREACHES TO THE ATHENIANS.

## CHAP. II.

*Christ is our advocate: we must keep his commandments, and love one another. We must not love the world, nor give ear to new teachers; but abide by the Spirit of God in the Church.*

MY little children, these things I write to you that you may not sin. But if any man sin, we have an advocate with the Father, JESUS CHRIST the just:

2 And he is the propitiation for our sins; and not for ours only, but also for those of the whole world.

3 And by this we know that we have known him, if we keep his commandments.

4 He who saith that he knoweth him, and keepeth not his commandments, is a liar, and the truth is not in him:

5 But he that keepeth his word, in him in very deed the charity of God is perfected: and by this we know that we are in him.

6 He that saith he abideth in him, ought himself also to walk, even as he walked.

7 Dearly beloved, I write not a new commandment to you, but an old commandment which you had from the beginning. The old commandment is the word which you have heard.

8 ᵃ Again a new command-ment I write unto you, which thing is true both in him and in you: because the darkness is passed, and the true light now shineth.

9 He that saith he is in the light, and hateth his brother, is in darkness even until now.

10 ᵇ He that loveth his brother, abideth in the light, and there is no scandal in him.

11 But he that hateth his brother is in darkness, and walketh in darkness, and knoweth not whither he goeth: because the darkness hath blinded his eyes.

12 I write unto you, little children, because your sins are forgiven you for his name's sake.

13 I write unto you, fathers, because you have known him, who is from the beginning. I write unto you, young men, because you have overcome the wicked one.

14 I write unto you, babes, because you have known the Father. I write unto you, young men, because you are strong, and the word of God abideth in you, and you have overcome the wicked one.

15 Love not the world, nor the things which are in the world. If any man love the world, the charity of the Father is not in him.

16 For all that is in the world is the concupiscence of the flesh, and the concupiscence of the eyes, and the pride of life, which is not of the Father, but is of the world.

17 And the world passeth away, and the concupiscence thereof. But he that doth

---

ᵃ John 13. 34. and 15. 12.

CHAP. II. Ver. 3. *We have known him. If we keep his commandments.* He speaks of that *practical knowledge* by love and affection, which can only be proved by our keeping his commandments; and without which we cannot be said to know God, as we should do.

Ver. 8. *A new commandment Viz.*, the commandment of love, which was first given in the old law, but was renewed and extended by Christ. See John xiii. 34.

ᵇ Infra, 3. 14.

the will of God, abideth for ever.

18 Little children, it is the last hour: and as you have heard that Antichrist cometh: even now there are become many Antichrists: whereby we know that it is the last hour.

19 They went out from us; but they were not of us. For if they had been of us, they would no doubt have remained with us: but that they may be manifest, that they are not all of us.

20 But you have the unction from the Holy One, and know all things.

21 I have not written to you as to them that know not the truth, but as to them that know it: and that no lie is of the truth.

22 Who is a liar, but he who denieth that JESUS is the Christ? this is Antichrist, who denieth the Father and the Son.

23 Whosoever denieth the Son, the same hath not the Father. He that confesseth the Son hath the Father also.

24 As for you, let that which you have heard from the beginning, abide in you. If that abide in you, which you have heard from the beginning, you also shall abide in the Son, and in the Father.

25 And this is the promise which he hath promised us, life everlasting.

26 These things have I written to you, concerning them that seduce you.

27 And as for you, let the unction which you have received from him abide in you. And you have no need that any man teach you: but as his unction teacheth you of all things, and is truth, and is no lie. And as it hath taught you, abide in him.

28 And now, little children, abide in him, that when he shall appear we may have confidence, and not be confounded by him at his coming.

29 If you know that he is just, know ye that every one also who doth justice is born of him.

## CHAP. III.

*Of the love of God to us; how we may distinguish the children of God and those of the devil. Of loving one another, and of purity of conscience.*

BEHOLD what manner of charity the Father hath bestowed upon us, that we should be called, and should be the sons of God. Therefore the

---

Ver. 18. *It is the last hour.* That is, it is the last age of the world.—Ibid. *Many Antichrists.* That is, many heretics, enemies of Christ and his Church, and forerunners of the great Antichrist.

Ver. 19. *They were not of us.* That is, they were not solid, steadfast, genuine Christians; otherwise they would have remained in the Church.

Ver. 20. *The unction from the Holy One.* That is, grace and wisdom from the Holy Ghost.—Ibid. *Know all things.* The true children of God's Church, remaining in unity, under the guidance of their lawful pastors, partake of the grace of the Holy Ghost, promised to the Church and her pastors; and have in the Church all necessary knowledge and instruction: so as to have no need to seek it elsewhere, since it can only be found in that society of which they are members.

Ver. 27. *You have no need, &c.* You want not to be taught by any of these men, who, under pretence of imparting more knowledge to you, seek to seduce you (ver. 26), since you are sufficiently taught already, and have all knowledge and grace in the Church, with the unction of the Holy Ghost, which these new teachers have no share in.

world knoweth not us, because it knew not him.

2 Dearly beloved, we are now the sons of God; and it hath not yet appeared what we shall be. We know that, when he shall appear, we shall be like to him: because we shall see him as he is.

3 And every one that hath this hope in him sanctifieth himself, as he also is holy.

4 Whosoever committeth sin, committeth also iniquity: and sin is iniquity.

5 And you know that he appeared to take away our sins: *a* and in him there is no sin.

6 Whosoever abideth in him, sinneth not: and whosoever sinneth, hath not seen him, nor known him.

7 Little children, let no man deceive you. He that doth justice, is just: even as he is just.

8 *b* He that committeth sin is of the devil: for the devil sinneth from the beginning. For this purpose the Son of God appeared, that he might destroy the works of the devil.

9 Whosoever is born of God, committeth not sin: for his seed abideth in him, and he cannot sin, because he is born of God.

10 In this the children of God are manifest, and the children of the devil. Whosoever is not just, is not of God, nor he that loveth not his brother.

11 For this is the declaration, which you have heard from the beginning, *c* that you should love one another.

12 Not as *d* Cain, who was of the wicked one, and killed his brother. And wherefore did he kill him? Because his own works were wicked, and his brother's just.

13 Wonder not, brethren, if the world hate you.

14 We know that we have passed from death to life, because we love the brethren. *e* He that loveth not, abideth in death.

15 Whosoever hateth his brother is a murderer. And you know that no murderer hath eternal life abiding in himself.

16 *f* In this we have known the charity of God, because he hath laid down his life for us: and we ought to lay down our lives for the brethren.

17 *g* He that hath the substance of this world, and shall see his brother in need, and shall put up his bowels from him: how doth the charity of God abide in him?

18 My little children, let us not love in word, nor in tongue, but in deed, and in truth.

19 In this we know that we are of the truth, and in his sight shall persuade our hearts.

20 For if our heart reprehend us, God is greater than

---

*a* Isaias 53. 9. 1 Pet. 2. 22.—*b* John 8. 44.

---

CHAP. III Ver. 4. *Iniquity*, ἀνομία, transgression of the law.

Ver. 6. *Sinneth not.* Viz, mortally. See chap. i. 8.

Ver. 9. *Committeth not sin:* that is, as long as he keepeth in himself this seed of grace, and this divine generation, by which he is born of God. But then he may fall from this happy state by the abuse of his free will, as appears from *Rom.* xi. 20-22. 1 *Cor.* ix. 27, chap. x. 12. *Philip.* ii. 12. *Apoc.* iii. 11.

*c* John 13. 34. and 15. 12.—*d* Gen. 4. 8.—*e* Lev. 19. 17. Supra, 2. 10.—*f* John 15. 13.—*g* Luke 3. 11. Jas. 2. 15.

our heart, and knoweth all things.

21 Dearly beloved, if our heart do not reprehend us, we have confidence towards God:

22 *a* And whatsoever we shall ask, we shall receive of him: because we keep his commandments, and do those things which are pleasing in his sight.

23 *b* And this is his commandment, that we should believe in the name of his Son JESUS CHRIST: and love one another, as he hath given commandment unto us.

24 *c* And he that keepeth his commandments abideth in him, and he in him. And in this we know that he abideth in us, by the Spirit which he hath given us.

## CHAP. IV.

*What spirits are of God, and what not. We must love one another, because God has loved us.*

DEARLY beloved, believe not every spirit, but try the spirits if they be of God: because many false prophets are gone out into the world.

2 By this is the spirit of God known. Every spirit, which confesseth that JESUS CHRIST is come in the flesh, is of God:

3 And every spirit that dissolveth JESUS is not of God: and this is Antichrist, of whom you have heard that he cometh, and he is now already in the world.

4 You are of God, little children, and have overcome him. Because greater is he that is in you, than he that is in the world.

5 *d* They are of the world: therefore of the world they speak, and the world heareth them.

6 We are of God. He that knoweth God heareth us. He that is not of God heareth us not. By this we know the spirit of truth and the spirit of error.

7 Dearly beloved, let us love one another: for charity is of God. And every one that loveth is born of God, and knoweth God.

8 He that loveth not, knoweth not God: for God is charity.

9 *e* By this hath the charity of God appeared towards us, because God hath sent his only begotten Son into the world, that we may live by him.

10 In this is charity: not as though we had loved God, but because he hath first loved us, and sent his Son to be a propitiation for our sins.

---

*a* Matt. 21. 22.—*b* John 6. 29. and 17. 3.—*c* John 15. 34. and 15. 12.

CHAP. IV. Ver. 1. *Try the spirits.* Viz. by examining whether their teaching be agreeable to the rule of the Catholic faith and the doctrine of the Church. For as he says, ver. 6, *He that knoweth God heareth us,* [the pastors of the Church.] *By this we know the spirit of truth and the spirit of error.*

Ver. 2. *Every spirit which confesseth, &c.* Not that the confession of this point of faith alone is, at all times and in all cases, sufficient; but that with relation to that time, and for that part of the Christian doctrine which was then particularly to be confessed, taught, and maintained against

---

*d* John 8. 47.—*e* John 3. 16.

the heretics of those days, this was the most proper token by which the true teachers might be distinguished from the false.

Ver. 3. *That dissolveth Jesus.* Viz. either by denying his humanity or his divinity.—Ibid. *He is now already in the world.* Not in his person, but in his spirit and in his precursors.

11 My dearest, if God hath so loved us, we also ought to love one another.

12 *a* No man hath seen God at any time. If we love one another, God abideth in us, and his charity is perfected in us.

13 In this we know that we abide in him, and he in us; because he hath given us of his spirit.

14 And we have seen and do testify, that the Father hath sent his Son *to be* the Saviour of the world.

15 Whosoever shall confess that Jesus is the Son of God, God abideth in him, and he in God.

16 And we have known, and have believed the charity which God hath to us. God is charity: and he that abideth in charity abideth in God, and God in him.

17 In this is the charity of God perfected with us, that we may have confidence in the day of judgment: because as he is, we also are in this world.

18 Fear is not in charity: but perfect charity casteth out fear, because fear hath pain. And he that feareth is not perfected in charity.

19 Let us therefore love God, because God first hath loved us.

20 If any man say, I love God and hateth his brother, he is a liar. For he that loveth not his brother, whom he seeth, how can he love God, whom he seeth not?

21 *b* And this commandment we have from God, that he who loveth God, love also his brother.

## CHAP. V.

*Of them that are born of God, and of true charity. Faith overcomes the world. Three that bear witness to Christ. Of faith in his name, and of sin that is, and is not to death.*

WHOSOEVER believeth that Jesus is the Christ is born of God. And every one that loveth him who begot, loveth him also who is born of him.

2 In this we know that we love the children of God: when we love God and keep his commandments.

3 For this is the charity of God, that we keep his commandments: and his commandments are not heavy.

4 For whatsoever is born of God overcometh the world: and this is the victory which overcometh the world, our faith.

---

*b* John 13. 34. and 15. 12. Ephes. 5. 2.

---

*a* John 1. 18. 1 Tim. 6. 16.

---

Ver. 18. *Fear is not in charity, &c.* Perfect charity, or love, banisheth human *fear*, that is, the fear of man; as also all *perplexing fear*, which makes men distrust or despair of God's mercy; and that kind of *servile fear* which makes them fear the punishment of sin more than the offence offered to God. But it in no way excludes the wholesome *fear of God's judgments*, so often recommended in holy writ: nor that *fear and trembling* with which we are told to work out our salvation. Phil. ii. 12.

CHAP V. Ver. 1. *Is born of God;* that is, is justified, and become a child of God by baptism: which is also to be understood; provided the belief of this fundamental article of the Christian faith be accompanied with all the other conditions, which, by the word of God and his appointment, are also required to justification; such as a general belief of all that God has revealed and promised: hope, love, repentance, and a sincere disposition to keep God's holy law and commandments.

Ver. 4. *Our faith:* not a bare speculative or dead faith, but a *faith that worketh by charity.* Gal. v. 6.

## I. OF ST. JOHN. CHAP. V.

5 ᵃ Who is he that overcometh the world but he that believeth that JESUS is the Son of God?

6 This is he that came by water and blood, JESUS CHRIST: not by water only, but by water and blood. And it is the Spirit which testifieth that Christ is the truth.

7 And there are three who give testimony in heaven, the Father, the Word, and the Holy Ghost. And these three are one.

8 And there are three that give testimony on earth: the spirit, and the water, and the blood, and these three are one.

9 If we receive the testimony of men, the testimony of God is greater. For this is the testimony of God, which is greater, because he hath testified of his Son.

10 He that believeth in the Son of God hath the testimony of God in himself. ᵇ He that believeth not the Son, maketh him a liar: because he believeth not in the testimony which God hath testified of his Son.

11 And this is the testimony, that God hath given to us eternal life. And this life is in his Son.

12 He that hath the Son hath life. He that hath not the Son hath not life.

13 These things I write to you, that you may know that you have eternal life, you who believe in the name of the Son of God.

14 And this is the confidence which we have towards him: That whatsoever we shall ask according to his will, he heareth us.

15 And we know that he heareth us whatsoever we ask; we know that we have the petitions which we request of him.

16 He that knoweth his brother to sin a sin *which is* not to death, let him ask, and life shall

---

ᵃ 1 John 4. 15.—ᵇ John 3. 36.

Ver. 6. *Came by water and blood:* not only to wash away our sins by the *water* of baptism, but by his own *blood.*

Ver. 8. *The spirit, and the water, and the blood.* As the Father, the Word, and the Holy Ghost, all bear witness to Christ's divinity; so the *spirit* which he yielded up, crying out with a loud voice upon the cross, and the water and blood that issued from his side, bear witness to his humanity, and *are one;* that is, all agree in one testimony.

Ver. 10. *He that believeth not the Son, &c.* By refusing to believe the testimonies given by the three divine persons, that Jesus was the Messias, and the true Son of God, by whom eternal *life* is obtained and promised to all that comply with his doctrine. In him we have also this lively *confidence,* that we shall obtain whatever we ask, according to his will, when we ask what is for our good with perseverance, and in the manner we ought: And this we *know,* and have experience of, by having obtained the *petitions* that we have made.

Ver. 16. *A sin* which *is not to death, &c.* It is hard to determine what St. John here calls a sin *which is not to death,* and a sin which is *unto death.* The difference cannot be the same as betwixt sins that are called *venial* and *mortal:* for he says that if a man pray for his brother who commits a sin that *is not to death, life shall be given him:* therefore such a one had before lost the life of grace, and been guilty of what is commonly called a *mortal* sin. And when he speaks of a sin that *is unto death,* and adds these words, *for that I say not that any man ask,* it cannot be supposed that St. John would say this of every mortal sin, but only of some heinous sins, which are very seldom remitted, because such sinners very seldom repent. *By a sin therefore which is unto death,* interpreters commonly understand a wilful apostasy from the faith, and

ST. PAUL'S DEPARTURE FROM EPHESUS.

be given to him, who sinneth not to death. There is a sin unto death: for that I say not that any man ask.

---

from the known truth, when a sinner, hardened by his own ingratitude, becomes deaf to all admonitions, will do nothing for himself, but runs on to a final impenitence. Nor yet does St. John say that such a sin is never remitted, or cannot be remitted, but only has these words, *for that I say not that any man ask* the remission: that is, though we must pray for all sinners whatsoever, yet men cannot pray for such sinners with such a *confidence* of obtaining always their *petitions*, as St. John said before, ver. 14.

Whatever exposition we follow on this verse, our faith teaches us from the holy scriptures that God *desires not the death* of any sinner, but that he be *converted and live*, Ezech. xxxiii. 11. Though men's *sins be as red as scarlet, they shall become as white as snow,* Isaias iii. 18. *It is the will of God that every one come to the knowledge of the truth* and be *saved*. There is no sin so great but which God is willing to forgive, and has left a power in his Church to remit the most enormous sins; so that no sinner need despair of pardon, nor will any sinner perish but by his own fault.—Ibid. *A sin unto death.* Some understand this of *final impenitence*, or of dying in mortal sin, which is the only sin that never can be remitted. But, it is probable, he may also comprise under this name the sin of apostacy from the faith, and some other such heinous sins as are seldom and hardly remitted: and therefore he gives little encouragement to such as pray for these sinners, to expect what they ask.

17 All iniquity is sin. And there is a sin unto death.
18 We know that whosoever is born of God, sinneth not; but the generation of God preserveth him, and the wicked one toucheth him not.
19 We know that we are of God, and the whole world is seated in wickedness.
20 And we know that the Son of God is come; *a* and he hath given us understanding, that we may know the true God, and may be in his true Son. This is the true God, and life eternal.
21 Little children, keep yourselves from idols. Amen.

---

*a* Luke 24. 45.

Ver. 19. *And the whole world is seated in wickedness,* i.e., a great part of the world. It may also signify, *is under the wicked one*, meaning the devil, who is elsewhere called the prince of this world, that is, of all the wicked. —John xii. 31.

Ver. 20. *And may be in his true Son. He is,* or, *this is the true God and life eternal.* Which words are a clear proof of Christ's divinity, and as such, made use of by the ancient fathers.

Ver. 21. *Keep yourselves from idols.* An admonition to the newly-converted Christians, lest conversing with heathens and idolaters, they might fall back into the sin of idolatry, which may be the sin unto death here mentioned by St. John.

# THE SECOND EPISTLE OF ST. JOHN THE APOSTLE.

*The Apostle commends ELECTA and her family for their steadfastness in the true faith, and exhorts them to persevere, lest they lose the reward of their labours. He exhorts them to love one another, but with heretics to have no society, even not to salute them. Although this Epistle is written to a particular person, yet its instructions may serve as a lesson to others, especially to those who, from their connexions, situation, or condition of life, are in danger of perversion.*

## CHAP. I.

*He recommends walking in truth, loving one another, and to beware of false teachers.*

THE ancient to the lady Elect, and her children, whom I love in the truth, and not I only, but also all they that have known the truth,

2 For the sake of the truth, which dwelleth in us, and shall be with us for ever.

3 Grace be with you, mercy, and peace from God the Father, and from CHRIST JESUS the Son of the Father, in truth and charity.

4 I was exceeding glad that I found of thy children walking in truth, as we have received a commandment from the Father.

5 And now I beseech thee, lady, not as writing a new commandment to thee, but that which we have had from the beginning, *a* that we love one another.

6 And this is charity, that we walk according to his commandments. For this is the commandment, that, as you have heard from the beginning, you should walk in the same.

7 For many seducers are gone out into the world, who confess not that JESUS CHRIST is come in the flesh: this is a seducer and an antichrist.

8 Look to yourselves, that you lose not the things which you have wrought: but that you may receive a full reward.

9 Whosoever revolteth, and continueth not in the doctrine of Christ, hath not God. He that continueth in the doctrine, the same hath both the Father and the Son.

10 If any man come to you, and bring not this doctrine, re-

---

Ver. 1. *The ancient;* that is, the ancient bishop St. John, being the only one of the twelve apostles then living. *To the lady Elect.* Some conjecture that *Electa* might be the name of a family or of a particular church; but the general opinion is, that it is the proper name of a lady so eminent for her piety and great charity as to merit this Epistle from St. John.

---

*a* John 13. 34. and 15. 12.

Ver. 10. *Nor say to him, God speed you.* This admonition is, in general, to forewarn the faithful of the dangers which may arise from a familiarity ceive him not into the house, nor say to him, God speed you.

11 For he that saith unto him, God speed you, communicateth with his wicked works.

12 Having more things to write unto you, I would not by paper and ink: for I hope that I shall be with you, and speak face to face, that your joy may be full.

13 The children of thy sister Elect salute thee.

with those who have prevaricated and gone from the true faith, and with such as teach false doctrine. But this is not forbidding a charity for all men, by which we ought to wish and pray for the eternal salvation of every one, even of our enemies.

---

# THE THIRD EPISTLE OF ST. JOHN THE APOSTLE.

*St. John praises Gaius for his walking in truth, and for his charity: complains of the bad conduct of Diotrephes, and gives a good testimony to Demetrius.*

## CHAP. I.

THE ancient to the dearly beloved Gaius, whom I love in truth.

2 Dearly beloved, concerning all things I make *it* my prayer that thou mayest proceed prosperously, and fare well as thy soul doth prosperously.

3 I was exceeding glad when the brethren came, and gave testimony to the truth in thee, even as thou walkest in the truth.

4 I have no greater grace than this, to hear that my children walk in truth.

5 Dearly beloved, thou dost faithfully whatever thou dost for the brethren, and that for strangers,

6 Who have given testimony to thy charity in the sight of the church: whom thou shalt do well to bring forward on their way in a manner worthy of God.

7 Because, for his name, they went out, taking nothing of the gentiles.

8 We therefore ought to receive such that we may be fellow-helpers of the truth.

Ver. 4. *No greater grace*: that is, nothing that gives me greater joy and satisfaction.

Ver. 7. *Taking nothing of the gentiles.* These ministers of the gospel are commended by St. John, who took nothing from the gentiles, lest they should seem to preach in order to get money by it.

9 I had written perhaps to the church, but Diotrephes, who loveth to have the preeminence among them, doth not receive us.

10 For this cause, if I come, I will advertise his works which he doth; with malicious words prating against us. And as if these things were not enough for him, neither doth he himself receive the brethren, and them that do receive them he forbiddeth, and casteth out of the church.

---

Ver. 9. *Diotrephes, who loveth, &c.* This man seemeth to be in power, but not a friend to the faithful; therefore this part of the letter might be an admonition to him from the Apostle.

11 Dearly beloved, follow not that which is evil, but that which is good. He that doth good is of God: he that doth evil hath not seen God.

12 To Demetrius testimony is given by all, and by the truth itself, yea and we *also* give testimony: and thou knowest that our testimony is true.

13 I had many things to write unto thee; but I would not by ink and pen write to thee.

14 But I hope speedily to see thee, and we will speak mouth to mouth. Peace be to thee. Our friends salute thee. Salute the friends by name.

---

THE

# CATHOLIC EPISTLE OF ST. JUDE THE APOSTLE.

---

ST. JUDE, *who wrote this Epistle, was one of the twelve Apostles, and brother to* ST. JAMES THE LESS. *The time it was written is uncertain, only it may be inferred from ver. 17, that few or none of the Apostles were then living except* ST. JUDE. *He inveighs against the heresies and wicked practices of the Simonians, Nicolaites, and Gnostics, &c., describing them and their leaders by strong epithets and similes. He exhorts the faithful to contend earnestly for the faith first delivered to them, and to beware of heretics.*

---

## CHAP. I.

*He exhorts them to stand to the faith first delivered to them, and to beware of heretics.*

JUDE, the servant of JESUS CHRIST, and brother of James: to them that are beloved in God the Father, and preserved in JESUS CHRIST, and called.

2 Mercy unto you, and peace and charity be fulfilled.

3 Dearly beloved, taking all care to write unto you concerning your common salvation, I was under a necessity to write unto you: to beseech you to contend earnestly for the faith once delivered to the saints.

4 For certain men are secretly entered in,(who were written of long ago unto this judgment,) ungodly men, turning the grace of our Lord God unto riotousness, and denying the only Sovereign Ruler, and our Lord JESUS CHRIST.

5 I will therefore admonish you, *though* ye once knew all things, that JESUS, having saved the people out of the land of Egypt, *a* did afterwards destroy them that believed not:

6 And the angels who kept not their principality, but forsook their own habitation, *b* he hath reserved under darkness in everlasting chains, unto the judgment of the great day.

7 As Sodom and Gomorrha, and the neighbouring cities, in like manner, having given themselves to fornication, and going after other flesh, were made an example, suffering the punishment of eternal fire,

8 In like manner these men also defile the flesh, and despise dominion, and blaspheme majesty.

9 *c* When Michael the Archangel, disputing with the devil, contended about the body of Moses, he durst not bring against him the judgment of railing speech, but said: The Lord command thee.

10 But these men blaspheme whatever things they know not: and what things soever they naturally know, like dumb beasts, in these they are corrupted.

11 Wo unto them, for they have gone in the way of *d* Cain: and after the *e* error of Balaam, they have for reward poured out themselves, *f* and have perished in the contradiction of Core.

12 These are spots in their banquets, feasting together without fear, feeding themselves, *g* clouds without water which are carried about by winds, trees of the autumn unfruitful, twice dead, plucked up by the roots,

13 Raging waves of the sea, foaming out their own confusion, wandering stars: to whom the storm of darkness is reserved for ever.

14 Now of these Enoch also, the seventh from Adam, prophesied, saying: *h* Behold, the Lord cometh with thousands of his saints,

15 To execute judgment upon

---

*a* Num. 14. 37.—*b* 2 Pet. 2. 4. Gen. 19. 20.—*c* Zach. 3. 2.

*d* Gen. 4. 8.—*e* Num. 22. 21.—*f* Num. 16. 32.—*g* 2 Pet. 2. 17.—*h* Apoc. 1. 7.

---

Ver. 6. *Principality,* that is, the state in which they were first created, their original dignity.

Ver. 8. *Blaspheme majesty.* Speak evil of them that are in dignity; and even utter blasphemies against the divine majesty.

Ver. 9. *Contended about the body, &c.* This contention, which is nowhere else mentioned in holy writ, was originally known by revelation, and transmitted by tradition. It is thought the occasion of it was that the devil would have had the body buried in such a place and manner as to be worshipped by the Jews with divine honours.—Ibid. *Command thee;* or, *rebuke thee.*

Ver. 11. *Gone in the way, &c.* Heretics follow the way of Cain, by murdering the souls of their brethren the way of Balaam, by putting a scandal before the people of God, for their own private ends; and the way of Core or Korah, by their opposition to the Church governors of divine appointment.

Ver. 14. *Prophesied.* This prophecy was either known by tradition or from some book that is since lost.

all, and to reprove all the ungodly for all the works of their ungodliness, whereby they have done ungodly, and of all the hard things which ungodly sinners have spoken against God.

16 These are murmurers, full of complaints, walking according to their own desires, *a* and their mouth speaketh proud things, admiring persons for gain's sake.

17 But you, my dearly beloved, be mindful of the words *b* which have been spoken before by the apostles of our Lord JESUS CHRIST.

18 We told you, that in the last time there should come mockers, walking according to their own desires in ungodlinesses.

19 These are they who separate themselves, sensual men, having not the spirit.

20 But you, my beloved, building yourselves upon your most holy faith, praying in the Holy Ghost,

21 Keep yourselves in the love of God, waiting for the mercy of our Lord JESUS CHRIST unto life everlasting.

22 And some indeed reprove, being judged:

23 But others save, pulling *them* out of the fire. And on others have mercy, in fear: hating also the spotted garment which is carnal.

24 Now to him, who is able to preserve you without sin, and to present you spotless before the presence of his glory with exceeding joy in the coming of our Lord JESUS CHRIST,

25 To the only God our Saviour through JESUS CHRIST our Lord, be glory and magnificence, empire and power before all ages, and now, and for all ages of ages. Amen.

---

*a* Ps. 15. 10.—*b* 1 Tim. 4. 1.   2 Tim. 3. 1.   2 Pet. 3. 3.

Ver. 17. *But you, my dearly beloved, be mindful, &c.* He now exhorts the faithful to remain steadfast in the belief and practice of what they had heard from the apostles, who had also foretold that in after times (Lit. in *the last time*) there should be false teachers, *scoffing* and ridiculing all revealed truths, abandoning themselves to their passions and *lusts*; who *separate themselves* from the catholic communion by heresies and schisms. *Sensual men*, carried away and enslaved by the pleasures of the senses.

Ver. 20, 21. *Building yourselves upon your most holy faith.* Raising by your actions a spiritual building, founded, 1st, upon *faith*; 2nd, on the *love of God*; 3rd, upon hope, whilst you are *waiting* for the *mercies* of God and the reward of *eternal life*; 4th, joined with the great duty of prayer.

Ver. 22, 23. *And some indeed reprove, being judged.* He gives them another instruction to practise charity in endeavouring to convert their neighbour, where they will meet with three sorts of persons. 1st, With persons obstinate in their errors and sins: these may be said to be already *judged* and condemned; they are to be sharply reprehended, *reproved*, and if possible, convinced of their error. 2nd, As to others, you must endeavour to *save them by pulling* them, as it were, *out of the fire*, from the ruin they stand in great danger of. 3rd, You must *have mercy on others in fear* when you see them, through ignorance and frailty, in danger of being drawn into the snares of these heretics; with these you must deal more gently and mildly, with a charitable compassion *hating* always, and teaching others to hate the *carnal garment which is spotted*, their sensual and corrupt manners, that defile both the soul and body.

Ver. 24, 25. *Now to him, &c.* St. Jude concludes his epistle with this doxology of praising God, and praying to *the only God our Saviour*, which may either signify God the Father or God as equally agreeing to all the three persons, who are equally the cause of Christ's incarnation and man's salvation, *through Jesus Christ our Lord*, who, being God from eternity, took upon him our human nature, that he might become our Redeemer.

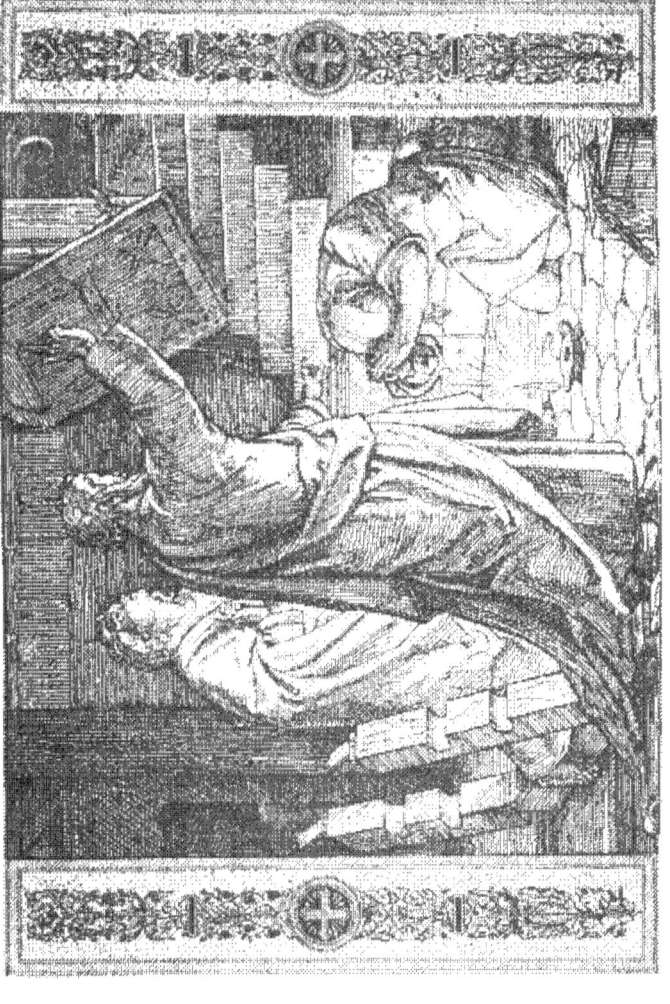

PAUL AND SILAS IN PRISON.—THE PRISON KEEPER BELIEVES.

# THE APOCALYPSE OF ST. JOHN THE APOSTLE.

*In the first, second, and third chapters of this Book are contained instructions and admonitions which St. John was commanded to write to the seven bishops of the churches in Asia. And in the following chapters, to the end, are contained prophecies of things that are to come to pass in the church of Christ, particularly towards the end of the world, in the time of Antichrist. It was written in Greek, in the island of Patmos, where St. John was in banishment by order of the cruel Emperor Domitian, about sixty-four years after our Lord's Ascension.*

## CHAP. I.

*St. John is ordered to write to the seven churches in Asia: the manner of Christ's appearing to him.*

THE Revelation of JESUS CHRIST, which God gave unto him, to make known to his servants the things which must shortly come to pass: and signified, sending by his angel to his servant John,

2 Who hath given testimony to the word of God, and the testimony of JESUS CHRIST, what things soever he hath seen.

3 Blessed is he that readeth and heareth the words of this prophecy: and keepeth those things which are written in it. For the time is at hand.

4 John to the seven churches which are in Asia. Grace be unto you and peace from him *a* that is, and that was, and that is to come, and from the seven spirits which are before his throne.

5 And from JESUS CHRIST, who is the faithful witness, *b* the first begotten of the dead, and the prince of the kings of the earth, who hath loved us, and washed us from our sins *c* in his own blood,

6 And hath made us a kingdom and priests to God and his Father, to him be glory and empire for ever and ever. Amen.

7 *d* Behold, he cometh with the clouds, and every eye shall see him, and they also that pierced him. And all the tribes of the earth shall bewail themselves because of him. Even so. Amen.

---

CHAP. I. Ver. 1. *The things which must shortly come,* and again it is said, ver. 3, *The time is at hand.* This cannot be meant of all the things prophesied in the Apocalypse, where mention is made also of the day of judgment, and of the glory of heaven at the end of the world. That some things were to come to pass shortly is evident by what is said to the Seven Churches, chap. ii. and iii. Or that the persecutions foretold should begin shortly. Or that these words signified that all time is short, and that from the coming of Christ we are now in the last age or *last hour.* See 1 John ii. 18.

*a* Exod. 3. 14.—*b* 1 Cor. 15. 20. Col. 1. 18.—*c* Heb. 9. 14. 1 Pet. 1. 19. 1 John 1. 7.—*d* Isaias 3. 13. Matt. 24. 30. Jude 1. 14.

CHAP. I.   THE APOCALYPSE.   CHAP. II.

8 ᵃI am alpha and omega, the beginning and the end, saith the Lord God, who is and who was, and who is to come, the Almighty.

9 I John, your brother and your partner in tribulation, and in the kingdom, and patience in CHRIST JESUS, was in the island which is called Patmos, for the word of God, and for the testimony of JESUS.

10 I was in the spirit on the Lord's day, and heard behind me a great voice, as of a trumpet,

11 Saying: What thou seest, write in a book: and send to the seven churches which are in Asia, to Ephesus, and to Smyrna, and to Pergamus, and to Thyatira, and to Sardis, and to Philadelphia, and to Laodicea.

12 And I turned to see the voice that spoke with me. And being turned, I saw seven golden candlesticks:

13 And in the midst of the seven golden candlesticks, one like to the Son of man, clothed with a garment down to the feet, and girt about the paps with a golden girdle.

14 And his head and his hairs were white, as white wool, and as snow, and his eyes were as a flame of fire.

---

ᵃ Isaias 41. 4. and 44. 6. and 48. 12. Infra, 21. 6. and 22. 13.

Ver. 8. *I am alpha and omega.* These are the names of the first and last letters of the Greek alphabet, and signify the same as what follows: *The beginning* and *the end;* the first cause and last end of all beings: *who is, and who was, and who is to come, the Almighty.* These words signify the true God only, and are here applied to our Lord and Saviour Jesus Christ, who is to come again to judge the living and the dead.

408

15 And his feet like unto fine brass, as in a burning furnace. And his voice as the sound of many waters.

16 And he had in his right hand seven stars. And from his mouth came out a sharp two-edged sword: and his face was as the sun shining in his power.

17 And when I had seen him, I fell at his feet as dead. And he laid his right hand upon me, saying: Fear not. ᵇI am the first, and the last,

18 And alive, and was dead, and behold I am living for ever and ever, and have the keys of death and of hell.

19 Write, therefore, the things which thou hast seen, and which are, and which must be done hereafter.

20 The mystery of the seven stars which thou sawest in my right hand, and the seven golden candlesticks. The seven stars are the angels of the seven churches. And the seven candlesticks are the seven churches.

## CHAP. II.

*Directions what to write to the angels or bishops of Ephesus, Smyrna, Pergamus, and Thyatira.*

UNTO the angel of the church of Ephesus write: These things saith he, who holdeth the seven stars in his right hand, who walketh in the midst of the seven golden candlesticks:

2 I know thy works, and thy labour, and thy patience, and how thou canst not bear them that are evil, and thou hast tried them who say they are apostles.

---

ᵇ Isaias 41. 4. and 44. 6. and 48. 12. Infra, 21. 6. and 22. 13.

and are not, and hast found them liars:

3 And thou hast patience, and hast endured for my name, and hast not fainted.

4 But I have somewhat against thee, because thou hast left thy first charity.

5 Be mindful therefore from whence thou art fallen: and do penance, and do the first works. Or else I come to thee, and will move thy candlestick out of its place, except thou do penance.

6 But this thou hast, that thou hatest the deeds of the Nicolaites, which I also hate.

7 He that hath an ear, let him hear what the Spirit saith to the churches: To him that overcometh, I will give to eat of the tree of life, which is in the paradise of my God.

8 And to the angel of the church of Smyrna write: These things saith the First and the Last, who was dead, and is alive:

9 I know thy tribulation and thy poverty, but thou art rich: and thou art blasphemed by them that say they are Jews and are not, but are the synagogue of satan.

10 Fear none of those things which thou shalt suffer. Behold, the devil will cast some of you into prison that you may be tried: and you shall have tribulation ten days. Be thou faithful unto death: and I will give thee the crown of life.

11 He that hath an ear, let him hear what the Spirit saith to the churches: He that shall overcome, shall not be hurt by the second death.

12 And to the angel of the church of Pergamus write:

These things saith he, that hath the sharp two-edged sword:

13 I know where thou dwellest, where the seat of satan is: and thou holdest fast my name, and hast not denied my faith. Even in those days *when* Antipas *was* my faithful witness, who was slain among you, where satan dwelleth.

14 But I have against thee a few things: because thou hast there them that hold the doctrine *a* of Balaam, who taught Balac to cast a stumbling-block before the children of Israel, to eat, and to commit fornication:

15 So hast thou also them that hold the doctrine of the Nicolaites.

16 In like manner do penance: or else I will come to thee quickly, and will fight against thee with the sword of my mouth.

17 He that hath an ear, let him hear what the Spirit saith to the churches: To him that overcometh, I will give the hidden manna, and will give him a white counter, and in the counter a new name written, which no man knoweth, but he that receiveth it.

18 And to the angel of the church of Thyatira write: These things saith the Son of God, who hath his eyes like to a flame of fire, and his feet are like to fine brass.

19 I know thy works, and thy faith, and thy charity, and thy ministry, and thy patience, and thy last works which are more than the former.

20 But I have against thee a few things: because thou sufferest the woman Jezabel, who

---

*a* Num. 24. 8. and 25. 2.

calleth herself a prophetess, to teach and to seduce my servants, to commit fornication, and to eat of things sacrificed to idols.

21 And I gave her a time that she might do penance, and she will not repent of her fornication.

22 Behold, I will cast her into a bed: and they that commit adultery with her shall be in very great tribulation, except they do penance from their deeds.

23 And I will kill her children with death, and all the churches shall know *a* that I am he that searcheth the reins and hearts, and I will give to every one of you according to your works. But to you I say,

24 And to the rest who are at Thyatira: Whosoever have not this doctrine, and who have not known the depths of satan, as they say, I will not put upon you any other burthen.

25 Yet that which you have, hold fast till I come.

26 And he that shall overcome and keep my works unto the end, I will give him power over the nations.

27 And he shall rule them with a rod of iron, and as the vessel of a potter they shall be broken,

28 As I also have received of my Father: and I will give him the morning-star.

29 He that hath an ear, let him hear what the Spirit saith to the churches.

## CHAP. III.

*Directions what to write to Sardis, Philadelphia, and Laodicea.*

AND to the angel of the church of Sardis write: These things saith he that hath the seven spirits of God, and the seven stars: I know thy works, that thou hast the name of being alive: and thou art dead.

2 Be watchful and strengthen the things that remain, which are ready to die. For I find not thy works full before my God.

3 Have in mind therefore in what manner thou hast received and heard: and observe, and do penance. If then thou shalt not watch; *b* I will come to thee as a thief, and thou shalt not know at what hour I will come to thee.

4 But thou hast a few names in Sardis, which have not defiled their garments: and they shall walk with me in white, because they are worthy.

5 He that shall overcome shall thus be clothed in white garments, and I will not blot out his name out of the book of life, and I will confess his name before my Father, and before his angels.

6 He that hath an ear, let him hear what the Spirit saith to the churches.

7 And to the angel of the church of Philadelphia write: These things saith the holy one and the true one, *c* he that hath the key of David; he that open-

---

*a* 1 Kings 16. 7. Ps. 7. 10. Jer. 11. 20. and 17. 10. and 20. 12.

CHAP. II. Ver. 26. *Power over the nations.* This shows that the saints, who are with Christ our Lord in heaven, receive power from him to preside over nations and provinces, as patrons, and shall come with him at the end of the world to execute his will against those who have not kept his commandments.

*b* 1 Thess. 5. 2. 2 Pet. 3. 10. Infra, 16. 15.—*c* Isaias 22. 22. Job 12. 14.

eth, and no man shutteth; shutteth, and no man openeth:

8 I know thy works. Behold, I have given before thee a door opened which no man can shut: because thou hast a little strength, and hast kept my word, and hast not denied my name.

9 Behold I will bring of the synagogue of satan, who say they are Jews, and are not, but do lie. Behold, I will make them to come and adore before thy feet. And they shall know, that I have loved thee.

10 Because thou hast kept the word of my patience, I will also keep thee from the hour of temptation, which shall come upon the whole world to try them that dwell upon the earth:

11 Behold, I come quickly: hold fast that which thou hast, that no man take thy crown.

12 He that shall overcome, I will make him a pillar in the temple of my God: and he shall go out no more: and I will write upon him the name of my God, and the name of the city of my God, the new Jerusalem which cometh down out of heaven from my God, and my new name.

13 He that hath an ear, let him hear what the Spirit saith to the churches.

14 And to the angel of the church of Laodicea write: *a* These things saith the Amen, the faithful and true witness, who is the beginning of the creation of God:

15 I know thy works, that thou art neither cold, nor hot. I would thou wert cold, or hot,

16 But because thou art lukewarm, and neither cold, nor hot, I will begin to vomit thee out of my mouth.

17 Because thou sayest: I am rich, and made wealthy, and have need of nothing; and knowest not, that thou art wretched, and miserable, and poor, and blind, and naked.

18 I counsel thee to buy of me gold fire-tried, that thou mayest be made rich: and mayest be clothed in white garments, and that the shame of thy nakedness may not appear: and anoint thy eyes with eye-salve, that thou mayest see.

19 *b* Such as I love, I rebuke and chastise. Be zealous therefore and do penance.

20 Behold, I stand at the gate, and knock. If any man shall hear my voice, and open to me the door, I will come in to him, and will sup with him, and he with me.

21 To him that shall overcome, I will give to sit with me in my throne: as I also have overcome, and am set down with my Father in his throne.

22 He that hath an ear, let him hear what the Spirit saith to the churches.

## CHAP. IV.

*The vision of the throne of God, the twenty-four ancients, and the four living creatures.*

AFTER these things I looked, and behold a door was opened in heaven, and the first

---

*a* John 14. 6.

CHAP. III. Ver. 14. *The Amen*, that is, the true one, the Truth itself; the Word and Son of God.—Ibid. *The beginning*, ἡ ἀρχη, i.e., the principle, the source, and the efficient cause of the whole creation.

*b* Prov. 8. 12. Heb. 12. 6.

CHAP. IV. THE APOCALYPSE. CHAP. V.

voice which I heard, as it were, of a trumpet speaking with me, said: Come up hither, and I will shew thee the things which must be done hereafter.

2 And immediately I was in the spirit: and behold there was a throne set in heaven, and upon the throne one sitting.

3 And he that sat was to the sight like the jasper and the sardine-stone: and there was a rainbow round about the throne, in sight like unto an emerald.

4 And round about the throne were four-and-twenty seats: and upon the seats, four-and-twenty ancients sitting, clothed in white garments, and on their heads *were* crowns of gold.

5 And from the throne proceeded lightnings and voices and thunders: and there were seven lamps burning before the throne, which are the seven spirits of God.

6 And in the sight of the throne was as it were a sea of glass like to crystal: and in the midst of the throne and round about the throne were four living creatures full of eyes before and behind.

7 And the first living creature was like a lion: and the second living creature like a calf: and the third living creature having the face, as it were, of a man: and the fourth living creature was like an eagle flying.

8 And the four living creatures had each of them six wings: and round about and within they are full of eyes. And they rested not day and night, saying, *a* Holy, Holy, Holy, Lord God Almighty, who was, and who is, and who is to come.

9 And when those living creatures gave glory and honour and benediction to him that sitteth on the throne, who liveth for ever and ever,

10 The four-and-twenty ancients fell down before him that sitteth on the throne, and adored him that liveth for ever and ever, and cast their crowns before the throne, saying:

11 Thou art worthy, O Lord our God, to receive glory, and honour, and power: because thou hast created all things, and for thy will they were, and have been created.

CHAP. V.

*The book sealed with seven seals is opened by the Lamb, who thereupon receives adoration and praise from all.*

AND I saw in the right hand of him that sat on the throne, a book, written within and without, sealed with seven seals.

2 And I saw a strong angel, proclaiming with a loud voice: Who is worthy to open the book, and to loose the seals thereof?

3 And no man was able, neither in heaven, nor on earth, nor under the earth, to open the book, nor to look on it.

4 And I wept much, because no man was found worthy to open the book, nor to see it.

5 And one of the ancients said to me: Weep not: behold the lion of the tribe of Juda, the root of David, hath prevailed to open the book, and to loose the seven seals thereof.

6 And I saw, and behold in the midst of the throne and of the four living creatures, and in

---

*a* Isaias 6. 3.

ST. PAUL'S ARRIVAL IN ROME.

the midst of the ancients, a Lamb standing as it were slain, having seven horns and seven eyes: which are the seven Spirits of God, sent forth into all the earth.

7 And he came and took the book out of the right hand of him that sat on the throne.

8 And when he had opened the book, the four living creatures and the four-and-twenty ancients fell down before the Lamb, having every one of them harps, and golden vials full of odours, which are the prayers of saints:

9 And they sung a new canticle, saying: Thou art worthy, O Lord, to take the book, and to open the seals thereof: because thou wast slain, and hast redeemed us to God, in thy blood, out of every tribe, and tongue, and people, and nation.

10 And hast made us to our God a kingdom and priests, and we shall reign on the earth.

11 And I beheld, and I heard the voice of many angels round about the throne, and the living creatures and the ancients: and the number of them was a thousands of thousands,

12 Saying, with a loud voice: The Lamb that was slain is worthy to receive power, and divinity, and wisdom, and strength, and honour, and glory, and benediction.

13 And every creature, which is in heaven, and on the earth, and under the earth, and such as are in the sea, and all that are in them: I heard all saying: To him that sitteth on the throne, and to the Lamb, benediction and honour and glory and power for ever and ever.

14 And the four living creatures said: Amen. And the four-and-twenty ancients fell down on their faces: and adored him that liveth for ever and ever.

## CHAP. VI.

*What followed upon opening six of the seals.*

AND I saw that the Lamb had opened one of the seven seals, and I heard one of the four living creatures, as it were the voice of thunder, saying: Come, and see.

2 And I saw: And behold a white horse, and he that sat on him had a bow, and there was a crown given him, and he went forth conquering that he might conquer.

3 And when he had opened the second seal, I heard the second living creature, saying: Come, and see.

4 And there went out another horse *that was* red: and to him that sat thereon, it was given that he should take peace from the earth, and that they should kill one another, and a great sword was given to him.

5 And when he had opened the third seal, I heard the third living creature, saying: Come,

---

a Dan. 7. 10.

CHAP. V. Ver. 8 *The prayers of saints.* Here we see that the saints in heaven offer up to Christ the prayers of the faithful upon earth.

CHAP. VI. Ver. 2. *White horse.* He that sitteth on the white horse is Christ, going forth to subdue the world by his gospel. The other horses that follow represent the judgments and punishment that were to fall on the enemies of Christ and his Church: the red horse signifies war, the black horse famine, and the pale horse (which has death for its rider) plagues or pestilence.

and see. And behold a black horse, and he that sat on him had a pair of scales in his hand.

6 And I heard as it were a voice in the midst of the four living creatures, saying: Two pounds of wheat for a penny, and thrice two pounds of barley for a penny, and see thou hurt not the wine and the oil.

7 And when he had opened the fourth seal, I heard the voice of the fourth living creature, saying: Come, and see.

8 And behold a pale horse, and he that sat upon him, his name was Death, and hell followed him. And power was given to him over the four parts of the earth, to kill with sword, with famine, and with death, and with the beasts of the earth.

9 And when he had opened the fifth seal, I saw under the altar the souls of them that were slain for the word of God, and for the testimony which they held.

10 And they cried with a loud voice, saying: How long, O Lord, (holy and true,) dost thou not judge and revenge our blood on them that dwell on the earth?

11 And white robes were given to every one of them one: and it was said to them, that they should rest for a little time, till their fellow-servants, and their brethren, who are to be slain, even as they, should be filled up.

12 And I saw, when he had opened the sixth seal, and behold there was a great earthquake, and the sun became black as sackcloth of hair: and the whole moon became as blood:

13 And the stars from heaven fell upon the earth, as the figtree casteth its green figs when it is shaken by a great wind.

14 And the heaven departed as a book folded up: and every mountain, and the islands were moved out of their places.

15 And the kings of the earth, and the princes, and tribunes, and the rich and the strong, and every bondman, and every freeman hid themselves in the dens and in the rocks of mountains.

16 And they say to the mountains and the rocks: ª Fall upon us, and hide us from the face of him that sitteth upon the throne, and from the wrath of the Lamb:

17 For the great day of their wrath is come, and who shall be able to stand?

## CHAP. VII.

*The number of them that were marked with the seal of the living God, and clothed in white robes.*

AFTER these things I saw four Angels standing on the four corners of the earth, holding the four winds of the earth, that they should not blow upon the earth, nor upon the sea, nor on any tree.

2 And I saw another Angel ascending from the rising of

---

Ver. 9. *Under the altar.* Christ, as man, is this altar, under which the souls of the martyrs live in heaven, as their bodies are here deposited under our altars.

Ver. 10. *Revenge our blood.* They ask not this out of hatred to their enemies, but out of zeal for the glory of God, and a desire that the Lord would accelerate the general judgment, and the complete beatitude of all his elect.

---

ª Isaias 2. 19, Osee 10. 8. Luke 23. 30.

the sun, having the sign of the living God; and he cried with a loud voice to the four Angels, to whom it was given to hurt the earth and the sea,

3 Saying: Hurt not the earth, nor the sea, nor the trees. till we sign the servants of our God in their foreheads.

4 And I heard the number of them that were signed, an hundred forty-four thousand were signed, of every tribe of the children of Israel.

5 Of the tribe of Juda *were* twelve thousand signed. Of the tribe of Ruben, twelve thousand signed. Of the tribe of Gad, twelve thousand signed.

6 Of the tribe of Aser, twelve thousand signed. Of the tribe of Nepthali, twelve thousand signed. Of the tribe of Manasses, twelve thousand signed.

7 Of the tribe of Simeon, twelve thousand signed. Of the tribe of Levi, twelve thousand signed. Of the tribe of Issachar, twelve thousand signed.

8 Of the tribe of Zabulon, twelve thousand signed. Of the tribe of Joseph, twelve thousand signed. Of the tribe of Benjamin, twelve thousand signed.

9 After this I saw a great multitude, which no man could number, of all nations, and tribes, and peoples, and tongues, standing before the throne, and in sight of the Lamb, clothed with white robes, and palms in their hands:

10 And they cried with a loud voice, saying: Salvation to our God, who sitteth upon the throne, and to the Lamb.

11 And all the Angels stood round about the throne, and the ancients, and the four living creatures: and they fell down before the throne upon their faces, and adored God,

12 Saying: Amen. Benediction, and glory, and wisdom, and thanksgiving, honour, and power, and strength to our God for ever and ever. Amen.

13 And one of the ancients answered, and said to me: These that are clothed in white robes, who are they? and whence came they?

14 And I said to him: My lord, thou knowest. And he said to me: These are they who are come out of great tribulation, and have washed their robes, and have made them white in the blood of the Lamb.

15 Therefore they are before the throne of God, and they serve him day and night in his temple: and he that sitteth on the throne shall dwell over them.

16 *a* They shall no more hunger nor thirst, neither shall the sun fall on them, nor any heat.

17 For the Lamb, which is in the midst of the throne, shall rule them, and shall lead them to the fountains of the waters of life, *b* and God shall wipe away all tears from their eyes.

## CHAP. VIII.

*The seventh seal is opened: the angels with the seven trumpets.*

AND when he had opened the seventh seal, there was silence in heaven, as it were for half an hour.

2 And I saw seven Angels standing in the presence of God: and there were given to them seven trumpets.

---

*a* Isaias 49. 10.—*b* Isaias 25. 8. Infra, 21. 4.

3 And another Angel came, and stood before the altar, having a golden censer; and there was given to him much incense, that he should offer of the prayers of all saints upon the golden altar, which is before the throne of God.

4 And the smoke of the incense of the prayers of the saints ascended up before God, from the hand of the Angel.

5 And the Angel took the censer, and filled it with the fire of the altar, and cast it on the earth, and there were thunders and voices and lightnings, and a great earthquake.

6 And the seven Angels who had the seven trumpets prepared themselves to sound the trumpet.

7 And the first Angel sounded the trumpet, and there followed hail and fire, mingled with blood, and it was cast on the earth, and the third part of the earth was burnt up, and the third part of the trees was burnt up, and all green grass was burnt up.

8 And the second Angel sounded the trumpet: and as it were a great mountain, burning with fire, was cast into the sea, and the third part of the sea became blood:

9 And the third part of those creatures died which had life in the sea, and the third part of the ships was destroyed.

10 And the third Angel sounded the trumpet, and a great star fell from heaven, burning as it were a torch, and it fell on the third part of the rivers, and upon the fountains of waters:

11 And the name of the star is called Wormwood. And the third part of the waters became wormwood; and many men died of the waters, because they were made bitter.

12 And the fourth Angel sounded the trumpet, and the third part of the sun was smitten, and the third part of the moon, and the third part of the stars, so that the third part of them was darkened, and the day did not shine for a third part of it, and the night in like manner.

13 And I beheld, and heard the voice of one eagle flying through the midst of heaven, saying with a loud voice: Wo, wo, wo to the inhabitants of the earth: by reason of the rest of the voices of the three Angels, who are yet to sound the trumpet.

## CHAP. IX.

*Locusts come forth from the bottomless pit: the vision of the army of horsemen.*

AND the fifth Angel sounded the trumpet, and I saw a star fall from heaven upon the earth, and there was given to him the key of the bottomless pit.

2 And he opened the bottomless pit: and the smoke of the pit arose, as the smoke of a great furnace; and the sun and the air were darkened with the smoke of the pit.

CHAP IX. Ver. 1. *A star fall.* This may mean the fall and apostacy of great and learned men from the true faith; or a whole nation falling into error and separating from the Church, not having the sign of God in their foreheads.—Ibid. *And there was given to him the key of the bottomless pit.* That is, to the *Angel*, not to the *fallen star*. To this Angel was given the power, which is here signified by a *key*, of opening hell.

3 And from the smoke of the pit there came out locusts upon the earth. And power was given to them, as the scorpions of the earth have power.

4 And it was commanded them that they should not hurt the grass of the earth, nor any green thing, nor any tree: but only the men who have not the sign of God on their foreheads.

5 And it was given unto them that they should not kill them; but that they should torment them five months: and their torment was as the torment of a scorpion when he striketh a man.

6 *a* And in those days men shall seek death, and shall not find it; and they shall desire to die, and death shall fly from them.

7 *b* And the shapes of the locusts were like unto horses prepared unto battle: and on their heads were as it were crowns like gold: and their faces were as the faces of men.

8 And they had hair as the hair of women; and their teeth were as lions.

9 And they had breastplates as breastplates of iron, and the noise of their wings was as the noise of chariots and many horses running to battle.

10 And they had tails like to scorpions, and there were stings in their tails: and their power was to hurt men five months. And they had over them

11 A king, the angel of the bottomless pit: whose name in Hebrew is Abaddon, and in Greek Apollyon; in Latin Exterminans *c(That is, destroyer).*

12 One wo is past, and behold there come yet two woes more hereafter.

13 And the sixth Angel sounded the trumpet; and I heard a voice from the four horns of the golden altar, which is before the eyes of God,

14 Saying to the sixth Angel, who had the trumpet: Loose the four angels, who are bound in the great river Euphrates.

15 And the four angels were loosed, who were prepared for an hour, and a day, and a month, and a year: for to kill the third part of men.

16 And the number of the army of horsemen was twenty thousand times ten thousand.

---

*a* Isaias 2. 19. Osee 10. 8. Luke 23. 30.

Ver. 3. *There came out locusts.* These may be devils in Antichrist's time, having the appearance of locusts, but large and monstrous, as here described. Or they may be real locusts, but of an extraordinary size and monstrous shape, such as were never before seen on the earth, sent to torment those *who have not the sign (or seal) of God on their foreheads.* Some commentators by these *locusts* understand heretics, and especially those heretics that sprung from Jews, and with them denied the divinity of Jesus Christ; as Theodotus, Praxeas, Noctus, Paul of Samosata, Sabellius, Arius, &c. These were great enemies of the Christian religion; they tormented and infected the souls of men, stinging them, *like scorpions,* with the poison of their heresies. Others have explained these *locusts,* and other animals, mentioned in different places throughout this sacred and mystical book, in a most absurd, fanciful, and ridiculous manner: they make *Abaddon* the pope, and the *locusts* to be friars, mendicants, &c. Here it is thought proper not to enter into any controversy upon that subject, as the inventors of these fancies have been already answered, and fully refuted by many controvertists: besides, those who might be imposed on by such chimerical writers are in these days much better informed.

*b* Wis. 6. 2.—*c* i.e., the destroyer.

And I heard the number of them.

17 And thus I saw the horses in the vision: and they that sat on them had breastplates of fire and of hyacinth and of brimstone, and the heads of the horses were as the heads of lions: and from their mouths proceeded fire, and smoke, and brimstone.

18 And by these three plagues was slain the third part of men, by the fire, and by the smoke, and by the brimstone, which issued out of their mouths.

19 For the power of the horses is in their mouths and in their tails. For their tails are like to serpents, and have heads: and with them they hurt.

20 And the rest of the men who were not slain by these plagues, did not do penance from the works of their hands, that they should not adore devils and idols of gold, and silver, and brass, and stone, and wood, which neither can see, nor hear, nor walk:

21 Neither did they penance from their murders, nor from their sorceries, nor from their fornications, nor from their thefts.

## CHAP. X.

*The cry of a mighty angel: he gives John a book to eat.*

AND I saw another mighty Angel come down from heaven, clothed with a cloud, and a rainbow *was* on his head, and his face was as the sun, and his feet as pillars of fire.

2 And he had in his hand a little book open: and he set his right foot upon the sea, and his left foot upon the earth.

3 And he cried with a loud voice as when a lion roareth. And when he had cried, seven thunders uttered their voices.

4 And when the seven thunders had uttered their voices, I was about to write: and I heard a voice from heaven, saying to me: Seal up the things which the seven thunders have spoken; and write them not.

5 ᵃ And the Angel, whom I saw standing upon the sea and upon the earth, lifted up his hand to heaven.

6 And he swore by him that liveth for ever and ever, who created heaven, and the things which are therein; and the earth, and the things which are in it; and the sea, and the things which are therein: That time shall be no longer.

7 But in the days of the voice of the seventh Angel, when he shall begin to sound the trumpet, the mystery of God shall be finished, as he hath declared by his servants the prophets.

8 And I heard a voice from heaven again speaking to me, and saying: Go, and take the book that is open, from the hand of the Angel who standeth upon the sea, and upon the earth.

9 And I went to the Angel, saying unto him, that he should give me the book. And he said

---

ᵃ Dan. 12. 7.

CHAP. X. Ver. 7. *Declared:* literally, *evangelized*, to signify the *good tidings*, agreeable to the *Gospel*, of the final victory of Christ, and of that eternal life which should be the reward of the temporal sufferings of the martyrs and faithful servants of God.

REVELATION OF JESUS CHRIST TO ST. JOHN (APOC. I.).

to me: <sup>a</sup> Take the book, and eat it up: and it shall make thy belly bitter, but in thy mouth it shall be sweet as honey.

10 And I took the book from the hand of the Angel, and ate it up: and it was in my mouth, sweet as honey: and when I had eaten it, my belly was bitter.

11 And he said to me: Thou must prophesy again to many nations, and peoples, and tongues, and kings.

## CHAP. XI.

*He is ordered to measure the temple: the two witnesses.*

AND there was given me a reed like unto a rod: and it was said to me: Arise, and measure the temple of God, and the altar, and them that adore therein.

2 But the court which is without the temple, cast out, and measure it not: because it is given unto the gentiles, and the holy city they shall tread under foot two-and-forty months.

3 And I will give unto my two witnesses, and they shall prophesy a thousand two hundred sixty days, clothed in sackcloth.

4 These are the two olive-trees, and the two candlesticks, that stand before the Lord of the earth.

5 And if any man will hurt them, fire shall come out of their mouths, and shall devour their enemies. And if any man will hurt them, in this manner must he be slain.

6 These have power to shut

---

<sup>a</sup> Ezech. 3. 1.

CHAP. XI. Ver. 8. *My two witnesses.* It is commonly understood of Henoch and Elias.

---

heaven, that it rain not in the days of their prophecy: and they have power over waters to turn them into blood, and to strike the earth with all plagues as often as they will.

7 And when they shall have finished their testimony, the beast, that ascended out of the abyss, shall make war against them, and shall overcome them, and kill them.

8 And their bodies shall lie in the streets of the great city, which is called spiritually Sodom and Egypt, where their Lord also was crucified.

9 And they of the tribes, and peoples, and tongues, and nations, shall see their bodies for three days and a half: and they shall not suffer their bodies to be laid in sepulchres.

10 And they that dwell upon the earth shall rejoice over them, and make merry: and shall send gifts one to another, because these two prophets tormented them that dwelt upon the earth.

11 And after three days and a half, the spirit of life from God entered into them. And they stood upon their feet, and great fear fell upon them that saw them.

12 And they heard a great voice from heaven, saying to them: Come up hither. And they went up to heaven in a cloud; and their enemies saw them.

13 And at that hour there was made a great earthquake, and the tenth part of the city fell: and there were slain in the earthquake names of men seven thousand: and the rest were cast into a fear, and gave glory to the God of heaven.

14 The second wo is past; and behold the third wo will come quickly.

15 And the seventh Angel sounded the trumpet: and there were great voices in heaven, saying: The kingdom of this world is become our Lord's and his Christ's, and he shall reign for ever and ever. Amen.

16 And the four-and-twenty ancients, who sit on their seats in the sight of God, fell on their faces and adored God, saying:

17 We give thee thanks, O Lord God Almighty, who art, and who wast, and who art to come: because thou hast taken to thee thy great power, and thou hast reigned.

18 And the nations were angry, and thy wrath is come, and the time of the dead, that they should be judged, and that thou shouldest render reward to thy servants the prophets and the saints, and to them that fear thy name, little and great, and shouldest destroy them who have corrupted the earth.

19 And the temple of God was opened in heaven: and the ark of his testament was seen in his temple, and there were lightnings, and voices, and an earthquake, and great hail.

## CHAP. XII.

*The vision of the woman clothed with the sun; and of the great dragon her persecutor.*

AND a great sign appeared in heaven: a woman clothed with the sun, and the moon under her feet, and on her head a crown of twelve stars:

2 And being with child, she cried travailing in birth, and was in pain to be delivered.

3 And there was seen another sign in heaven: and behold a great red dragon having seven heads, and ten horns: and on his heads seven diadems.

4 And his tail drew the third part of the stars of heaven, and cast them to the earth: and the dragon stood before the woman who was ready to be delivered; that, when she should be delivered, he might devour her son.

5 And she brought forth a man-child, who was to rule all nations with an iron rod: and her son was taken up to God, and to his throne.

6 And the woman fled into the wilderness where she had a place prepared by God, that there they should feed her a thousand two hundred sixty days.

7 And there was a great battle in heaven, Michael and his angels fought with the dragon, and the dragon fought and his angels:

8 And they prevailed not, neither was their place found any more in heaven.

9 And that great dragon was cast out, that old serpent, who is called the devil and satan, who seduceth the whole world: and he was cast unto the earth, and his angels were thrown down with him.

---

CHAP. XII. Ver. 1. *A woman.* The Church of God. It may also, by allusion, be applied to our blessed Lady. The Church is clothed with the sun, that is, with Christ: she hath the moon, that is, the changeable things of the world, under her feet: and the twelve stars with which she is crowned, are the twelve apostles: she is in labour and pain, whilst she brings forth her children, and Christ in them, in the midst of afflictions and persecutions.

10 And I heard a loud voice in heaven saying: Now is come salvation, and strength, and the kingdom of our God, and the power of his Christ: because the accuser of our brethren is cast forth, who accused them before our God day and night.

11 And they overcame him by the blood of the Lamb, and by the word of the testimony, and they loved not their lives unto death.

12 Therefore rejoice, O heavens, and you that dwell therein. Wo to the earth, and to the sea, because the devil is come down unto you, having great wrath, knowing that he hath but a short time.

13 And when the dragon saw that he was cast unto the earth, he persecuted the woman who brought forth the man child:

14 And there were given to the woman two wings of a great eagle, that she might fly into the desert unto her place, where she is nourished for a time and times, and half a time, from the face of the serpent.

15 And the serpent cast out of his mouth after the woman, water as it were a *river; that he might cause her to be carried away by the river.

16 And the earth helped the woman, and the earth opened her mouth and swallowed up the river, which the dragon cast out of his mouth.

17 And the dragon was angry against the woman, and went to make war with the rest of her seed, who keep the commandments of God, and have the testimony of JESUS CHRIST.

18 And he stood upon the sand of the sea.

## CHAP. XIII.

*Of the beast with seven heads; and of a second beast.*

AND I saw a beast coming up out of the sea, having seven heads and ten horns, and upon his horns ten diadems, and upon his heads names of blasphemy.

2 And the beast which I saw, was like to a leopard, and his feet were as the feet of a bear, and his mouth as the mouth of a lion. And the dragon gave him his own strength, and great power.

3 And I saw one of his heads as it were slain to death: and his death's wound was healed. And all the earth was in admiration of the beast.

4 And they adored the dragon, which gave power to the beast: and they adored the beast, saying: Who is like to the beast? and who shall be able to fight with him?

---

CHAP. XIII. Ver. 1. *A beast.* This first beast with seven heads and ten horns, is probably the whole company of infidels, enemies, and persecutors of the people of God, from the beginning to the end of the world. The seven heads are seven kings, that is, seven principal kingdoms or empires, which have exercised, or shall exercise, tyrannical power over the people of God; of these, five were then fallen, viz. the Egyptian, Assyrian, Chaldean, Persian, and Grecian monarchies: one was present, viz. the empire of Rome; and the seventh and chiefest was to come, viz. the great Antichrist and his empire. The ten horns may be understood of ten lesser persecutors.

Ver. 3. *One of his heads, &c.* Some understand this of the mortal wound, which the idolatry of the Roman empire (signified by the sixth head) received from Constantine; which was, as it were, healed again by Julian the apostate.

---

*Or flood.

5 And there was given to him a mouth speaking great things, and blasphemies: and power was given to him to do two-and-forty months.

6 And he opened his mouth unto blasphemies against God, to blaspheme his name, and his tabernacle, and them that dwell in heaven.

7 And it was given unto him to make war with the saints, and to overcome them. And power was given him over every tribe, and people, and tongue, and nation.

8 And all that dwell upon the earth adored him, whose names are not written in the book of life of the Lamb, which was slain from the beginning of the world.

9 If any man have an ear, let him hear.

10 He that shall lead into captivity, shall go into captivity: *a* he that shall kill by the sword, must be killed by the sword. Here is the patience and the faith of the saints.

11 And I saw another beast coming up out of the earth, and he had two horns, like a lamb, and he spoke as a dragon.

12 And he executed all the power of the former beast in his sight: and he caused the earth, and them that dwell therein, to adore the first beast, whose wound to death was healed.

13 And he did great signs, so that he made also fire to come down from heaven unto the earth, in the sight of men.

14 And he seduced them that dwell on the earth, for the signs which were given him to do in the sight of the beast, saying to them that dwell on the earth, that they should make the image of the beast, which had the wound by the sword, and lived.

15 And it was given him to give life to the image of the beast, and that the image of the beast should speak: and should cause, that whosoever will not adore the image of the beast, should be slain.

16 And he shall make all, both little and great, rich and poor, freemen and bondmen, to have a character in their right hand, or on their foreheads.

17 And that no man might buy or sell, but he that hath the character, or the name of the beast, or the number of his name.

18 Here is wisdom. He that hath understanding, let him count the number of the beast. For it is the number of a man: and the number of him is six hundred sixty-six.

*a* Gen. 9. 6. Matt. 26. 52.

Ver. 6. *His tabernacle, &c.* That is, his Church, and his saints.
Ver. 8. *Slain from the beginning, &c.* In the foreknowledge of God; and inasmuch as all mercy and grace, from the beginning, was given in view of his death and passion.
Ver. 11. *Another beast.* This second beast with two horns may be understood of the heathenish priests and magicians, the principal promoters both of idolatry and persecution.

## CHAP. XIV.

*Of the Lamb, and of the virgins that follow him: Of the judgments that shall fall upon the wicked.*

AND I beheld, and lo a Lamb stood upon Mount Sion, and with him an hundred forty-

Ver. 18. *Six hundred sixty-six.* The numeral letters of his name shall make up this number.

four thousand having his name, and the name of his Father written on their foreheads.

2 And I heard a voice from heaven, as the noise of many waters, and as the voice of great thunder: and the voice which I heard was as the voice of harpers harping on their harps.

3 And they sung as it were a new canticle, before the throne, and before the four living creatures, and the ancients; and no man could say the canticle, but those hundred forty-four thousand, who were purchased from the earth.

4 These are they who were not defiled with women: for they are virgins. These follow the Lamb whithersoever he goeth. These were purchased from among men, the first-fruits to God and to the Lamb.

5 And in their mouth there was found no lie: for they are without spot before the throne of God.

6 And I saw another Angel flying through the midst of heaven, having the eternal gospel, to preach unto them that sit upon the earth, and over every nation, and tribe, and tongue, and people:

7 Saying with a loud voice: Fear the Lord and give him honour, because the hour of his judgment is come: and adore ye him, *a* that made heaven and earth, the sea, and the fountains of waters.

8 And another Angel followed, saying: *b* That great Babylon is fallen, is fallen: which made all nations to drink of the wine of the wrath of her fornication.

9 And the third Angel followed them, saying with a loud voice: If any man shall adore the beast and his image, and receive his character in his forehead, or in his hand;

10 He also shall drink of the wine of the wrath of God, which is mingled with pure wine in the cup of his wrath, and shall be tormented with fire and brimstone, in the sight of the holy Angels and in the sight of the Lamb.

11 And the smoke of their torments shall ascend up for ever and ever: neither have they rest day nor night, who have adored the beast, and his image, and whosoever receiveth the character of his name.

12 Here is the patience of the saints, who keep the commandments of God, and the faith of JESUS.

13 And I heard a voice from heaven, saying to me: Write: Blessed are the dead who die in the Lord. From henceforth now, saith the Spirit, that they may rest from their labours, for their works follow them.

14 And I saw, and behold a

---

*a* Ps. 145. 6. Acts 14. 14.—*b* Isaias 21. 9. Jer. 51. 8.

---

CHAP. XIV. Ver. 8. *Babylon.* By Babylon may be very probably signified all the wicked world in general, which God will punish and destroy after the short time of this mortal life: or it may signify every great city wherein enormous sins and abominations are daily committed, and that when the measure of its iniquities is full, the punishments due to its crimes are poured on it. It also may be some city of the description in the text, that will exist, and be destroyed as here described, towards the end of the world.

Ver. 13. *Die in the Lord.* It is understood of the martyrs who die for the Lord.

white cloud; and upon the cloud one sitting like to the Son of man, having on his head a crown of gold, and in his hand a sharp sickle.

15 And another Angel came out from the temple, crying with a loud voice to him that sat upon the cloud: *a* Thrust in thy sickle, and reap, because the hour is come to reap, for the harvest of the earth is ripe.

16 And he that sat on the cloud thrust his sickle into the earth, and the earth was reaped.

17 And another Angel came out of the temple which is in heaven, he also having a sharp sickle.

18 And another Angel came out from the altar, who had power over fire: and he cried with a loud voice to him that had the sharp sickle, saying: Thrust in thy sharp sickle, and gather the clusters of the vineyard of the earth: because the grapes thereof are ripe.

19 And the Angel thrust in his sharp sickle into the earth, and gathered the vineyard of the earth, and cast it into the great press of the wrath of God.

20 And the press was trodden without the city, and blood came out of the press, up to the horses' bridles for a thousand and six hundred furlongs.

## CHAP. XV.

*They that have overcome the beast, glorify God. Of the seven angels with the seven vials.*

AND I saw another sign in heaven great and wonderful: seven Angels having the seven last plagues. For in them is filled up the wrath of God.

2 And I saw as it were a sea of glass mingled with fire, and them that had overcome the beast and his image and the number of his name, standing on the sea of glass, having the harps of God:

3 And singing the canticle of Moses the servant of God and the canticle of the Lamb, saying: Great and wonderful are thy works, O Lord God Almighty: just and true are thy ways, O King of ages.

4 *b* Who shall not fear thee, O Lord, and magnify thy name? For thou only art holy: for all nations shall come, and shall adore in thy sight, because thy judgments are manifest.

5 And after these things I looked, and behold the temple of the tabernacle of the testimony in heaven was opened:

6 And the seven Angels came out of the temple having the seven plagues, clothed with clean and white linen, and girt about the breasts with golden girdles.

7 And one of the four living creatures gave to the seven Angels seven golden vials, full of the wrath of God, who liveth for ever and ever.

8 And the temple was filled with smoke from the majesty of God, and from his power: and no man was able to enter into the temple, till the seven plagues of the seven Angels were fulfilled.

## CHAP. XVI.

*The seven vials are poured out: the plagues that ensue.*

AND I heard a great voice out of the temple saying to the

---

*a* Joel 3. 13. Matt. 13. 39.   *b* Jer. 10. 7.

THE BOOK SEALED WITH SEVEN SEALS IS OPENED BY THE LAMB (APOC. V.).

seven Angels: Go, and pour out the seven vials of the wrath of God upon the earth.

2 And the first went and poured out his vial upon the earth, and there fell a sore and grievous wound upon men, who had the character of the beast; and upon them that adored the image thereof.

3 And the second Angel poured out his vial upon the sea, and there came blood as it were of a dead man: and every living soul died in the sea.

4 And the third poured out his vial upon the rivers and the fountains of waters: and there was made blood.

5 And I heard the Angel of the waters saying: Thou art just, O Lord, who art, and who wast, the holy one, because thou hast judged these things:

6 For they have shed the blood of saints and prophets, and thou hast given them blood to drink; for they are worthy.

7 And I heard another from the altar, saying: Yea, O Lord God Almighty, true and just are thy judgments.

8 And the fourth Angel poured out his vial upon the sun, and it was given unto him to afflict men with heat and fire.

9 And men were scorched with great heat, and they blasphemed the name of God, who hath power over these plagues, neither did they penance to give him glory.

10 And the fifth Angel poured out his vial upon the seat of the beast: and his kingdom became dark, and they gnawed their tongues for pain.

11 And they blasphemed the God of heaven, because of their pains and wounds, and did not penance for their works.

12 And the sixth Angel poured out his vial upon that great river Euphrates, and dried up the water thereof, that a way might be prepared for the kings from the rising of the sun.

13 And I saw from the mouth of the dragon, and from the mouth of the beast, and from the mouth of the false prophet, three unclean spirits like frogs.

14 For they are the spirits of devils working signs, and they go forth unto the kings of the whole earth to gather them to battle against the great day of the Almighty God.

15 ᵃ Behold I come as a thief. Blessed is he that watcheth, and keepeth his garments, lest he walk naked, and they see his shame.

16 And he shall gather them together into a place, which in Hebrew is called Armagedon.

17 And the seventh Angel poured out his vial upon the air, and there came a great voice out of the temple from the throne, saying: It is done.

18 And there were lightnings, and voices, and thunders, and there was a great earthquake, such an one as never had been since men were upon the earth, such an earthquake, so great.

19 And the great city was divided into three parts: and the cities of the gentiles fell. And great Babylon came in remembrance before God, to give her the cup of the wine of the indignation of his wrath.

---

ᵃ Matt. 24. 43. Luke 12. 39. Supra, 3. 3.

CHAP. XVI. Ver. 16. *Armagedon*, i.e., the hill of robbers.

20 And every island fled away, and the mountains were not found.

21 And great hail like a talent came down from heaven upon men: and men blasphemed God for the plague of the hail, because it was exceeding great.

## CHAP. XVII.

*The description of the great harlot, and of the beast upon which she sits.*

AND there came one of the seven Angels, who had the seven vials, and spoke with me, saying: Come, I will shew thee the condemnation of the great harlot who sitteth upon many waters,

2 With whom the kings of the earth have committed fornication: and they who inhabit the earth have been made drunk with the wine of her whoredom.

3 And he took me away in spirit into the desert. And I saw a woman sitting upon a scarlet-coloured beast, full of names of blasphemy, having seven heads and ten horns.

4 And the woman was clothed round about with purple and scarlet, and gilt with gold, and precious stones and pearls, having a golden cup in her hand, full of the abomination and filthiness of her fornication.

5 And on her forehead a name was written: A mystery: Babylon the great, the mother of the fornications, and the abominations of the earth.

6 And I saw the woman drunk with the blood of the saints, and with the blood of the martyrs of JESUS. And I wondered when I had seen her with great admiration.

7 And the angel said to me: Why dost thou wonder? I will tell thee the mystery of the woman and of the beast which carrieth her, which hath the seven heads and ten horns.

8 The beast which thou sawest was and is not, and shall come up out of the bottomless pit and go into destruction: and the inhabitants on the earth (whose names are not written in the book of life from the foundation of the world) shall wonder, seeing the beast that was and is not.

9 And here is the understanding that hath wisdom. The seven heads are seven mountains, upon which the woman sitteth, and they are seven kings:

10 Five are fallen, one is, and the other is not yet come: and when he is come, he must remain a short time.

---

CHAP. XVII. Ver. 5. *A mystery:* that is, a secret, because what follows of the name and title of the great harlot is to be taken in a mystical sense.—Ibid. *Babylon.* Either the city of the devil in general, or, if this place be to be understood of any particular city, *Pagan Rome,* which then and for three hundred years persecuted the Church, and was the principal seat both of empire and idolatry.

Ver. 8. *The beast which thou sawest.* This beast which supports Babylon may signify the power of the devil; *which was and is not,* being much limited by the coming of Christ, but shall again exert itself under Antichrist. The seven heads of this beast are seven mountains or empires, instruments of his tyranny: of which five were then fallen, as above, chap. xiii. 1. The beast itself is said to be *the eighth and is of the seventh;* because they all act under the devil, and by his instigation, so that his power is in them all, yet so as to make up, as it were, an eighth empire, distinct from them all

11 And the beast which was, and is not: the same also is the eighth, and is of the seven, and goeth into destruction.

12 And the ten horns which thou sawest, are ten kings, who have not yet received a kingdom, but shall receive power as kings one hour after the beast.

13 These have one design: and their strength and power they shall deliver to the beast.

14 These shall fight with the Lamb, and the Lamb shall overcome them, *a* because he is Lord of lords and King of kings, and they that are with him are called, and elect, and faithful.

15 And he said to me: The waters which thou sawest, where the harlot sitteth, are peoples, and nations, and tongues.

16 And the ten horns, which thou sawest in the beast: these shall hate the harlot, and shall make her desolate and naked, and shall eat her flesh, and shall burn her with fire.

17 For God hath given into their hearts to do that which pleaseth him: that they give their kingdom to the beast till the words of God be fulfilled.

18 And the woman which thou sawest, is the great city which hath kingdom over the kings of the earth.

---

*a* 1 Tim. 6. 15. Infra, 19. 16.

Ver. 12. *Ten kings.* Ten lesser kingdoms, enemies also of the Church of Christ: which, nevertheless, shall be made instruments of the justice of God for the punishment of Babylon. Some understand this of the Goths, Vandals, Huns, and other barbarous nations, that destroyed the empire of Rome.

## CHAP. XVIII.

*The fall of Babylon: kings and merchants lament over her.*

AND after these things I saw another Angel come down from heaven, having great power: and the earth was enlightened with his glory.

2 And he cried out with a strong voice, saying: *b* Babylon the great is fallen, is fallen: and is become the habitation of devils, and the hold of every unclean spirit, and the hold of every unclean and hateful bird.

3 Because all nations have drunk of the wine of the wrath of her fornication: and the kings of the earth have committed fornication with her: and the merchants of the earth have been made rich by the power of her delicacies.

4 And I heard another voice from heaven, saying: Go out from her, my people: that you be not partakers of her sins, and that you receive not of her plagues.

5 For her sins have reached unto heaven, and the Lord hath remembered her iniquities.

6 Render to her as she also hath rendered to you: and double unto her double according to her works: in the cup, wherein she hath mingled, mingle ye double unto her.

7 As much as she hath glorified herself, and lived in delicacies, so much torment and sorrow give ye to her: because she saith in her heart: *c* I sit a queen, and am no widow: and sorrow I shall not see.

8 Therefore shall her plagues come in one day, death, and

---

*b* Isaias 21. 9. Jer. 51. 8. Supra, 14. 8.—*c* Isaias 47. 8.

427

mourning, and famine, and she shall be burned with the fire: because God is strong, who shall judge her.

9 And the kings of the earth, who have committed fornication, and lived in delicacies with her, shall weep, and bewail themselves over her, when they shall see the smoke of her burning:

10 Standing afar off for fear of her torments, saying: Alas! alas! that great city Babylon, that mighty city: for in one hour is thy judgment come.

11 And the merchants of the earth shall weep, and mourn over her: for no man shall buy their merchandise any more.

12 Merchandise of gold and silver and precious stones: and of pearls and fine linen and purple, and silk, and scarlet, and all thyine wood, and all manner of vessels of ivory, and all manner of vessels of precious stone, and of brass, and of iron, and of marble,

13 And cinnamon, and odours, and ointment, and frankincense, and wine, and oil, and fine flour, and wheat, and beasts, and sheep, and horses, and chariots, and slaves, and souls of men.

14 And the fruits of the desire of thy soul are departed from thee, and all fat and goodly things are perished from thee, and they shall find them no more at all.

15 The merchants of these things, who were made rich, shall stand afar off from her for fear of her torments, weeping and mourning,

16 And saying: Alas! alas! that great city, which was clothed with fine linen and purple and scarlet, and was gilt with gold and precious stones and pearls.

17 For in one hour are so great riches come to nought: and every shipmaster, and all that sail into the lake, and mariners, and as many as work in the sea, stood afar off,

18 And cried, seeing the place of her burning, saying: What city is like to this great city?

19 And they cast dust upon their heads, and cried, weeping and mourning, saying: Alas! alas! that great city, wherein all were made rich, that had ships at sea, by reason of her prices: for in one hour she is made desolate.

20 Rejoice over her, thou heaven, and ye holy apostles and prophets: for God hath judged your judgment on her.

21 And a mighty Angel took up a stone as it were a great millstone, and cast it into the sea, saying: With such violence as this shall Babylon that great city be thrown down, and shall be found no more at all:

22 And the voice of harpers, and of musicians, and of them that play on the pipe and on the trumpet, shall no more be heard at all in thee: and no craftsmen of any art whatsoever shall be found any more at all in thee: and the sound of the mill shall be heard no more at all in thee:

23 And the light of the lamp shall shine no more at all in thee: and the voice of the bridegroom and the bride shall be heard no more at all in thee: for thy merchants were the great men of the earth, for all nations have been deceived by thy enchantments.

24 And in her was found the blood of prophets and of saints,

## CHAP. XIX.

*The saints glorify God for his judgments on the great harlot. Christ's victory over the beast, and the kings of the earth.*

AFTER these things I heard as it were the voice of much people in heaven, saying: Alleluia. Salvation, and glory, and power is to our God.

2 For true and just are his judgments, who hath judged the great harlot, which corrupted the earth with her fornication, and hath revenged the blood of his servants, at her hands.

3 And again they said: Alleluia. And her smoke ascendeth for ever and ever.

4 And the four-and-twenty ancients and the four living creatures fell down and adored God that sitteth upon the throne, saying: Amen: Alleluia.

5 And a voice came out from the throne, saying: Give praise to our God, all ye his servants: and you that fear him, little and great.

6 And I heard as it were the voice of a great multitude, and as the voice of many waters, and as the voice of great thunders, saying: Alleluia; for the Lord our God the Almighty hath reigned.

7 Let us be glad and rejoice, and give glory to him : for the marriage of the Lamb is come, and his wife hath prepared herself.

8 And it is granted to her that she should clothe herself with fine linen glittering and white. For the fine linen are the justifications of saints.

9 And he said to me: Write: *a* Blessed are they that are called to the marriage supper of the Lamb. And he saith to me : These words of God are true.

10 And I fell down before his feet, to adore him: And he saith to me : See thou do it not : I am thy fellow-servant, and of thy brethren who have the testimony of JESUS. Adore God. For the testimony of JESUS is the spirit of prophecy.

11 And I saw heaven opened, and behold a white horse : and he that sat upon him was called Faithful and True, and with justice doth he judge and fight.

12 And his eyes were as a flame of fire, and on his head were many diadems, and he had a name written, which no man knoweth but himself.

13 *b* And he was clothed with a garment sprinkled with blood: and his name is called, THE WORD OF GOD.

14 And the armies that are in heaven followed him on white horses, clothed in fine linen white and clean.

---

*a* Matt. 22. 2. Luke 14. 16.—*b* Isaias 63. 1.

CHAP. XIX. Ver. 10. *I fell down before, &c.* St. Aug. (l. 20. contra Faust. c. 21) is of opinion that this angel appeared in so glorious a manner, that St. John took him to be God ; and therefore would have given him divine honour, had not the angel stopped him, by telling him he was but his fellow-servant. St. Gregory (hom. 8, in Evang.) rather thinks that the veneration offered by St. John was not divine honour, or indeed any other than what might lawfully be given; but was nevertheless refused by the Angel, in consideration of the dignity to which our human nature had been raised by the incarnation of the Son of God, and the dignity of St. John, an apostle, prophet, and martyr.

15 And out of his mouth proceedeth a sharp two-edged sword, that with it he may strike the nations. *a* And he shall rule them with a rod of iron: and he treadeth the wine-press of the fierceness of the wrath of God the Almighty.

16 And he hath on his garment and on his thigh written: *b* KING OF KINGS AND LORD OF LORDS.

17 And I saw an Angel standing in the sun, and he cried with a loud voice, saying to all the birds that did fly through the midst of heaven: Come, gather yourselves together to the great supper of God:

18 That you may eat the flesh of kings, and the flesh of tribunes, and the flesh of mighty men, and the flesh of horses, and of them that sit on them, and the flesh of all freemen and bondmen, and of little and of great.

19 And I saw the beast, and the kings of the earth, and their armies gathered together to make war with him that sat upon the horse, and with his army.

20 And the beast was taken, and with him the false prophet, who wrought signs before him, wherewith he seduced them who received the character of the beast, and who adored his image. These two were cast alive into the pool of fire burning with brimstone.

21 And the rest were slain by the sword of him that sitteth upon the horse, which proceedeth out of his mouth: and all the birds were filled with their flesh.

---

*a* Ps. 2. 9.—*b* 1 Tim. 6. 15. Supra, 17. 14.

430

## CHAP. XX.

*Satan is bound for a thousand years; the souls of the martyrs reign with Christ in the first resurrection. The last attempts of satan against the Church: the last judgment.*

AND I saw an Angel coming down from heaven, having the key of the bottomless pit, and a great chain in his hand.

2 And he laid hold on the dragon, the old serpent, which is the devil and satan, and bound him for a thousand years.

3 And he cast him into the bottomless pit, and shut him up, and set a seal upon him, that he should no more seduce the nations, till the thousand years be finished. And after that, he must be loosed a little time.

4 And I saw seats: and they sat upon them: and judgment was given unto them: and the souls of them that were beheaded for the testimony of JESUS, and for the word of God, and who had not adored the beast nor his image, nor received his character on their foreheads, or in their hands, and they lived and reigned with Christ a thousand years.

5 The rest of the dead lived not, till the thousand years were

---

CHAP. XX. Ver. 2. *Bound him, &c.* The power of satan has been very much limited by the Passion of Christ; *for a thousand years,* that is, for the whole time of the new testament: but especially from the time of the destruction of *Babylon* or Pagan Rome, till the new efforts of *Gog* and *Magog* against the Church, towards the end of the world. During which time the souls of the martyrs and saints live and reign with Christ in heaven, in the *first resurrection,* which is that of the soul to the life of glory; as the *second resurrection* will be that of the body, at the day of the general judgment.

THE SEVENTH SEAL OF THE BOOK IS OPENED (APOC. VIII.).

finished. This is the first resurrection.

6 Blessed and holy is he that hath part in the first resurrection. In these the second death hath no power: but they shall be priests of God and of Christ: and shall reign with him a thousand years.

7 And when the thousand years shall be finished, satan shall be loosed out of his prison, and shall go forth, and seduce the nations, which are over the four quarters of the earth, *a* Gog, and Magog, and shall gather them together to battle, the number of whom is as the sand of the sea.

8 And they came upon the breadth of the earth, and encompassed the camp of the saints, and the beloved city.

9 And there came down fire from God out of heaven, and devoured them: and the devil, who seduced them, was cast into the pool of fire and brimstone, where both the beast

10 And the false prophet shall be tormented day and night for ever and ever.

11 And I saw a great white throne, and one sitting upon it, from whose face the earth and heaven fled away, and there was no place found for them.

12 And I saw the dead, great and small, standing in the presence of the throne, and the books were opened, and another book was opened, which is the book of life: and the dead were judged by those things which were written in the books, according to their works.

13 And the sea gave up the dead that were in it, and death and hell gave up their dead that were in them: and they were judged every one according to their works.

14 And hell and death were cast into the pool of fire. This is the second death.

15 And whosoever was not found written in the book of life was cast into the pool of fire.

## CHAP. XXI.

*The new Jerusalem described.*

AND *b* I saw a new heaven and a new earth. For the first heaven and the first earth was gone, and the sea is now no more.

2 And I John saw the holy city the new Jerusalem coming down out of heaven from God, prepared as a bride adorned for her husband.

3 And I heard a great voice from the throne, saying: Behold, the tabernacle of God with men, and he will dwell with them. And they shall be his people: and God himself with them shall be their God.

4 *c* And God shall wipe away all tears from their eyes: and death shall be no more, nor mourning, nor crying, nor sorrow shall be any more, for the former things are passed away.

5 And he that sat on the throne said: *d* Behold, I make all things new. And he said to me: Write, for these words are most faithful and true.

---

*b* Isaias 65. 17. and 66. 22. 2 Pet. 3. 13. — *c* Isaias 25. 8. Supra, 7. 17. — *d* Isaias 43. 19. 2 Cor. 5. 17.

CHAP. XXI. Ver. 1. *The first heaven and the first earth was gone*, being changed, not as to their substance, but in their qualities.

---

*a* Ezech. 38. 14.

6 And he said to me: It is done: I am alpha and omega, the beginning and the end. To him that thirsteth I will give of the fountain of the water of life freely.

7 He that shall overcome shall possess these things, and I will be his God, and he shall be my son.

8 But the fearful and unbelieving, and the abominable, and murderers, and whoremongers, and sorcerers, and idolaters, and all liars, they shall have their portion in the pool burning with fire and brimstone, which is the second death.

9 And there came one of the seven Angels, who had the vials full of the seven last plagues, and spoke with me, saying: Come, and I will shew thee the bride, the wife of the Lamb.

10 And he took me up in spirit to a great and high mountain: and he shewed me the holy city Jerusalem coming down out of heaven from God,

11 Having the glory of God, and the light thereof was like to a precious stone, as to the jasper-stone, even as crystal.

12 And it had a wall great and high, having twelve gates, and in the gates twelve angels, and names written thereon, which are the names of the twelve tribes of the children of Israel.

13 On the east, three gates: and on the north, three gates: and on the south, three gates: and on the west, three gates.

14 And the wall of the city had twelve foundations, and in them, the twelve names of the twelve apostles of the Lamb.

15 And he that spoke with me had a measure of a reed of gold to measure the city and the gates thereof, and the wall.

16 And the city lieth in a four-square, and the length thereof is as great as the breadth: and he measured the city with a golden reed for twelve thousand furlongs, and the length and the height and the breadth thereof are equal.

17 And he measured the wall thereof an hundred forty-four cubits, the measure of a man, which is of an angel.

18 And the building of the wall thereof was of jasper-stone; but the city itself pure gold, like to clear glass.

19 And the foundations of the wall of the city were adorned with all manner of precious stones. The first foundation was jasper: the second, sapphire: the third, a chalcedony: the fourth, an emerald:

20 The fifth, sardonyx: the sixth, sardius: the seventh, chrysolite: the eighth, beryl: the ninth, a topaz: the tenth, a chrysoprasus: the eleventh, a jacinth: the twelfth, an amethyst.

21 And the twelve gates are twelve pearls, one to each: and every several gate was of one several pearl. And the street of the city was pure gold, as it were transparent glass.

22 And I saw no temple therein. For the Lord God Almighty is the temple thereof, and the Lamb.

23 *And the city hath no need of the sun, nor of the moon,

---

* Isaias 60. 19.

Ver. 17. *The measure of a man, i.e., according to the measure of men, and used by the angel. This seems to be the true meaning of these words.*

to shine in it. For the glory of God hath enlightened it, and the Lamb is the lamp thereof.

24 And the nations shall walk in the light of it: and the kings of the earth shall bring their glory and honour into it.

25 *a* And the gates thereof shall not be shut by day: for there shall be no night there.

26 And they shall bring the glory and honour of the nations into it.

27 There shall not enter into it anything defiled, or that worketh abomination or maketh a lie, but they that are written in the book of life of the Lamb.

## CHAP. XXII.

*The water and tree of life. The conclusion.*

AND he shewed me a river of water of life, clear as crystal, proceeding from the throne of God and of the Lamb.

2 In the midst of the street thereof, and on both sides of the river, *was* the tree of life, bearing twelve fruits, yielding its fruits every month, and the leaves of the tree were for the healing of the nations.

3 And there shall be no curse any more: but the throne of God and of the Lamb shall be in it, and his servants shall serve him.

4 And they shall see his face: and his name shall be on their foreheads.

5 *b* And night shall be no more: and they shall not need the light of the lamp, nor the light of the sun, because the Lord God shall enlighten them, and they shall reign for ever and ever.

---

*a* Isaias 60. 11.—*b* Isaias 6. 20.

6 And he said to me: These words are most faithful and true. And the Lord God of the spirits of the prophets sent his Angel to shew his servants the things which must be done shortly.

7 And, Behold I come quickly. Blessed is he that keepeth the words of the prophecy of this book.

8 And I John, who have heard and seen these things. And after I had heard and seen, I fell down to adore before the feet of the Angel, who shewed me these things.

9 And he said to me: See thou do it not: for I am thy fellow-servant, and of thy brethren the prophets, and of them that keep the words of the prophecy of this book. Adore God.

10 And he saith to me: Seal not the words of the prophecy of this book: for the time is at hand.

---

CHAP. XXII. Ver. 10. *For the time is at hand.* That is, when, compared to eternity, all time and temporal things vanish, and are but of short duration. As to the time when the chief predictions should come to pass, we have no certainty, as appears by the different opinions, both of the ancient fathers and late interpreters. Many think that most things set down from the 4th chapter to the end will not be fulfilled till a little time before the end of the world. Others are of opinion that a great part of them, and particularly the fall of the wicked Babylon, happened at the destruction of Paganism, by the destruction of heathen Rome, and its persecuting heathen Emperors. Of these interpretations, see Aksar. in his long commentary, see the learned Bossuet, Bishop of Meaux, in his treatise on this Book, and P. Alleman, in his notes on the same Apocalypse, tom. 13, who in his Preface says that thi., in a great measure, may be now looked upon as the opinion followed by the learned

11 He that hurteth, let him hurt still: and he that is filthy, let him be filthy still: and he that is just, let him be justified still: and he that is holy, let him be sanctified still.

12 Behold, I come quickly, and my reward is with me, to render to every man according to his works.

13 *a* I am alpha and omega, the first and the last, the beginning and the end.

14 Blessed are they that wash their robes in the blood of the Lamb, that they may have a right to the tree of life, and may enter in by the gates into the city.

15 Without are dogs and sorcerers, and unchaste, and murderers, and servers of idols, and every one that loveth and maketh a lie.

16 I JESUS have sent my Angel to testify to you these things in the churches. I am the root and stock of David, the bright and morning star.

17 And the spirit and the bride say: Come. And he that heareth, let him say: Come. And he that thirsteth, let him come: *b* and he that will, let him take the water of life, freely.

18 For I testify to every one that heareth the words of the prophecy of this book: If any man shall add to these things, God shall add unto him the plagues written in this book.

19 And if any man shall take away from the words of the book of this prophecy, God shall take away his part out of the book of life, and out of the holy city, and from these things that are written in this book.

20 He that giveth testimony of these things saith: Surely I come quickly. Amen. Come, Lord JESUS.

21 The grace of our Lord JESUS CHRIST be with you all. Amen.

---

*a* Isaias 41. 4. and 44. 6. and 48. 12. Supra, 1. 8. and 17. and 21. 6.

men. In fine, others think that St. John's design was in a mystical way, by metaphors and allegories, to represent the attempts and persecutions of the wicked against the servants of God, the punishments that should in a short time fall upon Babylon, that is, upon all the wicked in general: the eternal happiness and reward, which God had reserved for the pious inhabitants of Jerusalem, that is, for his faithful servants, after their short trials and the tribulations of this mortal life. In the meantime we meet with many profitable instructions and admonitions, which we may easily enough understand: but we have no certainty when we apply these predictions to particular events: for as St. Jerome takes notice, the Apocalypse has as many mysteries as words, or rather mysteries in every word. *Apocalypsis Joannis tot habet Sacramenta quot verba—parum dixi, in verbis singulis multiplices latent intelligentiæ.* Ep. ad Paulin. t. 4, p. 574, edit. Benedict.

Ver. 11. *Let him hurt still.* It is not an exhortation or license to go on in sin; but an intimation, that how far soever the wicked may proceed, their progress shall quickly end, and then they must expect to meet with proportionable punishments.

*b* Isaias 55. 1.

---

THE END OF THE NEW TESTAMENT.

AN
# HISTORICAL AND CHRONOLOGICAL INDEX
TO THE
# NEW TESTAMENT.

| A.D. | Sacred History. |
|---|---|
| 1 | CHRIST is born at Bethlehem. *Luke*, ii.<br>He is circumcized. *Luke*, ii.<br>The wise men come and adore him. *Matt.* ii.<br>He is presented in the temple. *Luke*, ii. Joseph and the Blessed Virgin mother fly with the child Jesus into Egypt. *Matt.* ii.<br>The massacre of the infants by Herod. *Matt.* ii. Joseph with the Blessed Virgin and her Son return from Egypt, but for fear of Archelaus, go to live at Nazareth in Galilee. *Matt.* ii. |
| 12 | JESUS is found in the temple disputing with the doctors when he was twelve years of age. *Luke*, ii. |
| 30 | St. John Baptist begins to preach penance, and to baptize. The chief of the Jews send messengers to ask if he was not the Messias. *John*, i.<br>JESUS himself is baptized by John. A voice from heaven declares him the beloved Son of God; the Holy Ghost comes down like a dove. *Matt.* iii. *Mark*, i. *Luke*, iii.<br>CHRIST is no sooner baptized, but he retires into a wilderness, where he fasted for forty days. The devil there tempts him. The angels come and minister to him. *Matt.* iv. *Mark*, i. *Luke*, iv.<br>CHRIST'S first miracle at Cana in Galilee, turned water into wine. *John*, ii. |
| 31 | St. John Baptist is cast into prison, and beheaded by Herod. *Matt.* xiv. *Mark*, vi. *Luke*, ix.<br>CHRIST makes choice of twelve of his disciples, whom he calls Apostles: Peter is the first of them. *Matt.* x. *Mark*, iii. *Luke*, vi.<br>CHRIST'S Sermon, or his instructions on the mountain. *Matt.* v. vi. & vii. He preaches in Judea and Galilee, casts out devils, cures all manner of diseases, and sometimes on the Sabbath days confutes and puts to confusion his adversaries, who blame him for it. *Matt.* xii. *Luke*, xiv. &c. |

# HISTORICAL INDEX.

| A.D. | Sacred History. |
|---|---|
|  | He raiseth to life the daughter of Jairus. *Matt.* ix. *Mark*, v. *Luke*, viii. |
|  | Also the son of the widow of Naim. *Luke*, vii. |
|  | He calms the sea by his word. *Matt.* viii. *Mark*, iv. *Luke*, viii. |
|  | He heals a man thirty-eight years ill of a palsy. *John*, v. |
|  | He sends his twelve Apostles to preach, with power of doing miracles. *Matt.* x. *Mark*, vi. *Luke*, ix. |
|  | He teaches them to pray. *Matt.* vi. *Luke*, xi. |
|  | He makes choice of seventy-two disciples. *Luke*, x. |
| 32 | He promises to make Peter the head of his Church, to build his Church upon him, to give him the keys of the kingdom of heaven. *Matt.* xvi. |
|  | He declares himself the Messias in plain terms to the Samaritan woman. *John*, iv. |
|  | He excuses his disciples for plucking the ears of corn on the second-first Sabbath. *Matt.* xii. |
|  | He feeds at one time five thousand men with five loaves. *Matt.* xiv. At another time four thousand with seven loaves. *Matt.* xv. |
|  | He promises to give them his body to be truly meat, &c. Many even of his disciples leave him, looking upon that doctrine as hard and harsh. *John*, vi. |
| 33 | His transfiguration. *Matt.* xvii. |
|  | The Sunday, or first day of the week, in which he died on the cross, he came riding upon an ass into Jerusalem. *Matt.* xxi. |
|  | In the beginning of that week he went daily into the temple, and in the evenings retired to Bethania, to pray in the garden of Gethsemani. *Luke*, xxi 38, &c. |
|  | On Wednesday, Judas made a bargain with the chief priests to deliver him up to them for a sum of money. *Matt.* xxvi. 15. |
|  | On Thursday he sent his disciples in the afternoon to bring the paschal lamb offered in the temple, which after sunset he ate with his twelve Apostles. *Matt.* xxvi. |
|  | He washed their feet. *John*, xiii. |
|  | After supper he instituted the Blessed Sacrament and Sacrifice of his Body and Blood. *Matt.* xxvi. |
|  | He gave his Apostles those excellent instructions set down by St. John, xiv. xvii. |
|  | CHRIST'S prayer in the garden three times repeated. |
|  | He is there seized, being betrayed by Judas. |
|  | He is led away to Annas, and then to Caiphas. |
|  | He is condemned as guilty of blasphemy, and death, for owning himself the Son of God. He is spit upon, buffeted, &c. |

THE ARCHANGEL MICHAEL'S VICTORY OVER THE DRAGON (APOC. XII.).

# HISTORICAL INDEX.

| A.D. | Sacred History. |
|---|---|

On Friday morning they deliver him up to the Roman governor, Pontius Pilate, who sees and declares him innocent, yet fearing not to be thought a friend to Cesar, condemns him to the death of the Cross.

He dies on the Cross, and is buried. For the history of his Passion, see *Matt.* xxvi. xxvii. xxviii. *Mark*, xiv. xv. xvi. *Luke*, xxii. xxiii. xxiv. *John*, xviii. xix. xx.

The miracles at his death. *Ibid.*

He riseth from death the third day. *Ibid.*

His different apparitions that very day: and others afterwards. *Ibid.*

He gives his Apostles power to forgive sins. *John*, xx. 23.

He gives to St. Peter the charge over his whole Church. *John*, xxi.

He promiseth to be with his Church to the end of the world. *Matt.* xxviii.

After forty days he ascends in their sight into heaven. *Acts*, i.

St. Matthias is chosen an Apostle in the place of Judas the traitor. *Acts*, i.

The day of Pentecost the Holy Ghost descended upon them and upon all present with them, in a visible manner. *Acts*, ii.

The wonderful change wrought in the Apostles by the coming of the Holy Ghost. Their undaunted courage. *Acts*, ii. &c.

They preach the resurrection of Christ, the necessity of believing in him, of repenting and doing penance.

St. Peter, the chief of the Apostles, converts on one day three thousand, on another five thousand. *Acts*, ii. 41, and *Ibid.* iv. 4.

He with St. John cures the lame beggar, that sat at the gate of the temple. *Acts*, iii. 6.

The new Christians have all things in common. Every one's necessities are supplied out of the common stock. *Acts*, iv. 32.

Ananias and Saphira for reserving some part of the money of a field sold, and for lying to the Holy Ghost, fall dead at St. Peter's feet. *Acts*, v.

The election of the seven deacons. *Acts*, vi.

Saul, by virtue of a commission from the chief priests, persecutes the Christians. *Acts*, ix.

St. Stephen was stoned to death. *Acts*, vii. 58.

The ministers of the gospel being dispersed, preach in Judea and Samaria, &c.

St. Philip in Samaria baptizeth Simon the Magician. He

# HISTORICAL INDEX.

| A.D. | Sacred History. |
|---|---|
| | offers money to St. Peter to have the power of giving the Holy Ghost. *Acts*, viii. |
| 34 | St. Paul is miraculously converted going to persecute the Christians at Damascus. *Acts*, ix. He presently preacheth JESUS. |
| | St. Peter cures Eneas at Lydda, and raiseth to life Tabitha at Joppe. *Acts*, ix. |
| | The very shadow of his body cures all diseases. *Acts*, v. 15. |
| 39 | He receives Cornelius the Centurion, and other Gentiles with him into the Church. *Acts*, x. |
| | He is thought to have gone about this time to Antioch in Syria, and to have founded the Episcopal See. |
| 41 | He preached in Pontus, Galatia, &c. |
| | St. Barnaby and St. Paul preach at Antioch, where the believers were first called Christians. *Acts*, xvii. 26. |
| 42 | Herod Agrippa puts to death St. James, the brother of St. John, and imprisons St. Peter, who was miraculously delivered. *Acts*, xii. |
| | St. Matthew, and afterwards St. Mark, wrote their Gospels. |
| 43 | St. Paul and Barnaby sent to preach in Pamphylia, Pisidia, Lycaonia. Afterwards in Pontus, Thracia, &c. *Acts*, xiii. xiv. |
| 48 | St. Peter about this time wrote his first Epistle. |
| 49 | A dispute between St. Paul and some zealous converts that had been Jews, about the obligation of making even the Gentiles observe the Jewish laws. *Acts*, xv. |
| | St. Paul and Barnaby are sent to Jerusalem, to have this question decided by the Apostles, &c. |
| | A council of the Apostles and bishops decide the question, St. Peter speaking first, and St. James joining with him. The letter of the council to their brethren the converted Gentiles. *Acts*, xv. |
| 51 | St. Paul and St. Barnaby separate. *Acts*, xv. |
| 52 | St. Paul with Silas goes to Asia. St. Timothy and also St. Luke become his companions. He goes to Philippi in Macedonia, to Thessalonica, to Berea, to Athens. Finds there an altar dedicated to the unknown God. *Acts*, xvi. xvii. |
| | He writes his first Epistle to the Thessalonians, and the second soon after. |
| | He stays eighteen months at Corinth. *Acts*, xviii. 11. |
| 55 | He goes to Ephesus. After a short visit to the brethren at Jerusalem, he goes to Antioch, and from thence again into Galatia and Phrygia, and stays three years at Ephesus, and thereabouts. *Acts*, xix. |
| 56 | He writes to the Galatians. |

# HISTORICAL INDEX.

| A.D. | Sacred History. |
|---|---|
| 57 | He writes his first, and soon after his second Epistle to the Corinthians. |
|  | He prepares to go to Jerusalem with alms he had gathered. *Acts*, xx. and xxi. |
|  | He writes to the Romans. |
| 58 | He comes to Jerusalem. *Acts*, xxi. |
|  | The Jews seize St. Paul in the temple; being beaten and in danger of being murdered by them, he is rescued by Lysias the tribune and his soldiers. *Acts*, xxi. |
|  | Lysias sends him to Felix, the governor of Judea, then at Cesarea, where he was two years a prisoner. |
|  | His discourse before King Agrippa, Felix, &c. *Acts*, xxv. |
| 60 | Having appealed to the tribunal of Cesar, he is sent to Rome with other prisoners. *Acts*, xxvii. |
| 61 | A description of his voyage and shipwreck on the coast of Malta. Every one in the ship is saved, being two hundred and seventy-six persons. *Acts*, xxvii. 44. |
|  | St. James about this time wrote his Catholic Epistle. |
|  | St. Paul's arrival at Rome. He is kept under custody for two years, with a soldier to guard him. *Acts*, xxviii. |
| 62 | He converts Onesimus, and sends him with his letter to Philemon. He writes to the Philippians and Colossians. |
|  | St. James, Bishop of Jerusalem, there martyred. |
|  | St. Paul, being set at liberty, writes to the Hebrews. |
| 66 | Goes again into Asia. Made St. Timothy bishop in Asia, and went into Macedonia, from whence he wrote his first Epistle to Timothy. |
| 68 | St. Peter about this time wrote his second Epistle. |
|  | About this time St. Peter and St. Paul came to Rome. See Tillemont, &c. |
|  | Not long after they were both put in prison, and suffered martyrdom. |
|  | St. John about this time came to live in Asia, and governed all those Churches for many years. |
|  | St. John was put into a cauldron of boiling oil at Rome, under Domitian, and banished to the island of Patmos, where he had those wonderful visions of his Apocalypse. |
| 96 | He returns to Ephesus, under the Emperor Nerva. |
|  | He writes his Gospel. |
|  | He dies at Ephesus, under Trajan, about the year 100. |

# A TABLE OF REFERENCES.

ABSOLUTION. The power promised and given to the pastors of the Church, St. Matt. xvi. 19. chap. xviii. 18. St. John, xx. 22, 23.

*Angels.* They have a charge over us, St. Matt. xviii. 10. Heb. i. 14. See also Exod. xxiii. 20, 21, &c. They offer up our prayers, Apoc. viii. 4, and pray for us, Zach. i. 12. We have a communion with them, Heb. xii. 22. They have been honoured by the servants of God, Josue v. 14, 15, and invocated, Gen. xlviii. 15, 16. Osee, xii. 4. Apoc. i. 4.

*Baptism.* Ordained by Christ, St. Matt. xxviii. 19. Necessary to salvation, St. John, iii. 5. Administered by the Apostles in water, Acts. viii. 36, 38. chap. x. 47, 48, also Ephes. v. 26. Heb. x. 22. 1 St. Peter, iii. 20, 21. For the baptism of infants, St. Luke, xviii. 16, compared with St. John, iii. 5.

*Christ.* He is the *only begotten*, the true, and natural *Son of God*, St. Matt. xvi. 16. St. John, i. 13. chap. iii. 16, 18. Rom. viii. 32. 1 St. John, iv. 39. The *same God* with his *Father, and equal to him*, St. John, v. 18, 19, 23. chap. x. 30. chap. xiv. 1, 9, &c. chap. xvi. 14, 15. chap. xvii. 10. Philipp. ii. 5, 6. *True* God, St. John, i. 1. chap. xx. 28, 29. Acts, xx. 25. Rom. ix. 5. Titus, ii. 13. 1 St. John, iii. 16. chap. v. 20. Also Isaias, ix. 9. chap. xxxv. 4, 5. St. Matt. i. 23. St. Luke, i. 16, 17. Heb. i. 8. He is the Creator of all things, St. John, i. 3, 10, 11. Coloss. i. 5, 16, 17. Heb. i. 2, 10, 11, 12. chap. iii. 4. *The Lord of glory*, 1 Cor. ii. 8. *The King of kings, and Lord of lords*, Apoc. xvii. 14. chap. xix. 16. *The first and the last: alpha and omega, the beginning and the end, the Almighty*, Apoc. i. 7, 8, 17, 18. chap. ii. 8. chap. xxii. 12, 13. *He died for all*, John, iii. 16, 17. Rom. v. 18. 2 Cor. v. 14, 15. 1 Tim. ii. 3, 4, 5, 6. chap. iv. 10. Heb. ii. 9. 1 John, ii. 1, 2. *Even for the reprobate*, Rom. xiv. 15. 1 Cor. viii. 11. 2 Peter, ii. 1.

*The Church of Christ stands for ever*, St. Matt. xvi. 18. chap. xxviii. 10. St. John, xiv. 16, 17. Psal. xlvii. 8. Psal. lxxi. 5, 7. Psal. lxxxviii. 3, 4, 29, 36, 37. Psal. cxxxi. 13, 14. Isaias, ix. 7. chap. liv. 9, 10. chap. lix. 20, 21. chap. lx. 15, 18. chap. lxii. 6. Jerem. xxxi. 35, 36. chap. xxxiii. 17, &c. Ezech. xxxviii. 24, 26. Dan. ii. 44. The Church is the *kingdom* of Christ, St. Luke, i. 33. Dan. ii. 44. The *city* of the great King, Psal. xlvii. 2. His *rest* and his *habitation for ever*, Psal. cxxxi. 13, 14. *The house of the living God*, 1 Tim. iii. 15. The *fold*, of which Christ is the *shepherd*, John, x. 16. The *body*, of which Christ is the *head*,

## A TABLE OF REFERENCES.

Coloss. i. 18. Ephes. v. 23. The *spouse*, of which he is the *bridegroom*, Ephes. v. 31, 32. Ever *subject* to him, and ever *faithful* to him, ver. 24, ever *loved* and *cherished* by him, v. 25, 29, and joined to him by an *indissoluble union*. v. 31, 32. The Church is the *pillar and ground* (or strong foundation) *of the truth*, 1 Tim. iii. 15. God's *covenant with her* is an *everlasting covenant of peace*, Ezech. xxxvii. 26, confirmed by a *solemn oath*, never to be altered; like that made to Noe, Isaias, liv. 9. A *covenant* like that of *the day and night*, to stand for all generations, Jeremias, xxxiii. 20, 21. God shall be her *everlasting light*, Isa. lx. 18, 19. Whosoever *shall gather together against her shall fall;* and *the nation that will not serve her shall perish*, Isa. lx. 12, 15, 17. The Church is always *one*, Cant. vi. 9, 10. John, x. 16. Ephes. iv. 4, 5. Always *visible*, Isa. ii. 2, 3. Micheas, iv. 1, 2. Matt. v. 14. Spread far and near, and teaching many nations, Psal. ii. 8. Psal. xxi. 27. Isa. xlix. 6. chap. liv. 1, 2, 3. Dan. ii. 35, 44. Malach. i. 11, &c. The Church *is infallible in matters of faith*. This follows from the premises, particularly see St. Matt. xvi. 18. chap. xxviii. 19, 20. St. John, xiv. 16, 17, 26. chap. xvi. 13. 1 Tim. iii. 14, 15. Isa. xxxv. 8. chap. liv. 9, 10. chap. lix. 19, 20, 21, &c.

*Church Guides*, and their authority, Deut. xvii. 8, 9, &c. St. Matt. xviii. 17, 18. chap. xxviii. 18, 19, 20. St. Luke, x. 16. St. John, xiv. 16, 17, 26. chap. xvi. 13. chap. xx. 21, &c. Ephes. iv. 11, 12, &c. Heb. xiii. 7, 17. 1 John, iv. 6.

*Communion in one Kind* sufficient to salvation, St. John, vi. 51, 57, 58. Body and blood of Christ now *inseparable*, Rom. vi. 9. Mention of one kind alone, Luke, xxiv. 30, 31. Acts, ii. 42, 46. chap. xx. 7. 1 Cor. x. 17.

*Confession of Sins*, Numb. v. 6, 7. St. Matt. iii. 6. Acts, xix. 18. St. James, v. 16. The obligation of confession is gathered from the judiciary power of binding and loosing, forgiving and retaining sins, given to the pastors of Christ's Church, St. Matt. xviii. 18. St. John, xx. 22, 23.

*Confirmation*, administered by the Apostles, Acts, viii. 15, 17. chap. xix. 6. See also 2 Cor. i. 21, 22. Heb. iv. 2.

*Continency*: possible, Matt. xix. 11, 12. The vow binding, Deut. xxiii. 21. The breach of that vow damnable, 1 Tim. v. 12. The practice commended, 1 Cor. vii. 7, 8, 27, 37, 38, 40. For reasons which particularly have place in the clergy, ver. 32, 33, 35.

*Councils* of the Church, gathered in Christ's name, are assisted by Christ, St. Matt. xviii. 20. And by the Holy Ghost, Acts, xv. 28. Their decrees are diligently to be observed by the faithful, Acts, xv. 41. chap. xvi. 4. See *Church Guides*.

*Eucharist*. The *real presence* of the body and blood of Christ, and *Transubstantiation* proved from Matt. xxvi. 26. Mark, xiv. 22, 24. Luke, xxii. 19. John, vi. 51. 52, &c. 1 Cor. x. 16. chap. xi. 24, 25, 27, 29.

*Eternity of Hell's torments*, Matt. iii. 12. chap. xxv. 41, 46. Mark, ix. 43, 44, 45, 46, 48. Luke, iii. 17. 2 Thess. i. 7, 8, 9. Jude, 6, 7. Apoc. xiv. 10,

## A TABLE OF REFERENCES.

11. chap. xx. 10. See also Isa. xxxiii. 14.

*Extreme Unction*, James, v. 14, 15.

*Faith.* True *faith* necessary to salvation, Mark, xvi. 16. Acts, ii. 47. chap. iv. 12. Heb. xi. 6. *Faith* without good works is *dead*, James, ii. 14, 17, 20, &c. *Faith alone* doth not *justify*, ver. 24. But *faith working by charity*, Gal. v. 6. *Faith* doth not imply an *absolute assurance* of our being in grace; much less of our eternal salvation, Rom. xi. 20, 21, 22. 1 Cor. ix. 27. chap. x. 12. Philip. ii. 12. Apoc. iii. 11.

*Fasting*, commended in Scripture, Joel, ii. 12. Practised by God's servants, 1 Esdras, viii. 23. 2 Esdras, i. 4. Dan. x. 3, i, 12, &c. Moves God to mercy, Jonas, iii. 5, &c. Is of great efficacy against the devil, Mark, ix. 29. And is to be observed by all the children of Christ, Matt. ix. 15. Mark, ii. 20. Luke, v. 35. See also Acts, xiii. 3. chap. xiv. 53. 2 Cor. vi. 5. chap. xi. 27. Christ's fast of forty days, Matt. iv. 2.

*Free-will*, Gen. iii. 7. Deut. xxx. 19. Eccles. xv. 14, &c. Often resists the grace of God, Prov. i. 24, &c. Isa. v. 4. Ezech. xviii. 23, 31, 32. chap. xxxiii. 11. Matt. xxiii. 37. Luke, xiii. 34. Acts, vii. 51. Heb. xii. 15. 2 Peter, iii. 9. Apoc. iv. 20.

*The Holy Ghost.* His divinity, Acts, v. 3, 4. chap. xxviii. 25, 26. 1 Cor. ii. 10, 11. chap. vi. 11, 19, 20. See also Matt. xli. 31, 32. Acts, xiii. 2. chap. xx. 28, &c. 2 Cor. xiii. 14. And the solemn form of Baptism, Matt. xxviii. 19, 20. He proceeds from the Father and the Son, John, xv. 26.

*Images*, commanded by God, Exod. xxv. 18, &c. Numb. xxi. 8, 9. And placed on each side of the mercy-seat in the sanctuary, Exod. xxxvii. 7. And in the temple of Solomon, 2 Par. iii. 10, 11. 3 Kings, vi. 23, 32, 35. And this by divine ordinance, 1 Par. xxviii. 18, 19. Relative honour to the images of Christ and the saints authorised, Heb. xi. 21. See also 2 Kings, vi. 12, 13, 14, 15, 16. 2 Par. v. 2, &c. Psal. xcviii. 5. Phil. ii. 10.

*Indulgences.* The power of granting them, Matt. xiv. 18, 19. The use of this power, 2 Cor. ii. 6, 7, 8, 10.

*Mass.* The sacrifice prefigured, Gen. xiv. 18. Foretold, Malach. i. 10, 11. Instituted and celebrated by Christ himself, Luke, xxii. 19, 20. Attested, 1 Cor. x. 16, 18, 19, 20, 21. Heb. xiii. 10. See *Eucharist*, &c.

*Matrimony.* A Sacrament representing the indissoluble union of Christ and the Church, Ephes. v. 32. See also 1 Thess. iv. 3, 4, 5. Marriage not to be dissolved but by death. Gen. ii. 24. Matt. xix. 6. Mark, x. 11, 12. Luke, xvi. 18. Rom. vii. 2, 3. 1 Cor. vii. 10, 11, 39.

*Holy Orders instituted by Christ.* Luke, xxii. 19. John, xx. 22, 23. Conferred by imposition of hands, Acts, vi. 6. chap. xiii. 3. chap. xiv. 22. Give grace, 1 Tim. iv. 14. 2 Tim. i. 6.

*Original Sin.* Job, xiv. 4. Psal. vii. Rom. v. 12, 15, 16, 17, 18, 19. 1 Cor. xv. 21, 22. Eph. ii. 3.

*Penance*, a sacrament. See *Absolution. Confession.*

*Pope*, or chief bishop, St.

THE NEW JERUSALEM (APOC. XXI.).

## A TABLE OF REFERENCES.

Peter, by Christ's ordinance, was raised to this dignity, Matt. xvi. 18, 19. Luke, xxii. 31, 32. John, xxi. 15, &c. See also Matt. x. 2. Acts, v. 29. Gal. ii. 7, 8.

*Prayers for the Dead*, 2 Machab. xii. 43, &c.

*Purgatory*, or a middle state of souls, suffering for a time, on account of their sins, is proved by those many texts of Scripture which affirm that God will *render to every man according to his works*: so that such as die in lesser sins shall not escape without punishment: for which also see Matt. xii. 36. Apoc. xxi. 27. Likewise Matt. v. 25. 26. chap. xii. 12. 1 Cor. iii. 13, 14, 15. 1 Pet. iii. 18, 19, 20.

*Relics*, miraculous, 2 Kings, xiii. 21. Matt. ix. 20, 21. Acts, xix. 11, 12.

*Saints* departed assist us by their prayers, Luke, xvi. 9. 1 Cor. xii. 8. Apoc. v. 8. We have communion with them, Heb. xii. 22, 23. They have power over nations, Apoc. ii. 26, 27. chap. v. 10. They know what passes amongst us, Luke, xv. 10. 1 Cor. xii. 12. 1 John, iii. 2. They are with Christ in heaven before the general resurrection, 2 Cor. v. 1, 6, 7, 8. Phil. i. 23, 24. Apoc. iv. 4. chap. vi. 9. chap. vii. 9, 14, 15, &c. chap. xiv. 1, 3, 4. chap. xix. 1, 4, 5, 6. chap. xx. 4. For their invocation, consult the texts quoted above with relation to Angels, and such as testify the great power which the prayers of God's servants have with him, and which authorise us to call for their prayers: for which see Exod. xxxii. 11, 14. 1 Kings, vii. 8, 9, 10. Job, xlii. 7. 8. Rom. xv. 30. Ephes. vi. 18, 19. 1 Thess. v. 25. Heb. xiii. 13. James. v. 16.

*Holy Scriptures*, hard to be understood, and wrested by many to their own destruction, 2 Peter, iii. 16. Not of private interpretation, 2 Peter, i. 20. Corrupted by heretics, St. Matt. xix. 11. 1 Cor. vii. 9. chap. ix. 5. chap. xi. 27. Gal. v. 17. Heb. xi. 21.

*Apostolical Traditions*, 1 Cor. xi. 2. 2 Thess. ii. 15. chap. iii. 6. 2 Tim. i. 13. chap. ii. 2. chap. iii. 14. See also Deut. xxxii. 7. Psal. xix. 5, 6, 7.

*Transubstantiation*. See *Eucharist*.

*Trinity* of persons in God, Matt. xxviii. 19. 2 Cor. xiii. 13. 1 John, v. 7.

*The B. Virgin Mary*. Her dignity, Luke, i. 28, 42, 43. All generations of true Christians shall call her blessed, Luke, i. 48. See, for her veneration and invocation, what is said above of angels and saints.

*Women*, must not preach nor teach. 1 Cor. xv. 34, 35, 37. 1 Tim. ii. 11, 12.

*Good Works*, meritorious, Gen. iv. 7. chap. xxii. 16, 17, 18. Psal. xvii. 11, 23, 24. Psal. xviii. 8, 11. Matt. v. 11, 12. chap. x. 42. chap. xvi. 27. 1 Cor. iii. 8. 2 Tim. iv. 8.

# A TABLE

## OF ALL

# THE EPISTLES AND GOSPELS

*For all Sundays and Holidays throughout the year; and also of the most notable Feasts in the Roman Calendar.*

*It must be observed, that the Verses at which the Epistle or Gospel begin and end, are set down after the Chapter.*

NOTE.—Ep. stands for Epistle, Gs. for Gospel.

ADVENT, 1 Sund. Ep. Rom. xiii. 11, 14. Gs. Luke, xxi. 25, 34.
2 Sund. Ep. Rom. xv. 4, 13. Gs. Matt. xi. 2, 10.
3 Sund. Ep. Philip. iv. 4, 7. Gs. John, i. 19, 28.
4 Sund. Ep. 1 Cor. iv. 1, 5. Gs. Luke, iii. 1, 6.
Christmas, 1 Mass, Ep. Tit. ii. 11, 15. Gs. Luke, ii. 1, 15.
2 Mass, Ep. Tit. iii. 4, 8. Gs. Luke, ii. 15, 21.
3 Mass, Ep. Heb. i. 1, 12. Gs. John, i. 1, 14.
St. Stephen, Ep. Acts, vi. and vii. 54, 59. Gs. Matt. xxiii. 34. 39.
St. John, Ep. Eccl. xv. 1, 7. Gs. John, xxi. 20. 24.
H. Innocents, Ep. Apoc. xiv. 1. Gs. Matt. ii. 13, 18.
St. Thomas Cant. Ep. Heb. v. 1, 7. Gs. John, x. 11, 17.
St. Silvester, Ep. 2 Tim. iv. 1, 9. Gs. Luke, xii. 35, 41.
New Year, Ep. Tit. ii. 11, 15. Gs. Luke, ii. 21, 22.
Epiphany, Ep. Isa. lx. 1, 7. Gs. Matt. ii. 1, 13.
1 Sund. Ep. Rom. xii. 1, 6. Gs. Luke, ii. 42, 52.
2 Sund. Ep. Rom. xii. 6, 16. Gs. John, ii. 1, 12.
Name of Jesus, Ep. Acts, iv. 8, 12. Gs. Luke, ii. 21.
3 Sund. Ep. Rom. xii. 16, 21. Gs. Matt. viii. 1, 13.
4 Sund. Ep. Rom. xiii. 8, 11. Gs. Matt. viii. 23, 28.
5 Sund. Ep. Colos. iii. 12, 18. Gs. Matt. xiii. 24, 31.
6 Sund. Ep. 1 Thess. i. 2, 10. Gs. Matt. xiii. 31, 36.
Septuagesima, Ep. 1 Cor. ix. 24, x. 5. Gs. Matt. xx. 1, 17.

## A TABLE OF ALL THE EPISTLES AND GOSPELS.

Sexagesima, Ep. 2 Cor. xi. 19. xii. 10. Gs. Luke, viii. 4, 16.
Quinquagesima, Ep. 1 Cor. xiii. 1, 13. Gs. Luke, xviii. 31, 34.
Ash-Wednesday, Ep. Joel, ii. 12, 20. Gs. Matt. vi. 16, 22.
1 Lent, Ep. 2 Cor. vi. 11. Gs. Matt. iv. 1, 12.
2 Lent, Ep. 1 Thess. iv. 1, 8. Gs. Matt. xvii. 1, 10.
3 Lent, Ep. Ephes. v. 1, 9. Gs. Luke, xi. 14. 29.
4 Lent, Ep. Gal. iv. 22. 31. Gs. John, vi. 1, 15.
Passion-Sunday, Ep. Heb. ix. 11, 15. Gs. John, viii. 46, 59.
Palm-Sunday, Ep. Phil. ii. 5, 11. Gs. Matt. xxi. 1, 10, and chaps. xxvi. xxvii.
Maunday-Thursday, Ep. 1 Cor. xi. 20, 33. Gs. John, xiii. 1, 15.
Good-Friday, Ep. Exod. xii. 12. Gs. John, xviii. xix.
Holy-Saturday, Ep. Col. iii. 1, 4. Gs. Matt. xxviii. 1, 7.
Easter-Sunday, Ep. 1 Cor. v. 7, 8. Gs. Mark, xvi. 1, 7.
Easter-Monday, Ep. Acts, xx. 37, 43. Gs. Luke, xxiv. 13, 35.
Easter-Tuesday, Ep. Acts, xiii. 26, 33. Gs. Luke, xxiv. 36, 47.
Low-Sunday, Ep. 1 John, v. 4, 10. Gs. John, xx. 19, 31.
2 Sund. after Easter, Ep. 1 Pet. ii. 21, 25. Gs. John, x. 11, 16.
3 Sund. Ep. 1 Pet. ii. 11, 18. Gs. John, xvi. 16, 22.
4 Sund. Ep. James, i. 17, 21. Gs. John, xvi. 5, 14.
5 Sund. Ep. James, i. 22, 27. Gs. John, xvi. 22, 30.
Ascension, Ep. Acts, i. 1, 11. Gs. Mark, xvi. 14, 20.
6 Sund. Ep. 1 Pet. iv. 7, 12. Gs. John, xv. 26. xvi. 4.
Whit-Sunday, Ep. Acts, ii. 1, 11. Gs. John, xiv. 23, 31.
Whit-Monday, Ep. Acts, x. 42, 48. Gs. John, iii. 16, 21.
Whit-Tuesday, Ep. Acts, viii. 14, 17. Gs. John, x. 1, 10.
Trinity-Sunday, Ep. Rom. x. 23, 36. Gs. Matt. xxviii. 18, 20.
Corp. Christi, Ep. 1 Cor. xi. 23, 29. Gs. John, vi. 56, 59.
2 Sund. Ep. 1 John, iii. 13, 18. Gs. Luke, xiv. 16, 24.

## A TABLE OF ALL THE EPISTLES AND GOSPELS.

3 Sund. Ep. 1 Pet. v. 6, 11.   Gs. Luke, xv. 1, 10.
4 Sund. Ep. Rom. viii. 18, 23.   Gs. Luke, v. 1, 11.
5 Sund. Ep. 1 Pet. iii. 8, 15.   Gs. Matt. v. 20, 24.
6 Sund. Ep. Rom. vi. 3, 11.   Gs. Mark, viii. 1, 10.
7 Sund. Ep. Rom. vi. 19, 23.   Gs. Matt. vii. 15, 21.
8 Sund. Ep. Rom. viii. 12, 17.   Gs. Luke, xvi. 1, 9.
9 Sund. Ep. 1 Cor. x. 6, 14.   Gs. Luke, xix. 41, 47.
10 Sund. Ep. 1 Cor. xii. 2, 11.   Gs. Luke, xviii. 9, 14.
11 Sund. Ep. 1 Cor. xv. 1, 10.   Gs. Mark, vii. 31, 37.
12 Sund. Ep. 2 Cor. iii. 4, 9.   Gs. Luke, x. 23, 37.
13 Sund. Ep. Gal. iii. 16, 22.   Gs. Luke, xvii. 11, 19.
14 Sund. Ep. Gal. v. 16, 24.   Gs. Matt. vi. 24, 33.
15 Sund. Ep. Gal. v. 25, vi. 11.   Gs. Luke, vii. 11, 16.
16 Sund. Ep. Eph. iii. 13, 21.   Gs. Luke, xiv. 1, 11.
17 Sund. Ep. Eph. iv. 1, 6.   Gs. Matt. xxii. 35, 46.
18 Sund. Ep. 1 Cor. i. 4, 9.   Gs. Matt. ix. 1, 8.
19 Sund. Ep. Eph. iv. 23, 28.   Gs. Matt. xxii. 1, 14.
20 Sund. Ep. Eph. v. 15, 21.   Gs. John, iv. 46, 53.
21 Sund. Ep. Eph. vi. 10, 17.   Gs. Matt. xviii. 23, 25.
22 Sund. Ep. Philip. i. 6, 11.   Gs. Matt. xxii. 15, 21.
23 Sund. Ep. Philip. iii. 17, 21.   Gs. Matt. ix. 18, 26.
24 Sund. Ep. Col. i. 9, 14.   Gs. Matt. xxiv. 15, 35.

# ON THE FEASTS OF THE SAINTS.

NOTE.—Ep. stands for Epistle, Gs. for Gospel.

St. Andrew, Ep. Rom. x. 10, 18. Gs. Matt. iv. 18, 22.
Conception of the B. V. M. Ep. Prov. viii. 22, 36. Gs. Matt. i. 1, 16.
St. Thomas, Ep. Eph. ii. 19, 22. Gs. John, xx. 24, 29.
Conv. St. Paul, Ep. Acts, ix. 1, 22. Gs. Matt. xix. 27, 29.
Candlemas, Ep. Malach. iii. 1, 5. Gs. Luke, ii. 22, 32.
St. Matthias, Ep. Acts, i. 15, 26. Gs. Matt. xi. 25, 30.
St. Patrick, Ep. Eccl. xliv. xlv. Gs. Matt. xxv. 14, 23.
St. Joseph, Ep. Eccles. xlv. 1, 6. Gs. Matt. i. 18, 22.
Annunciation, Ep. Isa. vii. 10, 15. Gs. Luke, i. 26, 38.
St. George, Ep. 2 Tim. ii. 8, 10; iii. 10, 12. Gs. John, xv. 1, 7.
St. Mark, Ep. Ezech. i. 10, 15. Gs. Luke, x. 1, 9.
SS. Philip and James, Ep. Wis. v. 1, 5. Gs. John, xiv. 1, 13.
Inv. Cross, Ep. Philip. ii. 5, 11. Gs. John, iii. 1, 15.
St. Barnaby, Ep. Acts, xi. 21, 27. Gs. Matt. x. 16, 22.
St. John Bapt. Ep. Isa. xlix. 1, 8. Gs. Luke, i. 57, 68.
SS. Peter and Paul, Ep. Acts, xii. 1, 11. Gs. Matt. xvi. 13, 19.
Visitation B. V. M. Ep. Cant. ii. 8, 14. Gs. Luke, i. 39, 47.
St. Mary Magd. Ep. Cant. iii. 2, &c. Gs. Luke, vii. 36, 50.
St. James, Ep. 1 Cor. iv. 9, 15. Gs. Matt. xx. 20, 23.
St. Ann, Ep. Prov. xxxi. 10, &c. Gs. Matt. xiii. 44, 52.
Transfiguration, Ep. 2 Pet. i. 16, 19. Gs. Matt. xvii. 1, 9.
St. Laurence, Ep. 2 Cor. ix. 6, 10. Gs. John, xii. 24, 26.
Assumption B. V. M. Ep. Eccles. xxiv. 11, 20. Gs. Luke, x. 38, 42.
St. Bartholomew, Ep. 1 Cor. xii. 27, 31. Gs. Luke, v. 12, 19.

## ON THE FEASTS OF THE SAINTS.

Nativity B. V. M. Ep. Prov. viii. 22, 36. Gs. Matt. i. 1, 16.
Exalt. Cross, Ep. Phil. ii. 5, 11. Gs. John, xii. 31, 36.
St. Matthew, Ep. Ezech. i. 10, 15. Gs. Matt. ix. 9, 13.
St. Michael, Ep. Apoc. i. 1, 5. Gs. Matt. xviii. 1, 10.
Angel-Guardians, Ep. Exod. xxiii. 20, 23. Gs. Matt. xviii. 1, 10.
St. Luke, Ep. 2 Cor. viii. 15, 24. Gs. Luke, x. 1, 9.
SS. Simon and Jude, Ep. Eph. iv. 7, 13. Gs. John, xv. 17, 25.
All Saints, Ep. Apoc. vii. 2, 12. Gs. Matt. v. 1, 12.
All Souls, Ep. 1 Cor. xv. 51, 54. Gs. John, v. 25, 29.
Presentation B. V. M. Ep. Eccl. xxiv. 14, 16. Gs. Luke, xi. 27, 28.

FINIS.